THIS IS SERVICE DESIGN DOING.

APPLYING SERVICE DESIGN THINKING
IN THE REAL WORLD

A PRACTITIONERS' HANDBOOK

THIS IS SERVICE DESIGN DOING

by Marc Stickdorn, Markus Hormess, Adam Lawrence, Jakob Schneider

Copyright © 2018 Marc Stickdorn, Markus Hormess, Adam Lawrence, Jakob Schneider. All rights reserved.

Printed in Canada.

Published by O'Reilly Media, Inc., 1005 Gravenstein Highway North, Sebastopol, CA 95472.

O'Reilly books may be purchased for educational, business, or sales promotional use. Online editions are also available for most titles (*oreilly.com*). For more information, contact our corporate/institutional sales department: (800) 998-9938 or *corporate@oreilly.com*.

Acquisitions Editor: Mary Treseler	**Indexer:** Lucie Haskins
Developmental Editor: Angela Rufino	**Cover Designer:** Jakob Schneider
Production Editor: Melanie Yarbrough	**Interior Designer:** Jakob Schneider
Copyeditor: Jasmine Kwityn	**Illustrator:** Ellie Volckhausen
Proofreader: Rachel Head	**Compositor:** Melanie Yarbrough

Revision History for the First Edition:

2021-02-12	Tenth release
2021-11-19	Eleventh release
2022-10-12	Twelfth release
2023-07-21	Thirteenth release

See *http://oreilly.com/catalog/errata.csp?isbn=0636920040354* for release details.

978-1-491-92718-2

[TI]

KPIs

[01] The four editors, Marc, Adam, Markus, and Jakob, are also the main authors and the designers of this book. All text that does not name a specific author was written by us. However, we were not alone. More than 300 people helped us to create this book. Besides the co-authors and contributors, many others had important roles. Have a look at the end of the book to find all of them.

[02] The 33 case studies describe how service design is used in various industries. They include many photos and key takeaways. Sometimes, we reference a specific case in a footnote as an example of how a specific tool or subject matter is used in practice.

[03] Detailed hands-on descriptions of all of the service design methods included in this book are freely available online at *www.thisisservicedesigndoing.com*. You'll also find short descriptions of the methods at the ends of Chapters 5, *Research*; 6, *Ideation*; 7, *Prototyping*; and 10, *Facilitating workshops*.

[04] Our 96 co-authors contributed 33 case studies and 105 expert comments and tips to this book, often going through several iterations of feedback from the editors and reviewers. Their names are always included with their contributions. Make sure to quote the right people when you refer to their work! Short bios and photos of all the co-authors can be found at the end of the book.

[05] We invited service design experts from academia and industry to critically comment on the chapters or to give tips on how to do it. You will find these tips and comments alongside the main text, with attributions.

[06] A total of 205 contributors reviewed the original text written by the editors chapter by chapter through separate Google Docs. They suggested changes, added passages and footnotes, and sometimes even had vigorous discussions on various topics. These critical reviews were our crit sessions. They helped us to broaden our view and incorporate diverse thoughts and sources. Even though this process was a lot of work and took much longer than expected, it vastly improved the quality of the book. Have a look at the Preface to learn more about the process of this book and to read the names of all 205 heroes who invested their time into this project.

[07] There are many footnotes in this book. Why so many? On the one hand, we do not expect that you will read this book cover to cover, so we wanted to highlight connections between the different chapters to guide you to other chapters you might be interested in. On the other hand, we wanted to show that service design is rooted in extensive academic work spanning many different disciplines. Even though the book is intended as a handbook for practitioners, we strove to keep a basic academic standard. As far as possible for a book like this, we have tried to mention and quote original texts or give examples for further readings where appropriate.

THIS IS SERVICE DESIGN DOING.

EDITED/COLLECTED/
WRITTEN/DESIGNED BY:

**MARC STICKDORN
ADAM LAWRENCE
MARKUS HORMESS
JAKOB SCHNEIDER**

WITH GENEROUS
SUPPORT FROM THE
GLOBAL SERVICE
DESIGN COMMUNITY

01
WHY SERVICE DESIGN?

02
WHAT IS SERVICE DESIGN?

O3
BASIC SERVICE DESIGN TOOLS

O4
THE CORE ACTIVITIES OF SERVICE DESIGN

05
RESEARCH

06
IDEATION

07
PROTOTYPING

08

IMPLEMENTATION

09
SERVICE DESIGN PROCESS AND MANAGEMENT

10

FACILITATING WORKSHOPS

11
MAKING SPACE FOR SERVICE DESIGN

12

EMBEDDING SERVICE DESIGN IN ORGANIZATIONS

MORE ONLINE ...
FIND DETAILED STEP-BY-STEP DESCRIPTIONS OF ALL METHODS ONLINE

This book includes short descriptions of some of the core service design methods in **Chapters 5, Research; 6, Ideation; 7, Prototyping;** and **10, Facilitating workshops.**

Besides these short method introductions, you can download detailed step-by-step descriptions including hands-on tips, method variants, and examples from the book's website.

Watch out for this icon:

www.tisdd.com

HELLO THERE!
PREFACE

Where we come from:
This book's predecessor

Back in 2010, our book *This is Service Design Thinking* captured the state of the art. Marc was looking for a comprehensive resource to teach service design to his students, but could only give them URLs and articles spread around the web. So he teamed up with Jakob to create the resource himself. At the very start, it wasn't even clear that the result would become a book, but it was clear that the project should be based on a real service design process – we wanted to practice what we preached.

So, we invited 23 co-authors and over 150 online contributors to create the most complete collection of basics, tools, and case studies possible. It soon became clear that only printed matter could inspire the perception of a standard reference. Even more importantly, it would be a snapshot, as we openly acknowledged that service design was and is an evolving field.

No one expected the book to become a best seller, but to our surprise it went on to be translated into multiple languages and even won several design awards. From the moment the book was printed, we received thousands of comments. The community responded to the book in an overwhelmingly positive way, but of course had plenty of fair criticism. To sum it up in three points: too fragmented, too academic, too theoretical.

Why this book is necessary

We heard you. It took us some years out in the field to finally produce the book's sequel. More importantly, we were lucky enough to expand the team with two exceptional service design doers: Adam and Markus. So here we are with the logical sequel of thinking → doing.

One of the reasons why we called our first book *Service Design Thinking* was to trigger a discussion in the community on whether what we do is service design or design thinking or something else – trying to go beyond labels. This didn't really work out as we hoped, and now there are agencies and design departments that call what they do service design thinking. Yes, we are flattered, and we still make jokes about it.

Service design (or design thinking, experience design, UX, CX, or whatever you might call what we're doing) is not just about *thinking*. Design in general is an act of *doing*. The feedback we received for #TiSDT often emphasized that the best part of the book was its second part: the service design toolbox. This book now takes that idea of a toolbox further.

This is Service Design Doing is a handbook of service design – a toolbox, a description of methods, a facilitation guide, packed with cases and examples – giving a clear picture of how you can put all those pieces together. It is a book for "doers," for people who want to improve customer experience as well as employee experience and the systems that connect all these stakeholders in an organization.

It is also a book that helps you pave the way to *doing* with both business and design audiences. It gives you enough theory and examples to explain why this approach actually works and how you can tie it into your organization.

The book you have in your hand concentrates on the bigger picture of setting up and running a service design initiative, and the details of facilitating both the project and the room. Many of the individual methods and tools involved – from visualization tools to specific research, ideation, or prototyping methods – are well known or already described in many other books and online resources. Instead of charging you for these "commodities," we have made the best descriptions we can, added plenty of expert tips, and put them online for free. If you need them, download them from *www.thisisservicedesigndoing.com*[01] and share the worksheets with your colleagues.

We may call it service design, but many organizations we work with call it something else. This book is not about labels, but about how to get stuff done. How to have an impact on employees, customers, citizens, all of us.

Who should read this book

This book is for everyone interested in customer experience, innovation, and collaborative creation. Put another way, if you have picked up this book, it is probably for you.

01 Or simply *www.tisdd.com*.

Perhaps you work in an organization which is trying to better help its customers (or citizens, or employees), and you want to create better or even new offerings that people will love to use and talk about. Perhaps your organization wants new ways to connect operational silos and work together more painlessly, using a "language" and toolset that everyone in the organization – and your stakeholders outside – can understand.

It might be that you want to run, lead, or participate in co-creative group sessions where people work together more effectively and enjoyably.

Maybe you have heard the term "service design thinking," or something like it, and want to understand more about it and why it works. Or you have already learned something about it and need to "connect the dots," moving from simple tool use to successful projects and strategy. You might even be a professional designer or consultant, looking to add to your knowledge or find material to use in your projects and sessions.

Who we are

We (Marc and Jakob) are the editors of *This is Service Design Thinking,* and we've been exploring this field since 2008, doing design work, design consultancy, teaching, and speaking. After working together for many years, we finally built two startups around service design: Smaply and ExperienceFellow. We couldn't be happier to team up with service design consultants and trainers Adam Lawrence and Markus Hormess from WorkPlayExperience – widely known as instigators of the Global Service Jam with its famous motto of "Doing, not talking."

In 2013, Marc, Adam, and Markus created an executive school called – surprise – This is Service Design Doing. Since then, hundreds of participants from all over the world and from a wide range of organizations have taken part, and the conversations with (future) service designers influenced much of what is contained in this book. The schools generated a co-created script that inspired us to write a sequel to #TiSDT.

Who is allowed to write this kind of book?

When we were discussing our plans to write a sequel to #TiSDT in 2014, we asked ourselves again: Who has the authority to write such a book? Who can decide which tools and methods should (or should not) be in the book? We came to the same conclusion as in 2009, when we wrote #TiSDT: it shouldn't be us, it should be the global service design community. We can only suggest, write drafts, promote, get a diverse group of people to review and to write parts of the book; it should be the community that actually decides what should be included and what shouldn't be. So as with #TiSDT, we decided to co-create #TiSDD with the community. Thankfully we found a publisher that supported us in this idea of co-creating a book together with a community: O'Reilly.

We were able to include the service design community in the shape of 200+ reviewers, cases from design agencies and in-house design departments, and as comments from both renowned service design experts and people from outside the community.

How to co-create a book

The content of this book has been through many iterations of writing, feedback, and rewriting. It started with the co-created handout from our *This is Service Design Doing Executive Schools.* More than 200 participants reviewed and added to our co-created script over 3 years, refining and reality-proofing it in real-world projects, creating the sh!tty first draft of what would turn into this book.

Based on this initial draft, we sketched out the content of this book and devised a co-creation strategy that led to a series of calls for contribution and co-creation. We invited leading service design practitioners from various fields and countries to submit case studies showing how specific tools and methods are applied in context. We asked the wider service design community for contributions through an open call on our temporary website, *tisdd.rocks.* Within an hour, 200 people had volunteered to review our drafts for the 12 chapters. We had intensive discussions and changes, and iterated our way forward.

Our publisher, O'Reilly, offered a pre-release version of this book as an ebook. Selected chapters were available for download from early 2016 on and we received feedback through the O'Reilly website, by email, and later also through *tisdd.rocks.* Our final draft was then sent out to invited experts from the service design community and beyond. They gave feedback on selected chapters and were invited to write comments, tips, or counter opinions, many of which are published under their own names next to the text. Finally, we invited 10 reviewers to read the whole manuscript end to end to review how the different parts fit together.

Overall, we tried to practice what we preach and used an iterative, co-creative, and "reader"-centered design approach to create this book. As you can imagine, such a process is time consuming and hard to plan. We missed many deadlines and had to postpone the publishing date several times. Luckily, we have a publisher who believed in these ideas and supported us all the way. And even now, this book is not "finished." It is just the beginning. It is a slightly less sh!tty first draft …

– *Your authors, Marc & Adam & Markus & Jakob*

Illustration: Mauro Rego

TIMELINE: HOW WE CO-CREATED THIS BOOK

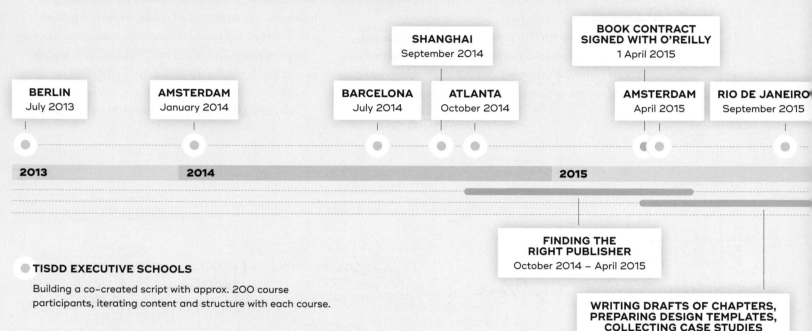

BERLIN
July 2013

AMSTERDAM
January 2014

SHANGHAI
September 2014

**BOOK CONTRACT
SIGNED WITH O'REILLY**
1 April 2015

BARCELONA
July 2014

ATLANTA
October 2014

AMSTERDAM
April 2015

RIO DE JANEIRO
September 2015

2013

2014

2015

TISDD EXECUTIVE SCHOOLS

Building a co-created script with approx. 200 course
participants, iterating content and structure with each course.

**FINDING THE
RIGHT PUBLISHER**
October 2014 – April 2015

**WRITING DRAFTS OF CHAPTERS,
PREPARING DESIGN TEMPLATES,
COLLECTING CASE STUDIES**
April 2015 – March 2016

CONTRIBUTORS: WHO CO-CREATED THIS BOOK

WE WOULD LIKE TO THANK THE 200+ REVIEWERS WHO VOLUNTEERED
TO HELP US CO-CREATE THIS BOOK. YOU FOLKS ROCK!

Adam Cochrane, Adriana Ojeda, Agnieszka Mróz, Ahmad Heshmat, Aimee Tasker, Alexander Staufer, Amy Barron, Ana Kyra Bekš, Ana Luis, Ana Osredkar, André Diniz de Moraes, Andreas Conradi, Andreas Kupfer, Anna Pfeifer, Anne Sofie Laursen, Ariane Fricke, Arthur Yeh, Barbara Niederschick, Beatriz Ricci, Belinda Garfath, Bengi Turgan, Brandon Ward, Bree Miller, Brian Clark, Camilla Bengtsson, Carlos Martinez, Carola Verschoor, Carolina López Tomás, Caroline Gagnon, Charles Woolnough, Chris Ferguson, Chris Roth, Christian Bessembinders, Christof Zürn, Claudia Brückner, Claudio Stivala, Clizia Welker, Daragh Henchy, Dariusz Paczewski, David Hernandez, Dennis Flood, Diego Passos, Diogo Rebelo, Dmitry Zenin, Do Hyeung Kim, Eerikki Mikkola, Elena Bernia, Elena Klepikova, Elizabeth Kimball, Eric Horster, Erik Flowers, Fabián Longhitano, Fabian Segelström, Felipe Montegu, Ferdinand Grah, Filipa Silva, Florian Egger, Francis Szilard Szakacs, Frank Danzinger, Fred Zimny, Frederic Dimanche, Gabriel Jiménez Andreu, Gerry Scullion, Graham Hill, Grete Haukelid, Guillaume Py, Hadas Arazi, Hajj Flemings, Henriette Søgaard Clausen, Ieva Prodniece, Ileana Manera, Ingrid Burkett, Irena Korcz, Iryna Prus, Ivan Boscariol, Izabela Piotrowska, Jaap Daalhuizen, Jane Vita, Jason Grant, Jens Wiemann, Jia Liang Wong, Jody Parra, Josef Winkler, Joseph McCarthy, Joumana Mattar, Juan David Martin, Juan Gasca, Juha Kronqvist, Julio Boaventura Jr, Kaja Misvær Kistorp, Karin Lycke, Katharina Ehrenmüller, Katharina Rainer, Kathryn Grace, Katrin Mathis, Kelsea Ballantyne, Kitjakaan Chuaychoowong, Kristin Low, Laura Mata Garcia, Lennard Hulsbos, Leon Jacobs, Leonides Delgado, Lina Arias, Lindsay Tingström, Linus Schaaf, Lisa Gately, Lucas Freed, Luis Francisco López, Luis Miguel Garrigós Escobar,

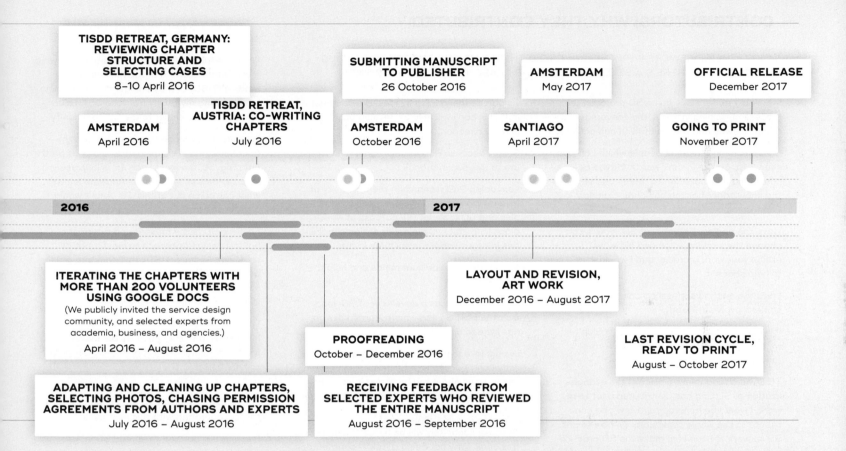

TISDD RETREAT, GERMANY: REVIEWING CHAPTER STRUCTURE AND SELECTING CASES
8–10 April 2016

AMSTERDAM
April 2016

TISDD RETREAT, AUSTRIA: CO-WRITING CHAPTERS
July 2016

SUBMITTING MANUSCRIPT TO PUBLISHER
26 October 2016

AMSTERDAM
October 2016

AMSTERDAM
May 2017

SANTIAGO
April 2017

OFFICIAL RELEASE
December 2017

GOING TO PRINT
November 2017

2016

2017

ITERATING THE CHAPTERS WITH MORE THAN 200 VOLUNTEERS USING GOOGLE DOCS
(We publicly invited the service design community, and selected experts from academia, business, and agencies.)
April 2016 – August 2016

ADAPTING AND CLEANING UP CHAPTERS, SELECTING PHOTOS, CHASING PERMISSION AGREEMENTS FROM AUTHORS AND EXPERTS
July 2016 – August 2016

PROOFREADING
October – December 2016

RECEIVING FEEDBACK FROM SELECTED EXPERTS WHO REVIEWED THE ENTIRE MANUSCRIPT
August 2016 – September 2016

LAYOUT AND REVISION, ART WORK
December 2016 – August 2017

LAST REVISION CYCLE, READY TO PRINT
August – October 2017

Lukasz Foks, Luke McKinney, Lysa Morrison, Mai Saito, Manuel Grassler, Manuela Boaventura, Manuela Procopio, Marcin Niewęglowski, Marco Di Norcia, Marianne Brierley, Mariusz Muraszko, Mark Cameron, Mark Goddard, Marlies Deforche, Marta Grochowska, Martha Valenta, Martin Heider, Martin Hrdlicka, Masaaki Nagao, Massimo Curatella, Matt Edgar, Maurice Vroman, Mauricio Manhaes, Mauro Rego, Max Niederschick, Megan Miller, Michael Darius, Michael Kacprzak, Mikael Seppälä, Mike Laurie, Mikkel Hansen, Mikko Väätäinen, Monica Puoli, Monica Ray Scott, Morten Skovvang, Natasche Padialli, Nathan Lucy, Nicola Giacchè, Nicolaas Bijvoet, Niels Corsten, Niels Verhart, Nurit Millo, Owen Hodda, Pablo Álvarez, Patricia Stark, Patti Hunt, Paul Flood, Pedro Moreira da Silva, Peesasadech Pechnoi, Peter Jaensch, Peter Jordan, Phillippa Rose, Primoz Mahne, Rafael Poiate, Ren Chang Soo, Ricardo Stucchi, Riccardo Ghignoni, Richard McMurray, Richard Tom, Richard Turner, Ron Bronson, Ross Robinson, Rui Quinta, Rupert Tebb, Seong-Eun Lee, Shahla Khan, Shaun Rolls, Simon Roberts, Sophie Buergin, Stefan Holmlid, Stefan Moritz, Stephan Pühler, Tadjine Nadim, Tenna Doktor Olsen Tvedebrink, Tero Marin, Tero Väänänen, Teun den Dekker, Thomas Sprangers, Tiago Nunes, Tiina Maria Honkanen, Tim Smith, Tiziano Luccarelli, Tomas Vergara, Trevor Jurgens, Tuan Huynh, Ulf Hücker, Valeria Adani, Valeria Grauso, Veronica Fossa, Vicky Tiegelkamp, Wilbert Baan, William Bakker, William Green, William Spiga, Yolanda Ladia, Yosef Shuman, Zuzanna Ostafin

CONTRIBUTORS: WHY THEY CONTRIBUTED

WE ASKED THE REVIEWERS WHY THEY INVESTED THEIR TIME AND ENERGY TO HELP US CREATE THIS BOOK. HERE'S A SELECTION OF THEIR REASONS FOR PARTICIPATING:

▷ I think SD rocks. I love doing SD projects, the process of gaining insights, the conversations along the way and the results you can achieve.

▷ Collaborate in a team of people which I always search for advice in their words. Maybe become also an inspiration to others and share the knowledge that the book has. Saludos! From Colombia

▷ I love the endless potential of SD. How it can change the world in small and big ways. I think your work is crucial and I would love to help shape it.

▷ I find the method supporting how homo-sapiens evolve brilliantly.

▷ If we preach design in co-creation, shouldn't we all then practice what we preach? (and it is fun too!)

▷ TISDT is a fundamental piece in the evangelization of SD and has contributed a lot to my work. I would be honored to review and contribute to the whole community on how to put SD to work. If I can help make the SD practice better, why not?

▷ I consider "this is SD thinking" the bible of SD, it really helped me in understanding the SD religion. Now I don't want to miss the chance to give my contribution to the New Testament :)

▷ Want to contribute based on my recent works in Japan

▷ As a relative newcomer to the field I can offer good perspective with respect to readers who are learning about SD for the first time. And admittedly I'm curious about the book as well!

▷ As part of the jam family I feel like contributing! This book will help us develop businesses in a SD direction.

▷ Simply because Russian SD wants to contribute to this superior book.

▷ I am doing PhD research in the University of Milano-Bicocca and exploring design principles and SD tools for the purpose of workplace innovation. Developing design capabilities in organisations is my main focus.

▷ Collaborate with brilliant minds and help the SD community

▷ I am a convert ...as a developer of 30 years over the past 8 years I have learned design has little to do with making it look pretty

▷ I would love to have the opportunity to modestly contribute to your Opus magnum :). I am very curious about the book and it would be great to be amongst the chosen ones that get a first glimpse.

▷ Because I definitely will be a f*ck*** user of this book. Why not being a f*ck*** contributor too? :) Plus I have some interesting experiences in: SD + Scrum (I'm also a Scrum Master) + In-house SD. You decide!!

▷ Because the book: "This is SD Thinking" is so great, and yesterday I listened to a UX podcast "Breaking down digital media silos!" with Donald Norman, where he talked also about "SD doing."

▷ I'm in the midst of a career transition, throwing myself into the world of SD. I'm learning by reading (TISD) and by doing. I'm also learning by relocating my family from the USA to London so I can be closer to the SD community.

▷ Your first book made me discover SD in the first place, and everything after that was pretty amazing. So, the least I can do, is help you guys review the second one. And who knows what can come out of this! P.s. And it would also be an honour.

▷ I believe SD is the present and future of a holistic design approach to most if not all problems we face. TISDT helped me to grasp this and started me down the path of implementing SD as a practice wherever I go. I'd love to help shape this new book.

▷ I have an innovation consultancy for small businesses and every day we are looking for new forms of inspiration to help our customers better.

▷ The first book is amazing and helped me to understand the power of SD. I need to return this collaborating with this next book.

▷ I have great passion to spread SD in Asia.

▷ Having set up two SD businesses operating in Asia I want to help represent this part of the world and offer a different perspective of our practice.

▷ Because I do design thinking and SD processes on a daily basis. Therefore I believe that I have something to contribute with, and at the same time I hope to get some learning and inspiration out of reading the book.

▷ I'd like to contribute to the creation of something that can be really useful for practitioners as well as for the people who want to know more about the discipline, the approaches and methods.

▷ I am passionate about moving the SD field forward, and very much looking forward to this book to build on the canon.

▷ I have been working with SD for several years within the public and private domain. Spreading the gospel and gathering practical experience. The latter I would like to contribute to the book.

▷ I want to decrease the gap between theory and practice, communicating practice in a pedagogic and clear way.

▷ Research in general is in B2B not very common. But lack of innovation opens up new doors - so B2Bs are discovering Design Research not only as a change of perspective but also a chance for cultural change.

▷ I'm an innovation consultant with a background totally different from a "typical SDer." I have a degree in economics/marketing/strategy but I believe in the power of combining design thinking with traditional business strategy.

▷ I'm passionate about service design and I begin my adventure with the first black book, and now working as a SDer (implementing projects for municipalities, hospitals and companies) so would love to have an impact on next book.

▷ Soy apasionado por el diseño de servicios. Estoy interesado que más personas tengan acceso a metodologías y herramientas de diseño de servicios.

▷ We have many copies of the first book and I've been in SD in govt for many years now. I would be so excited to be involved and believe I can contribute.

▷ For the past few years, I've been trying to implement SD principles into large organizations, but I was disappointed by the lack of real practical advice of the first This is SD book and would like to be able to ensure it in this follow up.

▷ I am a reader of the This is SD Thinking book and excited to make myself useful and contribute for the sequel. Met u guys in NYC during SDGC 2015, when I first heard the sequel was coming and I am eagerly awaiting its arrival.

▷ I'm a practitioner working in SD and have a strong bias towards doing over abstract thinking. I believe SD is a practical discipline that genuinely helps solve problems that other disciplines can't. I also loved the first book :)

▷ I believe that collaboration is the best way to improve and share experiences. TISDT is a book I refer to during work and it would be a great experience to be part of creating the new chapter for it.

▷ I'd like to help and give back from my experience from being a big enterprise company how I see this integrating.

▷ I've been managing a business R&D unit working with the use of Lean Startup, Design Thinking and SD. I have practical experience of introducing these methods in the corporate environment, I saw some good patterns and pitfalls while doing that.

▷ Doing is the hard bit!

▷ I've got about 18 years of experience in design and development. The last 8 years have been in a SD capacity. So I have plenty of insight to offer SD Doing, for sure. I'm particularly interested in techniques from (eco)system thinking.

▷ I am always looking to push SD to the next base. And to make it a bona fide part of business operations.

▷ I'm not that satisfied with current books. I also want to bring my experience with public SD in Brazil and NY!

▷ Because I'm part of a Public Innovation Team in Colombian Government. We have the SD as a core approach and we have to face complex challenges, both outside and inside of public organizations.

▷ We have set ourselves the goal of promoting the sector in Israel, to implement it in business and help organizations develop a better service strategy through design thinking.

▷ The TiSDD course changed my outlook not only for an important project at my current company, but also for what I want to do in my career. I believe TiSDD will be a great reference for marketers and content strategists.

▷ Excited about this book for a while. Would love to provide some support in return for yours.

▷ Want to be part of the future.

▷ My mission is to coach 1 billion people in Design Thinking.

▷ Keep the revolution going! Cheers!

01
WHY SERVICE DESIGN?

Silo-breaking, hands-on innovation that starts with the experience – why organizations adopt service design.

Expert comments ——————————————————

Chris Ferguson   Jeff McGrath   Lauren Currie   Mauricio Manhães

01
WHY SERVICE DESIGN?

This chapter also includes

1.1 WHAT DO CUSTOMERS[01] WANT?

In your childhood, you might have played a game called Pass the Parcel. Before a party, a mystery gift would be wrapped in gift paper, then wrapped again and again until it became impossible to guess more than the basic form of what was inside. The kids playing the game would unwrap layers and layers, impatient to get to the middle.

The offerings made by organizations – the products, physical and digital services[02] we want – are wrapped in much the same way. The outermost wrapping is the behavior, manner, and tone of the staff member (or technological interface) we are dealing with. Under this is a layer of subject and system expertise made of that person's or system's knowledge of the offerings and operations. Then there is a layer of processes carried out by staff – for example, the sales or refund routines. Next, we have the systems and tools run by the organization – logistics systems, billing, and point of sale systems. And at the core is the offering itself, like a telephone contract or a pair of running shoes.

As a customer of an organization, you are like the child playing Pass the Parcel. The only way to get to the offering you want is through all those layers – they all contribute to your experience. Disinterested staff, misinformed employees, byzantine processes, and clunky systems can all make it less satisfying to buy or interact with the offering, making it less valuable to you.

Traditionally, companies have focused heavily on the content at the core of the parcel, and perhaps the few innermost layers that let them deliver it. They concentrate on technical and operational excellence and they want to

The experience of our offering is filtered by customers' perception of our behavior, expertise, processes, systems, and tools. They only perceive our solutions through the veils of all these layers, usually starting with the outermost.[03]

01 In this book, we will generally use the word "customer" in its broadest sense as someone who receives the value we produce. In your world, you might use other words like "client," "user," "colleague," "citizen," "stakeholder," or "boss." When it is important to differentiate – for example, in a B2B case between a "user" who directly interacts with an offering and a "customer" who buys it – we will make a clear distinction. For more detail, see the textbox *Stakeholder terminology* in 3.4.

02 The term "products" describes anything a company offers – no matter if this is tangible or not. In academia, products are often divided into goods and services. However, products are usually bundles of services and physical/digital products. As "goods" is colloquially understood as referring to something tangible, we prefer to speak of physical/digital products. Read more on this in the textbox on *Service design and service-dominant logic* in 2.5.

03 This six-level model is the authors' adaptation of Swisscom's 5 Step Model. See, for example, Oberholzer, G. (2011, May 05). " Customer Experience – wie vermittle ich das meinen Mitarbeitenden? – CEN-Xchange Mai," at *https://stimmt.ch*.

CUSTOMER EXPERIENCE

BEHAVIOR

SUBJECT MATTER EXPERTISE

PROCESSES

SYSTEMS AND TOOLS

OFFERINGS

"get it right." To them, their job is to optimize the nuts and bolts of their activity – like the hamburger restaurant that invests heavily in new recipe development. Or they work hard at sales, telling the world that they have just what the customer needs to solve his problem – like the bank that strives to present a consistent image of trustworthiness.

But is this core offering what the customer really cares about? In one study, researchers asked tens of thousands of patients about the factors that led to their hospital stay feeling satisfying or not.[01] Now, most of us would expect the "medical outcome" – the successful healing of the ailment – to be one of the most important things to patients. After all, "healing" is the key value proposition of hospitals; it's why people go there. But in the study, none of the top 15 satisfaction factors related to whether or not the patient's health improved while at the hospital. Instead, the top factors usually related to interactions with personnel, including things like information flow, complaint handling, empathic and polite nursing staff, patient inclusion in decision making, a pleasant hospital environment, and the feeling of being cared for by a well-motivated team.

Of course, if someone did not experience a good medical outcome, the situation might be different. When we become more sick, the medical part of the experience becomes eminently important. But until then, it seems that the core competency of the hospital – healing – is taken for granted by the patients.[02] It's not hard to imagine this in other situations. If you are a tourist, you don't talk about your hotel room having a door, window, or bed until one is missing. If you are a CFO, you don't rate your corporate accountants on their arithmetic skills until they lose you money. And at that point, the deficit becomes an issue. But otherwise, customers rate organizations on other factors.

So at the hamburger restaurant, eaters actually care *more* about a warm greeting than an exciting new burger recipe. At the bank, clients worry *more* about the awful login process on the website than about trusting the institution.[03] As customers, it seems that we are less influenced by the core offering than by the layers of experience around it. So how might organizations understand better what their customers value, and use their knowledge of customers to systematically make that experience better?

01 Frampton S., Gilpin L., & Charmel P., eds. (2003). "National Patient Satisfaction Data for 2003." In *Putting Patients First: Designing and Practicing Patient-Centered Care*. San Francisco, CA: Jossey-Bass.

02 This phenomenon has been well documented and researched since the 1960s – e.g., Herzberg's theory on motivators and hygiene factors: hygiene factors only contribute to dissatisfaction if they are missing, but do not contribute to satisfaction if they are present, while motivators contribute to satisfaction if hygiene factors are fulfilled. Source: Herzberg, F. (1964). "The Motivation-Hygiene Concept and Problems of Manpower." *Personnel Administration*, 27, 3–7. See also the textbox *The Kano model* in 6.3.

03 Burger and bank examples both from Tincher, J. (2012, May 31). "The First Key to Creating a Great Customer-Inspired Experience," at *https://heartofthecustomer.com*.

Services? Products? Experiences?

This book has the word "service" in the title, but the first few paragraphs talk about hamburgers and sports shoes. Are they services? Many business people make a big fuss about the difference between services and goods (often colloquially called "products"), and where exactly the distinction lies.

"If my company offers it, it's our product," says one. "It's only a product if you can drop it on your foot," says another. There are approaches which sidestep this discussion. Within service-dominant logic[04] you will hear that tangible goods are merely distribution mechanisms for service

provision – goods have been called "service avatars." Or, the jobs-to-be-done approach suggests that customers "hire" a certain product or service to get a specific job done.[05] Within these discussions, there are further questions around emotional, relational, and functional aspects of services and products.

In this book, the word "product" is used to describe anything a company offers – no matter if this is tangible or not. To avoid confusion, instead of "goods and services" we often talk about "physical and digital products" as well as the products we call "services."

What all these terminology discussions have in common is that customers just don't care. They pay their money (or spend their time, or give their attention, or exchange something else they value, like data or votes or permission), and they want organizations to co-create value with them – by helping them, by taking away their problems, or by realizing their goals. And while that is happening, they expect organizations to provide an experience that reaches or exceeds their expectations, fits in with their lives, and meets their emotional needs. ◄

04 See the textbox on *Service-dominant logic* in 2.1. See also Vargo, S. L., & Lusch, R. F. (2004). "Evolving to a New Dominant Logic for Marketing." *Journal of Marketing,* 68(1), 1-17.

05 See Christensen, C. M., Anthony, S. D., Berstell, G., & Nitterhouse, D. (2007). "Finding the Right Job for Your Product." *MIT Sloan Management Review,* 48(3), 38.

1.2 THE CHALLENGES FOR ORGANIZATIONS

1.2.1 Empowered customers

The digital revolution has made customers' demand for good experiences even more powerful. Where they once were often forced to take what they could get locally or find in the newspaper, they now have a huge choice. Indeed, it is often easier to buy from the other side of the planet than from the store across town. Customers have many channels for information or for purchase, even within one provider, and will switch between them at their convenience. They have more information, with price comparisons, alternative sources, trusted reviews, and a wealth of other data just a screen away.

Social media amplifies this change, as customers seize the opportunity to share experiences with potentially millions of others. Conversations online are reshaping business,[01] as users trust the words of peers far more than expensive advertising campaigns. Business-to-business (B2B) services may be less sensitive to social media, but word of mouth (WOM) seems to fulfill the same role here, with employee and customer referrals often named as the most effective sales generator.[02] Whatever the numbers, we agree that when an organization messes up, the world will be told – and people will believe what they hear.

Customer experience makes a difference to the bottom line, as plenty of studies have shown. As early as 2009, it was estimated that poor customer experiences led to $83 billion of lost business in the United States alone.[03] Companies that excel at customer experience outperform the market[04] and are are more likely to be recommended by customers and more likely to see customers return and buy again;[05] also most customers are willing to pay more if they are sure of a better experience.[06]

It seems obvious that focusing on customer experience is crucial, so why do so many organizations get it wrong? They are made up of intelligent people who are doing good jobs, but they still manage to infuriate, anger, confuse, disappoint, or simply fail to impress customers.[07] One of the answers is the way organizations are set up.

01 This was already pinpointed in *The Cluetrain Manifesto* back in 1999. See Levine, R., Locke, C., Searls, D., & Weinberger, D. (2010). *The Cluetrain Manifesto.* Basic Books.

02 Implisit, reported for example in eMarketer. "Referrals Fuel Highest B2B Conversion Rates." (2015, February 10) at *https://www.emarketer.com.*

03 See, for example, "The Cost of Poor Customer Service: The Economic Impact of the Customer Experience and Engagement in 16 Key Economies" (September 2009) Genesys, e.g., at *www.ancoralearning.com.au.*

04 See, for example: Watermark (2015). "The Customer Experience ROI Study." Retrieved from *http://www.watermarkconsult.net/docs/Watermark-Customer-Experience-ROI-Study.pdf.*

05 See, for example, Temkin Group (2012). "The ROI of Customer Experience." Retrieved from *https://temkingroup.com/research-reports/the-roi-of-customer-experience/.*

06 See, for example, RightNow/Oracle (2011). "Customer Experience Impact Report." Retrieved from *www.oracle.com.*

07 Research findings support the conclusion that customers have lost their faith in business practices. Why? "Many marketers should confess that deep in their hearts consumers are never top priority". In their book *Marketing 3.0,* Philip Kotler et al. describe the development of marketing from being product-driven (1.0) to customer-centric (2.0) to human-centric (3.0), and later also 4.0 to include every aspect of the customer's journey). This includes a shift in product management from "The Four Ps (product, price, place, promotion)" to "Cocreation." (source Kotler, P., Kartajaya, H., & Setiawan, I. (2010). *Marketing 3.0: From Products to Customers to the Human Spirit.* John Wiley & Sons, p. 31).

1.2.2 Silos

Since industrialization, through movements like Taylorism[08] and total quality management,[09] organizations have focused on operational excellence and efficiency. In a mechanistic paradigm, they have understood their activities as a series of operational processes, and looked at optimizing each individual step, usually in terms of costs. After all, cost and efficiency are fairly simple concepts that offer convenient "levers to pull" for management. Whole organizational units (we often say "silos") have been constructed around work functions that make sense to the company, with a dedicated collection of business tools set up to understand, track, and manage these functions and optimize them within the silo and from the company's perspective – not the customer's. It sometimes seems that anything outside the basic offering and the processes necessary to deliver the core value is mostly seen as an overhead, a cost center, or as a "soft factor" – something to be streamlined, cut away, perhaps left to chance or to the "soft factor specialists" in advertising and HR.

So, these organizational silos reflect many of the layers of experience, putting them in the hands of separate teams. For example, when I buy my running shoes, the advice process might be designed by the Sales department, and the salesperson's soft skills and specialist knowledge trained by HR. The salesperson will use sales and stock

systems developed by IT, explain a returns procedure drawn up by Legal, and finally sell me a pair of shoes designed by R&D or bought in by Purchasing. The situation becomes even more knotted when my relationship with the company grows longer and more silos come into play.

All these people are good at their jobs, so their work inside their silos becomes more efficient from year to year while helpless customers bounce between them. Of course, there are calls and efforts to work together – but how exactly should this happen? People in different suborganizations have their own viewpoints on what is important, their own measures of success, their own key performance indicators (KPIs). There are tools like process diagrams which can indicate the contributions of different departments to the process, but these generally only include the customer if she is necessary for part of the process, or even exclude her completely. They can be used to promote efficient cooperation between silos, but not the understanding of the effect on the consumer. Even "Voice of the Customer" charts and quotes are often so widely shared that they lose all context and real customer needs are forgotten. And crucially, there are many parts of the customer journey that are important to the customer, but which do not appear at all on traditional process visualizations. These are the parts of the journey which are not directly influenced by the organization, but which are an important part of the

08 Taylorism, or scientific management, is a production efficiency methodology from the early 20th century. It was based on dividing work into the smallest meaningful subdivisions, each of which could be measured and optimized to ensure the perfect flow of actions by the worker.

09 Total quality management is a business methodology most famous in the 1980s and 1990s that attempted to continuously improve the quality of products and services using feedback loops and the systematic analysis of work processes.

(A) Dave Carroll has been a professional singer-songwriter for over 25 years.

(B) His "United Breaks Guitars" YouTube videos are often used as an example of the impact one customer can have on a brand.

(C) Dave now speaks regularly at international conferences.

(D) Dave's book, *United Breaks Guitars*.[01]

United Breaks Guitars

BY DAVE CARROLL

I have been a professional singer-songwriter for over 25 years now, and on March 31, 2008, I was traveling to Nebraska with our band Sons of Maxwell. We'd stopped in Chicago to deplane and catch our connector when a fellow passenger looked out her window and declared, "Oh my God, they're throwing guitars out there." It turned out that my $3,500 Taylor guitar was badly damaged, and this began my entry into a frustrating customer service maze with United Airlines. After 9 months, I was told that because I did not open a claim within the first 24 hours and instead waited 5 or 6 days, United's policy of taking responsibility for the damage was excused.

I responded by promising to write three songs and create three music videos that I would post to YouTube with a goal of receiving one million YouTube views in one year, with all three videos combined. While I followed through on the promise and the "United Breaks Guitars" trilogy

was, in fact, completed in just over one year, the first video went viral immediately and reached one million views in just four days. It became the #1 music video in the world for the month of July 2009 and the center of a mainstream media frenzy. Today it has nearly 16 million views. United Airlines stock was reported to have been affected by a 10% drop in market capitalization, or a decrease of $180 million in value, and that report made the music video relevant to businesses everywhere. It was clear that social media was now more than just videos of a cat flushing a toilet. A single dissatisfied customer could affect the profitability of one of the world's most recognizable brands with a $150 music video.

My story was featured on CNN, and virtually every major Western news agency. "United Breaks Guitars" was also an inspiration to countless unsatisfied consumers and I was inundated with

thousands of encouraging and grateful emails from customers around the world.

"United Breaks Guitars" has become a textbook example of the new relationship between companies and their customers, and has demonstrated the power of one voice in the age of social media. It has become a benchmark case study in the customer service and music industries, as well as branding and social media circles. Another unexpected outcome of my story is that it led to a busy career as a speaker on the topic of customer experience, branding, and the power of story. In sharing my message in over 25 countries to date, I discovered that I am a passionate advocate that companies become more compassionate to avoid problems altogether, and I enjoy teaching others how to become more effective storytellers in today's frenetic and noisy environment. ◄

01 Carroll, D. (2012). *United Breaks Guitars*. Hay House, Inc.

customer experience – like waiting, third-party reviews, or discussions with friends.[01]

So, put a cross-functional team in a room together, and where should they start? Usually the basic tool of such cooperative attempts is the meeting, and the teams are faced with the colossal task of reconciling different worldviews and different terminologies by basically talking about it. It is no wonder that cross-functional cooperation is extraordinarily difficult, as each delegate honestly argues for his own point of view using his own specialized language.

How can we make it easier for these people to cooperate and create new value together, so that each department sees the results as its own and is invested in their success? And how can we help them to orchestrate experiences across their silos, working together to create real satisfaction?

1.2.3 The need for innovation

Most organizations feel a great pressure to innovate. They see innovation as something necessary and desirable, and prioritize it as a goal in their work. It is often closely linked to generating a unique selling proposition (USP), and the innovation might be in terms of creating unique offerings – but it might also be in the internal processes that enable those offerings or even in the business model of the organization. Whichever of these

applies, the need for innovation is driven by a changing and super-connected (business) world, an immense shortening of business cycles, and a general ubiquity of technology and information which makes it easier than ever to copy. If an offering has value and is easy to reproduce, then it will be copied directly or indirectly, legally or illegally by people who have not had the development costs and can offer it cheaper. Even if they offer it at the same price, the result is the same – commoditization. There will be two or more similar offerings on the market, and a price war will loom.

Innovation is often focused on pleasing the customer, because new features are not new for long. In various models of customer satisfaction,[02] it's clear that aspects of an offering that are initially seen as delightful soon become expected. One vivid example is wireless internet in hotels at the start of the 21st century. Initially, travelers were surprised and delighted to be able to use WiFi in hotels and were happy to pay for it. Soon, they expected to find it in every hotel, and began to grumble that the price was higher than at home. As we write, with WiFi available for free in coffee shops, cabs, and cheap buses, hotel guests "compare WiFi to hot water, electricity, or air"[03] and are often annoyed or angry to see a charge for it on their hotel bill. In terms used by proponents of the Kano model,[04] an *excitement* factor has degraded to

---

[01] Read more on proposition-centered journey maps and experience-centered journey maps in 3.3.1, *A typology of journey maps*.

[02] See Oliver, R. L. (1977). "Effect of Expectation and Disconfirmation on Postexposure Product Evaluations: An Alternative Interpretation." *Journal of Applied Psychology*, 62(4), 480 (as well as Oliver's subsequent publications). In this book, see the textbox *The Kano Model* in 6.3.

[03] White, A.C. (2015, July 6). "Free Hotel Wi-Fi Is Increasingly on Travelers' Must-Have List." New York Times.

[04] See the textbox on *The Kano model* in 6.3.

💬 COMMENT

"Every day, we all use services that are broken – and this needs to change. Service design is designing services that work."

– Lauren Currie

💬 COMMENT

"B2B companies continue to move into services as a means of growing their markets. This is especially true with traditional product companies where they are creating new service businesses – sometimes in cooperation with other organizations – to complement and/or increase the value of industrial products from jet engines and locomotives to power generation. These service businesses represent significant opportunities for many B2B companies, and a great application area for service design."

– Jeff McGrath

a performance factor and then a basic factor. Yesterday's innovation is already out of date – a new one is needed.

All this means that many organizations prioritize innovation as a key success factor. And as service becomes more and more visibly important for every business, the focus of their innovation turns to services. They attempt to meet the multilayered needs of users, not just impress with flashy new ads or product extensions.

So, today's companies look for ways to understand the needs of their customers in a way that will provide useful insights and spark interesting ideas. And they want a way to work on those ideas in cross-silo (or cross-organizational) teams, diversifying, filtering, testing, and evolving concepts until they are implemented as new or improved offerings, operations, or even business models. The innovation might be incremental or disruptive, so we need techniques that work for both of these.

1.2.4 Organizations are reacting

It's clear that many organizations today – from startups to governments – understand the importance of innovating customer experience for their success. And this awareness is growing fast. Back in 2014, one study already predicted that 89% of companies expected to be competing mostly on the basis of customer experience by 2016 – in comparison to a meager 36% in 2010.[05]

When organizations understand the importance of customer experience, they often start tracking satisfaction. The most visible tools are online and offline surveys, or the Net Promoter Score (NPS)[06] in particular, with thousands of organizations asking "How likely is it that you would recommend our company/product/service to a friend or colleague?" This valuable metric faces the challenge of many quantitative measurements: when your NPS slumps, you know that you have a problem, but not why. Strong Voice of the Customer loops and listening points can show more, but do not in themselves offer solutions. They tell you how big your problem is, and perhaps where it comes from, but not how to fix it or how to innovate.

NPS and similar metrics can help show problem areas – often they pinpoint silo thinking as a source – but there is an old adage that *weighing the goose will not make it fatter*. So, organizations are looking for new, reliable, and scalable ways to move beyond measurement and innovate experiences strategically across silos. Increasingly, they turn to what we call service design.[07]

05 Sorofman, J. (2014, October 23): "Gartner Surveys Confirm Customer Experience Is the New Battlefield," at *www.blogs.gartner.com*.

06 Reichheld, F. F. (2003). "The One Number You Need to Grow." *Harvard Business Review*, 81(12), 46-55.

07 Service design? Other people might talk about design thinking, service design thinking, new marketing, UX design, holistic UX, CX design, human-centered design, customer experience management, experience design, touchpoint management, lean UX, new service development, new product development, customer journey work, or innovation, to name a few. Others will notice similarities with lean startup and agile development methodologies. We don't care what you call it – what matters is what you do and how you do it. Still, you might want to watch out, because some people have very strong opinions about what exactly terms like service design and design thinking and all those others really mean. Other people are quite relaxed – for example, some people will use the term "service design" to refer to almost any kind of service development work, while others will point out that strictly the phrase refers to one particular approach with its historical origins in the design studio. It might get a bit tricky when these people try to have a conversation about "service design," without realizing they mean very different things. With "design thinking," the situation is even worse. Does the person mean this great approach, or that splendid version, or do they mean every way of applying design principles to business challenges? There are certainly many flavors available – fortunately! – and they all have something to offer. But dwelling on the differences is not always useful. On the whole, unless you really enjoy this kind of discussion, we think you are better off just getting on with doing it.

WHY I CHOOSE SERVICE DESIGN

PRACTITIONERS SPEAK

"Service design applies design thinking to services and focuses on doing (not just talking). Service design skills are useful because they can transform employees and managers to be truly user-centered."

– Julia Pahl-Schoenbein
Senior project leader for
business development, Germany

"I got interested because design thinking and service design put customers and users at the center of their methodology and framework – they provide a holistic view of the solution and make it easy to identify gaps in the experience."

– Musa Hanhan
Executive at a business software company, US

"I love the fast, iterative cycle of the process, and that you don't need to get it right the first time. 'Sh!tty first drafts' are powerful!"

– Soo Ren Chang
HR professional, Malaysia

"My challenge was how to collaboratively generate service ideas that work; and how to guide/facilitate that process. Service design meets these challenges."

— Carola Verschoor
Creativity and change professional, Netherlands

"The challenge I was facing was to build a coherent multi-channel service. I needed a way to visualize the stages and parts of the service in order to identify and communicate the issues, as well as trying to improve matters for all concerned. Service design answered all of this through its toolset, specifically service blueprints, user journeys, and stakeholder maps, and allowed me to bring in others to understand the overall picture. Service design also helped set a base for research that was needed and then provided guidance on how to distill that information to a manageable format."

— Stuart Congdon
Infrastructure systems executive, UK

"While service design is quite often thought of in a B2C context, I find it very useful in a B2B environment. Here, we employ service design tools such as customer journey maps and stakeholder maps for the company we are doing business with, as well as for their customers. The biggest benefit is leveraging the designer's mindset in framing the problem or opportunity. We spend a lot more time up front framing the problem, making it more likely we will design a service that results in a better experience for our customers and their customers."

— Jeff McGrath
Business advisor, US

"Service design helps policymakers focus their minds on the impact a policy is likely to have on the people who use government services. It lets us prototype policies early in the process, to learn where a policy is likely to fail, and to design improvements that we can be confident will work in the real world."

— Andrea Siodmok
Designer in government, UK

1.3 WHY A SERVICE DESIGN APPROACH?

💬 **EXPERT TIP**

"It is critical to frame the problem or opportunity carefully. Many companies fail because they address the wrong problem or miss an opportunity altogether. It seems they spend too little time framing (and asking questions) up front, resulting in a *jump* to the solution based on their biases and not on the customer's needs or desires."

– Jeff McGrath

There are many ways to create or improve the value generated by an organization. People working on this challenge might call what they do service engineering, or marketing, or quality, or simply management. A few of them – a growing minority – refer to this work as service design. They share a certain outlook and often a common toolset.[01] Service design adopts the mindset and workflow of the design process, combining an active, iterative approach with a flexible and relatively lightweight set of tools borrowed from marketing, branding, user experience, and elsewhere.

It is its patchwork background that makes service design powerful. As a design discipline, it is focused on solving the *right* problem – by framing the problem or opportunity in the right way. So service design usually starts by investigating the needs of the user or customer. It is inquiring and inquisitive, using a range of mostly qualitative research methods to explore the "how and why" of the opportunity space. Understanding needs, instead of jumping straight to a "solution," makes true innovation possible.

Next, service design adopts the designer's approach of rapid experiments and prototyping to test possible solutions quickly and cheaply while generating new insights and ideas. Prototypes evolve into pilots, and then into implemented new offerings – and along the way there is always iteration. With this strong emphasis on iterations of research, prototyping, and even implementation, service design projects have a firm foundation in reality. They are built on research and testing, not on opinion or (rapidly outdated) authority. And the iterative approach makes decision making in service design a low-stakes activity. Instead of worrying about getting it right the first time, we can evolve a range of options, and rely on the structured process of prototyping and testing to test and improve our work.

Many organizations are looking for an effective way of working which makes it easy for people with different backgrounds and responsibilities to work together meaningfully and productively – they are looking for a "silo breaker." Because the tools of service design have been filtered through a design mentality, they are visual, fast, lightweight, and easy to grasp. They form a common language for collaboration, so cross-functional teams are happy to pick them up and get on with it. The tools can look very simplistic at first sight – they make no effort to encompass the entire complexity of a service system (there are already excellent tools for that). Instead, they filter complexity through the lens of various customer experiences. This makes the approach very powerful: even complex multichannel services become manageable for the team when they can understand them on both a practical and a human, empathic level.

Service design is not only useful to create value for the "end user" or "customer." It addresses the entire value ecosystem, and might focus on offerings aimed at end users, other businesses, internal partners, or colleagues. In other words, service design works for public services, B2C, B2B, and internal services.

Service design is an intensely practical and pragmatic activity, and this makes it inherently holistic. To create valuable experiences, service designers must get to grips with the backstage[02] activities and business processes that enable the frontstage success, and address the implementation of these processes. They must tackle the end-to-end experience of multiple stakeholders, not just individual moments. And they must find a way to make it pay, considering the business needs of the organization and the appropriate use of technology.[03]

With these characteristics, it is no wonder that many organizations are implementing service design methods under whatever name, and that many more are employing service design agencies. Examples in this book alone include banks, airlines, hospitals, manufacturers, telcos, nonprofits, educational institutions, tourism operators, energy companies, governments, and more – with more organizations turning to this approach every day.

Organizations are faced with the challenge of providing new and better services and end-to-end customer experiences across multiple channels. Service design's borrowed toolset and pragmatic iterative approach uses research and sensemaking tools to focus on stakeholder needs, and prototyping to test and evolve possible solutions before making large investments. Organizations can use service design to improve the services that they offer now and to develop whole new value propositions, perhaps based on new technology or new market developments. It gives organizations a way to balance their experiential, operational, and business needs in a robust but approachable manner, offering an unusually powerful common language and toolset for projects that include, empower, and mobilize a wide range of stakeholders.

02   "Backstage" refers to processes or actions that are normally not visible to the customer, such as checking in the store room or emptying the trash. "Frontstage," then, refers to the parts of the process that a customer can see.

03   In the epilogue of their book *Marketing 4.0*, "Getting to WOW!," the authors and Setiawan state that "In a Marketing 4.0 world where great products and great services are commodities, the WOW factor is what differentiates a brand from its competitors." A WOW moment is a surprising, personal, and contagious experience a customer has. "Winning companies and brands are those that do not leave WOW moments to chance. They create WOW by design." See Kotler, P., Kartajaya, H., & Setiawan, I. (2016). *Marketing 4.0: Moving from Traditional to Digital.* John Wiley & Sons, p. 168.

O2
WHAT IS SERVICE DESIGN?

Setting out the basics: what service designers do,
and what they don't.

Expert comments ————————————————————

| Arne van Oosterom | Birgit Mager | Jeff McGrath | Mauricio Manhães |

02
WHAT IS SERVICE DESIGN?

This chapter also includes

2.1 DEFINING SERVICE DESIGN

Service design can help solve some important challenges faced by organizations. You hold a book in your hand which tells you how to do service design. But what does that term mean? It is something about customer experience, and innovation, and collaboration – but does it include everything related to those concepts, or is it just part of those worlds? Is every activity concerned with creating, planning, fixing, and shaping services part of "service design"? Do service designers even agree on what they do? Some people like to start with a definition, so in mid-2016 we asked 150 service designers to share and vote on their favorites. Here are the most popular:

→ "Service design helps to innovate (create new) or improve (existing) services to make them more useful, usable, desirable for clients and efficient as well as effective for organizations. It is a new holistic, multi-disciplinary, integrative field." – *Stefan Moritz*[01]

→ "Service design is the application of established design process and skills to the development of services. It is a creative and practical way to improve existing services and innovate new ones." – *live|work*[02]

→ "Service design is all about making the service you deliver useful, usable, efficient, effective and desirable." – *UK Design Council*[03]

→ "Service design choreographs processes, technologies and interactions within complex systems in order to co-create value for relevant stakeholders." – *Birgit Mager*[04]

→ "[Service design is] design for experiences that happen over time and across different touchpoints." – *Simon Clatworthy, quoting* servicedesign.org[05]

→ "When you have 2 coffee shops right next to each other, selling the exact same coffee at the exact same price, service design is what makes you walk into the one and not the other, come back often and tell your friends about it." – *31Volts*[06]

01 Moritz, S. (2005). *Service Design: Practical Access to an Evolving Field*. Köln.

02 live|work (2010). "Service Design." Retrieved 10 August 2010 from *http://www.livework.co.uk*.

03 UK Design Council (2010). "What Is Service Design?" Retrieved 10 August 2010 from *http://www.designcouncil.org.uk/about-design/types-of-design/service-design/what-is-service-design/*.

04 See for example "Meet Birgit Mager, President of the Service Design Network." Retrieved 3 August 2017 from *https://www.service-design-network.org*.

05 *servicedesign.org* is no longer accessible, but see Clatworthy, S. (2011). "Service Innovation through Touchpoints: Development of an Innovation Toolkit for the First Stages of New Service Development. International Journal of Design, 5(2), 15–28.

06 See 31Volts, "Service Design" (original quote from 2008 extended in 2016). Retrieved 3 August 2017 from *http://www.31volts.com/en/service-design/*.

And the most popular definition with our panel of 150 colleagues:

→ "Service design helps organizations see their services from a customer perspective. It is an approach to designing services that balances the needs of the customer with the needs of the business, aiming to create seamless and quality service experiences. Service design is rooted in design thinking, and brings a creative, human-centered process to service improvement and designing new services. Through collaborative methods that engage both customers and service delivery teams, service design helps organizations gain true, end-to-end understanding of their services, enabling holistic and meaningful improvements."[01]

– crowdsourced by Megan Erin Miller

COMMENT

"Lumpers will often argue it is all about the mindset. Being open, empathetic, asking questions, starting with 'I don't know,' and learning by doing. You can call yourself anything you like, but if you share this mindset you are a service design thinker … or rather a service design do-er."

– Arne van Oosteroom

Other names

Listen in on a group of service design practitioners – whether they consider themselves "designers" or not – and you will hear two types of conversation when it comes to terminology. Just like when paleontologists discuss taxonomy, you will find the "splitters" and the "lumpers."

The splitters will talk about the differences between service design, experience design, design thinking, holistic UX, user-centered design, human-centered design, new marketing, and even more.

The lumpers will point out that these approaches have far more in common than they have differences, and suggest that names matter far less than the principles that these practices all share. The authors of this book belong very firmly in the "lumpers" camp. Honestly, we don't care what you call it, as long as you are doing.

Many service design tools are mind hacks that help us reframe problems in a way that humans can handle better. We shape slippery data into human forms and visual stories which we can understand from any viewpoint – technical, specialist, or simply empathic. Instead of designing complex systems directly, we try to answer simple "How might we …?" questions. And rather than trying to interpret each other's words, we communicate by building prototypes.

01 Miller, M. E. (2015, December 14). "How Many Service Designers Does It Take to Define Service Design?" at *https://blog.practicalservicedesign.com*.

2.2 DIFFERENT VIEWS

Service design can be explained in many ways. In different situations, each of these can be useful – or misleading. Each one, however, is only part of the picture.

2.2.1 Service design as a mindset

If a mindset is a collection of attitudes that determine our responses to various situations, service design can easily be thought of as the mindset of a group of people or even an entire organization. A group with a service design mindset will talk about users first, will see "products" as the avatars of a service relationship, will respond to asserted assumptions by suggesting some research, will reject opinions and endless discussion in favor of testing prototypes, and will not consider a project finished until it is implemented and already generating insights for the next iteration. As a mindset, service design is pragmatic, co-creative, and hands-on; it looks for a balance between technological opportunity, human need, and business relevance.

2.2.2 Service design as a process

Design is a verb, so service design is often described as a process. The process is driven by the design mindset, trying to find elegant and innovative solutions through iterative cycles of research and development. Iteration – working in a series of repeating, deepening, explorative loops – is absolutely central, so practitioners aim for short cycles at the outset, with early user feedback, early prototyping, and quick-and-dirty experiments. As the process continues, the iteration may slow down but it never goes away, as prototypes iterate into pilots and pilots iterate into implementation.

2.2.3 Service design as a toolset

Ask anyone to imagine service design, and they will usually imagine a tool – perhaps a customer journey map hanging on the wall, or simply people pointing at sticky notes. Those templates and tools sum up service design in many people's thoughts. Talk about tools seems to dominate talk about service design, so it's tempting to imagine service design as a sort of toolbox, filled with fairly lightweight and approachable tools adopted from branding, marketing, UX, and elsewhere. This is not the whole story, by any means – without a process, mindset, and even common language, those tools lose much of their impact and may even make no sense. Used well, however, the tools can spark meaningful conversations; create a common understanding; make implicit knowledge, opinions, and assumptions explicit; and stimulate the development of a common language.

One of the main aims of service design, or design thinking, or whatever we call it, is to break down silos and help people co-create. Do we want to set up our own silos at the same time, saying "This is service design," "That is design thinking," "This is UX," and so on? That makes no sense.

2.2.4 Service design as a cross-disciplinary language

💬 **COMMENT**

"Everyone likes to focus on processes and toolsets because they can see, touch, and use them. But without the service design *mindset*, people go right back to employing the processes and tools just like they used BPM and other 'improvement' approaches. Then they end up with the same internally focused solutions with the same awful customer experiences they have today."

– Jeff McGrath

Service design is almost dogmatically co-creative, and many practitioners pride themselves on their ability to connect people from different silos, bringing them together around some seemingly simple tools that they all find meaningful and useful. These tools and visualizations – sometimes called *boundary objects*[01] – can be interpreted in different ways by the different specialists working on them, allowing them to collaborate successfully without having to understand too much of each other's worlds. They are simple enough to be easily – even empathically – understood, yet robust enough to provide a good working foundation. In this way, service design can be seen as a common language or even "the glue between all disciplines,"[02] offering a shared, approachable, and neutral set of terms and activities for cross-disciplinary cooperation.

2.2.5 Service design as a management approach

When service design is sustainably embedded in an organization, it can be used as a management approach to both the incremental innovation of existing value propositions and radical innovation for completely new services, physical or digital products,[03] or even businesses. An iterative service design process always includes collaborative work in a series of loops. In this way, service design as a management approach has some similarities to other iterative management processes.[04] However, service design differs through using more human-centric key performance indicators, more qualitative research methods, fast and iterative prototyping methods for both experiences and business processes, and a specific approach to leadership. Its inclusion of internal stakeholders and view across the customer journey often results in changes to organizational structure and systems.[05]

[03] The term "products" describes anything a company offers – no matter if this is tangible or not. In academia, products are often divided into goods and services. However, products are usually bundles of services and physical/digital products. As "goods" is colloquially understood as referring to something tangible, we prefer to speak of physical/digital products. Read more on this in the textbox on *Service-dominant logic* in 2.1.

[04] Compare a service design process, for example, with the iterative four-step "PDCA" (Plan–Do–Check–Adjust, or sometimes also Plan–Do–Check–Act) management process. This is often used in business for project management and the continuous improvement of processes, products, or services. While both PDCA and service design processes describe an iterative sequence, PDCA focuses on improving defined KPIs that can be measured quantitatively. This means iterations only occur from loop to loop, but not within a loop. A design process, however, does not restrict iterations at any moment.

[05] Read more on this in Chapter 12, *Embedding service design in organizations*.

[01] See the textbox *Boundary objects* in 3.2.

[02] Arne van Oosterom on design thinking, as written on the wall at the Design Thinkers premises in Amsterdam.

2.3 ORIGINS AND PROGRESS

People – especially ones with a design school background – often speak of service design as if the term included all activities involved in planning and designing services. But if we look at the history of service design, we see that it is just one approach to working on services, one which grew out of design methodology in the 1990s and 2000s and was developed by designers. Crucially, service designers represent only one of many professions that create and shape services, including systems engineering, marketing and branding, operations management, customer service, and "the organization."

That list of important service makers comes from Brandon Schauer of Adaptive Path, who back in 2011 did some rough calculations[06] and estimated that around $2 billion was spent each year in the United States on the planning and design of services, but only $70 million (about 3.5%) of this was spent on "service design." The other 96.5% of the work was done by people who did not consider themselves service designers, and had possibly never heard the term.

Things are changing. More recently, customer experience has become overwhelmingly important for many organizations, and design (more usually, "design thinking") has become a key innovation and management methodology. Sitting firmly at the intersection of design thinking and customer experience, service design is now more visible than ever. Service, as it is traditionally defined, is often said to make up the lion's share of most developed economies.[07] And design is the process of making sure something fits its purpose – so service design can potentially be applied to the shaping of much of human activity. At the very least, it has a place in incremental and radical service development, in innovation, in the improvement of services, in customer experience work, in education, in empowerment, in government, and in the strategy of organizations.

COMMENT

"Today, design plays a major role in solving wicked problems. Organizations are trying to use the capabilities of design to move beyond the given and to infuse a different way of working and thinking into systems.

Often referred to as *design thinking* or *service design,* commercial organizations all over the world hire design agencies, build in-house capacities, and merge with and buy design agencies. They create innovation labs and change the physical working environment to foster and symbolize a new way of thinking and working."

– Birgit Mager

---

06 Brandon Schauer, presentation at SDN conference San Francisco 2011 and available at Schauer, B. (2014). "The Business Case for (or Against) Service Design," at *https://www.slideshare.net*.   07 From the point of view of service-dominant logic, it's basically everything.

2.4 WHAT SERVICE DESIGN ISN'T

Even in closely related fields, there is confusion about what service design should and can do. So here are a few things which service design certainly is not.[01]

2.4.1 It is not simply aesthetics or "putting lipstick on a pig"

The aesthetics of a service are not unimportant, but they are not the primary focus of service design. Service designers are much more concerned with whether a service works, whether it fulfills a need and creates value, than details of what it looks or sounds like. The aesthetics can be a part of those questions, but only a part.

Service design does not only address superficial, "cosmetic" aspects of services – the frontend, or the usability. In fact, service design looks not just at how a service is experienced, but also how it is delivered and even whether it should exist. It almost always goes far beyond the visible, to challenge and reshape everything from operations to the business model.

2.4.2 It is not simply "customer service"

"Customer service" – the cliché in stock photos is a toothsome model with a headset – could be the subject of a service design project. We could look at the customer needs and how the hotline specialist fulfills them, how she fits into the structures of her organization, what technology she uses to help customers, and how she creates value for the organization. But we would also ask ourselves how the company's offering might be better delivered to make her task unnecessary or unrecognizable. Service designers do not (only) solve customer problems; they design value propositions, processes, and business models.

2.4.3 It is not simply "service recovery"

Service design does not only come into play when things go wrong. It is not an "after sales" cost center or optional extra. Service design addresses the entire customer or employee journey, from becoming aware of a need all the way to becoming a regular customer or leaving the service relationship. It asks what service should be offered, how it should be experienced, and yes, even what happens when things go wrong. But it is fundamentally concerned with creating services that people value, not just repairing mistakes.

01 Ask Adam about the term "service design" and he will say, "I hate-hate-hate the term. It's made up of two simple words which most people misunderstand. 'Service,' they think, is being nice to customers, or fixing stuff. And 'design,' of course, is making things look nice. So 'service design,' they think, must be ... something which involves being nice to customers and making things look nice. So they smile, and nod, and walk away."

2.5 THE PRINCIPLES OF SERVICE DESIGN, REVISITED

2.5.1 The original

In the 2010 prequel to this book, *This is Service Design Thinking*,[02] the authors collected five principles of service design thinking which have been widely quoted (and misquoted) ever since. Should they be re-examined? The principles were:

1   User-centered: Services should be experienced through the customer's eyes.

2   Co-creative: All stakeholders should be included in the service design process.

3   Sequencing: The service should be visualized as a sequence of interrelated actions.

4   Evidencing: Intangible services should be visualized in terms of physical artifacts.

5   Holistic: The entire environment of a service should be considered.

Many of these principles have stood the test of time quite well, though they have evolved with the evolution of service design. Others bear re-examination.

Service design remains a highly "**user-centered**" approach. Some people ask, "What about the employees?" But in the 2010 version of the principles, the term "user" referred to any user of a service system, certainly including customers and staff. It might be clearer to say "human-centered," clearly including the service provider, the customer and/or the user, as well as other stakeholders and even non-customers who are impacted by the service.

In choosing the word "**co-creative**," the authors included two different concepts. One was the technical meaning of "co-creation" in terms of the value generated by services – a service only exists with the participation of a customer, so value is *co-created* together. The second concept was the idea of "co-design" – the process of creation by a group of people, usually from different backgrounds. People who practice service design have concentrated on this latter meaning.[03] They emphasize the collaborative and cross-disciplinary nature of service design, and the power of service design as a language to break down silos.

COMMENT

"Services are co-created, in the sense that different stakeholders are involved in innovating services. Working together, understanding the way people perceive services, how they use them and how they would love to use them is a driver for change."

– Birgit Mager

02 Stickdorn, M., & Schneider, J. (2010): *This is Service Design Thinking*, Amsterdam: BIS Publishers.

03 Many designers use the terms "co-creation" and "co-design" interchangeably. If in doubt, it's best to ask for more detail.

With the term "**sequencing**," we were reminded of the key role of the experience in service design, and of the interplay and relationships between the various moments, steps, or "touchpoints"[01] that make up a service experience. Journey mapping is still the most visible and well-known tool in the field. The term "sequencing" is an unusual one which causes some people to stumble. In everyday conversations, the more common word "sequential" is often adopted.

"**Evidencing**" was an acknowledgment of the intangibility of many parts of a service offering, and of how we can draw attention to the value created by a service, even if the activity takes place out of sight. The classic example of evidencing has always been the folded toilet paper in a hotel bathroom, signaling to you that your room has been cleaned since the last visitor was there. Evidencing – showing value – remains an important role and motor of service design, connecting it strongly to branding.

"**Holistic**" was another choice that combined several concepts in one word. One was the relevance of all our senses to an experience; another was the wide variety of individual journeys that one service can engender; the last was the relevance of service design to the corporate identity and goals of the organization. Today, the word "holistic" is often used to remind us that service designers aspire to shape the entirety of a service, not just patch individual problems (though that might be a good starting point). They also aim to address the complete needs of the customer, not only superficial symptoms.

2.5.2 The new

So what is missing in the original five principles? What has changed in service design, which is not shown here?

One key characteristic of the service design approach which we cannot see in these principles is the emphasis on *iteration* – starting with small, cheap attempts and experiments, allowing them to fail, learning from the failure, and adapting the process along the way. This is often hard for people to grasp, as many of us come from a decide-plan-do background. It is an essential characteristic of a design-led approach.

Another missing point might be service design's pragmatic foundation on research and prototyping, not on opinions or lofty concepts. It is an essentially practical approach, as we can see when Stanford colleagues describe design thinking as having a "bias toward action," or when participants at jamming events[02] wear T-shirts emblazoned with "doing, not talking" in many languages.

But perhaps the most important point not explicitly listed in 2010 is the imminent and central need for service design to be relevant to business. Although it is based on creating better experiences, it does this by understanding backstage processes and technological opportunities as well as the business goals of the organization. No service design can be successful or sustainable if it does not make sense on the spreadsheet, as well as in the sketchbook.

---

01 See the textbox *Steps, touchpoints, and moments of truth* in 3.3.

02 The Global Service Jam (*http://www.globalservicejam.org*), an international volunteer-run design event that takes place in around 100 cities each year, has played an important part in disseminating the service design approach worldwide.

So we offer the new principles of service design doing:

1 **Human-centered:** Consider the experience of all the people affected by the service.

2 **Collaborative:** Stakeholders of various backgrounds and functions should be actively engaged in the service design process.

3 **Iterative:** Service design is an exploratory, adaptive, and experimental approach, iterating toward implementation.

4 **Sequential:** The service should be visualized and orchestrated as a sequence of interrelated actions.

5 **Real:** Needs should be researched in reality, ideas prototyped in reality, and intangible values evidenced as physical or digital reality.

6 **Holistic:** Services should sustainably address the needs of all stakeholders through the entire service and across the business.

Service design is a practical approach to the creation and improvement of the offerings made by organizations. It has much in common with several other approaches like design thinking, experience design, and user experience design, has its origins in the design studio, and harmonizes well with service-dominant logic.[03] It is a human-centered, collaborative, interdisciplinary, iterative approach which uses research, prototyping, and a set of easily understood activities and visualization tools to create and orchestrate experiences that meet the needs of the business, the user, and other stakeholders.

03 While we often refer to service-dominant logic in this book, we do not understand this as a school of thought superseding other theories, but rather as a valuable component within a growing, changing, and patchy body of knowledge. As Achrol and Kotler say: "Some philosophers like Popper, Feyerabend, and Lakatos forcefully argue for theoretical diversity and against dominant paradigms [...]. Popper (1959) points out that because we never know for certain that our theories are correct, we should proliferate our theories as much as possible to encourage the growth of scientific knowledge." Achrol, R. S., & Kotler, P. (2006). "The Service-Dominant Logic for Marketing: A Critique." In R. F. Lusch & S. L. Vargo (eds.), *The Service-Dominant Logic of Marketing: Dialog, Debate, and Directions* (pp. 320-333). M.E. Sharpe, p. 331.

**The evolution of the principles
of service design**

2010

1. USER-CENTERED

Services should be experienced through
the customer's eyes.

2. CO-CREATIVE

All stakeholders should be included in
the service design process.

3. SEQUENCING

The service should be visualized as a
sequence of interrelated actions.

4. EVIDENCING

Intangible services should be visualized in
terms of physical artifacts.

5. HOLISTIC

The entire environment of a service
should be considered.

2017

1. HUMAN-CENTERED

Consider the experience of all the people
affected by the service.

2. COLLABORATIVE

Stakeholders of various backgrounds and functions should be
actively engaged in the service design process.

3. ITERATIVE

Service design is an exploratory, adaptive, and experimental
approach, iterating toward implementation.

4. SEQUENTIAL

The service should be visualized and orchestrated as a
sequence of interrelated actions.

5. REAL

Needs should be researched in reality, ideas prototyped in reality,
and intangible values evidenced as physical or digital reality.

6. HOLISTIC

Services should sustainably address the needs of all stakeholders
through the entire service and across the business.

Service design and service-dominant logic: A perfect match

BY MAURICIO MANHÃES

Whatever economic sector an organization operates in, its core activity is service. Whether it produces screws, shampoos, cars, or chairs, its product is a service. All these products are created through service design processes, whether organizations are aware of it or not.

To better understand these statements, we need to get to know service-dominant logic, proposed back in 2004 by marketing professors Steven Vargo and Robert Lusch.[01]

Service-dominant logic

Service-dominant logic (SDL) is more than a snapshot of the current world context. It presents an interesting review of human economic history, showing clearly that "services are the beginning, middle and end"[02] of all economic activity. SDL offers 11 foundational premises, which are grouped under 5 insightful axioms as a general framework to understand service (singular, as the common trait among all products) and services (plural, as the output of specific service provisions).

These five axioms are:

1 Service is the fundamental basis of exchange.

2 Value is co-created by multiple actors, always including the beneficiary.

3 All social and economic actors are resource integrators.

4 Value is always uniquely and phenomenologically determined by the beneficiary.

5 Value co-creation is coordinated through actor-generated institutions and institutional arrangements.[03]

Put briefly, the axioms let us see all products as service, blurring the boundaries between tangible or intangible products (1). They help us understand that value can only be created through the interactions of multiple actors, which include and go beyond the obvious direct customer and the service provider (2). We also see that any service is only made possible by all the actors providing resources for it, not only the service provider (3). Products (goods and/or services) have no intrinsic values, only the ones perceived by a beneficiary (4). Finally, the co-creation of value only occurs through the coordination of human-created institutions and institutional arrangements (5).

01   Vargo, S. L., & Lusch, R. F. (2004). "Evolving to a New Dominant Logic for Marketing." *Journal of Marketing*, 68(1), 1–17.

02   Bastiat, F. (1964). "Selected Essays on Political Economy," (1848), Seymour Cain, trans, George. B. de Huszar, ed. Reprint, Princeton, NJ: D. Van Nordstrand.

03   Institutions are rules, norms, meanings, symbols, practices, and similar aides to collaboration. Institutional arrangements are assemblages of interdependent institutions. See Vargo, S. L., & Lusch, R. F. (2016). "Institutions and axioms: an extension and update of service-dominant logic." *Journal of the Academy of Marketing Science*, 44(1), 5–23.

What does this serve for?

To help understand the axioms, let's take a look at one apparently simple product: a chair. When someone comes into contact with any object for the first time, what question does he ask? Probably "What is this for?" or "What does this serve for?" Right? So, what does a chair serve for? Is it just a separate seat for one person? Must it have a specific form, with a back and four legs? And what if a "chair" is not meant to be a seat, but is a historical object or a work of art? Is it still a "chair"? These kinds of questions can go on indefinitely.

At the end, it turns out to be surprisingly difficult to define any object precisely. Most likely, when people try to describe an object, they do it through the perceived services provided by it. It's almost impossible to objectively define any object without tapping into the possible potentials for action that we perceive it offers us. In other words, without understanding the set of possibilities of services that can be

What, exactly, is a "chair"?
It's an orchestra of possibilities, different for each beneficiary.

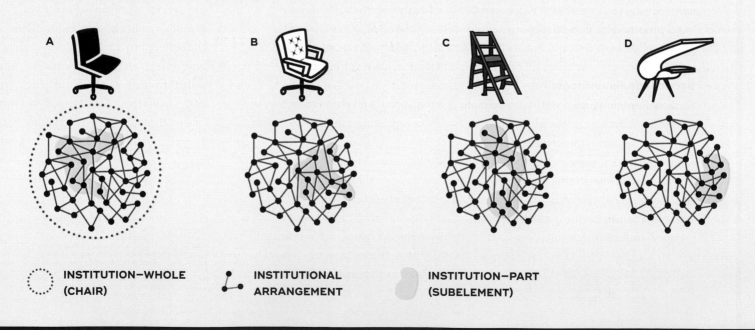

INSTITUTION—WHOLE (CHAIR)

INSTITUTIONAL ARRANGEMENT

INSTITUTION—PART (SUBELEMENT)

provided by a certain "object," it is not even possible to understand it. So, when the plain word "chair" is used by someone, it really represents an orchestra of possibilities, a large number of potential services, different for each beneficiary.

As shown in the picture, a chair can represent (A) an ergonomic support for working hours, (B) a symbol of status, (C) a ladder, or (D) a work of art. Are they all "chairs"?

By going back to the axioms, it becomes possible to understand a chair by understanding its potential to act – that is, the services it provides (1). These services can only be co-created by a concerted effort of a multitude of actors, like designers, engineers, production managers, decorators, salespeople, shop owners, and influencers – always including a specific beneficiary (2). As a matter of fact, a vast array of social and economic actors must integrate all sorts of resources to enable every product (good and/or service) that exists (3). What exactly each of these products is can only be determined by the perception of a specific beneficiary (4). In all these cases, the potential services that a product provides can only be understood as a designated coordination of institutions and institutional arrangements (5). Basically, this is why all existing products were created by a service design process, whether intentional or unintentional.

Service design

So, as well as offering an interesting review of human economic history with service at its center, SDL also sheds light on the role of service design. Specifically, it's possible to build a definition of service design on axiom 5, stating that "service design is the process of coordinating designed institutions and institutional arrangements to enable the co-creation of value."[01]

Therefore, for various reasons, SDL is the perfect match for service design. SDL's constant development continues to shed light on several important aspects relating to service as a broad concept, and also on specifics of service design. As well as providing a consistent discourse to understand service, it also guides us to perceive any product (good and/or service) as an orchestra composed of a large number of players and instruments, of a large number of potential services. It makes the effort to designate innovative arrangements for it far clearer and more effective. In other words, it provides an immense creative energy for service design to create service innovations. This is one of the major contributions made by SDL to service design. ◄

01 This is an interesting definition of service design, because it puts together a particular set of concepts: 1. "value co-creation" focuses service design on enabling value co-creation; 2. "coordination" establishes service design as a coordination process; 3. "institutions" acknowledges institutions and institutional arrangements as the fundamental and intangible structures of all designed products; and 4. "actor-generated" permits us to define design, understood as a process that delivers evolutionary actor-generated results, as the ideal process to create institutions and institutional arrangements.

THE 12 COMMANDMENTS OF SERVICE DESIGN DOING

1 CALL IT WHAT YOU LIKE

Service design? Design thinking? Service design thinking? Customer-centric innovation? It doesn't matter what you call it. It matters that you do it.[01]

2 MAKE SH!TTY FIRST DRAFTS

Don't waste time on making early versions beautiful. In the early parts of a project, you are going for quantity, not quality. Ideas don't need to be complete, just good enough to be explored and thrown away. The more beautiful you make them, the harder they are to abandon. So be sh!tty, not pretty.[02]

3 YOU ARE A FACILITATOR

Your clients' knowledge beats yours – so keeping a diverse team of employees, experts, and even customers working together is the best thing a service designer can do. Help them by embracing mind hacks. Shape customer data into personas; explain processes as stories; break complex ideation down to "How might we …?" questions; build it, don't describe it. Hack tasks into units you can deal with rationally and instinctively, but never forget the true complexities.[03]

4 DOING, NOT TALKING

Opinions are great, and everyone always has at least one. But service design is based in reality. Instead of talking about something for a long time, build stuff, test it, understand what needs to be improved, build it again. Show me, don't tell me. Stop comparing opinions, start testing prototypes.[04]

5 "YES, BUT …" AND "YES, AND …"

To open up your options and get some rough ideas to work on, use divergent thinking and methods ("Yes, and …"). To close down and get real, use a convergent approach ("Yes, but …"). Both of these are valuable. Design your own design process as a sequence of diverging and converging methods. And change your group cooperation patterns to fit what you are trying to do.[05]

6 FIND THE RIGHT PROBLEM BEFORE SOLVING IT RIGHT

When we see a problem, we want to jump right in and create a solution. But are we tackling the real problem, or just a symptom of something deeper? Get out on the street and challenge your assumptions with research, before you consider how to change things.[06]

7 PROTOTYPE IN THE REAL WORLD

Ideas always work in our heads (or in shiny presentations), and we always love our own ideas too much. Forget "good ideas" – aim for plenty of ideas and build good experiments to test and evolve those ideas through prototyping.[07] Get out of the studio as soon as you can, moving on to interactive prototypes that you can explore and test with real users in the original context of your service.

8 DON'T PUT ALL YOUR EGGS IN ONE BASKET

Triangulate your research with different research methods, researchers, and data types. Go for a big pile of ideas, not just one "killer" idea. And never, ever, have just one prototype. Prototypes are made to fail, and to teach you by failing.[08]

9 IT'S NOT ABOUT USING TOOLS; IT'S ABOUT CHANGING REALITY

A new journey map does not mark the end of a service design project. An ideation workshop is not co-design. A survey of your employees does not reveal their real needs. Just like building a house shouldn't end with an architect's plan, a service design project shouldn't end with ideas on paper.[09]

10 PLAN FOR ITERATION; THEN ADAPT

Service design is explorative, so you can never plan exactly what you will be doing each day. But you will need to plan your time investment and financial budget – so make plans that are flexible enough to allow you an adaptive and iterative process in the time you have.[10]

11 ZOOM IN AND ZOOM OUT

As you iterate, keep switching your focus between small details or momentary exchanges, and the holistic service experience.

12 IT'S ALL SERVICES

You can apply service design to anything – services, digital and physical products, internal processes, government offerings, employee or stakeholder experience … It's not just about making "customers" happy.[11]

01   See Chapter 2, *What is service design?*, and Chapter 12, *Embedding service design in organizations.*

02   See Chapter 6, *Ideation*, Chapter 7, *Prototyping*, and Chapter 10, *Facilitating workshops.*

03   See Chapter 3, *Basic service design tools*, Chapter 9, *Service design process and management*, and Chapter 10, *Facilitating workshops.*

04   See Chapter 10, *Facilitating workshops.*

05   See Chapter 4, *The core activities of service design*, and Chapter 10, *Facilitating workshops.*

06   See Chapter 4, *The core activities of service design*, and Chapter 5, *Research.*

07   See Chapter 4, *The core activities of service design*, and Chapter 7, *Prototyping.*

08   See Chapter 5, *Research*, Chapter 6, *Ideation*, and Chapter 7, *Prototyping.*

09   See Chapter 8, *Implementation*, Chapter 9, *Service design process and management*, and Chapter 12, *Embedding service design in organizations.*

10   See Chapter 4, *The core activities of service design*, Chapter 9, *Service design process and management*, and Chapter 12, *Embedding service design in organizations.*

11   See Chapter 1, *Why service design?*, Chapter 3, *Basic service design tools*, Chapter 7, *Prototyping*, and Chapter 8, *Implementation.*

03
BASIC SERVICE DESIGN TOOLS

A toolbox gathered from various disciplines, combined to research, create, prototype, and test services.

Expert comments —————————

Alexander Osterwalder   Hazel White   Mike Press

03
BASIC SERVICE DESIGN TOOLS

TOOLS VS. METHODS

In this book, we differentiate between tools and methods.

Tools are concrete models, such as journey maps, spreadsheets, and storyboard templates. They usually follow a specific structure or are built on given templates.

Methods are particular procedures to accomplish or approach something, such as conducting contextual interviews as a research method or doing desktop walk-throughs as a prototyping method.

Tools represent "what" we use, while methods usually describe "how" we create and work with certain tools in service design projects, such as interviewing, synthesizing, and prototyping. This chapter introduces some of the basic tools we use in service design. We describe what these tools look like, their structure, their components, alternatives you have for these tools, and when and why you can use them. On this basis, Chapters 5–8 give detailed instructions on various methods that explain how to work with these tools in a service design project.

This chapter also includes

3.1 RESEARCH DATA

Research data is one of the core tools of service design. Data is made up of facts that can be collected, synthesized, interpreted, and analyzed to answer research questions, to communicate findings, or even to help to predict future outcomes. Research activities collect countless facts, observations, and a variety of materials. This empirical data can be divided into raw data and interpreted data, also called first-order and second-order concepts, respectively.[01] Raw data is any data collected during research that has not been filtered by a researcher, such as pure statistics like how many people enter a shop or videos of customers using a product.[02] Raw data describes a situation without reflecting interpretations of the data by a researcher.

Interpreted data, on the other hand, includes the researcher's attempts to explain or understand the raw data. It summarizes patterns that researchers see in raw data or underlying concepts they find. As interpreted data reflects the reasoning of the researcher, it is affected by the researcher's education, beliefs, and experience – but also by potential cognitive biases the researcher has. Interpreted data should be backed up by sufficient raw data to minimize potential cognitive biases.

Although researchers should strive to be agnostic during their research, it is almost impossible to collect completely unbiased data. Every decision from the moment a researcher plans the fieldwork – the sampling, the methods applied, and so on – is a conscious or unconscious choice that influences the dataset and ultimately the research results.

> **EXPERT TIP**
>
> "As a design researcher you should *own* your bias. Be explicit about the values that determine your research agenda. And think of data collection as a process that is as creative as design itself."
>
> **— Mike Press**

TYPES OF RAW DATA
(first-order concepts)

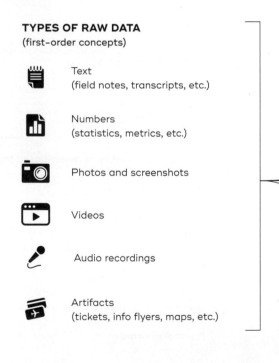

Text
(field notes, transcripts, etc.)

Numbers
(statistics, metrics, etc.)

Photos and screenshots

Videos

Audio recordings

Artifacts
(tickets, info flyers, maps, etc.)

---

01 More on first-order and second-order concepts can be found in 5.1.3, *Data collection*.

02 The term "products" describes anything a company offers – no matter if this is tangible or not. In academia, products are often divided into goods and services. However, products are usually bundles of services and physical/digital products. As "goods" is colloquially understood as referring to something tangible, we prefer to speak of physical/digital products. Read more on this in the textbox *Service design and service-dominant logic* in 2.5.

EXAMPLES OF INTERPRETED DATA
(second-order concepts)

JOB-TO-BE-DONE

When I have to travel for business

situation

I want to **lose as little time as possible**

motivation, forces

so that I can **maximize my work time.**

expected outcome

KEY INSIGHTS

Alan

persona, character, role

wants **to eat less chocolate**

action, situation

because **it makes him fat**

aim, need, outcome

but **it makes him feel safe.**

restriction, obstacle, friction

USER STORIES

As **a regular customer of SaaS products**

persona, role, type of user

I want **invoices to be sent directly to my accounting**

action

so that **I don't have to care about this every month.**

outcome

RESEARCH REPORTS

Assumption–based vs. research–based tools

The first thing you should do when you have to work with a tool prepared by someone else (e.g., a journey map or persona) is to ask whether it is based on research or on mere assumptions. If it just based on assumptions, challenge it.

Recognizing whether the content of tools used in service design is based on assumptions or based on research helps you to understand how solid and credible a piece of work is. In particular, when you look at work by others, this factor indicates how much you should challenge what you see. Pinpointing the research behind the contents of a tool, for example as footnotes or a caption, increases the credibility of the content. Typically, the research statement contains all the important aspects of the underlying research design, including which research methods were used, how many interviews or observations were conducted when and where, and whether basic rules of theoretical saturation and triangulation were applied.[01]

The information expressed using any service design tool, such as personas, journey maps, system maps, Business Model Canvases, and many more, can be based on assumptions or research.

→ **Assumption-based**

The content of these tools is based on assumptions and not research data. The quality of the information depends on the creator's knowledge of the subject matter. Often, you can further distinguish between tools that are made "ad hoc," a quick sh!tty first draft mostly used for research planning, and tools that have been created during a co-creative workshop. The quality of the latter can be quite good, if the people who participated in the workshop have profound knowledge of the subject matter and the workshop was properly facilitated.

→ **Research-based**

The content of these tools is based on research data. If the research was done properly, research-based tools have a greater significance than assumption-based tools. Often assumption-based tools develop into research-based tools over time, as assumptions are challenged and research gaps are identified and closed through iterative research loops. This needs more time and resources, but of course tools that are made to represent the current state of something are more robust and closer to reality if they are derived from real research. ◄

01   Read more on this in 5.1, *The process of service design research.*

3.2 PERSONAS

A persona is a profile representing a particular group of people, such as a group of customers or users, a market segment, a subset of employees, or any other stakeholder group. This profile is not a stereotype, but is an archetype based on real research. Personas, although fictional, help make groups with similar service needs more understandable. However, note that people with specific service needs and goals will not necessarily align with traditional segments in marketing. Rather, the needs expressed in personas will often cut across several groups, thus breaking down marketing silos that may hinder service design efforts. Whenever possible, personas should be based on research and represent a group of people with shared needs or common behavior patterns.[02]

Personas can be used to share research findings and insights within your team and outside your team, across different departments or even across organizations. They are "characters" with which design teams can engage, and can serve as boundary objects to align an interdisciplinary team.[03] They help a team to get onto the same page, to build empathy with customer groups, and to step into the shoes of different stakeholders, understand their needs, and review their tasks. Personas are a useful reference throughout the whole design process. They can develop into shared, empathic descriptions of a company's

customer or target groups, described in a form that everyone can work with. Some companies even have life-sized cardboard cutouts of their personas. They can bring them to meetings to include a certain perspective.

(A) Portrait image

A representative photo or image. Avoid using images of celebrities to prevent prejudice and to increase authenticity. Alternatively, gender-, age-, and ethnicity-neutral sketches or photos showing common attributes, goals, motivations, tasks, or behaviors can be used to avoid stereotypical assumptions.

(B) Name

A name often reflects a persona's heritage and social environment. Sometimes, archetypes are added as subheadings or used as an alternative to describe the represented stakeholder or target group.

(C) Demographics

Demographic information, such as age, gender, or geographics, gives context to a persona and immediately creates a specific image of a certain target group for a design team. This often also leads to stereotypical assumptions, so it should be used carefully. Demographics are often less meaningful for target group segmentation than they initially appear and in fact can be misleading when predicting tastes or behavior.

> 💬 **EXPERT TIP**
>
> "Personas should have an *expiry date* of around 12 months. In a year, a lot can change in terms of technology, organisational, and policy shifts – and you don't want to design based on old data."
>
> **– Hazel White**

02 For a case study on how to use personas in a service design project, see 5.4.3, *Case: Developing and using valuable personas.*

03 See the upcoming textbox *Boundary objects* for more details.

PERSONA

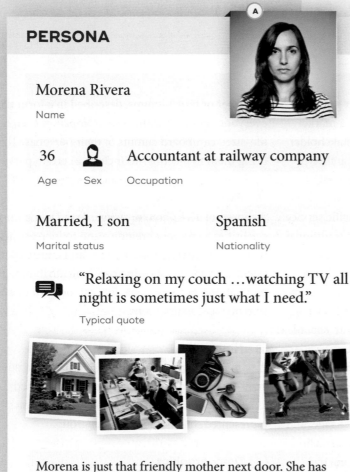

Morena Rivera
Name

36   **Accountant at railway company**
Age   Sex   Occupation

Married, 1 son   **Spanish**
Marital status   Nationality

💬 "Relaxing on my couch …watching TV all night is sometimes just what I need."
Typical quote

Morena is just that friendly mother next door. She has a secure job at the national railway company. Together with her husband Marco, she earns a monthly income of 5,000 after tax. Marco loves the outdoors, so whenever possible, the couple takes long hiking tours with Josh, their nine-year-old son. **Morena is not very interested in technology, she wants things to just work.**

General description

20,000   **24 %**   **3**   **377**

D Quote

A quote summarizes your persona's attitude in one sentence. This is easy to remember and helps team members to empathize quickly with a persona.

E Mood images

These photos or sketches enrich a persona with context. They illustrate a persona's environment or behavior patterns, as well as goals and motivations. One common type of contextual image shows items that personas always have with them in their pocket, purse, or bag. Mood images can also be used to add illustrative material to a written description.

F Description

The description can reveal characteristics, personality, attitudes, interests, skills, needs, expectations, motivations, goals, frustrations, brands or technologies the persona likes, or background stories. This information should include details that are important in the context of the research question or the company the persona is related to. Try to avoid using personas that don't have information relevant to the specific design challenge or research question.

G Statistics

Visualized statistics summarize relevant quantitative information. Representative statistics can increase the reliability of a persona – in particular when used in a more quantitative-based management or marketing context. Statistics can be a starting point for personas or used to substantiate the more qualitative descriptions.

Boundary objects

"Boundary objects are objects which [...] have different meanings in different social worlds but their structure is common enough to more than one world to make them recognizable, a means of translation. The creation and management of boundary objects is key in developing and maintaining coherence across intersecting social worlds."[01]

Sometimes people with different skills can understand each other better if they have a common artifact to look at.

Let's take the example of a journey map. A service design team comprised of an expert in service design, a business person, and a software developer will probably all see different things in the map: opportunities for a better experience, chances for cross-selling, or potential technology challenges. The interesting fact is that all three of them are looking at the same journey map, but each of them can extract what they need for their part of the project – information which might not be explicit in the journey map itself, but which

their specialist eyes can see. While all of them look at the same object, they all identify different problem areas, come to different conclusions, and generate different ideas. In this case, the journey map acts as a "boundary object." It helps people from different backgrounds and communities of practice[02] to collaborate on a common task.[03]

Boundary objects work best when they employ language and models that are easily understood across disciplines and functions. The artifacts act as a simple language, providing a unified form of communication across stakeholders. The service design tools

presented in this chapter can be used as boundary objects during various activities in the service design process for different purposes. However, they do not always necessarily serve as boundary objects continuously. While boundary objects are useful to co-create a shared understanding of a concept, at some point specialists also need to work within their own domain using their own technical language. Some of these service design tools can be used with very discipline-specific (technical) language that others do not understand. To bring their specific work back to the entire design team, specialists can modify existing service design tools or create new ones that serve again as boundary objects with a common language that is accessible for everyone. ◄

01 Star, S. L., & Griesemer, J. R. (1989). "Institutional Ecology, Translations' and Boundary Objects: Amateurs and Professionals in Berkeley's Museum of Vertebrate Zoology, 1907–39." *Social Studies of Science*, 19(3), 387–420.

02 Wenger, E. (1998). *Communities of Practice: Learning, Meaning, and Identity.* Cambridge University Press.

03 Rhinow, H., Köppen, E., & Meinel, C. (2012, July). "Prototypes as Boundary Objects in Innovation Processes." *Proceedings of the 2012 International Conference on Design Research Society*, 1–10.

3.3 JOURNEY MAPS

💬 **EXPERT TIP**

"Journey maps are the most flexible tool we use with clients. We use them in three ways:

1. To visually and transparently gather user stories when interviewing.

2. To understand how existing services work and uncover pain points and opportunities for improvement.

3. To envision future services."

— Hazel White

A journey map visualizes the experience of a person over time. For example, an end-to-end customer journey map can visualize the overall experience a customer has with a service, a physical or digital product, or a brand. This might include recognizing a need, searching for a specific service, booking and paying for it, and using the service, as well as maybe complaining if something goes wrong, or using the service again.

As a human-centered tool, journey maps not only include steps where a customer is interacting with a company, but reveal all the key steps of an experience. Journey maps help us to find gaps in customer experiences and explore potential solutions. They can be used to visualize existing experiences as well as potential future experiences. Just as a movie is structured as a sequence of scenes, a journey map is structured as a sequence of steps (often also referred to as events, moments, experiences, interactions, activities, etc.).

Journey maps can have various scales and scopes, and you will usually need several to represent different aspects of one experience or service: from a high-level map showing an end-to-end experience, to more detailed maps focusing on one step of a higher-level journey, to very detailed step-by-step descriptions of micro-interactions. The idea of different scales applies to any map. For example, when you are driving your car across the country, you need a larger-scale map showing the main express routes between cities. But when you get to your destination you need a smaller-scale street map to find a particular street and building.

Different "zoom" levels of journey maps work just like this. A journey map can show 30 years of a mortgage-loan experience including searching for a house, signing contracts, living in the house, and making loan payments until the loan is paid off. Another one can zoom in even further and only illustrate a one-hour consultation meeting in detail. You can include different types of information in maps, depending on their purpose. When you compare different geographic maps, they might share some general information, but also contain very specific data. For example, street maps might highlight data you need to drive, nautical maps will contain information for sailing, or mining maps will show exact positions of mineral resources. You can find similar patterns in journey maps. They can contain specific information for different purposes, while sharing general data.

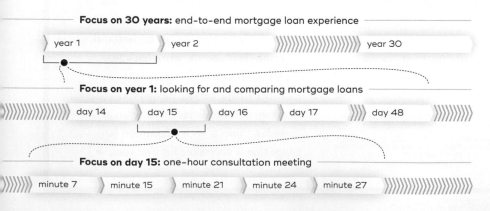

Focus on 30 years: end-to-end mortgage loan experience

| year 1 | year 2 | year 30 |

Focus on year 1: looking for and comparing mortgage loans

| day 14 | day 15 | day 16 | day 17 | day 48 |

Focus on day 15: one-hour consultation meeting

| minute 7 | minute 15 | minute 21 | minute 24 | minute 27 |

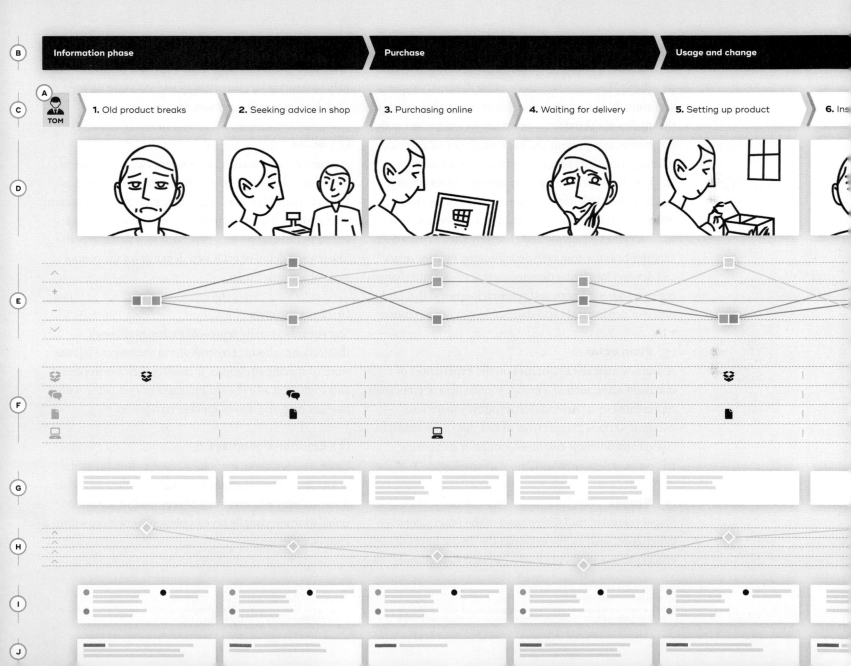

Information phase

Purchase

Usage and change

TOM

1. Old product breaks

2. Seeking advice in shop

3. Purchasing online

4. Waiting for delivery

5. Setting up product

6. Ins

Journey maps make intangible experiences visible and facilitate a common understanding between team members. They are a way to visualize data in a simple and empathic way, but the quality of any map depends on the quality of the data it is based on. Journey maps make no attempt to represent the full complexity of a service offering with all its options, such as decision trees or "if/then" loops. Instead, a journey map shows one typical or particularly interesting instance of a service. It forms a boundary object[01] that allows diverse teams to work together efficiently and creatively with a customer's experience as the common denominator. Journey maps can develop into living documents that evolve and change over several workshops and research loops and that bridge different departments and stakeholders in organizations.[02]

(A) Main actor

A journey map always focuses on the experiences of one main actor, such as a group of customers or employees represented by a persona. Some journey maps also combine various perspectives in one map – for example, comparing different customer groups or comparing customer experiences with those of employees.

(B) Stages

Stages represent the main phases of the main actor's experience, such as, for example, the classic buyer decision process stages of "Problem/Need Recognition,"

"Information Search," "Evaluation of Alternatives," "Purchase Decision," and "Post-Purchase Behavior." Stages help to structure a journey map and visualize its scale. Each stage normally contains several steps.[03]

(C) Steps

A journey map visualizes experiences as a sequence of steps from the perspective of the main actor. A step is any experience the main actor has, such as an interaction with another person, a machine, or a digital interface; but steps can also be activities, such as walking or waiting. The level of detail of each step depends on the overall scale of a journey map.

(D) Storyboards

Storyboards visually represent each step through illustrations, photos, screenshots, or sketches to tell the story of specific situations, including their environment and context. A storyboard increases our empathy with a journey map and allows quicker navigation.

(E) Emotional journeys

Emotional journeys are graphs representing the main actor's level of satisfaction at each step, often on a scale from −2 (very negative) to +2 (very positive). An emotional journey visually reveals obvious problems within a specific experience.

---

01 See the textbox *Boundary objects* in 3.2.

02 For case studies on how to use journey maps in service design projects, see 5.4.4, *Case: Illustrating research data with journey maps*, as well as 5.4.5, *Case: Current-state (as-is) and future-state (to-be) journey mapping*.

03 See Engel, J.F., Kollat, D.T., and Blackwell, R.D. (1968). *Consumer Behavior*, 1st ed., New York: Holt, Rinehart and Winston.

(F) Channels

Channels refer to any means of communication involved at a specific step, such as a face-to-face interaction, a website, an app, a TV advertisement, or a print advertisement. Specifying which channels the main actor is using helps us understand cross-channel experiences. A high-level map showing all possible channels provides a comprehensive overview of alternative end-to-end journeys.

(G) Stakeholders

A list of stakeholders involved at each step of a journey map reveals which internal or external stakeholders are part of – or even responsible for – certain steps. This helps you to identify potential key actors that should be included in research, prototyping, and implementation.

(H) Dramatic arc

A dramatic arc illustrates the level of the main actor's engagement at each step – for example, from 1 (very low) to 5 (very high). Such arcs of tension are a common concept in storytelling used in theater, movies, and books; in service design these arcs are often used to reflect on the pace and rhythm of an experience.

(I) Backstage processes

Backstage processes connect frontstage experiences visualized as steps of the main actor with backstage processes that are often visualized as flowcharts. Backstage processes reveal which departments and systems are involved or triggered at specific steps. A journey map that includes backstage processes can provide the same information as a service blueprint. Often there are overlaps or hybrids of these two tools.

(J) What if?

The "What if?" lane asks at every step, "What could possibly go wrong?" This helps to check if appropriate service recovery systems are in place. Important scenarios or problems that happen can then be visualized as separate journey maps.

Job to be done

The lane for jobs to be done (JTBD, sometimes also called user/customer jobs) describes what a particular service or product, whether physical or digital, helps the customer to achieve – either for the entire journey map or for specific steps of it. This helps to move away from the current solution and create a new frame to look for opportunities or to discover steps that do not provide value to a customer, but only exist due to the provider's processes.

Conversion funnel

A conversion funnel visualizes conversion rates between relevant steps – for example, how many people enter a shop, how many take a look at a specific product, how many interact with staff, and how many actually buy it. Conversion analyses can be done for on- and offline journey maps. They reveal at which step the main actor leaves a certain process and prompt questions for further research into why the actor leaves at this specific moment.

Dramatic arcs

Dramatic arcs (more usefully, "arcs of tension") are a well-known lens in the world of show business. They describe the sequence and rhythm of high and low engagement in a piece or performance. From Aristotle to Hollywood to dance club DJs, insiders know that the dramatic arc can make or break the experience.

But let's talk services: considering the dramatic arc of a service journey can give us new insights into how it is experienced and why users might value or reject it. By marking moments of high and low engagement[01] along a journey map, we can visualize the dramatic arc of an experience, and use it to understand the experience and focus our ideation.

The classic "boom-wow-Wow-WOW-BOOOM"[02] arc of a Bond film (or rock concert) is strikingly similar to the arc of a

commercial experience like an ocean cruise or a visit to a Disney park, as you can see in the figure. It is a great example of how successful arcs work, with a strong beginning ("Boom!"), rising engagement with breaks for breath ("wow!, Wow!, WOW!"), very strong crescendo ("BOOOM!!"), and a closing human moment ("Ah …"). In the wild, you will encounter many other arcs – the possible variations are infinite, and many work well while others flop.

Service experiences also have dramatic arcs which are often unique, but which can benefit from analysis and variation even if they do not fit a common pattern. It's important to remember that high engagement does not only come at exciting, loud, or "flashy" moments. A very quiet moment can be highly engaging too, if it is very relevant to the customer (or audience). Crucially, a high point on the dramatic arc is not necessarily "good" and a low point is not necessarily "bad." The height of the dramatic arc represents *engagement*, not satisfaction.

We might think of a high value as "thrill" and a low value as "chill." Both have their place – it is the interplay which makes the difference.

Try adding a visualization of the dramatic arc to your journey map. Is it overloaded? Frontloaded? Are early promises fulfilled? Are the periods of low or high engagement too long? Must a highlight be added, or – this is often more practical – should a less engaging step be spotlighted to increase engagement and show value more clearly? Compare the arc with a visualization of the emotional journey. If a moment is unsatisfying (a low dip on the emotional journey) *and* also highly engaging (a high peak on the dramatic arc), this is especially dangerous. For example, it's annoying if a waiter spills soup on you at the diner (low satisfaction, low engagement). But if a waiter spills soup on your dress on your wedding day (low satisfaction, very high engagement), it's a catastrophe. Ideally, your most pleasing experiences will be at moments of high engagement. ◄

---

01 These can be identified by observing customers' body language and facial expressions, by using survey techniques, or even using physical measurements (like lie detectors – this method is, of course, highly intrusive). Often, it is useful enough for ideation purposes if a team looks at the journey map and honestly – perhaps even cynically – assesses the user's engagement at each step.

02 For more on dramatic arcs and 007, see Lawrence, A. & Hormeß, M. (2012). "Boom! Wow. Wow! WOW! BOOOOM!!!: James Bond, Miss Marple and Dramatic Arcs in Services." *Touchpoint* (4)2.

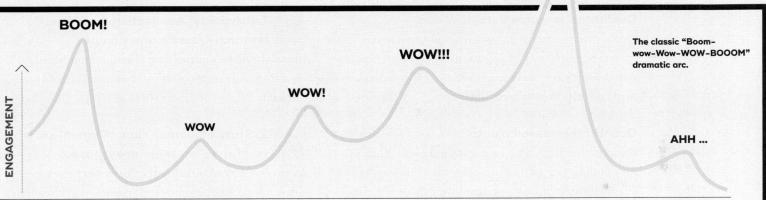

BOOOM!!!

BOOM!

WOW!!!

WOW!

WOW

AHH ...

The classic "Boom-wow-Wow-WOW-BOOOM" dramatic arc.

ENGAGEMENT

	First stunt scene	Credits and briefing	New location and risk	New location	James in danger	New location	James in danger	Enter evil headquarters	Save the world		James fails at the end
JAMES BOND	First stunt scene	Credits and briefing	New location and risk	New location	James in danger	New location	James in danger	Enter evil headquarters	Save the world		James fails at the end
CRUISE SHIP	Arrival and first ball	Sleeping in private cabin	Visit port, evening shows	Sleeping in private cabin	Visit port, evening shows	Sleeping in private cabin	Visit port, evening shows	Sleeping in private cabin	Captain's ball and dinner	Sleeping in private cabin	Goodbyes, ship departs
DISNEY PARK	View down Main St	Short pee break	Visit interesting Weenie	Shop and eat	Visit interesting Weenie	Shop and eat	Visit interesting Weenie	Shop and eat	Big parade and fireworks		Stream out, talk with strangers

SOME SHOWBIZ DRAMATIC ARCS ALSO SEEN IN CUSTOMER EXPERIENCES:

1 The Epic
(slow start, engaging crescendo) can be seen in house building services or cosmetic surgery. Like in Tolkien's *Lord of the Rings* book, the slow start may lead to doubt and abandonment of the project.

2 The Miss Marple
(thrilling mystery at the opening, slow middle building to an exciting reveal at the close) resembles a well-designed educational offering, where an engaging start or "taster" of future highlights carries us over the mid-term routine toward our final exams.

3 The Soap Opera
(regular, smaller arcs punctuated by thrilling "season finales") is very similar to the arc of your local Irish pub (Saturday, Saturday, Saturday, St Patrick's Day!), a church (Sunday, Sunday, Sunday, Easter!), or your phone contract (bill, bill, bill, new phone!).

Qualitative research data

Qualitative research data – such as quotes from customers or employees, observations from researchers, or videos, photos, and screenshots – enriches a journey map and improves its credibility.

Quantitative research data

Quantitative data such as statistics and metrics of, for example, satisfaction surveys for specific steps or channels can improve the reliability of a journey map and substantiate qualitative research data.

Custom lanes

Further lanes can be added to visualize project-specific content; for example, key performance indicators (KPIs), references to other journey maps or documents (files, links, etc.), responsibilities, or indicators of reliability (assumption-based vs. research-based).

3.3.1 A typology of journey maps

Even though most journey maps share the described structure, you will still find a wide variety of different types of journey maps. What a journey map represents, its quality, its focus, and its level of detail depend on many factors.

The following list summarizes four useful factors worth considering when you create a journey map or when you need to evaluate or work with journey maps created by others.

1. Reliability: Assumption-based vs. research-based journey maps

Always check if a journey map is assumption-based or research-based, as this is one of the crucial factors for its reliability.[01]

2. State of journey map: "Current-state" vs. "future-state" journey maps

A journey map can visualize the current experience (a "current-state" journey map) or can be used to visualize future experiences (a "future-state" journey map).[02]

Current-state maps describe how someone experiences an existing service or physical/digital product. Current-state journey maps are mostly used to find gaps in an existing experience and identify opportunities to improve services and physical or digital products. They can serve as boundary objects between team members or departments of an organization, between diverse members of an interdisciplinary co-creative team, or between an agency and its client to clearly communicate the gaps within the customer experience.

Future-state journey maps visualize the potential experience someone might have with a not-yet-existing service or physical/digital product. Future-state journey maps help people to imagine, understand, and even experiment with the potential experience and context of use. They can help to select which aspects or specific steps should be prototyped and tested.

01 See the textbox *Assumption-based vs. research-based tools* earlier in this chapter for more details.

02 See 5.4.5, *Case: Current-state (as-is) and future-state (to-be) journey mapping,* for an example of how to use both current-state and future-state journey maps in a service design project.

COMMENT

"Journey maps represent powerful boundary objects that enable conversations about services. In fields such as healthcare where communication can be challenging, they can move clinicians and patients toward mutual understanding."

– Mike Press

3. Main actor/perspective: "Customer" vs. "employee" journey maps

Although journey maps are mostly used to visualize customer experiences, they can also be used to visualize experiences of other stakeholders such as employees. Well-motivated staff is a key factor in delivering good customer experiences, so considering the employee experience can be a very valuable exercise. An employee journey map might cover the daily routines or monthly sales cycle, and strive to understand how the employee experience could be enhanced.

Other journey maps actually combine the experience of a customer with the experience of an employee. Here, interactions between customer and employee become visible as well as the employee actions that take place backstage (e.g., while the customer is waiting). On the other hand, these combined journey maps can also help to reveal problems customers experience during activities beyond the reach of employees – for example, what do customers do when they have to wait for an hour while their car is repaired?

4. Scope and scale: High-level vs. detailed journey maps

One of the biggest questions when creating journey maps is how to select the scale: Where do you start? Where do you end? What should you focus on? Which "zoom level" should your map have?

This depends on where you are in your project and why you are creating that specific journey map. If your journey map is being made to structure your research, you will probably want it to be quite comprehensive. But if your goal is to communicate an idea or a problem, it can be useful to concentrate on a key part that tells you a lot about the needs of the customer and how your idea meets them. This can give a powerful emotional message, which is why storytellers like filmmakers concentrate on key scenes.

Just as a play or movie can show us a lifetime in a few selected scenes, a journey map can show many of the overarching values and the tone of voice of a service using a partial view. The scale of a customer journey could range from a few seconds (think of the check-in experience a hotel) to some decades (think of the end-to-end experience of a property loan). The more you zoom out, the longer the experience you illustrate – though with less details. The more you zoom in, the shorter the time span becomes of the experience you illustrate, but with more details. Often this is not an "either/or" decision, but you have to constantly move between different zoom levels.

5. Focus: Product-centered vs. experience-centered journey maps

A product (or provider/brand)-centered journey map is a journey map containing only touchpoints[03] – in other words, only steps representing an interaction between a customer with a service, physical or digital product, or brand. These journey maps leave out all steps outside the reach of a company. In some cases, product-centered

03 See the textbox *Steps, touchpoints, and moments of truth* in 3.3.

journey maps are useful to visualize a specific and rather detailed experience, such as the onboarding experience to a piece of software, or to visualize a very high-level experience, such as a customer lifecycle map. Sometimes, however, these journey maps arise because people create them as if their customers think about nothing else than their company. For example, an energy provider might create a journey map for how new customers sign up for their electricity services when they move into their region. If they only map out touchpoints (collect information on the website, sign up online, receive and sign a contract, etc.) without considering all the other steps their customers have to do while they are moving home (packing, moving in, creating a redirection order for their former postal address, etc.), the map will miss many potential problems and opportunities, and clearly will not reflect the situational context.

Experience-focused journey maps reflect the situational context and show how touchpoints are embedded in the overall experience. In many cases, using a service or product is not the main goal of a customer. You probably know the famous saying by Harvard marketing professor Theodore Levitt: "People don't want to buy a quarter-inch drill. They want a quarter-inch hole." But in fact, people rarely want a hole in the wall either; they want a comfortable living room. To achieve this goal, they need to do a series of activities, such as agreeing on a painting with their partner, buying that painting, drilling a hole in the wall, and screwing in a hook to hang up the painting. Focusing only on the drill or the painting or the hook would miss the main point of why people use these items.[01]

Referring to the electricity example, people simply don't want to "become a customer" or handle any of these things. They probably only want to have light at home when they turn on the switch. An experience-centered journey map can lead to better insights about what people really want to achieve and not only how they interact with a company.

This also changes the design challenges companies strive to solve. For example, instead of just asking "What is the onboarding experience for our customers?" (a more product-centered question) we move to questions like "What is the overall experience of people moving house?" "What is the role of the energy provider in this context?" and "What is the role of an energy provider in this context in comparison with other basic infrastructure providers, like water, gas, phone, internet, etc.?" (a more experience-centered question).

6. Lanes and level of depth: Adding various lanes in journey maps

Journey maps can be enhanced by a variety of optional lanes. The lanes outlined in this chapter are just some examples without any claim to comprehensiveness. Which ones are useful depends on the subject matter of the project, and often lanes must be altered to serve the project's purpose.

---

01 Often this is visualized through an additional *Job-to-be-done* or *User/customer jobs* lane in a journey map.

Experience-centered journey maps visualize the overall experience from a customer perspective (e.g., moving from one apartment to another). In contrast, **product-centered** journey maps only focus on touchpoints, the interaction between a customer and a product/service/brand.

EXPERIENCE-CENTERED JOURNEY MAP

Decision	Preparation		Move		Set up utilities		
Renting new apt	Planning move	Changing utilities	Packing boxes	Moving belongings	Receiving package	Setting up phone	Reading m

PRODUCT-CENTERED JOURNEY MAP

We have no idea	Purchase of new phone contract		We have no idea	Installation at home		Troublesh
	Comparing online	Purchasing online		Receiving package	Plugging in phone	Calling se

3.3.2 Service blueprint

Service blueprints can be understood as an extension of journey maps. They are set up to specifically connect customer experiences with both frontstage and backstage employee processes as well as support processes.[01] "Frontstage" refers to people and processes with which the user has direct contact. "Backstage" represents people and processes that are invisible to the user. Support processes are activities executed by the rest of the organization or external partners.

A service blueprint builds on the frontstage experience visualized in a customer journey map, but adds layers of depth showing relationships and dependencies between frontstage and backstage processes. It illustrates how activities by a customer trigger service processes and vice versa: how internal processes trigger customer activities.

A service blueprint can also detail the processes of single departments or even employees/roles and how these processes are connected with each other and with customer activities. Moreover, a service blueprint illustrates physical evidences that show up in specific steps, such as tickets or receipts.

(A) Physical evidences

Physical evidences are physical objects that customers come in contact with and that can be designed. Besides tangible artifacts, messages that are delivered through non-physical channels (such as email, SMS, or interactive voice response systems) are often included here.

(B) Customer actions

Customer actions describe what a customer does at each step of a customer journey map. A customer action can include multiple physical evidences. They can be connected to both frontstage and backstage interactions when a customer action triggers a frontstage or backstage process or when a process results in a customer action.

(C) Line of interaction

The line of interaction divides customer actions and frontstage interactions. If a customer interacts with a frontline employee, the blueprint shows a connection across the line of interaction.

(D) Frontstage actions

This lane shows the activities of frontline employees that are visible to the customer. Optionally, different frontline employees can be detailed out to describe their various activities – these are often visualized as individual swimlanes.

(E) Line of visibility

The line of visibility separates frontstage and backstage actions by frontline employees. If a frontline employee goes backstage, what he does next is shown in the backstage action lane. If a frontline employee interacts with

---

01 One often-cited scholarly publication on service blueprints is Stostack, G. L. (1984). "Designing Services That Deliver." *Harvard Business Review*, 62(1), 133–139. Another is Bitner, M.J., Ostrom, A. L., & Morgan, F. N. (2008), "Service Blueprinting: A Practical Technique for Service Innovation," *California Management Review*, 50(3), 66–94. For an example of a service blueprint, see 5.4.1, *Case: Applying ethnography to gain actionable insights.*

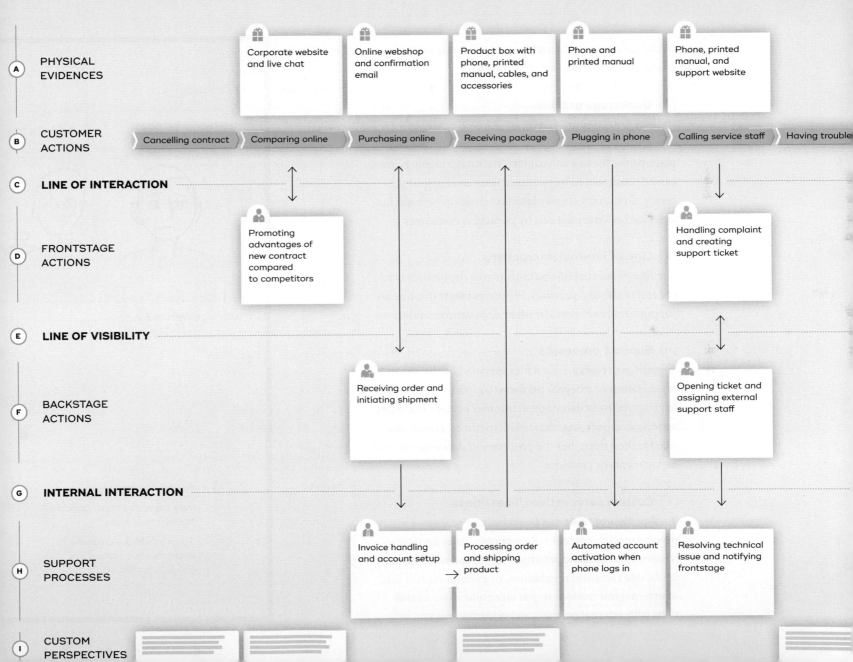

A PHYSICAL EVIDENCES

Corporate website and live chat

Online webshop and confirmation email

Product box with phone, printed manual, cables, and accessories

Phone and printed manual

Phone, printed manual, and support website

B CUSTOMER ACTIONS

Cancelling contract › Comparing online › Purchasing online › Receiving package › Plugging in phone › Calling service staff › Having trouble

C LINE OF INTERACTION

D FRONTSTAGE ACTIONS

Promoting advantages of new contract compared to competitors

Handling complaint and creating support ticket

E LINE OF VISIBILITY

F BACKSTAGE ACTIONS

Receiving order and initiating shipment

Opening ticket and assigning external support staff

G INTERNAL INTERACTION

H SUPPORT PROCESSES

Invoice handling and account setup

Processing order and shipping product

Automated account activation when phone logs in

Resolving technical issue and notifying frontstage

I CUSTOM PERSPECTIVES

backstage or support employees, the interaction in the blueprint crosses the line of visibility.

(F) Backstage actions

Backstage actions are activities by frontline employees that are not visible to the customer; these activities take place below the line of visibility. Backstage interactions can be connected to frontstage actions and support processes. Optionally, a swimlane visualization here might describe backstage actions by particular employees.

(G) Line of internal interactions

The line of internal interactions marks the boundary to the rest of the organization. Processes below this line are support processes done by other departments and teams.

(H) Support processes

Support processes are activities executed by the rest of the organization or external partners. Support processes can be triggered by or can trigger customer actions, frontstage actions, and backstage actions. Sometimes, a swimlane visualization describes the processes of different external departments or partners.

(I) Custom perspectives/lines/lanes

Further lines or lanes can be added to visualize project-specific content – for example, lanes for digital frontend and backend activities, lists of technical systems, applicable rules and regulations, or even an explicit line of external interactions to put an emphasis on interactions with external partners and organizations.

(A) ⟶

1. Old product breaks

2. Seeking advic

(A) All of these are steps.

(B) Very important steps are called "moments of truth."

(C) Steps in which a customer interacts with a brand are called "touchpoints."

Steps, touchpoints, and moments of truth

A journey map describes an experience as a sequence of steps from the perspective of one main actor. The main actor can be, for example, a user, a customer, an employee, a target group, a persona, and so on. Not all of these steps are interactions with a brand. Often, important things happen outside the reach of a brand. To differentiate between these, clear language is helpful. Unfortunately, there are no generally accepted definitions for these terms and sometimes even people within a team talk at cross purposes. This is how some of the core terms regarding journey maps are used in this book.

Steps

A step is any experience the main actor has. A step can be, for example, a conversation with another person, an interaction with a machine, or using a digital interface; but steps can also be activities, such as walking or waiting. The level of detail of each step depends on the overall scale of a journey map. Sometimes a step might comprise experiences of several days (e.g., waiting for the delivery of an ordered item), while other times a step might represent only a few seconds (e.g., greeting the receptionist).

Touchpoints

All interactions of a customer with a brand are called "touchpoints."[01] These touchpoints can involve different channels, such as watching an advertisement on TV or reading more about a product online. Touchpoints can be direct, such as calling a hotline or retrieving information from a company website, or indirect, such as reading reviews on third-party websites.

Moments of truth

Steps that are decisive for a user, customer, or organization are often called "moments of truth" (MoT).[02] These are steps in which the impression of a customer changes regarding a brand, service, or physical or digital product – for example, when a customer first hears about a new product (driving expectations) or sees a product in real life for the first time (driving anticipation), or when a customer uses a product for the first time (comparing expectations with actual quality and customer experience). ◄

01   The term "touchpoint" has been used in branding literature since the early nineties to describe any point of contact between a customer and a brand. In a literature review on service design, Jeff Howard summarizes when the term was first used and how it developed in service design. Read more on this in Howard, J. (2008). "On the Origin of Touchpoints," at *http://designforservice.wordpress.com*.

02   Note that our definition of "moments of truth" differs from its original meaning. The term was originally coined by Richard Normann in the 1980s and later popularized by Jan Carlson see Carlson, J. (1987). *Moments of Truth: New Strategies for Today's Customer-Driven Economy.* Ballinger). While Carlson refers to a MoT as any interaction a customer has with a business, the meaning of MoT has developed since this time. There are dozens of online articles and conference discussions on this topic. We follow the common use, where moments of truth are only those critical touchpoints where customers have a high involvement; ones that can make or break their overall experience.

3.4 SYSTEM MAPS

A system map is a visual or physical representation of the main constituents of the system in which an organization, a service, or a digital/physical product is embedded. They can include a huge variety of constituents, such as people, stakeholders, processes, structures, services, physical products, digital products, channels, platforms, places, pathways, insights, causes, effects, KPIs, and more. System maps are usually visualized on paper, as physical models, or as constellations with real people.

A visualization of a system usually takes a specific perspective at a specific moment in time. As ecosystems change over time, either several maps are needed to represent different states of a system or a dynamic approach can be used to illustrate changes over time.

By visualizing all the main components of a system, the interplay between these can be analyzed and designed. Complex systems become more comprehensible when they are visualized, which is particularly useful for wicked design problems. System maps can be used to map out not only existing ("current-state") systems, but also various scenarios of future ("future-state") systems to understand the impact of decisions, new components, or changed relationships. A system map can be used to find or predict intended or unintended benefits as well as disadvantages in the system. Affected stakeholders can be revealed and involved early in a project to increase buy-in and chances of success.

"System map" is a collective term for different visualizations that are often based on systems theory and/or systems thinking. The names of these visualizations may vary depending on your background or organization. The following three types of system maps are often used in service design:[01]

→ **Stakeholder maps**

A stakeholder map illustrates the various stakeholders involved in a specific experience. These maps can be used to understand who is involved, and how these people and organizations are connected.

→ **Value network maps**

A value network map is an extension of a stakeholder map. It illustrates the network of value exchanges between stakeholders. Value network maps are used to understand the flow of values, such as money, goods, services, information, or trust.

→ **Ecosystem maps**

An ecosystem map is a further extension of a stakeholder map or value network map. These maps are used to visualize complex systems that involve various constituents, such as humans, machines, interfaces, devices, platforms, systems, and so on, as well as their relationships and interdependencies.

01 Besides the three types of system maps described in this book, there are many more, such as process maps, flowcharts, or technical maps. Depending on your project, it might make sense to also use one of these other types.

3.4.1 Stakeholder maps

A stakeholder map illustrates the various stakeholders involved in an experience. It basically answers the question: "Who are the most important people and organizations involved in an experience?" By representing different customer groups or personas, frontstage and backstage employees or departments, partner organizations, as well as other stakeholders that might have a direct or indirect impact on the experience, the interplay between these various groups can be charted and analyzed. Stakeholder maps help us to understand which stakeholders are involved in this ecosystem, help to reveal existing relationships between these stakeholders and identify informal networks or frictions between stakeholders, and help us to find unseen business opportunities.

During a customer journey, customers interact with various internal and external stakeholders. Often customers don't realize which stakeholders are involved as they interact with websites, apps, machines, platforms, and more, not thinking about who is responsible for maintaining these systems and who is involved in handling their information.[02] Stakeholder maps enable a design team to actively redesign a system by adding or eliminating certain stakeholders; by creating, changing, or eliminating relationships between stakeholders; or by deliberately strengthening or weakening relationships.

💬 COMMENT

"Even quick-and-dirty system maps are useful in both suggesting cause and effect and – perhaps more importantly – where we have gaps in our understanding and need to do more research. They highlight our knowledge – and our ignorance!"

– Mike Press

1 Sectors

The background of a stakeholder map depends on the purpose. A simple and very generic option is to have three circles representing different stakeholder groups: (A) customers, (B) internal stakeholders, and (C) external stakeholders. Alternatively, the three circles could refer to the level of impact stakeholders have: (A) essential stakeholders, (B) important stakeholders, and (C) other stakeholders.

2 Stakeholders

Stakeholders are positioned on the map in a particular sector and can be arranged according to departments or groups (e.g., depending on how customers perceive them). Customer-centered organizations often put the customer in the center of a map, but depending on the purpose of the stakeholder map it can also be centered around a specific department for projects on internal services or around a specific employee for projects on employee experience.

3 Relationships

Relationships between stakeholders are visualized and should be detailed out in a description. Relationships can illustrate both formal and informal networks; they can show which stakeholders act as a hub or bottleneck in a system, and also reveal formal and informal decision-making authority or power structures.

---

02 Often stakeholder maps are derived from a journey map. This is why some journey maps include a lane for stakeholders.

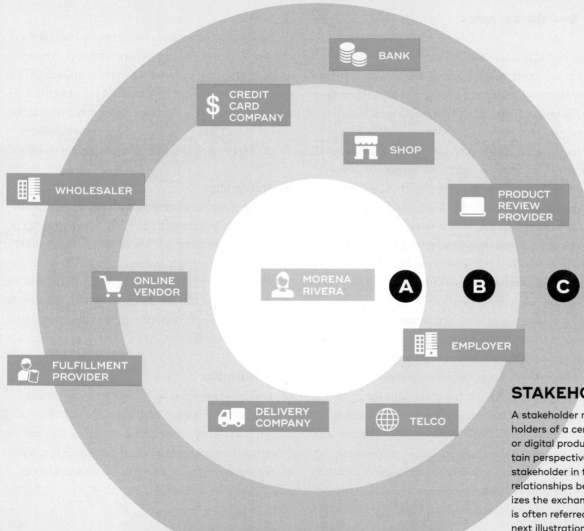

BANK

CREDIT
CARD
COMPANY

$

SHOP

WHOLESALER

PRODUCT
REVIEW
PROVIDER

ONLINE
VENDOR

MORENA
RIVERA

A B C

FULFILLMENT
PROVIDER

EMPLOYER

DELIVERY
COMPANY

TELCO

STAKEHOLDER MAP

A stakeholder map visualizes all major stakeholders of a certain experience, service, physical
or digital product, or system. It takes a certain perspective, often exemplified through the
stakeholder in the center of the map. You can add
relationships between actors. If a map visualizes the exchange of values between actors, it
is often referred to as a value network map (see
next illustration).

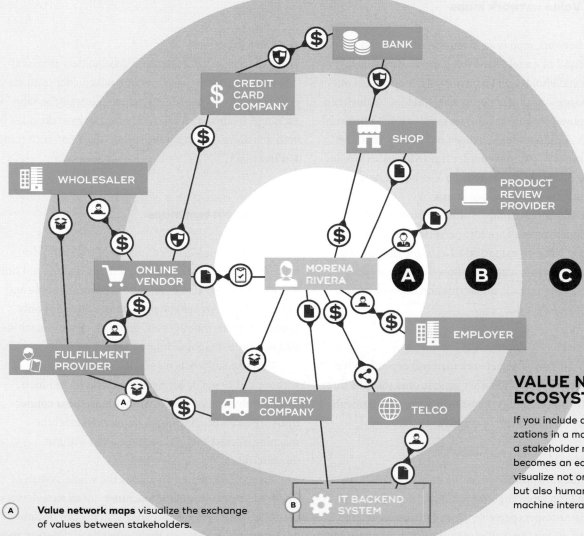

VALUE NETWORK MAP/ ECOSYSTEM MAP

If you include actors beyond people and organizations in a map, such as "IT Backend System," a stakeholder map or value network map becomes an ecosystem map. This allows you to visualize not only human–human interactions, but also human–machine and machine–machine interactions.

(A) **Value network maps** visualize the exchange of values between stakeholders.

(B) **Ecosystem maps** can include actors beyond classic stakeholders (people and organizations), such as interfaces, platforms, systems, places, etc.

3.4.2 Value network maps

A value network map is an extension of a stakeholder map. Instead of merely describing the relationships between stakeholders, a value network map details out the exchange of value between stakeholders. "Value" can refer to physical products and services as well as financial values. A simple value exchange could be: stakeholder A gives money to B, stakeholder B provides a service in return to A. Values exchanged can also be less tangible, such as information, trust, or status.

Like stakeholder maps, value network maps visualize systems from a specific perspective at a specific moment in time. In extension to a simple stakeholder map, value network maps can show the flow of values through a system, such as information flows or financial streams in a network.

1 Sectors
The template of a value network map will depend on the project: from simple and rather generic ones (like the three circles) to backgrounds visualizing different departments or geographies like a city or country.

2 Stakeholders
Stakeholders are positioned on the map in a particular sector and can be arranged according to departments or groups as customers perceive them. Customer-centered organizations put the customer in the center of a map, but a map can also be centered around a specific department or a specific employee.

3 Value exchanges
The exchanges of values between stakeholders are visualized with separate arrows from one stakeholder to another. Beside a description, icons help to illustrate the value exchange. In almost all cases, value exchanges take place in both directions, reflecting the saying "there's no such thing as a free lunch."

3.4.3 Ecosystem maps

An ecosystem map is an extension of a stakeholder map or value network map. Such maps include not only stakeholders, but also other actors beyond people and organizations. An ecosystem map includes not only human–human interactions, but also human–machine and machine–machine interactions.

Nowadays, there is no service or physical product without additional or connected services or products, whether physical or digital. Sometimes, these connections are established through automated machine–machine interactions – sometimes even without any interfaces.

An ecosystem map visualizes the whole system of involved actors – humans, machines, interfaces, devices, platforms, and systems. Because systems can become very complex, ecosystem maps often need different zoom levels, from system overviews without any details to very detailed views of subsystems.

Ecosystem maps show the following:

1   Sectors

Ecosystem maps can use a variety of sectors to structure a map depending on its focus. Besides generic templates (like the three circles), backgrounds can also represent different organizations, departments, or geographies (e.g., a building, city, or country).

2   Actors

Actors in an ecosystem map can be whatever makes sense to visualize a system: people, departments, organizations, places, machines, interfaces, devices, platforms, systems, and so on.

3   Relationships or value exchanges

Ecosystem maps can use anything to describe the interaction between actors, from simple descriptions of relationships to illustrations of value exchanges.

Stakeholder terminology

The terminology used in service design differs across organizations and cultures – particularly when it comes to the different players involved. As this can be confusing, this list shows how terminology is used in this book:

→   **Stakeholder**

A person, group, or organization that is somehow connected to or has an interest in a project, organization, or product (including everyone listed here).

→   **User**

A person who uses a service or physical/digital product.

→   **Customer**

A person who buys services or physical/digital products.[01]

01   Here's a simple example to illustrate the difference between a *user* and a *customer*: if you buy cat food for your cat, your cat is the user of cat food when it eats the cat food, but you are the customer as you are the one buying the cat food.

→ **Client**

Although "customer" and "client" are often used synonymously, differentiating these terms often makes work easier. In a service design context, a client is a person, group, or organization that orders and purchases (service design) services from an agency, in-house design department, or consultant.[01]

→ **Service delivery team**

A person, group, or department within an organization that is responsible for providing services to users or customers.

Employee

A person employed by an organization.

Frontline staff

A person, group, or department within an organization that provides services in direct interaction with users and customers.

Support staff

A person, group, or department within an organization that supports frontline staff without direct interaction with users and customers.

→ **Design team**

A group of people that is involved in the service design process.

Core (service) design team

A (small) group of people that manage a service design project, including process and activity planning, tools and methods selection, and facilitation. They are typically experts on service design.

Extended (service) design team

A (larger) group of people that are involved in different activities of a service design project. They are typically cross-functional and multidisciplinary experts with specific competences related to the subject matter of a service design project.

Agency

A person, group, or organization that provides services (design, facilitation, consultation) for other persons, groups, or organizations (i.e., the client) in the development or assessment of a service.

In-house design department

A person, group, or department within an organization that provides (service design) services (design, facilitation, consultation) for other persons, groups, or organizations within the organization (i.e., the client) in the development or assessment of a service.

Consultant

An internal or external person, group, or organization that temporarily provides (service design) consultation. ◄

---

01 Note that in this context, as in all kinds of B2B services, "the client" is rarely just one person. You might have to look at the people who actually own the issue, the people who contacted you, or even the manager who is responsible for the department you are going to work with.

3.5 SERVICE PROTOTYPES

COMMENT

"Prototyping is crucial to test ideas. As Linus Pauling said, '*The best way to have a good idea is to have a lot of ideas.*' Prototyping enables lots of ideas to be tested out in parallel in a low–fi way, so that the bad ideas can be killed off and the stronger ideas developed further."

– Hazel White

Service prototypes are staged experiences and processes (e.g., rehearsals, walkthroughs, simulations, or pilots) that replicate any chosen part of a service from frontstage to backstage – often with increasing fidelity and in varying contexts.[02] They contain or might even zoom in on other forms of more traditional physical or digital prototypes as important props or stages, such as physical mock-ups, scale models, wireframes, or click-models.

The term prototype derives from the Greek *prototy-pon*, which can be interpreted as "first or early form" of something – in our case, of a service or product, whether physical or digital. A service prototype needs to create a first or early experiential form of the service or the service experience.[03]

→ Purpose

Prototypes are prepared and used to explore, evaluate, and communicate service ideas during different activities within the service design process. By engaging with prototypes, the design team can quickly identify important aspects of a new concept, and then explore different alternative solutions and evaluate which one might work in everyday reality. Additionally, prototypes can be used as a communication tool to enhance collaboration and to present, persuade, or inspire.

As you go along, they allow you to systematically learn and evolve toward implementation and even refine during service operations.

→ Prototyping questions

Prototypes implicitly or explicitly address questions around the whole service, a specifically chosen part of the service, or the experience around a physical or digital product or artifact. A prototype can focus on the holistic end-to-end customer experience or a single step within that journey, or it can zoom in on specific backstage processes, issues, or technologies. In that respect, all prototypes are consciously set up and built in such a way that we can learn from them when they are run or used. Later, we step back and reflect and make sense of the results.[04]

→ Fidelity

Prototypes come in different forms, stages of refinement, and levels of detail, reflected onto the entire service or any of its intangible, physical, or digital parts. Depending on the purpose and prototyping questions, prototypes might be "more rough than ready" or be quite polished even at early stages. Examples of lower-fidelity prototypes include desktop walkthroughs to explore essential steps in the customer journey, cardboard prototypes to get a first idea about the shape of a future product, or sketches on paper to visualize

---

02 "Staged" in this context denotes experiences that are consciously put on before a selected audience and are accompanied by research activities to learn from them. This implies that if you do not set it up to learn from it, it's no (service) prototype.

03 See Chapter 7, *Prototyping*, for an in-depth description of how to prepare, plan, and manage your prototyping activities.

04 In other words: to be able to understand and analyze the feedback and data you get from a prototype, it is essential to know the prototyping question.

the early stages of a digital user interface. Higher-fidelity prototypes might include contextual simulations or pilots to test technical and feasibility aspects, 3D prints or immersive digital 3D models to evaluate a detailed look and feel, or actual code already closing the gap toward implementation.[01]

→ **Context and audience**

It is a conscious choice where and when prototypes are used/run and who is experiencing them to get feedback and other data. For example: do you want to simulate in

---

01   See *Fidelity* in 7.1.4 for an in-depth discussion on the fidelity of prototypes.

---

your actual shop environment with real customers during a peak period, or do you want to run a session in a safe studio environment with internal colleagues? The question of audience is also connected to fidelity, as, for example, low levels of fidelity will often require an audience accustomed to or even proficient in "reading" the prototype and learning from it.

Even though early prototypes are often created and used in the design studio, contextual prototypes (e.g., at home with potential users, at the workplace, or on the go) should be considered as early as possible. The more similar the context of the prototype is to the future

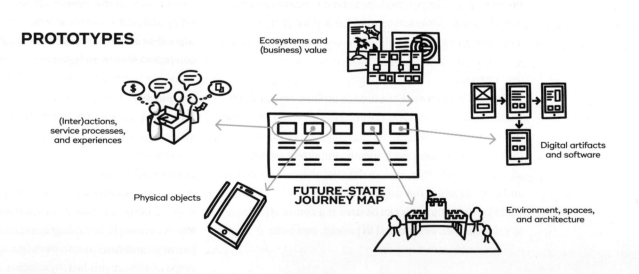

PROTOTYPES

Ecosystems and (business) value

(Inter)actions, service processes, and experiences

Physical objects

FUTURE-STATE JOURNEY MAP

Digital artifacts and software

Environment, spaces, and architecture

context of use, the more reliable feedback you will get from your prototype.[02]

→ **Methods**

Prototypes can be created with many different methods or techniques. Well-known methods include paper prototyping, cardboard prototyping, or theatrical techniques. Prototyping methods replace actual implementation techniques during the design task to allow you to create faster and cheaper, and to maximize learning – or simply because you might still need to figure out properly what and how to implement at all.

The precise form and shape of a prototype also depend on *what* you actually need to prototype: which parts of your future services and physical or digital products do you need to make or build to get answers to your prototyping questions?

In this book, we differentiate between and concentrate on the following:

→ **Prototypes of (inter)actions, service processes, and experiences**
→ **Prototypes of physical objects**
→ **Prototypes of environments, spaces, and architecture**
→ **Prototypes of digital artifacts and software**
→ **Prototypes of ecosystems and (business) value**

[02] Also see *Audience* and *Prototyping context* in 7.1.4.

3.5.1 Prototypes of (inter)actions, service processes, and experiences

Service prototypes are staged experiences and processes focusing on a certain part of a service experience. They can take the shape of a simple storytelling session, a quick step-by-step walkthrough or talkthrough, a more in-depth theatrical rehearsal session, or even a set of complex service simulations involving many different people from all parts of your organization, from frontstage to backstage. They contain other forms of more traditional physical or digital prototypes as important props or stages, such as physical mock-ups, scale models, wireframes, or click-models.

Sticking to the original meaning of the word "prototype," service prototypes create a first or early experiential form of the service or the service experience. This is connected to how staff, customers, or other stakeholders do and experience things, and how they behave in new service situations. Specifically, they address how things should be done differently – and experienced differently – in the future.

Ⓐ **Actors**

Actors enact the given roles in a service story or (inter)action – for example, as customers, staff, or other stakeholders. They use stages, props, and costumes to support their performance. In early or explorative prototypes it is often members of the project team who slip into the shoes of customers and staff, trying to emulate their behaviors. In

Service prototyping: This is how you learn, and always have

If you – as an individual – want to learn how to do something new, like learning a language, playing an instrument, or cooking a meal, what do you do? You might start to read about it, talk to your friends or some experts, observe how they do it, and at some point get started yourself. You might take a course, or find some online community to help you. Then you practice. You do it. You take your teetering first steps. You fall. You adapt. You take some feedback and advice. You try again. This is how you learn.

And essentially this is also how you learn as a team or an organization if you need to do something new. Suppose you need to better understand the language of your customers, or introduce a new system into your daily workflows, or learn how to work together with new colleagues in a different way. What do you do? You might do some training together, or find a consultant to help you through those teetering first steps. You fall. You adapt. You learn from the people who are interacting with you and your team. You sit down and reflect in your group. You take some feedback and advice. You try again. This is how you learn as a team or organization.

There are many different names that describe these learning journeys. Some might call it practice. Tryout. Runthrough. Rehearsal. Pilot. Trial. Test flight. Demonstration. Simulation. Experiment. Or simply preparation.

All of these examples can be seen as a first or early experiential version of something we want to do really well at some point later. All of these examples are service prototypes. In that sense, most organizations already create service prototypes almost every day. However, they usually create them quite late in the process, and they do not always plan them systematically. And they give them lots of different names. ◄

more evolved prototypes, it is key to use real customers or actual staff as the actors of a service prototype.

In those cases, the word *actor* should be understood to mean "the person acting" rather than "a person pretending to act as someone else."

(B) Props

Props are objects and artifacts that are not part of a fixed architecture. They usually are actively handled or at least somehow involved during the staging of the story. The prototype should answer questions about their role and meaning in the context of your prototyping question. Props can be physical or digital and often include signs and symbols.

(C) Stage

The stage of a service prototype is the actual room or space where the action of the service is happening. This includes the interior design and architecture and also the (sensory) environment, like lighting or even smell. A stage can be quite informal. When doing an early-stage investigative rehearsal or a bodystorming session, an empty workshop room can serve as the stage. Over time, stages might be made more complex and more real by adding more and more elements. In contextual prototyping the actual business environment is used, turning an existing shop or office into the stage of your prototype. In contrast to props, stage elements are usually fixed to the stage and rarely moved.

(D) Service story, (inter)action, and dialogue

The service story, (inter)action, and dialogue describe any kind of action which is (visibly) acted out. They represent the core of a service prototype. In essence, they describe what is happening on stage over time – for example, what actors say and do (including basic movement, dialogue, or interaction with other actors) and how the environment or props react to them. A service story can be improvised on the spot, follow a journey map as a guideline, or be prepared through a meticulous script.

(E) Subject matter content

Subject matter content is the information or knowledge that is discussed, used, or dealt with in interactions, in dialogues, or as part of physical or digital props. This becomes visible in the content of flyers, manuals, books, apps, etc., and extends to expert knowledge and skills actors need to be able to do the job.

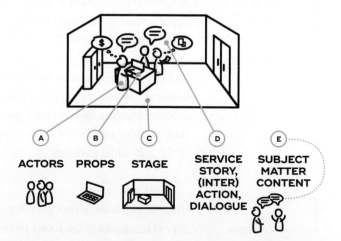

ACTORS | PROPS | STAGE | SERVICE STORY, (INTER) ACTION, DIALOGUE | SUBJECT MATTER CONTENT

3.5.2 Prototypes of physical objects

In industrial or product design, a prototype is an early, often lower-fidelity version of the product itself. We can, for example, create a "looks-like" prototype that gives an impression of the shape and style of the physical product and show them to an audience to get feedback. Or we can create a functional, "works-like" prototype and have people test it. Furthermore, embedding the physical prototype into a more holistic service prototype helps to explore or evaluate the role of the product in the life of its user.

(A) Function
Prototypes can exhibit different levels of functionality. The function of a prototype defines what it can do or what a selected audience can do with the prototype. The functions available in a prototype might be real, simulated, or faked. In proof-of-principle prototypes, only key functional aspects are prototyped, while a working prototype already tries to capture most of the functionality.

(B) Form
The form of a physical prototype describes the shape and aesthetics of a future physical product or artifact, including color and texture. Beyond basic geometry it also helps to look at wider aspects like balance, proportion, or emphasis of the individual elements.

(C) Size and scale
The size and scale of your prototype defines how the prototype is compared to the future physical product or artifact.

Small-scale models in service design are often used in connection with desktop walkthrough approaches or when they need to be combined with architectural models. Full-scale models are often used as stage elements or props in contextual walkthroughs or rehearsal techniques.

(D) Materials (and tools)
Physical prototypes can be created with different materials and tools. Early prototypes often use materials that are easy to work with and do not require specialized tools or knowledge (e.g., cardboard or wood). Evolved prototypes often use more resilient materials like plastics to create function, or explore a wider selection of materials to find the right aesthetics for the final product. Working with more advanced materials often requires special tools like 3D printers, CNC cutting/milling machines, molding equipment, and eventually the actual production toolchain.

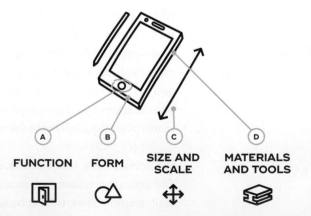

A	B	C	D
FUNCTION	**FORM**	**SIZE AND SCALE**	**MATERIALS AND TOOLS**

3.5.3 Prototypes of environments, spaces, and architecture

Prototypes of environments, spaces, and architecture essentially are a special case of prototypes of physical objects. In architecture, those prototypes often are scale models of a space or a building to test and communicate our ideas. Also, digital 3D models allow you to dive into new spaces using virtual reality headsets.

(A) Layout and space
Architectural models deal with aspects like orientation or layout of buildings and structures within a given fixed space. In contrast to physical products, architecture rarely can be easily moved around. Thus, architectural models often reflect how the future buildings or structures are embedded in surrounding spaces, nature, lighting situations, and so on.

(B) Form
The form of architectural prototypes or models describes the shape and aesthetics of future buildings or structures, including color and texture. Beyond basic geometry it also helps to look at wider aspects like mass, space, volume, texture, light, shadow, and materials of the individual elements.

(C) Function
Architectural prototypes and models can exhibit different levels of functionality. The function of a prototype defines what it can do or what a selected audience can do with the prototype. Functions explored or evaluated in architectural prototypes include the support of daily routines, influencing emotions, or at a basic level, dealing with climate, heating, cooling, and ventilation.

(D) Size and scale
The size and scale of your models defines how the models are compared to the future spaces, buildings, or structures. Small-scale architectural models are often used in desktop walkthrough approaches. Full-scale models are used in contextual walkthroughs or rehearsal techniques.

(E) Materials (and tools)
Prototypes of spaces and architecture can be created with different materials and tools. Early prototypes often use materials that are easy to work with and do not require specialized tools or knowledge (e.g., paper and cardboard). Evolved prototypes are often done using computer simulation and immersive 3D environments or explore a wider selection of actual materials to find the right aesthetics and feel.

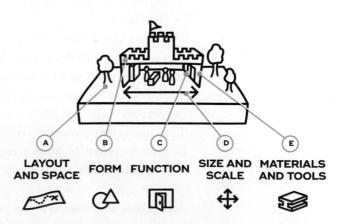

LAYOUT AND SPACE   FORM   FUNCTION   SIZE AND SCALE   MATERIALS AND TOOLS

3.5.4 Prototypes of digital artifacts and software

In software or web development, prototypes can be anything from rough scribbles of the interface, actors playing devices, and digital mock-ups or click-models up to working pieces of experimental code that already run on your target (mobile) device. They also might be embedded into a more holistic service prototype to explore or evaluate the role of the artifact or software in the life of its user.

Many productive prototyping tools and frameworks exist that push the boundaries of how real you can get with your prototype in a short amount of time. The creation of prototypes of digital artifacts or software is no longer limited to people with technical expertise only. Leveraging easy-to-use/fast-to-learn prototyping software, almost anybody can now quickly learn how to create early versions of software or web projects.

(A) Display
The display area of your prototype represents the display[01] of the future device (e.g., the screen of a smartwatch, smartphone, tablet, computer, or other machine).

(B) Screens
The screen is the canvas where content and interactive elements are placed. Multiples screens are created and linked together using interaction elements like hotspots or buttons.

When clicked or tapped, the display simply switches to another screen. In more elaborate prototypes, screens can also contain layers to model more complex behaviors.

(C) Interaction elements
Interaction elements are placed onto a screen. Common elements include visible navigational or interactive elements like buttons, links, sliders, input fields, and so on. Interactive prototypes of touch interfaces might also involve gestures, invisible hotspots, or other ways of interaction.

(D) Content elements
Content elements are placed onto the display area. They allow the subject matter content to be filled in, usually through traditional text elements like headings, subheadings, textboxes, images, audio, or video. Content elements also include labels used for interaction elements (e.g., defining the language on buttons or other navigational elements). Using actual data, copy, diagrams, visualizations, or photo material can make a huge difference as opposed to just using sample content and should be tested as early as possible.

(E) Structure and flow
How the screens or different elements of an interface are linked together defines the basic structure of your prototype. It allows you to figure out the flow of single features or the overall user experience. This includes the discussion of the underlying information architecture (IA) and data model, as inflexible data models or information architecture can create barriers for the future vision of a digital product.

01 More generally, you can, of course, replace "display" with alternative interfaces such as audio or tactile interfaces.

Ⓕ Function

The function of a prototype defines what it can do or what a selected audience can do with the prototype. It is closely tied to the interactive and content elements. The functions available in a prototype might be real, simulated, or faked. In proof-of-principle prototypes, only key functional aspects are prototyped, while a working prototype already tries to capture most of the functionality of the final artifact or software. Functional prototypes are built to assess feasibility and experiential aspects, and help to evaluate/guesstimate necessary effort.

Ⓖ Look and feel/graphical elements

The look and feel adds aesthetics and experience to the visible or perceptible elements and transitions/reactions of the system. This touches on overall style, layout, key graphics, key imagery, color schemes, and patterns as well as wider aspects like balance, proportion, or emphasis of the individual elements, or timing and responsiveness. Early look-and-feel prototypes might be very similar to mood boards when trying to capture a direction with perspectives like playfulness, gravity, lightness, or emotions.

Ⓗ Media and prototyping environment

Prototypes of digital artifacts and software can be created in different media. Early prototypes often use pen and paper. They are easy to work with and do not require specialized knowledge. More evolved prototypes use specialized digital prototyping tools like page-based or layer-based prototyping environments. Alternatively, (dummy) code can be used to assess design questions in different environments or stacks: from exploring different toolchains early in the process to running experiments on feasibility in actual development and test environments or on production systems.

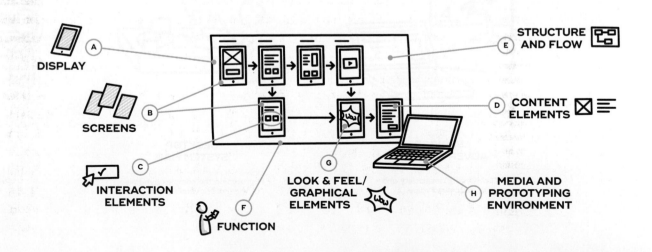

DISPLAY · SCREENS · INTERACTION ELEMENTS · FUNCTION · LOOK & FEEL/GRAPHICAL ELEMENTS · STRUCTURE AND FLOW · CONTENT ELEMENTS · MEDIA AND PROTOTYPING ENVIRONMENT

3.5.5 Prototypes of ecosystems and business value

Since all services and physical/digital products are part of a complex ecosystem and exposed to various (market) forces, there need to be many different types of prototypes. Each prototype is specifically tailored to understand and explore a certain perspective on those complex networks and relationships. Common tools include *service advertisements* (prototypes of desirability and perceived value), *desktop system maps* (prototypes of complex dynamics of the holistic business systems), *Business Model Canvases* (early prototypes of the core business model), or even *business experiments* or *pretotypes* (prototypes that follow a fake-it-before-you-make-it approach and help to explore and validate the core value proposition).[01]

01 See 7.3.6, *Case: Using multifaceted prototyping to create and iterate business and service models*, for an example of how learning from ongoing prototyping activities might allow you to gain confidence in business models that others might consider radical.

EXAMPLES

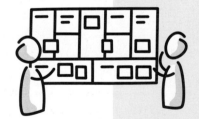

SERVICE ADVERTISEMENT

Prototyping desirability and perceived value.

DESKTOP SYSTEM MAP

Prototyping the complex dynamics of the (holistic) business system.

BUSINESS MODEL CANVAS

Prototyping early versions of the core business model.

Physical evidences

Physical evidences, or service evidences, are physical or digital artifacts that are related to a service (e.g., letters, emails, brochures, signs, souvenirs, text messages, tickets, bills, receipts, giveaways, stickers). One often-used example is the folded toilet paper in your hotel room as a physical evidence that your bathroom has been cleaned.

Sometimes, these physical evidences are an integral part of a service. However, they are often not designed intentionally and lead to unnecessary frustration in customers. As an example, an Austrian credit card company used to send out a text message once per month to its customers to inform them that their monthly invoices had been created. Unfortunately, it sent out this message in the middle of the night, waking up thousands of customers just to inform them about an invoice in their email inbox. Understanding if existing physical evidences provide value to customers is often part of the first service design initiatives that organizations undertake.

Physical evidences can be also added to existing experiences, for example to deliberately add further steps to a customer journey. One example might be giving out free souvenirs or giveaways in hotels with the intention that guests remember their stay when they arrive at home and unpack their luggage. In this context, physical evidences, like giveaways, can be used to intentionally prolong a customer journey and trigger certain customer actions (for example, when they are combined with a message intended to increase positive online reviews). They can also be used to make backstage processes visible to the customer, as in the case of the folded toilet paper.[02] ◄

The folded toilet paper in your hotel bathroom is a classic example of physical evidence of an otherwise intangible backstage process (room cleaning).

[02] See 8.6.1, *Empowering employees for sustainable implementation of a service design project,* for some nice examples of how the redesign of physical evidences – such as the final group photo after an organized motorcycle tour – can impact the overall experience.

3.6 BUSINESS MODEL CANVAS

The Business Model Canvas[01] is a simple template to sketch out a business model using nine core building blocks. Considering business models is an inherent part of any service design process: any changes to organizational structures, processes, software, physical or digital products, services, stakeholder relationships, or customer groups affect different parts of your business model. In return, changes to your business model affect the employee and/or customer experience.

The Business Model Canvas and similar canvases can be used to understand the influence of various options on the employee and customer experience as well as on the business impact. It can also be used to map competitors and compare their business models with your company's. This might give you insights into where you need to differentiate from your competition.

The upper seven building blocks of the Business Model Canvas are directly connected to the previous basic service design tools. By including "hard facts" such as resources, revenue streams, and cost structures, this framework creates a common ground for designers and managers to talk about new service concepts within any organizational structure. The financial blocks (*Cost structure* and *Revenue streams*) allow a design team to estimate the potential profitability of a business model.[02]

EXPERT TIP

"Experienced users of the Business Model Canvas will not just use it as a checklist to fill out the boxes. They will use the BMC to design business models that outperform competitors' with a powerful business model story in which all business model building blocks reinforce each other. Great examples of business model stories are Nespresso, IKEA, or the Nintendo Wii, which succeeded not just based on a great value proposition, but based on a powerful business model."

– Alexander Osterwalder

1 Value propositions

Value propositions[03] summarizes the offering of a company, such as its services or products (whether physical or digital), including the unique selling proposition that distinguishes that offering from its competitors'. This block describes the frontstage parts of a customer journey that a company actually offers to the customer, including services and physical/virtual products as well as intangible values customers may base their purchase decisions on.

The block *Value propositions* is connected with:
— **Journey maps:** Customer journey maps visualize the key experience from a customer's point of view. Often, they focus on a main benefit or the job to be done (i.e., why a customer uses a specific service or product, whether physical or digital). A summary of this describes the value proposition.
— **Prototypes:** Prototypes of services or physical/digital products can make a value proposition tangible and testable.

2 Customer segments

Customer segments describes the different market segments a company identifies as its core target groups. These target groups are normally marked by similar needs and attributes, and their respective size can be estimated.

---

01 For more information on the Business Model Canvas see Osterwalder, A., & Pigneur, Y. (2010). *Business Model Generation: A Handbook for Visionaries, Game Changers, and Challengers.* John Wiley & Sons.

02 See Chapter 7, *Prototyping*, for details on how to work with the Business Model Canvas.

03 See also the Value Proposition Canvas, described in Osterwalder, A., et al. (2014). *Value Proposition Design: How to Create Products and Services Customers Want.* John Wiley & Sons.

THE BUSINESS MODEL CANVAS

Designed for:

Designed by:

Date:

Version:

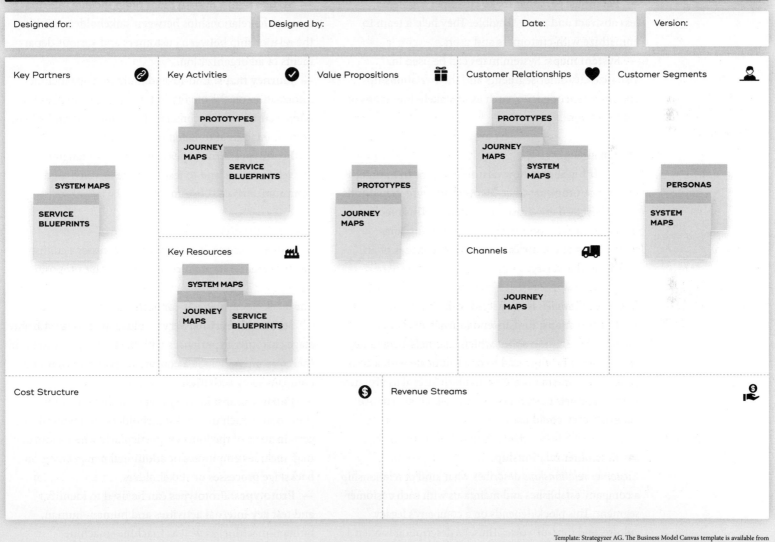

Key Partners

SYSTEM MAPS

SERVICE BLUEPRINTS

Key Activities

PROTOTYPES

JOURNEY MAPS

SERVICE BLUEPRINTS

Key Resources

SYSTEM MAPS

JOURNEY MAPS

SERVICE BLUEPRINTS

Value Propositions

PROTOTYPES

JOURNEY MAPS

Customer Relationships

PROTOTYPES

JOURNEY MAPS

SYSTEM MAPS

Channels

JOURNEY MAPS

Customer Segments

PERSONAS

SYSTEM MAPS

Cost Structure

Revenue Streams

The block *Customer segments* is connected with:
— **Personas:** Personas make customer segments less abstract and more tangible. They help a team to empathize with customers and users.
— **System maps:** System maps can be used to visualize customer segments and their relationships and interdependencies, such as in stakeholder maps or value network maps.

3 Channels

Channels highlights how customers want to interact throughout the customer lifecycle and which methods work best and are most cost-efficient. This block includes on- and offline channels used for communication and distribution across all stages of an end-to-end journey.

The block *Channels* is connected with:
— **Journey maps:** End-to-end journey maps often include information about which channels a customer uses to buy a product and to communicate with a company. Swimlane maps are particularly useful to visualize which channels customers use and which alternative channels they could use.

4 Customer relationships

Customer relationships describes what kind of relationship a company establishes and maintains with each customer segment. This block depends on a company's legacy, culture, and tone-of-voice. Thus, its description is often a bit more vague than the other blocks.

The block *Customer relationships* is connected with:
— **System maps:** System maps often include information on the relationships between stakeholders, such as the relationship between customers and various departments of an organization.
— **Journey maps:** End-to-end journey maps include information on the quality of relationships, such as how often a customer has contact with a company and whether the contact is automated or personal.
— **Prototypes:** Prototypes can be used to tangibilize relationships and to test the tone of voice used to communicate with customers.

5 Key activities

Key activities summarizes backstage processes a company needs to execute to produce or offer its value proposition.

The block *Key activities* is connected to:
— **Service blueprints:** Service blueprints connect frontstage customer experiences with backstage processes and therefore often include a comprehensive overview of a company's key activities.
— **Journey maps:** Journey maps can include information about which internal stakeholders are involved in certain steps of the journey, particularly when a journey map includes employees or additional perspectives on backstage processes or stakeholders.
— **Prototypes:** Prototypes can be used to identify and test key internal activities and human–human, human–machine, as well as machine–machine interactions that happen internally and externally.

6 Key resources

Key resources summarizes what a company needs to sustain and support the business, such as physical, intellectual (brand patents, copyrights, data), human, or financial assets. In a business model, key resources often include decisions regarding make-or-buy or in-/outsourcing.

The block *Key resources* is connected to:
— **System maps:** System maps can include detailed information on the involved internal stakeholders (stakeholder maps or value network maps) as well as other key resources (ecosystem maps).
— **Service blueprints:** Service blueprints mostly include detailed information on involved internal stakeholders.
— **Journey maps:** Journey maps can include information about which internal stakeholders are involved in certain steps of the journey and which of them might be considered as key resources, particularly when a journey map includes employees or additional perspectives on backstage processes or stakeholders.

7 Key partners

Key partners describes the direct ecosystem in which a company operates, including stakeholders that are needed as suppliers for key resources and key activities as well as other important strategic partners.

The block *Key partners* is connected to:
— **System maps:** System maps can include detailed information on the involved internal and external stakeholders. Stakeholder maps or value network maps are particularly useful to understand the relationships between a company and its external stakeholders and which of these might be considered as key partners regarding the business model.
— **Service blueprints:** Service blueprints include detailed information on involved external stakeholders, some of whom are key partners.

8 Cost structure

Cost structure outlines the most important fixed and variable cost factors of a business model and whether these can be affected by economies of scale and scope.

The block *Cost structure* is connected to the **upper seven building blocks** of the Business Model Canvas.

9 Revenue streams

Revenue streams describes how a company generates income from each customer segment or from key partners. It includes how much each customer segment pays, for what, how, and how much this contributes to the overall revenue through sales, usage or subscription fees, licensing, brokerage fees, or advertising.

The block *Revenue streams* is connected to the **upper seven building blocks** of the Business Model Canvas.

04
THE CORE ACTIVITIES OF SERVICE DESIGN

A flexible framework to tailor your service design process to your people, goals, and organization.

Expert comments —————————————————————————————————

Christoph Zürn   Francesca Terzi   Jamin Hegeman   Simon Clatworthy

04

THE CORE ACTIVITIES OF SERVICE DESIGN

This chapter also includes

4.1 IN SEARCH OF A PROCESS FOR DESIGNING A SERVICE

In this chapter and the ones that follow, we sketch out a framework that will help you understand the underlying activities and the overall process of designing a service. It will also help you to get a sense of its limitations. We'll consider questions like:

→   How much can you plan for, and how can you professionally manage expectations and uncertainty in the remaining parts?

→   How can you stay on time and on budget while the process still needs to be iterative and explorative?

→   How much structure is necessary? When will too much structure have a negative effect on the quality of the results?

These questions have no easy answer, and not surprisingly, there is no one process to rule them all, no step-by-step checklist, no silver bullet. However, it is one of the beauties of service design that it allows or even demands flexibility. The best design processes are those that adapt to the problem you want to solve – and not the other way around. Instead of a rigid theoretical process, we have something much more powerful: emerging patterns and

activities from real-world projects that are the strategic building blocks for any service design process.

The specific process you need to adopt for a project will vary depending on your organization, the challenge, the complexity of the challenge, the people involved, the underlying ideas or problems, and of course (and not least) the available budget, time, and other resources.

Designing the process and choosing the right methods and tools are core skills in service design. Even though you will see a lot of process charts and agendas in this book, be very aware that it won't be enough to simply copy them. Always adapt the process to the people, culture, and goals of the project you are working on.

💬 **EXPERT TIP**

"I always think of the design process like a music studio with a huge mixer desk. Each project needs a different mix of both instruments and levels (degree of use). Its always good to ask at the start, '*What mix is this project?*'"

– Simon Clatworthy

Iterative and adaptive design in a VUCA world

The adoption of iterative and adaptive design processes is in no way a fringe phenomenon.

It is taking place in major organizations – including the very conservative ones and very pragmatic ones, such as the US military. Faced with an operational context that is increasingly VUCA (volatile, uncertain, complex, and ambiguous), the US Army adopted a new approach in 2010 with its field manual *FM 5-0*. The manual "is a set of guidelines to be adhered to by military commanders when planning and decision-making for the battlefield. *FM 5-0* is unique, as it is the first time that design – and specifically 'design thinking,' the iterative process of problem-solving that is considered by some typical of design – was introduced into the vocabulary of the military field manual."[01] ◄

As our world is cranking out innovations at an unprecedented rate, more and more industries are being shaken up by disruptive shifts. The business world is increasingly described as VUCA – volatile, uncertain, complex, and ambiguous.[02] With that much pressure, you also need to be able to quickly adapt your problem-solving, innovation, and design skills. You need to be flexible and grow with the ever-changing challenges – and so does your process.

This book provides a framework for flexible service design process planning. It provides a set of proven tools to create and manage exactly the service design technique that your project and organization needs. As you evolve in your service design journey you might discover better ways to do things for yourself within your own context. However, getting to this point requires practice, skill, and a lot of experience.

To add to this, we challenge you to be critical as you read through the following chapters – and when you first apply the TiSDD framework. We challenge you to build your own customized service design process and give it a go. And we also challenge you to always stay critical of your own process. Always ask yourself: What worked? What didn't work? Why didn't it work? How might we do it better in the next project?

---

01 In its foreword, the manual states: "With [...] the introduction of design into our doctrine, we highlight the importance of understanding complex problems more fully before we seek to solve them through our traditional planning processes." From US Army (2010). *The Operations Process FM 5-0*. Headquarters Department of the Army.

02 For example, see Bennett, N., & Lemoine, J. (2014). "What VUCA Really Means for You." *Harvard Business Review*, 92(1/2), 27.

4.2 CORE PATTERNS IN THE DESIGN PROCESS

4.2.1   Divergent and convergent thinking and doing

At the core of any design process is the recurring pattern of creating and reducing options:

A During research activities, you generate a lot of knowledge through research methods which is then focused again through organizing and extracting key insights.

B During ideation activities, you create many opportunities that you filter through decision-making processes to arrive back at a handful of promising ideas.

C In prototyping and implementation, you open up by exploring and building potential solutions and then focus again through evaluation and decision making.

These patterns can be described as divergent and convergent thinking and doing; they are some of the most important patterns within any design process. The terms *divergent thinking* and *convergent thinking* were first coined by psychologist Joy Paul Guilford in 1956[03] and were introduced into the field of design and architecture by Paul Laseau in 1980.[04] In essence, both found that successful design and problem-solving processes can be described as an interplay between divergence (where we seek or create opportunities) and convergence (where we make decisions).[05]

From the perspective of a team member who is part of this kind of design process, divergent and convergent thinking require different skills and often come with a different mindset. On one side, you have many people who exhibit a bias toward divergent thinking and doing. They just love to create and explore new ideas. On the other side, there are others who look at an idea and instantly see the risk and potential problems: "Won't work here. Too expensive. Too political. Not legal." etc. They spot instantly why something might not work in the world they know. Those two sides are often called the "Yes, and …" (trying to find new solutions) and "Yes, but …" modes (instantly challenging or reality

The design process as interplay between divergent phases (seeking opportunities) and convergent phases (making decisions).

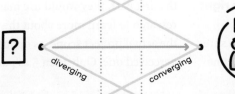

diverging   converging

03 Guilford, J. P. (1956). "The Structure of Intellect." *Psychological Bulletin*, 53(4), 267.
04 Laseau, P. (1980). *Graphic Thinking for Architects and Designers.* John Wiley & Sons.
05 Sometimes also called *elaboration* and *reduction*.

checking every idea).[01] However, be careful before judging whether one of them is better than the other. Divergent ("Yes, and...") and convergent ("Yes, but...") skillsets are both essential in service design.

For a successful project, you will always need both: divergent skills to create enough base material to have great results or breakthrough concepts, and convergent skills to help you to stay legal, stay within the budget, or manage real risks and – in the end – come to a decision. The key is to consciously plan and manage when to do which, which specific methods to use, and who to involve. This holds true for both the workshop level and the service design process as a whole.

Divergent and convergent thinking can be used as a generic, high-level lens when planning for or managing a service design process: Which of the activities or methods you use are divergent or convergent. When inviting stakeholders for your co-creation activities, this can be an additional perspective: What is the required mindset in terms of divergent and convergent thinking? Which mode should you currently be in? Is everybody on the same page?

4.2.2 Make sure you are solving the right problem before solving the problem right

Design processes are consciously designed to make sure you identify the right problem first before wasting time

and money on solving the problem right. This sounds almost trivial, but it is indeed fundamental and does not always come naturally. Many organizations are trained to solve problems and implement immediately as part of their DNA – which in many situations might even be considered a good thing. But when facing new problems, how can you be really sure that you are working on the right problem? Or, if you were asked to solve the problem by someone else, how can you be sure that the project sponsor or client has indeed accurately identified the problem in the first place? That you are not being asked to solve just a symptom? Or whether or not she herself actually has access to all the relevant information and has given it to you?

This is what sets design approaches apart: rather than jumping right in – which also often leads to obvious solutions – you first take a step back. You make sure you identify and understand the *right problem* before you move on and then are able to come up with genuinely better solutions.

In 2005 and 2007, the British Design Council conducted research[02] on how successful design teams across many industries work, and they found that the designers were following this very approach. The teams would split their projects into two major parts. During the first part, they would use market/user/design research to learn more about the problem and define the actual project scope, as opposed to the assumed or perceived one. Only then – as part two – would they

💬 **EXPERT TIP**

"The more expertise and experience you have, the greater the likelihood you'll find yourself in the 'Yes, but ...' category. This is why it's sometimes good to bring in an external or naive perspective, as naiveté naturally leads to 'Yes, and ...' behavior."
—Jamin Hegeman

---

01 See the "*Yes, and ...*" *warm-up* method in Chapter 10, *Facilitating workshops.*

02 Design Council (2007). "11 Lessons: Managing Design in 11 Global Companies: UK Design Council.

Yes, and ...

Yes, but ...

Patience, young Padawan, your time will come

Most people have encountered situations in meetings where half the team is in "Yes, and ..." mode but the other half is already in "Yes, but ..." mode, ready to shoot down every idea that the others come up with. And, hey, you have some friction. The good news is that the friction often can be addressed simply by explaining and acknowledging those two modes of working and clearly establishing which one the team is supposed to be in right now. For example, if you are running an ideation session, explicitly ask the team to switch to "Yes, and ..." mode and defer judgement and negative comments. This becomes even more effective when you also mention that there will be a session afterward where the group can filter, review, and critique those ideas – and kindly ask the "Yes, but ..." people in the room to be patient, as "Your time will come!"[03]

"Yes, and ..." and "Yes, but ..." attach a simple language to the divergent and convergent thinking modes and – if introduced right – soon become symbols for the associated behaviors and frictions within your team: "Hey guys, are we still in 'Yes, and ...' mode? Or are we already 'Yes, but-ing' each other? Let's align!" ◄

03 Consider using the "Yes, and ..." warm-up to introduce the two modes of working to a group. See *Yes, and..." warm-up* in Chapter 10, *Facilitating workshops.*

start to work on a solution using multidisciplinary approaches, visual management, prototyping, and testing until they implemented and launched the new service or product, whether physical or digital,[01] and received the first feedback from the market.

It is a good rule of thumb to challenge initial assumptions and kick off with some planned research. But even though this will often mean starting with research activities, keep in mind that there might be exceptions to that rule (e.g., when you start working on projects that are based on previous research or existing opportunity areas).

4.2.3 All design processes are alike... different

Over the last couple of decades, a plethora of different design processes have either been published by practitioners or described in literature.

This is also true in the field of service design. There might be differences in the exact wording and the number of activities, steps, or phases – usually between three and seven. But they ultimately share the same mindset and the same principles of service design we described in the previous chapter. Here are just a few examples:

| A | Discover, Define, Develop, Deliver[02] |

| B | Explore, Create, Evaluate[03] |

| C | Exploration, Creation, Reflection, Implementation[04] |

| D | Identify, Build, Measure – or – Orientate and Discover, Generate, Synthesize and Model, Specify, Measure, Produce, Transfer and Transformation[05] |

| E | Insight, Idea, Prototyping, Delivery[06] |

| F | Discovering, Concepting, Designing, Building, Implementing[07] |

One thing that becomes obvious very quickly is that at this level there are few (if any) differences in the core design process between service design and other design disciplines. The difference is rather in the specific set of tools and methods service design uses (e.g., customer journeys, service blueprinting, service prototyping), not in the design process itself. No matter what you design, you always need to understand user needs, you always work iteratively, you always have diverging and converging phases, and so on. So we need to look more deeply at exactly how these service design projects are run and what the underlying patterns and activities are.[08]

02 Design Council (2007). "11 Lessons: Managing Design in 11 Global Brands," UK Design Council.

03 Dark Horse Innovation (2016). *Digital Innovation Playbook*. Murmann Publishers.

04 Stickdorn, M., & Schneider, J. (2010). *This is Service Design Thinking*. BIS Publishers.

05 Overview and broken-down stages of Engine's service design process. See Engine (n.d.). "Our Process." Retrieved December 27, 2012, from *http://www.enginegroup.co.uk/service_design/our_process*.

06 Reason, B. (2009). "Service Thinking for Health Services" [slides]. Retrieved from *http://liveworkstudio.com*.

07 DesignThinkers Academy (2009). "DesignThinkers Service Design Method" [slides]. Retrieved from *http://www.slideshare.net/designthinkers/designthinkers-service-design-method*.

08 This leads to a discussion about the difference between goods, services, products, and experiences. See the textbox *Services? Products? Experiences?* in 1.1 for more details.

01 The term "products" describes anything a company offers – no matter if this is tangible or not. In academia, products are often divided into goods and services. However, products are usually bundles of services and physical/digital products. As "goods" is colloquially understood as referring to something tangible, we prefer to speak of physical/digital products. Read more on this in the textbox on *Service-dominant logic* in 2.5.

💬 COMMENT

"Visualizations of the service design process are like a lead sheet in jazz. It just shows the basic idea that is needed to get the band playing."

– Christof Zürn

💬 EXPERT TIP

"Our best practice is to brainstorm on processes and tools adaptation at the beginning of each project, with the aim to tailor our very own design process as much as we can to the project with all its challenges we will face."

– Francesca Terzi

THE DOUBLE DIAMOND

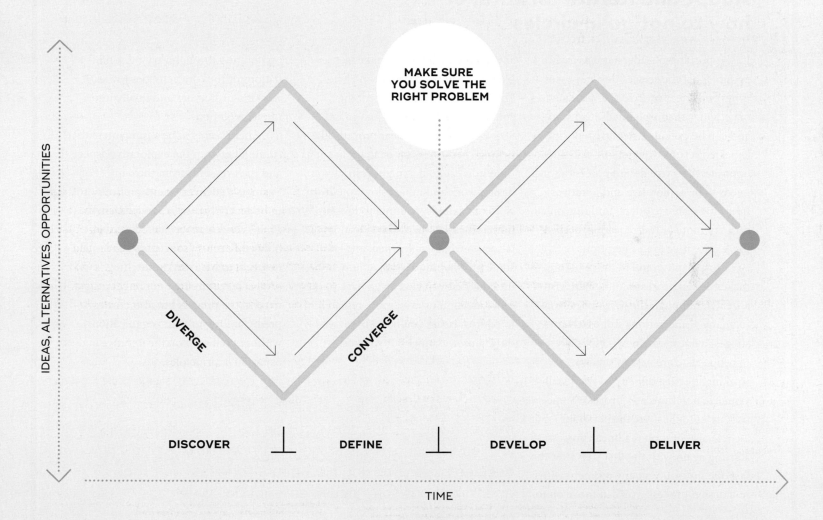

Adapt and iterate forward, or how to not go in circles

It is important to understand as early as possible that the service design process is never a linear process (i.e., a sequence of activities that is planned in advance and can be executed step by step with expected results). In fact, it's quite the opposite. A service design process always needs to be explorative and iterative. It has to be able to adapt, building on a series of more or less repeating, deepening, explorative loops: iterations.

This adaptive and iterative nature makes design processes difficult to visualize. Even though they are not meant to, many visualizations still somehow suggest a linear structure – especially to people who are new to this way of working. It is just difficult to graphically visualize iterations as a process. Some use circles to illustrate the iterations – but a circle also describes a linear process, starting again with the first step after the last one. In reality, at any moment within a design process, you can move on to

any other activity – if it makes sense. Design processes do not go in circles. They do not go back. Instead, they constantly move forward and adapt. Strictly following a linear process, like ticking checkboxes off of a task list or a rigid how-to-guide, might restrict your design work and in fact slow you down.

For example, you might do some initial research, then some ideation based on what you learned, and start some prototyping activities, only to find out that you have to go back to do more ideation or even more research to address issues you have discovered during prototyping. But you keep

on iterating through varying combinations of the core activities toward working prototypes and finally into implementation.

There seems to be a fundamental friction between the explorative aspects and the pressures from the daily business to deliver results on time and in budget. Chapter 9, *Service Design Process and Management*, describes how you can use concepts like planned iteration to build an overarching project structure that not only creates trust in the process but also creates predictability for your organization without giving up on the iterative and explorative principles. ◄

You will soon notice that while there might be useful patterns between the various core activities, there is no generally implied sequence. This is the reason why in this book we have decided to stop talking about core "phases" or "stages," and talk about core "activities" instead.

4.3 INTRODUCING THE CORE ACTIVITIES OF THE TISDD SERVICE DESIGN FRAMEWORK

We will discuss the four core activities of the service design process in Chapters 5–8 before moving on to explain the detailed mechanics of the overarching service design process in Chapter 9.

→ **Chapter 5, *Research*:** In service design, research is used to understand people and their behavior in relation to a service or product, whether physical or digital. Design research enables a design team to *empathize* with the people they design for and build up a genuine understanding of their practices and routines. This allows the team to work from a user-centered perspective throughout a project and potentially also include people they encounter during research at a later stage to ideate or prototype concepts.

→ **Chapter 6, *Ideation*:** Producing ideas is a vital part of a service design project – but it is not as all-important as many people seem to think. In service design, ideas are just starting points within a bigger evolutionary process. They need to be, however, generated systematically en masse, mixed, recombined, culled, distilled, and evolved or parked. Their real value often lies not in the ideas themselves but in the outcome(s) that stem from them.

→ **Chapter 7, *Prototyping*:** In service design, prototyping is used to explore, evaluate, and communicate how people might experience or behave in future service situations. Prototyping enables the design team to identify important aspects of a new concept, explore alternative solutions, and evaluate which one might actually work in the everyday business reality.

→ **Chapter 8, *Implementation*:** Implementation describes the step beyond experimenting and testing, moving into production and rollout. The implementation of service design projects can involve various fields, such as change management for organizational procedures and processes, software development for apps and software, and product development or engineering for the production of physical objects, as well as architecture and construction for the creation of environments and buildings.

→ **Chapter 9, *Service Design Process and Management*:** Research, ideation, prototyping, and implementation are the major building blocks of a working service design project. This chapter provides a framework to plan and prepare as well as to manage and continuously adjust your iterative approach to build trust and deliver results for your organization.

Four core activities
of the service design process

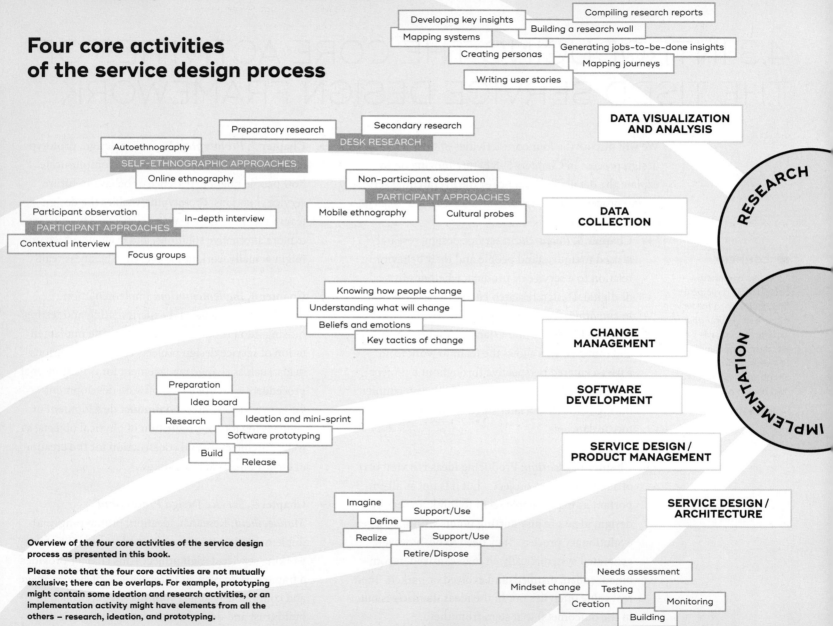

Developing key insights

Compiling research reports

Mapping systems

Building a research wall

Generating jobs-to-be-done insights

Creating personas

Mapping journeys

Writing user stories

Preparatory research

Secondary research

DESK RESEARCH

Autoethnography

SELF-ETHNOGRAPHIC APPROACHES

Online ethnography

Non-participant observation

PARTICIPANT APPROACHES

Participant observation

In-depth interview

Mobile ethnography

Cultural probes

PARTICIPANT APPROACHES

Contextual interview

Focus groups

**DATA VISUALIZATION
AND ANALYSIS**

**DATA
COLLECTION**

Knowing how people change

Understanding what will change

Beliefs and emotions

Key tactics of change

**CHANGE
MANAGEMENT**

Preparation

Idea board

Research

Ideation and mini-sprint

Software prototyping

Build

Release

**SOFTWARE
DEVELOPMENT**

**SERVICE DESIGN /
PRODUCT MANAGEMENT**

Imagine

Support/Use

Define

Realize

Support/Use

Retire/Dispose

**SERVICE DESIGN /
ARCHITECTURE**

Needs assessment

Mindset change

Testing

Creation

Monitoring

Building

RESEARCH

IMPLEMENTATION

**Overview of the four core activities of the service design
process as presented in this book.**

**Please note that the four core activities are not mutually
exclusive; there can be overlaps. For example, prototyping
might contain some ideation and research activities, or an
implementation activity might have elements from all the
others – research, ideation, and prototyping.**

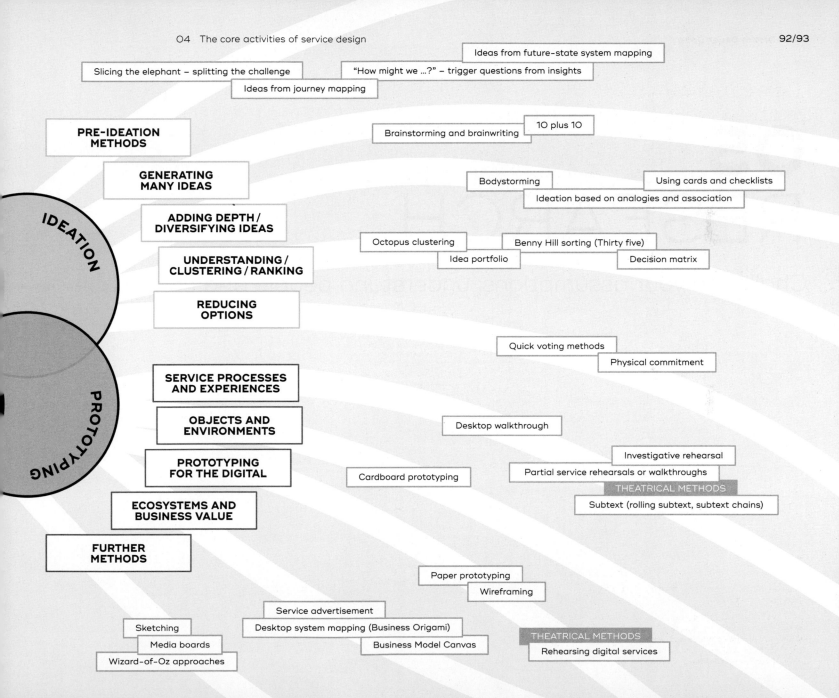

Ideas from future-state system mapping

Slicing the elephant – splitting the challenge

"How might we …?" – trigger questions from insights

Ideas from journey mapping

PRE-IDEATION METHODS

Brainstorming and brainwriting

10 plus 10

GENERATING MANY IDEAS

Bodystorming

Using cards and checklists

Ideation based on analogies and association

ADDING DEPTH / DIVERSIFYING IDEAS

UNDERSTANDING / CLUSTERING / RANKING

Octopus clustering

Benny Hill sorting (Thirty five)

Idea portfolio

Decision matrix

REDUCING OPTIONS

Quick voting methods

Physical commitment

IDEATION

PROTOTYPING

SERVICE PROCESSES AND EXPERIENCES

OBJECTS AND ENVIRONMENTS

Desktop walkthrough

PROTOTYPING FOR THE DIGITAL

Investigative rehearsal

Partial service rehearsals or walkthroughs

Cardboard prototyping

THEATRICAL METHODS

ECOSYSTEMS AND BUSINESS VALUE

Subtext (rolling subtext, subtext chains)

FURTHER METHODS

Paper prototyping

Wireframing

Service advertisement

Sketching

Desktop system mapping (Business Origami)

Media boards

Business Model Canvas

Wizard-of-Oz approaches

THEATRICAL METHODS

Rehearsing digital services

05
RESEARCH

Challenge your assumptions; understand people and context.

Expert comments _____

Anke Helmbrecht   Geke van Dijk   Jürgen Tanghe   Maik Medzich   Mauricio Manhães

Phillippa Rose   Simon Clatworthy

05
RESEARCH

This chapter also includes

MOVE BEYOND ASSUMPTIONS

In service design, research is used to understand people, their motivations, and their behavior. Usually research is one of the first activities in a service design project, but it's not uncommon for ideation, prototyping, or implementation to send a team back to research activities when new questions arise. **Design research enables a team to:**

→   Empathize with the people they design for and build up a genuine understanding of their practices and routines.

→   Immerse themselves in an unfamiliar area or subject and learn about the specific context they will be working in – which might be quite technical and specialized.

→   Step away from established routines and assumptions, looking at a certain topic with fresh eyes.

Mostly, researchers strive to find out how customers experience a specific physical or digital product, service, or brand (customer experience). Furthermore, research is used to study the experiences and behavior of different employees (employee experience) as well as other involved stakeholders. More generally, it can be used to reveal the ecosystem in which a certain theme, service, good, or product is embedded, including other players, places, artifacts, processes, platforms, and stakeholders, and to see how they are connected.

Research is crucial in service design, as it helps a design team to move beyond assumptions. There's a continuum from simple research for the inspiration of a design team to solid data that can reveal (valid) discoveries. Research can be divided into quantitative methods and qualitative methods. Both types are useful in service design. Quantitative research is often a good way to gain insights into the "what" and "how" of an experience, while qualitative research provides insights into the "why" – people's motivations and needs. However, research can be used in various forms at different stages within a service design project. We might see initial research identifying user needs, discovering experience gaps and other problems. Then we have research testing prototypes, validating implemented solutions and assisting ideation (by systematically gathering existing ideas and avoiding reinventing the wheel). In all stages research is used to inform decisions based on real data and insights, rather than on assumptions that may be biased.[01]

Service design research is a structured process with planned iterations. It starts with a research topic or one or more research questions and often aims to derive insights. Design research is based in user/human-centered design and usually includes ethnographic research methods.[02] When you start to explore this field, you might find that the methods and vocabulary used are often quite fuzzy or non-defined – it's an issue that academics and designers often criticize themselves for. Also, this type of qualitative research feels a little unsafe for people who are more accustomed to quantitative research in a business context, but usually a qualitative approach turns out to be really valuable.[03] Instead of looking for "the" truth, qualitative research can provide insights into "a" relevant truth. Insights from qualitative research are often more actionable than mere quantitative data as they provide answers to the "why" questions. New perspectives and nuances come up. Communicating insights with quotes, photos, or videos of user realities can initiate change in organizations by creating a common understanding of the problem and motivating people to do things differently.

As this book is about doing, this chapter presents an actionable framework for service design research, based on common academic standards.

COMMENT

"We view the research phase as a way to understand the world in the same way that the customer or employee does. If you feel that you do this, then you have a platform that makes your ideas and concepts better and more relevant."

– Simon Clatworthy

---

01 See 5.4.2, *Case: Using qualitative and quantitative research in service design,* for an example of how to use both quantitative and qualitative research in a service design project.

02 Strictly speaking, these are often more "ethnographically inspired" research methods. In "real" ethnographic research projects, ethnographers usually immerse themselves much more deeply into an organization or culture than designers do. It is not uncommon for ethnographers to spend months or even years in the field researching one particular topic. For a comprehensive introduction to how designers practice ethnographic research, see Nova, N. (2014). *Beyond Design Ethnography.* Geneva: SHS Publishing.

03 While your research should be heavily rooted in (and maybe start with) a qualitative approach, it should include quantitative data as necessary and useful. Following a a more holistic, mixed-method approach in design research often increases buy-in from other stakeholders.

THE BASIC PROCESS OF SERVICE DESIGN RESEARCH

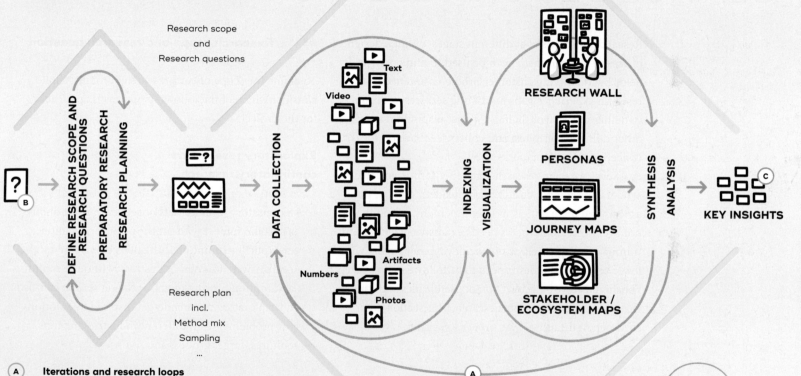

Research scope
and
Research questions

Text

Video

RESEARCH WALL

PERSONAS

JOURNEY MAPS

Artifacts

Numbers

Photos

STAKEHOLDER /
ECOSYSTEM MAPS

DEFINE RESEARCH SCOPE AND
RESEARCH QUESTIONS

PREPARATORY RESEARCH

RESEARCH PLANNING

DATA COLLECTION

INDEXING

VISUALIZATION

SYNTHESIS

ANALYSIS

KEY INSIGHTS

Research plan
incl.
Method mix
Sampling
...

A　**Iterations and research loops**
Design research is an iterative process – a sequence of
research loops within and between activities.

B　**Starting point**
Usually research starts with a brief from an internal or
external client. Based on some preparatory research, you
define research questions and start research planning.

C　**Output**
There are various potential outputs of design research,
from informal inspirations to formal research reports.

Research activities are embedded in an
iterative sequence with other activities of
ideation, prototyping, and implementation.

5.1 THE PROCESS OF SERVICE DESIGN RESEARCH

Research can be used at different stages within a design process. Design research can be used to find opportunity fields by identifying customer problems and needs; to research experience gaps in existing services or products (whether physical or digital);[01] to get inspiration from other domains; or to test and collect feedback on ideas, concepts, and prototypes.

Service design research can benefit from a clearly articulated research design that considers some of the aspects and main criticisms of ethnography.[02] Even though not every research process needs extensive planning, this framework might help you to achieve richer results with fewer resources. It doesn't need to be followed step by step, but should serve as a collection of useful rules of thumb that can be applied to your research. This section describes each step in detail.

---

01 The term "products" describes anything a company offers – no matter if this is tangible or not. In academia, products are often divided into goods and services. However, products are usually bundles of services and physical/digital products. As "goods" is colloquially understood as referring to something tangible, we prefer to speak of physical/digital products. Read more on this in the textbox *Service-dominant logic* in 2.5.

02 For a description of a well-articulated research design see, for example: Peffers, K., Tuunanen, T., Rothenberger, M. A., & Chatterjee, S. (2007). "A Design Science Research Methodology for Information Systems Research." *Journal of Management Information Systems*, 24(3), 45–77. For a brief scholarly discussion of problems of internal and external reliability and validity of ethnographic research see, for example, LeCompte, M. D., & Goetz, J. P. (1982). Problems of Reliability and Validity in Ethnographic Research. Review of Educational Research, 52(1), 31-60.

5.1.1 Research scope and research question

To define the scope of your research, it might help to consider which of the following options is applicable for the project.

Exploratory research vs. confirmatory research

→ Exploratory research sets out to learn more about a specific subject without the prior formulation of explicit assumptions. The objective is often to find answers to "Why" questions without a sound assumption of what might be the cause. You can also do exploratory research to get inspired by solutions (or problems) from different industries, regions, cultures, target groups, and so on.

→ Confirmatory research is intended to validate specific assumptions you have generated before you start research. The objective is often to find out if an assumption or hypothesis is supported by research findings. For example, assumption-based journey maps you created during a workshop might now need to be challenged with solid data on customer experience.

Research into existing services and physical or digital products vs. new ideas/concepts

→ Research that focuses on existing physical/digital products or services is mostly done in the existing situational context through fieldwork using ethnographic approaches. Customers, employees, and other stakeholders are observed or interviewed when they interact with the service or physical/digital product in question, or with one another in reality.

→ Research which could lead to new ideas or concepts uses similar ethnographic methods, but as there are no existing physical/digital products or services to be researched, we often use prototypes or experiments to get results that are as close as possible to the results we would get from the future situational context of this idea or concept.

Start by formulating a research question to make sure that your team (and your potential client) has a common research aim. An initial research question might derive from a (client) brief, from customer complaints, from a workshop, or somewhere else. Often you need to do some preparatory research before or during defining your research scope and phrasing research questions.[03]

A research question could have various aims: perhaps to understand customer needs ("Why do people

use selfie sticks?"), to find gaps in an existing customer experience ("Where do customers have problems or leave when they are in our shop?"), to confirm steps of an assumption-based journey map ("Which steps are missing in our journey map when our customers go through our software onboarding? And which ones do they skip?"), or to understand the ecosystem of a physical/digital product or service ("Which players are directly and indirectly involved in our procurement process?").

When developing your research question, always remember to think ahead and ask yourself what you will do with the answers. You know what the next activity of your project will be, so you can test a question by asking "How will the answer to this question help us generate a range of insights and ideas to create new (or more) value?"

Research questions are often rather broad and vague in the beginning, but then narrow down to one or more specific questions throughout the iterative process. It is like finding a path through a jungle: you don't know the way when you set out. You have a vague aim and move in that direction. Then, if you stumble over a creek, it's best to follow it as it might take you somewhere interesting much faster.

Be aware that research questions often need to be refined over time due to the iterative and explorative character of design research. In general, you should avoid questions that could be answered with a simple "yes" or "no" – otherwise your research might come to an end very fast, and you won't learn much. Often research questions are open-ended, sometimes followed with a follow-up "Why" question to gain more detailed insights. It

03 See *Preparatory research* in 5.2.

usually helps if you write down not only one question in the beginning, but 10 or 20 and then select one or more you like.[01] With a little practice, you will get better at developing questions. But you will always need to iterate and refine them.

Based on your progressive understanding of the subject matter, you'll be able to gradually rephrase the question better, improve your process and methods of collecting data during your fieldwork, and also refine the focus of your documentation.

5.1.2 Research planning

When planning your research, you should think of research methods that are most likely to give you fruitful answers for your proposed research questions. On the other hand, your research must fit within certain business constraints, as you always have to consider how to best allocate time, money, and people within a project.

A good starting point is to take a look at what is already out there so you are "standing on the shoulders of giants." Take a look at previous research and existing data on the subject matter. Ask the Market Research or Innovation department if they have any relevant data, get statistics that might be useful for your research, and get an overview of what has been done in this field by other departments in the organization. Besides existing research within the organization, also invest some time into classic desk research: use (academic) research platforms to look for scholarly papers published on that topic. In many cases, you might invest an hour or so to screen the research landscape until you have a good idea whether it is worth spending more time reading published research. If you find interesting research, it will save some time and budget by focusing your research on the really useful parts.

Besides conducting some preparatory research, your research planning will include decisions regarding research loops, sample selection, research context, sample size, and method selection.[02]

Research loops

Always plan qualitative research as an iterative process with a sequence of research loops. Fruitful design research often starts with a broad focus and aims to narrow it as soon as possible. The first loops can be really short: something between one hour and one day.

Through iterative research loops, it is possible to be more confident that the research is effectively targeting the important questions.

Each loop should include data collection with various methods as well as at least a simple form of data synthesis and analysis.

---

01 You'll find some helpful methods for creating many research questions with your design team in Chapter 6, *Ideation*.

02 Iteration does not mean doing the same thing over again. It means reflecting on your new data, adapting your approach, and starting another experiment. For more, see the textbox *Adapt and iterate forward* in 4.4.

Sample selection

Sampling is the definition of who you want to take part in your research. Who participates in your research and how you select them is a critical question for the reliability of any study. A skewed selection of research participants may distort your results – for example, when you ask only a specific age group, or only happy customers (the "sampling bias"). There are various strategies that aim either to get a representative dataset for large-scale quantitative research (probability sampling) or to get richer data from a specific group for in-depth qualitative research (non-probability sampling). Results based on quantitative probability samples can usually be generalized, but with data from qualitative non-probability samples that's not the case. Mostly service design research uses qualitative research methods and selects participants with non-probability sampling techniques, like these:

→ **Convenience sampling:** Find some people to participate in your research (the simplest, but also most biased sampling approach).

→ **Self-selective sampling:** Let participants decide to take part in your study without defining specific criteria or quotas – for example, through a link on a company website (also a very biased approach).

→ **Snowball sampling:** Find a few relevant people for your research purpose and ask them to recommend others (e.g., users of electric cars can get you in touch with other users from their network).

→ **Quota sampling:** Find out how a population is structured according to certain criteria, set a quota for how many participants you would like to have for each criterion (e.g., gender) and randomly select participants for each quota.

→ **Extreme case sampling:** Find very unusual participants to understand extreme positions (e.g., very early adopters of interesting technologies, or the opposite: people who are radically against or have never thought about using your service/product/technology).

→ **Emergent sampling:** Follow new leads during fieldwork as they unfold, to flexibly take advantage of new knowledge.

→ **Maximum-variation sampling:** Find participants with a wide range of variation on dimensions of interest with the aim to discover central themes or shared dimensions across a diverse sample (e.g., people who use a product in very different ways than it was intended).

→ **Maximum-input sampling:** Find participants with a comprehensive overview of an entire experience or system in order to get a maximum of input from the selected participants (e.g., people who have just followed a complete customer life cycle).

💬 **EXPERT TIP**

"Good practice is to regard the first one or two interviews as *pilots* to test out your script and materials. If all goes well you include the data in the research; if there are serious changes needed you may want to consider doing some extra pilot interviews."

– Geke van Dijk

💬 **COMMENT**

"When we were working with CarGlass in Belgium we discovered huge differences between the experience of changing a windshield during the day and at night. A well-designed process for the daytime was rather frightening for female customers during the night considering the dark and lonely location outside the city and the different emotional state the customers were in."

— **Jürgen Tanghe**

💬 **COMMENT**

"Theoretical saturation is important, but difficult to predict in advance. Usually it is based on prior experiences and rules of thumb in proposals, while keeping flexibility to extend the fieldwork when data and results indicate that saturation has not yet been reached."

— **Geke van Dijk**

Probability sampling can also be useful for service design research, especially when you need larger sample sizes or even representative samples for large-scale quantitative research. Here are just a few examples for probability sampling techniques:

→ **Simple random sampling:** Randomly pick participants from a sampling frame.

→ **Systematic random sampling:** Select a random number, such as 10, and pick every 10th person from a flow of people as your participants.

→ **Stratified random sampling:** Separate your sampling frame into groups based on specific criteria and use simple or random sampling to select participants within these groups.

→ **Cluster sampling:** Create a list of clusters based on specific criteria and randomly choose some of these clusters, then randomly choose participants within the selected clusters.

Most projects use a combination of different sampling techniques, for example systematic random sampling in combination with snowball sampling. Often you need to set certain selection criteria as screening questions (e.g., "Do you drive an electric car?"). Emergent sampling is something we should always do anyway in design – if you find something interesting, don't ignore it. The aim of a sound sampling strategy is to avoid a sampling error,

like systematically excluding a certain group of people that should have been considered.

Research context

Besides the "who," it is also crucial to define the context of your research: "when" and "where" to conduct the research. This might seem obvious – but think, for example, of the people you'd meet at a train station on weekdays in the morning (commuting to work/school?), weekdays around noon (lunch break?), weekdays in the afternoon (commuting from work/school?), or weekdays in the evening (leisure activities?). And compare this to the same times during the weekend. Also, seasons are important: consider how hard it would be to research customer experience at a ski resort during the summer season.

It often helps to engage participants in their natural surroundings or in a specific situational context of interest. Interviews are often done at people's homes, because they are most at ease when at home. Observations or contextual interviews should be done at places where people often use the specific service or physical/digital product, as they can relate to their experience more easily in that environment and maybe even point out certain aspects of it that they like or dislike. Also consider the effect of external factors on the experience and behavior of people, such as weather, public holidays, major events, and so on.

Sample size

You might decide to fix the sample size (how many participants your research has) before data collection, or you might choose to stay flexible. This is mostly a question

Sample size in service design is determined using an ethnographic research approach based on the concept of theoretical saturation. In other words, you stop collecting data when new data does not bring additional insights to the research questions.

researchers Nielson and Landauer published an article revealing that usability tests with only 5 users found 85% of all usability problems, while they needed at least 15 users to find all problems. Since service experiences are more complex, a good rule of thumb is to start with a small but culturally diverse set of participants. If you already see patterns emerging, use the next batch to confirm the patterns you spotted and see if you've already reached theoretical saturation for these patterns.[01]

of the research objective and methods used, as well as the resources and time available.

In quantitative statistics, your sample size depends on whether the data need be representative for a defined group of people (the population). In qualitative research – and particularly in ethnographically inspired design research – researchers instead look for recurring patterns. You do enough research – such as interviews or observation – to let you identify patterns. When more research only confirms the patterns you have already identified, you have reached theoretical saturation. This means doing more research would only confirm what you already know and will not bring any new knowledge. Just like a usability test that is designed to find the biggest bugs in software, service design research is used to find the biggest bugs (or opportunities) in a physical or digital product, a service, or any (customer) experience. Unlike quantitative statistics, service design is not especially interested in accurate percentages of exactly how many people struggle with one issue, but rather needs a ranking or just a shortlist of bugs to fix, a list of inspirations as a basis for ideation, or a hit list of features customers would like to have.

When you set your sample size, it should be large enough to identify recurring patterns. In 1993, the usability

5.1.3   Data collection

There are a huge variety of research methods you can use to collect meaningful data in service design. We use quantitative methods like surveys (offline and online), any form of automated statistics (e.g., conversion rate analysis), and manually collected quantitative data (e.g., frequency of shop visitors through simple counting). However, we mostly use qualitative methods and particularly methods based on ethnography. Select and line up a sequence of research methods to collect and to visualize, synthesize, and analyze your research data. See this section and 5.1.4 for details.

[01] "How many interviews are enough?" Theoretical saturation helps us understand when we have done enough, but it doesn't help us to define a sample size a priori. For example, when you have interviewed 20 (randomly selected) participants and identified patterns, the probability that the next 20 will tell you something completely different is negligible (i.e., theoretical saturation). However, you don't know how many people you will have to ask before you start seeing these patterns – it could be 10, 20, 30, or even more. See, for example, Guest, G., Bunce, A., & Johnson, L. (2006). "How Many Interviews Are Enough? An Experiment with Data Saturation and Variability." *Field Methods*, 18(1), 59-82. For an academic review of theoretical saturation, see for example, Bowen, G. A. (2008). "Naturalistic Inquiry and the Saturation Concept: A Research Note." *Qualitative Research*, 8(1), 137-152. For a more critical reflection on this topic, see O'Reilly, M., & Parker, N. (2013). "'Unsatisfactory Saturation': A Critical Exploration of the Notion of Saturated Sample Sizes in Qualitative Research." *Qualitative Research*, 13(2), 190-197).

Overt vs. covert research

When you use research methods that include any direct contact with people – that is, with your research participants, your "research subjects" – you can decide if you want to conduct overt or covert research.

For research methods such as autoethnography, contextual interviews, online ethnography, and non-participant and participant observation, this is an especially important decision with certain advantages and disadvantages, as well as ethical implications.[01]

Overt research describes a situation where researchers are open about their research intentions and make sure that the research subjects are aware of what is happening. This has some advantages – researchers can be honest and open about their work, avoiding ethical issues such as deception or lack of informed consent. It also helps researchers avoid getting too close emotionally to the people they study. An important disadvantage of any overt research – even online research – is the "Hawthorn effect" or "observer effect." This is when subjects change their behavior to act in a way that they believe is expected by the researcher, or by society in general (this is often referred to as the "social desirability bias").

Covert research is when researchers do not share their research intentions with the research participants; they go "under cover." Even though covert research obviously has an advantage of avoiding or at least minimizing potential observer bias, it almost automatically leads to ethical concerns as researchers might deceive research participants or lack informed consent. If you decide to use covert research in a project, always consider the ethical and even legal framework in the country and organization where you plan to do your research.

You might decide in advance if overt research is in or out of scope for your project, and sometimes you might switch between both in your research. If in doubt, always choose overt research as the increased validity of your research (often) is not worth the risk of potential legal consequences of covert research. ◄

01 For a brief academic discussion on the ethics of covert research, see Van Deventer, J. P. (2009). "Ethical Considerations During Human Centred Overt and Covert Research." *Quality & Quantity*, 43(1), 45-57. For a more general scholarly literature review on overt and covert research in ethnography, see Amstel, H. R. V. (2013). "The Ethics and Arguments Surrounding Covert Research." *Social Cosmos*, 4(1), 21-26.

Research methods

You should always consider a mix of methods as each research method has its own inherent potential bias. "Actions speak louder than words" is a common saying, and indeed you often observe that people behave differently than they say they would. This can have different causes, like the "interviewer effect," when the style and personality of the interviewer affects interviewees; the "Hawthorne effect," when people modify their behavior simply based on their awareness of being observed; or "confirmation bias," when researchers tend to search for information that confirms their beliefs or assumptions and thereby ignore other data that contradicts their beliefs. However, a good mix of research methods levels out potential biases.

As a rule of thumb, for a good mix of research methods pick one method from each of the following categories:[02]

→ **Desk research**, like preparatory research, secondary research

→ **Self-ethnographic approaches**, like autoethnography, online ethnography

→ **Participant approaches**, like participant observation, contextual interviews, in-depth interviews, focus groups

→ **Non-participant approaches**, like non-participant observation, mobile ethnography, cultural probes

→ **Co-creative workshops**, like co-creating personas, journey maps, and system maps

Method triangulation

When we are selecting the "right" research methods – ones that yield a lot of useful data – we always face the question of how many research methods we should use. Given a limited budget, researchers often need to decide whether they should put their budget into one method and do this rather well, or distribute their budget to use a variety of research methods. We always suggest the latter, based on the concept of method triangulation.[03] Triangulation is based on classic navigation and land surveying techniques. In simple terms, with triangulation you can estimate your own position by measuring the directions of at least two distinct landmarks. Based on basic principles of geometry, the more landmarks we measure, the more accurately the position can be calculated. Similarly, researchers can improve the accuracy and richness of their research by using different methods to collect data on the same phenomenon.

If different methods lead to the same outcome, you can be more confident about these findings. However, in design research, triangulation is not used as much to seek validation or verification of research results,

💬 **EXPERT TIP**

"A mantra we use is to *see* the customer (observation), *hear* the customer (dialogue), and *be* the customer (self-ethnography) – three complementary methods to understand customers or employees."

– Simon Clatworthy

---

02 All of these methods are described in detail in 5.2.

03 Denzin (1978) refers to four types of triangulation: method (methodological) triangulation, data triangulation, researcher (investigator) triangulation, and theory triangulation. For more information, see Denzin, N. K. (1978). "Triangulation: A Case for Methodological Evaluation and Combination." In N. K. Denzin (ed.), *Sociological Methods: A Sourcebook* (pp. 339–357), Routledge.

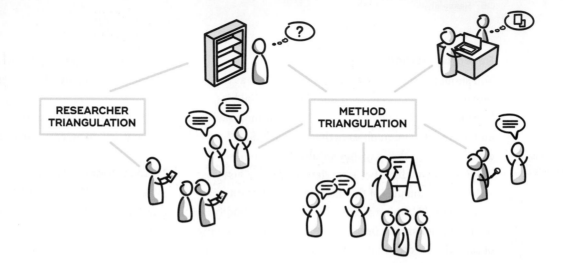

RESEARCHER TRIANGULATION

METHOD TRIANGULATION

but rather to ensure that insights are based on a rich and comprehensive dataset that is robust enough to provide a foundation for design decisions. In particular, when you do exploratory research to get inspiration for new ideas, richness of data and perspectives is key.

In a research context the fundamental idea of method triangulation is to cross-check findings with different methods.

Data triangulation

Different research methods generate different types of data as output, such as text (e.g., field notes or interview transcripts), photos, videos, artifacts (e.g., tickets or info flyers), as well as statistics. Some methods can generate different or even multiple types of data, and researchers should plan what kind of data they need. Again, following the principle of triangulation, you should strive to create different types of data in your research process.

Data triangulation enables researchers to support findings with different underpinnings and makes your dataset richer and more comprehensible. One advantage of using different types of data can be explained with a simple example. Imagine the situation of a contextual interview. If researchers only take field notes, they only write down what they regard as important. If they add photos of the situation, others can understand the situational context of the interview. If they do an audio recording of the interview and transcribe it afterwards, others have a chance to interpret the interview as well. If they take a video of the situation, others can also interpret body language and situational context. Different data types can help you to get a richer dataset and reduce the subjectivity of researchers.

Another differentiation is the distinction between primary and secondary data. Primary data is data collected by a researcher for a specific purpose. Secondary data is data that has been collected by someone else for

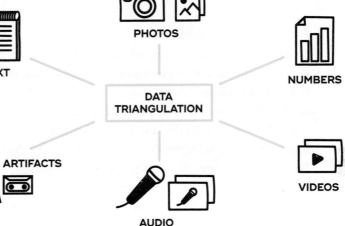

TEXT

PHOTOS

NUMBERS

DATA TRIANGULATION

ARTIFACTS

AUDIO

VIDEOS

—Use different types of triangulation to offset different forms of research bias:

—Researcher triangulation to avoid prejudices and predispositions.

—Method triangulation to get different perspectives on the same subject matter.

—Data triangulation to get a richer and more comprehensive dataset.

💬 **EXPERT TIP**

"Providing sufficient raw data speeds up the decision-making process and helps avoid endless discussions within your team and with superiors. Instead of [questions] like 'Is this really like this?' our team accept a fact when they see it with their own eyes – or even better, when they experience it themselves. They then move on and work on actionable solutions instead of pointless discussions."

– Anke Helmbrecht

other purposes, but is being used by a researcher for a new purpose. If your organization will be conducting several service design projects, it makes sense to integrate a data or knowledge management system. The outcomes from primary research in one project can serve as secondary data for another project and thereby save time and money. Researchers can build on the outcomes of prior research (i.e., secondary data) and so might be able to use a given research budget for more focused primary research, "standing on the shoulders of giants."[01]

The differentiation between first- and second-order concepts (not the same as primary and secondary data) is an important factor which affects how other researchers can work with the data. Basically, first-order concepts are the "raw data" (e.g., the direct transcript of an interview), while second-order concepts include interpretations by researchers. In practice, first-order concepts might be

any original evidence of research that researchers gain from observations or interviews – for example, interview transcripts, but also photos or videos. Second-order concepts might be summarized field notes or any other form of data filtered or biased by a researcher striving to identify patterns.[02] While both are useful, it is important to collect enough raw data (first-order concepts) that does not include interpretations by researchers, as only this raw data can be interpreted by other researchers at a later stage. Recorded data like photos or videos preserves to a large extent the raw content, which is often more convincing when presenting your results than any second-order concept. When you can do only field notes, distinguish between an accurate description of a situation studied and your personal interpretation, so that you can always go back and refine your interpretation.

01 See 12.5.6, *Case: Building up service design knowledge across projects,* for an example of how to reuse previous research.

02 The second-order concepts are the "theories" an analyst uses to organize and explain these [first-order] "facts" (p. 39), and "theories are tested, retested, and tested again in the field" (p. 51). Quotes from Van Maanen, J. (1979). "Reclaiming Qualitative Methods for Organizational Research: A Preface." *Administrative Science Quarterly,* 24(4), 520-526.

Researcher triangulation

As a (design) researcher using ethnographic methods, it is important to step into someone else's shoes. However, to be able to walk in the customer's shoes, you first need to take off your own. All researchers have their individual background, knowledge, and prejudices. It's almost impossible to get rid of this "researcher bias," but it helps if you become aware of your own tendencies regarding your interpretations and conclusions (e.g., through peer reflection by other researchers regarding potential biases and predispositions).

Researchers should also be aware of their "researcher status" – the social position a researcher holds among the studied group. Depending on your status, participants will react differently to your questions. This is something to consider in your research planning. How do you communicate the research to participants? Which research aim do you communicate? What expectations do your participants get through this and which hidden intentions might arise as a consequence?

One way to tackle researcher bias is by including various researchers, both during the collection of data and during synthesis and analysis. This researcher triangulation can help to reduce the level of subjectivity in ethnographic research and keep the team on a consistent knowledge level throughout the project. One way to increase the number of researchers involved is to use methods of data collection that actively integrate participants as researchers (e.g., diary studies or mobile ethnography) or methods that put researchers in the roles of participants (e.g., service safari or autoethnography).

In general, you'll have more informed conversations and increase buy-in from clients or management if your design process includes people from the client organization or management as well as other stakeholders. Invite them to participate in your fieldwork – even if they only have limited time. In most cases, contact with customers and other research participants will increase appreciation for research, and attention to customer needs.

Sometimes the downside can be that invited clients or management use such opportunities to explain or even promote their offerings to interviewees, or to prioritize single users or responses. One way of supporting less-knowledgeable clients could be by assigning them a clear role, such as a supporting interviewer or observer, while the members of the key project team lead the fieldwork.

Indexing

During your research, it is important to index your data so that you can trace insights back to the data sources they are based on. A simple way of indexing could be to label data with a short index, such as "i6.17" for interview 6, line 17, or "v12.3:22" for video 12, at minute 3:22. This allows you to later base your design decisions not only on insights you have generated, but on raw data. You might even be able to include the participants who reported a specific phenomenon in your prototyping of solutions to improve the original situation.[01]

💬 **COMMENT**

"Jürgen Habermas described a [...] way to apprehend reality in a way that may reduce research bias [...]:

1. Use research tools to produce/collect numbers (dry quantitative data) about the intended context of research;

2. Cast the most accepted or the researchers' preferred interpretation (what these numbers 'obviously' say);

3. Based on the same numbers, develop contrasting/alternative interpretations (what these numbers could also say);

4. Reflect upon the different interpretations in order to fine-tune the researcher's perception."

— **Mauricio Manhães**

---

01 See 5.4.1, *Case: Applying ethnography to gain actionable insights*, for a nice example of how to use indexing with a coding system to consistently trace every step of a design process to the research results.

5.1.4   Data visualization, synthesis, and analysis

💬 **EXPERT TIP**

"It is often iterating within stages, as well as between techniques: coding data then sifting and filtering and then analyzing to draw out insights. For example, in diary studies we write up all comments in a spreadsheet, look for common patterns and highlight/color code, then dig deeper again on specific issues and reanalyze comments. The issues identified are then explored further in exit interviews."

– Phillippa Rose

There are many ways to synthesize and analyze data (also known as sensemaking) in design research. In general, we can see two major ways to do this: the academic way and the practitioner's way. Although we'll focus mostly on the practitioner's approach, we can learn a lot from academic approaches.

The academic way to work with qualitative data mostly includes codifying data and then searching for patterns within this codified data. This process is often referred to as *content analysis* – there are various methods and even software[02] to support researchers in doing this, but of course pen and paper will often also do the job. For example, a researcher could codify the data by going through transcribed interviews and tagging sentences with specific labels. In a second step, the researcher then counts how often specific labels occur – or rather a software tool does this automatically.[03] This process takes some time, but is particularly useful when you have to cope with a huge amount of data because it lets you split up a set of data and work your way through it step by step. This happens often when you plan research design with a classic project management approach: one period of data collection followed by one period of data analysis.

However, if you follow an iterative research design with a rather visual synthesis and analysis process, you won't be drowning in data as you will have multiple iterations of data collection, synthesis, and analysis.

Visualizing data

Visualizing data helps teams get an overview of the amount of information, brings structure into complex data, identifies patterns, and uncovers existing gaps in the data. It also deepens their understanding of a topic and develops empathy with the people who were the subject of the research. There are many ways to visually work with and present research, and what makes sense depends on your aim. The following list summarizes some common ways to visualize research data in service design, with a brief description of why each might be useful:[04]

→ **A research wall**[05] to give you an easy overview of your data and your mix of research methods and data types; the wall may contain any of the other assets listed here.

→ **Personas** to exemplify different groups of people, such as customers or employees, and their individual characteristics, goals, and/or tasks.

→ **(Customer) journey maps** to visualize customer experiences happening over time.

---

02 Researchers use a huge variety of software to synthesize and analyze data, from simple spreadsheets or documents to sophisticated qualitative research software, such as ATLAS.ti, MAXQDA, NVivo, or QDA Miner, to name but a few. There is a wide selection of very specialized research software for different purposes.

03 Some methods require transcribing audio and video files so that researchers work only with text files. With new software, various data types can be codified using the same software: text can be coded at certain lines, audio and video files at certain timestamps, and photos at certain positions.

04 All of these methods are described in detail in 5.3.

05 Keep your research wall separate from your idea wall, if you have one. The concept of an idea wall is explained in Chapter 6, *Ideation*.

Generic stages of a customer journey

This is a list of generic elements of a high-level customer journey. This list can act as a pragmatic checklist to see whether you have already included all the main steps, or if you need to do more research to fill any potential gaps.

PRE-SERVICE

1 Wake up: Become aware. The customer becomes passively aware of the service provider and/or their services.

2 Wise up: Find out more, understand, consider. The customer looks for more information. This includes first direct interactions with peers, review sites, or the service provider as well as the decision-making process.

3 Join up: Enter the (service) system. The customer co-designs and/or negotiates the service or contract, and signs up or makes the purchase.

SERVICE

4 Set up: Prepare the project or service, prepare the use of the product. The customer sets up the service and prepares for first use.

5 Start up: Do the first real runthrough, use the product for the first time. The customer experiences the service. At this stage, some support systems for new customers may still be in place, while others for experienced customers may not yet be offered.

6 Keep up: Co-create value repeatedly (habitual use). The service co-creates the planned value and is experienced on a regular basis.

7 Mess(ed) up: Resolve incidents or problems. Something goes wrong; perhaps the customer reports an issue. The customer's questions or issues are answered and resolved.

8 Grow up: Grow the service or use of the product. Upgrade. Add. As the customer becomes experienced, she may start to extend her usage or add more service offerings to the existing package.

9 Pay up: Pay for the service. The customer pays for the service, perhaps with money, data, attention, or another value exchange.

10 Close up: Shut down the service or stop using the product. The customer decides to stop using the service (or signs up again).

POST-SERVICE

11 Speak up: Share your experience. The customer shares her experience with others.

12 Listen up: Stay in the loop. The customer receives advertisements, occasional phone calls, or invites to events to stay in the loop even though he is not actually a client at this time. This closes the loop, returning to the step "Wake up: Become aware." ◄

→ **System maps** to show relationships between stakeholders and product-service ecosystems.

→ **Key insights** to highlight the biggest customer problems or potentials customers have regarding a certain physical/digital product or service.

→ **Jobs to be done** to emphasize the big picture of what customers strive to achieve.

→ **User stories** to ensure a common language with software developers.

→ **Research reports** to ensure a comprehensive research overview, often including many of the tools above.

It is important to consider the target audience for your visualization and ask yourself what exactly you want to share. Different audiences will have different needs – do they need pithy research insights or lots of raw data? Do you need something rather formal and self-explanatory so your outcomes can be used in different departments or organizations? Or are your outcomes only needed for your internal team? Any research outcome that you need to communicate beyond your own team needs more polish.

Peer review and co-creation

One simple way to increase the quality of your research is through peer review. Include other researchers, customers, employees, and stakeholders to benefit from multiple perspectives and reduce the risk of confirmation bias. If you want to include others at this stage, they must be able to understand your data and draw their own conclusions. So, aim to collect as much raw data (i.e., first-order concepts) as possible and compare your own interpretations with those of your peers. Make sure that insights are always trackable to your raw data (use indexing), so that reviewers can understand the translation from data to insight and second it.

As a rule of thumb, it is easier to include other people early on during the synthesis and analysis stage, so that you can cluster your data and generate categories using a co-creative approach instead of only inviting others to review your work. However, sometimes co-creative workshops are not possible; then, peer-review is a way to limit subjectivity and research bias.

Codifying data

One major question when you're codifying data[01] is this: where do the categories for these codes come from? Mostly, qualitative research is understood to follow an inductive approach in which researchers "immerse" themselves in the data and generate categories and insights from the data itself. On the other hand, sometimes researchers follow a deductive approach and start with a defined set of categories derived from literature or other research, but then eliminate or add categories

01   Note the difference between *codifying data* and *indexing data*. Labels used for indexing data are often rather cryptic and only serve to find a specific piece of data within the raw dataset (e.g., "i6.17" or "o12.3:22"). Labels or tags used for codifying data are often keywords to summarize or interpret parts of the data. This could be categories of customer problems or phrases that customers repeatedly mentioned (e.g., "ticket machine" or "too little time to choose"). However, in practice, indexing and coding are often mixed up or used interchangeably.

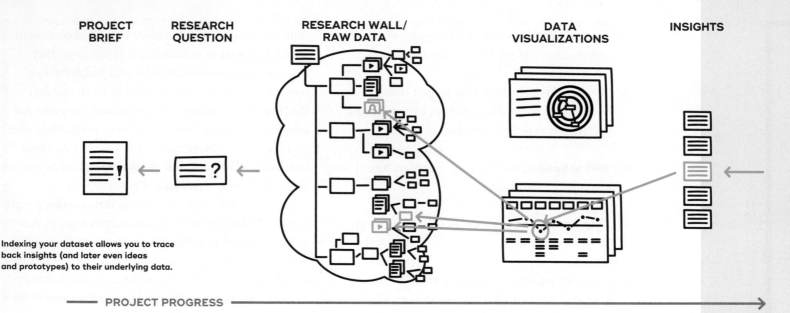

PROJECT   RESEARCH   RESEARCH WALL/   DATA   INSIGHTS
BRIEF   QUESTION   RAW DATA   VISUALIZATIONS

Indexing your dataset allows you to trace back insights (and later even ideas and prototypes) to their underlying data.

PROJECT PROGRESS

through their data synthesis. Deductive qualitative analysis strives to test specific assumptions or concepts and therefore often categorizes data in previously defined categories. While design research to identify customer experience gaps or people's needs is mostly inductive, research to test prototypes is often rather deductive.

5.1.5 Using research outcomes

The outcome of service design research usually serves as input for other service design activities, such as ideation or prototyping. In some cases, research output can even be used directly in implementation activities. For example, research can sometimes reveal simple

usability improvements for a piece of software that can be described as user stories and directly implemented during software development.[01] The usual case, however, is that topics identified during the research process are visualized with personas, journey maps, system maps, key insights, jobs to be done, user stories, or research reports. These can be used to identify problems or opportunities in subsequent ideation activities.[02] If you already have some immediate ideas of how to solve discovered issues, you might also directly try to prototype these in prototyping activities.[03]

---

01 See *Writing user stories* in 5.3 for a description of user stories and 8.3, *Service design and software development*, on how to use these in software development.

02 See Chapter 6, *Ideation*.

03 See Chapter 7, *Prototyping*.

Problem space vs. solution space

Immediate solutions usually just fix a symptom, but not the deeper problem (or opportunity) underneath.

Typically, during research activities, you explore in detail the existing problems of an experience, a process, or a system. You try to question what you see and challenge your assumptions. At least, this is what you should do. Unfortunately, one problem is that we as humans are trained to solve problems. When we see a problem, we immediately start thinking about potential solutions.

This is unfortunate, as these are probably not solutions for the root cause. To be able to work on that, you need to invest more effort into understanding the problem. You need to remain longer in the problem space, without jumping into the solution space too soon.

Sometimes it helps a design team if they clearly understand where they are. Are you in the problem space trying to understand someone's problem in more detail and depth, exploring this from various perspectives and trying to dig deeper and discover the root cause of it? Or are you in the solution space striving to find ideas on how to solve a well-defined problem? You can make this clear using visual clues such as a poster on the wall wherever your design team works, by clearly articulating where you are in your meetings and workshops.

Of course, a design team will have many ideas during research activities and it would be a shame to lose them. If ideas come up during research, capture them on an idea wall[04] and then let go.

Or, you might want to see the idea as a hypothesis and rephrase it into its underlying assumptions – this feeds into your next research iteration as a new research question. Also, you might want to brief your team before the next steps of the design process, such as ideation activities that might follow your research. ◄

04 See Chapter 6, *Ideation*, for more on dealing with ideas that come up at unexpected times.

O5
RESEARCH
METHODS

THESE
ARE
SERVICE
DESIGN
METHODS.

THIS IS
SERVICE
DESIGN
DOING.

Read more on methods and
tools in our free online resources at:

www.tisdd.com

5.2 METHODS OF DATA COLLECTION

This section provides a wide selection of potential research methods to collect data in service design research. Many more methods exist, and often the same method has several inconsistent names. We can only give a very brief introduction for each method, but if you want to dig deeper, there is plenty of literature – and for some methods, even whole books – with detailed descriptions and examples.[01] The research methods are structured in five categories:

These categories are not an academic standard, and as there are many variations and names for each research method, the boundaries between the categories might be rather fluid. However, as a rule of thumb, we suggest you use at least one method from each category in your research to give better method triangulation.

→ **Desk research:** Preparatory research, secondary research

→ **Self-ethnographic approaches:** Autoethnography, online ethnography

→ **Participant approaches:** Participant observation, contextual interviews, in-depth interviews, focus groups

→ **Non-participant approaches:** Non-participant observation, mobile ethnography, cultural probes

→ **Co-creative workshops:** Creating personas, journey mapping, system mapping

01 See also the more detailed online versions of these methods at *www.tisdd.com.*

(A) "Prep" research often includes an online search for certain keywords, companies, and competitors as well as searching for scholarly research on specific topics.

(B) When doing secondary research, keep notes and explore potentially interesting topics iteratively.

(C) A smartphone and/or a simple notepad is often the best tool to document autoethnographic research.

DESK RESEARCH
Preparatory research 👆

Your own preparation before you start your actual research or fieldwork.[01]

Preparatory (or simply "prep") research often includes digging deeper into an industry, an organization, competitors, or similar products, and also the client's perspective of what the research problem is, their context, perceptions, internal conflicts or interplays, and so on. Prep research is less about finding answers, and more about finding the right questions to ask in your research. Prep research can result in a summary of text snippets and/or a collection of photos, screenshots, or videos, perhaps visualized as a mood board.

Preparation: Often prep research starts with very wide research questions or topics, from soft topics such as "How does *home* feel?" to rather specific topics such as "Where else is this technology used?"

Use: Prep research can include conducting internal interviews; screening social media; listening to podcasts, online videos, or conference talks; and reading industry-specific scientific or special-interest publications along with newspapers or general-interest magazines.

Expected output: Text, statistics, photos, and videos, as well as mind maps, mood boards, and the like

01 See 9.2.2, *Preparatory research*, for a brief description of the importance of prep research for the overall service design process.

DESK RESEARCH
Secondary research 🖱

The collection, synthesis, and summary of existing research.[02]

In contrast to primary research, secondary research (often also simply called "desk research") uses only existing secondary data – information collected for other projects or purposes. The main idea is to check whether research regarding a topic already exists. This helps us to formulate a research question more precisely and identify promising methods of data collection, visualization, and synthesis. Desk research should always be the starting point of a research process, simply to avoid reinventing the wheel and to stand on the shoulders of giants when you start your primary research.

Preparation: Collect a list of potentially promising internal and/or external sources such as academic papers, white papers, and reports, as well as experts on your research topic.

Use: Search for qualitative and quantitative secondary data regarding your research topic using online search engines, scientific databases and journals, libraries, conferences, and expert talks and interviews.

Expected output: Text, statistics, mind maps and the like

SELF-ETHNOGRAPHIC APPROACH
Autoethnography 🖱

Researchers explore a particular experience themselves and self-document this using field notes, audio recordings, videos, and photographs;[03] also called self-ethnography/documentation.

Besides "real" (i.e., rather academic) autoethnographic research where researchers immerse themselves for months within an organization, service design often applies shorter versions of this: team members explore a particular experience themselves in the real situational context, mostly as customers or as employees. Variants of this include mystery shopping, mystery working, service safaris, explorative service safaris, or diary studies.

Preparation: Autoethnography is often one of the first research methods undertaken as it helps researchers to interpret behaviors when they conduct interviews or observations. Decide when and where you will conduct your research.

Use: Autoethnography can address one or more channels as well as actions with or without other people and/or machines. If you take field notes, write up first-level ("raw data") and second-level concepts ("interpretations") separately: for example, what you see and hear on the left page and what you interpret from this or how it feels on the right.

Expected output: Text (transcripts, field notes), audio recordings, photos, videos, artifacts

02 For a description and discussion of a more systematic process to use secondary data in research see, for example: Johnston, M. P. (2017). Secondary data analysis: A method of which the time has come. *Qualitative and Quantitative Methods in Libraries*, 3(3), 619-626.

03 For a more comprehensive introduction to how autoethnography can be used as a qualitative research method see, for example, Adams, T. E., Holman Jones, S., & Ellis, C. (2015). *Autoethnography: Understanding Qualitative Research* (Oxford University Press).

SELF-ETHNOGRAPHIC APPROACH

Online ethnography 🖳

An approach to investigate how people interact with one another in online communities,[01] **also known as virtual or cyber ethnography.**

Online ethnography can be done as self-ethnographic research, non-participant ethnography, or participant ethnography – however, it always focuses on online experiences. It can look at many different aspects, such as social interactions within an online community or the differences between the self-perception of people when they are online and in real life.

Preparation: Based on your research question, define which online communities might be suitable for your research question. Decide how you will document your experiences; e.g., through screenshots or screencasts, system or journey maps, or simply field notes.

Use: Often online ethnographies include a mix of methods, such as observations, contextual interviews conducted online with screen sharing, or in-depth retrospective interviews with other community members.

Expected output: Text (quotes, transcripts, field notes), screenshots, recordings (screencasts or audio recordings)

PARTICIPANT APPROACH

Participant observation 🖳

Researchers immerse themselves in the lives of research participants.

Participant observation is an umbrella term for a variety of methods, such as shadowing, a day in the life, or work-along.[02]

Preparation: Based on your research question, select suitable interviewees and plan when and where you will conduct your research and how you will document it. How will you approach your participants? How will you start and end? How will you manage the "observer effect"? How much time will you plan for it?

Use: Observations might be at the participant's workplace, in their home, or even following them throughout a process like a holiday trip. Use the situational context and ask participants to explain specific activities, artifacts, behavior, motivations, needs, pains, or gains. Sometimes contradictions between what people say and what people do can be very revealing if you mirror behavior back to participants. During participant observations it is important to observe not only what people are doing (by interpreting their body language and gestures) but also what they are not doing.

Expected output: Text (transcripts, field notes), audio recordings, photos, videos, artifacts

01 One of the most-cited descriptions of virtual ethnography is Hine, C. (2000). *Virtual Ethnography*. Sage.

02 According to one of the seminal books on participant observation from 1980, there's a continuum in the level of researcher involvement from non-participatory to passive, moderate, active, and complete participation. See (new edition) Spradley, J. P. (2016). *Participant Observation*. Waveland Press.

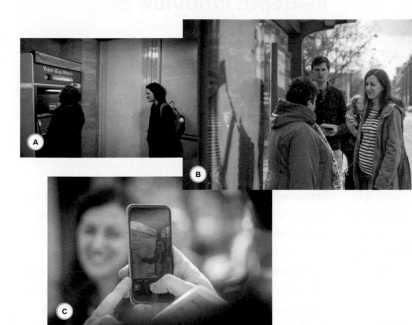

(A) When researchers conduct participant observations, they often switch between more passively observing situations and actively asking questions to get a deeper understanding of user needs.

(B) Contextual interviews help interviewees to articulate problems and needs as they are in the situational context, and they can simply show things right where they are.

(C) During contextual interviews or observations, take audio or video recordings to enable data triangulation, if possible.

PARTICIPANT APPROACH
Contextual interview 🖰

Interviews conducted with customers, employees, or any other relevant stakeholders in a situational context relevant to the research question,[03] also known as contextual inquiry.

Contextual interviews are used to understand a certain group of people better (their needs, emotions, expectations, and environment – useful for personas), to reveal formal and informal networks and hidden agendas of specific actors (useful for system maps), or to understand particular experiences (useful for journey maps). Contextual interviews can be done, for example, with employees at their workplace or with customers during a specific moment of the customer experience.

Preparation: In contrast to studio interviews, contextual ones are conducted "in situational context," so that researchers can observe the surroundings and interviewees can point to elements in the environment. Based on your research question, define who, when, and where you will interview and how you will document the situational context – including the interviewee's mood, gestures, and body language.

Use: Try to ask your interviewees to demonstrate details of the concrete experience of interest. It is often easier for people to articulate their motivations and experience when they can refer to concrete examples.

Expected output: Text (transcripts, field notes), audio recordings, photos, videos, artifacts

03 See, for example, Beyer, H., & Holtzblatt, K. (1997). *Contextual Design: Defining Customer-centered Systems.* Elsevier.

(A) Pay attention to your interviewees' body language and gestures and write down interesting observations. This often leads to further questions.

(B) Try to differentiate between concrete observations and your own interpretations (first-level/second-level concepts).

PARTICIPANT APPROACH
In-depth interview

A qualitative research technique of conducting intensive individual interviews.

In-depth interviews are often conducted with relevant stakeholders or external experts to understand different perspectives on a specific subject. These interviews can help researchers learn more about particular expectations, experiences, products, services, goods, operations, processes, and concerns, and also about a person's attitude, problems, needs, ideas, or environment.

Preparation: In-depth interviews are mostly done in a semistructured way to collect useful data. For example, interview guidelines can be based on an empathy map.[01] In-depth interviews are mostly done face to face, allowing researchers to observe body language and create a more intimate atmosphere. They can also be conducted online or by telephone.

Use: These interviews can be supported by co-creating boundary objects, such as scribbles or mind maps, or using personas, journey maps, system maps, or other useful templates. They can also include tasks like card sorting to understand user needs or storytelling supported by tangible touchpoint cards to visualize experiences.

Expected output: Text (transcripts, field notes), audio recordings, photos, videos, artifacts

01 The original empathy map includes the topics of *Who are we empathizing with?*, *What do they need to do?*, *What do they see/say/do/hear?*, and *What do they think and feel (pains and gains)?* In 2017, *Who are we empathizing with?* and *What do they need to do?* were added to the original template. See Gray, D., Brown, S., & Macanufo, J. (2010). *Gamestorming: A Playbook for Innovators, Rulebreakers, and Changemakers.* Sebastopol: O'Reilly.

PARTICIPANT APPROACH

Focus groups 👆

A classic qualitative interview research method in which a researcher invites a group of people and asks them questions on specific products, services, goods, concepts, problems, prototypes, advertisements, etc.

With a focus group, researchers strive to understand the perceptions, opinions, ideas, or attitudes toward a given topic. Although focus groups are often used in business, they have only limited applicability in service design. They typically lack the situational context and usually do not co-create boundary objects, such as personas or journey/system maps. This often leads to limited informative value as results depend solely on the moderated discussion and are biased by issues like observer effect, group think, social desirability bias, etc.[02]

Preparation: Focus groups are mostly carried out in a rather informal setting, like a meeting room or a special room where researchers observe the situation through a one-way mirror.

Use: Researchers often ask only an initial question and then observe the group discussion and dynamics. Sometimes a researcher acts as a moderator guiding the group through a set of questions.

Expected output: Text (transcripts, notes), audio recordings, photos, videos

NON-PARTICIPANT APPROACH

Non-participant observation 👆

Researchers collect data by observing behavior without actively interacting with the participants.

In non-participant observation, researchers do not interact with research participants; they behave like a "fly on the wall." Research subjects are often customers, employees, or other stakeholders, observed in situations that are relevant to the research question. Often, non-participant observation is used to level out researcher biases in other methods and to reveal differences between what people say and what they actually do.

Preparation: Plan who will do the research, when, where, and with whom. Sometimes when researchers do covert non-participant observation they pretend to be customers or passers-by, or even use one-way mirrors, minimizing the risk of the "observer effect."[03]

Use: During non-participant observations, it is important to observe not only what people are doing (for example by interpreting their body language and gestures), but also what people are not doing (perhaps ignoring instructions or refraining from asking for help or assistance).

Expected output: Text (field notes), photos, videos, audio recordings, sketches, artifacts, statistics (e.g., counting customers per hour)

---

02 You might realize a certain bias regarding focus groups in this text. Here's why: "Focus groups are actually *contraindicated* by important insights from several disciplines," says Gerald Zaltman, Emeritus Professor, Harvard Business School. "The correlation between stated intent and actual behavior is usually low and negative." Source: Zaltman, G. (2003). *How Customers Think: Essential Insights into the Mind of the Market*. Harvard Business Press, p. 122.

03 You can also do overt non-participant observation, for example, when researchers sit in on meetings or workshops on site, but do not actively participate in it. They behave like a "fly on the wall". See also the textbox *Overt vs. covert research* in 5.1.3.

NON-PARTICIPANT APPROACH
Mobile ethnography 🖱

Aggregated multiple self-ethnographies, taking place in a guided research setting where data is collected with mobile devices such as smartphones.[01]

A mobile ethnography research project can include anywhere from a handful to thousands of participants. Usually users, customers, or employees are included as participants, self-documenting their own experiences on their own smartphones with text, photos, videos, or quantitative evaluations, as well as date, time, and location. Researchers can review, synthesize, analyze, and export the collected data in real time.

Preparation: Plan to offer incentives for your participants (recruiting is often the hardest part!). In your invitation, provide clear and short instructions on how to join the project and how to document. Define questions for your participant profile so that you can cluster participants into groups matching your personas.

Use: Mobile ethnography works well for longer research over one or a few days. Once you have started your data collection, you can start to synthesize and analyze.

Expected output: Text, photos, videos, audio recordings, date and time information, geolocation data, statistics of participant profiles

NON-PARTICIPANT APPROACH
Cultural probes 🖱

Selected research participants collect packages of information based on specific tasks given by researchers.[02]

In cultural probes, research participants are asked to self-document certain experiences with field notes and photos, and/or to collect relevant artifacts. Cultural probes are often also done virtually using online diary platforms or mobile ethnography apps.

Preparation: Prepare and send a package to participants, which might include a set of instructions, a notebook, and a single-use camera. You might want to prepare a simple script for participants to follow, or instruct them to take photos of how they use specific products in various contexts.

Use: The aim of cultural probes is to gain unbiased data that has been collected by participants themselves in context, without having a researcher present. They help researchers to understand and overcome cultural boundaries and bring diverse perspectives into a design process. Cultural probes are often a mix of various approaches and may be combined with in-depth interviews to review the collected data retrospectively. They can include diaries kept over a day, a week, or even several years.

Expected output: Text (self-documented notes, diaries), photos, videos, audio recordings, artifacts

[01] For a comparison of mobile ethnography with other ethnographic approaches, see Segelström, F., & Holmlid, S. (2012). "One Case, Three Ethnographic Styles: Exploring Different Ethnographic Approaches to the Same Broad Brief." In *Ethnographic Praxis in Industry Conference Proceedings*, 2012 (1), 48-62. For more examples of applied mobile ethnography in tourism, see Stickdorn, M., & Frischhut, B. (eds.) (2012). *Service Design and Tourism: Case Studies of Applied Research Projects on Mobile Ethnography for Tourism Destinations.* BoD–Books on Demand.

[02] For an introduction on how to use cultural probes in design see, for example, Gaver, B., Dunne, T., & Pacenti, E. (1999). "Design: Cultural Probes." *interactions*, 6(1), 21-29.

Co-creating personas 👆

Using the know-how of a group of invited participants to create a set of personas.

The quality of results of a co-creative persona workshop depends on the research data you bring to the workshop and on how much participants know about the group of people you want to exemplify with personas – for example, a workshop with frontline employees is often quite useful to create personas of customers. For less biased results, avoid inviting only people with abstract knowledge of the subject matter. The results might look convincing, but often they are very biased.

Preparation: Invite and incentivize your workshop participants and describe the aim of the workshop. Select participants with in-depth knowledge of the stakeholder group you are creating the persona for. Write a facilitation agenda to create a safe space during the workshop.[05]

Use: These workshops often follow a structure similar to this: welcome and split into smaller groups, create initial personas, present and cluster, discuss and merge, visualize and validate, iterate.

Expected output: Drafts of personas (physical or digital), workshop photos, quotes of participants (audio or text), videos of workshop progress

(A) Participants use a mobile ethnography app on their smartphones to report on and evaluate their experiences step by step. Researchers see the data in real time and can start analyzing it immediately.[03]

(B) The content of a cultural probe (the observation package) to research flight travel experiences.[04]

(C) Even though age and gender is always an easy start for a persona, demographics might be quite misleading. Instead, think of factors that differentiate the groups you would like to represent with your personas.

03 Photo: ExperienceFellow.

04 Photo: Martin Jordan.

05 See 3.2, *Personas*; see Chapter 10, *Facilitating workshops*, for hands-on tips on facilitation and how to build a safe space.

CO-CREATIVE WORKSHOP

Co-creating journey maps 🖱

Using the know-how of a group of invited participants to create one or more journey maps or service blueprints.

Invite participants who have solid knowledge about the experience you are mapping. If you want to create a journey map about customer experiences, this might be customers (yes, real ones!) and/or frontline employees. The outcomes of co-creative workshops are often assumption-based. The results might look convincing, but often they are biased. These outcomes should be understood as tools in development, as a common starting point to design the research process, or to evaluate and enhance collected data.

Preparation: Think about inviting workshop participants with either a shared perspective (such as customers of a particular target group) or from differing perspectives (such as customers of various target groups or customers and employees). Clearly communicate the scope of the journey map, such as a high-level journey map vs. a more detailed map of one specific situation within a high-level journey map.

Use: Define your main actor and journey scope, welcome and split into smaller groups, identify stages and steps, iterate and refine, add perspectives such as the emotional journey (optional), discuss and merge, iterate.

Expected output: Drafts of journey maps (physical or digital), workshop photos, quotes of participants (audio or text), videos of workshop progress

CO-CREATIVE WORKSHOP

Co-creating system maps 🖱

Using the know-how of a group of invited participants to create system maps.[01]

For each system map, define a specific perspective and invite participants with a sound knowledge of this. With your decision on who to invite and who to leave out, you also decide which perspectives might be interesting enough to include. Constantly challenge your assumptions with solid research. Over time, assumption-based maps should develop into research-based ones.

Preparation: In addition to the know-how of the workshop participants, a second important factor is the qualitative research you do beforehand and bring to the workshop, for example through a research wall.

Use: Setting a clear scope and situational context helps workshop participants to get on the same page. Often these workshops follow a structure like this: welcome and split into smaller groups, create initial stakeholder maps (1. list stakeholders, 2. prioritize stakeholders, 3. visualize stakeholders on map, 4. illustrate relationships between stakeholders), present and compare, discuss and merge, iterate and validate, test different scenarios within the ecosystem (optional).

Expected output: Drafts of system maps (physical or digital), workshop photos, quotes of participants (audio or text), videos of workshop progress

01 See also 3.4, *System maps*, and Chapter 10, *Facilitating workshops.*

5.3 METHODS OF DATA VISUALIZATION, SYNTHESIS, AND ANALYSIS

This section introduces methods used in service design to visualize, synthesize, and analyze data collected as described in the previous section – sometimes this process is also called "sensemaking." This is just a brief overview; there are many more approaches to visualize data, and plenty of appropriate ways to communicate the data and insights. Also, often the same method is known by several (perhaps inconsistently used) names. If you want to dig deeper, there is plenty of literature, and for some methods even whole books with detailed descriptions and examples.

This section presents eight methods of data visualization and analysis:

→ **Building a research wall**
→ **Creating personas**
→ **Mapping journeys**
→ **Mapping systems**
→ **Developing key insights**
→ **Generating jobs-to-be-done insights**
→ **Writing user stories**
→ **Compiling research reports**

(A)   Visualizations, such as a journey map, help participants to understand the context of each step and enable them to navigate quicker.

(B)   Paper templates often help participants to get started and to take a task seriously. The more familiar they become with a tool, the less important templates are for them.

(C)   Value network maps quickly can become quite messy. Try to give a map a specific focus to keep an overview.

Building a research wall 📑

Creating personas 📑

Synthesizing and analyzing research data through a visual arrangement of research data on a wall.[01]

You can imagine a research wall as a more complex version of how detectives structure their crime scene data in many thrillers (think of any *CSI* episode). You'll find many types of data on these walls (quotes, photos, screenshots of websites or videos, statistics, artifacts, etc.). This enables you to identify patterns within your data, while also providing a place to share your research with others as it develops.

Preparation: Prepare a wall space or large cardboard sheets to hang up your research data. Also, think about who should join you to create a research wall.

Use: Hang the material on the wall and start synthesizing data by clustering it according to specific topics, like certain customer segments, common problems, steps along the journey map, etc. Name these clusters and look for connections between clusters as well as connections between single materials (be aware of a potential confirmation bias). The various patterns you identify can then be further explored with tools like personas, journey maps, system maps, key insights, and so on – all of which also become part of the research wall.

Expected output: A visual arrangement of research data

Creating a rich description of a specific fictional person as an archetype exemplifying a group of people, such as a group of customers, users, or employees.[02]

Personas focus on particular types of customer motivations and behaviors, and help to achieve empathy with a group of people to create solutions that address real problems. You can create them for existing market segments or to challenge an existing segmentation.

Preparation: Persona templates or empathy maps are sometimes helpful when creating personas. You often mix different approaches – for example, starting with assumption-based personas developed during a co-creative workshop with frontline staff, then enriching and backing these with research.

Use: Create approximately three to seven core personas representing your main market segments. Following the principle of "design for the average – test with extremes," create many more "edge-of-the-curve" personas to test ideas and prototypes with people from more extreme ends of your user spectrum.

Expected output: Personas

---

01 See 8.3, *Service design and software development* for an example of how a research wall is used to connect different service design activities of research, ideation, prototyping, and implementation.

02 For a comprehensive introduction to creating and using personas see, for example, Goodwin, K. (2011). *Designing for the Digital Age: How to Create Human-centered Products and Services.* John Wiley & Sons.

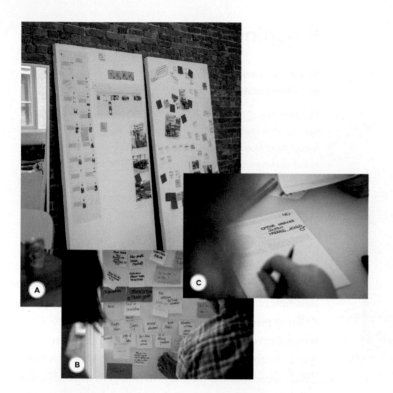

(A) Using foam boards as research walls helps a research team to keep research data (such as quotes, photos, screenshots, artifacts, etc.) with them when they have to move between rooms.

(B) Structure your research wall by clustering and adding headings to the different sections.

(C) Starting personas with demographics, like age, gender, nationality, job, and so on, carries the risk of stereotyping. Instead, try to build your personas from your research, perhaps starting with behavioral patterns you find within your data.

Mapping journeys 🖱

Visualizing specific experiences of a main actor, often exemplified by a persona, over time.

Journey maps can visualize[03] existing experiences (current-state journey maps) or planned experiences (future-state journey maps). The basic structure of a journey map consists of steps and stages defining the scale of the visualized experience, from a high-level journey map that shows an end-to-end experience to a detailed journey map showing only a few minutes.

Preparation: Even though assumption-based journey maps are relatively easy and fast to do, they can be very misleading. If you start with assumption-based journey maps, constantly challenge your assumptions. Over time, assumption-based journey maps should develop into research-based ones with a solid foundation on research data (beware of confirmation bias).[04]

Use: Often a process to create a journey map looks like this: prepare and print out data, choose a main actor (persona), define scale and scope, create steps, iterate and refine, add lanes.

Expected output: Journey maps

03 There are many ways to visualize experiences as maps. See, for example, Kalbach, J. (2016). *Mapping Experiences: A Complete Guide to Creating Value through Journeys, Blueprints, and Diagrams.* O'Reilly.

04 For case studies detailing how to use journey maps in service design projects, see 5.4.4, *Case: Illustrating research data with journey maps*, as well as 5.4.5, *Case: Current-state (as-is) and Future-state (to-be) Journey Mapping.*

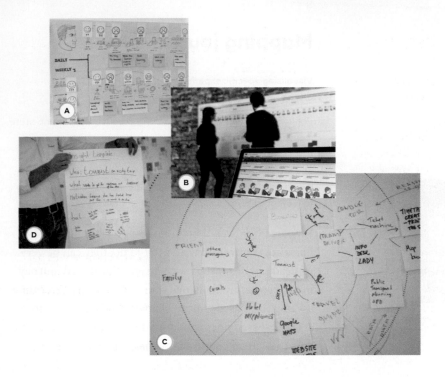

Mapping systems 👆

Visualizing the ecosystem around services and physical or digital products.

"System maps" is an umbrella term for different visualizations, such as stakeholder maps, value network maps, or ecosystem maps. All of these can be created from various perspectives. A system looks different from a customer's perspective compared with a business internal perspective. System maps have obvious relationships to other tools in service design, such as personas and journey maps.[03]

Preparation: As system maps can become very messy, it is important to define a clear focus for a map. Don't try to visualize every stakeholder you can think of on the same stakeholder map; it's more useful to make various maps for different purposes. System maps are an excellent tool to synthesize research data, so it is useful to prepare research data beforehand. Remember that research is iterative, and it makes sense to use these maps to find gaps in your research, which you can investigate in later research iterations.

Use: Often, creating system maps looks like this: prepare and print out data, collect stakeholders, prioritize stakeholders, visualize stakeholders on map, illustrate relationships between stakeholders (optional), find gaps and iterate.

Expected output: System maps

(A) A journey map visualizing two different scales of daily and weekly user activities. The map includes a sketched storyboard, an emotional journey, and user needs.[01]

(B) Journey mapping software helps you to quickly create professional journey maps with dispersed teams.[02]

(C) System maps are often hard to understand for people outside of your core team. Reduce them to the most important facts when you use them for communication.

(D) Using templates or a specific structure helps to develop key insights, but constantly ask yourself if every aspect of your insight is specific and clear enough and if it is backed by sufficient research data.

01 Photo: Wuji Shang and Muwei Wang, MDes, Service Design and Innovation, LCC, University of the Arts, London.

02 Photo: Smaply.

03 The mapping of systems is particularly useful in the context of product service system innovation. See, for example, Morelli, N. (2006). "Developing New Product Service Systems (PSS): Methodologies and Operational Tools." *Journal of Cleaner Production*, 14(17), 1495-1501.

Developing key insights 🖱

Summarizing main findings in a concise and actionable format for communication within and across project teams.[04]

Key insights are built on research and supported by raw data. They often include a situational context, and an intended outcome, as well as a restriction, obstacle, or friction. First insights are often generated based on patterns you find while you are collecting data, building your research wall, or codifying your data. If you don't have enough data to critically reflect on an assumption, collect more data. Design research is iterative!

Preparation: There are many ways (and templates) to formulate insights, such as: … *[actor] wants to … [action] because … [motivation], but … [tension]*. It helps to write down initial ideas for insights at any stage of the research process and then critically reflect on them using your research data.

Use: Often, key insights are developed from initial assumptions, hypotheses, and intermediate insights (try to avoid confirmation bias). The process often goes like this: prepare and print out data; write initial insights; cluster, merge, and prioritize; link key insights to data; find gaps and iterate. Key insights should be carefully phrased, as they will serve as points of reference for the further design process.

Expected output: Several key insights

Generating jobs-to-be-done insights 🖱

Summarizing the bigger picture of what customers want to achieve when they use certain services or physical/ digital products.

Jobs to be done (JTBD) is a specific way to formulate insights based on a framework by Clayton Christensen.[05] JTBD describes what a product helps the customer to achieve. It can be formulated for an entire physical/digital product or service (the main aim behind a journey map). Alternatively, formulate it for certain steps within a journey map by asking yourself what a customer or user wants to get done and adding your discoveries as an additional lane on a journey map. JTBD can help a team to break away from a current solution and discover new solutions based on what customers really want to achieve.

Preparation: Often, JTBD are developed based on this structure: *When … [situation], I want to … [motivation or forces], so I can … [expected outcome]*. To phrase JTBD, prepare and print out research data, personas, and journey maps.

Use: JTBD insights can be created iteratively together with data collection and can follow a process like this: write down initial JTBD insights; cluster, merge, and prioritize; link JTBD insights to data; find gaps and iterate.

Expected output: Jobs-to-be-done insights

---

04 "In contrast to this abundant data, insights are relatively rare. […] When they are generated, though, insights derived from the smart use of data are hugely powerful. Brands and companies that are able to develop big insights – from any level of data – will be winners." Kamal, I. (2012). "Metrics Are Easy; Insight Is Hard," at *https://hbr.org/2012/09/metrics-are-easy-insights-are-hard*.

05 Clayton, M. C., & Raynor, M. E. (2003). *The Innovator's Solution: Creating and Sustaining Successful Growth.* Harvard Business School Press.

Writing user stories 👆

Summarizing what customers or users want to be able to do; used to bridge design research with defining requirements for software development.[01]

User stories are used in software development to define requirements from a user perspective, instead of more product-based requirement documents. User stories are often formulated like this: *As a … [type of user/persona/role], I want … [action], so that … [outcome].* In service design, they are used to connect design research with actionable input for IT development to turn insights and/or ideas into productive software. User stories can also be used beyond software development to define the requirements of any physical/digital product or service.

Preparation: Just as journey maps have different zoom levels, software requirements also have different scales. While user stories typically describe detailed requirements, a set of user stories can be combined into an "epic," a longer, less detailed description of the big picture of what software can do. It's important to define this scale level beforehand.

Use: User stories should be formulated without IT-specific language, using simple, concise words, so that everyone can understand them. Writing user stories often follows a process like this: write initial user stories, cluster user stories into epics, link user stories to data, find gaps and iterate.

Expected output: User stories

01 User stories are used in many agile software development frameworks, such as Extreme Programming, Scrum, and Kanban. Mind that different approaches often use specific templates for how to phrase user stories. See, for example, Schwaber, K., & Beedle, M. (2002). *Agile Software Development with Scrum (Vol. 1)*. Upper Saddle River: Prentice Hall.

Compiling research reports 👆

Aggregate research process, methods, research data, data visualizations, and insights. Reports are often a required deliverable.

Research reports can have many forms, from written reports to more visual collections of photos and videos. Depending on the project a research report can serve various purposes, such as providing actionable guidelines to improve a physical/digital product or service, a "shock report" to get internal buy-in for a service design project, proof of work that justifies the budget spent on research, a compendium of research data that can be reused in other projects, and more.

Preparation: Have your research process and your research data, as well as different visualizations (personas, journey maps, system maps) and insights (key insights, JTBD, user stories), at hand. Think who you could invite to peer-review your report.

Use: Write a first draft of your research report. Ask yourself: who was involved, which methods and tools did you use, and how many iterations did you do? Add a summary of your key findings and key visualizations, add raw data as evidence, and use indices to show that there's much more data these are based on. Then invite other researchers or participants of the research to peer-review your report and iterate.

Expected output: Research reports

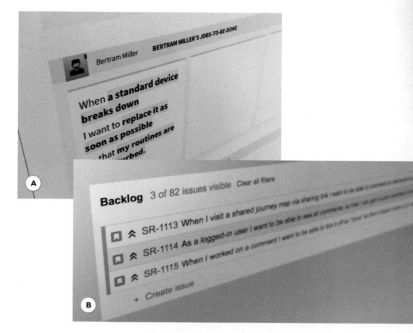

(A)   Jobs-to-be-done integrated as an additional lane
      in a journey map.

(B)   Example of a backlog in software development
      for an "epic" (i.e., a new feature) consisting of
      three user stories.

05
RESEARCH
CASES

→

The following five case studies provide examples of how service design research is done in practice: how to apply ethnography to gain actionable insights in a service design project **(5.4.1),** how to use both qualitative and quantitative research in service design projects **(5.4.2),** how to develop valuable personas and use these in a service design project **(5.4.3),** how to illustrate research data with journey maps and use these in a service design project **(5.4.4),** and how to use current-state (as-is) and future-state (to-be) journey mapping in service design **(5.4.5).**

5.4.1 CASE: APPLYING ETHNOGRAPHY TO GAIN ACTIONABLE INSIGHTS

Zahlhilfe program: An intersectoral cooperation to prevent electricity cutoffs

AUTHORS

Nina Weschenfelder
Senior Service Designer,
minds & makers

Michael Wend
Senior Customer
Experience Manager,
E.ON

minds &
makers

e·on

The challenge

Every year, the electricity supply is turned off in approximately 350,000 households in Germany[01] because the electricity bill cannot be paid. For those affected, the effects are dramatic and often lead to further social problems. For energy suppliers, cutting off the supply incurs costs, and it negatively affects the company's image. Energy-related debts are often just one aspect of a complex debt issue and must therefore be addressed holistically. In view of this, there is no viable alternative to a cooperative effort involving institutions from the public, private, and social sectors.

Project objectives

The project was intended to avoid electricity cutoffs, reduce energy debts, and prevent their recurrence. To reach these goals, the various perspectives of all stakeholders in the arena of energy poverty had to be taken into account. The project sought to establish and consolidate intersectoral cooperation between job centers, debt counseling charities, and the energy provider.

The goal is to develop services for customers, job centers, and counseling charities that have an immediate impact as well as long-term benefits, and to implement them throughout Germany.

Our project process: From briefing to evaluation in six phases

We started the Zahlhilfe project in 2014. It consists of six key stages. Following the *Identification, Understanding,* and *Developing* phases, we tested the service concepts with approximately 300 real customers, job centers, and counseling charities over a period of six months in the *Testing* phase.

The joint minds & makers and E.ON project team is currently developing the necessary skills and resources within E.ON to prepare processes and employees for the implementation of the service system. Additionally, we are steadily involving more job centers and debt counseling charities with the aim of rolling out the service system throughout Germany (*Implementation* phase). In a continuous monitoring process, qualitative and quantitative data from the company operation are being analyzed to make the social and economic effects of the services visible and communicable (*Evaluation* phase).

01 Bundesnetzagentur (2015). *Monitoring Report*, p. 192.

(A) In contextual interviews, the dramatic situation of people is visible in the form of the demands and cutoff notices.

(B) Based on service concepts that are linked to insights and opportunity areas, the project team develops first prototypes in a co-creation workshop.

(C) The service blueprint, complemented by insights, opportunity areas, and prototypes of the individual touch-points, makes the service tangible for all stakeholders.

Systematic approach: A guarantee for accountability, a basis for decision making

Our systematic approach is particularly useful in meeting the special challenges of the complex stakeholder cooperation and the long timescale of this project. We systematically integrate our research results into all stages of our innovation process. To this end, we use a precise coding system to be able to consistently trace every step of our work process to our research results at any time: from the original experiences and statements of our respondents to the insights derived from these, right through to the identified opportunity areas, subconcepts, and concepts and to final implementation.

Our stringent coding system is a vital prerequisite to keeping the context of the innovation and service concepts transparent and communicable. For example, we always link the code of an insight to that of the original quotes it is derived from. In concept descriptions, we always quote the insights and opportunity areas the concept is based upon. This high traceability does not apply only linearly to one single project phase and the previous step; thanks to our methodology we can trace back from any project phase to any other project phase.

Our carefully designed research system prevents adaptations of our innovation and service concepts that are not strictly based on our insights and thus contradict our consistent people-centered perspective. The entire content of a project is always transparent and comprehensible for any of the stakeholders so that decisions are made on the basis of verifiable research results instead of opinions or taste.

Results

Job centers, counseling charities, and energy suppliers are working together closely so that E.ON can offer its customers suitable aid at different points of the customer journey: through a separate hotline, counseling charities and job centers can directly reach out to E.ON contact staff who have the authority to take action and suspend cutoff orders immediately. Customers in emergency situations receive initial external debt counseling via telephone, helping them to work on solutions. Interest-free installment plans with realistic payment levels now reduce energy debts for the customers as well as the loss of revenue and other costs for the energy provider. These are just a few examples of our overarching, intersectoral service system that is now being applied throughout Germany and is in the process of consolidation.

The three stakeholders – job centers, counseling charities, and energy provider – are addressing the complex societal problem of energy poverty simultaneously at complementary levels. Finally, to ensure positive outcomes from the project, an accompanying social impact evaluation monitors the service system in the long term, so that potential for optimization can be recognized and implemented continuously.

Because of the Zahlhilfe project, the issues of energy poverty, payment problems, and cutoffs have been given a sustainably firm place within the company structure.

KEY TAKEAWAYS

01 **A high degree of transparency:** Using this approach ensures that solutions are very transparent and easy to understand. This is particularly important in more complex cooperations, such as those in which not all stakeholders are involved in all steps of the project.

02 **Ongoing verification of completeness and effectiveness:** In this approach it is continuously verified that the interests of the various stakeholders are being taken into account and whether the services that are offered solve the identified problems.

03 **Flexible application:** The original quotes of customers and other stakeholders' views make their concerns tangible; in this approach findings serve to support decision-making processes undertaken by the responsible bodies.

04 **A foundation of research:** By building upon the initially conducted research work, this approach makes concepts less vulnerable to ad hoc changes or process dilution.

05 **Ongoing effort:** This approach is slightly more elaborate in the beginning, but especially in the case of complex, long-term projects it reduces the overall error rate, as well as the time and effort needed for subsequent phases.

◀

5.4.2 CASE: USING QUALITATIVE AND QUANTITATIVE RESEARCH IN SERVICE DESIGN

Policy Lab Work & Health Project

AUTHORS

Cat Drew
Senior Policy Designer,
Policy Lab

Laura Malan
Senior Consultant,
Uscreates

uscreates

The problem
Around 2.5 million people receive health-related benefits in the United Kingdom, which costs about £15 billion per year,[01] and the wider economic costs of sickness absence and worklessness associated with working-age people in ill health are estimated to be over £100 billion.[02] The longer people are on these benefits, the less likely it is that they will return to work, and being out of work can have a big impact on people's health and well-being. On the other hand, finding the right work can be actively good for people's health.

The approach
The UK government's Policy Lab and the joint Work & Health Unit (a joint unit sponsored by the Department of Health and

01 Black, C., & Frost, D. (2011). "Health at Work – An Independent Review of Sickness Absence," Annual Report of the Chief Medical Officer.

02 Department of Health (2013). "Annual Report of the Chief Medical Officer 2013."

Department for Work and Pensions) created a multidisciplinary team with the service design agency Uscreates, ethnography agency Keep Your Shoes Dirty, and data science organization Mastodon C, and involved around 70 service providers, users, and stakeholders to solve the problem. After a three-day sprint to properly diagnose the problem, we embarked on a discovery phase of ethnography and data science, and a develop phase where we co-designed and prototyped ideas which we are now taking to scale.

We conducted ethnography with 30 users and people that supported them: doctors, employers, Jobcentre staff, and community groups.

The insights
We used data science techniques (Sankey analysis and *k*-means clustering) to look at patterns of people surveyed through the

Understanding Society survey. It validated the existing insight that once people move onto long-term sickness benefits, they tend to stay on them and that people on health-related benefits also have non-health-related needs. It also revealed fresh insights. For example, the clustering showed two groups of people on health-related benefits who reported comparatively good health, meaning non-health-related interventions must be more important for them, and these two groups were distinct (one high previous salary, the other low). Therefore, we need to personalize responses to support people in different ways.

We used a combination of techniques, including spending time with people in their homes or places of work, conducting interviews based on photos that participants had taken, and doing user-journey interviews.

Two key insights were:

→ People have to tell their stories multiple times to many different services that do not share information, meaning no one has a complete picture about someone's needs.

→ Individual line managers and confidence are big factors in whether people stay in or get back to work.

Idea generation

We turned these insights into evidence-based challenges to which users, doctors, employers, and policymakers brought their different perspectives at a co-design workshop. Ideas formed around a Work & Health coach who could signpost people to different non-health services, liaise with their employers to make adjustments, and build their confidence. We knew we could not build a whole new service from scratch, so local Jobcentres and community groups prototyped elements of it to see how it could fit in with their existing services.

In Penzance, the Jobcentre tested a website and posters which would allow employers to refer their employees to its service. One employee said: "Something like this would have been useful while I was still in work. I wasn't as quick as some other staff because of my condition but they didn't understand that. It might have helped me talk to my manager better about my health and what help I needed from him."

In Southend, the Jobcentre tested offering its services to the local doctors, so doctors could easily refer patients to them. In East London, the Jobcentre and a local community group tested how they could work together to provide Work & Health coaches with their combined knowledge of local services. In Bournemouth, the Jobcentre tested a Health & Work book for users to keep their information all in one place. One user said: "It helped me organize the situation and focus on what I need to do to get where I need to be."

Scaling

The qualitative feedback from the prototyping showed that these

(A) A photograph taken by one of the ethnographic research participants to show her daily experiences.

(B) A prototype of what the digital Health & Work book could look like.

(C) Participants at the co-design day exploring the evidence to inspire new ideas.

(D) The *k*-means clustering technique used to segment those reporting to be on health-related benefits.

prototypes had real value. We are now taking the ideas to scale, and the project has prompted wider systems change. The insights gained have informed a more positive and holistic conversation for new applicants for health-related benefits. We are creating a digital version for people who are still in work, preventing them from falling out of work. And the project has played an important part in the creation of the Work & Health Unit (set up halfway through the project) and the subsequent £40 million Work & Health Innovation Fund.

Lessons learned

A valuable lesson was how the insights from the data science informed the ethnography (e.g., revealing how mental and physical health are related), and how the ethnography informed the data science (e.g., highlighting the non-health needs of those on health-related benefits). There is huge power in using these two techniques together, with the data science giving the broad, large-scale "what" and the ethnography providing the deep, rich "why."

KEY TAKEAWAYS

01 Data science can inform ethnographic insights (and vice versa) through correlation of different events.

02 Combine data science to understand the large-scale context with ethnography to determine the deeper meaning or "why" of your research.

03 When conducting research, speak with people from all ages, levels, and perspectives.

5.4.3 CASE: DEVELOPING AND USING VALUABLE PERSONAS

Met Office app: A goal-based persona case study

AUTHOR

Phillippa Rose
Service Designer and
Facilitator, current.works

≋ Met Office

THE APP BUSINESS

I recently led user research for the new Met Office[01] app, replacing its old weather app. I worked closely with The App Business design team and the Met Office over six months on a range of research interventions. The use of goal-directed personas proved to be the most consistent and impactful tool.

Traditional demographic metrics were not fit for purpose. It was far more critical to deepen understanding of user behavior patterns, and motivations were key.

What do we need to understand?

In terms of target audiences for the new app, we were asked to design for almost everyone. As ever, we needed to make sure we really understood the problem before we could design solutions.

The weather affects everyone to varying degrees, and increasingly more and more people have smartphones and use them to access weather information – so in designing an experience for almost everyone, we needed to understand people's levels of interest in the weather and their motivations. We needed to make sense of user tasks and goals. We also needed to consider technical considerations, and of course human behaviors and skill levels, ensuring the app provided just enough of the right information, quickly and easily.

In order to answer some of these questions we chose to create goal-driven personas. This approach was key in identifying and meeting user needs, engaging a wider range of stakeholders, and informing design decisions.

Step 1:
Use what you have – what do we know already?

We collated and analyzed existing Met Office desk research and reports, analytics of the old Met Office app, and websites, plus feedback from the Met Office Public Weather Desk. We reflected on the data to get a sense of any common goals, tasks, or correlations between behaviors and motivations.

Step 2:
Distilling data into value curves

Next, we distilled evidence from this body of research with recent insights from our own user research – including over 500 interviews, online surveys, and field research – to produce a set of common user tasks and activities influenced by the weather. We then ranked them against key considerations to create a set of value curves of 11 common tasks/scenarios.

01 The Met Office is the United Kingdom's national weather service.

Step 3:
Testing assumptions through card sorting

We also needed to test our assumptions about what information is most important to people, so we conducted an online card sorting exercise with 139 responses.

Step 4:
Value curve trend analysis

We plotted the 11 value curves together and looked for commonalities and patterns between them. Three cluster groups emerged from the value curves one of the accompanying illustrations shows an example of four value curves forming one broad cluster group.

Step 5:
Affinity mapping exercise

We then reviewed all our findings and did an affinity mapping exercise to drill down further into the various tasks, looking at behaviors and considerations for individual tasks/goals.

The basic premises of three goal-directed personas emerged from this process:

Flexible planners: people adapting plans/timing/locations depending on the forecast conditions (prepared to wait for or seek out the best weather)

— **Be prepared:** people preparing for and making provision for weather conditions in order to stick to their overall plans, or adapting their plans to incorporate forecast weather conditions

— **High stakes/high impact:** high-risk outdoor activity/event planning requiring decisions based on long-term forecasting with others involved

Step 6:
Persona development workshop

We ran a goal-driven development workshop to flesh out the personas further using a persona template by Lucy Kimbell as a starting point. We adapted Lucy's template to focus less on individual characteristics and more on goals, environments, and issues.

Here's the final list of what we found most useful to flesh out each of the personas in turn:

— Goals
— Situations and considerations (can relate to time frames, logistics, or mindset)
— Environment and resources (can include people, information sources, and physical environment)
— Ties and associations (including people and organizations/brands)
— Issues/challenges (what's stopping them?)
— Workarounds/opportunities (possible solutions, problem solving)

We also used this session to further develop a set of user needs for each persona based on the guidelines from the Government Digital Service:[02]

A As a … [who is the user?]

B I need to … [what does the user want to do?]

C So that … [why does the user want to do this?]

02 This template is often called a "user story." See also: *Writing user stories* in 5.3.

Step 7:
Sharing

We then distilled the data down even further and wrote it up using a mix of text and images. We shared our refined personas with the wider Met Office teams and stakeholders, and stuck them on the wall in the project room.

Step 8:
Ongoing iteration

During ongoing user research the personas are being continuously reviewed and adapted as necessary. Persona profile characteristics have directly informed recruitment of participants for week-long diary studies using Dscout and ExperienceFellow. In usability lab testing interviews we have asked questions to test assumptions and uncover examples of goals, tasks, and behaviors associated with the different personas.

We also ran a series of ongoing design ideation workshops to generate ideas for future app updates and features during 2016 based on the needs and goals of our three core personas, and created a dedicated Trello board to document the ideas with color-coded labels corresponding with the relevant personas.

Learnings and next steps

What is distinct about this approach to previous personas I've worked on is that we deliberately concentrated on goals and tasks at the expense of characterization. Each of these three personas is distinct and people may identify with one more than the others, but it is likely that each one of us has experienced user needs similar to at least two of these personas in different situations or at different times in our lives.

A second distinction is that these personas have evolved over a six-month period, whereas often I work with teams on persona development in shorter, sharper iterations. A significant amount of time was dedicated to developing them and evolving them, in a close collaboration between myself, Rob Jung, and Dima Shvedun from The App Business with support from Chris Frost and Jay Spanton at the Met Office.

KEY TAKEAWAYS

 01 Consider focusing the approach on common goals, instead of solely personas, to help identify with user needs.

 02 Customer personas can evolve over a period of time as more insights are uncovered.

 03 Don't forget to use existing data that can help provide information.

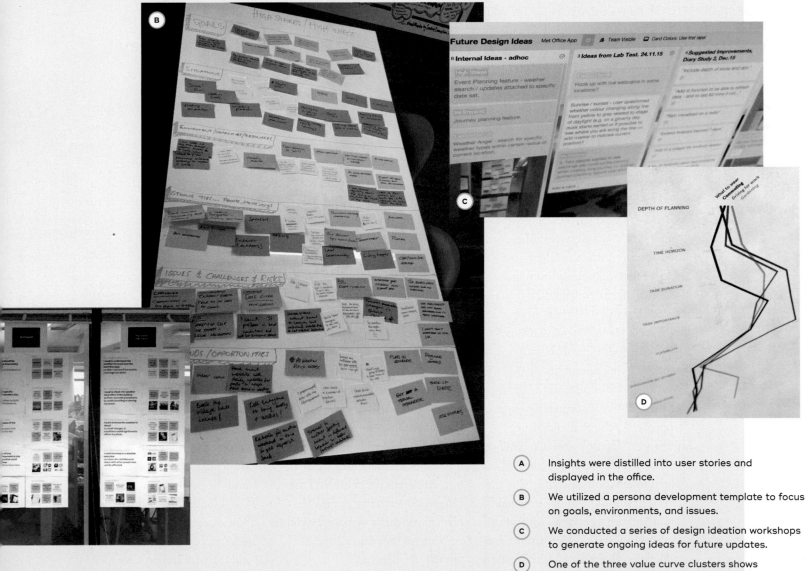

(A) Insights were distilled into user stories and
     displayed in the office.

(B) We utilized a persona development template to focus
     on goals, environments, and issues.

(C) We conducted a series of design ideation workshops
     to generate ongoing ideas for future updates.

(D) One of the three value curve clusters shows
     patterns between data.

5.4.4 CASE: ILLUSTRATING RESEARCH DATA WITH JOURNEY MAPS

Promoting youth mental health: The impact of mapping the journey

AUTHOR

Jamin Hegeman
Design Director,
Adaptive Path

The challenge

How can we help youth with mental health issues in a challenged community within San Francisco? What services might they need? How can we best deliver them? How can we inform policymakers to get the funding for such services? These are the questions that the Edgewood Center for Children and Families' Organizational Consultation team faced in early 2014 when they contracted with Mo' MAGIC, the Western Addition collaborative of youth-serving nonprofits.

The Edgewood team sought to bring a human-centered design approach to the challenge. They engaged 29 youths who attend Magic Zone, an after-school program located in the southeastern area of the Western Addition, and conducted 24 qualitative interviews with adult community stakeholders from 15 organizations from within the Western Addition and city-wide.

After a discovery and research phase, Edgewood reached out to Adaptive Path for service design expertise in creating a journey map and facilitating an ideation and prioritization session with community stakeholders. The Adaptive Path team, consisting of one service designer and one visual designer, designed two three-hour workshops: one focused on gathering data to create a journey map, another to generate ideas based on the journey framework.

Journey mapping workshop

For the first workshop, we gathered a small group of subject matter experts, people who worked with the youth in different capacities or on different programs and the Edgewood team that conducted primary research with the 29 youths who attend the Magic Zone after-school program.

The information we sought included the stages of the journey, actions, thoughts or expectations, feelings, people, services, and locations relevant to the stages. We also wanted to identify the high points and low points of each stage. To simplify data collection, we created large butcher paper templates (one for each stage) for the data we needed.

Journey map visualization

After the workshop, we synthesized the data both editorially and visually. We transferred the data into a spreadsheet, grouped like items, and applied an editorial lens to the information. We did this to focus the information and make it succinct and digestible.

In the workshop, we used custom worksheets to capture the essence of what needed to be communicated to aid the editorial process.

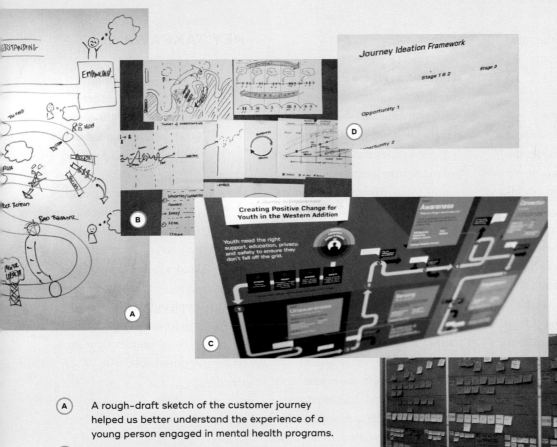

Our visual design process started on paper to quickly explore ideas. We then moved to Illustrator and continued exploring visual constructs. Once the visual matched the story we wanted to tell, we layered in the content. Several rounds of internal critique and share-outs with our stakeholders for feedback followed.

Applying an editorial lens to the content of a journey map is a skill and art in itself.

The keys to a successful journey map include:

1 Gathering the right content (then editing that for clarity, conciseness, and priority)

2 Articulating a point of view through communication design

3 Establishing an effective information hierarchy to ensure key messages are communicated and readers can access information at different levels of zoom

(A) A rough-draft sketch of the customer journey helped us better understand the experience of a young person engaged in mental health programs.

(B) Journey sketches showed the different layers of the story.

(C) The Mo' MAGIC journey map illustrates the complete journey with roadblocks that youths face on the path to empowerment.

(D) The ideation session generated 140 new, broadly defined concepts that were then prioritized.

(E) We gathered all the data points of the customer journey and analyzed them to tell a complete story.

In other words, follow the core principles of effective communication design.

Journey map outcome

The journey is broken into five stages, or phases. Each phase is signified by a one-word title: *Unawareness, Sensing, Awareness, Connection,* and *Engagement.* Within each phase, there is a quote that represents the overarching feeling or belief of the youth. This is followed by more of a matter-of-fact statement regarding the situation – for example, "Youth is not considering change." Each roadblock includes dialogue boxes containing language the youth might use. Dark gray arrows reinforce that youths often drop off the path to empowerment at all phases of the journey.

For the ideation and prioritization workshop, we created an ideation framework modeled after the stages of the journey. It contained a matrix of journey stages and opportunities. A cross-organizational team drew solutions for each box in the ideation framework for a set period of time.

Impact

This project achieved impact in several ways. First, it provided a common tool and language for various organizations and exposed stakeholders to a new way to tackle old problems. Second, stakeholders found the map useful when engaging youths to discuss where they might be in the journey. Finally, the journey map provided a new way to see a complex issue and make the case for funding several initiatives.

"Issues have been studied to death," says Mo' MAGIC executive director Sheryl Davis. Creating a journey map to understand the complexity of servicing youths with mental health issues was "very different," she said. It showed stakeholders where the gaps were and led to new ideas for action. Armed with our journey map and new service concepts, the organization received $200,000 in funding from the Office of the Mayor. That's service design making an impact.

KEY TAKEAWAYS

 01 A successful customer journey map includes gathering the right content (then editing that for clarity, conciseness, and priority).

 02 A customer journey map provides a common tool and language for various organizations and exposed stakeholders to solve problems.

03 Applying an editorial lens to a journey map can help make a complex issue more approachable.

▶

5.4.5 CASE: CURRENT-STATE (AS-IS) AND FUTURE-STATE (TO-BE) JOURNEY MAPPING

The bigger picture: Projects building up to more long-term and strategic value

AUTHORS

Geke van Dijk
Strategy Director, STBY

Ozlem Dessauer-Siegers
Sr. Service Experience
Design Lead, Vodafone

..STBY...

O vodafone

Introduction

Over the past four years the Service Design Lead at Vodafone has developed and fine-tuned a Service Experience Design methodology that was used for all Vodafone's customer journeys in the Netherlands, and later also in the rest of the Vodafone countries. STBY contributed to this by doing deep-dive design research on several of these journeys.

Each project focused on a particular set of customer journeys with the aim to better understand the experiences, behaviors, motivations, preferences, latent needs, and pain points of customers. At the same time, considerable extra value has been created across these projects through a structured way of working. The results of this approach have led to a company-wide change program. The key added value of this approach is that customer journeys mapped for specific projects can be linked up to customer life cycles with a more strategic scope. In this way, service design contributes to strategic value for a business on a larger scale than just the individual customer journey projects.

"Customer journeys linked up into a customer life cycle can deliver a more strategic overview with relevance to the wider organization."
— *Ozlem Dessauer-Siegers, Sr. Service Experience Design Lead, Vodafone*

Customer journey maps illustrating as-is and to-be service experiences[01]

Customer journeys are one of the key tools in the service design approach. In many service design projects, customer journeys are mapped to explore the experiences of people and their interactions with service providers. These customer journey maps offer an important foundation to analyze existing situations and to identify recurring patterns, pain points, and opportunities. A similar format can also be used for a different purpose – to visualize how service experiences could be improved in future offerings.

During each project with various teams in Vodafone the typical dynamic and project flow would be as follows: during the fieldwork stage, customer journeys are mapped to investigate how they actually recently happened (as-is). This leads to insights on aspects that could be improved (low-hanging fruit) and also on opportunity areas for substantial service innovation (new propositions). After a strategic prioritization of the identified

01   In this book, as-is and to-be journey maps are referred to as "current state" and "future state," respectively. See *Mapping journeys* in 5.3.

opportunities with stakeholders from several departments, the ideation stage in these projects then leads to ideas for new service concepts. These concept directions are expressed in new customer journeys (TO BE) that highlight where and how the customer experience can be improved for both new and existing customers, typically illustrated with sketches to indicate what these new service concepts would add to the customer experience. The concept ideas and sketches are then progressed in implementation projects that further specify and build the new service offerings.

Examples of focus points for the various projects STBY and Vodafone worked on include:

— New contracts for consumers (choosing a new contract or renewing a contract, and choosing a new phone)
— New contracts for businesses (complex process of stakeholder communication and decision making)

— Expenditure (monitoring and managing usage and costs during the contract period)
— Connectivity (experiences with the network during the contract period)
— International usage (traveling abroad during the contract period)
— Multiple contacts (complex interactions between customers and provider)
— Multiple contracts (adding other people or other features to a contract)

"To enable comparison across several projects, it is important to use a systematic approach."
— *Geke van Dijk, Strategy Director, STBY London & Amsterdam*

Systematic approach generating progressive deliverables

To enable cross-comparison between the results of various projects, it was important to use a systematic approach and to make sure that the project deliverables were created in a similar way that allowed for progressive understanding and

CUSTOME

CHANGING

OPTIMIZING

FIXING

NEGLE

Ⓐ

As Is

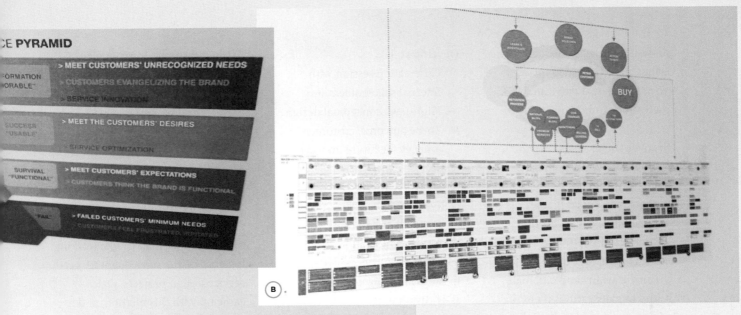

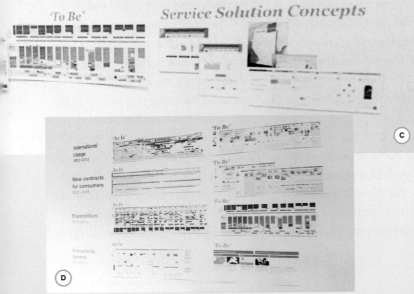

B

C

D

(A) Customer Experience Pyramid
© Ozlem Dessauer (2015).

(B) McKinsey's consumer decision journey, or customer life cycle, is projected from left to right on the customer journey map. The pain points and insights from the design research, channel analysis, and financial analysis are listed from top to bottom.

(C) The systematic set of project deliverables allows for progressive understanding and follow-up.

(D) Examples of some of the as-is and to-be customer journeys documented for the project. Printed posters (±5 meters long) were put up on the wall for the team to work with.

follow-up. The activities across the various stages included quantitative analysis, qualitative analysis, co-creation, and design.

Discover stage:
— Quantitative insight analysis: identify pain points and weak spots in the current offering
— Qualitative data collection: conduct in-depth interviews with a sample of customers (mix of young and old, male and female, various types of phones and contracts)
— Documentation: co-create customer journeys of recent and relevant service experiences, illustrated with photos, videos, and audio recordings
— Design research analysis: perform content analysis to identify patterns in customers' experiences

Define stage:
— As-is outcome: aggregated customer journey poster, illustrated report with key insights and recommendations, and trail of evidence to original data

Develop stage:
— Co-creation session with internal stakeholders
— High-level conceptual design
— To-be outcome: customer journey for future improved service experience

Deliver stage:
— Detailed design for implementation

In the *Define* stage, the aggregated as-is customer journey is developed, based on the recurring patterns of customer behavior and pain points found in the individual customer journeys. Relevant insights are then drawn out that lead to both direct improvements for the existing service offering and concept directions for substantial new service offerings. Each to-be customer journey delivers three levels of service solution outcomes: Fix (operational fixes), Optimize (improvements), and Change (service innovations).

From customer journeys to customer life cycles

Although produced for specific projects and specific project teams, customer journeys can also deliver a more strategic overview of consumer–provider interactions and offer relevance for the wider organization. This is done by linking the various customer journey maps into a customer life cycle map. While working together on the subsequent focused service design projects, Ozlem[01] came up with this method, and it turned out to work really well.

Customer life cycles are a key tool in the field of business strategy. The scope of a customer life cycle is wider than that of a customer journey, as it includes the entire relationship from the first day of formal interaction between a customer and an organization (e.g., a new customer requests a quote) until the last day (e.g., the customer stops being a client). In the case of Vodafone, the customer life cycle spans from the first contract

01 Ozlem Dessauer-Siegers, Sr. Service Experience Design Lead at Vodafone.

offered to a customer to the day that a contract ends and is not renewed.

For customer journeys, the start and end points of the process are less well defined. They usually start when a customer has identified a specific need and engages in activities to fulfill this need, and go until the point that this need is sufficiently fulfilled (or the customer decides to abort the process). This means that there can be a few different customer journeys within a customer life cycle.

Mapping customer journeys according to the focus of what customers are trying to accomplish is very useful for empathizing with their perspective and improving specific service concepts, but from the point of view of the organization these journeys need to be added up to create a more tactical and strategic overview that can be matched with the overall operations and the way the business is run. This is what a customer life cycle offers.

The wider scope of the customer life cycle needs to be taken into account while developing specific project assets. To be able to link the outcomes from each project into an overall customer life cycle, it is important to use a basic similar structure across projects. While doing this, the service design team needs to not only focus on the deliverables for the project at hand, but also anticipate how these deliverables can later be linked up to be useful to a more long-term and strategic view. A firm understanding of the link between customer journeys and customer life cycle maps enables this.

KEY TAKEAWAYS

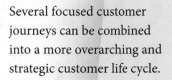

01 Several focused customer journeys can be combined into a more overarching and strategic customer life cycle.

02 Customer journeys can be formatted to express both the current as-is state of customer experiences and the envisioned to-be state of future improved customer experiences.

03 Customer journey–based analysis and ideation leads to both direct improvements for existing service offerings and concept directions for substantial new service offerings.

04 A systematic approach to customer journey mapping is needed in order to be able to link up into a customer life cycle.

06
IDEATION

Generating, diversifying, developing, sorting, and selecting ideas.

Expert comments ————————————————————————

| Chris Ferguson | Belina Raffy | Jürgen Tanghe | Mauro Rego | Satu Miettinen |

06
IDEATION

This chapter also includes

WHERE IDEAS COME FROM

The world will tell you that creativity is *all* about having the best ideas. People who work in arts or any type of creative profession – even designers – are always being asked, "Where do your ideas come from?" And when organizations initially approach service designers for help, they often say something like, "We want to kick off by generating some good ideas." Ideas are seen as the precious starting point of value generation.

Let's start by challenging that belief. Of course, producing ideas is a vital part of any service design project – but it is not as all-important as many people seem to think.[01] In service design, ideas represent one point (or usually several points) in an evolutionary process, and are a critical part of problem solving. They concretize aspects of what has come before, and are the sparks of what comes after them. Ideas are not especially valuable in themselves – they are neither good nor bad, but they might be useful.

So, to the surprise of many newcomers, service design does not set out to find one killer idea as a starting point. Instead, ideas are generated en masse at various stages in the process, mixed, recombined, culled, distilled, and evolved or parked. We call this process *ideation*, and it never stops.

---

01 In his 2015 TEDTalk "The Single Biggest Reason Why Startups Succeed," (*https://www.ted.com/talks/bill_gross_the_single_biggest_reason_why_startups_succeed*) Ted Gross suggests that the main success factor is not idea quality, but the timing and skills of the team. Timing is especially relevant to us, as service design can get prototypes and pilots on the road earlier.

6.1 IDEAS

Although ideation is often shown as a discrete process step – you will usually see a main phase of idea generation marked on the project plan, and it's there in the visualizations in this book – it is not the only time we generate ideas. We will have ideas all through the project. Our brain's determination to churn out ideas is valuable, but we should differentiate carefully between ideas from different contexts, as each context brings its own bias. Very early ideas might be useful – but do we really understand the challenge yet? Ideas often pop up in research – but is the data or situation which prompted that idea valid or representative? For many "tinkerers," the prototyping bench is the ultimate idea generator as we think with our hands – but are we in love with a clever prototype feature, or are we addressing a real customer need?

So all through the project, we will be creating ideas which might be useful – we should make sure we preserve them. Our idea management system might be as simple as an idea wall – a simple sticky note "parking place" – or a more structured layout. More ambitiously, we can adopt collaboration platforms and techniques from knowledge management. We might note the original context of each idea, so it can carry the appropriate bias warnings. It's wise to treat all unproven ideas with skepticism anyway.

Apart from the inevitable spontaneous ideas, there will be times when we deliberately try to generate ideas or fixes. These are generally the divergent phases of our project, and we use divergent techniques, aiming for

quantity, not quality – at least at first. It is often said that a high quantity of ideas leads to later success.[01] Whether this is true or not, it's not the only reason to aim for idea volume in a service design project.

The process of generating ideas is a valuable way for participants to begin to explore a theme cognitively. Aiming for quantity will help them move beyond the obvious to more interesting, radical ideas. Group ideation is also a good way to develop shared ownership of ideas, as participants build on each other's input. Later, no one can say whom the idea belongs to. Generating many ideas can be good training for divergent thinking, as the team practice temporarily suspending judgment. And, crucially, it can help break habits of perfectionism and ownership. If project participants are encouraged to generate a heap of ideas in a short time, they find it easier to accept that many of those ideas will be sketchy and imperfect, though perhaps still useful. And if we start with a big pile of ideas, it is easy to abandon most of them. Learning to let go of ideas to make way for new ones is a crucial skill of service design, and one that needs practice.

💬 **EXPERT TIP**

"Don't get attached to individual ideas. You are there to broaden the field of possibility. Later, you will come back and might find treasure – but for now, keep planting seeds."

– Belina Raffy

---

01 The link between idea quantity and idea quality is still debated (for example, see Paulus, P. B., Kohn, N. W., & Arditti, L. E. (2011). "Effects of Quantity and Quality Instructions on Brainstorming," *The Journal of Creative Behavior*, 45(1), 38-46) – partly because it is very hard to determine what constitutes a "good" idea without launching all of them. In service design, the question is whether or not an idea is useful in moving forward. Even incomplete, flawed, or impractical ideas can be valuable if they generate useful questions or prototypes.

THE BASIC PROCESS OF IDEATION

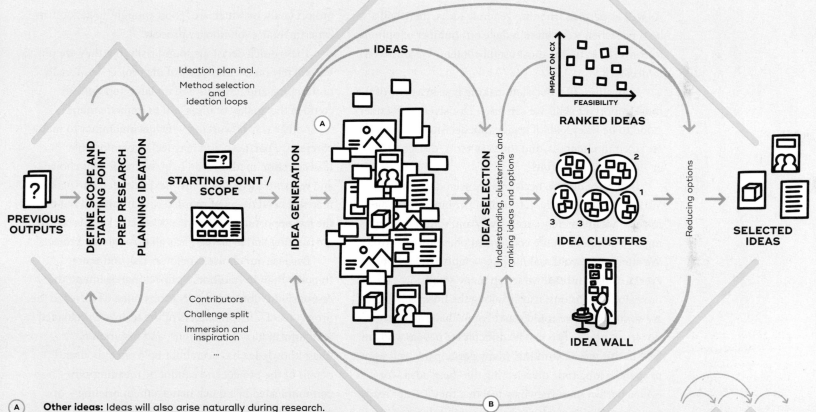

PREVIOUS OUTPUTS

DEFINE SCOPE AND STARTING POINT

PREP RESEARCH

PLANNING IDEATION

Ideation plan incl.
Method selection
and
ideation loops

STARTING POINT / SCOPE

Contributors
Challenge split
Immersion and
inspiration
...

IDEA GENERATION

IDEAS

(A)

IDEA SELECTION
Understanding, clustering, and
ranking ideas and options

IMPACT ON CX
FEASIBILITY
RANKED IDEAS

1
2
3
3
1
IDEA CLUSTERS

IDEA WALL

Reducing options

SELECTED IDEAS

B

(A) **Other ideas:** Ideas will also arise naturally during research. They can be parked, then added to the pool of ideas generated in formal ideation. Ideas which arise during prototyping can also be parked and added to a later ideation iteration, or they can be immediately prototyped.

(B) **Iteration and ideation loops:** Ideation is often an iterative process with a sequence of loops – iterations within one activity, such as idea generation – as well as loops which return to idea generation after selection or prototyping takes place.

Ideation activities are embedded in an iterative sequence with other activities of research, prototyping, and implementation.

6.2 DECISIONS

As well as periods when we generate ideas, there will also be times when we want to reduce our number of options, to converge in on the most useful content. We will need to decide.

In business life, decision making is seen as one of the most important skills we can have. Decisiveness is understood to be a key skill of leadership; decisions in business are often momentous, and the very term "decision maker" implies a senior role.

In service design, decisions are seen differently. We are not deciding the future of our company or project. Instead, we are merely successively and routinely narrowing down options in the convergent phases of our work. We attempt to avoid making big, weighty choices whenever possible. Instead, we set up many small, low-risk, provisional decisions, usually along the lines of "Where are some places we could start?" or "What experiments do we try next?" This can be difficult for people who are new to this way of working. Many participants will want to spend a long time on selecting the "best" idea – or even a perfect one. They may feel that they are not ready to make a choice or do not have enough information. Teams will need to learn that in a design process, we are not trying to choose the perfect idea, the silver bullet, then immediately investing massive resources in implementing it. Instead, we are trying to quickly spot a few ideas which are interesting, which seem to fit the project goals, or which are "good enough" to kick off an experimental, evolutionary process.

These quick decisions sound risky, but they are not. We will rely on the later parts of the project – especially prototyping and testing – and on later iterations to confirm the quality of ideas and to improve them.[01] It's another way of working which is unfamiliar to many co-creative partners, and may feel uncomfortable.[02] Idea selection methods can help formalize that choice and reassure them, but some inexperienced partners may still need frequent reminders that this will not be the last opportunity to change or replace key ideas – we are ideating and evolving ideas all through the project.

Because our choices are lower risk and more frequent than in traditional project management, the responsibility for making decisions often devolves to the project team.[03] The members of the team are preloaded with information, impressions, and inspiration. Their knowledge has been built up from a thousand details of the project and cannot be meaningfully communicated in a quick management briefing – or even in a lengthy document or discussion – because it is implicit, emergent, empathic, or abstract.

---

01 See 6.5.2, *Case: Co-design with hybrid methods*, for an example of successful postlaunch ideation.

02 In (company) politics, sticking to your ideas is usually seen as a positive characteristic. But in innovation, being ready and willing to switch focus is a key skill. In startups, we talk about the pivot, the "structured course correction designed to test a new fundamental hypothesis about the product, strategy, and engine of growth," as a key success factor. Quote from Reis, E. (2011). *The Lean Startup.* New York: Crown Business, p. 149.

03 The role of the design facilitator in decision making is discussed in Chapter 10, *Facilitating workshops*.

Abductive thinking

BY JURGEN TANGHE

One particular way of thinking differentiates design from other forms of working, thinking, and decision making, and that is abductive thinking.

Abductive thinking is the logic of what might be.[04] It's about synthesizing the data and making sense of it in a way that possibly hasn't been done before and thus finding a new, best plausible explanation given the observations and based on your own personal and professional experience. The foundations of abduction are laid when you formulate your challenge – specifically, the value you want to create for your customer, or for the world.

For most people, it is best done in a "low-tech," small-team context with sticky notes stuck to a wall. This large working space is useful, even necessary, because abduction involves pattern recognition. These are the first steps: summarize your data, spread it out and digest it, interpret it, and find out what appeals to you and how everything would make sense. This is where insights come from that allow you to take a fresh point of view that is suggested by the data.

Abductive thinking is intuitive – intuition *combined* with data from research. Its intuitive nature also means it is by definition not certain; it's a proposal of what *could* be going on. You will have to accept that: it's not about what's "right," it's about what's "probable" and "possible."

Abductive thinking often takes place in a low-tech environment.

This viewpoint, a novel perspective on the situation, consists of hypotheses about the human experience, the mechanisms of the design challenge, and a belief that this explanation of the situation helps to create value. Sometimes it is captured in a metaphor.

This new perspective is very inspirational and energizing, fueling ideation and paving the way for design and innovation. ◄

04 See Dorst, K. (2011). "The Core of 'Design Thinking' and Its Application," *Design Studies*, 32(6), 521-532. See also Kolko, J. (2010). "Abductive Thinking and Sensemaking: The Drivers of Design Synthesis., *Design Issues*, 26(1), 15-28. And see Martin, R. L. (2009). "The Design of Business: Why Design Thinking Is the Next Competitive Advantage," *Harvard Business Press*.

This necessity to keep implicit knowledge inside the process leads to one of the key concepts of decision making in service design: the people who are close to the project and who understand both the origin and implications of the choices need to be involved in all major decisions.

The difficulty of communicating implicit knowledge – especially across silos – is the reason why a continuity of personnel is crucial in service design projects.

Decision time is often a critical moment for a team as it moves from a divergent phase into a convergent phase.[01]

While the relative makeup of the team may shift throughout the project, we make sure that at least some of the people who will implement the project are there in the earliest phases, and that the people who understand the customer needs are still around during implementation. In a digital project, at least one coder needs to sit on the customer's sofa in the initial research; and at least one customer insights specialist should be there when the software is built and rolled out.

They might not be alone, as the decision will sometimes need to involve people who were not part of the ideation or prototyping process. Experts on technical, strategic, or brand issues, senior management, the legal team, and more might be brought in at particular moments, but these valuable "outsiders" should not decide in a vacuum.

The rich supply of details and strength of impressions carried by the team is valuable, but it can also make decision making cumbersome. How can they sift through the data to focus on what is important? How can they

step back and leave behind ideas they love? We need a set of tools and methods to protect the team from decision paralysis, and to help them co-decide with outsiders while making the most of their hard-won knowledge and empathy. These tools can be relatively lightweight – there is rarely need for complex analysis when you are merely deciding "which five ideas do we try next?".

6.3 THE PROCESS OF IDEATION

Even if many "spontaneous" ideation activities will often be carried out without extensive planning, systematic ideation can still benefit from a clearly articulated process.

6.3.1   Planning ideation

When you are setting up a divergent ideation activity, it pays to lay some groundwork. In a service design project, you will usually have done some research beforehand and will be well prepared for ideation, perhaps after insight generation. Or you might be coming back from a prototyping phase, ready to use what you have learned. Your starting point will be some kind of ideation challenge or question, made by reframing your insights. In planning your ideation activities, you will often be building from observations and data through insights and questions towards ideas, and then diversifying and filtering those ideas in a series of loops. Here are some things to think about when planning.

Ⓐ Starting point/scope
Re-examine the previous work (e.g., research or proto-typing results) – it can be helpful to immerse the core project team in it. Then decide on the starting point and scope of your ideation.[01] At times, you may like to leave some fuzziness within the scope, to increase the chance of disruptive or more novel solutions. For example, you might explicitly *not* brief some contributors on your research, add activities which use random input, allow opportunities for productive misunderstanding,[02] and so on. Based on your starting point, you might do some additional preparatory research to check for existing solutions or analogous problems.[03]

Ⓑ Immersion and inspiration
Consider how to bring in the essence and raw data from your previous work. Apart from including people who were active in the research or prototyping phase, you might show artifacts, videos, and quotes, keeping the raw data hidden but accessible. You could also develop key insights from your data. Also consider which inspiration elements or activities can be valuable prior to the actual ideation session.

Ⓒ Split the challenge
You do not need to think about everything at once, and you will probably want to split your ideation (and indeed the whole project) into multiple manageable tracks. Use "slicing the elephant" techniques, or cluster "How might we …" questions into opportunity areas that suggest directions for potential ideation.[04]

---

01 The scope of ideation activities is sometimes defined during the previous activity in your project, often research or prototyping.

02 For example, see 6.5.5, *Case: Supporting creativity with trigger visuals*.

03 Again, you should make a conscious decision about when to share this knowledge with the team.

04 See 6.4, *Ideation methods*.

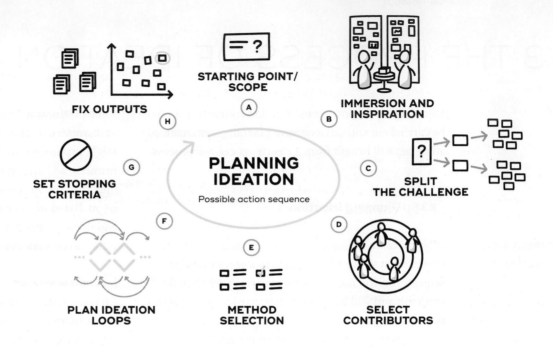

FIX OUTPUTS

(H)

STARTING POINT/
SCOPE

(A)

(B)

IMMERSION AND
INSPIRATION

SET STOPPING
CRITERIA

(G)

**PLANNING
IDEATION**

Possible action sequence

(C)

SPLIT
THE CHALLENGE

(F)

(E)

(D)

PLAN IDEATION
LOOPS

METHOD
SELECTION

SELECT
CONTRIBUTORS

(D) Select contributors

Do a stakeholder mapping session for each of the opportunity areas to find out who could meaningfully contribute to that area. Make sure you are balancing the needs of end users, key participants, and your own organization. A mix of insiders, outsiders, experts, and users works well. Our natural tendency is to make heterogeneous groups – but homogeneous groups will often get you more extreme ideas. And while experts are good at spotting minefields, they can sometimes be too dominant. You might mix and remix the groups in different sessions to get the best from the people you have.[01]

(E) Method selection

Line up a sequence of ideation and decision methods to fill your idea portfolio and select them.[02]

(F) Plan ideation loops

Ask yourself how the different ideation and decision-making sessions feed into each other. Be ready to be flexible, changing methods during the sessions if necessary. Remember to plan time between the activities and sessions for reflection and ideation "out of action."[03]

01 See *Extended project team* in 9.2.3 for more on team mixes.

02 See 6.3.2, *Idea generation*, and 6.3.3, *Idea selection*.

03 See the textbox *Reflection out of action* in 6.3.

(G) Set stopping criteria

It can be useful to define criteria for when to stop. This can be as simple as setting the number of ideas you want to achieve, or deciding to rely on expert assessment. Like with theoretical saturation in research, you might stop when further ideation produces (essentially) no new original ideas.[04] You should also assess the dependencies for doing prototyping or further research as you can be sure new questions will arise.

(H) Fix outputs

Decide how many selected ideas you will eventually need (e.g., how many prototypes you want to later build) and what format the ideas need to have so they can be pushed forward.

6.3.2   Idea generation

Briefing and inspiring participants

If there has not been formal research – or if you are in a preparatory ideation phase and research will come later in the project – you might fall back on other methods to connect with reality. You can give the participants homework – perhaps *not* to generate ideas,[05] but to put themselves in the shoes of the customers.[06] An alternative

is storytelling, where participants share their own experiences or listen to customers or colleagues from the front line.

You can also introduce participants to the theme of your ideation activity by giving them background information on what is happening currently in that field and in other useful contexts, and letting them explore this information – for example, using a World Café format.[07] As well as sparking ideas, this can also help put participants "on the same page," giving them all at least a basic grounding in the important themes.[08]

Method selection

Always consider a mix of methods. Like research methods, many ideation methods have their own inherent bias, perhaps allowing different types of people to contribute to varying degrees. While many people feel comfortable writing ideas on sticky notes, others might be more creative when you allow them to express themselves using visuals (e.g., sketching), mock-ups,[09] or movement (e.g., bodystorming).

A good mix of ideation methods levels out potential biases and invites the diverse talents of your contributors. Depending on the complexity of your ideation challenge or problem, pick one or more methods from the following categories.[10]

EXPERT TIP

"Participation in ideation – and the design process in general – can be confusing and exhausting for non-practitioners. There are many new terms and activities that are mentally taxing, and the process can be unpredictable and uncomfortable. Prepare people with one-on-one meetings or comfort calls ahead of time. Let them know that they are being selected to participate because they are creative (even if they don't think they are!) and important to the success of the project."

– Chris Ferguson

---

04 See 5.1.2, *Research planning* for more on theoretical saturation.

05 It can be useful to give some ideation homework after this research homework. The ideas participants generate at home, outside the groupthink of the sessions, will be diverse and considered. There is a risk that they may fall in love with these ideas, so frame them as springboards for further ideation, or prototype them fast so they can fail and start to evolve.

06 Essentially, this is research. Indeed, many research techniques make great homework – such as autoethnography, service safaris, diary work, cultural probes, or interviews.

07 See *http://www.theworldcafe.com*.

08 But think twice before tasking *all* your participants to look at existing solutions, as this can actually reduce the diversity of their ideas. See for example Smith, S. M., Ward, T. B., & Schumacher, J. S. (1993). "Constraining Effects of Examples in a Creative Generation Task." Memory & Cognition, 21(6), 837-845.

09 See several of these methods used in 6.5.3, *Case: Building on solid research*.

10 All of these methods are described in detail in 6.4, *Ideation methods*.

Reflection out of action

BY SATU MIETTINEN

Group or team ideation using "reflection in action" is an everyday practice in designer's work and focuses on generating new ideas and solutions.

Yet, Becky Currano from Stanford has discovered[01] that a major part of the innovative ideas of Silicon Valley designers were produced during reflection *out of action* in situations such as in the park, in the shower, or while doodling or jogging.

When we work with ideation in service design, it would make a lot of sense to mix in methods and processes to support not only in-action time but also out-of-action reflection.

The combination of in-action ideation with a team or group and out-of-action solo reflection helps you to understand and process large information clusters and do the slow thinking[02] that is supported by enjoyable out-of-action activities. You can have an idea log in your phone, window pens in the bathroom, or a notebook in a car where you can note the innovative ideas when they pop up. ◄

Intentionally plan time for out-of-action reflection during workshop situations. For example, include solo outdoor activities between sessions.

01 Currano, R. M., Steinert, M., & Leifer, L. J. (2011). *Characterizing Reflective Practice in Design – What About Those Ideas You Get in the Shower?* In *DS 68-7: Proceedings of the 18th International Conference on Engineering Design* (ICED 11), *Impacting Society Through Engineering Design*, Vol. 7: *Human Behaviour in Design*, Lyngby/Copenhagen, Denmark, 15.–19.08. 2011.

02 Kahneman, D. (2011). *Thinking, Fast and Slow.* Macmillan.

→ **Pre-ideation:** Slicing the elephant, ideas from future-state journey mapping or future-state system mapping, "How might we …?" questions from insights

→ **Generating many ideas:** Brainstorming, brainwriting, 10 plus 10

→ **Adding depth and diversity:** Bodystorming, using cards and checklists, ideation based on association and analogies

Simple challenges can be approached with a quick 15-minute ideation session with a simple activity. More complex questions might involve sessions with different stakeholders spread over a couple of weeks, perhaps first splitting up the challenge into distinct development directions, then running multiple ideation sessions with employees, customers, and experts. Each session might build directly on the output from the previous ones to diversify and evolve ideas.

Managing energy

There is growing evidence that boredom can lead to good ideas.[03] While this deserves exploration (perhaps you can use a long drive or repetitive preparation tasks as part of your process), deliberately boring participants will not make your project popular. Instead, warm-ups can help us feel more energetic and productive – they

are especially valuable before ideation sessions. Just as importantly, they can also help us establish the safe space[04] which makes us more ready to fail and helps us with more radical thinking. In each ideation workshop, you should choose one or more suitable warm-ups for your group, and consider carefully when to place them. It's usual to do warm-ups at the very beginning of a workshop, but there is plenty of evidence[05] that delay or deliberate distraction can improve the results of ideation sessions.[06] This might suggest placing the warm-up after you set the challenge for the ideation, but before you start to generate ideas.

6.3.3   Idea selection

The groan zone

Many representations of the service design process, like the famous Double Diamond,[07] show convergent phases following immediately on the heels of divergent phases. This abrupt change can be very hard, or even distressing, for project participants. Often, participants do not feel ready to start abandoning these fresh new options yet.[08]

Before participants feel ready to make a decision, they might need to develop a mutual understanding of

---

03 For example, see Mann, S., & Cadman, R. (2014). "Does Being Bored Make Us More Creative?" *Creativity Research Journal*, 26(2), 165-173.

04 For more on safe space, warm-ups, and idea facilitation, see Chapter 10, *Facilitating workshops*.

05 See, for example, work by Jihae Shin, reported in Grant, A. M., & Sandberg, S. (2016). *Originals: How Non-Conformists Move the World*. Viking.

06 It is usually suggested that distraction or delay gives the participants' subconscious time to work on the problem. More modern "honing" theories of creativity suggest that it is more about forgetting barriers. Whichever you prefer, it works.

07 See Chapter 4, *The core activities of service design*.

08 These participants will be in "the groan zone" – see the accompanying illustration.

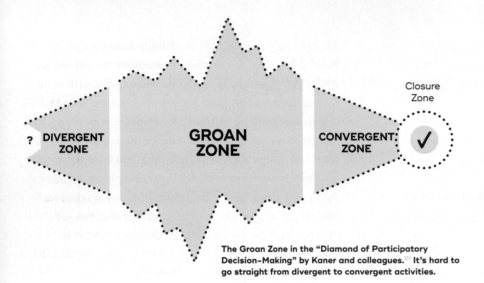

Closure
Zone

? **DIVERGENT
ZONE**

**GROAN
ZONE**

**CONVERGENT
ZONE**

✔

The Groan Zone in the "Diamond of Participatory
Decision-Making" by Kaner and colleagues.[01] It's hard to
go straight from divergent to convergent activities.

the options open to them. Their ideas will probably be at different levels – some will be concepts or systems, some features or details. Some might be reframed needs, some might be very concrete solutions. Teams might need to explore and organize their thinking by asking each other questions, sorting items, or perhaps developing some boundary objects[02] to bring clarity. Or participants might just need a break, a game to distract them, or a good night's sleep. Consider this when planning your process.

But don't give them too long. The more time we spend considering, explaining, and shaping our thoughts, the more we feel invested in them – and the more we fall in love. If the team has difficulty letting go

of ideas, this can be a problem. So sometimes it makes sense to acknowledge that other ideas also deserve more time, but to keep moving anyway, taking just a few ideas forward and asking participants to park the others. Even if you don't come back to them formally, the best aspects of abandoned ideas will bubble up in the DNA of future iterations.

Physical context of decisions

The physical context of decisions is important. Many people like to have a "clear head" and make decisions in a relatively neutral environment – which is why we take walks in the woods and cogitate on beaches. But in service design projects, it is less about making a single weighty decision, and more about running a decision-guiding process and the conversations it throws up. It's going to be useful to have our assets nearby, so we can quickly return to any points which come up, pointing at the sticky notes and turning the prototype around once more. It also seems that visually complex environments lead to better cognitive function, and ultimately to better decisions.[03] See what works for your team.

Agreeing to decide and selecting methods

Many decision-making tools do not actually make a decision. Instead, they prepare the ground by sorting information, flagging favorites, or slicing the big decision elephant into smaller, more manageable questions. In

01 Kaner, S. (2014). *Facilitator's Guide to Participatory Decision-Making*. John Wiley & Sons.
02 See the textbox *Boundary objects* in 3.2 for more information.
03 Davidson, A. W., & Bar-Yam, Y. (2006). Environmental complexity: information for human-environment well-being. In A. Minai & Y. Bar-Yam (eds.), *Unifying Themes in Complex Systems*, Vol. IIIB (pp. 157–168). Springer Berlin Heidelberg.

some cases, the method will make the decision very clear, and a glance around the room will show that you can just move on. But often there will still be the need for some discussion or voting before the course is clear.

One of the best things that a group can do in this situation is to decide in advance how and when the decision will be made, and what happens to the ideas left "on the cutting room floor." *Before* using a method, participants can decide what decision factors will be most important, and how long they will spend on the decision. Several of the methods presented in this section will be helpful – but no method in the world should decide for you. They can only support and facilitate your decision process.

As a rule of thumb, if you want to reduce friction it makes sense to break down the decision-making process into several steps and select one or more methods from each of the following categories:[04]

→ **Understanding, clustering, and ranking options**
such as octopus clustering, Benny Hill sorting ("Thirty-Five"), idea portfolio, decision matrix

→ **Reducing options** such as quick voting methods, physical commitment

6.3.4 **Documentation**

Ideation is a process which soon becomes complex and rather wasteful as you abandon far more ideas than you use. The ultimate documentation of your ideation process is the prototypes which come out of it, but they can never contain all the complexity of what has gone before. It is worth thinking about keeping track of what ideation activities you have done, and mapping where your idea assets are.

At the simplest level, you might just keep the physical artifacts of your ideation on display, evolving ideas along the wall – like a research wall, this supports conversations and the discovery of connections. You might digitize the results of each round for future reference. Or, you might use more complex indexing methods, connecting ideas to their project origins. It's very powerful when you can say, "This prototype comes from this idea, which comes from this partial idea, which comes from this 'How might we …' question, which comes from this strategic opportunity area, which comes from this insight, which comes from this original customer statement.[05] Let me play you the recording." On the other hand, indexing also takes a lot of work.[06] Find what…

---

04 All of these methods are described in 6.4 *Ideation methods*.

05 See the illustration "A breadcrumb chain of evidence" in 9.2.8.

06 You can find more on indexing in 5.1.3, *Data collection*.

Illustration: Mauro Rego

Illustration: Mauro Rego

The Kano model

When we are deciding which ideas to explore, understanding *how* customers
value the various aspects of our services and physical or digital products[01] is very useful.
The Kano model[02] can tell us where to start.

The Kano model is a theory of customer satisfaction. It gives us useful insights into what customers care about, and how this changes as expectations change. It is often represented as a graph, mapping customer satisfaction against the degree of implementation (level of technical development or ubiquity of the offering) of a value proposition. The curved lines on the graph represent different categories[03] of value proposition.

Some features of an offering can be considered basics (Kano calls them Must be Qualities). If these features are not there, the customer is dissatisfied – but endlessly improving the implementation will never be enough to delight the customer. For example, if a phone cannot connect to a network, the owner will be angry. But having a phone which always connects is nothing special unless you live in a very remote place.

Other attributes are performance factors (One-Dimensional Qualities) – the better they are, the higher the customer satisfaction. Battery capacity is one example – the longer my phone runs between charges, the more satisfied I am.

The third type are sometimes called delight or excitement factors (Attractive Qualities). These are not missed if not resent, but can lead to high customer satisfaction if implemented. On a phone, a 3D screen is a good example. While most phones have 2D screens, a 3D display would be something to be proud of – but not having one does not mean you are disappointed with your phone.

The Kano model shows how the satisfaction gained from a value proposition decays with time, as excitement factors become performance factors, then basics. One great example is a camera on a mobile phone. When cameras were first added to phones, they were an excitement factor – not expected, and great fun to have. Some years later, manufacturers were caught up in a "pixels race." As we write this book, most phones can record better pictures than most of us need. A good 2D phone camera is fast becoming a basic factor – for most of us, it only affects our satisfaction if it's missing.

01 The term "products" describes anything a company offers – no matter if this is tangible or not. In academia, products are often divided into goods and services. However, products are usually bundles of services and physical/digital products. As "goods" is colloquially understood as referring to something tangible, we prefer to speak of physical/digital products. Read more on this in the textbox *Service-dominant logic* in 2.5.

02 Kano, N., Seraku, N., Takahashi, F., & Tsuji, S. (1984). "Attractive Quality and Must-be Quality from the Viewpoint of Environmental Lifestyle in Japan." In H.-J. Lenz, P.-T. Wilrich, & W. Schmid (eds.), *Frontiers in Statistical Quality Control 9* (pp. 315–327). Physica-Verlag HD.

03 The categories often have different names depending on the translation from Japanese, or the influence of other authors.

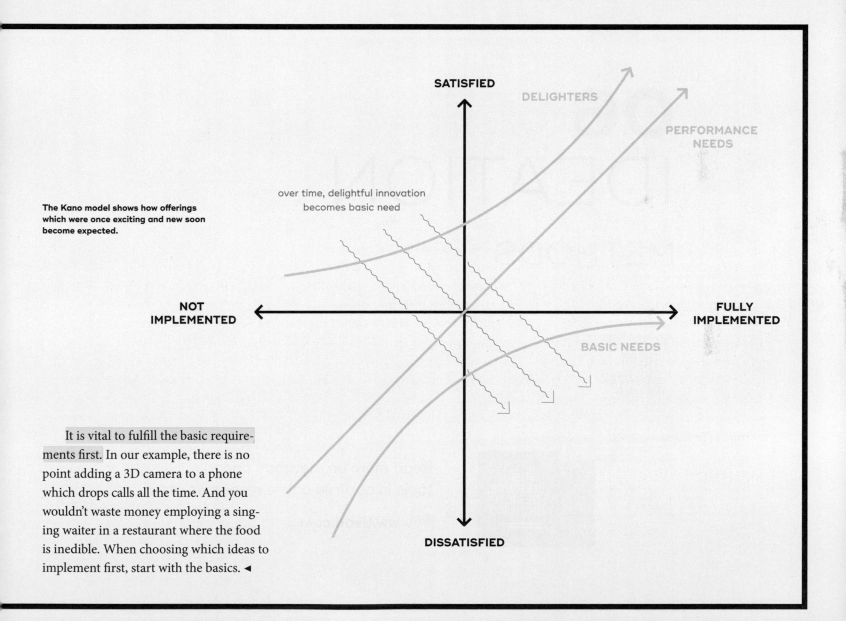

The Kano model shows how offerings which were once exciting and new soon become expected.

SATISFIED

DELIGHTERS

PERFORMANCE
NEEDS

over time, delightful innovation
becomes basic need

NOT
IMPLEMENTED

FULLY
IMPLEMENTED

BASIC NEEDS

DISSATISFIED

It is vital to fulfill the basic requirements first. In our example, there is no point adding a 3D camera to a phone which drops calls all the time. And you wouldn't waste money employing a singing waiter in a restaurant where the food is inedible. When choosing which ideas to implement first, start with the basics. ◄

06
IDEATION
METHODS

**THESE
ARE
SERVICE
DESIGN
METHODS.**

**THIS IS
SERVICE
DESIGN
DOING.**

Read more on methods and
tools in our free online resources at:

www.tisdd.com

6.4 IDEATION METHODS

EXPERT TIP

"Deciding in advance how decisions will be made is essential for process transparency, security, and perceived fairness. Who will decide, and how? We know from research that design by committee is often a recipe for poor design, yet service design is at its core participative and inclusive, so it is somewhat of a paradox. Some organizations use *adults* – lead designers or executives who can set direction and decide from options presented by the team."

– Jurgen Tanghe

There is a whole industry around idea generation and selection. Ideas are usually seen as the cornerstone of creativity and countless methods exist, often under multiple names, to create, filter, and select them. Here, we introduce some favorites, structured into categories:

→ **Pre-ideation:** Slicing the elephant and splitting the ideation challenge, ideas from journey mapping, ideas from system mapping, "How might we …?" questions from insights and user stories

→ **Generating many ideas:** Brainstorming and brainwriting, 10 plus 10

→ **Adding depth and diversity:** Bodystorming, using cards and checklists, ideation based on analogies and association

→ **Understanding, clustering, and ranking options:** Octopus clustering, Benny Hill sorting ("Thirty-Five"), idea portfolio, decision matrix

→ **Reducing options:** Quick voting methods, physical commitment

PRE-IDEATION
Slicing the elephant and splitting the ideation challenge 🖐

Making one big ideation challenge into a series of more manageable ones.

Often, the theme of ideation is too large or abstract to get a grip on. You can help the team by using techniques to limit or split ideation into more manageable subtasks. Famous examples include the *Six Thinking Hats*, where participants ideate from different viewpoints (process, facts, feelings, creativity, caution, and benefits); *attribute listing*, where you start with the attributes (physical, procedural, etc.) of a challenge; *5 Ws + H*, which invites teams to start from the who, where, what, why, when, and how; and the *Five Whys*, where we ask ourselves "Why?" five times. Each answer is a starting point for ideation.

Prepare and use: The process depends on the method used. Generally start by inviting the right people (people who know the background or will implement and deliver the service, experts, users, management, etc.). Prepare the participants[01] and run the method. Now examine your ideas. What do they suggest? Should you repeat? When ready, move into idea selection.

Expected output: More manageable challenges, more diverse approaches.

01 For more, see 10.3.4, *Creating a safe space.*

(A) Throw together some quick new future-state journey maps to start exploring your ideas.

(B) Look for opportunities to add value by strengthening relationships shown in system maps.

(C) Generating some first "How might we ...?" questions, based on the insights in the background.

PRE-IDEATION

Ideas from journey mapping 👆

Using the classic visualization tool to generate ideas around experience and process.

Starting with a current-state map, or using your research and experience, you create new future-state journey maps. On the way, you generate many ideas which may be diversified or prototyped. With groups who are comfortable thinking in journeys, this lets you think about orchestration and expectations early on.[01]

Prepare and use: Let the group look at your current-state journey maps and, if practical, the research behind them. (If you have no maps, storytelling offers a weaker alternative). Taking one map at a time, use the best information you have to spot critical steps in the journey by referring to your research, stepping into the shoes of your personas, or simulating process and experience using desktop walkthroughs, investigative rehearsal, or bodystorming. Use other ideation techniques to ideate around each critical step, recording insights, ideas, and new questions. Now draw some rough new maps with your most promising ideas. How does the change affect the rest of the journey (technology, process, experience, dramatic arc, expectations)?

Expected output: Idea descriptions (text), idea sketches (visualizations).

---

01 See 6.5.5, *Case: Supporting creativity with trigger visuals*, 6.5.4, *Case: Mixed-method ideation* (for examples), and 6.5.2, *Case: Co-design with hybrid methods* (for a modified version).

PRE-IDEATION

Ideas from system mapping 🖱

Using a classic visualization to generate ideas based on relationships.

The group try to add value to an existing (or quickly created) system map by adding, removing, or replacing elements, and examining the exchange between stakeholders.

Prepare and use: Let the group look at some current-state system maps and, if practical, the research behind them (a weaker alternative is to make some quick assumption-based maps). Take one map at a time – it's faster if you physicalize using Business Origami or a stakeholder constellation[02] – and ask: Can we strengthen a relationship? How could a key person become a hero? Which exchange could we facilitate? How could the network still function if some elements were removed, added, or changed?

Write down your insights, ideas, and questions. Use other ideation methods to diversify, then draw up new future-state system maps for the most interesting ideas. How can you make each map work? Is something still missing or imbalanced? Dig deeper using new journey maps, service blueprints, or prototyping.

Expected output: Idea descriptions (text), idea sketches (visualizations)

PRE-IDEATION

"How might we ...?" questions from insights and user stories 🖱

A systematic method to base ideation on research and knowledge.[03]

Use this systematic method when you have research or experience to build on, or when you need to step back from ideas and return to needs and opportunities.

Prepare and use: Start with the insights or user stories developed in your research activities. Look at the individual parts within each insight or user story, and convert each insight or story into several trigger questions, perhaps starting with "How might we ..." Sort and group the questions into useful clusters or "opportunity areas." Invite strategic specialists and senior management to help you prioritize them.

Look at the questions inside the clusters and decide what specialists you should invite to enrich your usual ideation cast of researchers, people who will implement and deliver the service, users, management, etc. Ideate around the questions inside your most important clusters, then move to idea selection.

Expected output: Trigger questions (text), map of idea clusters

---

02 A stakeholder constellation is a physical model where people represent different stakeholders, standing arranged in a room just like on a system map. See the online description of this tool for more details.

03 This version of the exercise is based on IDEO's 2009 *Human-Centered Design Toolkit* (*https://www.ideo.com/post/design-kit*), as evolved by minds & makers and others.

GENERATING MANY IDEAS

Brainstorming and brainwriting 🖐

Two famous methods which help teams stay in divergent mode while generating ideas quickly.

Use verbal brain*storming*[01] to find a starting point for your work, to get to grips with the theme, to boost energy, or to add options. Use the silent, more thoughtful brain*writing*[02] when ideas are more complex, when diversity is key, when the group is large, or to empower quiet participants.

Prepare and use: Prepare your group with information[03] and remind them to refrain from criticism, be open to wild ideas, focus on quantity, and build on the ideas of others. Show the ideation theme, then do a distracting warm-up before the exercise starts. In brainstorming, ask the group to shout ideas while you write them on the board. In brainwriting, ask participants to silently and individually write or sketch their ideas, one idea per page. They can pass them on to others for development, post them on a wall, or keep them secret for a while. At the end, display the ideas on the wall, cluster, discuss, and begin selection.

Expected output: Idea descriptions (text), idea sketches (visualizations), map of idea clusters

GENERATING MANY IDEAS

10 plus 10 🖐

A fast visual ideation method which combines breadth and depth of ideas.

The 10 plus 10 exercise[04] is a strong method for ideating around physical or digital situations and interfaces. It helps teams to quickly generate a broad variety of concepts, and to get some depth in understanding. The very visual approach helps them be specific.

Prepare and use: Pick a challenge and do a warm-up before dividing into table-sized teams. Give the teams just a few minutes to individually, silently, and very roughly sketch 10 concepts per team that address the challenge. They should draw real-world implementations, not metaphors or concepts. When the time is up, they can each briefly explain their sketches to their immediate team members. Then each team should quickly choose one sketch which seems interesting, before sketching silently again, making 10 variations of this. After sharing the results, they now have 20 sketches from two rounds – one broad, and one deep – to take into idea selection.

Expected output: Idea sketches (visualizations)

01 Osborn, A.F. (1963). *Applied Imagination*, 3rd ed. New York, NY: Scribner.

02 For more on brainwriting see Rohrbach, B. (1969). "Kreativ nach Regeln – Methode 635, eine neue Technik zum Lösen von Problemen," *Absatzwirtschaft* 12, 73-53.

03 See *Briefing and inspiring participants* in 6.3.

04 Greenberg, S., Carpendale, S., Marquardt, N., & Buxton, B. (2011). *Sketching User Experiences: The Workbook*. Elsevier.

ADDING DEPTH AND DIVERSITY

Bodystorming 🖑

A physical ideation method, sometimes called "brainstorming for the body."[05]

Use this physical exploration method to help understand, ideate, and show problems. It is very useful when the challenge has physical or interpersonal aspects, or when a session needs empathy, energy, or a highlight. Bodystorming is simpler and faster than investigative rehearsal,[06] but has less depth.

Prepare and use: Immerse the group in the context of the challenge via research or site visits. If the group know the context well, storytelling might be enough. Make a list of interesting situations or ideas. In the original context or in a workshop space, take one situation at a time and act it out.[07] There will be lots of laughter at the beginning, but remember that this is work and challenge the group if they make their lives too easy or slip into discussion mode. As alternatives come up, try them out or park them. Take notes to help the group remember what they discovered, and repeat for other situations or ideas. Reflect, and take ideas forward into idea selection.

Expected output: Video/photo documentation of bodystorming sessions, documentation as idea descriptions (text), bug lists (text) or idea sketches (visualizations)

(A) Brainwriting in silence produces more diverse output than brainstorming, and gives less assertive team members a voice.

(B) 10 plus 10 sketching produces a wide range of concrete ideas rapidly. Go for quantity, and encourage sh!tty first drafts.

(C) Bodystorming ideas for a machine interface by playing through some quick scenarios. Ideas come thick and fast, so one team member is busy recording them.

05 Gray, D., Brown, S., & Macanufo, J. (2010) *Gamestorming*. O'Reilly.

06 See Chapter 7, *Prototyping*.

07 Safe space is especially important for this method. See 10.3.4, *Creating a safe space*.

ADDING DEPTH AND DIVERSITY
Using cards and checklists 🖱

Cards (and checklists) focus an ideation session on one question or inspiration, with surprising results.

Ideation, creativity, brainstorming, and method cards (there are many names) can be used when the group feels stuck, or can't move away from familiar thinking. They promote discussion, to suggest new avenues of exploration, to structure thinking, and to spark ideas. There are many sets – and similar lists – available, or you can make your own. Card sets can also function as a checklist – work through the cards, and you won't forget anything important. The cards can also be used to prioritize by sorting out the most important ones, or they can form the headings around which you cluster your ideas and observations.

Prepare and use: The process will vary, so read the instructions. Warm-ups will be useful if you aim to ideate, especially warm-ups around making associations and building on each other's ideas. To push beyond the obvious, spend a little longer on each card than the group wants to.

Expected output: Idea descriptions (text), idea sketches (visualizations)

ADDING DEPTH AND DIVERSITY
Ideation based on analogies and association 🖱

Ideate by translating existing solutions or looking for links to random stimuli.

Analogies are a way to translate ideas which already exist. Instead of struggling with new Problem A, adapt known solutions to the essentially similar (analogous) but familiar Problem B.[01] Associations work in a similar way to analogies, but help us reframe the problem and think in new ways by trying try to find associations with a randomly chosen word or image. These methods are best used after other, simpler methods.

Prepare and use: Good analogies are powerful, and preparing them gets easier with experience. Basically, you reduce the challenge to its essential characteristics, separate it from its context, and look for problems with similar characteristics in other fields. Choose the best analogies, and think about the analogy, not the initial challenge. What worked there? Make notes, and try various analogies. Can the ideas and experience be translated?

Random association has the same basic process, but starts with a random word, phrase, or image. Open a book at random, or use one of the many random word and image generators online.

Expected output: Idea descriptions (text), idea sketches (visualizations)

01 See, for example, 6.5.3, *Case: Building on solid research.*

(A) Octopus clustering. In a very large group, five highly engaged rows of participants sort hundreds of sticky notes in minutes.

(B) Card packs can help focus or diversify an ideation session – or break a deadlock.

(C) Random words or images can be used to diversify and unblock ideation.

Octopus clustering 🖱

A very quick group method to sort and cluster ideas or information. Everyone gets to know the ideas.

Use octopus clustering to sort large numbers of ideas, insights, data – anything which fits on a sticky note. As well as sorting, everyone gets an overview of what the material is and starts to share ownership of ideas.

Prepare and use: Stand people in clear rows in front of a wall of sticky notes. The front row actively sorts the notes; the second row advises, and other rows have various support functions. Every 30 seconds, the front row moves to the back, and everyone steps forward into a new role. Remind them to watch out for "orphans" and break up overlarge clusters. After a few cycles, the notes are sorted and the group knows the content.

In this exercise, people work fast and close to each other, so it also acts as a great warm-up. Also, everyone touches many notes, leaving them crumpled and tired – we lose attachment to the ideas. The new clusters might help us understand the overarching structure of the material, or suggest different directions for the next step.

Expected output: Idea clusters, photo documentation of idea wall

(A) Benny Hill sorting (based on "Thirty-Five") –
Mixing up the papers.

(B) Sharing out the points in Benny Hill sorting.

(C) A typical idea portfolio. You will see some quick wins at
the top right (circled), but might also choose to explore
some long-term goals (top left), and perhaps some
important infrastructure tasks which will open up future
opportunities (lower left).

UNDERSTANDING, CLUSTERING,
AND RANKING OPTIONS

Benny Hill sorting ("Thirty-Five") 🖱

**A fast, high-energy way to choose the most interesting or popular
from a large group of options.**

This method[01] for bigger groups takes a large number of items
and quickly ranks them by whatever criteria you decide. Use it to
select ideas or pitches which the group finds most interesting.
Or use it to agree on priorities for the session, rules of cooperation,
and so on.

Prepare and use: Everyone is standing, each holding a
piece of paper, perhaps with a very clear sketch of their
idea. When music plays, they move quickly through the
group, swapping papers with everyone they meet. When
the music stops, they form random pairs, compare their
two unfamiliar papers, and have 45 seconds to share 7
points between the ideas. The exercise repeats five times
and the results are summed. As well as ranking the
items, this exercise also thoroughly mixes them, starts to
establish co-ownership, and leaves the idea papers looking
tired and used – helpful if the group have trouble letting
go. Perhaps you can use a *physical commitment* method to
form work groups around the most interesting ones.

Expected output: Ranked ideas

01 We use a name which is more familiar to many service designers, but this is actually just a version of the
excellent game Thirty-Five by Thiagi. See Thiagarajan, S. (2005). *Thiagi's Interactive Lectures.* American Society
for Training and Development.

UNDERSTANDING, CLUSTERING,
AND RANKING OPTIONS

Idea portfolio 🖱

A slightly more analytical selection method for quick but reliable sorting.

Ideas are ranked according to two variables and arranged on a portfolio or graph.[02] Because two variables are used, the method can balance different needs and appeals to analytical mindsets. It prepares the groundwork for an informed decision, and even allows a strategic view of the options.

Prepare and use: Decide on your criteria: "Impact on customer experience" against general "Feasibility" works very well. Mark up a portfolio (graph) on the wall or floor. Taking one idea at a time, ask the group (or a subgroup) to assign 0 to 10 points for each variable and position it on the portfolio. The discussion they have now is as important as the tool. When all ideas are laid out, talk about which to investigate. Often the ideas with high impact and high feasibility are the most interesting, but you need a varied selection, so you might include some other ideas for their long-term benefits, or for idea diversity. Take the shortlisted ideas into further exploration, perhaps via journey maps, blueprints, or prototyping.

Expected output: Ranked ideas, visual idea portfolio

UNDERSTANDING, CLUSTERING,
AND RANKING OPTIONS

Decision matrix 🖱

A more analytic, multiple-factor approach to decision making.

This MCDA (multiple criteria decision analysis) method[03] is welcomed by analytical thinkers. It includes several criteria in the decision, but lets us consider them one at a time.

Prepare and use: Collect your options and list them down one side of a table. Write the decision factors as headings for the columns of the table. If you want, give each decision factor a weighting. Be careful – small differences in weighting will strongly affect the outcome. For each idea, assign a value for each factor. Multiply the value by the weighting and write it in the box. The idea with the highest total value is the one to consider first, but you should choose a mixed group to take further.

Like with many "decision" tools, the discussion while using the tool – even while selecting decision factors and weighting – is as important as the tool itself. This tool can lead to very long discussions, where teams are basically guessing values. Point this out, and use the tool to highlight the gaps in understanding, then use research or prototyping to inform or replace the discussion.

Expected output: Ranked ideas or options

02 The idea portfolio adapts the thinking behind similar decision grids, matrices, or portfolios. See for example Martilla, J. A., & James, J. C. (1977). "Importance-Performance Analysis." *The Journal of Marketing*, 77-79. See also the Impact & Effort Matrix in Gray, D., Brown, S., & Macanufo, J. (2010). *Gamestorming: A Playbook for Innovators, Rulebreakers, and Changemakers.* Sebastopol: O'Reilly.

03 Pugh, S. (1991). *Total Design: Integrated Methods for Successful Product Engineering.* Addison-Wesley.

REDUCING OPTIONS
Quick voting methods 🖰

Quick ways to get the majority view, for larger groups and small teams.

Often, groups faced with options or decisions will slip into discussions, simply out of habit. Adopt quick techniques to explore which ideas, insights, or datapoints are most interesting or see if the group has already made a decision.[01]

Prepare and use: Dot voting gives each team member a fixed number of sticky dots or pen marks to show favorites. Barometers let us assess every option by marking ratings on paper labels or holding a stickynote in the air to show approval or disapproval (perhaps with a Likert scale from +2 to –2). "Nose picking" lets teams or small groups see if they already agree. Each team member puts one finger on their nose, and they all count together to three and quickly put that finger on their preferred item. Anyone who hesitates has lost her vote.

Before using techniques like these, you might want to (quickly!) agree on criteria. If in doubt, ask, "What is most promising right now?" Then apply these techniques to support decisions, or see if one has already been made, not to make them. They should not replace important discussions, but can quickly reveal if discussion is necessary.

Expected output: Revealed decisions, ranked ideas or favorites

REDUCING OPTIONS
Physical commitment 🖰

A way to quickly pinpoint popular ideas and form teams for the next step.

These physical choice methods let everyone see who supports an idea and who wants to be in which group, and any changes are quick, easy, and obvious.[02]

Prepare and use: In a floor gallery, participants browse papers laid out on the floor. They show support or join a group by standing on a piece of paper. Use this when the items are larger or need time to read – like elevator pitches, idea sketches, or service ads.

In Coraling, group members look at items on the wall and put their finger on a favorite. Others join by touching the shoulder of the first person, forming lines and branches like coral. Use this variant for anything which is tricky to take off the wall, like clusters of sticky notes.

If you are forming groups, now look at the groups. Are they viable? Too small, too large? Who might change groups and help out elsewhere? Which important ideas are the group ignoring? If you are selecting ideas, is there enough balance and variation? Which important ideas are missing? What needs more attention?

Expected output: Ranked or selected ideas, new working groups (if used for group forming).

---

01 See also the *bull's-eye* sorting method used before an idea portfolio in 6.5.4, *Case: Mixed-method ideation.*

02 Groups formed this way might be unbalanced (often beneficial in the short term), so use these activities to split up the group for the next task of a workshop, not to form long-term teams for a project.

(A) A floor gallery. The options are spread out on the floor, and team members stand on the ones they are interested in.

(B) Coraling to form workgroups. Participants at a workshop start to choose clusters which interest them and place hands on others' shoulders to "join up."

(C) A decision matrix. Like all decision tools, this does not make the decision, but supports the process and the conversation around it.

06
IDEATION
CASES

⟶

The cases in this chapter show how formal and informal ideation combines with other activities within a successful project. They discuss ideation and co-design with customers **(6.5.1),** how ideation methods can be hybridized to fit a project **(6.5.2),** solutions emerging from research **(6.5.3),** idea generation through a mix of methods **(6.5.4),** and the use of visualizations and misunderstandings to encourage creativity **(6.5.5).**

6.5.1 CASE: OPENING THE DESIGN STUDIO TO YOUR CUSTOMERS

KLM cares: Developing ideas through co-creation with customers

AUTHOR

Marcel Zwiers
Founding Partner,
31Volts

31VOLTS

KLM

Over the last decade or so, many airlines – including KLM – have focused on providing more and more self-services, empowering their customers to take control of their travel experiences. Services that used to be delivered by the ground stewardesses now belong to the customer, from printing out your boarding pass to labeling and checking in your luggage. Checking passports, printing boarding passes, and lifting suitcases onto conveyor belts became a thing of the past for KLM staff. But what would the future look like? If the the team were no longer depended on to do these tasks, what then?

In many projects, a question or challenge is often answered by a solution. In this case, the idea was to provide the staff with more freedom to provide the KLM customers with a positive travel experience. But what does freedom look like? How much freedom are we talking about? And, even more difficult, who will be managing this newly acquired freedom?

Our main goal was to use (service) design in order to learn as much as we could from the people that KLM cares deeply about: the world travelers entering, leaving, or just transferring through Amsterdam Airport Schiphol. We tried to understand what it was they valued, what was important to them, and what it meant to travel the world.

Let me take you one step back … In 2010, the Eyjafjallajökull volcano in Iceland erupted, putting huge amounts of ash into the atmosphere. For five days, most flights to and from Europe were canceled, leaving many people stranded in airports. The Amsterdam Airport Schiphol was also closed. But something interesting happened – most of the KLM staff headed to the airport. Not because they had to – there were no flights leaving – but because they cared. The KLM staff took their freedom not for their personal benefit but to be there for the people stranded at Amsterdam Airport Schiphol.

This event and the many things that happened afterward meant a lot for KLM. It was also, although indirectly, the starting point of several service design projects we started. from the "Wall of Inspiration," to the "Idea Canvas," to the SurpriseUs game, to designing the book *No Day Is the Same,* for which we collected more than 100 stories.

Service Design Studio

All these small projects led to the Service Design Studio we created for KLM, right in the middle of all the buzz at the airport. For two months in the spring of 2013, we were open almost 24/7 to talk to people. The Service Design Studio was an open space without doors, so everybody could drop by to ask questions and participate.

Design as the language

Talking to people in design means engaging them in activities, using design to help people to express themselves. Every week we picked a relevant topic to work on, from "Traveling with kids" to "Peace of mind" to "Connectivity." With the studio as a context and using small designerly assignments, we had KLM staff engage with the people traveling through Amsterdam. The design approach and the way of working was new to them. However, the goal was to work together with the people visiting the airport, which was familiar territory.

The combination of the new way of working within a comfortable environment worked surprisingly well. The Service Design Studio turned out to be a safe haven for both the staff and the passengers to have conversations about an even better customer experience.

(A) The beautiful Service Design Studio was created in the middle of the airport to engage customers.

(B) The KLM staff worked together to understand their customers.

(C) Customers shared their input about their travel experiences.

(D) Eriano Troenokarso, a designer from 31Volts, made a visual summary at the end of every week.

(E) The staff took ownership of all projects.

Conclusion

What about the freedom? All project teams were built around KLM staff taking ownership of the goals we set. They were the true designers.

We are very proud of the Service Design Studio and the things we accomplished together with and for KLM. It hasn't been an easy path. For an organization that is highly dependent on doing things fast, safely, and on time, the explorative and creative nature of a designerly approach is hard to incorporate – especially when the outcome of the project isn't clear from the start. And when we finally delivered the more than 50 insights, the question remained, "Who would take the next step?"

Together with KLM, we learned a lot during this time. The most important practical lesson might well be the value of a designerly approach in an open environment to engage people. Talking to people by way of doing things together creates a deep understanding of the relationship your organization has with its customers.

KEY TAKEAWAYS

01 When a customer-centric organization or customer-centric culture is a key aspect of your service design project, make the project room stand out and ensure that it is accessible to everyone who wants to participate. Make it a project in itself.

02 Designing out in the open and for everyone to see might feel uncomfortable at first. Don't worry – your vulnerability is your strength. Any discomfort will pass faster than you expect.

03 Provide service design tools for the non-designers from your client organization to guide them. Conversations about innovation are different from daily reality.

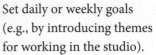

04 Set daily or weekly goals (e.g., by introducing themes for working in the studio).

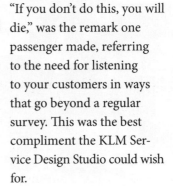

05 "If you don't do this, you will die," was the remark one passenger made, referring to the need for listening to your customers in ways that go beyond a regular survey. This was the best compliment the KLM Service Design Studio could wish for.

◀

6.5.2 CASE: CO-DESIGN WITH HYBRID METHODS

From vision to reality in 90 days

AUTHORS

Florian Vollmer
Partner and Chief
Experience Officer/CXO,
InReality

Chris Livaudais
Creative Director,
InReality

Project background

Imagine you are in need of a new kitchen faucet. Where do you start? For many, the answer may be to visit a local kitchen and bath showroom. Once there, you are faced with a sea of options. Shiny fixtures of all shapes and sizes cover the walls. Tiny nameplates, manufacturers' part numbers, and features too technical to understand flood your senses. Eventually, you might be greeted by a sales associate who, if willing and engaged themselves, begins to help you through this process toward the selection of your dream kitchen faucet. The process leaves consumers overwhelmed and unlikely to stay loyal to any one brand.

The journey just described happens repeatedly, in variations, all over the world. This was the situation facing Danze, an "affordable luxury" brand in the kitchen and bath space. Danze wanted to become a recognized leader in the industry. They envisioned an innovation that served

two purposes: (1) to create such a dramatically better customer experience that (2) a new channel partner is compelled to implement the experience on the showroom floor.

The people and the design brief

A key driver for this project was visionary CEO Michael Werner. He and his team approached InReality, and collaborated actively at all stages of the project. His energy also invigorated his internal sales and marketing team, as well as his operations group – we had a base level of buy-in from the beginning. Outside collaborators such as advertising agency and trade association representatives were important partners early on. In an industry where innovation is moving slowly, this shared authorship helped pave the way to quicker adoption of service innovation. How did we build the vision for this new, reimagined showroom experience?

It was clear that the traditional presentation of products on slat walls left little room for imaginative customer experiences or brand building beyond a simple logo on the wall.

Together, we evaluated the latest innovations in automotive showrooms, best-in-class retail, and leading museum experiences (London's V&A, amongst others). Interviews with some of the creators of these experiences helped our client understand what it takes to make a bold vision a reality. Observational research and interviews with sales associates rounded out the first phase.

From understanding to creating: Service design tools "out in the wild"

Using co-creation methods, the team at InReality facilitated a collaboration workshop with key stakeholders. Activities moved us quickly from the sharing of objectives into a collaboration space, one that empowered every single participant in the room to contribute and share their voices. The culminating event was a bodystorming/customer journey hybrid – essentially a stop motion of a typical customer journey where our customer would act out journey steps and then state their feelings at each moment in the journey. Participants watching each scene were asked to share insights from *their* perspectives: brand, product, marketing, operations, sales, and so on.

During a series of pre-meetings, it became clear that we would have to plan for a way to infect all project stakeholders with a passion for what would be possible.

Taking an approach of live journey mapping versus presenting a static slide deck resulted in a heightened level of empathy not only for the user but also for other (internal and external) stakeholders. Participants shared freely what they loved about various steps in the process and what they found challenging, forming a rich design brief for subsequent phases.

The solution

Our co-created customer journey evolved into a service blueprint, outlining requirements for the physical form and digital components. Customer-centric thinking, stakeholder awareness, and a sophisticated interpretation of brand form language were merged with a deep understanding of digital technologies.

Product samples are mounted on RFID-enabled, removable bases. Customers or associates can place the product on a "Smart Shelf" containing an RFID reader mounted below the touchscreen display, delivering dynamic content based on the product placed on the shelf. From there, shoppers can navigate through product details, material finishes, coordinating products, and more. The solution allows for a "three-way conversation" between the physical product, the digital content, and the people interacting with it all. When not in use, the screen works as a brand-centric messaging platform, attracting customers and reinforcing top-of-mind brand awareness with showroom representatives.

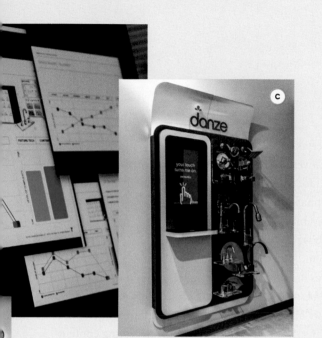

(A) Throughout our research, we directed the focus on "service design grit" – the hard work of making a service vision a reality. The findings, along with the strategic business requirements, made for a robust design brief from the onset of the project.

(B) The workshop was nothing short of amazing: the energy in the room was immense and a feeling of shared accomplishment by all truly was deep-felt.

(C) The buying experience for the customer and the selling experience for the showroom representative were so dramatically different that our client was easily able to break into the new sales channel, strategically widen- ing its distribution base. The adoption by the show- room partner happened in greater numbers and at a faster pace than initially projected.

The solution requires less linear wall space (less money spent for products on display) and adds a level of engagement previously not seen in these showroom environments. And the digital interactions can be tabulated and analyzed in a way that was never possible before.

Making it a reality

We produced and deployed the system to hundreds of locations in three months. Yet, initial usage of the smart shelf was not as high as anticipated. What was going on? Rather than pointing blame, our collaborative client–agency relationship allowed us to proac- tively seek a solution. A quick round of heuristic ideation revealed that perhaps the attract loop content did not have the immediate stopping power we desired. We suggested a change to the screen content with a stronger call to action. Working with an agency partner, we redeveloped the narrative and quickly pushed changes to the field. This improved usage rates dramatically.

Using service design tools tightly integrated with traditional marketing and industrial design tools resulted in a rapid development cycle and an industry-leading experience, ultimately exceeding the client's business goals.

KEY TAKEAWAYS

01 Live journey mapping can lead to amazing levels of participation and buy-in.

02 Digitally driven experiences offer great value – we can now enter the market with a minimum viable product (MVP) and iterate on it afterward.

03 True partnership with all stakeholders builds a trust and long-term mutual respect that encourages pro- active thinking and problem solving.

◀

Creating digital tools for mental health and employment support in the UK

AUTHORS

Sarah Drummond
Co-Founder and
Managing Director,
Snook

Valerie Carr
Creative Director,
Snook

SNOOK™

THE POINT PEOPLE

Department
of Health

Department
for Work & Pensions

Mental health in the UK is costing the government around £70 billion per year,[01] and that figure continues to increase. In 2014, the Department of Health (DoH), Department for Work and Pensions (DWP), and RAND Europe report outlined existing evidence around mental health interventions and made a call to "provide access to online mental health and work assessments and support."[02]

Snook was commissioned in partnership with The Point People to conduct research to explore future opportunities for digital products and services, specifically looking at the potential of digital to scale up access to frontline services that exist to support positive mental well-being, and also at self-management and how processes like cognitive behavioral therapy (CBT) could be scaled.

The project was undertaken with sponsorship by the Government Digital Service (GDS) and focused on executing a discovery phase, outlined in the GDS Service Manual.[03] During this phase, our focus was on identifying opportunities and user needs across varying stages of employment that could then be taken forward by design teams to later work up solutions.

As a research and design team, we were focused on not producing "solutions" for two reasons:

1 The discovery phase is about the identification of user needs aligned at core stages of employment, such as "As a line manager, I need tools to recognize my employees' mental well-being so that I can support them before they reach crisis points" and

"As someone who is unemployed, I need encouragement and tools that give me belief in my own abilities, because I have low self-esteem."

2 The system we were designing for was more complex than one or two products of the Government Digital Service. Our results could end up being used in a variety of contexts, from suggesting content and tools housed on NHS Choices, to creating principles to stimulate the private sector market, to developing digital tools that meet needs.

"If someone is off work with broken arms and legs, people rally around them. If someone is off work with mental health problems, they're like 'Oh, they will pull themselves together' sort of thing ... A lot of places need to understand it a little bit more."

— *Charles (research participant),*
45 years old

01 Elliott, L. (2014). "Mental Health Issues 'Cost UK £70bn a Year,' Claims Thinktank." Retrieved March 26, 2016, from *http://www.theguardian.com.*

02 RAND Europe. (2014). "Psychological Wellbeing and Work: Improving Service Provision and Outcomes." Retrieved March 26, 2016, from *https://www.gov.uk.*

03 Government Digital Service (n.d.). "Service Manual" at *https://www.gov.uk/service-manual.*

We conducted user research with people throughout the UK, from Dundee to Brighton, to gain understanding of their experience of being in and out of work and the impact on their mental well-being. The people we interviewed were not diagnosed with mental health conditions and a full breakdown of demographics can be found in the project report, including the ability to use technology.

Phases of research

Snook's research was in two phases:

1 **Discovery phase:** User research investigating people's experiences of accessing support for mental well-being and their current use of digital platforms

2 **Pre-alpha phase:** Co-designing digital platforms and tools that could support people to maintain mental well-being throughout their employment journey

Snook's sessions included in-depth interviews, focus groups, and workshops, all using bespoke tools developed specifically for the project. These helped in the creation of visual maps of people's employment history, clearly illustrating highs and lows of mental well-being and opportunities for digital innovation in service delivery.[04]

As a discovery project, our core findings were vast, so we split these down according to core stages of employment and user groups. Within the "in work" stage, our core findings highlighted the need for a greater set of resources and tools within the workplace for both line managers and staff to discuss and manage well-being. Our research highlighted key moments where and when this would be needed, from embedding tools into email accounts to annual review processes.

In the "finding work" phase, we highlighted a need to support people in thinking proactively about job searching, including alternative options like networking and skills development and how other people had achieved this in practical terms. Our

research therefore picked up both macro and micro needs/insights across the employment journey.

The focus was on three main phases of employment: finding work, being in and out of work, and managing work. Based on extensive user research, we created a set of design briefs presenting needs, insights, and challenges, each with its own case study. In addition, we outlined a list of design principles relevant to anyone developing digital tools in this field.

Key tools and processes

There were three key tools and processes utilized in the project – use cases, life journeys, and low-fidelity wireframes. These were chosen so a product development team could easily build on our framed user needs with deeper research and subsequent service designs by understanding the context to design for.

The ideation sessions included a variety of methods, like sketching, looking for analogies in other industries, and creating journey maps and low-fi mock-ups. The designers brought form to ideas through sketching, all of which corresponded to the

04 Throughout the project, Snook held workshops with the funding partners (Department of Health, Department for Work and Pensions, and Government Digital Services) to present findings and identify priorities for research and development.

(A) Showcasing high-fidelity prototypes to user groups.

(B) A high-fidelity wireframe showcasing the data hierarchy and a profiling tool to deliver tailored information for user groups.

(C) Mock-ups produced to highlight our strategic recommendations on integrating with existing employment journey tools in the system.

(D) A high-fidelity mock-up showcasing our alpha stage formed concepts from user-led content to tips on reducing anxiety at key moments in the "out of work" stage.

identified use cases. They developed ideas in timed sessions, working through each use case, identifying useful content for users, or sometimes joining several needs and use cases to form a standalone product or service opportunity.

We developed concepts through discussion, utilizing sketching to bring basic form to ideas. We identified one or two key features so we could recognize each idea later on, focus on the function of the concept, and quickly articulate it to others. We also looked for examples of innovations and existing products and services that were used to inspire similar concepts, but applied within the context of mental health and the scenarios we were designing for.

To further concepts, we sketched journeys of users and the concepts we were developing to articulate features of the service concepts and the delivery mechanisms that might be involved to make them a reality. This helped us not only to provide service and product design propositions, but to articulate stakeholders within the system of government, employment, and health who could be the delivery mechanisms.

After our core ideation sessions, we produced low-fidelity mock-ups, focusing only on features. The mock-ups did not include any visible aesthetic design features like color or defined fonts. We used this process to come to concrete design decisions on the core features of the different ideas we were creating and, through this whole process, consider how they might work together in tandem as a system of products and services.

"This research into likely user groups, needs, and preferences for a potential online mental health and work assessment and support tool provides invaluable insight into experience and need within our population. It provides information on people's experiences of living with a mental health condition and service provision. The research outlines where a digital service could benefit particular groups and through the early design and testing of prototypes provides a range of ideas for potential online tools."

— *Lauren Jones, Policy Lead for Mental Health and Work, Department of Health*

Looking ahead

This project was a new way of working for the DoH, which has historically employed market research techniques to inform digital development. The depth of insights generated through this user research exceeded the clients' original expectations and have been carried forward into various work packages through NHS Choices, the DWP, and the DoH.

The ongoing projects our clients were undertaking at the time were able to utilize the strategic recommendations, ideas, and wider user needs and insights we identified to inform the products and services in current development. Throughout every stage, we sought to ensure there were projects already instigated that could utilize the results to inform their work.

While this was a research project specifically for a digital tool, some of the findings have been useful for informing wider policy decisions and have been presented to Nesta, NHS Choices, and the wider GDS teams. The DoH welcomed these reports and has made them publicly available so that they can inform the future design of mental health and employment support.

KEY TAKEAWAYS

01 When undertaking discovery research, ensure that you are not forming solutions before identifying user needs and that insights are clearly identified and communicated.

02 Utilize journeys to consider the wider end-to-end remit of where a product or service moment fits in context with the wider system. Use this when researching to uncover insights and also to present needs at a later stage.

03 When "working live," make sure you understand the wider system of organizations, people, other stakeholders, and ongoing programs of work. This is so you can identify as you go where your developing project knowledge can be fed into (and how) and you can strategically position your work to increase the likelihood of positive impact.

04 Focus on function, not form, especially when testing prototypes. Keep everything low fidelity for as long as you can to ensure you test the proposition.

05 There is no silver bullet to "solve" mental health. The problem of service support is not owned by one department or organization, and you cannot design a "solution." Ensure the insights about how to design a product or service are clearly articulated and useful for a follow-on team or funder to learn from when embarking on their development within one part of the wider system.

6.5.4 CASE: MIXED-METHOD IDEATION

Opportunities for innovation in patient experience

AUTHORS

Marc Garcia
Professional Questioner,
We Question Our Project

Itziar Pobes
Project Brain,
We Question Our Project

WE QUESTION
OUR PROJECT

SJD
Sant Joan de Déu
Barcelona · Children's Hospital

Sant Joan de Déu–Barcelona Children's Hospital is locally seen as a synonym for innovation and empathic care of patients and families. In their own words, it is "a humanistic hospital."

In 2015, Sant Joan de Déu was the first hospital in Spain to set up a Patient Experience department to systematically rethink – and redo – its care model by involving patients, families, and staff through service design thinking methods.

Uncovering opportunities
Barcelona-based service design studio We Question Our Project collaborated in one of the new department's foundational projects. It comprised a broad study of the experience of several types of patients and their families: children and young adults up to 18 years old with diabetes or complex chronic conditions, international children with oncological and orthopedic diseases getting specific treatment unavailable in their countries of origin, and pregnant women. The research was aimed at uncovering opportunities for new digital and face-to-face services.

"This is the first time we have seen the patient's treatment process as a whole."
—Head of Diabetes Care

Fieldwork included observations, mobile ethnography, and in-depth interviews with families, patients, and almost all the range of professionals that work within the hospital: nurses, doctors, staff of support services (admissions and reception, customer service, social service, coordination of volunteers and donors, communication, digital marketing, and management). We then synthesized all that data into detailed – and valuable – user journey maps.

Due to the very tight schedules of hospital staff, it was challenging to involve them actively. We had to fix workshops months in advance and squeeze them into two-hour slots, which included putting everyone back on track, moving forward, and collecting results – there was almost no time left to create a safe space!

We started by having professionals related to each type of patient observe their corresponding user journey and make an individual traffic light assessment – what was already working (green), what could be improved (amber), and what was not working at all (red) – with an additional round of what was missing. After sharing and clustering everyone's notes, they translated the categories into ideation questions starting with "How might we …" At that point, we noticed that most of the issues they had identified in separate user journeys were surprisingly similar. There were eight big opportunity areas across patient types and services, such as managing fear and

(A) Special facilities, such as this image diagnosis room, and procedures have been part of the Sant Joan de Déu's efforts to
ease children's time in hospital for years, even before the Patient
Experience department was created.

(B) While doing ethnographic research with the Patient Experience
team, our project room was set in the hospital nursing school.
On the wall, clusterings of pregnant women's verbatim statements. On tables, early structures of two treatment processes.
On the floor, the complex chronic user journey in the making.

(C) We shared preliminary research results in the form of user journeys with relevant stakeholders and asked them to contribute
with additional knowledge. In some cases, reading patients' own
words was a shock, but it sparked meaningful conversations
around the need to change procedures or attitudes.

(D) Hospital staff integrated the research results by doing a traffic
light assessment of user journeys, and moved into ideation by
translating emerging topics into "How might we …?" questions.

expectations or making children feel normal (as opposed to sick) while in the hospital.

Ideas to prototypes

From that moment on, we no longer worked in patient-related teams, but mixed staff from different units. We generated tons of ideas through brainwriting rounds with different angles and prioritized them using a bull's-eye: most relevant in the center, least relevant outside. Ideas were developed into concepts by quickly sketching and describing how they would work; identifying who would be involved; and considering how innovative, feasible, and impactful they would be.

"I feel hope every time we meet. We are actually working to improve problems I see on a daily basis."
— Case manager for international patients

Finally, staff also contributed to taking concepts further through prototyping. Some teams sketched new systems and procedures in detail. Others focused on digital tools and were able to produce early versions of interactive mock-ups. We refined those prototypes just enough to check them with patients and families in guerrilla tests around the hospital.

A long-term vision and action

After prioritizing the projects again with an idea portfolio, some are already being put into practice by Patient Experience and the relevant stakeholders – for example, context-sensitive ways for communicating bad news and a resource center for families.

This case also proved the value of a service design approach to the management. Beyond discrete projects, patient experience has become one of the foundations of the new strategic plan of the hospital.

Taking a broader approach was key to building a long-term vision with projects for the next few years. Involving staff from different units and levels both as informants during research and as co-creators since then developed a shared understanding and a goodwill for change.

KEY TAKEAWAYS

01 Don't be discouraged if the conditions for collaborating with stakeholders and users of your service design project are not ideal. Embrace the constraints and make the most of people's commitment.

02 No matter how rigid your schedules, be prepared to come across unexpected results – and to adjust your work accordingly.

03 Participants with little experience in innovation or design tend to mix up opportunities and solutions. Make sure you frame clearly what stage you are at in the ideation process and what you expect to produce.

04 When generating ideas in teams that work together usually, they may have discussed the same topics over and over. Let them express themselves, but make them go beyond complaints and ordinary solutions by asking for more alternatives.

6.5.5 CASE: SUPPORTING CREATIVITY WITH TRIGGER VISUALS

Using customer journey mapping to understand cookstove users in Kenya

AUTHORS

Fiona Lambe
Research Fellow,
Stockholm Environment
Institute

Hannah Wanjiru
Research
Associate-Energy,
Stockholm Environment
Institute Africa Center,
Nairobi, Kenya

Sophie Andersson
Senior Service Designer,
Transformator Design

Per Brolund
Senior Concept Designer,
Transformator Design

Erik Widmark
Co-Founder and
Service Designer,
Expedition Mondial

Susanna Nissar
Co-Founder and CEO,
Expedition Mondial

Despite decades of donor and government financing, three billion people worldwide still cook on smoky traditional stoves and open fires, and a large-scale shift away from the traditional use of biomass for cooking has yet to occur in many developing countries. This results in 4.3 million annual deaths from respiratory illnesses. Still, typical methods for understanding behavior tend to be quantitative and tell us little about exactly how and why households adopt (or fail to adopt) and use improved cookstoves and cleaner fuels. Service design methods helped to shed new light on the needs and wider contexts of improved cookstove users in Kenya. The work led to concrete insights for the specific context, but could also be used to improve the way in which better cookstove programs are designed and implemented in other developing country settings in the future.

In September 2015, a mixed team of service designers and SEI researchers conducted 19 in-depth interviews with households in Kiambu County, Kenya, with focus on the adoption and usage of a biomass pellet stove from Philips. We partnered with SNV Netherlands Development Organisation, which distributed the stove, and with a local micro-finance institution, VEP (Visionary Empowerment Programme), which provided loans to the women to afford the stove.

"It was really useful for us to see the full journey for the women – not just receiving the stove, but how they get information, how they learn to use the stove, and how they cope if something goes wrong. This helps us to see where problems might pop up now and in the future, and how we might solve them together with our partners."

— *VEP field staff*

The interviews were conducted with the help of a local translator, and in order to overcome language barriers we used visual material showing different situations and suggestions related to cooking. This visual material triggered the respondents to share stories and helped us facilitate the interviews. When displaying the visuals, we asked "What is this?" "How would you use this?" or "What if things looked/worked this way?" and they started to share their stories. After our first set of initial interviews, we could see patterns within the customer journey that were not ideal for them as end users. In order to understand more about those problem areas, we used other visual material to show the respondents new situations, new services, or different stove designs.

The overall ideation process
In the first round of interviews, the users claimed to be happy with the

EXPEDITION MONDIAL

SEI STOCKHOLM ENVIRONMENT INSTITUTE

Transformator design

usage of the stove and had no suggestions for improvements. But when shown images of stoves with different simple variations in height, width, or fabrication materials, suddenly something happened. Users spontaneously started talking about the pros and cons of the different designs, which also gave clues on how they experienced using the current stove: for example, "Oh, I would love if it was higher, then it wouldn't burn the food," or "A wider stove would definitely make less pellets go to waste at the bottom."

They even started coming up with new suggestions for designs, services, and solutions. When different respondents were presented with ideas for alternative stove designs over and over again, they automatically refined relevant ideas and sorted out the irrelevant ones.

"This was useful for us to understand the daily logistic challenges faced by our field staff in trying to deliver the stoves and how we can address these challenges together to make the system smoother for the customer."
— *VEP Managing Director*

Misinterpretations, assumptions, and evaluations of what they saw in the visuals were encouraged. This was an important part of the ideation process, where simple, rough drawings left space for interpretation and allowed the respondents to fill it with their own needs and wishes. The core activity within the ideation process, as any service designer would know, is not to confirm ideas generated by "designer geniuses," but really to co-create together with the users. Ideas and innovations have no value on their own unless the ideas meet the needs of the user.

Thanks to the iterative process of interviews and ideation, we could both co-define the challenges connected to adopting improved cookstoves and co-create the solutions together with the end users.

Some of the challenges for the end users were hands-on practicalities, such as the logistics of getting the new fuel and stoves to their homes. Others faced challenges in lack of support during the crucial startup phase, where their new habits are beginning to be formed. It was also difficult for the end users to compare and evaluate

(A) The use of half-finished visual material invited respondents to fill in the gaps. Here, respondents were presented with a mock product presentation leaflet. In response, they would speak about what aspects of the product they would want information about.

(B) Trigger material was used that pictured products, situations, and themes.

(C) After respondents had built their own customer journey out of pictures and words, they were asked to draw their emotional journey, which resulted in more nuanced and in-depth stories.

(D) The customer journey map incorporated the experience of stove users, their families and friends, the distributors, NGOs, and the government to fully understand their perspectives.

different types of fuels because of different usage and payment models.

"Starting from the customer journey map is good because it shows how everyone – the stove users, their families and friends, the distributors, NGOs, and even the government – fits into the system and how we can collaborate to improve the user experience."
— SNV program officer

The CJM as a communication tool for stakeholders

The user's experience of acquiring and using an improved cookstove was summarized and visualized in a customer journey map. This map showed bottlenecks and thresholds for achieving widespread adoption of improved cookstoves. We used the map in a stakeholder workshop as a base for sorting out roles and relations between stakeholders. It proved to be a crucial communication tool, as it created a common understanding with the end user's needs and experience as the unifying focus.

Based on the outcomes from this case we were invited to apply the same methods for a cookstove company working in Zambia in spring 2016.

KEY TAKEAWAYS

O1 When interviewing across language barriers, use visuals to start the conversation and make sure translators have an understanding of the methodology.

O2 Visual material showing artifacts, situations, or themes related to the topic of interest can help respondents open up and verbalize their thoughts and experiences.

O3 The ideation process should not be an isolated phase for designers exclusively. It needs to be embedded within the research phase and end users should be invited in order to find the most relevant solutions.

O4 Using the end users' experience as a reference point helps sort out which actors and aspects in the surrounding service ecosystem are relevant to understand and improve the service or system. ◀

07
PROTOTYPING

Explore, challenge, and evolve your ideas in reality.

Expert comments ———————————————————————————————————————

Alexander Osterwalder   Carola Verschoor   Francesca Terzi   Johan Blomkvist   Kristina Carlander

07
PROTOTYPING

This chapter also includes

Experiential aspects: Getting concrete   217

Wishlists and hostages   220

Two types of service prototyping:
Direct experience vs. indirect imagination   227

Dealing with failure of prototypes and critique   229

From specialized approaches to your
own living prototyping lab   242

REDUCING UNCERTAINTY

In service design, prototyping is used to explore, evaluate, and communicate how people might behave in or experience a future service situation. **Prototyping helps the design team to:**

→ Quickly identify important aspects of a new service concept and explore different alternative solutions.

→ Systematically evaluate which solutions might work in our everyday reality.

→ Effectively create a shared understanding of initial ideas and concepts, enhancing communication, collaboration, and participation of interdisciplinary stakeholders.

Prototyping is an essential activity to reduce risk and uncertainty as early and as cheaply as possible, to improve the quality of your final deliverable, and to eventually implement your project successfully. Usually prototyping is done after some initial research and ideation in a service design project, but it can also be used to kick off a project, especially when working on existing products. Prototyping activities often uncover new questions and send the team back to research or ideation, which leads to even more options you might decide to prototype and test.

By turning your ideas into prototypes and testing them with real customers and stakeholders in realistic contexts, you keep your personal biases[01] in check. Through prototyping you produce work which is grounded in reality, not in assumptions and opinions.

Practically, over the course of a whole service design project you will use a wide range of methods, from quick-and-dirty prototyping to simulating and testing close-to-reality prototypes that deliver solid and valid (market) data. Prototyping is a structured but in itself iterative process. It often starts with exploring a simple idea or question and leads to iterating between working on specific parts of the service and exploring the effects of those changes on holistic end-to-end experiences.

Service prototyping uses walkthroughs, theatrical rehearsals, or process simulations as well as traditional model making and testing techniques from a wide range of disciplines. While the scope of prototyping in service design might vary, it should always balance holistic perspectives across multiple steps with a detailed focus on single touchpoints or experiences. You employ ethnographic research methods to evaluate and make sense of the gathered data. In many ways – especially when used for explorative and validating purposes – service prototyping can be seen as research focused on future service situations.

COMMENT

"One of the key challenges in service prototyping is the constant interplay between prototyping of single touchpoints vs. consistent and iterative development of holistic service experiences."

– Johan Blomkvist

01 As we are now working in solution space, we – the proud creators of a service concept or solution – are especially prone to confirmation bias. In other words, we want our babies to succeed. So, our assumptions and estimations about how our ideas will perform when implemented will most certainly be much too optimistic. Be mindful of this bias, especially when creating tests for your prototypes. Always try to really break your prototypes. Remember: if you do not break them, your clients will (or the board will during the final presentation).

THE BASIC PROCESS OF SERVICE PROTOTYPING

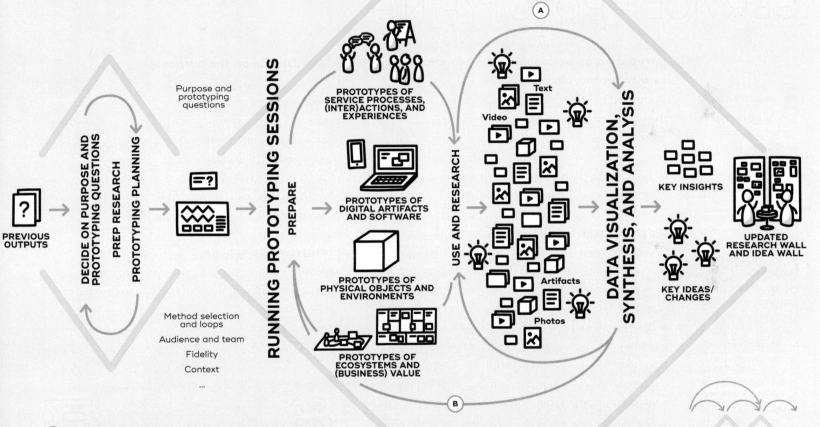

PREVIOUS OUTPUTS

DECIDE ON PURPOSE AND PROTOTYPING QUESTIONS

PREP RESEARCH

PROTOTYPING PLANNING

Purpose and prototyping questions

Method selection and loops
Audience and team
Fidelity
Context
...

RUNNING PROTOTYPING SESSIONS

PREPARE

PROTOTYPES OF SERVICE PROCESSES, (INTER)ACTIONS, AND EXPERIENCES

PROTOTYPES OF DIGITAL ARTIFACTS AND SOFTWARE

PROTOTYPES OF PHYSICAL OBJECTS AND ENVIRONMENTS

PROTOTYPES OF ECOSYSTEMS AND (BUSINESS) VALUE

USE AND RESEARCH

Video
Text
Artifacts
Photos

DATA VISUALIZATION, SYNTHESIS, AND ANALYSIS

KEY INSIGHTS

KEY IDEAS/ CHANGES

UPDATED RESEARCH WALL AND IDEA WALL

(A) **Research-based:** The creation of the prototype itself is only the starting point which allows us to focus on using and testing prototypes and learn from them.

(B) **Iterations and prototyping loops:** Prototyping is an iterative process with a sequence of prototyping loops. The challenge is to find a balance between prototyping the details of a single (inter)action, object, or app and the wider end-to-end experience.

Prototyping activities are embedded in an iterative sequence with other activities of research, ideation, and implementation.

7.1 THE PROCESS OF SERVICE PROTOTYPING

Introducing an actionable framework for service prototyping

Compared to prototyping in other (design) disciplines, the prototyping of services or product experiences is more holistic. It starts with the wider context of how services and physical or digital products[01] are experienced and used, but also encompasses traditional prototyping work on key assets like (physical) products, software, architecture, or actual content, making it more complex to work with. This chapter presents an actionable framework for service prototyping in practice.

Just like any other core activity of the service design process, prototyping[02] can benefit from a clearly articulated design. Even though not every prototyping activity needs extensive planning, the following framework might help you to achieve richer results with fewer resources. It doesn't need to be followed step by step, but provides a collection of useful principles that you can apply to your prototyping efforts.

7.1.1 Decide on the purpose

Your first step in prototyping is to clarify your purpose: Why you are prototyping and what you want to achieve. There are three main reasons why prototyping is used in service design: to explore, to evaluate, and to communicate.[03] Be aware that this is not a strict distinction and often the activities can be mixed – to some degree even within a single prototyping session.

Prototyping to explore

Explorative prototyping (or prototyping to explore) is used to create new options and new future solutions

03 See Blomkvist, J., & Holmlid, S. (2010). "Service Prototyping According to Service Design Practitioners." In *Proceedings of the Service Design and Innovation Conference* (pp. 1–11). Linköping University Electronic Press. Interestingly, this research also showed a lack of shared concepts and language in service prototyping. So, when you talk to colleagues, do not assume but ask about what they are actually doing and why they are doing it.

Prototyping is used to explore, evaluate, and communicate at various stages in the process.

01 The term "products" describes anything a company offers – no matter if this is tangible or not. In academia, products are often divided into goods and services. However, products are usually bundles of services and physical/digital products. As "goods" is colloquially understood as referring to something tangible, we prefer to speak of physical/digital products. Read more on this in the textbox *Service-dominant logic* in 2.5.

02 Interestingly, the process of service prototyping also works nicely for other forms of prototyping. One reason is that a service prototype often contains physical or digital products as props or architecture for its stage. So, to create a full-service prototype we also need to include all other forms of prototyping.

based on a given initial service concept or idea (or a previous prototype). Think of it as a form of ideation, or "thinking with your hands." You learn more about the opportunities and the challenges of the solution space.

Explorative prototyping is mostly done for yourself or the core project team.[04] Prototypes are created in parallel to quickly compare different options and perspectives. Explicitly, they are built to be thrown away, so you might want to use prototyping materials or platforms that are geared toward creating prototypes fast. Early in the process, these are typically things you have lying around your workspace already. Explorative prototyping creates many insights, new questions, and hypotheses about how a future service might create value, might work, or might feel.[05]

Prototyping to evaluate

Evaluative prototyping is used to understand how people experience the future that our prototyping suggests. Sometimes you will carefully evaluate your hypotheses in formal testing, and sometimes you will do more lightweight tests on the fly.[06] Whether formal or informal, evaluative prototyping helps you to converge again, to start reducing the number of options you have and decide what to focus on. Evaluative prototyping sessions are created with a specific set of questions or hypotheses

in mind that need to be tested. Prototypes are often built for potential customers or other carefully selected stakeholders from outside the team.[07]

During formal evaluative prototyping, you strive to create prototypes that mimic aspects of reality as closely as possible. If you are interested in the emotional responses to a service (or part of a service), you must let the customers experience it. For the evaluation part, this form of prototyping is heavily supported by qualitative research and analysis methods that can provide some hard facts and metrics, such as contextual and in-depth interviews as well as various forms of observation.

Prototyping to communicate and present

Communicative prototyping is used to communicate important aspects of your project to selected audiences. Specifically tailored prototypes and prototyping activities help you to reduce misunderstandings and ignite meaningful discussions around the key design questions within the team or organization, or with other stakeholders. This facilitates collaboration, supports decision making, and reduces friction in your project right from the start. Different personal perspectives and potential conflicts become clearly visible and can be openly addressed. In addition to creating a safe space for experimentation, these activities are a great tool for team formation.

For a wider audience, presentational prototypes can be used as props for well-rehearsed storytelling

COMMENT

"We use prototyping sessions instead of traditional idea generation on sticky notes when we start working with highly interdisciplinary teams. Every one of them has their own specialist jargon and this leads to many misunderstandings. Prototyping is the universal language that helps them to understand each other much faster."

– Francesca Terzi

04 This does not mean, however, you cannot or should not include an audience from outside your team (i.e., customers or other stakeholders) in the explorative prototyping sessions as co-creators. See for example 6.5.1, *Case: Opening the design studio to your customers*, for a great example of how to engage with your customers.

05 It can also be used as a tool during research to better understand users' needs or desires using a physical representation of their ideas. For example, see Buchenau, M., & Suri, J. F. (2000). "Experience Prototyping." In *Proceedings of the 3rd Conference on Designing Interactive Systems: Processes, Practices, Methods, and Techniques* (pp. 424–433). ACM.

06 Note that a prototype itself can be seen as an implicit way of expressing a hypothesis which is otherwise hard to articulate. The prototype is the hypothesis.

07 Note that even early in the process and even with rough, lo-fi prototyping you will still use evaluative prototyping. It is used whenever you need to make decisions or have to reduce the number of prototypes you want to work on.

presentations. In those cases there is little to no interactivity of the audience with the prototype.[02] The prototypes are adapted from previous prototyping activities and are usually quite polished. Used with care, presentational prototypes are a valuable strategic tool to present, persuade, and inspire management or key stakeholders.

7.1.2 Decide on your prototyping questions

At each iteration, you need to clearly state what you want to learn or achieve through your prototyping activities by formulating one or many prototyping questions. Think about these prototyping questions as the research questions[03] of the prototyping stage. In our prototyping work, we have found *value, look and feel, feasibility,* and *integration* to be especially helpful perspectives in generating initial prototyping questions and focusing on key aspects of a service concept during prototyping.[04]

As Stephanie Houde and Charles Hill point out, "prototypes provide the means for examining design problems and evaluating solutions. Selecting the focus of a prototype is the art of identifying the most important open design questions."[05] By formulating one or many prototyping questions you make sure that your team (and your potential client) have a common prototyping aim.

Start with a value prototype

Value prototypes are often a great start. Usually it is easier to find a suitable technology or business model if you already have a strong value proposition than the other way around. Be aware that look-and-feel and especially technical feasibility prototypes can take a lot of time and effort to create. This is easily wasted if the value proposition is still changing rapidly. You can spend a lot of effort and money creating a great look and feel, but if you don't build it on top of a solid value proposition that is backed by research or prototyping, you are very likely to burn money.

Assess idea and project context

Keep in mind that your actual starting point always depends on your individual project. In the fashion industry, look-and-feel prototyping will get more focus than in B2B business consulting, where there is a stronger focus on value. In projects where a specific technology stack has to be used, feasibility prototypes should be given a higher priority as they define the playing ground for many solutions. Your decision will also depend on whether the project needs to deliver immediate results or is used to explore innovative future solutions as inspirations for future developments – like concept cars in the automotive industry.

01 Maeda, J. [@johnmaeda on Twitter, 5 Oct 2014]. *"If a picture is worth 1000 words, a prototype is worth 1000 meetings." – saying at @ideo.* Retrieved September 27, 2016, from *https://twitter.com/johnmaeda.*

02 The presenter usually follows well-prepared steps through the different aspects of a prototype (e.g., like showing precreated click paths through an app prototype). Some people would refer to this as a demo.

03 See 5.1.1, *Research scope and research question.*

04 The model presented here is adapted from Houde, S., & Hill, C. (1997). "What Do Prototypes Prototype?" *Handbook of Human-Computer Interaction, 2,* 367–381. It uses a set of high-level perspectives that is tailored toward a more general prototyping approach. While we (the authors) have found using it to be quite insightful in most of our own projects, we are aware that these perspectives certainly are not the only ones you could use. For example, another widespread set is people-business-technology, which might work for some.

05 Houde, S., & Hill, C. (1997). "What Do Prototypes Prototype?" *Handbook of Human-Computer Interaction, 2,* 367–381.

VALUABLE PERSPECTIVES TO IDENTIFY PROTOTYPING QUESTIONS

START HERE

VALUE

INTEGRATION

FEASIBILITY   **LOOK & FEEL**

HOW DO WE CREATE VALUE?
What can this future service do for the customer?
What kind of needs and pain points do we address?
How will our service eventually fit into the
bigger context of our customers' or stakeholders' lives?

HOW DO WE MAKE IT WORK?
What does our organization need to do to deliver this service?
What are the requirements for scalability and performance?
Is there a business model?
Is it feasible technically, financially, legally?

WHAT DOES IT LOOK AND FEEL LIKE?
What does the service as a whole or in part look like?
Who do we interact with and how does it feel?
What are the physical or digital objects we interact
with and how does this feel?

HOW DOES IT ALL WORK TOGETHER?
What is the whole customer experience when we bring
together value, look and feel, and implementation?
How do the different aspects of the service work together?
How do we need to balance and resolve constraints?

Iterate

As you move forward, iterate between value, look and feel, and feasibility on one side and integration prototypes on the other to make sure you are not wasting time and effort on concepts that might not work in the implementation context. Identify dependencies between the different aspects early and learn how to integrate them into your design. Staying with value prototypes for too long tends to result in concepts that are hard to implement – which makes it challenging for short-term projects. On the other hand, this might be spot on when you are looking for inspirational concepts as a guidance for future work.

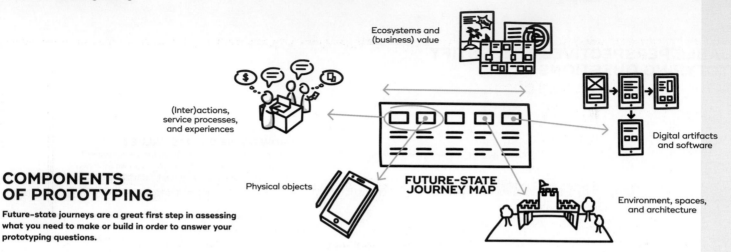

Ecosystems and
(business) value

(Inter)actions,
service processes,
and experiences

Digital artifacts
and software

Physical objects

**FUTURE-STATE
JOURNEY MAP**

Environment, spaces,
and architecture

COMPONENTS
OF PROTOTYPING

**Future-state journeys are a great first step in assessing
what you need to make or build in order to answer your
prototyping questions.**

7.1.3   Assess what to make or build

It can be helpful to first assess which parts of your future
services and physical or digital products you actually need
to make or build in order to get the answers you need, and
then get concrete. Future-state journeys of customers or
key stakeholders are a great first step.[01] Often, this allows
you to break your prototyping challenge down to a mix of
the following major components:

→ (Inter)actions, service processes, experiences
→ Physical objects
→ Environments, spaces, architecture
→ Digital artifacts and software
→ Ecosystems, (business) value

01   Note that your chosen scope can be frontstage as well as backstage. Usually you would start by looking at the
journeys of customers and frontstage staff, but this can and should be extended to other key stakeholders
depending on your specific purpose and prototyping questions.

For some prototyping questions this can be straightforward. If for example you are working on a new home
automation system, your questions about hardware
and software might suggest that you build a functional
prototype of a piece of software together with a physical
prototype of an internet-enabled gadget.

However, more complex questions – for example,
whether your home automation service actually creates
a meaningful value for your customers and makes them
happier people – cannot be answered directly.

In this context, experiences with services or products,
whether physical or digital, can be likened to an (interactive) theater play. While theatermakers cannot design the
emotions of an audience directly, there are things they can
do. They can create a compelling story, write gripping
dialogue, create great costumes and stage design, develop
systems and technologies for special effects, and rehearse
with actors and staff (front- and backstage). They can keep

Experiential aspects: Getting concrete

You will find that breaking down complex concepts into simple but concrete questions like *Who? What? Where? When? and How?* makes them much easier for people to understand and relate to – and helps you to identify what you need to build or make tangible through your prototyping activities.[02] Consider the following:

→ **Scope and scale**: Which part of the overall journey do you need to look at (i.e., which detail and in which time frame)?

→ **Actors**: Who are the main actors or stakeholders you choose to look at? Who can you influence?

→ **(Inter)actions, process, activities**: What is happening across the whole journey? What is happening at a specific step? What are the (inter)actions with other actors, objects, or the environment?

→ **Stage – interior design, architecture, (sensory) environment**: What is your stage? What does the "stage" look like? What is the spatial layout? What is the architecture like? What are the ambient conditions as perceived with your five senses? What does it smell like? How is the lighting?

→ **Props – physical objects or artifacts**: What physical objects are involved, actively handled, or merely present? What role do they play? What signs and symbols are used?

→ **Props – interactive digital or electronic objects or artifacts**: What digital objects (or software) are involved, actively handled, or merely present?

→ **Visible content or topics**: What do people talk or think about? Is there specific content visible as part of other artifacts (e.g., in an app, a brochure, etc.)?

→ **Location and geographical context**: Where is your stage located? What are the other places involved? Think about different geographies or markets.

→ **Temporal context**: When does this happen? In summer? In winter? At the start of a business day? At the end of it? At the beginning of a customer relationship or at the end?

→ **Quantities**: How much? How many? How many people are there? How large or small are things? How many products are in your lineup? How many consulting sessions do you plan for? How much is the merchandise? ◄

02 Note that the experiential aspects of an idea or concept are closely related but not limited to the concept of physical evidences (see textbox *Physical evidences* in 3.5). The experiential aspects go beyond physical or digital artifacts and also include interactions, processes, and activities as well as other aspects that can be experienced directly by an audience using suitable prototyping/simulation methods.

doing this until they can deliver an engaging interaction that evokes the emotional response and creates the value they are striving for in both the actors and their audience.

Prototyping tackles the same challenge with the same basic approach. We cannot design the actual experiences of our future services and physical or digital products directly, but we can design and prototype many concrete aspects around them to gather valuable feedback and other data from the people involved.

However, since it is usually impossible to prototype every aspect, you will need to make a decision about which aspects are most important. One way to do this is to use a prototyping portfolio (based on an idea portfolio) to discuss and prioritize the parts and elements of your service that you want to explore, evaluate, or communicate through prototyping.[01]

7.1.4 Planning prototyping

When planning your prototyping activities, you should think of the ways that are most likely to give you fruitful answers for your proposed design questions within your chosen purpose and goals. Just like anything else you do, prototyping activities must fit within certain business constraints, as you always have to consider how to best allocate time, money, and human resources within a project. Specifically, prototyping planning includes decisions about

audience, authors, fidelity, context, prototyping loops, multitracking, and method selection. We'll explore them further here.[02]

Audience

Like in research, you have to think about your sample:[03] Who will be experiencing or testing your prototypes? Who do you want to observe? Who should participate in your prototyping sessions and how do you select them? These questions are critical for the reliability of what you are going to learn during prototyping and how valid the results will be. Use stakeholder mapping to get a clear picture about the sampling strategy for your prototyping activities.[04]

In prototyping you will typically move between different groups of stakeholders acting as your audience: e.g., members of your project team, colleagues, current staff, internal/external experts, clients, (potential) users, customers, and future staff.[05] As a rule of thumb, the closer people are to the project team the easier (and faster) it gets to recruit them for your prototyping sessions. However, you will find stronger bias in those groups than with people from outside. Of course, your goal should always be to show your prototype to actual users and customers as soon as possible.[06]

EXPERT TIP

"Prototyping is serious business, that should be used systematically and may require a notable amount of planning. But don't forget the ability to quickly create lo-fi prototypes of your ideas, also in later stages. You will learn a lot just by taking a step from *thinking* to *doing*. If you get stuck in a discussion, a simple role-play (acting out the problem) may in that moment suggest the solution you need. And that role-play is also a prototype others can react to. Nurture a prototyping culture!"

— **Kristina Carlander**

---

01 See *Idea portfolio* in 6.4. Useful dimensions for an efficient prototyping portfolio are complexity ("How hard is it to actually implement or test this aspect of the service?") and importance ("How important in the overall context of your service concept is it to get this aspect right?").

02 Please note that you do not have to work through those aspects in the order presented here, or in any other particular sequence. This is more like a checklist to help you ask the right questions when planning prototyping activities.

03 See *Sample selection* in 5.1.2 to learn more about sampling and the different strategies you can use there.

04 Also see *Stakeholder maps* and *Ideas from system mapping* in 6.4 *Ideation methods*.

05 See 7.3.2 *Case: Using prototyping and co-creation to create ownership and close collaboration between the designers, project group, and staff* for an example of how to rethink behind-the-scenes processes with multiple stakeholders from a customers or users perspective.

Roles in the team

While the audience has a huge impact on the outcome of the prototyping activity, so too do the people who drive the prototyping process, who prepare and build the prototypes, run the sessions, and observe the reactions of the chosen audience.[07] Typical roles in prototyping activities include:

EXPERT TIP

"Nurture a sustainable prototyping process. Some of us work with services as a project, which has an end. But the service should be continuously tested and improved. Provide the staff with training and easy-to-use tools and formats for prototyping. Prototype together, to make it easy for the staff to continue prototyping when the project is over."

– Kristina Carlander

→ **Concept owner:** The concept owner is the person who came up with the concept you are prototyping.

→ **Writer or (model) maker:** The writer scripts or sketches out a starting point for the experiences, (inter)actions, or scenarios that you are going to prototype. The (model) maker builds all necessary (physical and digital) props, sets, and stages for the prototyping session.[08]

→ **Facilitator:** The facilitator is responsible for the process and guides the selected audience through a prototyping session.[09]

→ **Actors and operators:** Actors and operators assist the facilitator in creating an experience during the prototyping session. This involves people acting as staff or other customers during service simulations, or manually operating an interface that is tested. When preparing your prototyping sessions, always ask yourself: Who will be taking on which role during the prototyping process? What are the biases and motivations each person brings to the table?

→ **Researcher:** The researcher independently observes the audience during the prototyping session and records her insights.

→ **Subject matter experts and key stakeholders:** Subject matter experts and key stakeholders complete the prototyping team, adding special skills and in-depth knowledge about the subject matter and target contexts suggested by scope and prototyping questions.

Note that especially early in the project, one person can be concept owner, maker, facilitator, and researcher all rolled into one. Later, when you have a clearer picture of your service concept, you might make the decision to involve specialists for each necessary craft or discipline (e.g., model makers, UX specialists, experience directors, ethnographers, etc.).

Always be aware of your role, bias, and associated influence on the audience at every step of the prototyping process. For example, concept owners and makers

06 Or in the words of Hazel White: "Show your prototypes to the people who will use the service – they'll add to them, turn them upside down, tear them apart, and challenge your assumptions. Listen."

07 Prototyping might never stop. In a running service, needs, systems, and access to resources are changing constantly – so it's valuable to ask yourself early on how you can involve the people who will be responsible for running and adapting the future service. See 7.3.3, *Case: Enabling staff and stakeholders to prototype for continuous evolution,* for an example of how to enable staff to take over the prototyping and design process, without the need for a skilled designer or any special tools.

08 Possible starting points are an exposé (text), sketching up a sh!tty first draft of a storyboard (visualization), defining a set of rules for the improvisation game (guidelines/ruleset), or filming part of a desktop walkthrough (hands-on simulation documented on film).

09 Because the facilitator's involvement can actively influence the audience, it's important to be as neutral as possible when acting as the facilitator. See Chapter 10, *Facilitating workshops,* for more on different kinds of neutrality.

Wishlists and hostages

BY JOHAN BLOMKVIST

Note that some people might see your prototypes as wishlists ("an opportunity to push *my* ideas and agenda into the project") or even as hostages ("if I put this in the prototype they'll have to include it in the result").

In order to avoid unrelated agendas interfering, be specific about the purpose and extent to which the prototyping session will influence the project as a whole *and* the role/function of the prototype. Then capture participants' ideas and put them into your idea portfolio to be prioritized and checked against research and other ideas and concepts at the next iteration planning session. ◄

often want their concept to survive – consciously or unconsciously – because they have already invested some time into the concept or prototype. This obviously has an influence on the audience, and the results become biased.[01] One way to tackle this *prototyper bias* is to be open about your role and acknowledge that there is a bias. This lets you consciously put down your concept owner or maker hat and take a more objective position. Other options include inviting an independent facilitator or researcher for your testing sessions, or changing roles within the existing team between iterations.

Fidelity

Decide how refined your prototype needs to be. What level of detail is needed? What resolution does it make sense to achieve for your given scope and research question? How much effort do you need or want to put into this prototype? The question of fidelity is closely connected to the economic principle of prototyping by Lim, Stolterman, and Tenenberg: "The best prototype is one that, in the simplest and most efficient way, makes the possibilities and limitations of a design idea visible and measurable."[02]

The economic principle seems to suggest starting with low-fidelity prototypes like paper or cardboard prototypes and then gradually increasing the level of detail as you get closer and closer to implementation. However,

01 This very much relates to the problem of researcher bias. See *Researcher triangulation* in 5.1.3.

02 Lim, Y. K., Stolterman, E., & Tenenberg, J. (2008). "The Anatomy of Prototypes: Prototypes as Filters, Prototypes as Manifestations of Design Ideas." *ACM Transactions on Computer-Human Interaction (TOCHI)*, 15(2), 7.

the world is slightly more complex than simply dividing the prototyping world into lo-fi or hi-fi.

While fidelity is often connected with visual fidelity (look and feel), you can also talk about fidelity in other dimensions, like fidelity of the implementation.[03] You can even find those different levels within one single prototype. The prototype of a website can be low fidelity with respect to look and feel, but quite high fidelity with respect to content or information structure. Hence, try to be specific about which parts of your prototype are really needed at which level of fidelity. This will help you manage your prototyping resources efficiently. It also is a great tool to guide the attention of your audience.

It is important to understand that the fidelity of your prototype has an impact on the quality and type of feedback you get from your test audience. Low-fidelity prototypes tend to inspire more open discussions while high-fidelity prototypes seem to lead the discussion more to the details of a concept because the prototype looks finished – and therefore decided.

The right fidelity for your prototype also depends on where you are in the process and what your purpose is. Earlier in the process, especially during explorative prototyping you would lean toward lower fidelity, while later in the process or during evaluative and communicative prototyping you usually lean toward higher fidelity. However, this needs to be reassessed for each project on an individual basis. Value prototypes like a service advertisement – which can be done quite early in the process – can already show high fidelity in a few essential perspectives (e.g., the value propositions), even though the rest of the business model is still quite raw.

In any case, always make sure the fidelity fits your audience. For example, people new to prototyping approaches usually need higher-fidelity prototypes together with clear guidance on purpose and scope. On the other hand, also make sure you are not over-promising. High-fidelity prototypes often are perceived as "finished" even if the underlying concept is still raw and basically untested.

Prototyping context

Choose the environment and context in which you run your prototyping sessions carefully. There are two major approaches:

→ **Contextual prototyping:** Contextual prototyping happens where the final service or product, whether physical or digital, would be used or be produced – for example, in the actual shop, tourism destination, or in one of your own offices where you run your consulting practice. By doing the prototyping session

---

03 See 7.3.4, *Case: Minimum lovable products, living prototypes, and high-fidelity sketching in code,* for an example of how to use sketching with code in a service design project.

Low-fidelity prototypes usually allow you to work blazingly fast. However, if you put too much emphasis on speed and low fidelity, your prototypes become meaningless. Try to find the sweet spot – the lowest meaningful fidelity at any given time – and move to high fidelity when you really need it.

DIFFERENT FLAVORS OF FIDELITY

Fidelity comes in different flavors depending on what you are prototyping. While it is often connected with visual fidelity (look and feel), you can also talk about fidelity in other dimensions, like fidelity of the implementation.

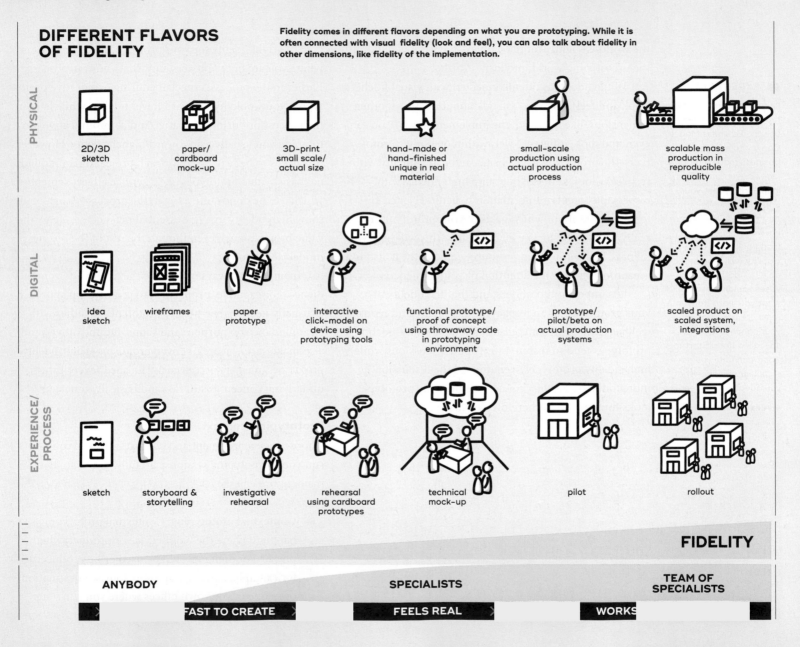

PHYSICAL

- 2D/3D sketch
- paper/cardboard mock-up
- 3D-print small scale/actual size
- hand-made or hand-finished unique in real material
- small-scale production using actual production process
- scalable mass production in reproducible quality

DIGITAL

- idea sketch
- wireframes
- paper prototype
- interactive click-model on device using prototyping tools
- functional prototype/proof of concept using throwaway code in prototyping environment
- prototype/pilot/beta on actual production systems
- scaled product on scaled system, integrations

EXPERIENCE/PROCESS

- sketch
- storyboard & storytelling
- investigative rehearsal
- rehearsal using cardboard prototypes
- technical mock-up
- pilot
- rollout

FIDELITY

ANYBODY	SPECIALISTS	TEAM OF SPECIALISTS

FAST TO CREATE | FEELS REAL | WORKS

in context you can very efficiently assess whether or not a prototyped solution is a fit for that context or not. You also quickly learn what might work and, especially, what might not work. Just as in contextual research (e.g., contextual interviews, participant and non-participant observations, work-alongs, self-ethnography, etc.), you get a much better feel for the nuances that are needed to implement a working solution.[01]

→ **Lab prototyping:** Lab prototyping is done within the safe confines of a lab environment or any place that is out of context. Choose lab prototyping when the real context is not available to you, does not allow any changes, does not exist yet, or simply is too expensive to use.

It is important to note that *context* can include not only the space or location but also the time when you are prototyping, the availability of key resources, or even environmental conditions. For example, prototyping new hospitality services for a winter sport destination in winter can be contextual, while to test the same activities in summer you will have to fall back on lab prototyping.

As a rule of thumb, the closer your prototyping environment and contexts are to the intended implementation contexts, the more reliable feedback you will get during evaluative prototyping. Similarly, during explorative prototyping, ideas generated in similar contexts

tend to be more transferable from the prototype to the intended implementation context.[02]

Prototyping loops

Always plan prototyping as an iterative process with a sequence of prototyping loops. Each loop should have a clear purpose; a clear set of prototyping questions; and include (a) building or preparing a prototype, (b) running the prototyping session, as well as (c) at least a simple form of data synthesis and analysis. The first loops are often explorative and might only take a couple of hours or a day. Use them to open up and create a shared understanding of the opportunity space. After those first loops, you might want to validate the proposed value propositions before eventually moving toward systematically exploring and validating the different aspects and dimensions of the selected concepts further and further. Continually check whether the chosen methods deliver meaningful results and whether your hypothesis or research questions for the prototyping stage need adjustments.

Depending on the skill set of your prototyping teams, you might have to involve specialists and split the work into separate work streams to achieve higher fidelity – for example, UX designers working on improving an existing app, service designers prototyping human-to-human interactions or required business processes, and an architect redesigning the office space. Even though they will work at different iteration speeds,

💬 **EXPERT TIP**

"Even if you have only a limited budget, do your best to stretch the scope to allow at least a few iterations, to make use of the learnings from the prototyping. It is better to make a few less ambitious prototypes than a bigger one-shot prototype."

– Kristina Carlander

01 See 7.3.1, *Case: Enabling effective co-creation through prototyping minimum viable solutions and contextual mock-ups,* for an example of simulating workflows in day-to-day working environments.

02 Blomkvist, J., & Holmlid, S. (2011). "Existing Prototyping Perspectives: Considerations for Service Design." In *Proceedings of the Nordic Design Research Conference* (pp. 29–31).

💬 **COMMENT**

"Just as there is theoretical saturation in design research, there is practical saturation in prototyping. Prototyping is great to help us understand by doing. At each iteration, you pivot into a new version by integrating the learnings of the previous version of the prototype. However, when any new learnings or insights have no significant or meaningful impact on the next version of your prototype anymore, you have effectively reached practical saturation. You are now ready to move on to the next phase on your service design journey."

– Carola Verschoor

it is still important to plan in regular sessions (e.g., weekly or biweekly) to give feedback and to adjust the prototyping plan. Depending on the complexity of your prototypes, you might also want to consider establishing a first sprint-like structure.[01]

Keep iterating between the details of a single (inter)action, object, or app and the wider picture of the end-to-end experience.

Multitracking

Decide how many prototypes you want to work on in any given segment. Multitracking your efforts helps you to reduce risk by not putting all your eggs into one basket. It also allows you to strategically manage uncertainty in your concept portfolio and expectations of stakeholders:

→ How many of the prototypes seem to be **in reach for a quick win?**

→ How many of them seem to have **potential mid/long term?**

→ How many of them are lined up for a **disruptive breakthrough?**

→ How many of them are a **shot from the hip?**[02]

Also, decide whether you want to have different teams working on individual prototypes or have one team sequentially work through them.

The prototyping stage consists of a number of exploratory or evaluative prototyping sessions that can be lined up in parallel or in sequence. At certain points, you might add communicative prototypes to involve external stakeholders.

Method selection

Reflect on your chosen scope (including which elements of the service need to be prototyped), fidelity, and target context and choose the methods for your prototyping activities accordingly.

A helpful starting point is to do a quick assessment of the resources you have at your disposal. Before spending too much effort on creating complex prototypes, you might want to do some quick desk research[03] to find existing prototypes or research on similar questions or an appropriate prototyping platform you can leverage. Are there any elements you can simply reuse? Ask your Innovation department if they have already done something similar.

Desk research might quickly reveal similar services or products, whether physical or digital, which you can use as a basis to create your own prototypes so you do not have to start from scratch.

When you are selecting the "right" prototyping methods – ones that give you a lot of useful data, support your decisions, or communicate the concept well – you always face the question of how many methods you should use. Given a limited budget, you need to decide whether you should put all your budget into one method

---

01 See 9.5.2 Case: *Managing strategic design projects* for an example of how to adopt agile methodologies like sprint structures in a service design project.

02 Out-field prototypes which are thought to have a low chance of success but which help teams think bigger are often called "dark horse" prototypes.

03 Also see *Desk research* in 5.2.

"It is easy to like a prototype, even a mediocre prototype of a mediocre idea, as long as it addresses and solves an important problem in some way. It is therefore valuable to challenge one prototype with another, to make sure to get the best ideas. Therefore, make different prototypes, representing different ideas or directions of your idea. It is often valuable to stretch different directions to extremes (more or less), to provoke and learn rapidly. This is mostly relevant in early stages, where lo-fi prototypes are cheap to do and test."

– Kristina Carlander

and do this rather well, or distribute our budget to use a variety of prototyping methods. Just like in research, you should also apply the concept of method triangulation during prototyping.[04]

As a rule of thumb, you might want to consider to including at least one method from each of the following categories:

→ An experience prototyping approach to **validate the core value proposition**.

04 Also see *Method triangulation* in 5.1.3.

→ Some methods that allow the **exploration and assessment of a holistic/end-to-end perspective** on the service, like desktop walkthroughs, contextual walkthroughs, Business Model Canvases, Business Origami, minimum viable services/products or service simulations, and so on.

→ Some methods that focus on **key elements** within the holistic perspective, like paper prototyping, cardboard prototyping, digital mock-ups, and so on.

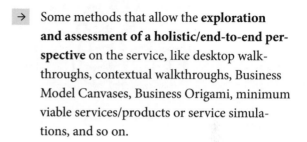

AUDIENCE

FIDELITY

METHOD SELECTION

MULTITRACKING

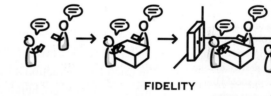

PLANNING PROTOTYPING

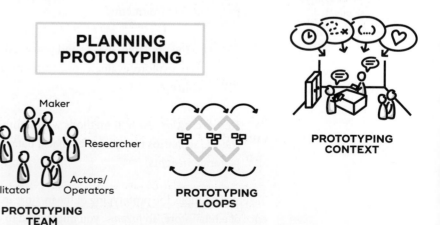

PROTOTYPING CONTEXT

Maker

Concept owner

Researcher

Facilitator

Actors/ Operators

PROTOTYPING TEAM

PROTOTYPING LOOPS

OVERVIEW OF PLANNING COMPONENTS

The planning of prototyping includes making decisions about audience, authors, fidelity, prototyping context, prototyping loops, multitracking, and method selection.

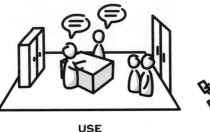

PREPARATION

USE

RESEARCH

Running prototyping sessions: preparation, use and research. The creation of the prototype is only the starting point, which allows us to focus on using and testing the prototype and learning from it.

7.1.5 Running prototyping sessions

💬 **EXPERT TIP**

"Make sure you do not get stuck on solving problems that only exist in your prototyping environment and not in the actual service system. Prototyping should be future oriented rather than task oriented."

— Johan Blomkvist

Prototyping methods share an underlying common structure. Any prototyping method can be broken up into the following three core activities:

→ **Preparation:** Prepare prototypes through setting up templates or canvases, scripting and practicing an intended interaction or walkthrough, making physical models, building stages/sets, and/or preparing environments.

→ **Use:** Use the prepared objects and practiced activities to explore, evaluate, or communicate a design concept.

→ **Research:** Use research methods while running the use scenarios to capture feedback, data and generate insights.

Take, for example, the prototyping of the in-store experience of a retail store. To *prepare*, you might need to create a first sketch of the intended customer journey, consider your roles, practice the key scenes, set up the stage, and create a handful of key props (like an app prototype, some mock-up advertising posters, or a new checkout desk made of foamcore). You then *use* the setup to test the resulting experience (e.g., the checkout process). By using *research* methods like observation and interviews with the participants of your prototyping sessions you can collect a lot of data and capture and generate valuable insights.

It is important to understand that prototyping is not just about *creating* a prototype.[01] Rather, the creation of prototypes is only the starting point, which allows us to focus on using and testing prototypes and learning from them.[02] As Michael Schrage (author of the book *Serious Play*) says, "the value of prototypes resides less in the models themselves than in the interactions they invite."[03] In this sense, prototyping indeed is research into future situations.

01 This is why some people refer to the creation of a prototype as *model making* to make a clear distinction. It is only after you have used the model and learned from it that it becomes a real prototype.

02 See 7.3.6, *Case: Using multifaceted prototyping to create and iterate business and service models,* for an example of how learning from ongoing prototyping activities might allow you to gain confidence in a business model that others might consider radical.

03 Schrage, M. (2013). *Serious Play: How the World's Best Companies Simulate to Innovate.* Harvard Business Press.

Two types of service prototyping:
Direct experience vs. indirect imagination

"When we use the term 'experience prototyping' we are talking about methods that allow designers, clients, or users to 'experience it themselves,' rather than witnessing a demonstration or someone else's experience."
— Marion Buchenau and Jane Fulton Suri on experience prototyping[04]

Experience prototyping

Experience prototyping (also called experience-like, do-like, interact-like, or act-like prototyping) uses prototypes that allow people to act in the way they would act – or use the thing they would use – in the future service, and in that way "experience it themselves."

The people might interact with low-fidelity versions of environments, objects, or other actors. While the interaction itself might be low fidelity (e.g., a "fast-forward" or walkthrough), the people still interact essentially in the same way, hence provoking a similar experience.

Experience prototyping is sometimes also referred to "direct," "experiential," or "embodied" prototyping.

Imagine-like prototyping

Imagine-like prototyping uses prototypes that only help us to rationally think through, imagine, or empathize with the intended (inter)action (it "scaffolds our thinking"). It is used when the actual interaction is not possible to do or not accessible. Here the interaction itself is different than in the future service. Imagine-like prototyping includes sketches and customer journey maps, as well as metaphorical simulations (e.g., during a role-play replacing an app interface with a real person doing the same job).

Imagine-like prototyping might also be referred to as "indirect," "empathic," or "disembodied" prototyping. ◄

04 Buchenau, M., & Suri, J. F. (2000). "Experience Prototyping." In *Proceedings of the 3rd conference on Designing interactive systems: processes, practices, methods, and techniques* (pp. 424–433). ACM.

7.1.6 Data synthesis and analysis

Running prototyping sessions generates a lot of data, insights, and new ideas about the future service. So, as a next step you need to synthesize and analyze that prototyping data (sensemaking). As prototyping can be interpreted as research into future service situations, the synthesis and analysis process in prototyping is technically the same as the synthesis and analysis process that was covered in Chapter 5, *Research*.[01]

7.1.7 Visualizing prototyping data

There are many ways to present your prototyping data, and once again what makes sense depends on your aim. Luckily, all the ways to capture research data in service design are also applicable for prototyping data. They include:[02]

→ **Research wall**
→ **Personas**
→ **(Customer) journey maps**
→ **Stakeholder maps**
→ **Key insights**
→ **Jobs to be done**
→ **User stories**
→ **Reports**

Additionally, since you are now essentially working in solution space, there are two more tools that are especially useful:

→ **Idea wall/portfolio:** To get a quick overview of new concepts and ideas to be prioritized and lined up for prototyping and testing

→ **The prototypes themselves:** To make the future service experience tangible, and replace tedious verbal documentation

Again, it is important to consider the target audience for your visualization: Do you need something rather formal and self-explanatory so your outcomes can be used in different departments or organizations? Or are your outcomes only needed for your internal team? Any prototyping outcome that you need to communicate beyond your own team needs more polish.

01 See 5.1.4, *Data visualization, synthesis, and analysis*, and 5.3, *Methods of data visualization and analysis*, for details.
02 See *Visualizing data* in 5.1.4

Dealing with failure of prototypes and critique

BY KRISTINA CARLANDER

Is a failed prototype a failure? I would say no. Sometimes a prototype brings to light legal, ethical, or other barriers that should stop a concept that seems to be good in theory. Embrace the fact that the barriers have now been discovered much faster and more cheaply than they would have been through any "thinking/talking/investigating" process. And all the learnings you have made are far from wasted.

But even when you consider the prototype a success, prepare to be criticized – especially if you work in an environment where prototyping is not everyone's normal way of working. No matter how much you emphasize that "this is just a prototype," you may get comments such as "Is it really going to look like that?" or "Have you not thought of *X*?" Just be patient, welcome the feedback, and make sure you have a chance to come back and show a new version, proving that prototyping is a very powerful tool to get quick results. ◄

07
PROTOTYPING
METHODS

Read more on methods and
tools in our free online resources at:

 **www.tisdd.com**

7.2 PROTOTYPING METHODS

This section provides concise descriptions of a selection of methods which allow you to prototype a broad range of services or products, whether physical or digital. As service design needs to provide a common language and support co-creation between different disciplines, we have chosen prototyping methods that do not require specialist skills. While this might sound limiting at first, this selection of methods allows you to push almost any concept to the point where you can make a safe decision on which experts you actually need to involve for which aspects of the project.

Many more methods exist and should be included in the planning and execution of your prototyping activities, but many of those require you to invite specialists from the respective field of expertise, like change managers, product designers, or software developers.

The prototyping methods selected for this book are structured in five categories:

→ **Prototyping methods for service processes and experiences:** Investigative rehearsal, subtext, desktop walkthrough

→ **Prototyping methods for physical objects and environments:** Cardboard prototyping

→ **Prototyping methods for digital artifacts and software:** Rehearsing digital services, paper prototyping, wireframing

→ **Prototyping methods for ecosystems and business value:** Service advertisement, desktop system mapping, Business Model Canvas

→ **General methods:** Mood boards, sketching, Wizard of Oz approaches[01]

There are many variations of and names for each prototyping method, and the boundaries between the chosen categories might be rather fluid. Often, a specific prototyping method can also be adapted to answer different prototyping questions. Reflect on your chosen scope (including which elements of the service need to be prototyped), fidelity, and target context and choose the methods for your prototyping activities accordingly. As a rule of thumb, you might want to consider including at least a few methods to account for method triangulation.[02]

---

01   General methods can be used across any of the above categories.

02   See *Method selection* in 7.1.4 for guidance on how to create a suitable mix of methods.

PROTOTYPING SERVICE PROCESSES
AND EXPERIENCES

Investigative rehearsal 🖱

Investigative rehearsal is a theatrical method to deeply understand and explore behaviors and processes through iterative rehearsal sessions.[01]

Based on forum theater, it is a structured, full-body way to clarify the emotional side of an experience and reveal many practicalities around physical space, language, and tone of voice.[02]

Preparation: Choose and quickly prepare a (key) scene as a starting point, e.g. from research or from a future-state journey map, and create essential props and a stage.

Use: Play through the initial scene, repeating and commenting until there is a deeper understanding on a physical and motivational level. Only then, change the scene. Review the effect of each change and explore alternatives. Iterate. Always keep a list of bugs, insights, and ideas.

Research techniques: Use-it-yourself (autoethnography), participant observation, co-creative workshops

Expected output: Research data (specifically a list of bugs, insights, and new ideas), raw video footage and photos

PROTOTYPING SERVICE PROCESSES
AND EXPERIENCES

Subtext 🖱

Subtext is a theatrical method that can reveal deeper motivations and needs by focusing on unspoken thoughts in a rehearsal session.[03]

We can think of subtext as the unspoken thoughts of a character – it is what we mean, but don't say. Bringing subtext into a rehearsal session can reveal deeper motivations, help us understand needs, and illuminate new opportunities to create value.

Preparation: In an investigative rehearsal, identify a key scene. Now, hold the scene at one key statement by a customer or employee.

Use: Ask, "What would be the subtext of that statement?" Continue with, "What would be the subtext of that subtext?" and repeat. As you go deeper, ask how the service could respond at each level.

Research techniques: Use-it-yourself (autoethnography), participant observation, co-creative workshops

Expected output: Research data (specifically documentation of the subtext chains, new insights, and ideas), raw video footage and photos

---

01 Investigative reheasal is based on Forum theater. See, for example, Boal, A. (2000). *Theater of the Oppressed.* Pluto Press. Investigative Rehearsal uses participants' own experiences, ideas, or prototypes as a starting point, and goes beyond Forum's focus on behavioral strategies to also examine and challenge the basic process, the architectural setting, support tools, and more.

02 See 7.3.5, *Case: Using role-plays and simulations in large-scale 1:1 prototypes,* for an example of how to use similar techniques to focus on the feasibility and desirability of the overall service as well as individual elements.

03 Subtext is a crucial concept in performing arts, and is especially important in the work of Stanislavski and his artistic heirs. On stage, the subtext is usually implicit, but in prototyping (as in some rehearsal techniques and improv games) it becomes explicit, making it easier for the workshop participants to focus on it. For more on subtext in theater, see Moore, S. (1984). *The Stanislavski System: The Professional Training of an Actor,* New York: Penguin Books. For a film where subtext becomes explicit for comedic effect, see *Annie Hall* (Woody Allen, 1977, MGM).

A A team "stress testing" the returns procedure of a retail service using investigative rehearsal. Two team members simulate the encounter, while others are ready to step in with alternatives to the process, setting, systems, or behavior.

B Simply moving figures around on a map and acting out the dialogues allows you to quickly simulate a service experience.

C Subtext: another actor speaks out loud the unspoken thoughts of one character as part of a rolling rehearsal scene – subtext is what we mean, but usually don't say.

D A visual sketch of a multilevel subtext chain.

PROTOTYPING SERVICE PROCESSES
AND EXPERIENCES

Desktop walkthrough 🖱

Desktop walkthroughs can be seen as interactive mini-theater plays that simulate end-to-end customer experiences.[04]

Using maps, figurines, and small-scale models of the service environment, you test and explore common scenarios and alternatives of a service process or experience.

Preparation: Create an overview map for all relevant locations. Pick a figurine for each key stakeholder in your service and create essential props using paper, cardboard, modeling clay, etc. Decide on a story as a starting point.

Use: Run through the story using the maps as the stage and the figurines as actors. Act out all dialogues and interactions with other actors, devices, etc. After each runthrough, reflect on what you would like to change or try. Always keep a list of bugs, insights, and ideas. Then iterate.

Research techniques: Participant observation, interviews, co-creative workshops

Expected output: Research data (specifically documentation of the simulated variants, new insights, and ideas), raw video footage and photos

04 See Blomkvist, J., Fjuk, A., & Sayapina, V. (2016). Low threshold service design: desktop walkthrough. In *Proceedings of the Service Design and Innovation Conference* (pp. 154-166). Linköping University Electronic Press.

(A) Early cardboard prototypes are cheap and easy to make. This has one of the lowest entry barriers of any of the prototyping methods.

(B) After each step the team reflects on what worked, what didn't work, and what they would like to change or try next. Keep it brief. Then move on.

(C) After creating hand-sketched versions, a user can easily test the interface by "clicking." An operator simulates the changes by replacing or adding parts of the interface.

PROTOTYPING PHYSICAL OBJECTS
AND ENVIRONMENTS

Cardboard prototyping 👆

Cardboard prototyping refers to prototyping 3D mock-ups of almost any physical object or environment out of cheap paper and cardboard.[01]

The prototypes – for example, the interior of a shop or a ticket machine – can be small scale or actual size. To explore the role the objects play in the context of the future service, cardboard prototyping is often used together with walkthrough approaches.

Preparation: Use simple materials to build the objects. Split your team into users, operators, and observers and give them some time to prepare.

Use: As the user starts to use the object (i.e., handling it, pressing buttons, etc.), the operators manually simulate the reaction of the object. Observe and keep a list of bugs, insights, and ideas. After each testing session reflect on what you would like to change or try. Then iterate.

Research techniques: Use-it-yourself, participant observation, interviews, co-creative workshops

Expected output: Research data (specifically bugs, insights, and new ideas), raw video footage and photos, documentation of the tested variants

01 For example, see Hallgrimsson, B. (2012). *Prototyping and Modelmaking for Product Design.* Laurence King Publishing. For a full-scale example of cardboard prototyping in service design see Kronqvist, J., Erving, H., & Leinonen, T. (2013). *Cardboard Hospital: Prototyping Patient-Centric Environments and Services.* In *Proceedings of the Nordes 2013 Conference* (pp. 293–302).

PROTOTYPING DIGITAL ARTIFACTS AND SOFTWARE
Rehearsing digital services 👆

Rehearsing digital services is a variant of investigative rehearsal that helps to prototype digital interfaces as if they were human conversations or interactions.[02]

Within an investigative rehearsal, your app or web page is replaced by a human actor. This method can be used even before creating any wireframes or paper prototypes.

Preparation: Choose a starting point, e.g. based on user stories from research, and prepare props and a space. Then, quickly familiarize yourselves with the chosen story.

Use: Run through the story and have a human play the app or web page. Don't think digital be a full human being, but one with superhuman access to knowledge and media, like a knowledgeable butler or "genie in a bottle." For example, a landing page can be simulated by a concierge asking, "What are you looking for?" then evolving the conversation naturally. Afterwards, consider how to digitalize the experience.

Research techniques: Use-it-yourself, participant observation, co-creative workshops

Expected output: Research data (specifically a list of bugs, insights, and new ideas), raw video footage and photos, updated wireframes or paper prototypes

02 See *Investigative rehearsal* in 7.2

PROTOTYPING DIGITAL ARTIFACTS AND SOFTWARE
Paper prototyping 👆

In paper prototyping, the screens of a digital interface are hand sketched on paper and presented to a user to quickly test interfaces.[03]

Users can now *use* the interface by "clicking" with their finger indicating what they want to do. A researcher simulates the operation of the computer simply by replacing the screen page or by adding "pop-ups" on smaller pieces of paper.

Preparation: Create hand-sketched versions of all key elements (e.g., pages, dialog boxes, and actual key content). Split your team to take on the roles of users, (computer) operators, and observers and give them time to prepare.

Use: As the user starts to use the interface, the operators simulate all changes in the interface by replacing or adding parts. Keep a list of bugs, insights, and ideas. After each testing session reflect on what worked, what didn't work, what you would like to change. Revise your prototype and iterate.

Research techniques: Use-it-yourself, participant observation

Expected output: Research data (specifically bugs, insights, and new ideas), raw video footage and photos, documentation of the tested variants

03 See, for example, Snyder, C. (2003). *Paper Prototyping: The Fast and Easy Way to Design and Refine User Interfaces.* Morgan Kaufmann.

PROTOTYPING DIGITAL ARTIFACTS AND SOFTWARE

Interactive click modeling 🖱

Interactive click modeling is a popular lo-fi method to create a first working digital prototype.

Special prototyping apps allow you to take photos of your hand-drawn sketches and link them together so you can test them on the actual device you are developing for.

Preparation: Hand-sketch all the different screens of the interface on paper, take photos of the sketches, and import them into the prototyping app. In the app you can now define click-areas that link between sketches, effectively creating a working interface.

Use: Ask a user to complete some tasks using the click-model and observe how she reacts to the interface. If you want to use the prototype for communication you can also film the use of the click-model for further reference.

Research techniques: Use-it-yourself, participant observation

Expected output: Research data (specifically bugs, insights, and new ideas), raw video footage and photos, documentation of the tested variants

PROTOTYPING DIGITAL ARTIFACTS AND SOFTWARE

Wireframing 🖱

Wireframing uses nongraphical schematics of digital interfaces and their structure to show how they fit together and create alignment within the design team.[01]

Most of the elements are more hinted at than explicit, which makes wireframes fast to create, requiring less specialized skills. Wireframes are often used to align the different disciplines within a design team and to map out user journeys or act as the starting point for paper prototypes or interactive click-models.

Preparation: Rough versions of the different screens of the interface are sketched on paper, on whiteboards, or in special wireframing apps. Leave out color, specific fonts, and aesthetics as much as possible. Use placeholder content.

Use: The wireframes are put up on a wall and discussed with the team or a selected audience. Annotations are added to capture the behaviors of the marked interface elements and details about the content or context in which the system might be used.

Research techniques: Co-creative workshops, interviews, concept tests

Expected output: Research data (specifically bugs, insights, and new ideas), raw video footage and photos, documentation of updated wireframes and annotations

01 See, for example, Brown, D. M. (2010). *Communicating Design: Developing Web Site Documentation for Design and Planning.* New Riders.

PROTOTYPING ECOSYSTEMS AND BUSINESS VALUE
Service advertisement 🖱

Service advertisements are prototype advertisements that allow us to (re)focus on the core value proposition and test the desirability and perceived value of a new offering.

Like simple advertisement posters, they use concise slogans, engaging visuals, and text to sell the new offering. Later, service advertisements can be created as online ads, web landing pages, or TV or video advertisements (including in-depth documentary-style variants).

Preparation: Do a brief brainstorming on ideas for emotional and factual content for the poster. What do you want to communicate in the ad? What could be suitable emotional hooks or narratives? What are the facts? Sketch out a couple of advertisements on big pieces of paper.

Use: Show your advertisements to people who do not yet know your project and collect their feedback. Keep a list of bugs, insights, and ideas. Discuss what worked or what didn't work, and what you would like to change. Revise your prototype and iterate.

Research techniques: Participant observation, interviews, co-design

Expected output: Research data (specifically bugs, insights, and new ideas), raw video footage and photos, quotes from the test audience

(A) Special prototyping apps allow almost anyone (even without prior knowledge) to create interactive click-models of your interface. They can be shown to potential users for testing or storytelling to gather valuable feedback.

(B) Wireframes help the design team to understand and explore how the different parts of software work together. They connect the conceptual structure, functions, or information architecture to the visual design.

(C) Service advertisement posters are a fast and engaging way to quickly explore, clarify, and test your value proposition.

Desktop system mapping (a.k.a. Business Origami) 🖱

Desktop system mapping is an approach which helps us to understand complex value networks using simple paper cutouts representing key people, locations, channels, and touchpoints.[01]

The cut-outs can be quickly placed, moved, and reconfigured again on a table or horizontal whiteboard. Relationships and value exchanges are visualized by grouping or drawing connections between different elements.

Preparation: Create, cut out, fold, and label the key elements of the service system using the paper templates.

Use: Create a draft of the service system by placing key elements to create a map. Reflect on relationships, value exchanges, (inter)actions, or basic material/money/information flows. Add those as arrows and consider grouping elements. Start to simulate the service system over time. Always keep a list of bugs, insights, and ideas. Then, revise your prototype and iterate.

Research techniques: Participant observation, co-design

Expected output: Research data (specifically bugs, insights, and new ideas), raw video footage and photos, documentation of the ecosystem

(A) Business Origami first looks at the system taking a holistic approach. Like with many other service design tools, the critical deliverable is not the model itself but the experience of modeling the service system in the team.

(B) Using the Business Model Canvas, you can quickly analyze existing business models and prototype new ones.

(C) Mood boards are collages of existing media to communicate an intended design direction.

01 See Hitachi Ltd. (n.d.). "Experiential Value: Introduce and Elicit Ideas," at *http://www.hitachi.com/rd/portal/contents/design/business_origami/index.html.* See also McMullin, J. (2011). "Business Origami," at *http://www.citizenexperience.com/2010/04/30/business-origami/.*

PROTOTYPING ECOSYSTEMS AND BUSINESS VALUE
Business Model Canvas 🖱

The Business Model Canvas is a high-level approach to co-create and visualize the key components of a business model that allows you to iteratively test and refine various options.[02]

Considered a strategic management tool, it is intended to be used in an iterative design process.

Preparation: Prepare the Business Model Canvas template. It helps if you have personas, stakeholder maps, customer journeys, and prototypes at hand as well.

Use: Fill in the upper seven boxes first. If available, use information from other service design tools to fill in information from previous work. Then fill in the lower two boxes, identifying cost drivers and potential revenue streams. Add numbers and estimate costs and revenues. Prototype and test whether your business model is sustainable. Then start creating alternative business models and test potential options. Compare different models and iterate; combine and refine them.[03]

Research techniques: Co-creative workshops, interviews

Expected output: Research data (specifically bugs, insights, and new ideas), photos

GENERAL METHOD
Mood boards 🖱

Mood boards are collages that help to visualize and communicate intended design direction.

Using a mix of text, sketches, visualizations, photos, videos, or any other media, they transport current or future experiences, style, or contexts.

Preparation: Start to collect inspiration and raw material (often photos or video footage) from magazines, stock photo libraries or your own media library, or quickly create new material yourself. Organize that material and set up a first collage. Iterate until you are happy. Your mood board can be a physical wall, or it can be an online media board, a more practical solution if you are working with video or interactive media.

Use: Present your mood boards either to each other within the design team or to an external audience to receive feedback and ignite discussions. During these presentation sessions, you can work on existing boards by adding annotations or adding, reshuffling, or removing media or even create completely new boards from a pool of data.

Research techniques: Studio interviews, focus groups, concept tests/discussions

Expected output: Research data (specifically bugs, insights, and new ideas), photos, collages

---

02 See 3.6, *Business Model Canvas,* for a summary of the canvas and its connection to other service design tools. Also see Osterwalder, A., & Pigneur, Y. (2010). *Business Model Generation: A Handbook for Visionaries, Game Changers, and Challengers.* John Wiley & Sons.

03 Eventually, a Business Model Canvas needs to be translated into experience prototypes or actual offers. See 7.3.6, *Case: Using multifaceted prototyping to create and iterate business and service models,* for an example of ongoing prototyping activities supporting confidence in a business model that others might consider radical.

GENERAL METHODS
Sketching 👆

Sketching refers to methods of visualization or representation of design ideas that support fast and flexible exploration.[01]

Sketches – low-fidelity visualizations of an idea – are flexible, quick, and inexpensive. Their explorative nature often makes them the first step in explorative prototyping.

Preparation: Sketches are usually created fast using only pen and paper. However, you can create sketches with almost anything as long as they are quick to produce, inexpensive, and support exploration – e.g., sketching in software,[02] hardware,[03] or with our bodies (bodystorming).

Use: Present sketches to others to receive feedback and ignite discussion. During these sessions, you can directly work on existing sketches (e.g., by adding annotations or changing them on the spot) or easily add new ones with the changes already included.

Research techniques: Studio interviews, focus groups, concept tests/discussions

Expected output: Research data (specifically bugs, insights, and new ideas), photos, video footage

GENERAL METHODS
Wizard of Oz approaches 👆

Faking it using invisible puppeteers.[04]
Wizard of Oz techniques manually create the responses from people, devices, apps, or the context/environment through invisible operators ("wizards") behind the scenes. The users are led to believe that they are dealing with an actual working prototype.

Preparation: Think of the operator ("wizard") as an invisible puppeteer for those objects and service elements. Prepare all relevant parts of the service or systems and rig them to allow the "wizards" to create realistic responses on the spot.

Use: A user is given specific tasks to use the prototype. The operator simulates the operation of backstage processes, devices, or the environment by operating behind the scenes and manipulating the objects and environment. Use this approach to explore and evaluate core functionality and value.

Research techniques: Participant/non-participant observation, contextual interviews

Expected output: Research data (specifically bugs, insights, and new ideas), photos, video footage, observations and interview transcripts

---

01 See 7.3.4, *Case: Minimum lovable products, living prototypes, and high-fidelity sketching in code,* for an example of how sketches and prototypes can make intent tangible and highlight hidden complexities.

02 See Reas, C., & Fry, B. (2004). "Processing.org: Programming for Artists and Designers." In *Proceedings of SIGGRAPH '04: Web Graphics* (p. 3). ACM.

03 For a first discussion, see Holmquist, L. (2006). "Sketching in Hardware." *interactions,* 13(1), 47-60. But it is possibly best to find a local makerspace, get your hands dirty, and make things!

04 Go watch *The Wizard of Oz* (Victor Fleming, 1939, MGM). Only then, get some more popcorn and read the seminal publication on Wizard of Oz techniques in design: Kelley, J. F. (1984). *An Iterative Design Methodology for User-Friendly Natural Language Office Information Applications. ACM Transactions on Information Systems* (TOIS), 2(1), 26-41.

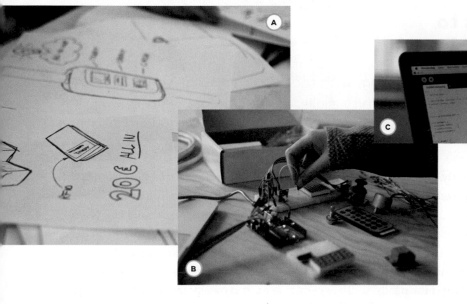

(A) Sketches using pen and paper provide a quick and low-fidelity visualization of an initial idea or concept.

(B) Open source prototyping platforms like Arduino allow you to sketch in hardware, creating first working prototypes of interactive devices.

(C) With the right prototyping platform, sketching in code lets you explore working prototypes early.

(D) In Wizard of Oz techniques, the responses from people, devices, apps, or the context/environment are manually created by invisible operators ("wizards") behind the scenes.

(E) Bodystorming, or "sketching with our bodies," is a very efficient lo-fi way to sketch (inter)actions using re-enactment.

From specialized approaches to your own living prototyping lab

Keep in mind that a prototyping lab is not just a room with tools in it. It needs to be a living lab – a vibrant combination of people, community, skills, methods, and tools all set in an accessible environment – that allows you to work fast and learn fast.

This methods section only provides a concise selection of prototyping methods, specifically chosen to *not require specialist skills*. This allows you to have a conversation within a broader team about where the project should be heading. It also allows you to make safer decisions about what kind of skills and expertise will be needed when moving toward implementation; e.g., when you dive deeper into change management, software development, product development/management, architecture, or other more specialist disciplines. You can now safely invite the relevant stakeholders with their expert methods.

Those specialists bring in specialized tools to tackle specific challenges quickly and efficiently, including but certainly not limited to:

→ Software prototyping tools and frameworks
→ CAD (computer aided design) and 3D printing
→ Change management toolsets and structures
→ VR (virtual reality) applications for architecture and experience prototyping
→ Fablab (fabrication laboratory) environments or makerspaces with access to tools that allow you to prototype almost any physical object

When you choose suitable methods for your project, carefully assess how quickly they will allow you to build and test the prototype. Your choice might also depend on the skills of your team and the tools they have access to.[01]

It can be useful to put together your own tailored prototyping pipeline or even create your own prototyping lab.

Where can you run a quick service simulation? Are you allowed to prototype in context? How fast do you get access to fabrication equipment, and are you able or even allowed to use it on your own? Do you have instant access to a user

01 See 7.3.3, *Case: Enabling staff and stakeholders to prototype for continuous evolution,* for an example of how to enable staff to take over the prototyping and design process – without the need of a skilled designer or any special tools.

community for a quick user research, or do you first have to go through a long purchase process? Where can you experiment with fresh ideas and grow them before you need to apply for funding?

Your own prototyping lab can start small and be quite informal. With iteration, it might develop into something useful enough to become an official internal institution.[02]

But remember, whatever you set up, always keep it accessible to your whole organization and stay fast.[03] ◄

Virtual reality environments and content can be highly engaging. Unfortunately, authoring VR content often still requires specialist skills – but as tools evolve this might change rapidly, making it one of the most exciting technologies not only for prototyping but also for documenting and revisiting field research data.

---

02 You might even consider including a network of supporters like internal/external development teams in other time zones that can finish your prototypes overnight. This can be very impressive to teams.

03 Also see Chapter 10, *Making space for service design.*

07
PROTOTYPING
CASES

→

The following six cases provide examples of how prototyping is applied in practice: how to enable effective co-creation through prototyping minimum viable solutions and contextual mock-ups **(7.3.1);** how to use prototyping and co-creation to create ownership and close collaboration between the designers, project group, and staff **(7.3.2);** how to enable staff and stakeholders to prototype for continuous evolution **(7.3.3);** how to create minimum lovable products, living prototypes, and high-fidelity sketches in code **(7.3.4);** how to use role-plays and simulations in large-scale 1:1 prototypes **(7.3.5);** and how to use multifaceted prototyping to create and iterate business and service models **(7.3.6).**

7.3.1 CASE: ENABLING EFFECTIVE CO-CREATION THROUGH PROTOTYPING
MINIMUM VIABLE SOLUTIONS AND CONTEXTUAL MOCK-UPS

Innovation on the shop floor: How to demonstrate the value of design thinking to a manufacturing organization

AUTHORS

Thomas Abrell
Innovation Manager,
Airbus

Dr. Markus Durstewitz
Senior Innovation
Manager, Airbus

Crafting a design thinking strategy and proving it in reality

Design thinking at Airbus emerged organically from different departments – workshops were conducted, training offered, and projects following human-centered approaches established, all labeled under the term *design thinking*. However, besides a core group of departments that formed a deep understanding of the power design thinking can have in product and service innovation, the majority of employees of Airbus have different understandings of design and design thinking, if they are acquainted with the concept at all. In July 2015, we crafted a strategy to infuse design thinking as part of the DNA of Airbus. One step on the ladder toward a broader understanding of design thinking was to engage in a grand challenge: we wanted to show, in an investment project of

strategic importance, the potential of design thinking. Airbus is currently extending its production capacity of its successful Single Aisle Family, A319, A320, and A321. To enable this ramp-up, Airbus has created an additional final assembly line in Hamburg. Our value proposition in this project was to co-innovate with the workers at the shop floor.

The project started in September 2015 and focused on problem framing and need finding from the workers' perspective. To ensure visibility and to reach the right level of awareness, it was important that design thinking was placed prominently in the project structure as one dedicated work stream. Being placed at this level gave us enough influence to push for creating real impact by achieving an end-to-end implementation.

"With design thinking, we are following a balanced approach that emphasizes early user engagement. The purpose is to make sure that we address the real needs and focus on doing the right things, which finally will make the difference to succeed with innovation in delivering added value to customers and users by going beyond the obvious."

— Dr. Markus Durstewitz

Prototyping plays a prominent role in the design process as a tool to make assumptions tangible and to involve users. We applied prototyping for gaining user insights, and for ensuring employee engagement and management buy-in. Our prototypes were often quite simple, rough mock-ups such as cardboard prototypes or clickable user interfaces. In general, these are good enough to test functionalities and to continuously involve users in the evolution of the concepts. In addition, we used the prototypes to better understand goals and the rationale behind requirements from different departments. Here, inter-disciplinary and cross-functional collaboration was essential to reach consensus between all stakeholders.

"Fast iterations in prototyping min-imum viable solutions are a key as-set for gathering user insights, for reducing the time to product, and for accelerating the innovation process."
— Dr. Markus Durstewitz

By having tangible prototypes and the possibility to interact with and alter them, we were able to gain deep insights, tapping into the tacit knowledge of the different stake-holders. We used the prototypes to test early and fail fast and cheap, in order to iterate to a solution that would ultimately be valuable to the end users and approved by all stakeholders. The simple proto-types helped us to perform early user tests and to reach a good level of maturity and alignment before making bigger investments.

From need finding to prototyping: Finding opportunities beyond the obvious and prototyping in design thinking

We started out with user research to understand how the production environment is perceived from a worker's point of view. We shadowed key people, going through their workdays with them, and we inter-viewed workers on the shop floor and other relevant stakeholders such as production support and manufac-turing engineers. The need-finding stage lasted three months, in which time we can to understand the final assembly line from the work-ers' point of view. We distilled our findings into four opportunity areas where design can make a change.

"Although it is tempting to shortcut in the early phase, crucial for the success was to conduct deep need finding prior to prototyping. Only through going into the field, observing and shadowing users, was it possible to look beyond the obvious and to ensure we are doing the right things."
— Thomas Abrell

After need finding, we selected two of the four opportunity areas to prototype in a timebox of eight weeks, from kickoff until the final prototypes were delivered. To master this tight timeline we built a team of internal and external experts with diverse skills, from industrial design and rapid prototyping to user research to coding.

We addressed two challenges in an iterative way, utilizing prototypes as a tool to co-create, to commu-nicate, and to iterate: information system interfaces on the shop floor and material delivery.

In building the team, we relied on experienced service designers from Airbus to manage the over-all design process, project and stakeholder management. For the information system side of the project, we chose an external partner with specialists in indus-trial design, design thinking, and user experience design. It was also important for us to bring in perspec-tives from a non-aerospace domain, bringing in diverse skillsets and design expertise.

(A) Prototype in the final assembly line.

(B) Sketch of the future system.

(C) Information system interface feedback session.

(D) Scale models as tools in the process.

Prototyping:
Making things tangible
on the shop floor

The project was set up in such a way that two teams worked in parallel, one focusing on the physical proto-type, the other on the information interaction prototype. It was important to co-locate the teams in a creative space: we used an aircraft fu-selage and built a workshop around it, so that our team had the possibili-ty to continually build things.

Our experiment was to see how digital and physical prototyping could work in parallel, involving all stakeholders. Workers were involved continuously. In addition, we scheduled three co-creation workshops to engage a wider group of stakeholders, a demo day, and an intermediate management presentation. We used a *build-measure-learn* cycle, but instead of measuring, we relied on qualitative evaluations and direct feedback from the users. The co-creation workshops were used to iterate the prototypes, and we moved from lo-fi mock-ups to functional us-ability mock-ups.

"It was an interesting experiment to run physical prototyping in parallel to digital prototyping. Ultimately, we designed a service for the workers, involving digital and physical touchpoints. Our aim was clearly to improve the work experience for our employees."

— *Thomas Abrell*

With the information system inter-faces, we complemented our need finding by researching what infor-mation workers really need – *and want to use* – to perform their work, and which *devices* would be suitable for interacting with the information. We therefore enriched our findings from the need-finding phase, and observed and interviewed the work-ers specifically with respect to the information they need. We mapped the necessary information and proto-typed it in rough concepts, showing screens on different devices such as tablets, smartwatches, smartphones, and large touchscreen displays.

In the first co-creation work-shop, we got user feedback on the devices and the functions. We

distilled the most important insights before going into the next prototype iteration, until a user interface was generated and a device concept was determined. Finally, we took the prototypes into one existing final as-sembly line, and let the users interact with them, simulating their very own workflow with the new prototypes in their current day-to-day working environment. These insights helped us to further iterate and refine them.

The material delivery units (MDUs) were addressed the same way. First, we went to the shop floor to see how material delivery works in practice – complementing the view we had from need finding, the planning documents, and internal logistics. Then, we conceptualized three material delivery units and built 1:5 scale models – in practice, three material trolleys for the same set of material, but with different conceptual considerations behind them – which were iterated in co-creation workshops.

One week later, we had the first 1:1 full-scale mock-up, which was brought to the final assembly line for feedback at the assembly station itself. With this feedback, and feedback gathered in the co-creation workshops, we built two more iterations of the full-scale mock-up. We added "smart" functionalities (connectivity) to the prototype, simulating how it would interact with its environment and the parts inside. The second prototype iteration got additional usability features such as a bumper and boxes for tools to make it more usable and more useful for the worker.

In the last co-creation workshop, we simulated a scenario incorporating both prototypes, the information system interface and the material delivery unit. Our project team simulated the situation together with the users, gathering feedback about the overall workflow, since material delivery and the information system interface are interrelated in their respective workflow.

At the editorial deadline of this book, we are doing a proof of concept of the material delivery unit, and integrating the information system interface into a larger project at Airbus changing the way

our manufacturing environment is set up and operations are performed. The learnings of the project are being used to propose a holistic design thinking approach for Airbus.

Learnings

Crucial for success were not only user engagement and user acceptance, but also the involvement of the Workers' Council as a key stakeholder. This entity, entitled to represent the workforce, can amplify a project's results in positive or negative terms. Only through continuous deep involvement of the council did we create a sense of ownership, involving them as a strategic partner for employee engagement implementing user-centered solutions.

"It's important to have a good balance between internal and external project team members. Only with a small internal core team is it possible to maintain continuity during the project, while external team members bring in specific expertise."
— *Thomas Abrell*

For the future, we will need a small internal core team with a wide array of skills to anchor the approach and leverage the expertise until implementation. In practice, it will be an interdisciplinary team consisting of aircraft manufacturing domain experts from Airbus, designers, method experts, and specialists for end-to-end support of the innovation project. We believe that collaboration with external partners from the design community (e.g., with freelancers and design agencies) will be necessary to keep up a high level of momentum and creativity.

"People are at the heart of our company. Let's complement the diversity of our employees and introduce a new way of working in cross-functional teams to deliver outstanding results. Let's team up for innovation! This may include all actors along the value chain, suppliers, customers, and users."
— *Dr. Markus Durstewitz*

Now, the next step is to go further in our endeavor to make design thinking part of the DNA of Airbus, by creating a specific design center to coordinate and steer the activities and to give creatives a home within the organization. In this organization-to-be, we want to educate service designers inside Airbus, and build up a strong network spanning Airbus.

KEY TAKEAWAYS

01 Deep need finding is necessary to ensure that you are "doing the right things." If this phase is bypassed, you run the risk of merely incrementally improving existing solutions instead of innovating.

02 Prototyping is a powerful tool for demonstrating to stakeholders the power of a design team. Designers are fast at making assumptions visible and tangible. This craft helps to make tacit knowledge of stakeholders explicit, and to get buy-in for design thinking as an innovation approach.

03 A combination of external and internal team members is crucial, but the right balance needs to be found. A team of experts is needed to be fast, and it should be complemented by a cross-functional team from the organization to make innovation happen.

04 A new way of working for users leads to a strong commitment to finding solutions. However, these solutions might be in conflict with traditional metrics in the company, and the speed of working might alienate parts of the organization. Although benefits such as increased usability can be related to KPIs such as increased performance, organizations also need to acknowledge "soft" experience-related factors as benefit.

05 It is crucial to create the right environment for design teams to work in. Having not only an inspiring workspace but also access to prototyping facilities is clearly necessary. Also, a shared location is mandatory for success, as much of the information otherwise gets lost in transmission.

7.3.2 CASE: USING PROTOTYPING AND CO-CREATION TO CREATE
OWNERSHIP AND CLOSE COLLABORATION

Reducing the waiting time for breast cancer patients

AUTHORS

Marie Hartmann
Design Director,
Designit Oslo

Kaja Misvær Kistorp
Lead Service Designer,
Designit Oslo

Emilie Strømmen Olsen
Senior Service Designer,
Designit Oslo

Designit®

Oslo
University Hospital

By reducing the waiting time for breast cancer patients from (up to) three months to seven days, Oslo University Hospital used service design methods to improve the lives of women facing a difficult period in their lives.

Women with a heightened risk of developing breast cancer typically faced a delay of up to three months before receiving an examination and diagnosis at the Oslo University Hospital, the largest hospital in Scandinavia. Supported by the Norwegian Design Council's Design-Driven Innovation Program (DIP), Designit worked together with a project team at the hospital to reduce waiting time and improve the overall patient experience. The collaborative, visual, and iterative process enabled the hospital staff to work more closely together and envision a new system.

Service thinking and co-creation

The project group and the designers facilitated a workshop with 40 employees across different departments within the hospital to map out a typical patient journey from their point of view. Afterwards, the patient journey was visualized in a detailed diagram demonstrating all the steps a patient goes through. This diagram was a valuable tool that enabled a common understanding across different departments of the complexity of a patient's journey.

After the workshop, in-depth interviews were conducted with patients. The designers used image cards to help the patients express emotional aspects of their journey, which are just as important as the logical steps. In order to gain deeper understanding of the staff's work process, the designers conducted contextual inquiry with the staff,

role-play with general practitioners (GPs), and phone interviews with stakeholders. Designit talked to a number of different actors that were involved in the patient's process, including oncologists, radiologists, radio technicians, nurses, patient coordinators, secretaries, private clinics, and GPs.

There was a lot of information gathered through these activities. This was used to identify the right opportunities for optimizing the process, ultimately reducing patient waiting time. The findings had to be inspiring and actionable. The key insight from all of this was that patients felt that they were patients from the day a lump was discovered, while the hospital considered them patients from the day the diagnostic work started.

The Oslo University Hospital decided to rethink the process. The ideal user journey was mapped out, completely removed from today's process and its challenges, and they worked backward from that. Together with the designers, the staff came up with solutions on how they could work differently with new routines that reduced the diagnosis period. The team then ran co-creation workshops with staff members where they developed prototypes, mainly in the form of scenarios and user stories. The scenarios were tested by presenting them to patients and staff. The designers did some alterations based on the test results in collaboration with the project team until they had a solution that was both feasible and met user needs (both backend and frontend). As a result, the team defined what the radiologist, the nurse, the pathologist, and the patient coordinator had to do to deliver this experience.

The solution aimed to improve cancer patients' lives by rethinking behind-the-scenes processes from a patient's point of view. The hospital staff played an important role in their patients' lives, and this had to be acknowledged. A large part of this included the hospital recognizing, accepting, and working on improving the customer service experience for the time leading to diagnosis.

The new Breast Diagnostics Centre (BDS)

The new process at the BDS was officially inaugurated at the Oslo University Hospital on November 4, 2013, with the Norwegian Minister of Health and the Norwegian Design Council attending the event.

With the new process, patients should feel confident that they are in the care of the hospital from the moment they leave their general practitioner's office. The goal was to create a straightforward path from the GP to diagnosis, getting the patient an answer as soon as possible

The journey toward a diagnosis has been radically reduced down to a total of seven days, a previously unthinkable goal. On day one, patients receive a brochure from their GP with information detailing the steps they will go through to diagnosis. They are also equipped with a direct phone number they can call in case they have any questions. On the backend, the hospital now assesses

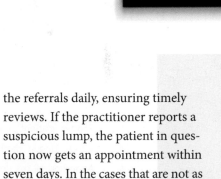

the referrals daily, ensuring timely reviews. If the practitioner reports a suspicious lump, the patient in question now gets an appointment within seven days. In the cases that are not as alarming, the patient may wait longer, but never more than four weeks.

On the day of the examination, the patient is greeted at the center by a radiographer. The patient then meets the radiologist and is given a preliminary diagnosis. The patient receives a follow-up appointment

(A) Today's patient journey.

(B) Conducting in-depth interviews with patients.

(C) Analyzing all the data gathered from
the insight phase.

(D) Ideation workshop with employees at the hospital.

(E) Developing analogue scenarios to lower the threshold
for patients and employees to give feedback.

(F) Patient flow with the new service.

(G) 90% waiting time reduction with the new
Breast Diagnostic Center.

the next day where the diagnosis is confirmed and, in the case of a positive diagnosis, a treatment plan is outlined.

Instead of meeting once a week, all the specialists involved meet every morning to discuss the patients. The test results are ready four days after the examination, and are evaluated in this meeting. This ensures that all patient cases are discussed in a timely manner and the waiting time doesn't accrue.

Prior to this, it could take up to 12 weeks before patients received a letter scheduling an examination at the hospital. Now, patients are contacted, either by phone or letter, just a few days after receiving their referral from their GP. All in all, the time from referral to diagnosis is now between 7 and 28 days, depending on the severity of the case. The new process represents a 90% reduction in waiting time.

Service design proved to be a valuable method in starting up this project and contributed to creating a real change. After the design phase, hospital staff drove the new process through implementation.

This combination enabled an ambition within the groups that led to the project's realization and impacted patients' lives. As a result of this success, it has now become the precursor to the national standardized procedures for breast cancer, introduced in January 2015.

KEY TAKEAWAYS

O1 The key to success throughout the project was the close collaboration between the designers, project group, and hospital staff.

O2 The designers brought the patient's perspective while the project group and staff identified where the pain points lay.

O3 In addition to the ownership created through co-creation and involvement from the staff, top management had committed from the beginning of the project to realizing the solutions.

7.3.3 CASE: ENABLING STAFF AND STAKEHOLDERS TO PROTOTYPE FOR CONTINUOUS EVOLUTION

Infinite prototyping

AUTHORS

Johan Dovelius
Head of Service
Design, Doberman

Henrik Karlsson
Creative Director,
Doberman

DOBERMAN®

EXPERIO LAB

Prototyping is often described as one of the core activities of the design process. But in service design, we need to embrace the prototype as the goal. There is no final service, it is just an infinite prototype.

Complex services need evolutionary improvements

Doberman was engaged by the healthcare innovation hub Experio Lab to redesign the different points of contact between people with chronic diseases and primary care clinics. Early in the process it became clear that smaller evolutionary improvements in the interface between patients and staff would have the most impact, as opposed to making one radical service innovation. And even more important, the improvements needed to be in constant evolution to be adapted to constantly changing needs, systems, and restricted resources. Enter infinite prototyping.

"I wish I had access to these tools when I got my diagnosis."

— *Sally Hjert, a participant in the design process living with chronic pain*

Collaborative insights

Through a collaborative insight and discovery approach, the design process identified five service improvement tracks that spanned events, artifacts, interactions, and organization:

— Holistic responsibility
— Empowerment in meetings
— Empowerment in the process
— Meeting equals
— Service overview

"A primary care center will never be 'ready' or 'final.' Instead, we must see it as an ever-evolving service."

— *Erik Almenberg, Strategist, Doberman*

All tracks needed prototyping, not just to evaluate ideas, but to establish viable and framed concepts that could be cultivated and evolved by the organization over time. The service will never be "done."

Staff taking over the prototypes

The design team developed a wide range of lo-fi prototypes that were tested and refined by staff and patients, in up to five iterations. As all prototypes were made in simple formats, like Word documents, so the staff could gradually adapt the process of prototyping, with no need for in-depth designer skills. As a side effect, the staff involved have embraced the concept of the complete service as an infinite prototype, and are now capable of approaching further challenges through design together with the patients.

"As we worked with lo-fi prototypes, we could iterate quickly, together with the staff and patients."

— *Therese Björkqvist, Service Designer, Doberman*

"As we see and spread the solutions as prototypes, they are easy to pick up, adjust, and integrate in other parts of the healthcare system. They also inspire staff to generate and prototype other solutions. Spreading the prototypes helps build courage and nourish a more innovative culture."

— *Thomas Edman, Experio Lab*

Scaling the prototypes

The innovation hub Experio Lab helps to distribute the solutions within Swedish healthcare, still in an open, prototyping-friendly format. Therefore, the solutions can be continuously tested, refined, and adjusted to different contexts within the Swedish healthcare system.

KEY TAKEAWAYS

01 Involve the staff in the prototyping process by letting them prototype, not just give input or feedback.

02 Use formats that can be easily used and evolved by the staff. They shouldn't need a skilled designer or any special tools to take over the design process.

03 Focus on artifacts that are relevant to many, that can be easily adjusted to specific needs.

04 Foster a prototyping and remixing culture.

05 Make the prototypes accessible and shareable.

(A) Collaborative insight and idea sessions with patients and staff were central to the prototyping process.

(B) Conversation cards help patients to set the agenda for the interaction with staff. Made in a simple format, the conversation cards can evolve over time.

(C) The Appointment Guide is a simple form used before, during, and after an appointment to help patients articulate their feelings and needs. The infinite prototype was designed in a simple format that can easily be adjusted to fit various situations.

(D) The Diagnosis Day is a meeting format to interact with other people with the same diagnosis – participants get further medical information and updates on the latest research and have an opportunity to ask questions. The actual agenda for the meeting was identified as the infinite prototype to synchronize the organization around the meeting and test relevance with patients. This simple agenda can evolve over time and functions as an organic guideline for the Diagnosis Day.

(E) A collection of prototypes. Experio Lab distributes the prototypes in formats that are easy to evolve, such as Word files, completed with instructions that encourage continuous evolution.

7.3.4 CASE: MINIMUM LOVABLE PRODUCTS,
LIVING PROTOTYPES, AND HIGH-FIDELITY SKETCHING IN CODE

ATO Partner Space case study

AUTHORS

Andy Polaine
Design Director,
Fjord Evolution APAC

Eduardo Kranz
Service Design Lead,
Fjord

Chirryl-Lee Ryan
Global Design and
Innovation Principal,
Fjord Evolution

Design and Innovation from
Accenture Interactive

Australian Government

Australian Taxation Office

In early 2015, the Australian Tax Office (ATO) embarked on a program called Reinventing the ATO, which outlined the future experience for ATO customers, partners, and staff. In partnership with the ATO, Fjord was engaged to help realize the Reinventing the ATO program through a subproject called *Working with Our Partners* – all the stakeholders who sit between the ATO and taxpayers, primarily tax and BAS (Business Activity Statement) agents and developers who create tax and accounting software that interacts with the ATO's systems and services.

As a result of the initial engagement, a group of prioritized service concepts were created to bring *Working with Our Partners* to life. One of these concepts was Partner Space, an online space where tax partners can easily access information and start interactions with the ATO.

Collaborative prototyping workshops are an excellent substitute for telepathy, because they make intent tangible. They help concrete discussion, highlight hidden complexities, and avoid participants talking at cross purposes.

Building a team of stakeholders
Looking beyond the online space, a combined team of ATO and Fjord staff visited tax partners to conduct contextual research and gather in-depth knowledge of their goals, pain points, and opportunities, as well as the way they work with taxpayers and businesses across Australia (e.g., such as how the ATO communicated with them and their clients, the status of queries to the tax office, keeping track of deadlines, and maintaining an overview of their clients' situations).

Additionally, tax software providers were involved in the research to ensure the ATO can support them

to deliver a consistent experience for tax partners. We co-designed activities with ATO stakeholders and combined insights with internal data to ideate initial concepts.

After refining these concepts, we ran a special prototyping workshop[01] with tax partners, ATO staff, and the project team. Such collaborative co-design workshops are used to discuss and develop initial concepts with a focus on making ideas tangible by building simple prototypes on the spot.

Creating a minimum lovable product
Developing the prototyping workshop outputs further, the team mapped out what a "minimum lovable product" would look like in terms of features and user journeys. We use "lovable" instead of "viable" because this shifts the focus

---

01 Fjord Makeshop is a proprietary co-design and prototyping workshop.

from the functional to the experiential. A bare-bones service that nobody likes using is not going to gain traction out in the world in its fragile early days.

Apart from the usual research and concept outputs at the end of this stage of a project, we created giant journey maps and roadmaps for the development of Partner Space. Since a focal point was a portal, Fjord's Creative Technologist built a living prototype. This was a case in which it was quicker to build something in HTML, CSS, and JSON than to design mock-up screens and annotate them. The prototype was created over the course of a couple of weeks. It used a pseudo-dataset that could be queried and filtered by a mocked-up frontend. Within the bounds of the fake data, we could demo filtering, searching, notifications, and responsive layouts and give a much greater sense of the power of the design than with just clickable pages. This provides an easier segue from concept to UX to delivery.

The fundamental ideas and needs for the portal had already been gathered and synthesized and concepts refined and iterated in workshops and in the weeks following. These were shared with the client team and external partner stakeholders – tax agents and software developers. The roadmap for the rollout of the features of the big picture experience was done based on a scoring system. The final scores from each group determined, more or less, which features were to be developed in phase one, which in phase two, and so on. The portal prototype was only part of a broader set of concepts, since it was a portal view onto several other deeper and more complex features. The prototype was intended more to explain how such a portal might work than to be a final design – a high-fidelity sketch in code rather than an end state.

Spreading the service design practice

The prototype was only part of a larger project involving several other features. The project has since moved into full design, development, and delivery. Alongside the design activities, Fjord held service design

(A) Workshop participants selecting and giving feedback on concepts.

(B) A territory map of tools and software used every day by agents and whether they love them or they're heartbreaking.

(C) Participants were given content elements in a co-design session to help define the information architecture and features.

(D) During the Makeshop, we quickly made our sketched ideas interactive in order to elicit immediate feedback and develop iterations.

(E) Taking over a public space in the ATO helped communicate the process. Here, the research and concepts are all on the wall and eventually covered by the minimum lovable product journey map poster and the roadmap poster.

(F) A prototype of the portal was the quickest way to describe the concepts in action.

learning sessions at the ATO as part of the knowledge transfer process. These sessions covered topics that were part of the design process in advance, so project members from the ATO could be aware of what was about to happen, and enabled them to collaborate effectively in the co-design exercises that took place throughout the project. Not only does this approach make working with our clients significantly more collaborative, it also ensures the impact of service design has long-term sustainability within the ATO by creating cultural change.

ATO staff who worked with Fjord have gained the confidence to drive internal projects as they continue the design learning experience, and those who worked on Partner Space have become joint guardians of the design vision as it heads into the delivery phase. The project has been extremely well received in the ATO, and it is exciting to work on a project with large-scale societal impact from conception right through to delivery as well as helping to shift the design culture within a large government enterprise.

KEY TAKEAWAYS

01 We conceive of a minimum "lovable" product instead of "viable" to shift the focus of the prototype from functional to experiential.

02 Collaborative prototyping workshops can help make intent tangible and highlight hidden complexities.

03 Creating artifacts – sketches and prototypes – is a powerful way of calming everyone's nerves by having something tangible to discuss and carry forward.

◀

Prototyping at scale: Redesigning Lufthansa's business class experience

AUTHOR

Barbara Franz
Senior Lead Design and
Research, IDEO

IDEO

 **Lufthansa**

Aiming to increase competitiveness through service, Lufthansa approached global design and innovation consultancy IDEO in October 2013 to redesign its long-haul business class experience. With an aggressive one-year time frame to roll out the new service, prototyping proved a vital tool throughout the process.

Learning by doing

The ambitious timeline demanded an iterative, hands-on approach from the get-go. After putting ourselves into the shoes of passengers and crew, and diving into what luxury means for today's traveler, we immediately began to prototype. The team mocked up a section of an airplane cabin in the IDEO Munich studio which was used for regular role-plays, helping us draft the initial service concept.

"Our goal was to improve service in these private moments so that the guest receives a totally new flying experience with much more quality time – time which they can use to work, relax, or be pampered."

— *Dorothea von Boxberg,*
Head of Customer Experience, Lufthansa

Designing the personal experience

Based on our insights, we created a more personal service experience, focusing on the interaction between crew and passenger. Crew should think of themselves as a traveler's trusted, knowing hosts, like at top-notch restaurants.

"Only if flight attendants understand and live the new service philosophy – being a host – will passengers feel the difference in the long run."

— *Stefan Wendland,*
Project Manager, Lufthansa

Prototyping, at scale

We then moved to a large-scale, 1:1 prototype – 92 seats, 3 galleys. Over four weeks IDEO and Lufthansa stakeholders, including crew, catering, and management, prototyped several versions of the new service, focusing on the feasibility and desirability of individual service steps, interactions, and the overall service flow from a passenger and flight attendant point of view.

Building for buy-in

The mock-up allowed us to run four- to five-hour simulations with real crew, watched by passengers and board members. The early involvement of key stakeholders created a sense of ownership and increased their confidence in shaping the design toward a common goal. During rollout, heightened awareness and buy-in from crew members helped ensured more willing adoption across all 18,000 flight attendants.

A The team mocked up a section of the airplane in
   IDEO's Munich studio.

B IDEO and Lufthansa prototyped the entire experience
   in a 1:1 model of a business class cabin.

C Flight attendants were among the key stakeholders.
   Involving crew in the design helped ensure adoption
   during the rollout.

D The experience was a more personal interaction
   between the crew and the passengers.

"We chose this holistic approach to trigger a new way of thinking about service quality and passenger experience at Lufthansa."

— Dorothea von Boxberg,
Head of Customer Experience, Lufthansa

KEY TAKEAWAYS

01 Challenge the system: If the organizational effort and lead time for change in your test follow the rigid rules of the current system, you won't operate freely and are limited in your creativity. Allow for flexibility in the test to enable you to experiment and iterate on your learnings.

02 Zoom in and out: When prototyping, pay attention to the details, but don't get lost in them. Balance that by constantly removing yourself to look at the bigger picture and the design intent.

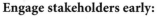

03 Take time to tell and listen: Brief your partners before each test, and debrief afterwards. Customer experience projects require us to listen to customers, but also to all those who deliver the service to them.

04 Engage stakeholders early: Leverage knowledge from different stakeholders and use the opportunity to create a sense of support and ownership by bringing people on board early. This will accelerate implementation and minimizes the risk of failure.

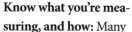

05 Know what you're measuring, and how: Many different factors impact a service, so agree beforehand on *what* you're testing and, just as importantly, *how* you're testing. Make sure to pick the appropriate technique for what you're trying to measure, and one that doesn't impact the overall service experience. ◀

7.3.6 CASE: USING MULTIFACETED PROTOTYPING TO
CREATE AND ITERATE BUSINESS AND SERVICE MODELS

Multifaceted prototype evolution over time

AUTHOR

Klara Lindner
Head of Customer
Experience, Mobisol

The company Mobisol started with a goal and an insight: having traveled around the globe, its founder Thomas Gottschalk came to understand that energy is an essential requirement for development, and thus set his heart on "plugging in the world." He also saw the potential of combining two seemingly unrelated trends: a steep cost decrease for photovoltaic (PV) solar, and the radical uptake of mobile networks and phones in the developing world.

Building on that, the initial business idea was quickly formulated: offer PV solar systems to people living off the grid, and let them pay for it over time via SMS.

Rather than working on a 50-page investor's deck, the first action was building a tangible prototype that illustrated the concept, which was used to get rich feedback and find partners to collaborate with. The prototype at this point was a light bulb and a solar panel connected to microchip with an embedded SIM card. By sending an SMS to that card, you could turn it on and off. Sized to fit in a suitcase, we could take it anywhere we wanted.

To better understand how to turn this idea into a solid business model, we jumped on a plane to visit the three countries that had adopted mobile most (Kenya, Tanzania, and Ghana). We hired a car and a translator to carry out intensive field research and get in touch with potential partners in those isolated areas.

What we brought home were four **main insights** that would help to shape our offer substantially:

— Even in the remotest village, the awareness about PV solar is quite high, but bad-quality products and lack of after-sales infrastructure have harmed its reputation in the past.

— Better lighting is of course nice to have, but what people really long for is a power source that is able to run larger electric appliances like stereos or TVs.

— The classic indicator – ability to pay – is not fixed number. Many people have three or four income sources and their monthly income fluctuates depending on seasonal factors and also how much they want something.

— The current spending on energy, which we could substitute with a solar system (lighting and getting the phone charged), adds up to approximately 15 €/month.

We used these insights to evolve our core offer: large PV systems coming in three different sizes, complete with battery, cabling, lights, etc. The offer also includes a three-year credit agreement and free maintenance throughout the repayment period.

A second prototype of the PV system was developed, now fully functional (but still very ugly):

we could remotely turn the PV system off and on based on incoming mobile money payments (M-Pesa), and gather performance and usage data in real time to foresee maintenance activities.

A hardware prototype made from DIY components helped to overcome cultural barriers and get honest feedback from our pilot customers.

During our trip, we had found a small, like-minded Tanzanian organization, with whom we started a field test soon after. In batches, we connected a total of 200 households (paying customers), gathered feedback on our technology, and prototyped different approaches to get the service ecosystem around the PV system right. There were many open questions about how to orchestrate different steps of the customer journey – let's zoom in on a few of these to better understand the iterative approach we chose.

"This is like having to put the engine into your new Mercedes-Benz!"

— Mama Baraka, *focus group member*

How can we assure proper system installation?

Since we are all trained as engineers, we did the system installation ourselves in the beginning – but quickly grasped that this would not be feasible for a commercial rollout.

Our first move was to develop a plug-and-play kit that customers could install themselves, and in co-creative sessions with real customers, we even managed to draft an accompanying manual that works. But we came to realize that even though our customers were now able to do the installation themselves, they simply did not want to.

People wanted someone knowledgeable to do the job. Our second iteration was the development of the "Mobisol Akademie," a two-week program through which technicians from the village (until then repairing houses, bikes, or phones) got trained and certified as Mobisol Installation Technicians.

And with that, we not only arrived at a feasible solution for us, but also made our customers even happier (because they know and trust their

local technicians) – and created jobs in the village.

What is the business model behind this?

Initially, we thought that Mobisol could become a manufacturer or maybe wholesaler, with local distributors buying in bulk and acting as the point of contact for the end users. But in our field test, we learned that there was neither a distribution nor a financing infrastructure to build on, and if we wanted this to work, we would have to build up our own structures and adapt our value proposition:

— We needed to take on the role of a micro-lender. This meant that on the one hand we had to borrow money from somewhere to bridge the three-year repayment period, and on the other, we had to carefully assess the creditworthiness of interested households. While the "switch off" mechanism helped us to get the necessary pre-finance more easily than we had thought, it took several iterations to come up with a credit survey that allowed us to find suitable customers.

(A) Cofounders Thomas and Klara meeting with village leaders in rural Kenya to better understand the role of energy in their village.

(B) We evaluated our pilot phase and gained insights for further development through home visits and focus group discussions.

(C) A Mobisol sales outlet right next to the regional market square.

(D) A screenshot of our web app remotely monitoring all systems installed.

— We needed to make sure that our customers could gain access, no matter how remote their homes were.

To come up with a cost-efficient distribution strategy, we looked into informal markets for inspiration: when a Tanzanian family build their new home, they go to the nearest market, buy the bricks, and find a means for transporting all the materials home – sometimes a bus with the right route, sometimes a car, sometimes a boat. Every village has a mason, who is hired to build the house.

We already had the local technicians, so we started to build up a decentrally organized network of sales outlets. Today, we have our "market hubs" at marketplaces that our customers regularly visit. We make sure the packaging is optimized for easy transport, and as soon as the papers are signed our customers handle transport over the final stretch, bringing the system components home, where a village technician is waiting to do the installation for them.

"Side effects" of our pilot research

Through close interaction with our first 200 customers, we found out that some of them were using the system productively and making quite a bit of money. We wanted to foster that and started to develop small business kits, so-called "business out of the box." In essence, these are electric appliances suited to our system together with entrepreneur-training materials and marketing materials for the customer to use. At the moment, we have a phone-charging kit and a barber shop.

Evolution of the business

Through our iterative process and being very close to our customers, we gained confidence about a business/service model that others considered pretty radical. As we pre-finance our technology for three years, we could only grow if we borrowed money. This confidence plus our "proof from the field" helped to make sure we found people who believe in it.

As I write this, Mobisol is about four years into the business and around three into commercial sales. We've grown to 500+ employees and provided access to electricity to more than 50,000 households. Having started in Tanzania, we went to Rwanda in 2014 and later started operations in a third country, Kenya.

KEY TAKEAWAYS

01 Be flexible with your business model – sometimes customer research can reveal the need to create new possibilities.

02 Through the Mobisol Akademie, we found a way to empower our users to not just be consumers but business-people as well.

03 When asking for feedback on our prototypes, we used a DIY hardware iteration, which helped to overcome cultural barriers and get honest feedback. ◄

08
IMPLEMENTATION

Service design should not end with a concept or
a prototype. The aim must be to have an impact on
people, organizations, and the bottom line.

Expert contributions and comments ———————————————————————

| Erich Pichler | Jürgen Tanghe | Julia Jonas | Kathrin Möslein | Klaus Schwarzenberger |

| Minka Frackenpohl | Patricia Stark |

08
IMPLEMENTATION

THE SHARP END
OF SERVICE DESIGN

💬 **COMMENT**

"To provide solutions, firms need to create service systems composed of physical components, technology, and data, including knowledge, communication channels, and networked actors. This equally applies to service systems in manufacturing, health-care, energy, or security and has been promoted especially in the context of the Internet of Things."

— Kathrin Möslein

Implementation – turning a prototype into a running system – is the sharp end of service design. Some commentators have criticized service design for being weak at implementation, and it is easy to understand these objections.

Many early service designers came from graphic or product design where, if they kept within set technical parameters, the realities of production did not concern them much. Or clients did not include implementation in the scope of the project, even if the designers wanted to address it. Perhaps because of this background, their mode of working might have been uncharitably perceived as: "Here is your design and an invoice, good luck making it happen."

Service design today is different. Service designers are invited to support projects end-to-end and a growing number of implementation projects even adopt a service design approach to replace their traditional project management methodologies from start to finish.

In any case, if our goal is to create a change which affects end customers, employees, processes, and even the business model, implementation always must be an indispensable core part of our work.

This chapter also includes

8.1 FROM PROTOTYPE TO PRODUCTION

8.1.1 What is implementation?

Implementation describes the step beyond experimenting and testing, to production and rollout. The implementation of service design projects can involve various skill sets, such as change management for organizational procedures and processes (including training, coaching, recruitment), software development or engineering for the production of physical objects, but also architecture and construction management for the creation of environments and buildings. Despite the different contexts, there are several similarities between these fields of implementation.

The boundaries between prototyping, piloting, and implementation are fluid. Full implementation might need us to initiate a large technical process, even refit a production line – steps which are very expensive to change later. Or implementation might just be a case of a handful of people doing their jobs differently. Whatever the scale of the change, there are some common patterns as we move into "everyday business":

→ Switching to production systems
New services or new products,[01] whether physical or digital, run within the real context, in a given environment and system.

→ Working with actual employees
Employees that were not involved in the service design process now have to execute new processes, even though they might not truly believe in them.

→ Main focus on business goals
Services and physical or digital products are sold at full price. The main focus shifts toward core business goals and away from innovation.

→ Integration into existing (eco)systems
The services or products, whether physical or digital, are embedded into existing (legacy) IT systems, environments, and legal frameworks, as well as functioning partner networks and (eco)systems.

→ Integration into existing KPI frameworks
New business metrics are integrated into existing and regularly monitored KPI frameworks.

→ "Business as usual"
The customer no longer perceives the offering as beta. Employees no longer perceive it as pilot.

→ Iterations/changes/adaptations get more expensive
As we progress toward implementation changes become increasingly difficult and expensive. Therefore, organizations tend to avoid changes at this stage.

COMMENT

"Cost and sales supervision, resource planning, and similar topics related to facts and figures are a crucial element of service implementation."

– Julia Jonas

01　The term "products" describes anything a company offers – no matter if this is tangible or not. In academia, products are often divided into goods and services. However, products are usually bundles of services and physical/digital products. As "goods" is colloquially understood as referring to something tangible, we prefer to speak of the term physical/digital products. Read more on this in the textbox *Service-dominant logic* in 2.5.

Pilots: Prototypes or implementation?

In a way, a pilot is a prototype of implementation, as it faces many of the challenges of communicating processes and intent to people who were not part of the earlier parts of the design project.

Pilots are the small-scale operation of new services and processes in a localized context. They can be seen as an overlap between prototyping and implementation. A pilot reveals many challenges a prototype faces during larger rollouts, as it includes employees who have never seen the concept before, as well as paying customers in a normal business context. We learn not only about how the service will work, but how it might be introduced and how it will affect other running services and systems.

On the other hand, a pilot is unlike full implementation. It is still a context for experimentation and learning, a test bed for trial and testing. [02] Everything is very new, the staff inexperienced, and some parts of the service might still be fakes or workarounds outside the standard business systems. More importantly, the design team are fully focused on the activity, and are always nearby to explain the "how" and – perhaps more importantly – the "why." In the wild, they will not be so near at hand. Management focus is also usually quite strong, which can have a noticeable effect on the staff members taking part. ◄

[02] See 8.6.4, *Case: Creating measurable business impact through piloting and implementing service design projects*, for a great example of the crucial role of piloting in gathering hard economic data to support your service design work.

8.1.2 Planning for human-centered implementation

It is often valuable to consider your implementation activities as a separate project within your service design project. In this *implementation project* you need to consider frontline and backstage staff, and all implementation partners, as your primary target audience. Think about:

→ **Research**
Who is or needs to be involved? What will the rollout/implementation experience look like? What are key obstacles or needs that need to be addressed?

→ **Ideation**
How might you create a great implementation or rollout experience? How might you effectively build the final offering? How might you scale?

→ **Prototyping**
How can you build a pilot – a working prototype of your implementation? How can you use prototyping to create a great implementation experience (rollout, launch) for your employees, customers, and partners?

→ **Implementation**
Based on the learnings from your prototypes and pilots, how are you now building, launching, and rolling out your final offerings (a unique mix of services, physical products, and digital products)?

8.1.3 Four fields of implementation

Implementation needs to vary from project to project. To reflect this, and to make principles and methods of implementation in various fields more tangible, in the following sections, four guest authors describe how service design can connect with four specific fields of implementation:

8.2 Service design and change management
How to implement new concepts and make lasting behavioral change happen in organizations

8.3 Service design and software development
How to give a common language to your development team, connect them to user needs, and answer the questions of what we should actually build and how it should be prioritized.

8.4 Service design and product management
How to integrate service design with product development and product management to balance UX, technology, and business requirements, and how to implement the value proposition of your product and service portfolio across the whole product lifecycle.

8.5 Service design and architecture
How to identify user needs related to people using space, co-create through prototyping with the later users, and enrich the architectural practice with approaches and tools from service design.

8.2 SERVICE DESIGN AND CHANGE MANAGEMENT

AUTHOR
Jürgen Tanghe

Some service designers consider their work done once they have proposed a new concept, in the form of a management pitch, a service blueprint, or a (working, functioning) prototype. They fail to fulfill the last phase of the service design process. This situation is akin to a product designer designing the most beautiful, ergonomic, functional, and ecological chair …then failing to produce it.

Artifacts of services come in a variety of forms, including physical, like a document or check-in desk, and digital, like a website or app. Also, in most services there is a human interaction element that is the essence of service: someone (the service provider) helping somebody (the customer) to achieve something.

This means the organization and the people in the organization become the "material" you are producing the service with. This section will help you work with this them to get your design fully implemented.[01]

Design involves desired behavior

Explicitly or implicitly, a designed service always involves establishing a desired way for both the customer and the service provider to behave. Therein lies the challenge for change management in service design.

How can we make people change their behavior, so that it is beneficial for the customer experience? Many traditional banks are redesigning their retail experience, for example, by creating a more open layout. But this only works when bank employees also change – they need to be more hosts than bankers, more advisors than tellers.

8.2.1 Know how people change

The reality is that organizations themselves don't change; only people do, and ideally an organization supports that behavior. This means that the only real measure of change is: "Do people act differently?"

Be change

While many claim that people hate change ("the only person who likes change is a baby with a wet diaper"), the truth is more complex. People change constantly, and they love some changes. Oftentimes, people are even willing to make big life changes to meet a goal, such as relocating to work for a particular employer.

You can't change people: Set up the context for change instead

Behavioral change is both simple and complex. On the one hand, people change all their lives, all the time – it is a rather natural activity. On the other hand, deliberately

---

01 The importance of design doing, craft, and material knowledge for making is nicely described by Jon Kolko. See Design Thinking Foundations (2012, January 26). "Design Thinking vs. Design Doing," at *https://vimeo.com/35710033*.

changing can be difficult, even if the stakes are really high. Just look at how difficult it is for people to adopt a healthy lifestyle even if they really want to or when their lives are at risk.

The probability of people changing their behavior depends on three factors: (1) how much they understand that they *must* change, (2) how much they *want* to change, and (3) how much they *can* change. In other words: MUST*WANT*CAN or Drive*Motivation*Ability. These three factors hold the ingredients to make individual, lasting behavioral change in organizations happen.

With this formula in hand we can draw up the circumstances and context that give people the biggest chance of changing their behavior in a way that is beneficial for the service. **Chances of success are biggest if we can:**

→ Start with motivation.
→ Do one small, specific, but significant thing differently.
→ Adapt the environment to make it as easy as possible.
→ Establish a relationship with a group of people accustomed to that behavior.
→ Grow from there to a new definition of your identity.

8.2.2 Understanding what will change

Before you can make any form of change strategy, you need to understand the consequences of the new service to the organization. What will need to work differently in the organization for the service to become real?

One classic and easy-to-apply analysis framework is Leavitt's Diamond, a model that is composed of four elements: task, people, technology, and structure. In essence, this model proposes that for an organization to be successful, the four elements need to be aligned and balanced. Imagine you have a sandwich bar, serving fresh, made-to-order sandwiches:

→ **Task:** This describes what the staff is expected to do. What is the job of each of the roles? In the sandwich bar, you might have someone to take orders, somebody to make the sandwiches, and somebody to collect the money.

→ **People:** Think about the people you need in your organization. What knowledge and skills do they need, and do they require any formal training or education? How many people do you need?

→ **Structure:** Structure is about how the organization is organized. This includes how departments are structured, but also what is measured and monitored, and how decisions and made? To be efficient, you could imagine that the decision rules would be flexible enough to allow staff to accommodate special requests for a sandwich that isn't listed on the menu (if the bar has the necessary ingredients) – staff shouldn't need to ask for permission to do this. Also, you will probably have some kind of monitoring system to assess customer satisfaction, the freshness of the food, and maybe the success of the daily specials.

→ **Technology:** These are all the tools, digital and analog, that are needed for the staff to perform their tasks efficiently and effectively. In our sandwich shop, this would include a decent knife and a cash register, but also maybe a checklist with instructions for how to make that daily special.

As a service designer, you can use this framework in multiple ways. First, you can see if you have thought of all the aspects of the service system. Second, any change introduced to the organization will impact one or more of these four elements; you can use this framework to map them, and thus to manage all of those potential impacts.

There are several ways to do this impact analysis. However, it is always important to involve the people who can judge the impact, because they know the current status. You can do this type of impact analysis:

1 As a checklist for yourself
Of course, you can just go over your concept and reflect on the impact on the different elements. This might work if you know the organization really well.

2 Based on a service blueprint
If you are accustomed to working with a service blueprint, it is a good basis for an impact analysis. Look at all the staff actions, and assess how they will be different from now, what support the staff will need, and what could go wrong. With the right people in the room, this is an interesting use of a blueprint in a workshop.

3 Using interviews
Based on the model, you can ask people what they think the impact would be. It is essential that they understand the concept well to make that judgment.

4 As part of prototyping and testing
You can integrate this model into your evaluation routines when prototyping and testing. In that way, you can not only test the desirability but also the feasibility of your prototype, and let it evolve to more fidelity.

8.2.3 Beliefs and emotions
There are two more things you should remember about change. First, for a long time we thought that the key to getting people to change was answering "What's in it for me?"

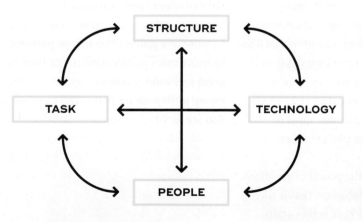

Leavitt's Diamond: an analysis framework
to understand elements of change

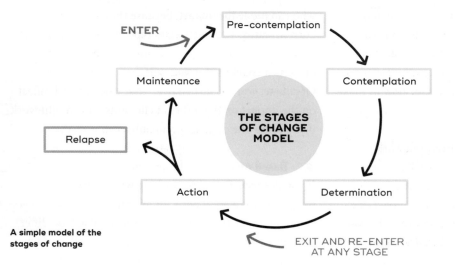

ENTER → Pre-contemplation → Contemplation

THE STAGES OF CHANGE MODEL

Maintenance

Relapse

Action

Determination

EXIT AND RE-ENTER AT ANY STAGE

A simple model of the stages of change

This not only is a very transactional way of looking at people, but has also been proven to be wrong. Actually, once you can establish the need for change and a minimal level of motivation, the most important question that people have is "How can I do this? How can I be good at it?"

The psychologists Carlo DiClemente and James Prochaska developed the transtheoretical model (TTM) of behavioral change. As the graphic shows, most of the steps are related to the belief that you are able to make the change.

Second, we need to remember the power of emotions. Emotions are the biggest driver of behavior; that is where the energy comes from and that is where action starts. It can be very hard, or nearly impossible, to convince people to take action or change based on pure rational arguments. One of the strengths of designers and design thinkers is being in contact with the emotions of people in an organization, and this strength should be utilized in change management efforts.

Based on this knowledge, there are three key tactics that are very powerful to both deal with organizational impact and support behavioral change:[01]

1   Use a human-centered and stakeholder-focused approach

Just as you would do a stakeholder map of the service environment, it is essential early in the project to map the internal stakeholders. You can use Leavitt's Diamond to get more richness in the descriptions of your stakeholders' organizational positions. Also, use the same empathy you used toward the customers to really understand your stakeholders. There is a lot of writing about "resistance to change" or "unwillingness." Sometimes there is a real resistance or unwillingness because of a political agenda or personal ambitions, but in many cases people have (from *their* perspective) very good and valid reasons to oppose changes that others are trying to impose on them. You can find those reasons, if you are willing to use your empathy.

01 See 8.6.1, *Case: Empowering employees for sustainable implementation of a service design project,* for an example of how some of those key tactics can be successfully applied to achieve outstanding service.

2   Participation and co-creation

Working co-creatively is one of the key principles of service design. Not coincidentally, participation in decision making has been proven to be essential in change management because basically there is a reverse correlation: high participation leads to low resistance; low participation leads to high resistance. This means you should see co-creation as part of both the creation and the implementation process; in addition, you should make deliberate use of those co-creative sessions to prepare the organization for implementation. One of the challenges is scaling. You cannot invite the whole organization to join a co-creation session, so you need to help the participants use their experiences within their own teams. You might also want to run more sessions than might be strictly necessary for your design process.

3   (Visual) storytelling

For all the ingredients that support change – transferring a sense of necessity, creating emotional appeal, giving instructions on what is the right thing to do – there is a method that people have been using since the beginning of human development. That is the power of the story. Stories and the heroes in them are also one of the basic elements of an organizational culture.

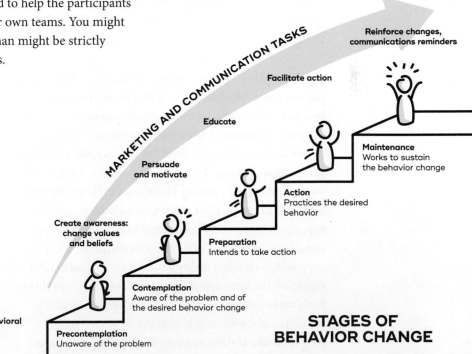

The transtheoretical model (TTM) of behavioral change, developed by psychologists Carlo DiClemente and James Prochaska

STAGES OF BEHAVIOR CHANGE

8.3 SERVICE DESIGN AND SOFTWARE DEVELOPMENT

AUTHOR
Klaus Schwarzenberger

How to create and maintain a meaningful development backlog

In this section we will explore how to connect service design methods with popular agile approaches in software development and engineering. Service design helps answer one of the most challenging questions at hand: what should we actually build and how should it be prioritized? As most agile methods today focus on the engineering team and the actual implementation, it's service design that helps to fill the backlogs with meaningful stories.

Today, almost all customer experiences include a digital experience at some point. The hard part is to harness those different channels and technologies and build a product or service that actually serves the customer's needs. Quite often, utilizing technology of all kinds makes stuff harder to use. Take, for instance, the early days of "car apps" that enabled you to open your car without a key. Instead of just pressing a button on the key (one step), users had to get out their phones, unlock them, open the app, and press a button (four steps) to achieve the same thing. This system had other flaws too: what are users supposed to do when their phones run out of battery, for example? The same applies to the Internet of Things (IoT) and connected devices. It's a cool thing if you are able to turn on a light with your phone, but again, an empty battery or broken phone can make the whole thing useless.

Because services and software are intangible and often inherently complex, it is crucial to make sure that all stakeholders are on the same page and involved in the process right from the start. If this principle were boiled down it would be: seeing is believing. Everybody in the team must do user research. To fully understand the customer's needs and provide a suitable solution, user stories, roadmaps, and fancy descriptions are not enough.

The alternative can be as easy as adding your lead developers and designers to the support email channel to make sure they see where customers get stuck. On top of that, empower them to actually make decisions based on their research results, and feature discussions will change immediately.

8.3.1 Basic factors

There are some basic "hygiene factors" that should be considered before you start applying a service design process to software projects. Some of them are technical, but most are more "people stuff."

We won't go into too much detail when it comes to the technical bits, since they may differ from industry to industry.

Agile

In software engineering the rise of Agile started in 2001, when Kent Beck et al. released the Agile Manifesto.[01] But before that, the CHAOS Report,[02] initially published by the Standish Group in 1994, brought awareness of failed projects in software development. The problem was that the same project management approaches that worked in the construction industry were used for software projects, but the complexity and changing requirements made a mess of things.

Instead of trying to plan ahead (and constantly rewriting the script as unexpected developments arise), the Agile Manifesto was a starting point for a different approach. Different methods, like Scrum, XP, ASD, Crystal, and APM, arose. Over the last couple of years most companies have followed one or a combination of these approaches with different levels of rigor. Everybody tweaked the methods to their needs, but no one admitted that they had "their own" system.

In 2015 Andy Hunt introduced the GROWS Method,[03] which actually boiled down all the different agile methodologies to their core principles. It's a set of methods from which a team can pick and choose for a given situation. No matter whether you are running a clean implementation of one of those methods or making your own version, they are based on these principles:

→ Adhering to timeboxes (sprints, iterations)
→ Maintaining a backlog of some sort (a list of features that is prioritized) for the next iteration
→ Following a meeting structure to collect feedback (daily stand-ups, weekly planning sessions, retrospective meetings)

Lean

Lean is more a mindset, and in our company we call it "entrepreneurial common sense."[04] In a nutshell, it's the organizational foundation for working with Agile. It emphasizes early feedback, experiments, and "cheap" failures. "Fail early, fail cheap" is one of its mantras. We think it's important to mention because it is really easy to be agile, but not lean. This means you can work in a way which is perfectly aligned with the Agile Manifesto while not actually aiming for a minimum viable product, collecting early user feedback, or following tracer bullet development.

Minimum viable product

A minimum viable product (MVP) in software development is a piece of software that contains just enough features to be deployed and tested by real users.[05] The idea is to boil down a product to the core problem that it solves and aim to find a minimum solution to the problem. It should be just useful enough to find out if the assumptions about the product idea are true, and how to improve it. Defining an MVP usually requires a lot of

01 Beck, K., et al. (2001) "Agile Manifesto," at *http://agilemanifesto.org*.
02 Standish Group (1994). The chaos report. *The Standish Group.*
03 See *http://www.growsmethod.com*.

04 There's an awesome German word for "entrepreneurial common sense": *Hausverstand.*
05 Ries, E. (2011). *The Lean Startup: How Today's Entrepreneurs Use Continuous Innovation to Create Radically Successful Businesses.* Crown Books.

discussion. What can help is to define the job that the user actually has to do (job to be done) as the job story,[01] derive the MVP from that definition, then validate the need with potential users. Work on a solution and create a sh!tty first draft. Ask again. Iterate on it. And accept that your assumptions will change.

However, keep in mind that you should still apply at least some basic technical hygiene factors when it comes to building a software prototype. The boundaries between throwaway code and actual production code can be blurry. If a tracer bullet development turns out to be a huge success, if you are not careful you might end up with temporary code runnning in production.

Early user feedback

For early user feedback you don't actually need an MVP. User feedback starts long before you have a digital product at hand. It can be a cardboard prototype, a desktop walk-through, a paper prototype, a click dummy, or anything else that is detailed enough to ask potential customers what they think about it. Make early feedback a habit and aim for testable products after every iteration.[02] Again, this is not something that only product managers should do; designers, engineers, and team members from other disciplines should be involved as well. Create teams of two or three people from different disciplines and give them a task – for instance, to collect feedback on feature *X*, or test assumptions on prototype *Y*. Then ask them to present

their research results to the rest of the team. This is an ideal foundation for ideation and again prototyping.

Tracer bullet development

Let's face it: some service innovations lead to technically challenging solutions. In order to tackle those big problems early on (and make sure they are solvable), it's best to follow the tracer bullet approach, initially published by Andy Hunt and David Thomas.[03] In their book, they propose that tracer bullet development is comprised of two components:

1 Address the most **technically challenging tasks** as soon as possible.
2 Deliver a **useful result** as soon as possible.

We will focus on the first of these, since the second is addressed via early user feedback and MVP development. Just as a tracer bullet gives an idea of the target area, the term in software engineering involves trying different approaches to challenging ideas as soon as possible, trying to figure out which one "might" work.

While prototypes are often just mocks that imitate functionality, a tracer bullet is "fired" to, for example, check the range of certain Bluetooth technologies very early in an IoT project. It contains code that might run in the final product. A tracer bullet is the engineers' version of a wireframe that is tested with users. It gives an idea of what might work and what doesn't – no more, but no less.

01 Klement, A. (2013) "Replacing the User Story with the Job Story," at *https://jtbd.info/replacing-the-user-story-with-the-job-story-af7cdee10c27*.

02 For an overview of prototyping methods see 7.2, *Prototyping methods*.

03 Hunt, A., & Thomas, D. (2000). *The Pragmatic Programmer: From Journeyman to Master*. Addison-Wesley Professional.

Technical hygiene factors

Rapid development, short iteration cycles, and the immediate application of changes pose huge challenges for the technical foundation of a project. When you apply a test-driven development approach to a very early (and still likely to change) prototype of an idea, you are facing a trade-off between maintainability and the risk of wasting time and money.

What can you – as a service designer – learn from these approaches? How do you do service design reviews? How do you keep track of changes in your designs? Have you set up or automated essential tasks to be able to prototype more quickly and collect feedback faster?

It is hard to go into detail here, since the technical hygiene factors differ from one programming language to another and are specific to your technology stack. There are, however, four technical factors that every project of any status should have implemented:

→   Code versioning
→   Code reviews
→   Build automation
→   Documentation (even if it is hard to do)

These are the minimum standards to incorporate in any project involving software, even at a very early stage.

In later stages of a project, those technical standards need to be elevated to a higher level and may include the following:

→   Style guides
→   Dependency management
→   Test-driven approach
→   Log, error, and performance monitoring
→   …

There is no definitive list of factors to implement at a particular stage. Just be aware of them and make conscious decisions on whether you want to implement certain standards.

8.3.2   Implementation

This section describes a typical lifecycle in a software project. It works both for an early-stage idea that is being tested for the first time and for the continuous improvement of a product. We will discuss implementation-specific concerns for software projects.

Preparation

Before starting a new iteration, you must define the scope. A good way to frame it is to define a user job; for example, "When I drive from my hometown to work, I want to be automatically notified about any traffic jams so that I can get to the office on time." Rather than focusing on specific target groups, the idea of user jobs is that anybody could be in that situation at some point. It moves away from the classic concept of user stories that define scope by focusing on a specific target group that wants something ("As a millennial I want notifications

THE PROCESS

Structured questions help you fill
the backlog in a reasonable way.

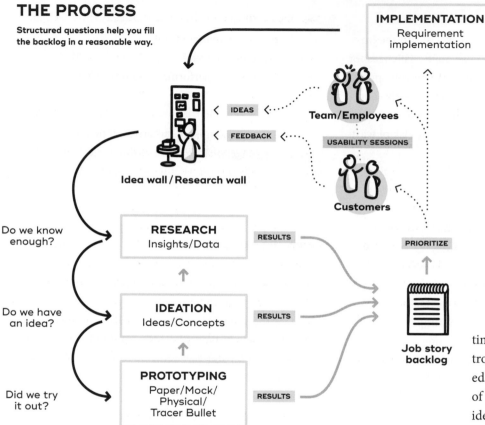

IMPLEMENTATION
Requirement
implementation

IDEAS

Team/Employees

FEEDBACK

USABILITY SESSIONS

Idea wall / Research wall

Customers

Do we know
enough?

RESEARCH
Insights/Data

RESULTS

PRIORITIZE

Do we have
an idea?

IDEATION
Ideas/Concepts

RESULTS

**Job story
backlog**

Did we try
it out?

PROTOTYPING
Paper/Mock/
Physical/
Tracer Bullet

RESULTS

Surviving in the agile world: Short daily
stand-ups with the development team help
align the process, checking the status of
individual tasks against the overall roadmap.

about all social media channels so I can stay up to date")
and focuses more on the context itself, instead targeting
particular situations that all users might experience. It's a
foundation and usually the job will change, or new jobs
will be added. At this stage, it is a starting point.[01]

01 See *Writing user stories* in 5.3.

While traditional sprints in software engineering are
timeboxed and take two or four weeks, the activities introduced here can have different lengths. The time needed for research, for example, depends on the complexity
of the research question being tested. On the other hand,
ideation is something that is usually done within a day.

If you aim to integrate service design into software
engineering long term, it's best to divide parts of the
processes into team activities and individual activities.
Workshops are an exhausting activity not just for the
facilitator, but specifically for developers. Carefully
separate activities like prototyping into team activities
(mini-hackathons) and individual tasks (tracer bullet
development) and give each team member time to work
on their own before jumping back to team activities.

Idea wall

Look out for any ideas that pop up, either during research for a different topic, in interviews with customers, or simply because you have used your prototype/software yourself and come up with an idea. You'll soon need a physical or virtual place to store your ideas and to collect user feedback that supports those ideas or contradicts them: an idea wall. Do a review of your idea wall before every iteration. Ask your team (or even better, your customers) to vote for their favorite ideas, and then prioritize and create job stories for each of those ideas that will go into development. Unless you implement faster than you generate ideas, you'll end up with a prioritized job story backlog. Before each iteration, choose the ones that you want to focus on during the next development cycle, again either by asking your team or your customers to vote for their favorites.

Research

When we start out with a user job, we follow a deductive approach. So, we have an assumption, and we search our database, logs, interview documentation, and other customer knowledge for data that falsifies our hypothesis. This can be a limiting factor because we might skip data that is unrelated but still very important.

In contrast, an inductive approach forces you to crawl your data for deeper structures. This can be as easy as checking recent support emails (say, going back about two months) to look for patterns that are mentioned more often or in combination with each other.

No matter which method you choose to implement, you'll need to find several team members that are responsible for the research phase. Ideally those people should have different backgrounds – for example, pair a backend engineer with a designer and let both individually do research on a topic. Make sure to brief them properly: research is not about "finding data that fits my idea." That's why deductive approaches can be risky. You have to find out what works best in your team. At the beginning, they might be overwhelmed by an inductive approach. While only a few are responsible for the research, bring the whole team on board if possible and let them contribute to the research results.

Usually research will have already started in the implementation/prototyping phase of a previous iteration. While it is important to focus on the research for the upcoming iteration, you should not forget the big picture. Usually after every second, third, or fourth iteration we ask ourselves: Are we still on track? Do we need to shift priorities? Did anything new and important emerge that changes our (bigger) plans? Team members then collect data from any available source, like:

→ Research data and insights from previous sprints or activities
→ Support conversations
→ Interviews with existing/potential customers
→ Usage data about an existing product
→ Analytics data from websites
→ External sources like studies
→ Desk research about competitors or the market
→ Conversations at conferences, meetups, and the like

The data is collected on a research wall in preparation for the next activity: ideation. Research works best if your team members have some time to do it. Depending on the size and complexity of the job/topic, allow up to four weeks for data collection.

To present the research results, have each of the team members that were involved in the research activities define their three to five key findings individually. Compare and discuss these together, and try to boil them down to five key findings.

Every single one of the following steps will contain another research/feedback activity at some point.

Ideation and mini-sprint

EXPERT TIP

"If you have a running product out there, you could also try *preto-typing*: add a button for that fancy new feature idea, but instead of implementing the actual functionality just add a feedback form that asks your customers what they would expect to find. You will easily find out two things: Will anybody click at all? And if so, what did they expect to happen?"

– Klaus Schwarzenberger

Set up a workshop and block off one day for it. Get everybody on the project team into one room. Present the research results to your team and let them know everything that you've learned. Answer all their questions, and also let them know about any doubts and limitations you have uncovered. This part usually takes up to one hour.

Now divide the team into several groups of two to four people. Give each team the chance to discuss the results and their views on them. Next, generate as many ideas as possible using whatever method you prefer. A round of 10 plus 10[01] works well and is a good combination of individual work and team effort.

At the end of the first ideation step, each team should come up with one idea to continue with. Depending on their knowledge about service design, a next step could be a journey map, a first paper prototype, or anything that illustrates the idea and makes it testable. Each team should aim for a sh!tty first draft.[02] Ideally, they will have the chance to test their first prototype with one of the other teams to see if it solves the problem.

At the end of this activity you will have gone through ideation, prototyping, and some research. Usually in software teams, these workshops are held on a monthly basis, depending on the status of the research activities.

Software prototyping

Prototypes are there to be tested.[03] Depending on the technical dependencies, prototyping activities are all about either tracer bullet development (to figure out which approach might technically work) or gathering early user feedback and data. So at the end of this iteration there should be a working digital prototype that can be tested with real users. The next step can be another set of research and ideation activities, or if the feedback is positive: implementation.

Depending on the complexity, this prototype can be the actual implementation or a rough sketch of an algorithm that is intended to solve a complex problem without touching edge cases of any kind. From a graphical point of view we can differentiate between low-fidelity (lo-fi) prototypes and high-fidelity (hi-fi) prototypes. Aim for lo-fi at first and add more details during the actual implementation.

01 See *10 plus 10* in 6.4.

02 See *Sh!tty first drafts* in 10.3.4.

03 Read more about how to further plan and use prototyping in Chapter 7, *Prototyping*.

HAZARD ZONE
getting lost

**TRACER BULLET
DEVELOPMENT**
early feedback

IMPLEMENT FAST
working results

WASTING TIME
burning money

COMPLEXITY

EFFORT FOR PLANNING/PROTOTYPING/ITERATING

MANAGING COMPLEXITY

Tracer bullet development is invaluable to get a first glimpse of technical feasibility in complex projects. One or two developers explore potential solutions for the most challenging problems. The result is not "production-ready" code but a better understanding of the problem.

It is actually a form of prototyping; even if it fails it produces valuable results.

Build and implement

It is essential to have a solid framework for your research, ideation, and prototyping activities when working on any bigger feature (they are usually called "epics") that is going into implementation. This section ends where most resources on Scrum, Kanban, and so on usually begin: with the product backlog. After finishing research, ideation, and prototyping, the results should be summarized in a requirements document. Together with the engineering team, schedule a planning session to create a list of tasks or stories that need be worked on to fulfill the requirements in the epic. Then follow whichever approach works best for your team and iteratively implement the features. Define deadlines, estimate the effort, and make sure that any area of uncertainty is touched as soon as possible to avoid blockers at the end of the development cycle.

Aim for a demo day at least once per week where product managers and lead developers check in on the progress and give early feedback. Again, seeing is believing. By collecting early feedback from stakeholders, you can avoid expensive feedback loops right before the feature release. The aim of every iteration should be a running, usable piece of software.

Release

The complexity of your release management activities will depend on the stage of your project. While in early prototyping you might just throw away everything and start from scratch, this will not be possible when users are relying on your product. What is a "test" for you is a finished product for them. As soon as you start to have users actually using your service, consider the following:

→ **Have a testing routine:** No matter if you go with automated tests from the start, have someone testing the features, or do it yourself, document your testing routine and do it carefully to avoid critical bugs appearing in production. Ideally, set up a "staging environment" where people can test everything, like for the "real thing" in production.

→ **Communicate properly:** Let users know what's going to happen. Will the update break something they were used to? Will your service go offline for some hours?

→ **Make releases robust:** Whether you're building a mobile app, a hardware product with integrated software, or a web-based tool, make sure that releases won't wreck your nerves. You should be able to easily roll back if something goes wrong. You should be able to release a new version within a couple of minutes and without downtime. Ideally, no manual work should be required for each new release, except pressing the button.

→ **Ask for feedback as soon as possible:** Again, this point can't be stressed enough.

Making the change

Giving a common language to teams is the biggest improvement that service design brings to software engineering. Scrum, Kanban, XP, and other methodologies focus on the engineering part while service design helps to answer the questions of what to build and how to prioritize that work. For people accustomed to being on the receiving end of requirements documents, the team approach can be quite uncomfortable. When you are in a facilitator role, try to aim for a slow transition with lots of guidance in the beginning, slowly making the tasks more open and challenging.

01 See 8.6.3, *Case: Implementing service design in a software startup*, for an example of how to implement the idea of an iterative process across your entire team.

8.4 SERVICE DESIGN AND PRODUCT MANAGEMENT

AUTHORS
Patricia Stark and Erich Pichler

One way to describe the essence of product management is shown in the product management Venn diagram by Martin Eriksson. You, as a product manager, are right in the center of negotiating the user needs (user experience or UX) against technological feasibility, business targets, and the strategic goals of the company.

For a great UX and to achieve the business goals, the role of services within the value proposition is becoming increasingly important. As a result, the role of the product manager is expanding from managing the product to managing the whole value proposition, including all the different services, over the product lifecycle.

The following sections outline the different phases of the product lifecycle, as illustrated in the diagram. They provide an overview of major challenges, typical tasks for a product manager, and some industry examples. In addition, possible use cases for applying service design in each phase are described.

Imagination phase

The very first phase in product management is all about imagining the future. You need to explore your current business model and strategy with regard to new solutions. The challenge is to find potential areas of innovation to generate value for your existing or future customers.

These areas will need to be aligned with your company's vision for the future. There is no one-size-fits-all approach and no turnkey solution when it comes to innovation. In a project manager's reality, there may be many reasons to urgently need something new, like perhaps a new competitor, a decrease in turnover, new technologies, or the end of life of an existing product.

As a product manager, you are expected to have a deep understanding of your customers, but also of the industry, data, and business. In order to get a deeper understanding of your customers and users and quickly evaluate ideas, service design or design thinking methods and tools play a major role in modern product management. Based on research and exploration, customer journey maps, personas, and early prototypes are often used in an industrial context and are the basis for any development. Although prototypes are built and refined in all phases of the lifecycle, the service design concept of early, rough prototyping adds value at this stage. The more concepts you can test and learn from in this early phase, the more likely it is that the right problems will be solved later on.

Lessons learned from service design

BY PATRICIA STARK

Beijing on a sunny morning in spring 2009. I got up early to see our product, an ATM machine, in a newly opened bank branch close to the hotel where I was staying. I was a young product manager responsible for the Chinese market and curious to see the new ATM location. The branch had already opened a few weeks before, so when I arrived I was surprised that the transportation legs (needed to allow transportation by forklift) were still installed on the ATMs. I was astonished for three reasons. First, the only purpose of those legs was for transportation; second, because the market requirement was to lower the user interfaces of the ATMs because users in China are a different height to users in Europe; and third, because Europe has rules and regulation about how an ATM has to be fixed to the ground. As I found out later that week, new ATMs in other Beijing branches were also still on these installation legs. I was curious to find the reason, so I talked to various people until I found the answer: the way of cleaning in China. Cleaning staff simply pour out a bucket of water and then wipe the floor. So, if they had removed the transportation legs, the ATMs would have been flooded on a regular basis. It took some time to realize that a deeper customer understanding, stakeholder maps, and customer journeys would have already brought this insight to light at the imagination stage. ◄

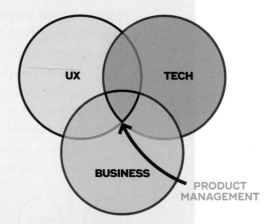

Product management Venn diagram: [01] product management sits at the intersection of UX, technology, and business.

Definition phase

Yet, before the actual realization phase starts (which often comes with a standardized process with a rather rigid project milestone concept and tight schedule), there is typically a definition phase, which can have the form of a pre-project. At this stage you need to verify the concepts, build further prototypes (e.g., for new inter-action concepts, new technology, new materials etc.), test them, and alter them. Within this phase the product manager builds the foundation for future developments. According to Vijay Kumar, "The next challenge is to combine compatible and valuable concepts into reliable and systemic solutions that are actionable for future successful implementation." [02]

A product requirement document has to be created for further development. This document contains all the requirements a certain product has to fulfill and helps everyone in the later development better understand what the product is expected to do. Depending on your preferences, this can be a "real" document, a spread-sheet, or a dedicated software solution. Besides customer requirements, as a product manager you have to prepare a holistic picture of the future solutions and combine concepts. Thus, the product requirement document also includes the context – like industry standards (e.g.,

size of machines, maximum weight etc.), any relevant regulations (e.g., regarding security or usability), and also the business side. These requirements should also be accompanied by the prototypes and the learnings from early evaluation.

This definition phase (or pre-project) is the basis for your realization phase, where the actual development of a physical product and/or service takes place. The definition phase is often conducted with a smaller team, but when it comes to realization the number of people involved increas-es rapidly, as do costs. Consequently, no matter whether your company has a waterfall approach or a more agile one, at some point you need a schedule, budget, and staff.

The deliverable of the definition phase is typically a product requirement document, tested prototypes, and a project plan for the realization phase.

Realization phase

When it comes to the development of new products, speed is of great importance. "Because we pursue inno-vation in a competitive marketplace, speed matters. The faster that great ideas get to market, the faster we earn money, build our brand, and extend our reach into the future." [03] In software development lean and agile devel-opment processes are widely followed already. [04]

01 Busuttil, J. (2015). *The practitioner's guide to product management.* New York, NY: Grand Central Publishing. p.7.

02 Kumar, V. (2013). *101 Design Methods: A Structured Approach for Driving Innovation in Your Organization.* Hoboken, NJ: John Wiley & Sons, p. 247.

03 Morris, L., Ma, M., & Wu, P. C. (2014). *Agile Innovation: The Revolutionary Approach to Accelerate Success, Inspire Engagement and Ignite Creativity.* Hoboken, NJ: John Wiley & Sons.

04 See 8.3, *Service design and software development.*

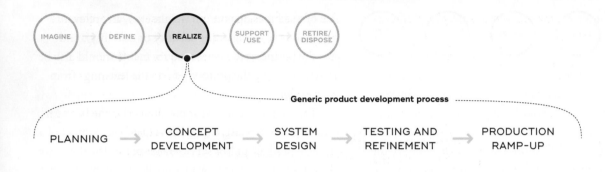

Generic product development process

PLANNING → CONCEPT DEVELOPMENT → SYSTEM DESIGN → TESTING AND REFINEMENT → PRODUCTION RAMP-UP

Yet, many companies still struggle to apply these concepts to the development of physical products. The reasons are manifold: sometimes it is just not possible to split the final solution into smaller pieces (think about some big machines in the recycling industry, for example) or test it without the whole system. Many companies have introduced standardized processes for recurrent tasks and consequently follow a classical, milestone-driven project management approach for the development of physical products.

A generic product development process during the phase of realization might look like the figure above, yet in practice it is never that linear and has iterations in it as well.

During realization the role of the product manager is crucial. One of the most important tasks is to constantly remind the development team of the user needs. Due to the growth of service design, more and more product managers are using personas in the early phases of product definition. One approach that has turned out quite well in practice is to have members of the development team adopt these personas during realization. Basically, each team member adopts one persona and has to take care of that persona's needs during the entire development process. In this context not only personas for customers are used, but personas for all kinds of stakeholders. In the case of an ATM, there might be personas for a service technician, a bank employee, or a third-party software provider. Whenever a new concept is reviewed or a milestone approached, each team member can assume the role of her persona and give feedback in the persona's name. This is a simple but effective method to apply a service design tool during the realization phase.

Support/use phase

When your product or solution is out in the market, you focus on market success and making profit. One model which can help you to decide which tasks are necessary for your product to stay successful is the classical marketing lifecycle model.

It distinguishes between different (sub)phases during the period when the product is offered to the market (the sales period). As a product manager it is crucial to monitor market success and to trigger the right actions during the market lifecycle in order to keep your product successful. In addition, you have to decide when a new product generation should be developed. Nevertheless, you have to keep in mind that in reality the lifecycle curve of your product might look very different from this idealized version and depends a lot on developments in the external environment (new competition, new regulations, overall economic situation, and more).

As outlined in the remainder of this section, your tasks as a product manager will vary during the lifecycle stages, and each stage offers chances to use different service design tools.[01]

1   Market introduction

When introducing a new product you will need to get references, improve your sales channels, and probably eliminate teething troubles in your products. You can surmount these challenges if you have additional services ready, not only the product itself. Your sales channels should be properly trained and ready to provide you with customer feedback. You should be able to offer the right consulting and support to your customers so that they

feel confident using your product as early adopters. An important tool to improve your offering at this stage is the customer journey map; monitor this closely so you can improve the customer experience by learning from your early customers. The example in the next section illustrates the importance of developing services related to the introduction of a new service and the importance of designing these services based on the needs of all stakeholders.

2   Market growth

Growth means that your product has gained traction. You now want to accelerate the growth rate. How could you grow your market share faster? How could you find new sales channels and optimize your offer for these new channels? How could you improve your customer relationships and your visibility? These are the questions you have to ask yourself. With new sales channels and new customers, you will feel the need to adapt and improve your product (new features, new variants). Think outside of the "product box" and consider services which could support these goals. Individualization becomes more and more important at this stage. After this, you will have to start again with the exploration of new customer groups and new applications for your products.

Example: An Austrian company developed a new innovative portable welding device, the first in its class. But after the market introduction they realized that people were reluctant to use the device and their customer base was growing slowly. So, the product manager decided that he had to offer more than just the product

---

01 The service design approach should not be limited to your product management activities. See 8.6.2, *Case: Implementing service design to create experiences, momentum, and results in sales,* for an example of how design thinking and doing can transform the way your sales team engages with your customers.

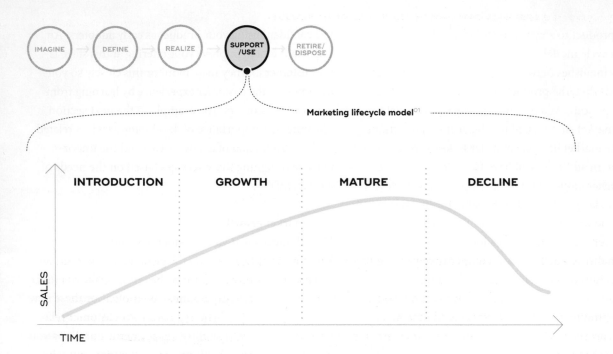

to customers and that another close look at the users was necessary. As part of a service design project, the company gathered new user insights and developed concepts for additional services. Now they offer a whole solution consisting of the welding device, an accompanying software service for better and easier adjustment of the device, and a ready-to-weld transportation package. With these additional services and offerings they have been able to significantly increase their market growth.

01 Polli, R., & Cook, V. (1969). "Validity of the Product Life Cycle." *The Journal of Business, 42*(4), 385.

3 Market maturity

You have reached a good market share and you are making sufficient profit with your product. But it would be a mistake to think everything is fine and you can lean back. Now you will have to deal with competition in the market. You will have to defend your market share and find measures to differentiate your offer from the competition and keep your business as profitable as before. Now the time has come when you should start thinking about your next-generation product. To increase the lifespan of your product, it might make sense

Lessons learned from service design

BY PATRICIA STARK

Co-created customer journey map

After my first workshop on service design with Prof. Birgit Mager from Cologne University, I immediately wanted to implement the approach. So I asked the sales staff at my company to organize a few meetings with some friendly customers to create some customer journey maps together.

These workshops were quite interesting. The most important pain point for the employees turned out to be the amount of time they spent explaining new ATM machines and their functions to customers. They said that they were unable to do their actual work because they were standing in the self-service area explaining all day. At the workshops it became clear that they wished for some assistants to explain new functions at ATMs.

So, we quickly recruited a dozen students from all over Austria, trained them intensively at our headquarters, and then offered our customers (the banks) a service which provided assistants when they ordered new ATMs.

How often do you think this service was sold? Not once. It turned out that our research had missed some important points. One was that bank managers don't want non-employees (our students) to approach their customers. We iterated and went back to exploration. We conducted contextual interviews and observed customers in the banks' self-service areas. The main finding was that if the bank employees are familiar with the ATMs and excited about their functions, the customers will be much more likely to use the machines as well.

So, instead of developing a new training program which showed employees how to best explain new functionalities, how to argue why customers should use ATMs, and so on, we simply made a basic flyer aimed at employees. We briefly explained the content of the training and wrote that we wanted to train the bank employees at our premises to get them excited about the ATM and the company behind it.

Drumroll! Within a couple of weeks, our sales staff were selling the service purely on the grounds of this flyer (which was our prototype). And since then the fully developed course has become a successful product-related service during the introduction phase. ◄

to relaunch the existing product or reposition your offer. By developing new, associated services and new revenue models you might be able to find new ways to differentiate your offer from the competition.

4 Market decline

The product is no longer attractive in the market. There are still customers buying it, but the profit is shrinking. Now your main goal is to avoid losses and hopefully prepare for the introduction of the next generation. To avoid losses you can reduce the internal and external support costs by eliminating product variants. You should also think about how you can keep or increase your service profits – for example, you could offer updates and retrofit solutions to the existing customers.

5 Support

The use/support phase does not finish with the sales decline. Customers are still using the products and they still expect some product support (repair, spare parts, retrofit solutions, and more). So, work together with the service department on revenue models for the support phase and find a way to capture user insights for the next generation of solutions.

Be aware that these stages might look different for your product. Nevertheless, service design offers product management a variety of tools and methods to make products even more successful during their lifecycle.

Retirement/disposal phase

The product has reached its "end of life" and the customer disposes of it. You should use this last touchpoint in the customer journey to introduce your new product generation and support the disposal process with useful services.

The role of services for product management

To sum up, the production, use, and circulation of products cannot be separated from associated services. Firms must not only focus on products or services, but should develop service–product combinations (solutions) to generate multiple revenue streams.

The transition from a product manufacturer to an organization that also offers services is challenging. It might implicate organizational and business model changes, new value propositions to customers, different pricing strategies, and innovative approaches to making services marketable.

Thus, today's product managers have to discover new mindsets and methods, such as service design, to to generate tomorrow's solutions by combining existing know-how and capabilities within the organization and along the whole supply chain.

01 Photo: Summer Design Summit/Florian Voggeneder.
02 Photo: Service Design Linz/Florian Voggeneder.

Lessons learned from service design

BY ERICH PICHLER

When I was product manager for an ATM product line we faced the challenge that the existing product generation had been on the market for more than five years and the development of the successor product had not started yet.

Our competitors had started to offer a new product generation and the competition was becoming much stronger. So we decided to relaunch the existing product line. We focused on two new aspects: improved security and economy. But the opportunities for technical product improvements were limited, so we had to offer not only the adapted product but also a complete new package with additional services. We offered new security services bundled together with the product.

The relaunch was a success and we were able to keep the product competitive in the market for another five years. ◄

(A) Making a video prototype during a service design workshop for the new welding services.

(B) Making insights visible for further development.[01]

(C) Referring back to personas during a concept review meeting.[02]

8.5 SERVICE DESIGN AND ARCHITECTURE

AUTHOR
Minka Frackenpohl

This section sets out to connect two disciplines that originate from a similar background. However, the way they are performed is quite different. The aim here is to identify opportunities where architecture and service design can learn from each other and outline chances for them to merge.

When graduating from architecture school in 2009, I presented a basic architectural structure. It consisted of a foundation slab and a concrete core, containing a bathroom, a kitchen, and a staircase. As well as the structure, a process was described to complete the basic house. In this process, the future inhabitants could build their houses themselves and develop them individually based on their needs and at their own pace. After the handover of this basic house to the residents, the new owners would decide how to use the building services offered. Within this service, clear anchor points were designed for the users to add material and build up knowledge or expertise. Overall, this project aimed at building the capacity of an ethnic group. The service created various touchpoints for inhabitants to use when needed.

My auditors greeted me with incomprehension. Why should people design and build their own houses when there is an expert (i.e., the architect)? This experience illustrates the dilemma of architecture: the claim of an almost universal knowledge of the subject and about the future users. User needs are rarely identified prior to planning, nor are stakeholders part of the design and planning process. This means their needs and creative input are seldom included in the development of a building. Classic architecture is understood as a manifested singular, to be used in its current form rather than being part of a process, used as one piece of a service ecosystem. The usage of a building may, however, change over time. Future-ready buildings need to be developed employing holistic building processes.

In many countries, the architectural process is divided into clearly defined phases, structuring the classical architecture project. The Royal Institute of British Architects (RIBA) has defined seven work stages, which are described in the Plan of Work Framework. They reach from preparation (appraisal and design brief) to use and aftercare (post-practical completion). Within this framework, however, there is still a need for some additional aspects that may lay the groundwork for enriching the profession of architecture. The equivalent phases are obligatory within the service design process and rich with highly developed methods and tools: a change of mindset from a singular to being one part of a system, identification of user needs, co-creation, and prototyping.

In the following sections, six stages will be described. These describe joint phases of the architectural or service

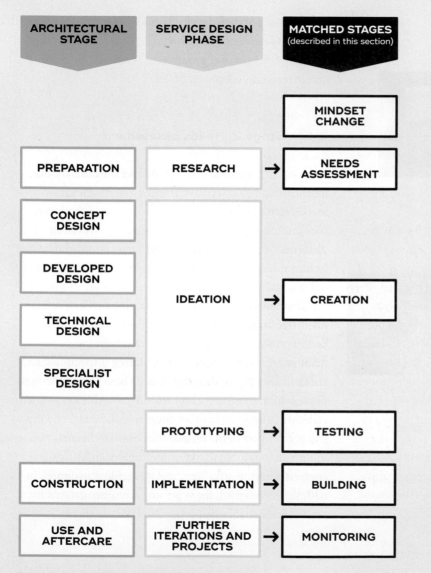

ARCHITECTURAL STAGE	SERVICE DESIGN PHASE	MATCHED STAGES (described in this section)
		MINDSET CHANGE
PREPARATION	RESEARCH →	NEEDS ASSESSMENT
CONCEPT DESIGN		
DEVELOPED DESIGN		
TECHNICAL DESIGN	IDEATION →	CREATION
SPECIALIST DESIGN		
	PROTOTYPING →	TESTING
CONSTRUCTION	IMPLEMENTATION →	BUILDING
USE AND AFTERCARE	FURTHER ITERATIONS AND PROJECTS →	MONITORING

Comparison of architectural and service design stages that are matched to the stages described in this section.

design process and are matched to both or one of them. They identify possible areas for enriching the architectural practice with approaches and tools from service design.

8.5.1   Stage 1: Mindset change

The first stage sets the groundwork. Architecture has been viewed since modernity as a single static building or conglomerate of various forms. There is a great opportunity in perceiving architecture as a process rather than a static building. In service design, we look at the whole system as the product, whereas in architecture the one product is the building. In order to make architecture part of a service ecosystem, the built environment must be redefined as one touchpoint and the building itself as a physical manifestation.

Stakeholder maps can be used to make sure all the people involved in the lifecycle of a building (everyone involved in designing, building, using, monitoring) are represented. This helps to set the groundwork for integrating all (built) needs during the process. Creating an architectural customer journey of people using the building identifies touchpoints, whether service, product, or built.

We worked with the team from Cowoki,[01] a Cologne-based startup that provides coworking combined with childcare. During this project, we defined the journey for

01 See http://www.cowoki.de.

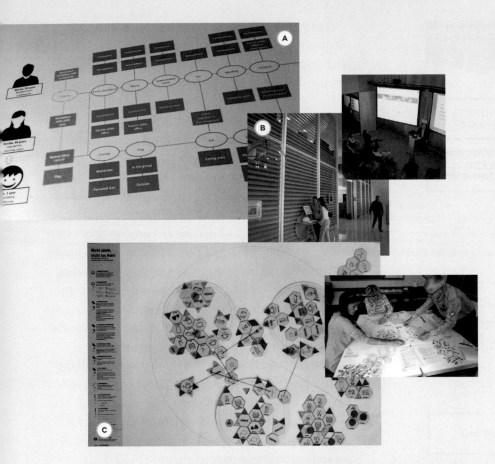

various users of their service and set the focus on what the built space needed to provide in order to match the needs of different user groups (e.g., community space, quiet areas, and telephone boxes).

Stage 2: Needs assessment

As architects, we should aim to deliver the best solution for the buildings' users. For this reason, it is fundamental to understand their specific needs. In the 1960s, the concept of programming, or briefing, evolved in America.[04] Programming is called Phase 0 in the architectural process and different tools are used during this phase to gain knowledge about the later users of a building. It is a research and problem-solving process, used to identify, examine, and elaborate various needs within a design project. Methods used are brainstorming, contextual interviews, benchmarking, building inspections, and relationship graphs. Programming is now part of the first phase within the American Institute of Architects' service catalogue. However, in other countries, such as Germany, it is not yet part of the official framework. This makes it difficult for a potential client to understand why to commission this extra step, and it is seldom assigned. In addition, if assigned, there are no recommendations for action or a structured approach to take the client along.

(A) Creating a customer journey of coworking with a child using three identified personas. The focus is on how the different spaces within the coworking space serve the needs of a coworker and a child.[01]

(B) User-centered spatial solutions at the Stanford Center for Innovations in Learning.[02]

(C) Stakeholders creating the Dream Space Map "Living and Residing as Seniors in Rural Areas."[03]

01 Photo: COWOKI, Cologne.

02 Photo: IDEO.

03 Photo: Baupiloten, Berlin.

04 For more information about programming, see William M. Peña, W. M., & Parshall, S. A. (2012) *Problem Seeking: An Architectural Programming Primer*, 5th ed. John Wiley & Sons. See also Kumlin, R. R. (1995) *Architectural Programming: Creative Techniques for Design Professionals*, McGraw Hill Professional. And see Sanoff, H. (1977) *Methods of Architectural Programming*. Dowden, Hutchinson & Ross.

As an example from the design perspective, IDEO worked together with the architect and staff members at the Stanford Center for Innovations in Learning. This project showed how the architectural process and the assessment of user needs can be united. The team did six weeks of research, including on-campus interviews, photo surveys, and shadowing, to understand the work process of the students and the Center's staff and faculty. "This work informed the design documentation IDEO delivered, including visualizations of every aspect from architecture and furnishings to information systems and protocols of use."[05]

8.5.3   Stage 3: Creation

When talking about new or creative methods in architecture, user engagement within the pre-design phase is often mentioned (as described earlier). But what about integrating the stakeholders into the design phase and handing over the pen?

Considerable efforts have been made to integrate stakeholders into the process of urban planning, reaching back to the 1940s, when the British government used reconstruction after World War II as an opportunity to engage the public. Planners created new techniques to communicate with laypeople such as mobilizing publicity, measuring public opinion, organizing exhibitions, and experimenting with new visual strategies.[06] For co-creation, various tools are conceivable (e.g., idea generation, design scenarios, or storyboards).

In the book *Architecture Is Participation* (*Partizipation macht Architektur*), the Berlin-based architecture company Baupiloten introduced their methods for participatory design.[07] "Negotiate the dream space" is one method they work with. This board game uses activity and atmosphere cards to co-design space. In their project "Living and Residing as Seniors in Rural Areas," stakeholders "negotiated a future life in the country. Initially each player developed a vision for their personal area and then they negotiated the communal facilities for all of them, there was both a great need for privacy as well as a willingness for neighborly interaction – such as through the connection of two units by a common area for communal cooking and eating." By creating a Dream Space Map, needs for spatial relationships and atmospheric qualities are revealed.

05 IDEO (n.d.) "Multistory Teaching Environment." Retrieved September 9, 2015, from *http://www.ideo.com/work/stanford-center-for-innovations-in-learning*.

06 Cowan, S. E. (2010). "Democracy, Technocracy and Publicity: Public Consultation and British Planning, 1939-1951," at *http://www.escholarship.org/uc/item/2jb4j9cz*.

07 Hofmann, S. (2015). *Architecture Is Participation: Die Baupiloten: Methods and Projects*. Jovis.

8.5.4 Stage 4: Testing

Building architectural models is essential to every building project. Working models are built to study aspects of an architectural design or to communicate design ideas. Thus, an architectural model might be something used as a first quick prototype. Models are, however, rarely used in this way in daily architectural practice. Mostly they are built during the very last design phase and act as a visualization and sales tool for the finished design. Looking at it from a design thinking perspective, the possibilities of a prototype are manifold. By introducing early-stage modeling, the design inevitably benefits. Working models help the architects to understand their own designs better while supporting communication with the stakeholders and hence strengthening the process and the trust between the parties. Tools used may include architectural staging, LEGO® SERIOUS PLAY®, or building prototypes.

Baupiloten uses an exploration game they call "Test scenarios." The game uses spatial modules in a specific architectural scale. "The aim is to enable users to adjust their needs and desires within the future built environment, using these building blocks, which transfer easily into the design process because of their scale."[01]

As another "doing" example, we undertook a semester project in cooperation with Deutsche Telekom. The students were to create ideas on smart housing, and prototyping was one part of the process. By creating prototypes, the students produced very deep, detailed ideas, and the concepts were truly enriched compared to the previous outcomes.

8.5.5 Stage 5: Building

After the building is planned, the architect functions as the touchpoint for contracting the craftspeople. Offers are collected, tested, and evaluated. Bidders are negotiated with and orders are placed. Additionally, the architect takes on the cost control of the building process. Once all tradespeople have been hired, the architect coordinates and supervises the implementation. One could say that building is a rather technical phase. So where are opportunities for service design in this stage?

A helpful tool that is often used is a "catalogue of intersections." This catalogue details the planning process and the intersections between all involved parties.[02] Though it is not part of the officially mandated working documents, this helps keep an overview during the long building phase. Combining the catalogue of intersections with a stakeholder map can have great effects on the smooth working of the building process.

The craftsmen form an important interest group at this point of the architectural process. They are dependent on the architect's planning, as well as obliged to fulfill standards within their fields of expertise. Speaking to them and enquiring what they need to render the best service they can should be in the architect's interest as

01 Hofmann, S. (2015). *Architecture Is Participation: Die Baupiloten: Methods and Projects.* Jovis.

02 Fritsch + Tschaidse Architects, Munich.

Relationship model of a community organizer; semester project on smart homes.[02]

Children building up a model for their own play area in "Le Buffet kids restaurant" based on their needs and imagination.[03]

well. However, the official requirements regulate contact between architect and craftsmen solely in terms of technical implementation. A structured assessment of the craftsmen's needs and a clear definition of the intersections between the trades can improve the process. For example, if there is a technical innovation within one craft, this novelty might have an impact on the design of the building and the architect might benefit from receiving early information on it.

The later users of the building don't play a role within the building phase. If you look at it from a technical point of view this seems quite logical. On the other hand, this stage marks the first visible touchpoint of the later building. At this point, users are eager to get engaged and receive information. This is a good time to reinvolve those parties, either by showing them the actual project status, confirming their needs (to abe able to adopt possible changes in the detailed planning as soon as possible), or even conducting a late co-creation workshop targeting aspects which can still be changed (e.g., detailed planning, interior design).

8.5.6 Stage 6: Monitoring

The last phase of the architectural process, monitoring, defines the use and aftercare activities after the building is finished. For example, for office buildings it is common to

02 Photo: HfG Schwäbisch Gmünd, in cooperation with Deutsche Telekom, Germany.

03 Photo: Baupiloten, Berlin.

hand over an operations and maintenance manual to the owner. This is a technical report which contains things like care instructions for the floors or operating instructions for the ventilation system as well as the built drawing. It generally does not include the human factors of using the building (e.g., why certain decisions were made and how rooms can be used flexibly). There is a lack of transfer from the findings of the needs assessment stage to the implemented use of the building. Within the German HOAI (the schedule of services and fees for architects and engineers), two obligatory services are described: assistance in the release of guarantees and the compilation of graphic and textual documentation. As an additional special service, the architect may offer site inspections for user groups after handover. However, this is the sole (perhaps contracted) post-build opportunity for the architect to re-engage with users. After this, once the building is in use, any earlier efforts in integrating stakeholders and especially users by assessing their needs are not reflected.

Changes and the in-use evaluation of residential and office buildings, for example, are not part of the classical architectural contract. Once a building is finished, the decisions made in planning are set in concrete. In a finished building one can't easily remove walls or change the structure as one can within a classical service. Thus, how would a post-occupancy evaluation be of value? There are at least two reasons to expand the classical architectural process here. First, catching up with users helps manage the expectations set earlier and opens an exchange for ongoing improvements to the building. Involving users could be done through feedback workshops using methods such as walkthroughs or "a day in the life". In addition, it is a great opportunity for the architect to learn for the next project.

8.5.7 On the other side: What can service design learn from architecture?

Although this section focuses on improving the architectural process by integrating service design skills, there are options for service design to learn from the field of architecture.

The title "architect" is protected, and it may only be used after intensive university study and evidence of practical experience. This ensures a consistent quality of delivered services. Due to the presence of architectural associations, architects have a united voice that allows them to address their needs in order to work professionally. The performance of the architect is structured within the work phases and the fees for the respective work phases are set in fee scales (e.g., HOAI in Germany). As these structures do not exist in the field of (service) design, there is a chance to establish an equal standard of quality in work and results.

We have seen that there are various fields of opportunities for service design doing in architecture. If designers are able to dismantle the fixed structures within the architectural process, there are many possibilities to enable innovative space solutions that represent great physical touchpoints within service ecosystems.

01 Photo: Fritsch + Tschaidse Architects, Munich.

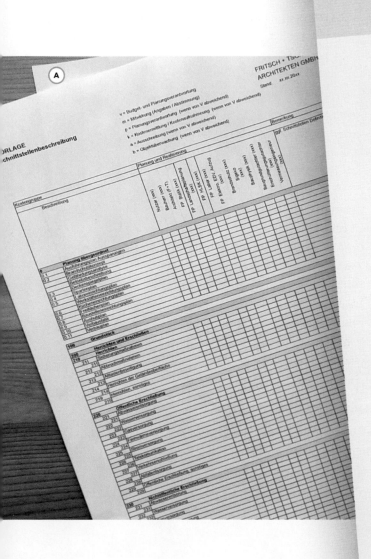

08
IMPLEMENTATION
CASES

⟶

The following four case studies provide examples of how service design implementation can take place in practice: how to empower employees for sustainable implementation of a service design project **(8.6.1),** how to implement design doing to transform customer and seller experiences **(8.6.2),** how to implement service design in a software startup **(8.6.3),** and how to create measurable business impact through piloting and implementing a service design project **(8.6.4).**

8.6.1 CASE: EMPOWERING EMPLOYEES FOR SUSTAINABLE
IMPLEMENTATION OF A SERVICE DESIGN PROJECT

Best ride there is! How to create and maintain a perfect customer experience

AUTHOR

Mario Sepp
Founder, Gastspiel

Edelweiss Bike Travel set out to orchestrate an even better experience for their customers. With the help of Gastspiel, Austria, they analyzed and improved their end-to-end customer journey. The most important factor was employee training.

Initial situation: A healthy company with tradition

Edelweiss Bike Travel – the world's leading company in guided motorcycle tours – has been providing motorcycle and scooter touring around the globe since 1980. Around 50,000 customers – mainly from the United States, Brazil, Canada, and Germany – have been on an Edelweiss tour. Featuring the latest motorcycles, 12 different tour categories, from basic tours to luxurious vacations, are offered in 75 locations.

Design challenge and project goals

Edelweiss Bike Travel certainly provide great customer service, but it is "legendary" service that they strive for. Only when their clients' expectations are exceeded is a tour considered a success.

The service design challenge: after 35 years of doing motorcycle tours around the globe, Edelweiss Bike Travel decided to revamp and standardize the customer experience on all of their tours. The company was continuing to expand and the growing number of tour guides from all over the world – who are all freelancers – posed a real challenge to staging a continuously consistent customer experience for the equally growing number of new and loyal clients.

In particular, feedback from regular clients – who often booked the same tour a second or even a

third time and sometimes brought along acquaintances and friends to whom they had previously warmly recommended Edelweiss Tours – clearly demonstrated what enormous influence each individual tour guide ultimately has on the perceived quality of the customer experience.

But there was yet another factor that was rapidly gaining increasing importance. Since Edelweiss Bike Travel is the official partner for BMW, Ducati, Triumph, and Harley, it's important to recognize that these companies insist on a perfectly orchestrated customer experience for the clients when their motorcycles are used on the tours.

"We just don't run tours, we want to deliver the ultimate customer experience – and that is before the tour, during the tour, and of course after the tour!"

— *Rainer Buck, Managing Director,*
Edelweiss Bike Travel

The agency's approach:
A classic service design process

Gastspiel was selected to develop and co-create – together with a prestigious team from Edelweiss – the new "Edelweiss Customer Experience." After in-depth design research (which was carried out in the form of observations and ethnographic methods as part of the preparation, implementation, and follow-up of different motorcycle tours), devising and drafting a stakeholder map, the mapping of the customer journey and development of associated personas, and the design and implementation of the new customer experience finally took place.

Besides various improvements to the customer journey before and after the tour, the spotlight was clearly on the tour itself. Management recognized that the tour guides and their behavior are the absolute "make-or-break factor" for the individual guest experience. To launch and embed the new "Edelweiss Customer Experience" in a sustainable way, a new Tour Guide Training program has been implemented.

How implementation
worked in detail

The service design process has evolved tremendously over the last few years, but the biggest challenge has always been the sustainable implementation of the designed customer experience measures throughout the whole organization.

Employees with direct customer contact in particular have to be in the position to stage the designed customer experience in their daily routine, regardless of their length of affiliation with the company: "We are what we repeatedly do." To overcome this challenge, we have created a new method of video-based service training, where employees are not only taught to stage the perfectly designed customer experience step by step, but can also instantly experience the impact of these steps on the customer.

The service training video, which is divided into individual training segments, shows all the previously mapped out processes and procedures in real-life situations between company and client along the entire customer journey. Within the scope of the Tour Leader Training, a common reflection on the just – viewed situation was carried out after each video chapter and the most important details were recording. An appropriate "Quick Reference Guide" was developed, containing all the relevant information in compact print; this is carried by each tour leader for safety reasons, ease of reference, and in general in aid of carrying out all the appropriate tasks during a tour.

Talking to the employees

It is of utmost importance to stress the emotional aspect of the customer experience and make employees directly and equally experience what enormous importance each customer experience means to the company, and what incredible responsibility each employee carries and must therefore fulfill.

Anything that touches people on an emotional level will remain far more strongly rooted in their memories than mere situational experiences and procedures which are only taught or conveyed by means of printed matter. It is therefore necessary to take course contents to an emotionally tangible level.

(A) Comprehensive customer journey maps laid the foundation for the whole process. Used as a tool for convincing employees and developing new customer flows, it has been crucial throughout the project.

(B) Team members setting up checkpoints according to the newly developed guidelines.

(C) The back office team taking care of back-stage processes, on the basis of a story-board hanging in the background.

(D) The new employee guidelines: the foundation for all face-to-face interactions.

(E) A personal welcome: creating physical evidence for intangible services.

(F) Team coaching taken seriously.

The better each employee understands and grasps this reality and the better each employee comprehends the fundamental advantage for himself, the better and the more willingly he will focus his effort toward meeting and satisfying customer expectations in the interest of the business. From Service Design to exceptional Service Delivery!

Customers will not always remember in detail what they have been told or what has been done for them, but they will always clearly remember whether you made them feel good.

Measurable results after employee training

The feedback Edelweiss received from their customers from the first tours thereafter was overwhelming – and it was proved once again: great customer experiences create great business results. After completion of the project, Edelweiss Bike Travel was able to celebrate the most successful business year since its inception in 1980!

Key insights and learnings

Compared to static pictures, mere text, or spoken information, the video medium provides a far greater density of information, especially when individual modules are used. The tailor-made service training video – which was made authentic by filming actual clients and employees in real-life, everyday situations – not only depicts the training content in a visual and vivid manner but also conveys it on an emotional level, which in turn positively enhances the acquisition of knowledge and results in a significantly improved and sustainable anchoring of the learned content.

To communicate the required ways of conduct, necessary explanations, and specific actions and behaviors desired by the tour operators a sophisticated didactic concept was developed which was ultimately implemented in accurately adapted audiovisual material and finally compacted in the training video. The employees are consistently shown the correct procedures and each individual employee is guided by them in practice, obviously within their personal scope.

"What I get out of this – more than anything – after all the tours I've done, is the people. Not only the riders, but the tour guides. I just love this. So the combination ...it's the people more than anything. And I want to thank everybody for making my life more whole."
— Customer, Edelweiss Bike Travel

That way the company facilitates, for both new and longtime employees, a better understanding of which services are relevant at any given time and in any given manner for a perfect customer experience and further assists them by showing them how they can successfully implement these services in their immediate everyday work.

Because nothing must be left to chance, it is important nevertheless that any course of action must be perceived as authentic. Quite a challenge indeed! Especially in the field of soft skills, relevant video segments depicting interpersonal situations can be experienced in an emotional and authentic way as opposed to viewing mere text or graphic illustrations.

In particular, the fact that the team of tour guides comprises people of different nationalities makes it all the more important to ensure that each one of them equally understands the relevant training content. In fact, we were able to see the effects of the new service training video even before the first tour leader training sessions were carried out.

Gaining internal pride for the results

The presentation of the completed video to the owners, management, and the members of the project team met with equally incredible emotional reactions in all – they were truly moved, touched, and most of all incredibly proud! Proud of "their" company, proud of their personal performance and that of the entire team, and proud of their commitment and the honest effort of their employees in their daily interaction with clients.

Team emotions as driving factor

One thing is clear – such strong emotions are a huge motivational factor and strengthen loyalty to the company. It was therefore all the more gratifying that we received this "I'm really proud to be part of the Edelweiss Bike Travel Team!" as unanimous feedback from all employees at the end of the training sessions we conducted. This spirit of togetherness and the employees' convinced attitude and feeling of loyalty toward their company and its services are obviously also felt by the customers of Edelweiss Bike Travel. And it is exactly that which is without doubt the best and most sustainable basis for authentic and therefore unique customer experiences!

KEY TAKEAWAYS

 01 Visualization tools like customer journey maps are crucial for basic understanding of a common goal across the team.

 02 Outstanding services rely on empowered employees.

 03 For employees, not only training but also deep understanding of the idea of customer experience is important.

04 Dedicated training material, such as video and printed guidelines, can help with sustainable implementation of new concepts.

◄

8.6.2 CASE: IMPLEMENTING SERVICE DESIGN TO CREATE
EXPERIENCES, MOMENTUM, AND RESULTS IN SALES

Transforming customer and seller experience

AUTHORS

Jurgen De Becker
Vice President,
Global Solutions
Consulting, Genesys

Lisa Gately
Senior Director, Content
Strategy, Genesys

ꝏ GENESYS™

Today's digital revolution has fueled enormous customer engagement expectations. Nowhere is that more clear than in the contact center, where customer engagement models have rapidly transformed. Genesys, a popular global customer experience platform, knows this very well from 25 years of empowering companies to create exceptional omnichannel experiences, journeys, and relationships. With over 4,700 customers in 120 countries, Genesys orchestrates over 24 billion contact center interactions per year in the cloud and on-premises.

However, with its fast growth (acquiring 12 companies in 4 years), and entry into new market segments while expanding its portfolio, Genesys needed to transform its model for working with customers. A small core team was formed, with leaders from marketing, sales, and services, to solve what became a service design challenge. Genesys needed to accelerate customers' time to value and improve their buying journey by bridging the company's technology and expertise across all customer-facing teams. In particular, sales and services teams needed to drive repeatability and standardization with a common methodology and toolset, while also helping customers visualize and improve the customer experiences they deliver.

The challenge of increased complexity

For many companies, success is now about delivering connected customer experiences across multiple journeys and channels, including phone, interactive voice response (IVR) systems, email, social media, web chat, text, mobile applications, video, and other IoT automated services. At the same time, customers perceive value based on business outcomes, not necessarily the price of an offering, and they make comparisons to the best experiences they've had in any industry.

Anticipating these market shifts, Genesys's portfolio grew rapidly and its sales model began to evolve from a product-based to a solutions-based, consultative approach. But these changes introduced more complexity and inward, rather than outside-in, thinking. This complexity started affecting customers' experiences in their buying journeys, and the collaboration between Genesys teams.

A cross-functional team of sales, marketing, and services leaders created a mission to optimize both customer and Genesys outcomes with a consistent approach: creating and delivering memorable "wow" customer experiences. The SMART Method project was born, and it became a corporate transformation program, sponsored by the CMO and global sales and services leaders to break through departmental silos.

Creating memorable "wow" experiences

The first steps in change are often the most difficult ones, and this was true for the SMART Method. Stepping into the customer's shoes and moving beyond the limitations of current internal tools and processes for sales and services teams required a completely new mindset.

A key event in bringing the core team together was completion of the "This is Service Design Doing" course. The shared experience brought customer centricity to the forefront of all discussions, and shaped our use of common tools and language. Thereafter, conference rooms were decorated with journey maps, stakeholder maps, and service blueprints. The technique of "octopus clustering" even became part of a sales training exercise.

The "Double Diamond" (Design Council, UK) was an inspiration for the SMART Method's core design process, which starts with extensive research. The team confirmed the most important experience gap in the buying journey: the touchpoint when the customer requirements are being identified. While customers appreciated the Genesys CX vision, they perceived it as complex and often missed insights about how to achieve business outcomes. Therefore, the first design challenge focused on providing quantifiable value and a clear path to the target state. This became the basis for multiple iterations and prototypes.

The resulting service design–led approach specified that the sales team and the customer analyze the end customers' journeys together. Products become a means to an end, which is to help companies deliver great customer and employee experiences, with efficient operations. The historical focus on product features faded to the background, while building relationships, reimagined journeys, and great business outcomes gained the spotlight.

Implementing small steps to build momentum and results

Within six months of its inception, the SMART Method was introduced to the entire Genesys sales team during the annual sales conference. With the support of service design thinking (and doing) experts, we provided context and insights into the design process. The feedback was very encouraging, with 88% of the sales team agreeing that this method would reduce the customer's time to value and create new experiences.

After this introduction phase, the cross-functional team worked to guide expectations during the implementation with the Genesys teams. One of the first challenges we encountered was overcoming the sales team's hesitance of entering design doing conversations with customers, or the question "Am I creative enough?" We discovered that a design doing approach led to even better customer conversations, with customers sharing meaningful details and stories. Early experience also revealed that sometimes being simple and pragmatic is all you need. Finally, we learned how important it is to find the right journey when working with customers.

A customer lifecycle includes many journeys, and design thinking

(A)   Design doing in action: The Genesys team discusses customer touchpoints and potential approaches to a design challenge.

(B)   The SMART Method (initially called the WOW Method) was inspired by the UK Design Council's Double Diamond.[01]

(C)   Jurgen De Becker of Genesys presents early results and direction during the company sales conference.

01 Find out more at *http://designcouncil.org.uk*.

allows us to imagine many future possibilities. However, we needed to identify the most relevant journey in a customer's situation to start design doing, and not lose momentum. Working together in an agile manner, taking many small steps and learning across the sales team with some pilot customer projects, led to great initial results.

As the program grew, an important next milestone was to establish a small, dedicated team to facilitate design thinking in the customer lifecycle and implement new tools for sales teams. This team not only focuses on optimizing experience, but also on building and sharing knowledge across the sales and services teams. Each co-creation process conducted with customers generates valuable insights where new service capabilities can be added to the solution portfolio. Establishing a center of excellence was a critical step in implementing the program and making design thinking a core discipline.

Although the SMART Method is still in its infancy, we are achieving positive results. Service design has helped Genesys transform to creating more intuitive, personalized customer (and sales) experiences. What started as a small stealth-mode initiative has quickly gained momentum in helping the company reduce complexity, break down silos, and bring a thoughtful, human approach to our business.

"Service design has transformed how Genesys teams engage with our customers. We have changed the conversation with journey mapping becoming the vehicle to discover and co-create new, innovative customer experiences together. This approach has proven to be very effective, and clearly helps our customers transform how they create great customer experiences with their customers."

— Mark Turner, *Executive Vice President of Global Sales and Field Operations*

KEY TAKEAWAYS

 As a company grows, you can't let the focus shift away from the customer to internal changes. Never lose sight of the customer experience!

 Stepping into the customer's shoes requires a completely new mindset and, to act on this, a common culture across teams.

 The point where you identify customer needs can be the biggest experience gap in the customer journey.

04 Design thinking and doing can bring simplicity to your approach.

8.6.3 CASE: IMPLEMENTING SERVICE DESIGN IN A SOFTWARE STARTUP

From canvas to reality

AUTHORS

Klaus Schwarzenberger
CTO, More than Metrics

Jakob Schneider
CCO, More than Metrics

Marc Stickdorn
CEO, More than Metrics

**more
than
metrics**

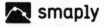 smaply

Starting a business with service design in its DNA

When we published our book *This Is Service Design Thinking*, we promised an app to work with the Customer Journey Canvas. However, we quickly discovered through contextual interviews and workshops that our initial idea was not enough. We understood that users need more than just a digital version of our paper canvas. They need a tool to quickly create entire journey maps that they can share and use in workshops – an insight that guided us throughout the whole development process. Based on feedback we received from our consulting clients and the wider service design community, we realized that we need to build web-based software that allows users to create professional journey maps (e.g., after a workshop to share with all participants and as an input for further iterations). What started as a simple side project to our service design

consulting developed into a startup. We even had a business plan …

Smaply became a web-based tool to visualize personas, stakeholder maps, and journey maps. This case focuses on our prototyping process and how we prototyped, tested, and changed our business model over the years.

Starting bootstrapped

Boosted by the sales of our book and the resulting interaction with service designers from across the globe, we felt the timing was right. In 2011 journey mapping started to become mainstream. In 2012, our founding team combined the most needed skills for a software startup: technology (Klaus), design (Jakob), and management (Marc). We were able to handle most tasks ourselves and had very close access to our potential users and customers. This made initial researching, prototyping, and testing very quick

and cheap. The actual concept and business model were still subject to permanent change.

We started with many assumptions based on our own service design consulting experience, but still needed to validate these through research.

As we needed to stay flexible, we combined our agile development process with a team-wide iterative service design process. So, not only was the software itself developed in repeating loops, but we also developed our underlying business model iteratively.

As the service design community was quite interested in our project, we originally planned to finance the development of Smaply through crowdfunding. Unfortunately, international crowdfunding platforms didn't support projects based in Austria in 2012. We had the naive 6notion to set up a crowdfunding platform ourselves. Unfortunately, we were fighting legal boundaries in Austria at that time and had to discard this approach for legal reasons.[01] To finally get started, we decided to bootstrap Smaply and finance everything out of our own pockets.

Developing our business model

We planned Smaply as a classic Software-as-a-Service (SaaS) product. The interesting aspect about these business models is their scalability: you maintain relatively stable costs, no matter how many products you sell.

One crucial aspect of SaaS business models is their pricing. In the beginning, our pricing was based on gut feeling. We are experienced SaaS users ourselves and asked ourselves what we would pay for this kind of software. So, we created a "Starter" and a "Regular" plan for €10 and €25 per month, respectively. The idea was simple: if we convinced 200 customers to buy the Regular plan, we'd be able to cover our basic costs. We had no employees at that time and

planned to develop a first version of the software ourselves.[02]

Selling alpha and beta access

Of course, we didn't just rely on our gut feeling when it came to market potential and product/market fit. Through early iterations and research phases during our closed alpha with selected users from the service design community, we already knew that the tool served a need for companies and agencies doing service design.[03] One research question we had though, was "Is this need big enough that users would actually pay for it?" To answer this question we took a more radical step and did some research through value prototyping.

We set up a prototype to test the market response and price sensitivity. We offered 100 "alpha accounts" for €30 each. This basically meant: "Hey, you can check out our sh!tty first draft, but you have to pay for

it! We were surprised when these accounts sold out in 24 hours, and decided to offer another 100 beta accounts for €50 each a few weeks later, experiencing similar success. Selling alpha and beta accounts helped us to identify and connect with our most engaged users.

E

01 The legal situation has since changed, and crowdfunding and crowd investing are now becoming popular in Austria.

02 Four years later, we are a team of 20.

03 In 2012/2013, we described the value proposition of Smaply as "Create professional journey maps in minutes." We described the user need we tried to fulfill as "Users need to quickly create presentable journey maps and be able to change these when they iterate with geographically dispersed teams." As our core target groups we defined "agencies and companies doing service design."

(A)   Draft for Smaply crowdfunding website that never went live.

(B)   Sh!tty first draft of a Business Model Canvas for Smaply as planned in 2012.

(C)   Prototyping market response and price sensitivity by selling alpha and beta accounts in 2013.

(D)   Original feedback we received from Markus in 2013.

(E)   The 2017 Smaply with increased flexibility.

(F)   Our idea wall: a physical board to collect ideas from our team and users that we use as input for our internal workshops.

(G)   A poster in our office to remind the team of our server overload.

Building a community

In 2013, we had about 50 invited closed alpha users, 100 paid alpha users, and 100 paid beta users. On that basis, we tried to establish a long-term relationship with the most engaged users. That basically meant we talked to everyone. Some users were thrilled when we sent them long and honest answers to their bug reports and feature requests, or when one of their ideas actually made it into the final product.

One core aspect of building a community was thinking beyond the mere software. We started to offer free downloads of persona, stakeholder map, and journey map templates for paper-based workshops, but also sold ready-made paper templates through our online shop "Mr.Thinkr." We rewarded our most engaged users with some free templates as physical evidences of the software.

Iterating product and pricing

We launched the public version of Smaply in December 2013. Within a few days we had the first few customers on board – most of them were alpha and beta users who converted their accounts. As we couldn't handle everything ourselves anymore, we hired our first two employees in 2013. With increasing costs, we had to work on our business model and pricing. However, we wanted to make sure that our customers would have the feeling that Smaply was "worth it," so we asked a few of them for their opinions. Backed with their feedback, we increased the pricing in 2014 to €25 for the Starter plan (limited to three projects and just one user) and €50 for the Regular account (unlimited projects and optional additional users).

Our initial concept was based on the idea of providing users with maximum guidance. This approach also includes limitations for users, like: "You cannot do this because it doesn't make sense." As our users got more and more skilled, we increasingly received complaints about this model. Users wanted to build maps in a more flexible way. We kept telling them how to work around problems, collecting more and more use cases. After two years of very iterative software development our code base looked like a patchwork rug. So, we decided on a complete rewrite of the software. Even though this was a major investment, this would increase stability and enabled us to finally tackle the flexibility issue of Smaply. We tested many new ideas with our most engaged users – often just roughly scribbled interface ideas on paper. Internal insight workshops brought together the learnings from our entire team through a healthy mix of analyzing research data, creating insights, generating ideas, paper prototyping, and creating digital mock-ups for further usability tests.

Connecting features with pricing in plans

Through intense dialogue with our users, we were able to learn about features and functions that appeared truly desirable. We were pretty surprised when users stated that a predefined storyboard image set (a rather simple thing for us) was much more important than real-time collaboration (a really complex thing to build).

Our most crucial instrument to understand needs and design features and pricing at the time (as well as today, after some growth) was a rather simple one: everyone in the team has meaningful conversations with our users. We don't have a dedicated support team.

Everyone talks with users: the founders, the developers, the marketers, etc.

In our company, we all deal with support, usability tests, software demos, bug reports, complaints, and the like, following our own slogan: "Talk to your f***ing customer!". This means everyone knows what the most prominent user needs are, and we discuss these every two weeks. We collect ideas for improvements, new features, plans, and pricing on our idea wall and regularly prioritize these with an idea portfolio based on impact on the users and impact on our business. This is how we co-create our backlog for future software development.

Growth
In March 2016, we stopped insisting on credit card details when new users signed up for Smaply. We underestimated how much this change

would affect the signup rate: our new signups per month increased instantly by 1200% - and just two weeks later our servers crashed. A poster in our office reminds us of this day, but we were able to learn from our mistake and set up a new server infrastructure for faster growth.

Lessons learned
Our whole development process is now based on the iterative activities of exploration (talk and work with users), ideation/prototyping (build simple prototypes and test them as soon as possible, and implementation (get it out and directly start testing again). This is part of our company culture and we strongly believe that our success so far is deeply rooted in this approach.

KEY TAKEAWAYS

01 Establish authentic relationships with your users and involve them in your innovation process. Reward them for their ideas and feedback.

02 Create a feeling of ownership among your customers and maintain a close dialogue with your most engaged critics – even if they have bad manners.

03 Implement the idea of an iterative process across your entire team. Make it clear that there is no "final" version of your product. Be prepared for the fact that people don't like that feeling.

04 Accept that you don't know that much about real use cases of your product. Don't rely only on numbers. Ask humans.

05 Stick to your principles. It is essential to talk to people and co-create with them – but you are responsible for the big picture, and for the nifty details.

8.6.4 CASE: CREATING MEASURABLE BUSINESS IMPACT THROUGH PILOTING AND IMPLEMENTING SERVICE DESIGN PROJECTS

Creating a vision for the future: Sustainable, high-quality care for the elderly

AUTHORS

Ingvild Støvring
Service
Designer, Livework

Rune Yndestad Møller
Senior Business
Designer, Livework

Melissa Gates
Communication
Designer, Livework

Marianne Rolfsen
Senior Service
Designer, Livework

live|work

Oslo is facing one of the major global challenges – a rapidly growing aging population who will need some provision of care. The city service providers needed to find ways of managing demand while ensuring that quality is not only maintained but, if possible, improved. They asked Livework to help them define a vision for elderly care in 2025 that would be achievable, sustainable, and inspiring.

The agency approach: The first phase is always "understand"

To complement the council's extensive data, Livework set about gaining insights via qualitative research. We conducted over 40 in-depth interviews with end users, their caregivers, admin staff, and care workers. We also made use of more covert techniques, including shadowing city staff engaged in home visits.

Desk research was also essential to widen our perspective and gain inspiration for different approaches from other sources. We conducted trend analyses in health and elderly care and researched best practices, looking at provisions in other countries. We also conducted an analysis of the economic impact of key needs and triggers, ensuring that service design walked hand in hand with the business perspective.

Developing and testing new approaches

After mapping existing customer journeys and running workshops with various stakeholders to gather further insights and generate ideas, we developed several tools which were integral to the project. The planning tools were used by all the various providers of elderly care, when they were planning their treatments. These enabled them to work across silos, using the same user needs–based tool irrespective of whether they were from the mental health department or the hospital, focused on nutrition or physiotherapy. The tools were designed not just to plan and deliver treatment in the immediate term but to plan and achieve longer-term goals, discussed and defined with the users.

We mapped users' needs on a matrix which clarified areas where needs could be better met, and created further potential customer journeys. A set of nine service principles was developed to inform and guide the future delivery of services.

Piloting was done in parallel with business as usual, testing new service propositions backstage and frontstage, gathering insights from

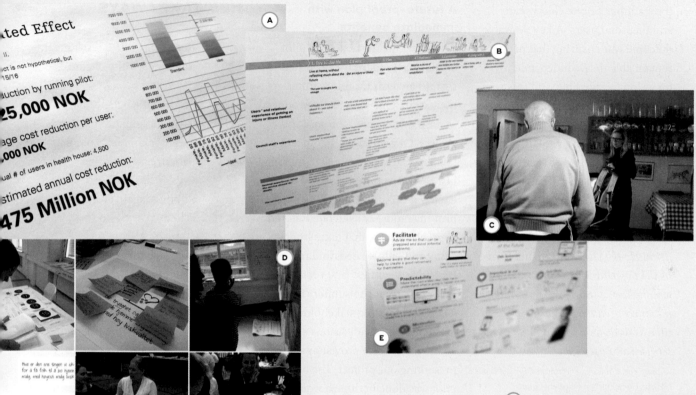

(A) One pilot program alone produced savings that covered the entire cost of the project.

(B) Livework mapped out the customer journeys of the people who used Oslo's elderly care services.

(C) We shadowed city staff who were engaged in home visits to the elderly.

(D) We ran several workshops with various stakeholders to gather insights.

(E) A set of nine service design principles was created to inform and guide delivery of future services.

the staff that deliver elderly care and their end users. A key desirable outcome was ensuring that people remain able to live independently for as long as possible, and this was achieved by designing systems that enable the council to target their services to meet individuals' needs more accurately and efficiently gain the best outcome for both the municipality and the users.

"Putting the user at the center was definitely the right thing to do. It gives us the opportunity to truly work differently in the future, [to] accomplish major cost reductions at the same time as we improve the quality of the services and user experiences."
— *Bjørg Torill Madsen, Director and Project Lead, Nursing Home Agency, Oslo City Council*

A future-proof plan with immediate benefits

Analyzing the impact of the pilot enabled us to make the projected savings analysis for future implementation. One pilot alone produced savings that covered the cost of the project. Of course, the significant financial savings are a big win – but just as importantly, the user experience was reported as being improved: a more considered, tailored approach to care that takes into account individual needs and respects individuals' wishes.

We continue to support the client by attending stakeholder meetings where policy decisions are made about elderly care provision and presenting our project. The original pilot was done in three boroughs and the tools and methods developed are now being shared across the other boroughs that make up the Oslo municipal district.

KEY TAKEAWAYS

 01 Reducing costs doesn't mean reducing quality of care.

 02 Finding the balance between pragmatic solutions and utopian ideals requires patience.

03 Piloting (again and again) is key.

04 How you present your insights and proposals can be as important, if not more so, as the work itself. In this case, having "the numbers" (hard economic data) to back up our work was crucial.

05 The road from having a vision to implementation is long. We are continuing to support the client into the future of implementing services, after the project's "close," because we want to see them succeed.

09
SERVICE DESIGN PROCESS AND MANAGEMENT

Understand, plan, and manage the adaptive and iterative activities of service design.

Expert comments ————————————————————————

Simon Clatworthy Jamin Hegeman Julia Jonas Kathrin Möslein

Giovanni Ruello Francesca Terzi Christof Zürn

09
SERVICE DESIGN
PROCESS AND MANAGEMENT

This chapter also includes

MANAGING ITERATIONS

In this chapter, we'll take an in-depth look at how the core activities of service design – research, ideation, prototyping, and implementation – can be planned and managed as an iterative service design process that fits your project, your stakeholders, and your team. **Here are a few familiar points from Chapter 4,** *The core activities of service design*, **to keep in mind:**

→   **Make sure you solve the right problem before solving the problem right:** Always challenge your initial assumptions. This is what sets design approaches apart: rather than jumping right in – which also often leads to obvious solutions – you first take a step back. You make sure you identify and understand the *right problem* before you move on to solutions.[01]

→   **Think in diamonds:** Divergent and convergent thinking and doing are key when managing a service design process. Which of the activities or methods you use are divergent or convergent? What is the required mindset in terms of divergent and convergent thinking? Which mode should you be in just now?[02]

→   **Iterate and adapt:** The service design process is never a linear process. In fact, it's quite the opposite.

A service design process always needs to be explorative and iterative. You have to adapt to what you learn along the way, building on a series of more or less repeating, deepening, explorative loops: iterations. Practically, this means creating a rhythm of planning, doing, reflecting, then re-planning.[03]

→   **Look beyond the individual tools and methods:** The service design process is more than a simple combination of its individual parts. Continuously reflect: How do the individual activities play together? How does the quality of the output of one activity affect the following activities? How can you build an overarching project structure that creates trust in the process but also creates predictability for your organization without giving up on the iterative and explorative principles?[04]

→   **Now, build your own:** This is a process framework, not a step-by-step checklist. We challenge you to build your own customized service design process and give it a go. And we also challenge you to stay critical of your own process. Always ask yourself: What worked? What didn't work? Why didn't it work? How might we do it better next time?[05]

01   See 4.3.2, *Make sure to solve the right problem before solving the problem right.*

02   See 4.3.1, *Divergent and convergent thinking and doing.*

03   See the textbox *Adapt and iterate forward* in 4.4.

04   See 4.3.3, *All design processes are alike …and different.*

05   See 4.2, *A toolkit to design your own process.*

9.1 UNDERSTANDING THE SERVICE DESIGN PROCESS: A FAST-FORWARD EXAMPLE

Let's revisit the core service design activities in a short exemplary walkthrough to get a better feel for how they connect and work together. Imagine you have discovered that the customer experience feedback rating (insert your favorite KPI here) of your business unit has dropped substantially. Your boss is worried and triggers a project within your organization to address the issue, and you decide to use a service design approach to tackle the project. Here is one path you might take.

Planning and preparation

To get started, you put together a rationale for *why you have chosen service design*.[01] You find a suitable management sponsor and a great team, securing you the necessary organizational support and *management buy-in*.[02] After a careful inquiry and analysis of the *project stakeholders and the wider ecosystem*[03] and their expectations for the project, you start *planning a service design process*[04] for them as well as for your core project team, adapting the approach to the context and the realities of your people, organization, and industry. You put in place an initial management and communication structure

to navigate and *manage the service design process*[05] on a daily basis and then officially kick off the project. You are now ready to dive into the content work.

Research[06]

Your first challenge is that the change in your feedback rating by itself does not tell you *why* it went wrong. So clearly, you need to look deeper, beyond the numbers. You ask yourself: What do I need to learn? What do I need to find out? What is my *research question*?[07] Then further: *Where* and *how* can I answer my research question? *Whom* do I need to talk to or work with?[08]

A great way to do all this is to go and find out, to leave the safe haven of the meeting room and get in touch with reality as quickly and as much as possible. To avoid a one-sided or biased approach, you use a mixture of different research methods; you might *try the service yourself*,[09] *observe*,[10] and *do interviews*[11] with customers, frontline staff, management – talk to as many stakeholders as possible. And don't forget your

01 See Chapter 1, *Why service design?*, for inspiration.

02 See Chapter 12, *Embedding service design in organizations*, for more information on how to establish service design inside your organization beyond management buy-in, raising awareness, and building up proficiency.

03 See 9.2.3, *Project team and stakeholders*.

04 See 9.2, *Planning for a service design process*.

05 See 9.3, *Managing the service design process*.

06 See Chapter 5, *Research*.

07 See 5.1.1, *Research scope and research question*.

08 See 5.1.1, *Research scope and research question* and 5.1.2, *Research planning*.

09 For example, see *Self-ethnographic approaches: Autoethnography* in 5.2.

10 See *Participant observation* in 5.2 and *Non-participant observation* in 5.2.

11 See *Contextual interview* in 5.2.

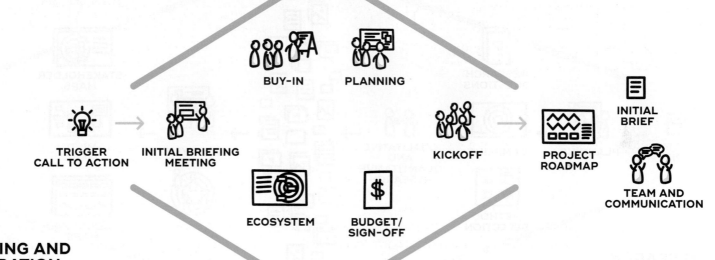

PLANNING AND PREPARATION

Getting a project off the ground

basic *desk research*:[12] Have any of your questions been answered before? Is there any existing data you could use to inform your research? Who are the giants whose shoulders you can stand on?

These activities provide you with a wealth of material about the initial challenge and your initial research questions – a lot of *real-world data*[13] to challenge your assumptions. You might have gathered photo and video footage from interviews or observations, original quotes from users and staff about pain points with an existing situation, basic step-by-step documentation

of their service experiences, deep knowledge about the context in which the user or customer is experiencing your service or product[14] (whether physical or digital), and so on.

However, this big pile of data and inspiration can be overwhelming. To make it accessible and manageable you need to break it down. One common way to do this is to create a *research wall*[15] and organize the data into mind maps (after you have identified useful categories[16]),

---

12 See *Preparatory research* and *Secondary research* in 5.2.

13 See *Data triangulation* in 5.1.3.

14 The term "products" describes anything a company offers – no matter if this is tangible or not. In academia, products are often divided into goods and services. However, products are usually bundles of services and physical/digital products. As "goods" is colloquially understood as referring to something tangible, we prefer to speak of the term physical/digital products. Read more on this in the textbox *Service-dominant logic* in 2.5.

15 See *Building a research wall* in 5.3.

16 Structuring the data using project-specific frameworks that emerge from the data itself can help you to understand the situation better and give you a fresh eye for the actual problem you need to solve.

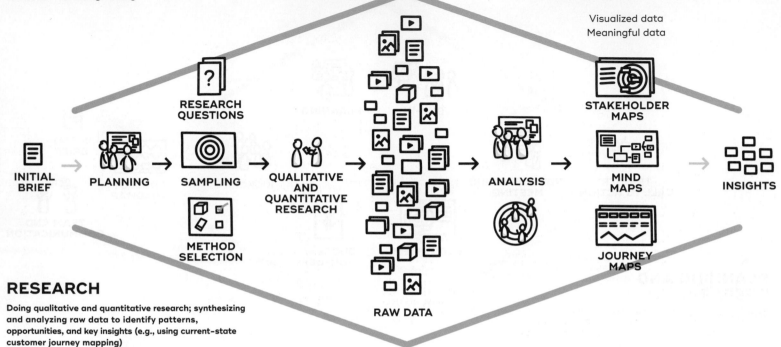

Visualized data
Meaningful data

RESEARCH
QUESTIONS

STAKEHOLDER
MAPS

INITIAL
BRIEF

PLANNING

SAMPLING

QUALITATIVE
AND
QUANTITATIVE
RESEARCH

ANALYSIS

MIND
MAPS

INSIGHTS

METHOD
SELECTION

JOURNEY
MAPS

RAW DATA

RESEARCH

Doing qualitative and quantitative research; synthesizing and analyzing raw data to identify patterns, opportunities, and key insights (e.g., using current-state customer journey mapping)

or to sort the material into models like *current-state system maps*[01] or *journey maps*.[02] Here, journey maps visualize the key experiences found during research, and help you to identify critical steps in each journey.

After you have had a hard look at all the data, you try to find patterns in your data: What are the actual needs, pain points, or wishes of the people involved? What are your *key insights*[03] about your users or customers that might help you to create a great service? What are

the underlying (business) problems and opportunities? But also: what might be better questions?

You might have to collect some more data to fill in those gaps, refining your insights or creating even more. After a few research loops, the newest data does not bring additional insights to your research questions – and you move on.

You can now use this knowledge to reframe your initial challenge statement(s), thus making sure that you are solving the right problem and addressing the right opportunities.

01 See *Mapping systems* in 5.3.
02 See *Mapping journeys* in 5.3.
03 See *Developing key insights* in 5.3.

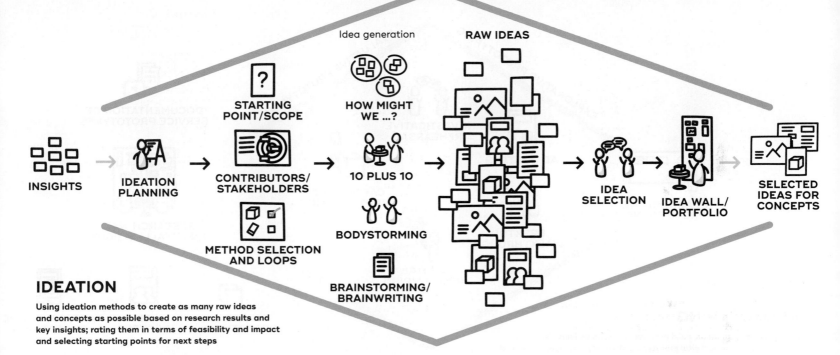

Idea generation

RAW IDEAS

STARTING POINT/SCOPE

HOW MIGHT WE ...?

10 PLUS 10

BODYSTORMING

BRAINSTORMING/ BRAINWRITING

INSIGHTS

IDEATION PLANNING

CONTRIBUTORS/ STAKEHOLDERS

METHOD SELECTION AND LOOPS

IDEA SELECTION

IDEA WALL/ PORTFOLIO

SELECTED IDEAS FOR CONCEPTS

IDEATION

Using ideation methods to create as many raw ideas and concepts as possible based on research results and key insights; rating them in terms of feasibility and impact and selecting starting points for next steps

Ideation[04]

During your research activities, you have consciously restricted yourself to exploring the problem space. Now that you have identified a real opportunity or challenge, you can move into solution space.

Your key question now is: how can I generate as many ideas as possible to maximize my chances of success? In order to achieve this, you look at the problem and assess *who you need to invite*[05] to contribute and co-create. And

then you choose a matching mix of methods to leverage the participants' knowledge and skills. For example, you break down your challenge into a set of trigger questions (*"How might we ...?"*)[06] and use *brainstorming or brainwriting,*[07] *10 plus 10 sketching,*[08] and *bodystorming*[09] to generate many, many, many ideas. At this point, judgment (e.g., in terms of feasibility) is momentarily deferred to maximize your output during this stage.

04 See Chapter 6, *Ideation*.

05 Ownership is key. As a rule of thumb, invite people who know about it, who have to do it, or who can stop it. See 9.2.3, *Project team and stakeholders*, for more details.

06 See *"How might we ...?" questions from insights* in 6.4.

07 See *Brainstorming and brainwriting* in 6.4.

08 See *10 plus 10* in 6.4.

09 See *Investigative rehearsal* in 7.2.

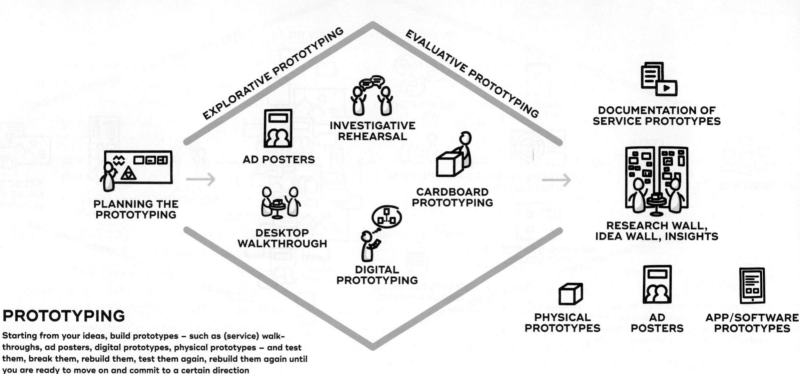

EXPLORATIVE PROTOTYPING

EVALUATIVE PROTOTYPING

INVESTIGATIVE REHEARSAL

AD POSTERS

DOCUMENTATION OF SERVICE PROTOTYPES

CARDBOARD PROTOTYPING

PLANNING THE PROTOTYPING

DESKTOP WALKTHROUGH

DIGITAL PROTOTYPING

RESEARCH WALL, IDEA WALL, INSIGHTS

PHYSICAL PROTOTYPES

AD POSTERS

APP/SOFTWARE PROTOTYPES

PROTOTYPING

Starting from your ideas, build prototypes – such as (service) walk-throughs, ad posters, digital prototypes, physical prototypes – and test them, break them, rebuild them, test them again, rebuild them again until you are ready to move on and commit to a certain direction

The next step is to work through all of those ideas and evaluate which ones should be developed further. One method that can help you to do this with a large number of concepts is the *idea portfolio*,[01] where all concepts are rated by two simple criteria[02] – often their impact on customer experience and their feasibility.

The idea portfolio helps your team to focus their discussions and supports the *decision-making*[03] process. Which ones are the concepts you would like to take forward and explore more deeply?

01 See *Idea portfolio* in 6.4.

02 Note that while the criteria mentioned here have proven to be useful, it often is the discussion you have while using the tool that is as important as the tool itself. Also, those criteria might change depending on your project. See *Idea portfolio* in 6.4 for more details.

03 See 6.3.3, *Idea selection*, or 6.2, *Decisions*, for some background on decision making and taking.

Prototyping[04]

You now have some promising ideas or concepts. That's great, right? The problem is that up until now, all those ideas live in the Land of Ideas – where everything works.

The bad news is, *we* do not live in the Land of Ideas, and neither do our customers. We need to face (business) reality. Thus, you take your ideas and concepts into the real world by prototyping and testing assumptions with real users and other stakeholders before it gets too expensive. A design process aims to find out what works and what does not as early in the process as possible. This makes the design process not only faster, but also more cost effective.

You might start by creating *explorative prototypes*[05] to better understand the important aspects and implications of an idea. You might do some *evaluative prototyping*[06] (e.g., to validate your core value proposition). For both these approaches, you will employ tools like *(service) walkthroughs,*[07] *service advertisements,*[08] *digital prototypes,*[09] or *cardboard prototypes.*[10] You build, use, and learn from your prototypes, you break them, you rebuild them again. You open new doors and along the way create many valuable insights about your future service, but also you develop much better questions.

💬 **EXPERT TIP**

"Try prototyping multiple touchpoints together to show the value of design-ing across channels and, likely, silos."

— Jamin Hegeman

Implementation[11]

After some iterations, you have achieved a handful of working prototypes supported by working business cases and positive feedback from actual users. The activities during implementation now depend heavily on your project and what exactly you need to implement. Do you need to *change internal or external operative processes, organizational structures, or procedures?*[12] Do you need to *develop and roll out software?*[13] Do you have to *develop and produce physical products*[14] or *change spaces and architecture?*[15] Or do you need to implement a mix of all of those measures in parallel?

The answers to these questions will guide the methodologies you apply during your implementation activities. Implementation will often involve a lot more people starting to work on the project. And also, as every practical aspect of the service has to be created, tested, and implemented, there still is a lot of conceptual and design work left. This tends to take over the major share of a project.[16] In itself implementation also includes research, ideation, and prototyping. Often the only difference is which stakeholders are involved, as you start working with real employees on real stages with more depth and fidelity than before.

---

04 See Chapter 7, *Prototyping.*

05 See *Prototyping to explore* in 7.1.1.

06 See *Prototyping to evaluate* in 7.1.1.

07 See *Investigative rehearsal* in 7.2 for an example of a full-sized walkthrough variant and *Desktop walkthrough* in 7.2 for a scale variant.

08 See *Service advertisement* in 7.2.

09 For more on common methods for prototyping digital artifacts and software see, for example, *Paper prototyping, Interactive click modeling,* and *Wireframing* in 7.2.

10 See *Cardboard prototyping* in 7.2.

11 See Chapter 8, *Implementation.*

12 Also see 8.2, *Service design and change management.*

13 See 8.3, *Service design and software development.*

14 See 8.4, *Service design and product management.*

15 See 8.5, *Service design and architecture.*

16 While your mileage might vary, many service design projects often experience a strong focus on change management and training during implementation.

Iterations

Your prototyping activities create new insights and questions which make you step back again and initiate further iteration. You do some more research on those questions. You take on some of the new insights for more ideation. And you do more prototyping to explore and evaluate those new concepts further, until you can filter down to solutions you want move on with.

Incidentally, the same can happen within or after any of your service design activities. Your ideation activities might not just prepare ground for prototyping but also uncover new topics and new directions for more research. Your research might reveal ideas that you take to prototyping straight away, but also give you more hypotheses and questions. And the same thing happens during implementation activities as you get concrete on so many levels.[01]

Almost any activity can create new insights and questions which make you step back again and initiate further iteration.

Another important aspect is that you are not trying to iterate on one *single concept* or *early prototype* that you then implement in a long and expensive implementation project. This puts a lot of pressure on that concept – and in turn on your project team. Instead, you try to avoid putting all your eggs in one basket. You keep a selected range of options in the game until you can make a reliable enough decision about which ones to take forward.[02] This not only reduces risk but also maximizes learning and thus the quality of your design. ◄

01 You can find iterations within almost any scope of the service design process. Iterations might happen within a method (e.g. iterating a customer journey to make it better), within a core activity (e.g. research or ideation loops), or between core activities, sprints, or even projects. See 9.2.4, *Structure: Project, iterations, and activities,* for more details on different iterative structures for your own service design process.

02 Also see 9.2.5, *Multitracking.*

9.2 PLANNING FOR A SERVICE DESIGN PROCESS

In this book, there is a conscious distinction between "planning *of*" and "planning *for*" a service design process or project. We usually talk about "planning *for*" because there are many details and activities in a service design project that you can prepare for, but cannot plan with precision beforehand. You will notice, however, that it is possible to set and keep milestones and – at the same time – keep an open mind to adapt the project as you go along. The planning of a service design project is actually the first iteration of your service design project.

When planning for your service design process, your activities must fit within given business constraints, as you always have to consider how to best allocate time, money, and human resources within the project.[03] Specifically, planning for a service design process includes various activities which we will explore further in the following sections:

→   Clarifying the brief
     (including purpose, scope, and context)
→   Doing some preparatory research
     (to inform your planning process)

→   Making decisions about project team and stake-holders, project structure (i.e., planned iterations and activities), project phases and milestones, outputs and outcomes, multitracking, documentation, budgeting and mindsets, principles, and style

Keep in mind that you might not need all of these, and you might not need them in this order. This is not a step-by-step manual but more a checklist to ask the right questions when planning for your process.

9.2.1   Brief: Purpose, scope, and context

The brief defines the actual starting point of your project and tries to capture the explicitly defined or implicitly assumed overall expectations about purpose, context, scope, and objectives. This also includes boundary conditions for the project in terms of budget, time, and other resources (and beyond). Often, however, you will not be approached with a perfect brief. Rather, people might have identified more of a rough starting point; an unmet need, a wish, a problem, or a seemingly brilliant idea like "We need to reduce the call volume in the call center by 10%," "Develop that new service idea," "We have this new technology, come up with something

03   In this book, we often speak about the service design process or service design projects almost interchangeably. In response to that, service designer and book contributor Matt Edgar argued that calling your service design work a "project" could limit its impact. Instead, we might want to consider terms like "engagement," "intervention," or "activity" to better reflect service design's formative, iterative, and open-ended potential through the whole service lifecycle. Edgar, M. (2016, October 11). Personal interview.

💬 EXPERT TIP

"Exploring the brief together with the project sponsor is important, since you can get a good feeling of both expectations and possibilities. Sometimes this can lead to the rewriting and rescoping of a brief."

– Simon Clatworthy

💬 EXPERT TIP

"Every project needs a scope. But the research and ideation should go beyond this scope, otherwise you may lose the most important parts."

– Christof Zürn

A design process does not end with a concept!

The later phases in the service design process are quite often neglected or misunderstood. Just to be clear. "It ain't over 'til it's over"[01] – a service design project does not end with a concept or a shiny presentation but with an implemented and operational service.

There is sometimes a misunderstanding when concept-specialist service design agencies deliver only research and concept work as part of a client's overall project. The agency will interpret the creation of the concepts as their own implementation stage, while the client organization still sees itself in the conceptual or prototyping stage.

It is important to keep in mind that a full service design project usually begins with an initial brief, and while the role of the service designer might change after the implementation of an initial solution, the iterations continue well beyond.[02] Then, the operations team is often on board and is scaling and adapting the solution to the ever-changing circumstances of the day-to-day business. More and more, service design becomes an ongoing activity embedded in the organization.[03] ◄

01 As heard on Lenny Kravitz (1991). *Mama Said* [CD]. Virgin.

02 See 7.3.3, *Case: Enabling staff and stakeholders to prototype for continuous evolution,* for an example of how staff can be enabled to prototype by themselves, with no need for in-depth designer skills.

03 See *How to set up service design as an ongoing activity in an organization* in 12.4.

so we can sell it," "Create new innovative business ideas," "Fix the 20% drop in our NPS score," "Improve the conversion rate of our online sales channel," "Redesign the employee onboarding," and so on. It usually is a good idea to clarify those together with the project sponsor and your team so everybody has a clear understanding:

→ **Purpose:** Why do we want to work on this challenge? Where does the challenge come from?

→ **Scope/objectives:** What do we want to achieve? What do we want to avoid?

→ **Context:** What is the context in which we want to achieve this? Where and when should the project happen?

→ **Resources:** What is the budget available? Who needs to be involved? Who will be able to contribute? What tools or materials are available?

→ **Time:** What are the expectations in terms of milestones and deadlines?

9.2.2 Preparatory research

Set up one brief iteration of preparatory research[04] to get a better feel for the size and complexity of the project, the

04 See *Desk research* and *Preparatory research* in 5.2.

ecosystem,[05] and potential research and development directions. This bit of research should deepen your insights about the content challenge as well as your understanding of the context, perceptions, and internal conflicts, or interplays that may emerge during the overall project.

Data collection for planning

Start with the inputs from the initial brief and do a quick brainstorm of potential research questions. It is not necessary to present them in a beautiful way, as they will only serve to support your planning session.

Select a couple of key questions and start your preparatory research sessions. It is important to remind yourself that this is not yet about *doing the research* and solving the challenge but *planning your research* and the rest of your service design process. You need to gather just enough data and insights to be able to set up a workable process structure.

If you have a bit more time for your planning, you can also add data from additional methods that deliver fast first results – for example, *current-state stakeholder mapping*, *secondary research*, *autoethnography*, *online ethnography*, or first *(contextual) interviews*.[06]

Assessment of potential development directions

Based on the data from your preparatory research, you should also create a first assessment of potential development directions. This can give you a sense of what you need to work on as likely outputs and outcomes, as well as whom you might need to involve during ideation, prototyping, and implementation. Of course, this can and will change as you go through your project, but it is important to have this first idea to discuss and allocate reasonable budgets, time, and resources. Hence, no matter what you find (or don't find, for that matter), it is key to truthfully acknowledge the level of uncertainty with respect to potential *types of solutions*. For example, if you know your project scope involves updating an existing app, you can plan and budget in the appropriate resources from your UX and development teams. But if you cannot yet tell what type of solution you will be implementing, it might be helpful to plan and budget for a pilot project, giving you the time and resources to clarify more concrete development directions first.

9.2.3   Project team and stakeholders

Assess who might be affected by your project and whom you need to include in which activity. This should be based on the insights from your brief as well as on your preparatory research and any initial planning efforts. "Where does the project brief come from?" and "Who needs to implement this?" are just two important questions you should always ask yourself when you start a project in an organization. You might, for example, learn about similar projects and identify people who were previously involved. They might be able to assist you in selecting your project team and managing important stakeholders.

💬 **EXPERT TIP**

"Consider visualizing your stakeholder map the same way you might create an ecosystem map. Show the relationship between stakeholders to understand whom to include during different parts of the process."

– Jamin Hegeman

05 See *Mapping systems* in 5.3 and 3.4.3, *Ecosystem maps*.
06 See *Secondary research*, *Autoethnography*, *Online ethnography*, and *Contextual interviews* in 5.2 and *Mapping systems* in 5.3.

Dealing with constraints

The more freedom you have, the more structure you need![01]

When planning and managing a project, you will often be hit by constraints. You will work with limited resources (especially budget or access to people), with tough deadlines and an ambitious scope or objectives. To make things worse, those constraints will influence each other. If you want to be cheap and fast, you might have to limit your project's scope or quality. If you need to achieve an ambitious scope at high quality, it won't be cheap or fast. The rule of thumb is that you can fix one or two of these constraints, but need to stay flexible on at least one of them.[02]

In many traditional projects the scope is fixed. That works well if the scope is built around a deterministic challenge. But every time you discover it is not as defined as you thought, the approach becomes painful. You can either hurriedly add more resources in an attempt to fix it (making it more expensive), or you might have to shift the delivery date (putting a dent in your reputation as a project manager).

Specifically, this approach does not work for service design, where you often challenge and change the scope of a project right from the start ("Make sure you solve the right problem before solving the problem right").

This poses a new problem: if you are dealing with complex challenges it is now very easy to lose track of all the different insights, opportunities, or ideas. You will soon waste a lot of time and resources, and your team might start to pull in different directions.

Keeping the scope variable adds a high degree of freedom to your project that needs to be managed very carefully. You will need to add structure which will allow for the necessary freedom in scope while letting you plan and manage the process. One proven model is the agile approach to planning, with a clear planned iteration or sprint structure.[03] This fixes both time and constraints, allowing you to work efficiently until your scope becomes more defined. ◄

---

01 Interestingly, this parallels what we find with seasoned improvisers, jazz musicians, or teachers: "Without the structure you do not have improvisation, you have anarchy or indulgence. Without the freedom you have suffocation." See Jackson, P. Z. (1995). "Improvisation in Training: Freedom within Corporate Structures." *Journal of European Industrial Training*, 19(4), 25-28.

02 See 9.5.1, *Case: Creating repeatable processes to continually improve services and experiences at massive scale*, for a great example of accepting that services and experiences will never be perfect, but can be continually improved – with constraints on an Olympic scale.

03 You can read more on how to embed service design in organizations with a sprint structure in 12.4, *Design sprints*.

04 Graphic adapted from Aljaber, T. (n.d.). "The Iron Triangle of Planning," at *https://www.atlassian.com/agile/agile-iron-triangle*.

PROJECT TRIANGLE
UPSIDE DOWN

Traditional project triangle ("iron triangle," on the left) versus agile, adaptive triangle.
Service design tends to work with the latter but it is important to stay adaptive and choose
the appropriate model at any given stage.[04]

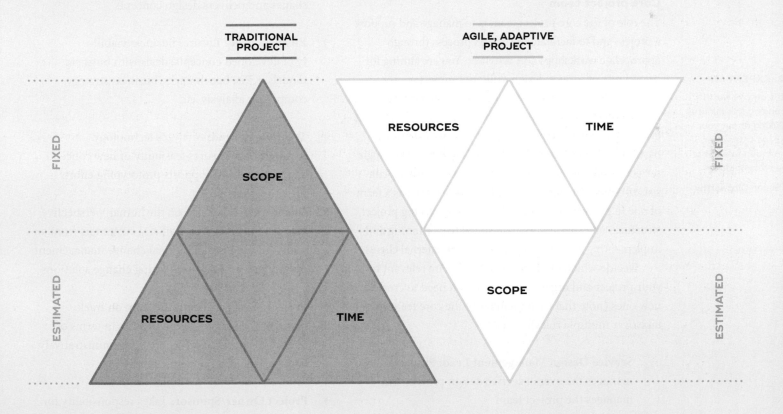

TRADITIONAL
PROJECT

AGILE, ADAPTIVE
PROJECT

FIXED

ESTIMATED

SCOPE

RESOURCES   TIME

RESOURCES   TIME

SCOPE

FIXED

ESTIMATED

In many ways, all the people on your project are the customers of your service design process. Reflect on their skills, needs, and pain points and design the process for them. Your design process should be there to support them and to leverage their knowledge, skills, and talents.

Core project team

The role of the core project team is to manage and support a project and to facilitate the design process through appropriate workshops and activities. You are aiming for a good mix of service design skills and subject matter expertise. However, not everybody on the core project team needs to be an expert in service design. Similarly, not everybody needs to be an expert in your industry or to have a deep knowledge of your organization.[01] For a single service design project, the core project team usually consists of a handful of people, but it can be as small as a team of one (e.g., working as a coach within an existing project structure) or as big as a football squad (e.g., running and implementing a project for an internal or external client).

Decide which of the following roles are relevant to your project and organization, or if you need to create new ones (note that each member of the core team might take over multiple roles):

→ **Service Design Management Lead:** Plans and manages the overall service design process and manages the project team

01 Also see 12.2.1, *The core service design team.*

→ **Facilitation Lead:** Ensures continuous feedback and learning, facilitates team collaboration, and provides design support or facilitation of co-creation workshops

→ **(Service) Design Lead:** Focuses on content and quality of service design outputs and deliverables; shapes and delivers design concepts

→ **Business Lead:** Ensures business viability of developed concepts; deals with business models, KPIs, benchmarks, business strategy, competitor analysis, etc.

→ **Technology Lead:** Analyzes technology requirements, ensures feasibility of new concepts, and manages and supports prototyping efforts

→ **Change Lead:** Focuses on the human perspective; assesses the impact on staff and customers from an individual and organizational change management perspective, and develops fitting change solutions

→ **Project Manager:** Keeps the team on track; manages the service design process in terms of budget, deadlines, and reporting; administratively backs up the project team

→ **Project Owner/Sponsor:** Takes responsibility for strategic direction and budget – the person who assumes this role is often a key decision maker

Extended project team

Most projects are also supported by an extended project team: a larger group of people with specific competencies that can be involved in specific sections or activities within the project.[02] Hence, the team size of an extended project team can vary over time and even change from workshop to workshop. Consider including:[03]

→   An internal selection of cross-functional members to ensure a holistic perspective.

→   External method or subject matter experts to manage the competencies that your organization does not have (e.g., ethnography, UX, change management, architecture, etc.).

→   Departments and/or external stakeholders that are responsible for earlier or later parts of your project, but also involved in daily operations.

→   Key decision makers from your organization. The success of your project might not just depend on the quality of your output but also on the hierarchical position of the decision makers who support it. Put careful thought into how to integrate them closely into your project team from the beginning.[04]

→   Users or customers, as ambassadors of their stakeholder group. This allows quick research and prototyping without a lot of planning.

→   Generally, any people who are directly affected by the project, or who have the power to stop it.

It is crucial that you involve affected staff as early as possible in the design process of their future daily work routines. This makes them co-owners of the new solution, a status which will help implementation and acceptance.

9.2.4   Structure: Project, iterations, and activities

Your project structure lays out how you want to create and advance the expected outputs and outcomes as defined in your brief.

Each higher-level iteration involves at least some activities of research, ideation, and prototyping. Just like in build-measure-learn cycles,[05] you create potential solutions in the shape of prototypes or implemented services, use them, and systematically learn from them. This implies that you most likely need to adapt your original planning or even change as you go along.

02   Also see 12.2.2, *The extended project team.*

03   Convincing people to contribute can be a challenge. See *Onboarding and communicating with co-creators* in 9.3.2 for more on how to address common questions stakeholders have when they join a new project.

04   When important stakeholders are pushing their own ideas into a project, you might experience the *ugly baby* bias: everybody says, "I'm not going to be the one who tells our CFO that her baby is ugly." One way to address this is to embrace their ideas, but then – as soon as possible – adapt your plan to push them into a prototype and test them with real users. The stakeholders then see their concepts fail with their own eyes (or succeed, but then it was you and your team that needed that validation).

05   Build-measure-learn cycles can be traced back at least as far as Galileo and the dawn of the scientific method, with incarnations like the Deming cycle from the 1950s or the more recent Lean Startup. See Moen, R. (2009). "Foundation and History of the PDSA Cycle," Ries, E. (2011) and *The Lean Startup: How Today's Entrepreneurs Use Continuous Innovation to Create Radically Successful Businesses.* Crown Books.

(Co-)team building

It is important to decide how to prepare your (core) project team to work together. Should this cooperation be planned or emergent? Should the team be involved in and co-create process, strategy, planning, management, and execution? Here are a few points to consider when you are aiming for a great team:[01]

→ Create a safe (team) space
To be able to adopt this new way of thinking and doing, decide how you can create a (psychological) safe space for each individual on your team – as well as for your team within your organization.[02]

→ Give structure and orientation
Always clearly explain the goals, background, and vision of the project when onboarding new team members so they can understand their role and the impact of their contributions to the project and the bigger organization.[03] Decide how to (co)create and share project plans/ roadmaps and how you are going to update them as you go along. Also decide on roles and clarify interdependencies within the team: Who is going to be responsible for what? Are there interdependencies between different team members? How will you communicate who is working on what at any given time?

→ Decide on how you work and how you decide
Consider sharing personal preferences and work styles within the team and adapting your planning accordingly. To reduce potential problems during the later process, decide early on how you are going to make decisions or resolve conflicts. This includes decisions on the content as well as decisions on the team and the way you work.[04]

→ Reflect and learn
Decide how to establish a clear and constant feedback routine within your team on (a) the work you are doing[05] and (b) how you are doing the work.[06] Learn from the feedback and act upon it. Short feedback cycles make sure that problems are addressed early enough, before they hurt. Consider keeping a record of your lessons learned.

→ Co-create a suitable kickoff
Especially with new teams, the first shared steps can be crucial. Team culture, once set, can be hard to change. Take your time to address and design those first steps in your project accordingly. Consider how co-creative project planning sessions or kickoff workshops can be used to share expectations,[07] create buy-in, establish trust, and ignite motivation within your (core) team.[08] ◄

---

01 The points here are presented from a service design perspective. For a great resource on building effective teams, check out Duhigg, C. (2016). "What Google Learned from Its Quest to Build the Perfect Team." *The New York Times Magazine.* See also re:Work (n.d.). "Guide: Understand Team Effectiveness." at *https://rework.withgoogle.com/guides/understanding-team-effectiveness/ steps/introduction.*

02 See 10.3.4, *Creating a safe space,* to learn more about the core principles of creating a safe space in the context of facilitation.

03 See *Onboarding co-creators* in 9.3.2.

04 See 6.3.3, *Idea selection,* or 6.2, *Decisions,* for some background on decision making and taking.

05 See *Content reviews* in 9.3.3.

06 See *Team retrospectives* in 9.3.3 as well as the textbox *The daily stand-up* in 9.3.1.

07 This will also allow you to acknowledge and share fears, hopes, and expectations about the project and individual performance early on.

08 Refer to Chapter 10, *Facilitating workshops,* when designing the perfect kickoff.

PLANNED ITERATIONS

Consider breaking up your project into a planned sequence of smaller projects to deal with uncertainty and reduce the risk involved.

Breaking up your project

It can be helpful to break up your project into a planned sequence of smaller projects to deal with uncertainty and reduce the risk involved. Sometimes a short but well-prepared iteration like a five-day service design sprint can be enough to have a great impact on your results.[09] This structure introduces clear points for reflection and decision in between projects that allow you to stop a certain development direction early if necessary.[10]

The different projects can also put a different emphasis on certain service design activities compared to others. The following options are certainly not a complete list, but might help to give you some basic orientation:

→ **Strategic research and innovation projects**

If you are quite far forward in your innovation funnel, you might want to set up a strategic research project. Strategic research and innovation projects are usually not intended for implementation, but instead help to create meaningful starting points for more incubation, or implementation-oriented service design projects. Their main focus is clearly on research even though they end with a first couple of steps into solution space – for example, creating validated opportunity areas, lighthouse concepts on a prioritized idea portfolio, and first early communication prototypes to make those concepts more tangible.

→ **Incubation projects**

If you are trying to explore and validate the market potential of one or more concepts, it makes sense to split your project into a sequence of incubation projects with growing budgets and resources. Incubation projects have a strong focus on experience prototyping, which delivers real data about the risks and market potential of each string of concepts.

→ **Implementation projects**

If the solution space is sufficiently defined, you can plan straight for prototyping and implementation in a series

💬 **COMMENT**

"Experiments and pilot projects truly matter: they can be a starting point for larger innovation initiatives [and] provide a fruitful context for testing tools, exploring processes, or experiencing new models of value creation. Learning from piloting can be a powerful driver for change in organizations and markets!"

– Kathrin Möslein

09 See 9.5.3, *Case: Using a five-day service design sprint to create a shared cross-channel strategy.*

10 Often you will observe a reluctance in organizations to kill projects. One of the reasons is that there are many stakeholders who might feel they will lose face, because they started the project it in the first place or because they invested time and resources. Breaking up a project from the start makes this decision easier, as it is clear that there will be decision points coming up. Also, the team will be able to reach a feeling of closure as the previous project has officially been finished.

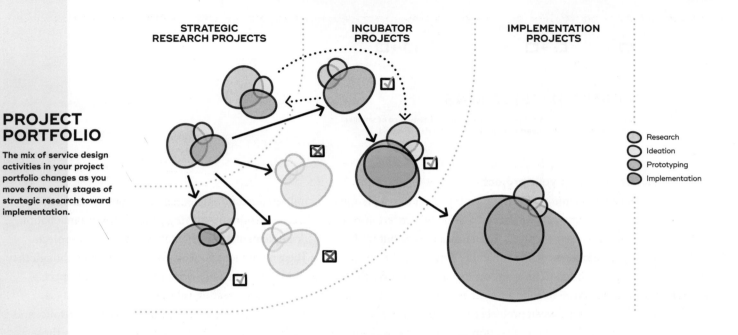

**STRATEGIC
RESEARCH PROJECTS**

**INCUBATOR
PROJECTS**

**IMPLEMENTATION
PROJECTS**

PROJECT PORTFOLIO

The mix of service design activities in your project portfolio changes as you move from early stages of strategic research toward implementation.

- Research
- Ideation
- Prototyping
- Implementation

of iterations within one project. Even though there still needs to be a strong emphasis on research and prototyping at the beginning, over the whole of the project most of the time and resources will go into implementation activities.

If you cannot yet see the shape of a potential solution,[01] there is no way you can safely create a sound implementation plan or project. This would depend too much on the intermediate results of your research and prototyping activities. Start with a strategic research/innovation project or incubation project first.

Planned iterations

Within your project, *planned iterations* are iterations you promise to do and deliver on time and within budget/resources.[02] Each planned iteration consists of three parts:

1 Iteration planning
2 Service design activities
3 Reflection on content and process

Planned iterations are the predictable timeboxes you set up for your design activities – a safe space to do, learn,

---

01 This does not mean you need to know what the exact solution will be. It only means, for example, that you know that you will need to build an app for a specific system, or create a change initiative within a certain part of the organization, so you can roughly plan for software development resources or change management skills.

02 See 12.4, *Design s*, for an overview of how planned iterations can be used within design sprints to go beyond individual projects.

When to involve service design experts

BY GIOVANNI RUELLO

At Bosch, a "user experience relevance check" must be performed before starting any standard development process. This assessment by project managers is mandatory whatever the goal of the project (services or products, whether physical or digital). If the result of the check reveals relevance to user experience, design experts are engaged in order to identify activities that can be executed as an integrated UX or service design project.

The design team has first talks with the specific division in order to understand the scope of the "technical" project and identify user-centered design activities that could be executed as "integrated" UX or service design project.

Such activities are categorized as "user experience design" or "service design" projects. In order to prevent a clash of working cultures, mindset, or terminology, the design team is free to decide on a different label and just refer to the scope as "improvement of the experience," no matter if the project is concerned with the use of new products and services or the establishment of a customer relationship. This re-labeling is not just related to the terminology, but also reflected in the activities and tools used in the design phase.

While executing the project, the core design team might prefer to add the user perspective on top of established production methods, rather than imposing specific design frameworks. In this case, elements of service blueprinting, stakeholder mapping, and value mapping can be combined with typical product or software development processes. They can be visualized together as "user or empathy enhanced tools." For example, instead of a customer journey, the design team could develop a sequence of user stories that are connected to a journey but are close to our customer's working processes and therefore easier to grasp and more actionable. By doing so, it is possible to provide non-designers a better understanding of the product lifecycle, process dependencies, and stakeholder synergies needed to achieve specific targets along the process phases, as well as the ultimate goal. ◄

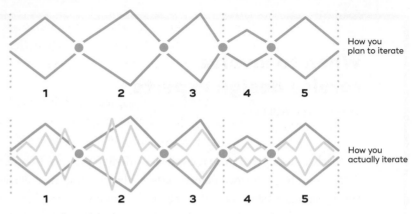

How you
plan to iterate

How you
actually iterate

The Squiggle:[01] **This famous illustration shows how people can experience the design process as strange, almost chaotic. Using planned iterations helps to bring a solid structure but at the same time leaves enough space for exploration.**

Planned versus actual iterations: Planned iterations create a formalized uber-structure for planning, service design activities, and reflection to stay iterative and adaptive at all stages of your service design process.

and adapt. They are the primary iterations you need to focus on during your planning activities as they also define ahead of time when you will invite stakeholders from outside the project team for co-creation and decision making. A prominent example of planned iterations is the sprint structure you find in agile software development methodologies like Scrum.[01]

With planned iterations, you create a formalized uber-structure which establishes a set rhythm of planning, service design activities, and reflection to stay iterative and adaptive within your service design process. This keeps your team on track, and especially helps stakeholders who are not accustomed to this way of working.

Still, people who are experiencing service design for the first time (or looking in from the outside) can perceive it as arbitrary and almost chaotic. "Explorative and iterative work" is often misunderstood as "playing around and doing what you want." Planned iterations help you to actively address and manage this perception.

The amount of freedom – or "wiggle room" – within your planned iterations depends on the experience of your design team. If you are working with inexperienced designers or an interdisciplinary team not accustomed to this way of working, keep the planned iterations tight and closely coach them through them until they pick it up.[03]

01 Newman, D. (2010). "The Squiggle of Design," at *http://cargocollective.com/central/The-Design-Squiggle*. The Process of Design Squiggle by Damien Newman, Central Office of Design, is licensed under a Creative Commons Attribution-No Derivative Works 3.0 United States License.
02 See Schwaber, K., & Sutherland, J. (2011). "The Scrum Guide," at *http://www.scrumguides.org/index.html. Scrum Alliance*. For details about software development methodologies in the context of service design, see 8.3, *Service design and software development*.
03 You can – where the cost of any major change is still low – use planned iterations formally or informally. In the end, it is up to you how much of the underlying structure you are going to share beyond your core project team.

If you are working with experienced designers, you can trust them to iterate within the given boundaries as necessary. The typical length of planned iterations often ranges between two to four weeks.

It is important to make space regularly for reflection sessions focused on your process and future iteration planning, taking time to adapt to what you have learned so far. Usually, reflection sessions are put at the end of a planned iteration. With shorter iterations they can be quite informal, but make sure you always also conduct formal review and planning sessions at least at the end of higher-level iterations.

In your reflection and iteration planning, you need to consider the content, tools, and methods as well as the way you collaborate within your team: What did you learn in terms of your project content, and what needs to happen in the next iteration in terms of tools and methods? How was the collaboration in the team and what can you do to become more effective as a team?[04]

The key driver for cyclical and iterative methodologies like the service design process is the desire to reduce the risk at each single step while at the same time maximizing learning to make subsequent steps more efficient.

Planning core activities

The most important aspect of this part of the planning process is to create a preliminary plan which accounts for continuous iteration planning and content/process reviews along the way. These activities will become the cornerstones of your adaptive and iterative process. In the following pages, we sketch out how to create a more detailed picture of your research, ideation, prototyping, and implementation activities. Initially this will help you to put together a proposal, including a roadmap, a list of resources you need, and a budget. Later on, this becomes a living document as you adapt and improve.

The planning of your service design activities is also iterative in itself. So, plan your first iterations quickly, then come back and adapt and improve. Chapters 5–8[05] give you in-depth descriptions on how to plan your research, ideation, prototyping, and implementation activities when you are about to do them. During the process of planning, however, you need to balance the uncertainty at the time of planning (pre-project) with the need for just enough detail to at least be able to create a budget and key milestones. For each iteration, it is helpful to be able to communicate a clear picture of how you want to work, creating trust in your process and your project team.

Be aware that at some stage it might become pointless to plan for an iteration which is too far into the future – even if your client is pressing for it. In those cases, it might be helpful to sketch out an exemplary project framework based on *a typical service design process*, knowing that you only will be able to properly plan it when you get there.

■ EXPERT TIP

"It's not just difficult to visualize, it's sometimes difficult to follow, unless you are used to it. Designers jump forward and backwards, zoom in and out, always on the hunt for something new, something that can inspire an innovation. If you are used to structure in everything, this may be challenging and difficult to follow. But ... there is method in the madness – give it time."

– Simon Clatworthy

---

04 This closely follows one of the principles of the Agile Manifesto: "At regular intervals, the team reflects on how to become more effective, then tunes and adjusts its behavior accordingly." (Source: "Principles Behind the Agile Manifesto" (n.d.), at *http://agilemanifesto.org/principles.html*. See Chapter 8, *Implementation*, for a more thorough discussion on the similarities between agile approaches and service design.

05 See 5.1.2, *Research planning*, 6.3.1, *Planning ideation*, 7.1.4, *Planning prototyping*, and 8.1.2, *Planning for human-centered implementation*.

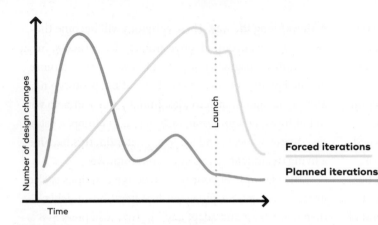

Forced iterations

Planned iterations

PLANNED ITERATIONS VS. FORCED ITERATIONS

In the forced iteration model, necessary changes are only forced onto the team by imminent implementation deadlines. The team is mostly reactive; changes are expensive.

Using systematic research, ideation, and prototyping loops, the planned iteration model pushes design changes toward the beginning of the project. The team operates proactively; the cost of changes is low.[01]

Plan for research

→ **Review** your initial research question(s), preparatory research, and high-level iteration structure.

→ **Select research methods:** Line up a sequence of research methods and decide how to analyze and visualize them. Roughly guesstimate typical setups in terms of sample selection, sample size, researcher team, data types, and triangulation strategy.

01 Adapted from Pugh, S. (1991). *Total Design: Integrated Methods for Successful Product Engineering.* Wokingham: Addison-Wesley, p. 206.

→ **Consider potential researchers:** Briefly refer back to your stakeholder map or do a quick informal brainstorming on potential stakeholders. How much of the research can be done by the project team? Where do you need external help?

→ **Split activities into planned research loops:** Sketch out how you want to arrange the selected methods into different research and analysis/visualization sessions and how they feed into each other. Add adaptive iteration planning and review sessions.

Plan for ideation

→ **Review** your initial assessment of potential development directions.

→ **Consider potential participants:** Very briefly (as this will certainly change after your research activities) refer back to your project stakeholder map or do a quick informal brainstorming on potential experts or stakeholders for key opportunity areas.

→ **Select methods:** Line up a sequence of ideation and decision-making methods to fill your idea portfolio and select them. Guesstimate how many ideas you might want to take forward into prototyping.

→ **Split activities into planned ideation loops:** Sketch out how you want to line up the selected methods into different ideation and decision-making sessions and how they feed into each other. Add adaptive iteration planning and review sessions.

Plan for prototyping

→ **Review** your initial assessment of potential development directions.[02]

→ **Assess what you might have to make:** Remember that at this point you might only be able to plan for approximate types of prototypes (e.g., if you already know you are going to work on an app, a consulting session, a physical product, etc.). It might also be impossible to say what needs to be prototyped just yet. However, in many projects the expected outputs are quite well defined and can guide your planning. It might be important to assess the uncertainty of your planning so you can adjust as you move forward.

→ **Select explorative and evaluative prototyping methods and plan supporting research:** Line up a sequence of explorative and evaluative prototyping methods. Roughly guesstimate the typical fidelity, multitracking, context, audience, and audience size

for each of those methods. Remember to select supporting research methods to learn from for each of your prototyping activities.

→ **Consider potential prototyping skills and team(s):** Do a quick informal brainstorming on potential skills you need and experts or stakeholders who have those skills to create the prototypes you need. Plan for interdisciplinary prototyping teams – who can make almost anything – at early iterations and include specialized skills later on.

→ **Split activities into planned prototyping loops:** Sketch out how you want to line up the selected methods into different explorative and evaluative prototyping sessions and how they feed into each other. Add adaptive iteration planning and review sessions.

Plan for implementation

→ **Assess what you might have to make:** Planning implementation means planning based on assumptions of what you might have to make. This will be based on your guesstimations of the prototyping activities and will share a similar uncertainty.

→ **Consider potential implementation skills and team(s):** Break down the implementation task into the involved disciplines. Do a quick informal brainstorming on potential skills you need and experts

💬 **EXPERT TIP**

"During planning, keep in mind that the project members and co-creators are embedded in organizational structures: your activities may have unforeseen effects going beyond your project environment. To avoid friction, carefully consider how these individuals perceive your service design activities and what effects their experiences may have."

– Julia Jonas

02 See *Assessment of potential development directions* in 9.2.2.

or stakeholders who have those skills to implement the project as it is planned today. Just like when you are planning for prototyping, it is often useful to plan for a core interdisciplinary implementation team – who can plan and manage almost anything – at early implementation iterations and move toward more specialized setups later on. Those might change, but having the interdisciplinary team at the beginning buys you the necessary time to adapt and communicate any changes as early as possible.

→ **Involve specialists to do implementation planning:** Line up seasoned project managers to give feedback on planning the implementation part(s). Co-create individual implementation plans together with the specialists.

→ **Split activities into planned iteration loops:** Sketch out how you want to line up the selected methods into different implementation loops and how they feed into each other. Add adaptive iteration planning and review sessions. As implementation activities are often done in parallel, make sure you sync those activities and continuously check the progress of single work packages against the holistic customer experience.

At any given stage, the higher the uncertainty in the outputs of your design process, the more parallel concepts or prototypes you should keep in the game.

9.2.5 Multitracking

Decide how many insights, ideas, prototypes, or services you want to work on. In bigger projects, it often makes sense to multitrack your iterations – for example, split the team and work in parallel.

Multitracking can be used to reduce risk by exploring a certain number of concepts or prototypes instead of just one. Not putting all your eggs into one basket allows you to strategically deal with uncertainty in your concept portfolio and manage the expectations of stakeholders.

Essentially, by working in this way you replace the old model of making one big bet on one concept with a series of smaller bets on a handful of promising prototypes. This reduces the risk associated with each individual decision and substantially reduces the risk associated with your overall innovation and design project.

Later, when you are closer to implementation, you can use multitracking to divide the work on different elements that need to be implemented into parallel work streams to speed up the time to delivery. For example, creating the interior design for a shop environment, creating training sessions for the staff, and implementing a support app can certainly run in parallel. Depending on the complexity of the development tasks, each work stream can also run at a different iteration speed. To keep the different work streams on track, regularly align the progress and make sure the output fits together.[01]

---

01 See 9.5.2, *Case: Managing strategic design projects,* for an example of how to adopt agile methodologies to manage strategic design projects.

9.2.6 Project phases and milestones

Gantt charts, project phases, and milestones are the currency of traditional project management. They have their roots in the world of more or less deterministic projects that could be planned and executed using basic work-breakdown structures, analyzing work package dependencies. While we strongly suggest you avoid using Gantt charts to plan and manage your project, you might still have to deliver milestones and a roadmap to comply with internal requirements.[02]

One way to deal with this situation is to use a black-boxing approach. You try to encapsulate the activities of your service design process in such a way that – from the outside – it almost looks like any other project. Ask yourself: how might we adapt our service design process to fulfill the (reporting/planning) requirements for projects within our organization, *without giving up* the iterative and adaptive nature of the service design process? Be careful with black-boxing service design projects, though, as it is just a workaround. It might be a starting point for service design within an organization, but it should not be the default.

The approach you choose will depend on your own experience and the previous experience of stakeholders with iterative and adaptive development approaches. Here are a few starting points.

COMMENT

"While it's tempting to want to check off the box and move on, designing a service is never done. It's only over when you go out of business."

— Jamin Hegeman

Identify and map project phases

Have a look at periods of iterations within your design process where you can identify a dominant activity or scope. Mark them as overarching project phases for your project. Often they combine a distinct mix of activities, methods, and deliverables. Map them to align with existing iterations. Sometimes it is useful to play with the naming of your project phases to match with existing terminology. For larger service design projects, mapping project phases onto your service design process can also be used to give a sense of orientation and progress. **Here are some examples of project phases:**

→ **Preparation phases, setup phases, scoping phases, or initial iterations** often include project planning and prep research, but sometimes also some first research, ideation, and even prototyping activities. You might even do a very quick first iteration including all these activities to better plan the entire project.

→ **Discover phases, insight phases, pre-project phases, or research phases** might package early, research-heavy high-level iterations, but will usually also contain some ideation and light-weight prototyping.

→ **Concept (development) phases, design phases, or ideation phases** might package ideation-focused high-level iterations but will also contain research and at least some lightweight prototyping.

02 As an outside agency – especially when you are called in for your expertise – you might make it an explicit point and take it as an opportunity for a change intervention: to challenge existing structures and do it the service design way. However, as a single designer or a small team within a big organization you might need to work differently (e.g., black-boxing your service design approach to initially fly under the radar, so to speak).

→ **Prototyping phases, build phases, or incubation phases** allow you to package prototyping-focused high-level iterations, but might also include some research and ideation activities.

→ **Internal alpha, local beta, beta, or rollout phases** allow you to plan phases around user engagement or the user learning curve.

→ **Delivery phases, implementation phases, pilot phases, or rollout phases** allow you to package different implementation-focused high-level iterations.

→ **Operation phases or in-production phases** allow you to package the continuous improvement iterations of the standard daily operations after your go-live. Service design is then set up as an ongoing activity in an organization and brings holistic cycles of research, ideation, prototyping, and implementation activities to the daily operations of your service.

Set outputs and milestones

Milestones mark specific points on your project timeline at which you reach an agreed status. They often are also the points in a project where you present to or involve a wider audience and communicate the progress and status of your project.

Set up your milestones to match your planned iterations – and carefully manage the expectations of what you can or cannot deliver at those points. The outputs you promise should be specific, measurable, and realistic and will often be called *deliverables* here.[01] **Typical milestones include:**

→ Intermediate research report done
→ Key insights identified and prioritized
→ Opportunity areas identified and prioritized
→ Ideation sessions done with key stakeholder groups
→ A defined number of ideas generated
→ A defined number of detailed concepts developed
→ A certain number of low-, mid-, or high-fidelity value/look-and-feel/feasibility/integration prototypes tested and feedback analyzed
→ A certain number of prototypes tested with real customers and feedback analyzed
→ Business cases for a defined number of prototypes validated
→ Pilot with frontline staff done and analyzed

In contrast to traditional projects, your deliverables stay living outputs. They will grow further and change as you go forward.

In some organizations these milestones might be squeezed into an existing stage-gate process, often consisting of phases like discover, scope, plan, develop, test, launch, and review. Even if this is not ideal, it unfortunately often reflects business reality. Between these stages,

01 Keep in mind that the examples given here are milestones when working in agile, adaptive mode. Later in a project, when you are working with a fixed-scope model, they might get more specific. To read more about how people perceive design processes, see *Planned iterations* in 9.2.4 and the textbox *Dealing with constraints*.

there are gates – decisions on whether a project will get a (conditional) go, be put on hold, be recycled, or be killed. Be aware that if you "black-box" an iterative structure with labels like these, you'll still need to meet existing hard criteria at each gate to get a go for the next stage. Often, you can define "must-have" and "nice-to-have" criteria for each project stage. Try to define the criteria mentioned in this chapter as "must-haves," since you can be certain you will meet them if you follow the process.

9.2.7   Outputs and outcomes

Going beyond the tangible

Many service design activities will have tangible outputs (e.g., research data, documented insights, idea sketches, prototypes, research and project reports, etc.). However, as we have seen throughout the previous chapters, sometimes the more intangible or implicit outcomes of your design activities will be more important for you. For example, early prototyping activities might primarily be used to create a shared understanding and alignment amongst the interdisciplinary project team – and are not just done for the ideas.[02] Or take qualitative research: while you collect a lot of concrete data on your research wall, one of the key goals might be to create empathy with your stakeholders within the design and management team. That's not something you can put into a report.

💬 **EXPERT TIP**

"Carefully manage expectations throughout the innovation process. Otherwise, especially after intensive innovation workshops, clients will demand that the specific individual solution they developed be delivered [too] soon afterwards."

– Julia Jonas

Even though the rest of your organization will usually be looking at the tangible outputs, it is equally important to carefully assess and plan your intangible outcomes. They often turn out to be the driving factors for successful co-creation, reducing resistance within the organization and increasing your chances to implement in the long run.

Flow of project knowledge, ideas, and insights

Key intangible outcomes (like empathy and deeper contextual knowledge and understanding of the stakeholders, the problem, and potential solutions) are almost inseparable from the people who developed these in your team. While some stakeholders are part of the project from beginning to end, many more will only join for some parts of the journey. This offers an opportunity for new ideas and perspectives and raises the challenge of passing on the important knowledge so they can meaningfully contribute. When people leave the project there is also a danger of losing essential parts of that hard-earned empathy, deep knowledge, and understanding. Plan to keep the flow of knowledge and empathy intact by building an unbroken chain of people across the project, supported by tangible documentation.

It can be helpful to map out the flow of people, key outputs, and outcomes across your design process to better understand where empathy, deep knowledge, and understanding are generated and how they are passed on to upcoming steps – through people or through tangible outputs like documentation or prototypes.

02 *See Prototyping to communicate and present in 7.1.1.*

FLOW OF EMPATHY

Handover through documents will not carry over empathy. Keep up the flow of empathy by keeping key people in the project from beginning to end.

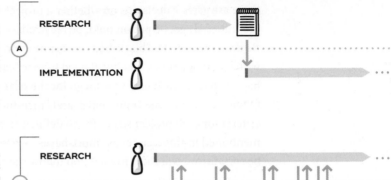

In a "classic" project handover empathy is lost during the handover – for example, when implementation merely builds on a consolidated research report.

Keeping a core project team avoids handovers and preserves the flow of empathy. At least one person responsible for implementation takes part in research, and at least one person responsible for research participates in implementation.

 **9.2.8 Documentation**

Decide early how you are going to organize and create your written[01] project documentation. Check (e.g., with your project sponsor) whether or not there are any requirements on form and content. Depending on the industry you work in, there might be strict rules and obligations. Documentation can be tedious and hard work, especially if it is done in retrospect, so plan this well ahead of time. Build it into the activities themselves as much as possible, or at least do it while your memory is still fresh.

Document your process and decisions

The service design process is adaptive and iterative. As you are constantly reviewing your progress and making changes, the real process will deviate from your original plan. As you go along, create concise documentation of the changes you made and the underlying reasons. This can be as simple as filing handwritten meeting minutes, or just taking photos of flipcharts or sticky notes that contain those details. However, it might also be necessary to prepare a glossy slide deck to run a decision past the board or to follow an official template for change requests.

Important decisions that are undocumented might be challenged, creating unnecessary discussions or, in the worst case, forcing you to do over.

---

01 By written documentation, we actually mean any kind of tangible documentation. Often this will be text and images, but it can be supplemented by other formats like video or interactive media as well.

Document your tangible outputs

Most activities in the service design process have tangible
outputs which in turn act as the inputs for the next
set of activities. These outputs are important for your
documentation as they allow you to trace back outputs
like prototypes to the underlying insights from research
or even back to the original quotes from your research
data.[02] A simple indexing system can help to connect the
original data from your research to your prototypes or
implemented solutions.

If a piece in the chain is challenged, you can retrace
some steps and re-examine the underlying assumptions or conclusions, or explain where it came from and
who contributed.[03]

Keep the documentation accessible

You should decide up front how and where to store
your tangible outputs so you can make them accessible quickly at any stage later in the project. In smaller
projects, a big project room with plenty of wall space
might be enough. There, you can sort all the assets onto
your research wall and idea/concept wall and exhibit
your prototypes on tables or in a distinct area. In more
complex projects, you should still keep a physical project
space for key assets, but also plan for a structured virtual
space where you keep the complete dataset.[04]

02 See *Indexing* in 5.1.3 for more information on indexing data. See also 5.4.1, *Case: Applying ethnography to gain
actionable insights*, for an example of how this works in practice.

03 Be careful: a complete documentation trail sometimes can amplify a "not invented here" syndrome within the
project team. New ideas are dismissed too quickly because they have not been through the whole process. It is
key to acknowledge bias and stay open to new ideas and challenges. However, always keep track of those gaps
or missing links to your insights and research data and close them if it becomes necessary.

04 For more on team spaces, see Chapter 11, *Making space for service design*.

Key outputs for documentation

→ Raw research data, research wall
→ Visualizations of research data
   (e.g., system maps, journey maps, etc.)
→ Key insights, jobs to be done,
   user stories
→ Research reports
→ Opportunity areas, including
   "How might we …?" questions
→ Ideas, idea/concept sketches, idea wall
→ Visualizations of future ideas and
   concepts (i.e., future-state system
   maps, future-state journey maps, etc.)
→ Prototypes, including visualizations/
   documentation (e.g., video documenta-
   tion, photos, descriptions)
→ Prototyping reports (including research reports on user tests)
→ Presentations (including presentation prototypes)
→ Implementation roadmaps
→ Documentation of implemented
   services and physical/digital products
   (e.g., process documentation, training
   manuals, etc.) ◄

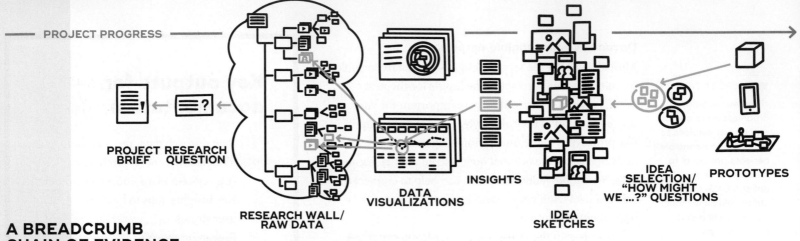

PROJECT PROGRESS

PROJECT
BRIEF

RESEARCH
QUESTION

RESEARCH WALL/
RAW DATA

DATA
VISUALIZATIONS

INSIGHTS

IDEA
SKETCHES

IDEA
SELECTION/
"HOW MIGHT
WE ...?" QUESTIONS

PROTOTYPES

A BREADCRUMB CHAIN OF EVIDENCE

As tangible outputs are the physical evidences of your service design process, your documentation trail becomes your chain of (physical) evidence, complementing your chain of empathy. Such a chain helps to find raw data revealing the problem your developed prototype strives to solve. Indexing helps to keep track.[01]

Documenting the intangible outcomes

Decide which of your intangible outcomes you want to add into the official documentation, and how. Many organizations have a bias toward the tangible outputs, and making sure you document the intangible outcomes can help you shift that focus toward a more balanced view. For example, you might include photos and use storytelling from a high-energy prototyping jam to underline the effects on interdisciplinary collaboration and alignment on shared goals ("We have never seen them work together before!").

Be careful though, since this is not always easy to do. Some of the effects can be quite subtle or hard to show. Reflect on this within your core project team and strategically include the parts you feel comfortable with.

9.2.9 Budgeting

After completing the first planning cycle, you should have a good first idea of your core project and planned iteration structure, an initial baseline of core activities, and a sense of the size of your core and extended project team.

Also, you can guesstimate the amount of travel, materials, and external services that are required. This gives you plenty of input for an initial draft of your budget. In that sense, budgeting for a service design project can be really easy, or it can be as hard as in any other project. **Here are a few tips:**

01 See *Indexing* in 5.1.3.

→ **Always start with a ballpark figure.** If you have a target range, you can make sure you are not over or under planning. Then get more detailed. Iterate.

→ **Break up big budgets to reduce risk.** If you aimed too high, consider breaking up the project into a sequence of smaller projects with increasing risk and budget. If you are too low, add depth or more iterations.

→ **Consider budget thresholds.** Make sure to check the budget thresholds of the organization you are working in/with. What is the maximum budget your project sponsor is allowed to sign off? If you have to aim higher, who else will have to be involved (and convinced) to sign off that budget?

→ **Plan with typical content.** As you cannot plan later iterations in detail, budget for *typical* work packages instead which are – from your experience – within the parameters of your project brief and the expected output and outcome.

→ **Use group estimates.** Seek out experts and experienced project managers to help estimate efforts and resources for each of your planned iterations. Use lightweight methods like planning poker[02] to create meaningful discussions and arrive at realistic group estimates to remove individual bias.

Tips for working on a shoestring budget

→ Start small.

→ Select an appropriate project to start with.[03]

→ Be clear if the project goal is for you to learn, or to convince others.

→ Don't expect others to change before you have. Follow the principles within your own circle of influence.

→ Use undercover budgets: asking for time is easier than asking for money.

→ Practice guerilla co-creation: go informal, do undercover coffee-corner workshops.

→ Ignore labels and piggyback on existing initiatives. ◄

03 Service design is not suitable for every challenge. It is most fertile if applied to wicked or ill-defined problems (especially if someone has failed to solve them before), rather than deterministic problems.

02 See Cohn, M. (2005). *Agile Estimating and Planning*. Pearson Education.

→ **Plan with an appropriate buffer.** Often people try to build in a buffer across the board to cater for unforeseeable challenges. While you can take the deviations from your mean estimates as an indication, 20% seems to be a frequently used value – but your mileage might vary. If your project budget is estimated by multiple people (e.g., subproject leads) make sure you are not adding buffers onto buffers.

→ **Manage expectations.** Make sure people understand that the content within your iterations *needs to be flexible.* Your budget accounts for overall time and resources, but you must to have a certain flexibility in how you actually spend your budget and allocate your people within the process. Clarify how to handle those changes.

→ **Understand calls for tender.** For big projects, make sure you have a clear understanding of the sourcing procedure/tender process of your client organization. Purchasing departments will try to haggle and bring the price down. Decide whether or not you want to play their game and set your prices accordingly.

9.2.10 Mindsets, principles, and style

Think about the "soft" side of *how* you do things. On paper and even in terms of the method mix, many design processes look the same. But people are different,

including the people working on your service design project. You will find a broad variety of mindsets, principles, and styles. While most practitioners with experience in service design share a common mindset and set of core principles, there will still be small but important differences. What is the vibe of the facilitation? Are you all speaking the same language? How do you interpret your role as a service designer?

Depending on the ecosystem you are working in and your role, there is broad range of styles that you can bring to the table. Are you the engaging ones in suits or the thoughtful ones in turtlenecks? Is your background in design or do you come from the technology or business side of service design? Are you an external agency that offers to create and implement breakthrough projects with a team of experts? Or are you a service design coach who enables people inside the client organization to do service design on their own? Or a project owner inside an organization who needs to figure out how to work with colleagues?

If you are shopping for an agency or consultant, this might be one of the key points for consideration: Is there a cultural fit between my organization and the agency? Or, if you are implementing a service design project within your own organization, what will be your way?[01]

---

01 A lot of the softer side has to do with your style of facilitation. See Chapter 10, *Facilitating workshops,* for more information.

9.3 MANAGING THE SERVICE DESIGN PROCESS

9.3.1 **Iteration planning**

Iteration planning regularly adapts your planned iterations and roadmap to the learnings of any previous activities. After completing a planned iteration, use a sped-up version of the planning process described in the previous section as a base to update your planning. Where necessary, use the planning sections in Chapters 5 through 8 to do detailed planning of core activities for in-depth research, ideation, prototyping, and implementation iterations. Typically, for most iterations of your project the iteration planning session of the next iteration will be combined with the iteration review of the previous one.

A planned iteration structure with fixed dates for iteration planning and review also helps to manage the ideas and change requests you will receive from project sponsors and stakeholders – often on a daily basis. Those requests can wreak havoc on your project if not managed carefully. Communicating a clear structure of review and planning sessions can help to channel most of those requests. If the next session is not too far off, people are often happy if their new ideas and change requests are officially documented, assessed, and prioritized during the next planning session.

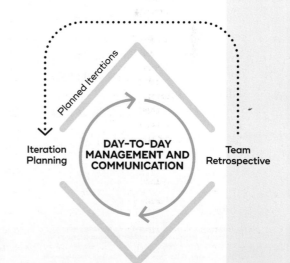

Discuss change requests or process feedback in your iteration review session. Put new questions, ideas, or changes onto your research wall or idea portfolio to be prioritized and added to your overall project funnel.

Overview of service design management activities: iteration planning, content reviews, team retrospectives, and day-to-day management and communication.

The daily stand-up

A daily stand-up is a regular daily meeting of your core team to quickly talk about what is happening and align the plans for the next 24 hours. It mainly helps to improve communication within your project team and uncover and solve problems as early as possible. The rules are simple: you meet (standing up), and everybody shares where they are going next and if they need help. It's over in 15 minutes. You repeat this every day at the same time.[01]

Here are a few recommendations based on recent research[02] on daily stand-ups:

→ **Focus on the future only.**
This is not about boring status reports (see below).[03] Prompt your participants to ask themselves, "What will I do next to help our team achieve its goals?" and "What problems do I know of that may prevent progress?" Allow others to help you answer these questions.

→ **Don't talk about progress. Visualize it.**
Tangible visualizations like burndown charts that you put up in your workspace can efficiently render boring status reports unnecessary. The project's status is constantly visible to everyone. Save the time for solving actual problems.

→ **Do discuss solutions. But do it briefly.**
Identify problems and try to solve or discuss how to avoid them. This is actually regarded as one of the most valuable activities in a stand-up meeting. But if the problem is too complex to solve in the given time frame, agree on a follow-up meeting to work on it with the right people. Do not break the timebox.

→ **Minimize disruption.**
Choose a time and place that's least disruptive for your participants, so no one has to wait or kill time. Pre-lunch often is the best time for a stand-up. Most people are there even if they had to work late the day before, and the prospect of imminent food will naturally keep the meeting short.[04]

01 This becomes even more important when you are working within a remote team. In those cases, use a stable videoconferencing system to set up your daily meetings.

02 Stray, V., Sjøberg, D. I., & Dybå, T. (2016). "The Daily Stand-Up Meeting: A Grounded Theory Study." *Journal of Systems and Software*, 114, 101–124.

03 The previously cited research shows that "What have I done since we last met?" should not be included in a daily stand-up. It often turns the stand-up into a boring status report, taking away from discussions on how to resolve real issues.

04 There is another advantage of having the meeting before lunch: people might have informal conversations over lunch and can easily arrange follow-ups or in-depth sessions when necessary.

→   **Be on time. Keep it brief.**
Start punctually. Swiss time. We mean
it. Wait for no one. And the meeting
should be 15 minutes *or less*. When
the 15 minutes are over, stop. If there's
nothing more to say before the 15 minutes are over, stop too.

→   **Don't facilitate.**
Try to teach your team the format,
but then withdraw. The daily stand-up
should turn into a self-organized ritual.
Also avoid determining who should
talk. This often leads to a one-way
communication between the facilitator
and the group. Instead, throw a die,
then go (counter-)clockwise from there.
This supports an egalitarian discussion
within the group. ◄

9.3.2 **Iteration management**

Manage focus between big picture and details
One of the key elements of service design is the constant
switching between different aspects of the service – from
the big picture to the details. Practically this means, for
example, going back and forth between a focus on details
(like single steps of the customer journey or even specific
user stories or jobs to be done) and the orchestration of
the end-to-end customer journey across all those steps.
Make sure to balance your attention between working on
single touchpoints versus consistent and iterative development of holistic service experiences.

When you are managing a service design process,
it is important to do this systematically. Decide which
perspective might be most valuable as a next organic step
in your process (e.g., customer experience, stakeholder
network, business model, organizational feasibility, or
technological feasibility). But then also check the effects
of the changes you've made on the service as a whole.
This is especially important when you have split up the
project team and started to work in parallel. Build those
checks into your regular project structure – for example,
by attaching them to specific milestones in the process.

Manage problem and solution
The same back-and-forth applies to the interdependence
of problem and solution. When navigating through your
iterations, make sure to keep a constant eye on both your
potential solutions and whether they trigger new problems which might lead to new, better solutions. These

kinds of iterations can be observed in the design behavior of experienced designers and often happen organically. If you and your team are new to this, you might have to explicitly step back and reflect on where you stand in this problem-and-solution space: "Proposed solutions often directly remind designers of issues to consider. The problem and solution co-evolve."[01]

Day-to-day project management

In terms of the daily tasks of project management, service design projects are not much different than other projects. Here are a few tips to help you stay sane:

→ **Do. Now.**
Service design is about doing. Refer to Chapters 5, 6, 7, and 8 for tips on how to do and manage specific activities.

→ **Talk briefly. But talk often.**
If you do not align with your fellow project team members, things can quickly go astray. But outside your core service design activities, try to keep coordination efforts lean and efficient. Consider introducing a daily stand-up meeting (see textbox) to align the team on a day-to-day basis and make sure problems get identified and solved quickly.

→ **Make process and progress visible –
preferably physically.**
One of the biggest problems in projects arises when activities are stuck and no one notices. Create visual process and progress boards and put them up in your workspace so everybody can see them and trigger action if necessary. Of course, if you are working with a distributed team you might have to switch to a virtual solution. But the rule stays: make sure it does not get buried in a file folder far, far away, but becomes visible in a popular virtual space (e.g., the start page of your internal social network).

→ **Keep your rhythm.**
When a project hits a tricky problem, it can be tempting even for experienced designers to lengthen the current iteration until team members feel they have the perfect solution. Resist this temptation! Timeboxed iterations with regular reviews[02] are even more valuable at times like this.

→ **Orchestrate quiet times and times of intense
collaboration/exchange.**
Service design can be used to seek solutions for wicked problems. This can be hard and requires a deep understanding of the matter. Try to create safe spaces of uninterrupted work time for people to dig into those challenges. During those periods, prefer asynchronous communication like email over instant or face-to-face communication. At the same time, make sure there are enough opportunities for formal exchange (i.e., workshops) as well as plenty of informal opportunities to just run into each other to lower the barriers for personal exchanges.

💬 **EXPERT TIP**

"Over time, not only the scope of the project but also the environment around it may change, for example through new employees or the launch of new projects. It is therefore advised to periodically update tools like your project stakeholder map to review the overall situation and reflect on such changes."

– Julia Jonas

01 Kolodner, J. L., & Wills, L. M. (1996). "Powers of Observation in Creative Design." *Design Studies*, 17(4), 385-416.

02 See *Content reviews* and *Team retrospectives* in 9.3.3.

"Why should I join your project?"

If service design (or whatever you call it) is new to your organization, you will have to sell your project twice to each participant: once for the work, once for the new way of working. It's not just a new project, it's a weird one.[03]

Here are a few common questions stakeholders have when they are invited to join or help with a new project, and what you can do about them:

→   **Why me? Why am I here?**
Explain why you invited them in the first place, so they get a sense about their role in the process and the expectations you have about their contribution.

→   **How does this help my organization? My team? Me?**
The project is *your* project, but not necessarily *their* project. Put yourself into their shoes and try to convey why they should care.

→   **Is this legit?**
Show that they are not wasting their time. Build trust by outlining where the project comes from, who sponsors it, and which key people you have already talked to.

→   **Aren't we already doing this?**
Research early on whether there have been similar or even just similar-looking projects within the company before and put your initiative into context.

→   **What do you need or expect me to know?**
Assess how much information really is necessary to join the co-creative process. Usually not everybody needs to know everything. Do not overwhelm or confuse them.

→   **What do you want me to do?**
Clearly communicate what you expect them to do. Also explain how their contributions tie into the overall process/project.

→   **What will happen to my contributions?**
Use a visualization of your service design process to give them a sense of what is happening to their contributions. Who will work with those outputs afterwards? Will they receive credit?

→   **How can I stay in the loop?**
Regularly update your co-creators on what is happening to ensure long-term buy-in. This can be a few emails sent out at specific points during the project, pointers to an online project platform, or concise presentations in selected meetings. ◄

03   For more on how to sell service design to colleagues or other stakeholders, see Chapter 1, *Why service design?*

→ **Choose your context.**

This sometimes is neglected, but try to choose wisely *where* you and your team plan to work. Working on location at your client's office will be different than just visiting every now and again. When do you need to limit external exposure? When do you need the (informal) exchange?[01]

→ **Deal with unavoidable conflicts in a timely manner.**
You will find that the service design approach has many built-in strategies that help you to avoid conflicts in the first place. You can find them in the overall approach (e.g., the strategic use of boundary objects or prototypes for communication and development of a shared understanding, and the iterative nature of the process to reduce risks) as well as in specific toolsets.[02]

Conflicts that are more emotional or arise from interpersonal relationships ("I just cannot stand that guy!") are harder to tackle and usually require a different skill set. Hence, in the long term, consider training your team in conflict resolution up front. That allows them to quickly notice and resolve conflicts themselves before they interfere with the atmosphere in the team. Consult with a professional mediator on how you should proceed or check the conflict resolution literature for an overview on available options.[03]

Onboarding and communicating with co-creators
Co-creation is at the heart of service design. Over the course of a project you might need to onboard many people to your extended project team. Make sure you plan for this, as it takes time. You might need to get permission before you can invite or work with people from other departments or external experts. In any case, almost everybody needs lead-in time to make space in their own schedule for your project. The people you might want to work with are probably *not* sitting around doing nothing and waiting for you to call. You even might have to get through their natural defense mechanisms ("Oh, another project …") before they will commit themselves to join your process – even if it is just for one workshop.

True co-creation means you also need to create and maintain a sense of co-ownership with your co-creators beyond their direct involvement. This implies that they are not just involved but can also see or at least sense the impact of their own contributions later on. Try to regularly update your co-creators on what is happening. This, in turn, ensures buy-in. There is a real danger in a "co-create-and-forget" mentality. Buy-in will only work if you keep people in the loop and give them the opportunity to see and experience the effects of their own contributions.

Be aware, however, that you still need to carefully manage expectations during your co-creation sessions so everyone understands that not all contributions will make it into concepts or prototypes, let alone the eventual service solution.

---

01 Also refer to Chapter 11, *Making space for service design*, for details on setting up a dedicated project space, even a temporary one.

02 See, for example, 5.3, *Methods of data visualization, synthesis, and analysis*, and 6.2, *Decisions*.

03 As a starting point, see Brown, D. M., & Berkun, S. (2013). *Designing Together: The Collaboration and Conflict Management Handbook for Creative Professionals*. Pearson Education. See also Shapiro, D. (2016). *Negotiating the Nonnegotiable: How to Resolve Your Most Emotionally Charged Conflicts*. Viking Adult. While it is important to learn about conflict resolution, remember that your main focus should still be to build a resilient team that works in a positive and engaging way and can handle problems and conflicts with energy and effectiveness (and even a bit of fun whenever appropriate).

EXPERT TIP

"Onboarding is import-
ant, but its also worth
thinking about a pos-
sible future where you
will not be so centrally
involved in the proj-
ect. Make sure ...that
you have managed to
hand over all of the key
premises and findings
for a successful project
during your project
communication. Many
of these are unspoken
in a project, and lead
the project to go off in
undesirable directions
once you have left."

– Simon Clatworthy

Regardless of how small the contribution is and whether it is used later or not, it is always good practice to track it and give credit. In its simplest form, this involves keeping lists of participants for all the activities you do during your process. Decide how you want to and can best give credit in your project – considering the realities within your organization – so it is actually meaningful to your participants.

9.3.3   Iteration review

In an iteration review, you step back and reflect on what happened during your last iteration(s). You try to make sense of what you learned, create options for what you would like to do, and make decisions on how to make necessary changes to move forward. Typically, iteration reviews will be combined with planning the next iteration.

Content reviews

At many steps in your service design process, you need to do a content review – that is, reflect on the quality of your outputs and make decisions based on that. Many of the core activities of service design have those key reflective elements already built in. In research, have a look at methods of data synthesis and analysis.[04] In ideation, especially check out the pre-ideation methods or any methods on selecting ideas.[05] And for prototyping,

there is reflection mainly in the evaluative prototyping methods and subsequent synthesis and analysis stages.[06]

Content reviews are usually done by the core project team together with selected stakeholders from the extended team. It can be useful to include an additional content review as part of your iteration review session before moving on to the team retrospective.

Team retrospectives

You also need to address your learnings on the process itself, your mindset, and the quality of your collaboration within the core or extended project team. This is done during team retrospectives, usually carried out within the core project team.

There are many ways to do an effective retrospective of past iterations, and there are many useful questions you can ask. See the textbox *Conducting a team retrospective* for one common approach.[07] In a project with people working full-time, a more formal iteration review should be done at least every couple of weeks.

Unless there is an escalation or your project sponsor requests formal documentation, your iteration planning and any of your intermediate documentation can usually be quite rough. Create visual notes on flipcharts that everyone writes on simultaneously or take photos of your sticky notes. It's important that you do it and learn from it. But do not try to make it pretty – it will change again too soon.

---

04 See 5.1.4, *Data visualization, synthesis, and analysis,* and 5.3, *Methods of data visualization, synthesis, and analysis.*

05 See methods for *pre-ideation* and *reducing options* in 6.4.

06 See 7.1.6, *Data synthesis and analysis,* which essentially again refers back to 5.1.4, *Data visualization, synthesis, and analysis,* and 5.3, *Methods of data visualization, synthesis, and analysis.*

07 See also Kerth, N. (2013). *Project Retrospectives: A Handbook for Team Reviews.* Addison-Wesley.

Conducting a team retrospective

"Regardless of what we discover, we understand and truly believe that everyone did the best job they could, given what they knew at the time, their skills and abilities, the resources available, and the situation at hand."
– Retrospective prime directive by Norman L. Kerth[01]

A good way to get started is to read the prime directive of retrospectives out loud to your team.[02] Then:

1 Remind your team what has happened so far, highlighting key outputs and outcomes since your last iteration(s). Consider doing the session in your project room, where your key outputs are visible or easily accessible (e.g., your research or idea walls).

2 On a wall, put up these key questions:[03] What did we do well? What did we learn? What should we do differently next time? What still puzzles us?

3 Ask your participants to silently write sticky notes answering those questions and put them up on the wall. If there have been change requests, feedback, or new ideas from outside the core team, add them here too. Cluster the answers and clarify any notes you don't understand.

4 Discuss the clusters step by step. Add ideas, learnings, and potential changes as you go along.

5 Ask participants to highlight the key drivers that need to be considered when doing your iteration planning session. Document your results.[04] ◄

01 Kerth, N. L. (n.d.). "The Retrospective Prime Directive," at *http://www.retrospectives.com/pages/retroPrimeDirective.html*.

02 This can be an essential part of creating the necessary safe space for an honest review. Over time, it becomes a ritual. To avoid it losing effect, take turns reading it. Always try to keep it honest and fresh.

03 Kerth, N. L. (n.d.). "The Key Questions to Be Answered During a Retrospective," at *http://www.retrospectives.com/pages/RetrospectiveKeyQuestions.html*.

04 Especially when times are rough within a project, you might turn to that documentation to show the team how much really already has happened to boost morale and motivation.

9.4 EXAMPLES: PROCESS TEMPLATES

FOUR- TO EIGHT-HOUR INTRODUCTION WORKSHOP

The shorter the format, the more detailed your plan can be. Workshops like this allow you to engage with stakeholders and can be used to kick off a project or act as an initial preparatory iteration for bigger projects or workshops.

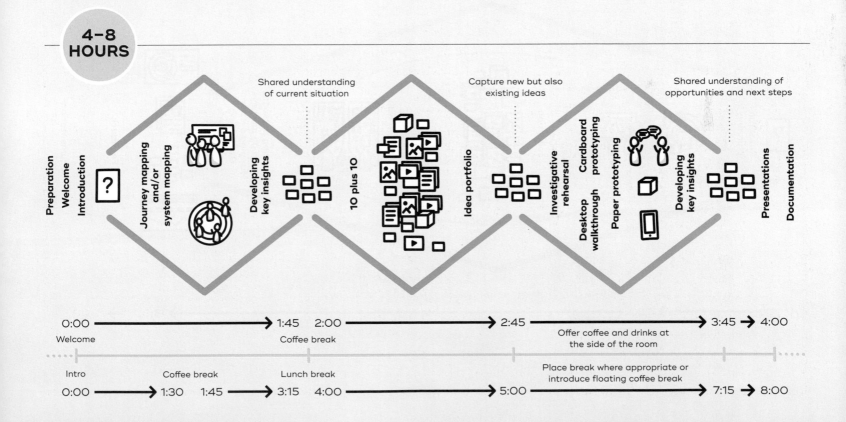

4–8 HOURS

Shared understanding of current situation

Capture new but also existing ideas

Shared understanding of opportunities and next steps

Preparation
Welcome
Introduction

Journey mapping and/or system mapping

Developing key insights

10 plus 10

Idea portfolio

Investigative rehearsal
Desktop walkthrough
Cardboard prototyping
Paper prototyping

Developing key insights

Presentations
Documentation

0:00 ⟶ 1:45   2:00 ⟶ 2:45   3:45 → 4:00
Welcome   Coffee break   Offer coffee and drinks at the side of the room

Intro   Coffee break   Lunch break   Place break where appropriate or introduce floating coffee break

0:00 → 1:30   1:45 → 3:15   4:00 ⟶ 5:00 ⟶ 7:15 → 8:00

THREE-DAY
SERVICE DESIGN SESSION

Compared to the short four- to eight-hour introduction, there is more time for actual iterations, especially within research, prototyping, and testing. In this example setup you can see the emphasis on customer-focused tools and methods.

DAY 1

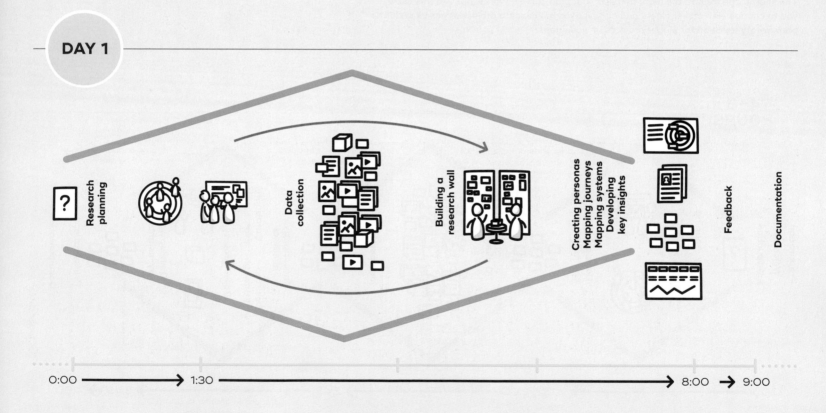

Research planning

Data collection

Building a research wall

Creating personas
Mapping journeys
Mapping systems
Developing key insights

Feedback

Documentation

0:00 → 1:30 → 8:00 → 9:00

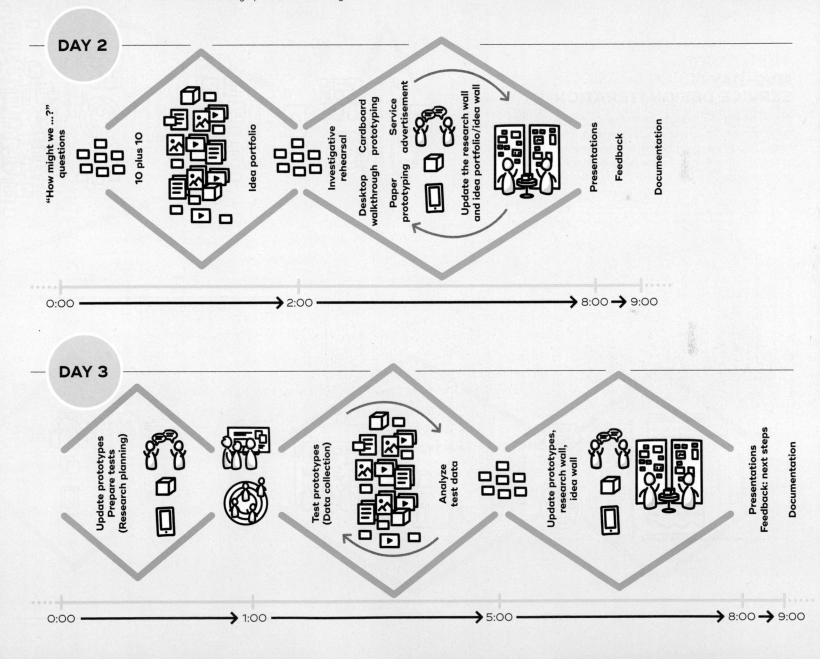

DAY 2

"How might we ...?" questions

10 plus 10

Idea portfolio

Investigative rehearsal

Desktop walkthrough

Cardboard prototyping

Paper prototyping

Service advertisement

Update the research wall and idea portfolio/idea wall

Presentations

Feedback

Documentation

0:00 — 2:00 — 8:00 → 9:00

DAY 3

Update prototypes
Prepare tests
(Research planning)

Test prototypes
(Data collection)

Analyze test data

Update prototypes, research wall, idea wall

Presentations
Feedback: next steps

Documentation

0:00 — 1:00 — 5:00 — 8:00 → 9:00

FIVE-DAY
SERVICE DESIGN ITERATION

Structurally, this is similar to the three-day variant, but with more iterations and depth during research, prototyping, and testing. It also creates a clearer business view with the addition of service blueprints and/or the Business Model Canvas on the last day.[01]

[01] Note that any given five-day sprint always has to be carefully prepared and adapted to the specific project. See 9.5.3, *Case: Using a five-day service design sprint to create a shared cross-channel strategy,* for an example of how this structure can be applied.

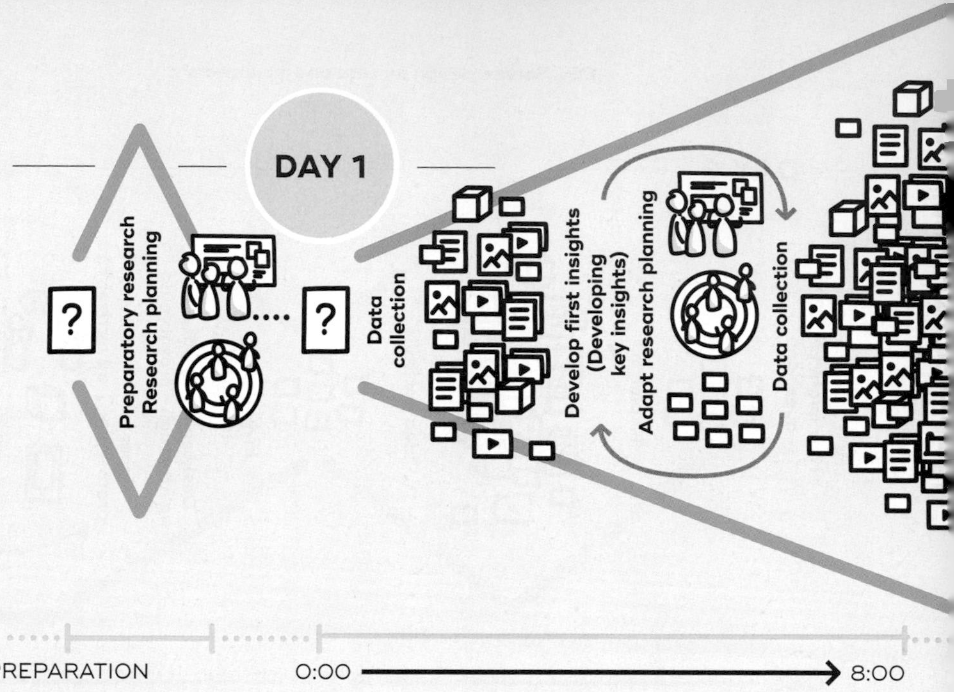

DAY 1

Preparatory research
Research planning

Data collection

Develop first insights
(Developing key insights)

Adapt research planning

Data collection

PREPARATION   0:00 ——————→ 8:00

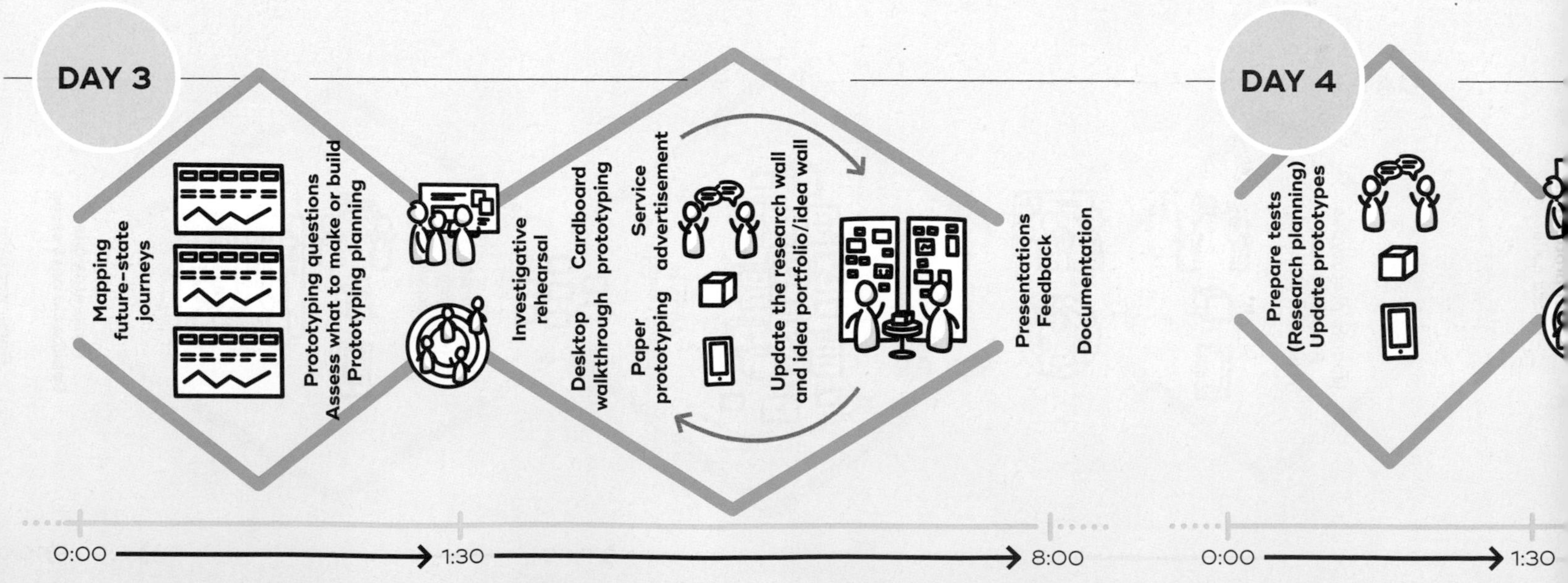

DAY 3

Mapping future-state journeys

Prototyping questions
Assess what to make or build
Prototyping planning

Investigative rehearsal

Desktop walkthrough
Cardboard prototyping

Paper prototyping
Service advertisement

Update the research wall and idea portfolio/idea wall

Presentations
Feedback
Documentation

0:00 ——————→ 1:30 ——————→ 8:00

DAY 4

Prepare tests
(Research planning)
Update prototypes

0:00 ——————→ 1:30

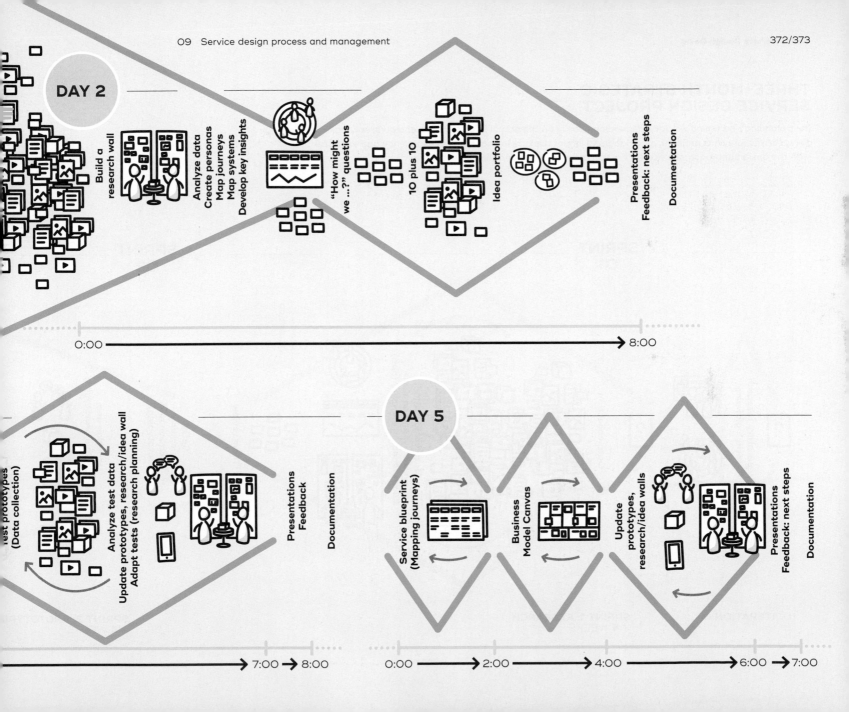

DAY 2

Build a research wall

Analyze data
Create personas
Map journeys
Map systems
Develop key insights

"How might we ...?" questions

10 plus 10

Idea portfolio

Presentations
Feedback: next steps

Documentation

0:00 ———————————————→ 8:00

Test prototypes (Data collection)

Analyze test data
Update prototypes, research/idea wall
Adapt tests (research planning)

Presentations
Feedback

Documentation

DAY 5

Service blueprint (Mapping journeys)

Business Model Canvas

Update prototypes, research/idea walls

Presentations
Feedback: next steps

Documentation

———————→ 7:00 → 8:00

0:00 ——→ 2:00 ——→ 4:00 ————→ 6:00 → 7:00

THREE-MONTH STRATEGIC SERVICE DESIGN PROJECT

Your planning and timing will vary, depending heavily on the actual brief, your stakeholders, strategic perspectives, previous projects, etc. Managing longer design projects requires experience and expertise with the design approach, the ecosystem you are working in, and the subject matter.[01]

01 For a model of ongoing development, also see 12.4, *Design sprints*.

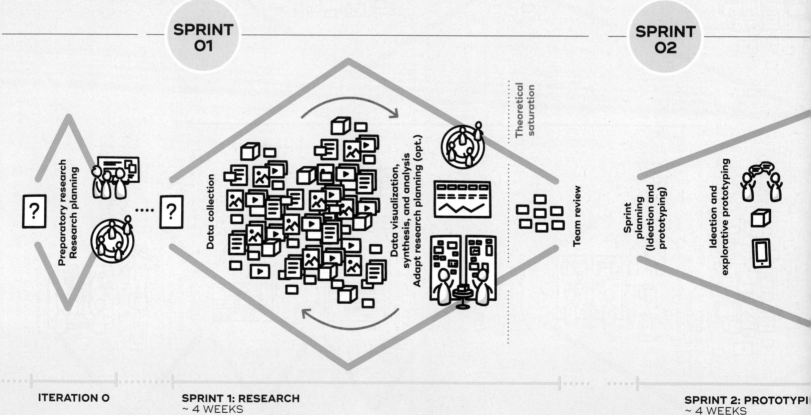

SPRINT 01

SPRINT 02

Preparatory research
Research planning

Data collection

Data visualization, synthesis, and analysis
Adapt research planning (opt.)

Theoretical saturation

Team review

Sprint planning (Ideation and prototyping)

Ideation and explorative prototyping

ITERATION 0

SPRINT 1: RESEARCH
~ 4 WEEKS

SPRINT 2: PROTOTYPI
~ 4 WEEKS

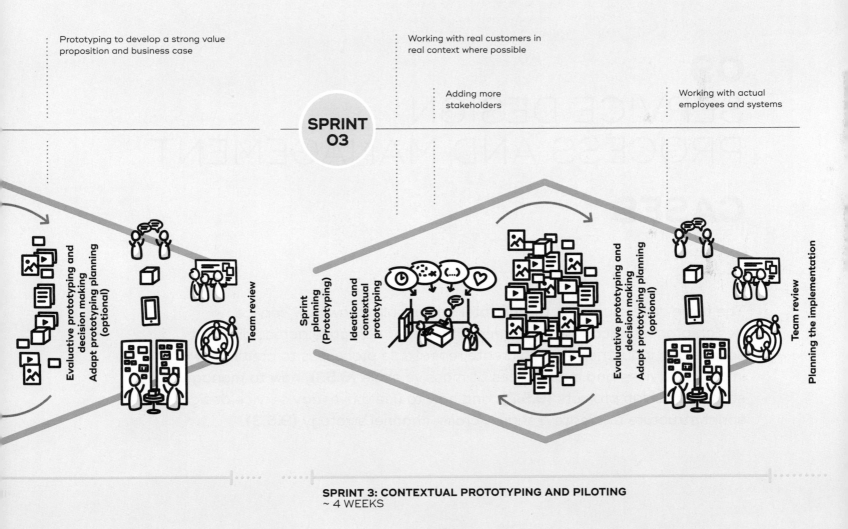

Prototyping to develop a strong value proposition and business case

Working with real customers in real context where possible

Adding more stakeholders

Working with actual employees and systems

SPRINT 03

Evaluative prototyping and decision making

Adapt prototyping planning (optional)

Team review

Sprint planning (Prototyping)

Ideation and contextual prototyping

Evaluative prototyping and decision making

Adapt prototyping planning (optional)

Team review

Planning the implementation

SPRINT 3: CONTEXTUAL PROTOTYPING AND PILOTING
~ 4 WEEKS

09
SERVICE DESIGN PROCESS AND MANAGEMENT
CASES

→

The three case studies in this chapter specifically show how service design processes can be structured differently in practice across different scopes and industries: how to create repeatable processes to continually improve services and experiences at massive scale **(9.5.1),** how to manage strategic design projects **(9.5.2),** and how to use a five-day service design sprint structure to create a shared cross-channel strategy **(9.5.3)**.

Continual improvement of the Olympic spectator experience (when you know it won't be right on day one)

AUTHOR

Alex Nisbett
Service Designer,
Spectator Experience,
London Organizing
Committee of
the Olympic and
Paralympic Games

When it finally came to game time, the organizers of the London 2012 Olympic and Paralympic Games were clear on one thing: that it wouldn't be right on day one. Or day two, or even day three. In fact, they were well prepared for things to go wrong (they did), and understood the value of continual improvement of the spectator experience.

As part of the team who designed and delivered the spectator experience at London 2012, one of my roles as Games time approached was to design for, and then support this continual improvement.

We created a *simple, repeatable process* to help identify the positive and negative experiences across the Games, which could be shared with venue and functional teams to help them make improvements to the services they were providing to the 12+ million spectators who made it to the Games:

1 Listen

Our research team had already planned daily questionnaires, some of which were conducted as exit interviews as spectators left venues after their events; more were delivered via email. The results of this research helped us generate a *hotspot map* showing where the main pain points were across the venues, along with numbers showing how venues were performing relative to each other. A healthy sense of competition between venues seemed totally appropriate!

Qualitative and quantitative

Observations from members of the spectator experience team in and around the venues combined with plain common sense from the venue teams helped us to define more exactly what the problems were and why they were happening. Additional detail also came from monitoring of social media (the use of geolocation tagging meant we didn't need tweets to include the name of the venue).

2 Learn

With so much data from so many sports and venues, daily analysis and synthesis was critical to help us create a high-level daily report (see the image) for senior stakeholders, plus additional details for the venue and functional area (FA) teams to help them make improvements. What we saw as the daily challenges and continued threats to the spectator experience (the insights) were matched up to practical and achievable improvements and mitigations (the service levers) to create a number of actions which we believed would make a difference.

Daily report

The daily report delivered to the main operations center also included

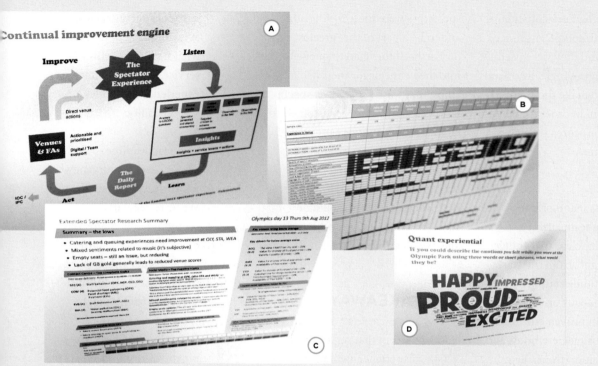

scores, ratings, and rankings to help identify the high and low performers, plus overall trends across the Games. The very highest scores were in fact on the days when Team GB won medals and when the weather was at its best, proving that sometimes there is more to an experience than what can be designed into it.

3 Act

Tangible actions, including their operational details, were refined and then prioritized by venue and FA leadership, before being shared with the teams on the ground who would implement them. These actions included changes to what already existed (e.g., adjusted behaviors for frontline staff, or additional water fountains as well as completely new additions (temporary digital signage to support new "day pass" ticketing, or the design and construction of Mascot House for the Paralympics).

Prototype early

Most teams were actually really well prepared for the changes they were asked to make; in fact, each

(A) The continual improvement engine operated each and every day of the games, involving multiple teams in the creation of data, analysis, reporting, and finally taking action to improve the spectator experience.

(B) Hot spot maps showing relative high and low performers were created each day using data from exit interviews and online questionnaires about the spectator experience in and around venues.

(C) A daily report created by analyzing detailed research results for each sporting venue and functional area helped those at the main operations center, and senior stakeholders, to quickly understand how well we were performing.

(D) A simple word cloud created from responses to one of the questionnaire prompts allowed us to see at a glance how spectators were really feeling. [01]

01 All images on this page: Alex Nisbett (2012).

and every team had previously run a test event (a prototype in service design speak) and they were used to learning and improving. Some teams were less able to make the changes required of them in order to increase their satisfaction scores – notably the catering team.

4 Improve

A sense of realism and pragmatism among the teams helped, and we were very clear that things "wouldn't be right" from the start. This healthy attitude meant that we were able to focus on continued and sustained improvement from Opening to Closing Ceremony, and across the transition from Olympics to Paralympics. In many ways, the Olympics were seen as a warm-up for the "Paras," and indeed, the Paralympics benefited from lessons learned a few weeks earlier.

Spectator satisfaction (met or exceeded expectations) rose from 90% on day one to 96% at the end of the Games. The spectator experience team could not claim responsibility for this, nor could service design alone as at the end of the day,

spectators were there for the athletes and to be a part of the "greatest show on Earth." If they had to queue to get into the venue or for their fish and chips, that wasn't so bad, as spectators, especially those accustomed to large-scale events, were prepared for that. It *is* the Olympics, after all.

However, improving the spectator experience continually, knowing that even the last day would be someone's first day, was what we had all signed up for.

KEY TAKEAWAYS

01 Accept that services and experiences will never be perfect and can be continually improved. Each and every day sees customers getting their first and (so the song goes) lasting impression. Don't miss your chance to make a difference.

02 Spend time on the front line watching and listening. Become part of customer-facing teams, even for just a day. Know what it's like to deliver a service. Make customer experience everyone's responsibility.

03 Define a deadline – create a sense of urgency, focus, and real purpose. We were regularly reminded how many "days to go" there were until Games time. This was initially motivating but subsequently frightening!

04 Everything can be prototyped, even sports events of Olympic proportions.

05 Finally, if you ever get the chance to work on your dream project, cause, or job, do it. Drop what you're doing and go for it; you'll have no regrets.

9.5.2 CASE: MANAGING STRATEGIC DESIGN PROJECTS

Vodafone: Retail meets service design

AUTHORS

Marta Sánchez Serrano
Head of Commercial
Strategy and
Operations, Vodafone

Jesús Sotoca
Consultant and
Strategic Design
Director, Designit

Vodafone, one of the world's leading multinational communications companies, was ready to transform its approach from focusing on sales to focusing on clients. As part of that plan, the company envisioned developing a new store concept focused on user experience. They wanted to interact with customers in a different way and increase customer satisfaction by creating a unique experience. Designit came on board to help them conceptualize, design, and implement the new service experience in their stores in Spain.

A multidisciplinary team of 12 people from both Vodafone and Designit led the project (although more than 90 professionals were involved in the extended team), in which 30 key processes in the shop and the back office were redesigned. Eight weeks of live prototyping were carried out after the first implementation.

Key challenge

The challenge was broken down into 350 micro tasks, which ranged from creating an express checkout process and tablet service to defining new incentive systems for employees. Therefore, flexible project management was needed, so the team adopted agile methodologies (e.g., daily stand-up team meetings and weekly reporting sessions, design sprints, validation sessions at the end of the week) and adapted new tools (dynamic lists, instant conversation groups). It was key to gather the team regularly in order to balance the outputs of each micro task with the holistic view of the future customer experience.

As with every strategic design project, the 10-week collaboration with Vodafone started with a research phase. During that phase, the Designit team conducted ethnographic research in Vodafone stores, interviewed users and commercial agents, held workshops with store managers and Vodafone leaders, and carried out research on trends and best practices in retail. Afterward, through a few co-creation sessions, the team and managers committed to developing new store principles, a new service experience, and improved customer journeys.

Prototyping methods

At a very early stage, it became clear that the project was defined by a "prototyping challenge." As the Vodafone store was a "new experience," it was in itself a kind of prototype. Using methods like role-plays and brief contextual walkthroughs in the shop environment, the Designit team was able to prototype the customer journeys. Many processes were modified before and after implementing them in the store.

During the prototyping stage, the team also created mock-ups, digital and physical prototypes of the interface's redesign, and new communication items such as a queue system, screen design, and set of commercial posters.

(A) Modular furniture allows flexibility to easily reconfigure the store layout.

(B) Sales assistants are not constrained to a specific area. Each of them has a tablet with access to Vodafone operations software so they can have a closer conversation with clients.

(C) The Apptualizador (Tech Expert) area is more prominent. High desks have been set up to offer customer service, and there are pods for payments and activations.

(D) Only live devices, no mock-ups. There's a top 10 table with the best-selling devices and more than 40 live devices in the shop.

(E) The working schedule was optimized according to the store footfall and in agreement with the store team.

(F) Communication is now simpler and more direct. A number of messages were simplified.

Rapid in-store testing of all of these ideas allowed the team to quickly validate and iterate and to observe and measure the success or failure of the ideas. For example, Designit proto-typed a "self-care kiosk" in the shop – a self-service point that allowed the customers to experience several services. Through iteration we identified the fastest way to be served there.

During the "live prototyping" stage, consisting of in-store tests with real customers, the team even prototyped different furniture for new products in Vodafone's portfolio such as the "connected home."

The project team collected quantitative and qualitative data (attention time, impact of using tablets during service, time per journey, satisfaction per journey, etc.) that helped them to take decisions and to further iterate on the design. Those were the seeds for defining today's key performance indicators of the Vodafone in-store experience. Finally, the team prepared all the material for the rollout.

Redesigned store
At the end of the ideation and pro-totyping phases, the store had been redesigned in every single aspect. New sales and experience models were created, new roles were defined, and new back office processes were developed. Designit generated a store manual with all of the information, documenting and detailing every single design specification for the new store experience.

In order to implement the service, Designit trained the commercial agents and coached them during the in-store testing. Training and teambuilding were emphasized to ensure that the new attention model was brought to customers as Vodafone had imagined it. Finally, they spent a few weeks monitoring and measuring the implementation, ensuring that everything was running as planned and fine-tuning some of the initiatives.

Other deliverables that the project included were new interfaces for the self-service kiosks and a KPI control dashboard for measuring store success.

Finally, a new innovation methodology was introduced to the Vodafone team. Ultimately, Designit and Vodafone have achieved three main objectives: reducing waiting time and service time by half, and reducing the number of people who leave the store without being attended to. As a consequence, there has been a significant increase in Vodafone's client satisfaction.

KEY TAKEAWAYS

01 Use user-centered innovation processes to enable the project team to act and think differently to obtain different results.

02 Collect qualitative and quantitative research to help make decisions and iterate on the design.

03 Include teambuilding activities when training staff to implement a service.

04 Be sure to monitor and tweak the new service in the first few months of implementation. ◄

9.5.3 CASE: USING A FIVE-DAY SERVICE DESIGN SPRINT TO CREATE A SHARED CROSS-CHANNEL STRATEGY

Itaú's design challenge: New brand's tone of voice for digital channels

AUTHOR

Clarissa Biolchini
Design Consultant
and Service Design
Specialist, Laje

A MARCA É, FAZ E FALA.

In December 2015, Ana Couto Branding and Laje, a Brazilian branding agency and its innovation cell, were invited by Itaú – one of the biggest private banks in Latin American – to develop a project for them.

The project's goal was to help Itaú's team to redefine their brand's tone of voice for digital channels. The bank's team would have to co-create their own results. The interesting detail of this project was the type of challenge to which we applied service design tools, since our client's main challenge was related to a communication problem, not a specific product or service issue.

Ana Couto Branding's team, for which I was one of the main facilitators, created a 5-day design sprint for 25 participants from across the organization and selected external stakeholders. This included participants from different areas of the bank and a couple of representatives from Itaú's advertising agencies; on top of that we requested 12 end users and a research mediator for the tests. We worked for a few weeks with a team of four people to prepare the sprint and align it with the sponsor.

Itaú is known to be an innovative company in Brazil, already very focused on customer experience with a strong design culture. As Danielle Sardenberg, Itaú's Marketing Channels Superintendent, said, "It was Itaú's request to have a co-creative sprint for this specific brand demand, in order to create a collaborative approach, with deep understanding of the problem and excellent results, in a much faster time frame, compared to normal agency processes."

Although Itaú's internal culture is familiar with new co-creative and innovative methods, this design sprint with a specific focus on branding required careful preparation. "One of our main challenges during the process was finding the right design thinking tools that would be effective in a co-creation approach to redesign the brand's tone of voice in its digital channels," said Danilo Cid, Creative Director and Partner at Ana Couto Branding.

At first, we created activities to help the participants empathize with the bank customers' needs, applying tools such as digital user-based personas, empathy maps, and expectation maps. The teams co-created their customer journeys based on a daily use of Itaú's digital channels, and another specific journey focused on one digital activity. This allowed them to analyze the bank's digital

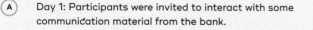

(A) Day 1: Participants were invited to interact with some communication material from the bank.

(B) Day 2: Participants were led through customer journey maps.

(C) Day 3: We brainstormed a plethora of ideas on words for the brand's tone of voice.

(D) Day 4: Participants did an energizer in which they had to draw their partner without looking at the person.

(E) Day 5: The team helped the participants to consolidate the results of the design sprint.

services in detail, giving us answers about the amount of time end users utilized the digital channels and also the appropriate tone of voice. We also used card sorting and a "physical voting" method, where the participants had to walk around in the room to vote "yes" or "no" using their body movements. This ultimately helped them to define some specific criteria regarding their brand's communications, like what expressions should or should not be used in the bank's digital channels when communicating with clients.

Regarding the customers, Sardenberg said, "Along the process we had great insights for communication from the perspective of the clients." We realized that the customers prefer red a more direct and friendlier tone, compared to the more formal one the bank had previously used in its communications. During the ideation phase, the teams co-created new rules and guidelines for the communication touchpoints and were able to build prototypes of the bank's communication items, such as ads, text replies to the digital devices, and customer service scripts. These

prototypes were tested with real clients on the fourth day of the sprint.

During the sprint days, "Itaú's teams reacted very well to the sprint, since the process involved many of the bank's departments that understood the complexity and relevance of the project," said Patricia Martins, Itaú's Marketing Channels Manager. We were easily able to notice the empowerment of the participants and their engagement with the project.

In just five days our team, together with the client's team, was able to deliver the new guideline for Itaú's communication across all digital channels and create a shared understanding of the tone of voice across all teams involved in the bank's communication and sales materials.

Our main takeaway from the project was to understand and be able to create a more assertive way for the bank to communicate, in a friendlier and less authoritative tone of voice. And from the organizational point of view, the project has inspired us and made it possible to apply its results in the bank's other divisions.

— *Patricia Martins, Marketing Channels Manager, Itaú*

KEY TAKEAWAYS

 01 A short five-day sprint can deliver unexpected results and serve as a valuable tool to deliver results.

 02 Service design tools are not one-size-fits-all. It's important to carefully assess and select the right tools for your specific project.

03 Even though a sprint may only take a few days, it requires careful, thoughtful, and professional preparation within a small team.

 04 Service design can be a powerful tool to create a shared understanding of communication tone and strategy toward implementation across all channels and teams involved.

10
FACILITATING WORKSHOPS

Workshops are the key working format of service design.
How can we keep them engaging, relevant, and productive?

Expert comments ————————————————

Arne van Oosterom

Arthur Yeh

Belina Raffy

Carola Verschoor

Ivan Boscariol

Renatus Hoogenraad

10
FACILITATING WORKSHOPS

WHY FACILITATE?

"Co-creation" (more strictly, co-design)[01] makes great sense. In engaging a diverse group of participants in a multidisciplinary team, we encourage a rounded approach to a project, keep it rooted in reality, and boost the buy-in from a wide group of stakeholders who have been involved from the beginning. We need that precious range of viewpoints and experience.

If service design is a truly co-creative activity, then facilitation must be the key tool of any practitioner.

But put some folks from marketing, some hotline staff, a financial wizard, some techies, some middle management, a couple of designers, a union rep, and a handful of customers in a room, then sit back and listen. It will immediately be clear that the people speak very varied languages, sometimes literally. They might not share the same level of education or powers of empathy, abstraction, expression, and comprehension. They certainly have different ways of working, diverse goals, and varied measures of success.

How can we get the most out of these people, and keep them moving forward together in a context where they all feel useful, engaged, and might even come again next time? How can we even help them get better at what they do? Figuring that out is the role of the facilitator.

01 For a descrption of the difference between co-design and co-creation, see 2.5.1, *The original.*

10.1 KEY CONCEPTS OF FACILITATION

A quick search online or a glance through your business library will reveal a lifetime's reading on the roles of the facilitator.[01] But most of this good advice arises from the context of meetings and similar work sessions – largely verbal activities which are usually set up to make big decisions. Service design, in contrast, is a creative, exploratory, and sometimes physical activity which has a very different process and outcome. Are the traditional business facilitation approaches enough? We suggest adding techniques used in other creative and exploratory processes, used by people who call themselves the *director*, *servant leader*, *Joker*, or *difficultator*.

A facilitator has a complex task, as she works at three levels simultaneously – process, group, and individual. She will facilitate the process, offering information, selecting activities, and consolidating results to guide the work toward a successful conclusion. She will facilitate the group, keeping them motivated, engaged, and productive while handling conflicts and tensions. And she will facilitate the individuals, helping them to be more empathic, analytic, creative, or skeptical as

needed, and perhaps helping them evolve in their skills and perspectives. To achieve this, she will need to consider three key concepts: consent, status, and neutrality.

10.1.1 Consent

Facilitating a process without the consent of the participants is an uphill struggle. Most facilitators prefer to get explicit consent before going far into the project – but that "I'm the facilitator" and simple nod on the first morning is never really enough. At first, all the participants know about an external facilitator is that she is an outsider, probably earns more per hour than most other people in the room, and was just seen laughing with the boss in the corridor. There is no trust at all, but nobody will speak up against her in the glare of C-suite attention. Lack of consent is more often not explicit, but is a creeping sickness of lethargic responses, sideways glances, and insupportable objections.

To counter this, it's not enough to throw in some (questionable) team-building exercises like trust falls. You will need the participants to truly trust you to guide work which is directly relevant to their business, and you will be asking them to fail in front of their peers. To build

💬 **COMMENT**

"The goal of facilitation, its primary purpose, is content driven and not process driven. So, while facilitators facilitate, they facilitate *toward* a result. On the way, they might do some teaching, some coaching, or different interventions to keep the group's energy going. But it is not enough to deliver on process if the results are not achieved."

— Carla Verschoor

---

01 Some experts distinguish between *the facilitator* and someone who is just facilitating. Others talk about a facilitator, a facilitative individual, a facilitative leader, and a facilitative group. See Doyle, M. (2014). "Foreword," in S. Kaner, *Facilitator's Guide to Participatory Decision Making*, 3rd ed. Jossey-Bass.

this trust, many facilitators slowly stack up implicit consent through a series of small agreements. They might start with consensus on the simple stuff like timings, breaks, and where to have lunch, then move on to agreements on the process and how to make group decisions. Later, depending on their style, there might be permission to step into disputes, to offer suggestions, even to determine the endpoint of the process.

10.1.2   Status

The status of a facilitator is complex. It is multipolar: she might be master of the process, but she is also a servant of the group and their bosses. It is variable: localized within a room or project, temporary, and limited even there. But as an outsider a facilitator can also say and do things which others cannot. Forum Theater[02] practitioners call their facilitator a Joker,[03] and the term fits well for any facilitator. Like a medieval fool, a facilitator is disqualified from holding real power, so she is free to ask the stupid question and name the elephant in the room.

Most people in organizations "have" status – through seniority, personality, and network, or a combination of these. For facilitators, it is more useful to see status as a tool which can be consciously applied and changed.[04]

10.1.3   Neutrality

There is a great expectation of facilitators to be fair, and one of the fastest ways to lose a group's consent is to behave in a way they see as biased. But different facilitators have different interpretations of neutrality, especially when it comes to content.

Some facilitators, especially external ones, only take care of the process, and remain firmly agnostic to the content and the final result. Others are happy to share their own knowledge in a carefully neutral way – "I saw it done this way at corporation X," "Professor Y wrote an interesting article on that" – but will not make a judgment or cast a vote. A third group feel able to grapple fully with the content, stating firm opinions while also owning the process. Whichever path they choose, facilitators will need to remain fair, and pay at least enough attention to the content to make sure that the group is making progress toward the goals of the workshop.[05]

---

02   Forum Theater is a facilitated, participatory theater form in which members of the audience explore potential strategies by stepping into a play themselves. For a similar technique adapted to service design, see *Prototyping service processes and experiences: Investigative rehearsal* in 7.2.

03   See more on Jokers in 10.2.1, *Adopting a role.*

04   See 10.4.9, *Changing status.*

05   [Here be another footnote just to raid the reading experience of our poor readers. And it's better for the layout, in this case.]

10.2 STYLES AND ROLES OF FACILITATION

10.2.1 Adopting a role

It is not always necessary or even advisable to "be yourself" as a facilitator. Like a manager, a facilitator steps into a role, and can choose how that role should be expressed. This does not mean pretending to be someone you are not (or copying another facilitator), as inauthenticity is bound to fail. Adopting a role is about deciding which aspects of your personality to emphasize.

Many disciplines offer premade roles which can be adopted or adapted for service design facilitation. A director in theater or film instructs and coaches her ensemble toward a new experiential offering.[01] Some directors have a clear vision of the final result, others let it emerge; some are very open to input from the ensemble, others are autocratic. But like many design superstars and many managers, a director takes primary responsibility for the final result – something that few service design facilitators would do. This can be a difficult model for design teams, as the participants can feel like servants of the facilitator, but some aspects of it are very useful – in particular, taking the audience's point of view and coaching team members to play to their strengths.

Another great facilitation model is the sports coach. He is no longer able to do what he asks the athletes to do, and perhaps he never could. But he helps identify problems and opportunities, guides the team to create the strategy, allocates resources and solves disputes fairly, and then lets the team's collective intelligence take the action and make the decisions on the field.

In Scrum, an approach to co-creation most usually seen in agile software development, the facilitation of the project is cleverly divided into two roles: the Product Owner and the Scrum Master.[02] The Product Owner is responsible for the successful output of the project – making sure that the needs of the sponsoring organization and the customer are met. He does not interact with the development team in technical matters. The Scrum Master is responsible for the success of the development process. She will "protect" the development team, making sure that they they have freedom to work and move forward.

01 Importantly, the director is not usually an actress himself, so he is leading a team of people who are capable of things he cannot do. This is very similar to the situation of software development managers, who are not usually coders. See Austin, R. D., & Devin, L. (2003). *Artful Making: What Managers Need to Know About How Artists Work*. FT Press.

02 Schwaber, K., & Sutherland, J. (2016). "The Scrum Guide," at *http://www.scrumguides.org/scrum-guide.html*.

Scrum Masters are sometimes described as "servant leaders,"[04] in that they serve the team by removing roadblocks. This makes them obviously valuable to the team – a great example for any facilitator.

If service design facilitators take inspiration from the agile model, they can consciously switch between the roles of Project Owner and Scrum Master – perhaps in different phases of the workshop – or can share them between co-facilitators.

Just like service design, improvisational theater takes a fundamentally unpredictable process and gives it form and direction by sticking religiously to some simple structures and principles. Among these is the idea of diffuse leadership, exemplified in the traditions of "Yes, and …"[05] or "follow the follower."[06] One variety of improvised exploration, Forum Theater,[07] has a facilitator role called the Joker which offers useful inspiration to service designers. As a Joker, practitioners accept that co-creative groups will often try to make their lives easy. They will assume that their ideas will be accepted quickly, that people will want to use them and will understand them, that the sun will always shine.

A Joker (or "difficultator") challenges these assumptions, representing the harshness of the real world and making things trickier for the design team. The name

03 A local design event, part of the Global Service Jam initiative, *http://www.globalservicejam.org.*

04 Greenleaf, R. (2007). "The Servant as Leader." In W. Zimmerli, K. Richter, & M. Holzinger (eds.), *Corporate Ethics and Corporate Governance* (pp. 79–85). Springer. See also Larry Spears's various writings on Greenleaf.

05 In "Yes, and …" exercises, an actor takes a colleague's idea and continues it with "Yes, and …", adding his own ideas to the story. This leads to exciting and interesting scenes. Substitute "Yes, but …," and the scene goes nowhere. See the *Yes, and … warm-up method* in this chapter.

06 Spolin, V. (1999) *Improvisation for the Theater: A Handbook of Teaching and Directing Techniques,* 3rd ed. Northwestern University Press.

07 Boal, A. (2000). *Theatre of the Oppressed,* 3rd ed. London: Pluto.

"Joker" is very well chosen. Just like the Joker in a pack of cards, he is fundamentally neutral. He is also changeable or apparently capricious, often using dark humor to flip between making life easier for the team ("facilitation") and the equally important task of making it more difficult by forcing the team to be realistic ("difficultation").

10.2.2 Co-facilitation

Facilitators often work alone, but it can be very effective to have a facilitation team. With large groups, there might be a lead facilitator with responsibility for the entire process while junior co-facilitators might step in for particular tasks, keep the records, or assist a subset of the group. It can also be fruitful to share the lead completely, taking turns to be in the spotlight. This gives the participants variation in delivery and style, which will help them pay attention. The facilitator who is less in focus can watch the group for potential misunderstandings, prepare the next task, work on documentation of the last step, or simply be ready to jump in as needed. It's enormously empowering to be facilitating in the knowledge that you can go as far as you need to go, try new ideas, or mess something up – your co-facilitator will get you out of trouble.

With two facilitators, one effective division is for one facilitator to be outcome-focused, while the other takes care of the needs of the group. This is similar to the division of Scrum roles, and it is not far from the TV thriller classic of "good cop, bad cop" – at least as far as the participants are concerned.[01] Sometimes, the backgrounds or organizational roles of the facilitators will offer other useful divisions, such as "frontstage/backstage" (user experience versus process). Or one "low-flying" person might take charge of the tools and exercises being run in the room, while another connects the outputs into the "high-flying" strategy and goals, showing the participants that they are on target for their organizational needs.

Having multiple facilitators also gives the facilitation team one very valuable tool – it's possible for the facilitators to publicly (but politely) disagree. This can help more passive groups understand that there is no one clear "answer" to the problem they face, and that their own input is just as valuable as the facilitators'.

10.2.3 Can a team member be a facilitator?

EXPERT TIP

"One intermediate solution is to *borrow* an experienced facilitator from another part of your organization. They will understand the organization's culture and limits, but will be able to be more neutral on the project itself. As they are a colleague, buy-in might be easier to achieve – but set the boundaries and responsibilities very clearly."

– Ivan Boscariol

It's a common question: "Can a team member be a facilitator?" In most situations, this seems difficult. A colleague working temporarily as a facilitator might have the consent of the group, but it is difficult to remain neutral if you are in the project because of your connection to the theme. It is even trickier to be perceived as unbiased when you represent a certain part of an organization. More crucially, an internal facilitator has a clear place in the hierarchy, and does not have access to the full range of status strategies which an external facilitator can adopt.

In everyday project work, budget constraints or timing often mean that one team member must take on the facilitator role. While challenging, it is not impossible to facilitate your colleagues. Look at the tricks of traditional meeting processes, where the chairperson is a temporary role given localized authority. That's an excellent model for facilitating colleagues – taking control of the agenda and timing, keeping some distance from the issues by perhaps standing at the flipchart while others sit, and only dipping into the content level when necessary or especially valuable, perhaps with a "casting vote."

A team *leader* in a facilitator role will have great difficulty ever being seen as neutral and will find it hard to effectively adopt a lower status. This makes it especially difficult to combine project leadership and facilitation tasks.

---

01 Colleagues with military experience have likened these roles to the duties of the second in command and the senior NCO; or they may even be likened to clichéd "mother and father" roles. One variation is where the "good cop" does the "fun" stuff in the divergent phases, and the "bad cop" knuckles down in the convergent parts.

10.3 SUCCESS FACTORS

10.3.1 Building the team

The selection of people in the room may vary at different stages of the project,[02] and may not be the choice of the facilitator. But a good rule of thumb is to include representatives of anyone affected by the workshop or project, anyone who will deliver on the outcomes and outputs, and anyone who can stop it – in other words, the key stakeholders.[03] Many organizations tend to restrict the invitation list for a workshop to the core project team, but they are usually quick to see the benefits of involving other parts of the organization, and these "guests" are often enthusiastic about being involved. This can cause budgeting issues – who is paying for that person's time? – so make sure to discuss this aspect in advance.

When it comes to customers, many organizations are unwilling to show their offerings in an incomplete state and to let customers look "behind the scenes" in co-design sessions. It's a pity, because this inclusive approach can be warmly greeted. When KLM set up a co-design lab at Amsterdam Airport Schiphol, they expected (and got) great insights. But they also benefited from their customers' positive reaction to actually being involved in a design process,[04] instead of just a satisfaction survey. One way to encourage unwilling teams toward more co-design with customers is to involve customers in other ways (e.g., in more street testing and contextual interviews) so that the team sees firsthand the value of including customers and is keen to bring them into the workroom.

In some B2B organizations especially, the relationship with customers is quite formal, contract-led, and stiff, so this kind of co-creation is seen as difficult. This is a missed opportunity, as B2B partners are often in a long-term relationship, and can be quite happy to reduce risks and get better value from the future service, perhaps by prototyping together.

10.3.2 Purpose and expectations

Before planning a workshop (or series of workshops), it is important to be clear what it is for. Often, your client (or boss, or colleague) will ask for a workshop without being clear themselves what they want to get out of it. They might feel a need for activity – but not much more than that. It's important to pin down what your sponsor needs, even if you might not share this information fully with the participants. Find out what outputs and outcomes are expected and choose methods to reach them. You should also share an honest assessment of what is possible with the time and people you are given.

---

02 See also (at the project level) 9.2.3, *Project team and stakeholders*, and (at the level of the entire organization) 12.2.1, *The core service design team*, as well as 12.2.2, *The extended project team*.

03 Don't forget people with any expert knowledge you need.

04 Marcel Zwiers, 31 Volts, presentation at the Service Design in Tourism Conference, Sarasota 2013; see also 6.5.1, *Case: Opening the design studio to your customers*.

💬 COMMENT

"There is sometimes a tension between the neutral role of a facilitator, and the expected role of a consultant. Consultants are generally expected to deliver the results that the sponsor asks for. But in a facilitation setting we know that we cannot promise results, because the final decision is made by the team."

– Arthur Yeh

Some sponsors have inflated ideas about the power of service design or design thinking to generate killer new business propositions or problem solutions in a very short time. It's important to explain that service design is an understanding and development process, not a single creativity technique.

Epic wins can happen at any time, but they can never be guaranteed. To make them more probable, you need to look behind the perceived problem or opportunity; to understand the needs; to generate, prototype, and test concepts; and to iterate. That's not one workshop.

The purpose of the workshop needs to be clear to the sponsor and (usually) to the participants.[01] If you decide to tell them, tell them clearly: "We are here today to find out what really goes on in this part of the call center."

10.3.3 Planning the work

Group facilitation takes place over various time frames, which we can think of as the project scale (months, weeks) and the session scale (hours, days). Planning the facilitation will be a matter of choosing activities and allocating resources along this timeline. Project-level planning will usually follow whatever innovation or design structure the organization and facilitator choose, such as the typical iterative process of research, ideation, prototyping, and implementation.[02]

Within a single session there might be less ground to cover, and thus more freedom for the facilitator. Your workshop might only be set up to fulfill one task – like mapping a value network or planning some research – or you might need to go through the entire service design process in just a couple of days[03] as a "taster" or as the first mini-iteration to kick off a project.

It's vital to remember that design is exploration, and it is both futile and counterproductive to try to plan everything, whether for a project or a session. You will have to adjust and pivot as you go along, confidently changing your plans to fit the reality of the discovery process but never losing sight of the time constraints.[04] There's no need to be afraid, as the workshop which goes off the rails sometimes has the most startling results. All a facilitator needs is some backup plans, or enough methods "on call" that he can launch as needed. Or you might consciously adopt an approach of sprints, reflection, and adjustment like in agile software development.

As well as considering project goals, a facilitator will also have to consider the human needs of participants, planning a sequence of activities which is not only effective but engaging, enabling, encouraging, and enjoyable.

---

01 Sometimes, surprise can be useful. See, for example, 10.6.1, *Case: The energizing power of the unfamiliar.*

02 See Chapter 4, *The core activities of service design.*

03 See *Innovation jams* in 12.2.

04 See for example 10.6.2, *Case: Pivot and focus.*

10.3.4 Creating a safe space

Many service design tools and methods seem uncomfortable and strange to people in organizations, especially because a creative process needs people to fail. This is a very unfamiliar way of working, and people need help to accept and welcome it.

One powerful way to do this is to pay attention to "safe space," the physical and mental environment which accepts and embraces failure. The idea of safe space is well developed in theater, where every actor knows that the rehearsal room is completely safe. He can try anything, will never be interrupted or mocked, and will be judged only on what he chooses to bring out of the room. That's the ideal atmosphere for innovation.

A safe space cannot be set up by simply declaring it. "Today, nothing we do goes beyond this room" is a statement which only works if there is full trust, and trust is not usually present at the beginning of a co-creative project. Instead, safe space is built up using a mix of techniques – both in the planning phase and during the session itself. Many of these techniques are based on giving a sense of security to participants who are going through an unfamiliar process. Others help the team members adopt different mindsets – catalogs of behavior and responses – which are unlike the usual work mindset and are more conducive to cooperative, creative work.

Own the space

A good co-creative session needs its own private space where the group is not overlooked. Close the door, uninvite guests ("no spectators today, sorry – you are welcome to join in or step out"), and paper up any windows which expose you to curious passersby. This need not be overt – a strip of flipchart paper at eye level gives privacy and holds your sticky notes later. You can extend the room ownership to the group by letting them rearrange the room themselves.[05]

Start in familiar territory

It's rarely helpful to plunge people into cold water. Start where they feel safe. For example, in a corporate environment you might wear a suit and welcome guests into a conservative room layout. Perhaps you start with a calm slide presentation showing which corporate strategy the project is part of. Orientation is important,[06] but people don't always perform best if they know exactly what is coming. Show an agenda which describes the coming session in conservative terms, without being dishonest. For example, an agenda point of "role-play session" or "live street research" will terrify some group members, but you can describe the same session as "understanding the customer" and no one will think twice.

Make sure you understand the organization's language – terms like "research," "insight," and "prototype," or even "customer," "user," or "stakeholder" can mean very specific things in some organizations. So use terms the way your participants use them, or take time to explain how you will use them differently, and why.

EXPERT TIP

"With a new team, people I did not know, I would wear a suit and tie. This communicated that I took people seriously and I was a professional. I would also use slides for presenting ideas and action plans. For the second meeting I would lose the tie and dress more casually. This would create a more relaxed and personal *among friends* atmosphere. I would also lose the slideware. People would be more relaxed, open, and less defensive."

– Arne van Oosterom

COMMENT

"Facilitation means holding the space so that group wisdom can come out."

– Arthur Yeh

---

05 See *Break with routine* later in this section.
06 See *Give orientation* later in this section.

Invoke authority

It's possible to establish ownership of the process with the right tone of voice, a look straight in the eye, and carefully chosen words of welcome. Saying, "I am the facilitator today, and I will make sure we get a result" will make roles clear and also show you accept responsibility. But you may need more.

If you have reference customers who are impressive and perhaps also conservative, you might name them when you introduce yourself to the group, and say in what context you were able to help them. If you have relevant qualifications which will mean something to the group (and if you can talk about them without sounding like a boaster), mention them early on. You might also name-drop some very conservative and traditional organizations that are using service design or design thinking, like Big Four consulting companies and their peers,[01] or the US military.[02] For a small nonprofit, you might choose other examples.

Best of all, get senior staff of your client organization to address the group by video message or in person and tell them which parts of the organization are behind the initiative, and which strategic goals it fits into.

Break with routine

Having started off in a conservative tone, it's time to show that the upcoming work session will be different and will have room for other kinds of ideas and behavior. Do something unusual but clearly useful (like an extreme warm-up,[03] complete with neurological explanation of why it's important; or have the group quickly rearrange the room for group work). It's impossible to win trust straight away, but you might generate some curiosity. If someone resists warm-ups as kid stuff, talk about the science and experience behind them and gently show that someone who rejects them is missing an opportunity to be more effective.

Ease in

Don't jump straight into the hard stuff, be too crazy, or put anyone in the spotlight yet. This is a good time to agree on or establish some ground rules. The Rules of Rehearsal are one example, but you might have your own. It's useful to establish early on how you will make decisions – the Rules of Rehearsal do this via the point "Doing, not talking." You might play a game to demonstrate useful behaviors or attitudes, like perhaps a "Yes, and …" round. Don't spend too long on this, though. After an intense warm-up, the team will want action, not discussion.

EXPERT TIP

"When I am facilitating co-creative groups, I often draw on the practical (but profound) principles of improvisational theater. There are many ways to express them, but I like Robert Poynton's *let go*, *notice more*, and *use everything* with a core of *yes, and*. That's a great foundation for any creative session – or project."

— Belina Raffy

---

01 *"Service design will be at the core of where we want to go."* Joydeep Bhattacharya, Managing Director, Accenture Interactive Financial Services at SDN Global Conference, Stockholm 2014. More professional services companies, banks, and other large organizations have bought up service design agencies in an attempt to benefit from their skills and capacities.

02 US Army (2012). *Army Doctrine Publication 5-0: The Operations Process.* Headquarters, Department of the Army. 03 See 10.4.1, *Warm-ups*, and the method *Three-brain warm-up* in 10.5.

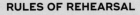

RULES OF REHEARSAL

→ **Use what you have.**
→ **Play seriously.**
→ **Doing, not talking!**

The Rules of Rehearsal use a term which seems odd in many workspaces – "play." In fact, play is a safe space in itself as it includes permission to fail. A serious, focused playfulness can be enormously effective in a creative context.

Give orientation
People always feel more comfortable if they know where they are in the process. But as service design is an explorative, iterative task, it's not always useful to post a method agenda – you can never be sure in advance when you will change it. Instead, a large visual of the whole process can be reassuring. Refer to your process visualization often, and especially to the divergent and convergent phases.[04]

Some phases of a design task are not comfortable, especially for inexperienced designers, and telling the group that it is OK to feel confused or out of control at these points will help them enormously. The end of a divergent phase can feel especially overwhelming. Participants thought they had a handle on a possible end result, and now suddenly there are so many new ideas, so many possible variations. This is a loss of control, which

is precisely what most organizational processes try to avoid. It's unsettling – so tell them "it's normal to feel like this," and show them that while the outcome is fuzzy, the process is perfectly clear. And try not to end a session on a divergent phase.[05]

Sh!tty first drafts
People who are new to creative work are usually far too careful. They think creativity is about having great ideas, so they spend too much time on their first ideas and run the risk of falling in love with them. Show them that in these early iterations, "lo-fi" – a rough, low-fidelity approximation of reality – is encouraged.

You could show them some of your own terrible sketches, present some very flimsy prototypes, make them use fat pens on small pieces of paper, or perhaps introduce the concept of sh!tty first drafts (this is based on Hemingway's observation that "the first draft of anything is sh!t").[06] That's a tough word to say in some corporate concepts, but there is no better way to express the idea.

In the executive schools which led to this book, the concept of the "sh!tty first draft" became a real favorite with participants returning to their companies, as it freed people from the desire to think everything through in detail and take responsibility for every spontaneous idea. Management folks in particular are often delighted to discover how fast they can get to actionable results with this attitude.[07]

05 If it happens (sometimes it can't be avoided), acknowledge it openly.

06 Ernest Hemingway's statement, and the term "shitty first draft", were popularized in Lamott, A. (1994). *Shitty First Drafts. Bird by Bird: Some Instructions on Writing and Life* (pp. 21–26). Anchor.

07 Another benefit: commentators seem to give more honest and sweeping feedback on lo-fi prototypes as they think we have not invested too much time in them.

04 The Squiggle (discussed in *Planned iterations* in 9.2.4) is also useful here.

To encourage this type of working, you can talk about sh!tty first drafts explicitly, or leave the term unsaid and instead encourage people toward them. One way is to use seemingly "impossible deadlines" which make the group worry about quantity instead of quality.[01]

Mix activities, make a mess

Different people appreciate and understand different types of activities, so keep the energy in the room and appeal to different audiences by including a broad mix.

Try to choose activities which make a clear contribution to the task at hand, but vary the location in the room, the media, the focus, and the physical position of participants. You can emphasize the explorative, "throwaway" nature of ideas and prototypes by creating a mess as you go on. Have candy in wrappers (rustling, noisy ones are best) which litter the room. Don't clean up (too much) overnight.[03] Have things like toys, gadgets, and old prototypes lying about – people will pick them up and fiddle with them while they think and talk. All these will help people remain sketchy in their thinking and presentation, until the time comes to focus down, make choices, and tidy the room. A key part of the design process is moving from productive messes to simplicity and clarity.

01 See 10.4.2, *Timing*.
02 See 6.3.1, *Planning ideation*.
03 Bruce Mau writes, "Don't clean your desk. You might find something in the morning that you can't see tonight." Mau, B. (2001). "An Incomplete Manifesto for Growth" at *http://www.manifestoproject.it/bruce-mau/*.

Safe space principles in practice

WORKSHOP STRUCTURE

The workshop is structured in three phases: a prephase, to fill in information gaps and even lower expectations; a main phase leading up to the key tool of investigative rehearsal; and a final reflection phase.

In this one-day design workshop for a group of mainly frontline staff or customers, the plan is to examine an existing experience, then generate and test many new ideas using investigative rehearsal[04] – a usually unfamiliar tool. We might spend about two hours establishing safe space and building energy before subtly slipping into the rehearsal phase, finally ending the day with a reflective phase.

1 **Slideware** presentation. (start in familiar territory, invoke authority / 20 mins)
2 **Three-brain** warm-up. (break with routine / 15 minutes)

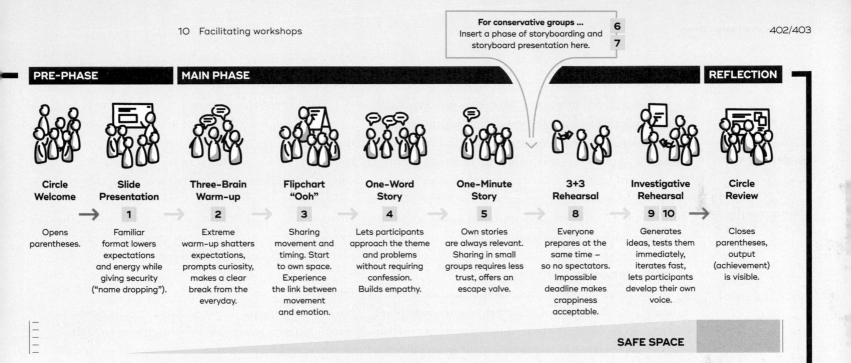

For conservative groups ...
Insert a phase of storyboarding and
storyboard presentation here. **6 7**

| PRE-PHASE | | MAIN PHASE | | | | | | | REFLECTION |

Circle Welcome
Opens parentheses.

Slide Presentation 1
Familiar format lowers expectations and energy while giving security ("name dropping").

Three-Brain Warm-up 2
Extreme warm-up shatters expectations, prompts curiosity, makes a clear break from the everyday.

Flipchart "Ooh" 3
Sharing movement and timing. Start to own space. Experience the link between movement and emotion.

One-Word Story 4
Lets participants approach the theme and problems without requiring confession. Builds empathy.

One-Minute Story 5
Own stories are always relevant. Sharing in small groups requires less trust, offers an escape valve.

3+3 Rehearsal 8
Everyone prepares at the same time – so no spectators. Impossible deadline makes crappiness acceptable.

Investigative Rehearsal 9 10
Generates ideas, tests them immediately, iterates fast, lets participants develop their own voice.

Circle Review
Closes parentheses, output (achievement) is visible.

SAFE SPACE

3 **Rules of Rehearsal** as participatory game; re-arrange room. (ease in / 10 minutes)

4 **Storytelling games** about the situation today to generate material for later. (ease in / 20 minutes)

5 **Teams choose** interesting stories to work on and give them a Hollywood title. (safety net / 5 minutes)

6 **Storyboard** the scenes on paper "in 8 minutes." (make a mess, doing not talking, sh!tty first draft / 10 minutes)

7 **Present** storyboards to the group – this is the first time anyone has spoken to the whole group, but it is a familiar situation. (ease in / 15 minutes)

8 **Prepare** to show the scene. Tell groups "We want to experience the scene here in the room, just a quick first version up to 3 minutes long. Decide where it will happen in the room, and what you will need. Decide who will be each person in your storyboard. You have 3 minutes to prepare and walk it through.

One rule: nobody plays himself." All teams prepare at once. Don't use the words "act" or "role-play." (avoid killer words, sh!tty first draft, doing not talking, offer safety net / 3 minutes)

9 **Watch** all the sh!tty first drafts, without comments but with applause. (avoid judgment / 10 minutes)

10 **Move** straight into real investigative rehearsal without a pause. (ease in) ◄

04 Investigative rehearsal is a research, ideation, and prototyping tool you can use to understand experiences, then quickly generate and test new ideas. See *Prototyping service processes and experiences: Investigative rehearsal* in 7.2.

Avoid killer words

Avoid words and phrases which force people to be overly analytical or which raise the stakes on ideas too early. Don't ask for "your best idea," just ask for "a heap of ideas to get us started." Don't ask people to "choose the best option," just tell them to "grab an interesting one to kick off with." Don't ask for a "presentation" or a "role-play," ask instead for a "quick status report" or say "Can you get up and show me quickly how it might look?"

Offer safety nets

Participants agonize about the quality of their ideas, but some simple safety nets will ease their worries. Help people learn to let go of ideas by generating so many of them that leaving some behind becomes easier (and remind them of the link between the number of ideas and the final success). Increase the willingness to let go by throwing nothing away. Ask teams to pin up *abandoned* ideas on the wall so they can come back to them later. Let subgroups choose which ideas and insights to take forward, so someone can quietly ask his subgroup, "Can we *not* take my suggestion, please?"

Avoid judgment

In most corporate contexts, quickly deciding what is good and what is not is a key skill. Service design encourages us not to rank and choose ideas, but to evolve them through prototyping and testing. So, it is helpful to avoid asking "Was that a good idea?" and instead ask "How did that feel?" or "What does that suggest?" In a co-creative environment, the words "good" and "bad" are rarely useful for content.

Notice more and adapt

Good facilitators develop good sensing skills, and are able to read the room and the people in it. They can see when the group is losing track, being dominated by certain members, or is lost, confused, or demotivated. Sometimes, you can ask the group directly. But they are not always willing or able to verbalize – and sometimes it is not the group which needs help, but particular individuals. This means sensing skills are very important, as is the flexibility to change the facilitation plan in response.

Fail first

It is no use telling participants that failure is welcome, then doing everything you can yourself to avoid it. If you mess up a part of your facilitation, be open about it. Laugh, and describe it as a learning opportunity (some irony is completely appropriate). Be clear that the whole session is explorative, and that some activities might fail. Give permission to be human by being human yourself.

10.3.5 Work modes in teams

Whether "brainstorming," talking, or prototyping, group work in teams has three basic forms. Look out for them in groups – consciously switching between them can be a useful technique, choosing the best one for the next task and the current group dynamic. We describe them as if the task was a written activity like drawing up new ideas, but the models apply equally well to working on a prototype.

(A) Sh!tty first drafts can be made very quickly.

(B) A sh!tty first draft of an app (here combined with a rough desktop walkthrough) gets across the basic idea in seconds, and starts the iteration process in minutes.

(C) A sh!tty first draft or guesstimation of the numbers can let teams rescope early.

(D) This looked much more roomy on paper ... a physical sh!tty first draft of a transport seating system immediately reveals problems.

(E) At the Hatch, participants are invited to get hands-on and messy.[01]

One page, one pen

All the group members are talking and one person is writing or sketching – either on a pad or device, or on a flipchart or board for all to see. Although status within the group plays a role, the "hands-on" person has a basic choice between being a servant or a king. If he chooses the servant option, he will record the group consensus and not take much part in the conversation.

Or he could choose to wait until he agrees before writing a point down, or shape his notes to his preferred slant on the discussion. With various degrees of subtlety and success, he could take the crown of the king.

"One page, one pen" is the mode you will see most often in your workplace and is the one most groups will default to. It is familiar, and has the advantage that the output has coherence, basic consensus, and is understood by the whole group, especially when the work has been visible to all. But more diverse ideas and opinions have already been ironed out. We have a narrow, "predigested" outcome – and this way of working is very slow in comparison with the other modes.

One page, many pens

In this mode, the whole group sit or stand around a shared work object. Everyone is writing, drawing, amending the same drawing or text. There might be discussion, or they might work in silence. They share their time between actively contributing and looking at what the others are doing, what they are changing.

01 See more on the Chick-fil-A design space in Chapter 11, *Making space for service design.*

OF PENS AND PAGES

Different ways of working in groups have different advantages and disadvantages. Most groups will default to one pen, one page, so encourage them to sometimes change their group cooperation pattern when they need diversity or speed.

ONE PEN, ONE PAGE   **MANY PENS, ONE PAGE**

MANY PENS, MANY PAGES

Completeness
Shared understanding

Speed
Diversity

This mode also works digitally: when writing publications, the lead authors of this book often use online platforms to write simultaneously in the same document. We don't have any verbal channel open – we simply write, or sit back, and watch the other cursors before dropping in to rearrange, rewrite, or add emphasis and examples.

"One page, many pens" is reasonably consensual. Afterward, there may be a need to tidy up and explain some of the work to each other, but there is usually a basic understanding of the shared ideas. The technique is messy, but quite fast. Conflicts and differences of opinion are usually readily visible on the page as crossings-out or notes and might be the start for a good discussion afterward.

Many pages, many pens

The group consciously split up and work as individuals. Each person writes on their own pages, usually writing or sketching one idea per page. Often, the group tries for an ambitious number of ideas in a fixed time period, so they keep searching after the obvious ideas have been recorded. When the time is up, they come back together and each show the group their results.

"Many pages, many pens" is a fast way to develop many ideas and particularly empowers more introverted participants. Some ideas will probably occur several times from different group members, but there will still be far more diversity than with either other mode. This method does not bring a shared understanding – some ideas will need to be explained to the rest of the group, and this will take some time. The group will also need to decide which ideas to take forward, either by discussion, voting, or using selection matrices or portfolios.[01]

01 See, for example, *Idea portfolio* in 6.4.

10.4 KEY FACILITATION TECHNIQUES

10.4.1 Warm-ups

Warm-ups and energizers can be enormously valuable or a colossal waste of time and good will. They can help to "break the ice" in a group, help members get to know each other, get people comfortable in a space, make ideation more effective, help teams let go of ideas, help people to be happy failing, and wake people up in the natural low points of the day. Badly chosen or framed, they can also cost you the respect and consent of the group.

If possible, pick warm-ups which have a secondary effect, and explain the thinking behind your choice.[02] Some warm-ups, for example, are great models of communication patterns or show us valuable behavior for group cooperation. Others demonstrate a point. Nearly all of them are ideation boosters.[03] This chapter contains descriptions of several warm-ups we like to use.

Rather than doing warm-ups automatically at the start of the day and after lunch, think about placing them more carefully. In particular, people are usually pretty fresh directly after lunch, so do a warm-up 45 or 60 minutes later, when they are really battling their biorhythm. A powerful warm-up can also be a great way to start opening a safe space, after the introductory talks are over and the

VIPs have left. In ideation activities, give the ideation challenge first, then move straight into a warm-up which demands complete concentration *before* you start generating ideas. This will stop the participants thinking about the challenge for a few minutes, with a positive effect[04] on the ideation which follows.

Combine warm-ups with other functions to be doubly efficient. Rearranging the room into a new configuration is a great way to mark a new step in the process. Add some fun music and a tight deadline and it becomes a great warm-up too (the same goes for tidying the space). Or, instead of boring introduction rounds, have the participants map out their organization, skills, or physical world by where they stand in the room. A game like Thirty-Five or Benny Hill sorting is a highly efficient work process that also works as a warm-up. If you have one of these activities coming soon, a warm-up might not be necessary.

If you can, go for warm-ups with a physical, spatial, and mental component, and with a fun factor. If people are concentrated, moving, and laughing, it's going to be a good warm-up. And if we are having fun failing, we show a shared humanity and open a door to successful failure in our work.

---

02 This might happen after the warm-up, in a short reflection – consider warm-ups as experiential learning tools in themselves. See Kolb, D. (1984). *Experiential Learning as the Science of Learning and Development*. Prentice Hall.

03 Got a sketching activity coming up? Try a sketchy warm-up like "draw your neighbor in 30 seconds without looking at the paper." These games are remarkably effective. See for example Worinkeng, E., Summers, J. D., & Joshi, S. (2013). "Can a Pre-sketching Activity Improve Idea Generation?" In M. Abramovici & R. Stark (eds.), *Smart Product Engineering* (pp. 583-592). Springer, Berlin, Heidelberg.

04 See *Managing energy* in 6.3.2.

10.4.2 Timing

One of the most powerful tools of the facilitator is time. Use deadlines throughout the day to keep the team moving forward and to adjust the level of detail and polish in their work. Very tight or "impossible" deadlines can help teams avoid wasting time on talking too much. Time pressure will encourage them to go for quantity instead of quality. It will prevent them considering details too early in the process and promote creating the sh!tty first drafts mentioned earlier in this chapter.

An occasional countdown through a task will help teams use their time wisely and keep up energy in the room, and counting out the last seconds (or playing a "time's up" song with a clear end) means no one gets stopped mid-sentence. If a deadline must cut people off in mid-presentation, find a supportive way to interrupt – a vigorous round of applause hurts least.

But be careful with impossible deadlines, though. They are very powerful up to a certain point, but there is a minimum time below which the task becomes meaningless. Play around with deadlines and see what works for your group. Give them 3 minutes, and they will gasp but knuckle down. Give 10 minutes and they will expect 15, but give 8 minutes and they will focus. Give 20 minutes and they will step out to fetch a coffee first; give 18 or 21 and they might not.

Not everything can be done at a sprint. Like a project, a workshop also needs slower times for reflection, recovery, and to make a satisfying dramatic arc.[01] Decide if you need a visible clock in the room. If you don't have one, you can use "liquid time" – secretly shorten deadlines to add pressure and increase energy; secretly lengthen deadlines if important discoveries are made, or if people have trouble with a task or need to feel productive.

10.4.3 The room

The room itself is a tool, and a crucial one. We will talk about dedicated spaces in Chapter 11, *Making space for service design,* and much of that applies here. But let's consider temporary spaces first.

It's easy to consign this kind of work to expensive off-site locations with a "creative atmosphere" that help us "think outside the box"; but that can signify to some people that service design is detached from everyday concerns, and needs a specialized environment. It's fun, useful, and perhaps more sustainable to take a normal conference room and transform it temporarily into a more flexible and stimulating space. It shows that we can do this anytime and anywhere, and means that our colleagues' expertise and experience is just a short walk away.

If you have a choice of rooms, think about light, privacy, acoustics, and flexibility. Everyone loves light and air, and facilitation in a low-ceilinged, gloomy room is always much more difficult as the day wears on.[02] But no one wants to work in a fishbowl either, and a feeling of

> **💬 EXPERT TIP**
>
> "Make sure you keep the pressure high, even though the real timing may be *liquid*."
>
> **– Renatus Hoogenraad**

01 See the textbox *Dramatic arcs* in 3.3.

02 In experiments, high ceilings seem to put test participants in a mindset of freedom, creativity, and abstraction, while low ceilings help them limit and focus. See, for example, Meyers-Levy, J., & Zhu, R. (2007). "The Influence of Ceiling Height: The Effect of Priming on the Type of Processing That People Use." *Journal of Consumer Research,* 34(2), 174–186.

being "on display" can seriously inhibit creativity. So if the room is very glassy, encourage participants to use the glass as a work and display surface, and perhaps hang blank paper at eye level to shield them until the windows fill up.

Music can be an incredibly useful tool. Use it to energize, speed up, relax, calm, create urgency, have fun. Play light, jangly music during group discussion rounds, so the participants cannot listen in on other groups. Play quiet music to help create an atmosphere of concentration in solo work. Establish rituals like a set of songs to count down to a deadline, the start of the next session, or to a break.

Practitioner's experiments[03] have found that the most effective furniture for creative groups seems to be a combination of high tables and bar stools – they are restful for the legs but also make it easier for people to get up and move around. A flexible selection is ideal, with light but sturdy furniture which can be moved quickly and even folded away. Rearranging the room several times throughout the day helps punctuate the activities[04] and mark the process, as well as mixing up groups and breaking up hardening social structures in the space. If they do it themselves, it also helps the participants "own" the space.[05]

💬 **EXPERT TIP**

"If high tables and bar-stools are not available (talk to the manager of the staff restaurant before you give up), ask yourself if you even need chairs. Try a fluid *standing* space with some tables near the walls to perch on and perhaps a few chairs for those who really need them. Ideally, there would be a comfortable sitting area for reflective phases nearby."

– Renatus Hoogenraad

10.4.4 Tools and props

Tools and other tangible items can enrich a room. One option is to have a core toolkit (standard pens, scissors, knives, tape, note paper, sticky notes) on each workspace, and a central pool of shared resources like templates, cardboard, building bricks, figurines, and other prototyping material. Add to the mix by spreading some random portable objects around the room – toys, gadgets, ornaments, puzzles, even little bits of costume (or rubber chickens). They can help establish a safe space by prompting other playful, curious, empathic, or experimental mindsets.

You can never have enough wall space in a room.[06] Participants should keep their material visible by hanging it on the wall, letting them constantly discover new connections and trace ideas back to their origins in research insights. This consumes wall space very fast, so expand it with wheeled pinboards or simply big sheets of cardboard which can be moved around fast, rested against tables, and laid to one side when not needed. If the space is very high, use a ladder to have another row of key material hanging high above the active area. It's a great visual reference and stimulus, but it's never in the way.

10.4.5 Visualization

With so much service design DNA coming from the world of product and graphic design, visualization will always have a key place in the design process.[07] Appropriate visuals speed up the process, allow for easy iterations, and get people on the same page very quickly. Compare

03 Doorley, S., & Witthoft, S. (2012). *Make Space: How to Set the Stage for Creative Collaboration*. John Wiley & Sons.

04 For an example of changing the room to great effect during a workshop, see 10.6.2, *Case: Pivot and focus*.

05 For more on this topic, see 10.3.4, *Creating a safe space*.

06 Read more on this in Chapter 11, *Making space for service design*.

07 See the comic strip section on visualization in Chapter 6, *Ideation*.

(A) Timing to the second. The facilitator counts down
the final eight seconds of a lighting presentation.
Tight deadlines, used lightly, keep the room engaged
and help participants escape the urge to be perfect.

(B) A quick visualization tells a thousand words ... and
provides the perfect support for storytelling or explaining
an insight. That's why so many key service design tools
are visualizations.

(C) As well as promoting a playful, humane mindset,
random objects spread through the room will often
become part of a prototype or a group's identity.
They will even help some people think better.[01]

a 4-page text document with many open questions to 10
quick sketches: only the latter will help you in a workshop
setting. Visuals help enormously to make things tangible,
helping participants move away from theoretical thinking
into practical doing. Not least, you will rely on documentation after your workshops, and visualizations of any quality
will be extremely helpful and authentic in this context.

If you want participants to draw, don't show them
your exquisitely drafted flipcharts first. Use scrappy
visuals and scribbled templates yourself, tell them that
stick figures are welcome, or give them a crash course in
simple visualization techniques. Remind them that most
of the visualizations they create will be only for the team,
and will be left behind soon.

10.4.6 Post it or lose it: The expert's guide to sticky notes

If there is one tool which has become the epitome – or
cliché – of service design it is surely the sticky note. In
fact, those notes are enormously useful – they each hold
a bite-sized piece of information and let us organize and
sequence it easily, then change our mind. But they can be
even more powerful if we use them intelligently.

Encourage participants to both choose and mark
their sticky notes consciously, not just grab the nearest
one. Encourage them to use one color and size of note,
and one color and thickness of pen for the same level of

01 Karlesky, M., & Isbister, K. (2013). "Fidget Widgets: Secondary Playful Interactions in Support of Primary
Serious Tasks." In *CHI'13 Extended Abstracts on Human Factors in Computing Systems* (pp. 1149-1154). ACM.

information. (Make this easier for them by only having one type of pen in the room and specifying the note color for each task or step.) This makes it easier to find connections and groupings within the clusters of notes.

If you use many colors, shapes, and pen sizes, participants may feel themselves distracted by searching for patterns among the colors, even if their conscious minds know that the format is meaningless. It can also make it very easy to see which ideas come from the boss …

On the second day of a workshop, or after lunch, the floor will usually be littered with notes which have fallen off the wall.[02] It's annoying and it costs us data. Teach your team to pull sticky notes "like a pro" so they stick better. A flat note will stay on the wall far longer, and your "million-dollar idea" will be safe from the fifty-dollar vacuum cleaner.

COMMENT

"I use my sticky notes one color at a time, as it seems to work best and I think it encourages shared ownership of ideas. Other colleagues use chaotic mixes of colors and pens when they think the group needs this shock treatment or craves a release from gray thinking. That's a valuable point, but I find the cost of the colorful inspiration is a slower process, and irritation for some people who like structure."

– Belina Raffy

10.4.7 Space, distance, and positioning

As a facilitator, one of your most powerful tools is your own body and physicality, using the entire room as a three-dimensional stage. Do you sit with the participants, hover near them, or have your own territory? When will you step firmly into the center to get attention and focus, withdraw into a corner to let them get on with it, or fade into the group to do something together? To help someone pay attention, you can stand closer to her, step into her personal space (directly behind her is most effective), or, if appropriate, lay a hand on her shoulder to really make the point.

02 Those extra-sticky notes are a good investment.

STICKY NOTE 101

(A) A facilitator remains standing, available but not intruding, while her group works. On the table, her mobile phone counts down the time remaining for the task.

(B) The facilitator leans in, occupying the neutral space of the table and naturally taking the group's attention.

(C) Sticky note 101, pulling like a pro. Pull up, and your note will curl and soon end up on the floor. Put your thumb high under the top note and pull down toward your belly to *snap* off a flat note. Later, when the pad is thin, peel from the side or turn the pad over and start at the back.

POSITION AND CONVERSATION

Parallel and triangular positioning, for a very different conversation.

PARALLEL POSITIONING

TRIANGULAR POSITIONING

Be conscious of relative height as well – there are times when you should stand when the group sits, times when you should sit or stand with them, times you should sit while they stand. When would you stand on a chair, squat beside someone, even sit on the floor? When do you make eye contact, and when do you let it slip away? When do you spread out your arms, or put your head in your hands? When is your body language open, critical, engaged, relaxed? Observe others and you will soon see what works.

Most positioning strategies come down to two basic arrangements called parallel or triangular positioning. *Parallel positioning* is where two people (or two groups, or a person and a group) stand or sit directly facing each other, their shoulders forming two parallel lines. It is the position of the interviewee to the interviewer (or the police officer), the two negotiation teams, the two tough guys about to fight. This is an unnatural and uncomfortable position which feels confrontational. *Triangular positioning* is different. The two parties stand at two points of a triangle, facing the third point. The third corner holds (or represents) the material being discussed, the

challenge, the problem. It is a more cooperative position, like two friends fishing in one ice hole, or mechanics discussing how to fix a dent in a car.

A parallel position is not always bad, and a triangular one is not always good. Sometimes a parallel position can give authority, like the judge in court or the nightclub doorman. It can be a powerful position to take charge of a group, to call a halt to unacceptable behavior, or to punctuate the day.[01]

10.4.8 Feedback

Feedback is a very versatile facilitation tool. Quick team feedback from a "passing" facilitator or mentor can help teams stay on track, break deadlocks, or quietly suggest methods and tools. More public feedback – perhaps from the whole room or from visitors (e.g., users, customers, frontline staff, or other stakeholders) – can give a team a broad selection of new ideas and input, help them focus, and can also be used to divide up the day.

Feedback sessions can be weighted differently to fit your needs. To keep teams on track and to diversify their options, keep feedback low-key and ask for "a one-minute status report in five minutes." Teams will see this as a brief interruption in their workflow and an opportunity to get some input, but will not see it as a goal in itself, or a "gate" in the process.

01 A critique session, or simply "crit session," is often used in design and art schools, where the term describes a session in which either peers or faculty critically evaluate a student's work. In service design, crit sessions refer to inviting people who are not familiar with your project to critically reflect on your work. This often includes asking the really stupid questions no one within the design team dares to ask anymore – similar to the approach of "rubber duck debugging" in software development. See, for example, Hunt, A., & Thomas, D. (2000). *The Pragmatic Programmer: From Journeyman to Master.* Addison-Wesley Professional.

If you want teams to filter and converge their ideas more strongly and perhaps make some tough decisions, present the feedback opportunity as a more significant event. Warn teams well in advance that they will be asked to pitch or present their ideas more formally to the group, to another team, or to a visitor. This is a huge opportunity for valuable discovery, so you can even present it as a kind of research.

Feedback can be enormously time consuming, especially if open feedback methods lead to discussion. When planning, remember that closed feedback methods are faster. If there are several teams, decide if they get feedback in parallel (e.g., by pairing teams) or in series (e.g., in plenum).

To make a feedback round into a real point of convergence, hold a "dragon's den" or "shark tank" session with visiting experts and perhaps a facilitator. These work best as a formal session in a separate room. Other groups should be excluded, to strengthen the impression that the feedback will be especially tough and honest. Teams can be quite shell-shocked after this experience, so don't end a session with this.

10.4.9 Changing status

A facilitator's unique role as a leader of the process and a servant of the group gives him the ability to use his status as a tool, varying it as needed. The ability to elegantly move along a spectrum between "high" and "low" status can be a crucial tool and form part of a facilitator's personal style.

Our choice of words and use of artifacts can play a part, but because we are monkeys, much of this can be done with voice and three-dimensional positioning in the room.

At your next trip to the zoo, spend some time watching the baboons. The one sitting still, high up on the rock and looking everyone in the eye is the boss. He's a power-dresser, with broad shoulders, a laconic loud voice, and head held high. Around him we have the main group looking busy, chattering and stealing sideways glances at him and at one another. And at the edges, we have the youngsters playing and one or two smaller individuals who sit quietly with their backs bent, eyes on the floor. That's about all you need to know about status in one scene. There are always exceptions, and a lot will depend on your own physical stature, gender, and personal style in the context of your local culture. But as a rule, to raise your perceived status, go physically higher up (stand straighter, or closer to a seated person to seem higher), look at people directly, keep movements purposeful, and speak in a lower voice, using shorter, firm phrases and words. To decrease your perceived status, go lower, look down, move aimlessly or fidget, speak quietly and higher, and don't finish your sentences.

It's important to remember that taking a low status does not mean surrendering control of the process (even if you claim you are doing exactly that). Sometimes, it is useful to go lower status to regain control. The Status/Control Matrix described in the following textbox shows some strategies for keeping a tight or loose rein on a process from different status levels.[02]

02 Developed by Samuel Pickands and Adam Lawrence, based on experiences as a military officer and biker-bar doorman, respectively.

The Status/Control Matrix

It's possible to lead from low status, and to allow others to lead without giving up high status. In one design session, the facilitator felt he was losing control of the group and the situation was getting critical.

Raising his status would have led to confrontation in that context, so he went low. From a standing position, he sighed and slumped suddenly into a chair, scanned the floor with his eyes, fiddled with his pen, and then looked up at the group with a hangdog expression. "You guys are killing me today," he said quietly. "What do you suggest I do?

Shall I cancel the session for today, or … well … (shrug)." After letting the group react – mostly by looking at each other in silence – he began to take control of the situation again by saying, "Is there any reason we can't move past this today? Are there any facts we don't have? OK, so … what can I do which will help us crack this in the next half an hour?" In effect, he consciously crashed from peer status down to very low status, then moved through the bottom row of the Status/Control Matrix, from left (low status, low control) to right (low status, high control). ◄

A A facilitator (wearing spectacles) has chosen a taller chair. His relative height separates him from the group, and gives him authority. He could stand to increase the effect; this is more subtle.

B Later, the facilitator takes a physically lower position to emphasize his role as the servant of the group – still leading, but now from a lower status and using humor.

	RELAXING CONTROL, GATHERING IDEAS	CHECKING WHERE WE ARE	CONTROLLING THE PROCESS
SPEAKING FROM HIGHER STATUS	What options do you see?	Did you have something you wanted to talk about?	I see you have concerns. Let's hear them.
SPEAKING FROM PEER STATUS	What ideas do we have?	What I think I hear you saying is …	You had another idea? Let's see if it improves the plan.
SPEAKING FROM LOWER STATUS	What would you do in this situation?	What's on your mind? What do you need?	How can I help you?

DOING, NOT TALKING

Some tips on the many facets of "doing, not talking" from the Global Service Jam community. The table suggests alternate, "doing" ways to keep a process moving.

GOAL OR TASK	THE "TALKING" WAY	THE "DOING" WAY
Create ideas by ...	talking about it.	thinking with your hands: making sketches, playing around with rough models, acting it out.
Evolve ideas by ...	talking them through, comparing opinions.	building and testing them, comparing prototypes.
Make decisions by ...	discussing the opinions.	building fast prototypes, trying them.
Share information by ...	telling me about it.	showing me, letting me try it, letting me experience it.
Break a deadlock by ...	discussing it, arguing.	testing, asking an outsider, playing a game, tossing a coin.
Present your work by ...	creating a presentation.	showing a prototype, letting people experience and try a prototype.

10.4.10 Doing, not talking

At Stanford's d.school, you will often hear of a "bias toward action."[01] At the Global Service Jam,[02] where thousands of people in a hundred cities try to create new services in just a few hours, the cry is a simpler one: "Doing, not talking!" As well as being a great way to keep moving forward, this attitude can help a facilitator in many critical situations. Often, an effective way to break past a creative or interpersonal lock-up is to change the working method or communication channel – leaving the verbal and switching to other ways forward.[03]

In a "doing, not talking" mindset, ideas are evolved by pragmatically iterating on the prototype, instead of making hypothetical leaps through discussion. A "bias toward action" in any co-creative session will usually keep things moving more smoothly, as well as giving more opportunity to the team members who are less verbally dominant. Play with the balance between doing and talking, and with

the sequence. Do you talk first, then build? Or do you build first, then talk? Do you need to understand something before you build it, or can you build it to understand it?

10.4.11 Growing as a facilitator

As a practicing service designer, facilitation will always be a key factor in your success or failure. You will invariably discover and experiment with different facilitation styles and techniques. Learn from other experts, such as agile coaches, therapists, sports coaches, hosts of jams and other innovation events, practitioners of applied improvisation, and more. It's valuable to ask participants for feedback on your facilitation style after each session or project.

As you spread service design through your professional context, you will develop a community of practice not just for design tools and methods, but also for facilitation. You will find that every facilitator is different, and that what works for one will not work for others. Embrace this diversity – we can all learn from each other as we develop our own styles of facilitation.

01 See, for example, "Bias toward action" at *https://dschool.stanford.edu.*
02 See *http://www.globalservicejam.org.*
03 See, for example, 10.10.1, *Case: The energizing power of the unfamiliar.*

10
FACILITATING
WORKSHOPS

METHODS

THESE
ARE
SERVICE
DESIGN
METHODS.

THIS IS
SERVICE
DESIGN
DOING.

Read more on methods and
tools in our free online resources at:

www.tisdd.com

Three-brain warm-up 👆

An unusually intensive, effective, loud, and very popular warm-up where participants have fun failing.

Description: A volunteer stands between three other people. From her right, she is asked simple mathematical questions. From her left, she is asked the color of familiar objects. In front of her, a fourth person makes very precise movements that she has to copy. The people asking questions are insistent, constantly repeating them until the right answer is given: "Two plus two! Two plus two! Hurry up! Two plus two!" After half a minute or so, the participants trade roles.

Essentials: Stand in groups of four (or groups of three with a shared 'conductor' making the movements). Explain the roles and make sure the questioners are very insistent. They can reuse questions, but should never stop talking. When the subject is warm (eyes bright, face full of life, usually after about 30 seconds), change so everyone gets a new job.[01] Once the team know the warm-up, it can be performed in a couple of minutes.

Outcomes: Warmed-up and excited participants who have been distracted from their previous thinking; an equalized group of people who have just had fun failing

Color-chain warm-up 👆

A fun team warm-up which includes a lesson on communication.

Description: A group of 7 to 11 people stand in a ring. Led by a captain, they "pass" words to each other in endless, simultaneous chains: perhaps one chain of colors, one of animals, and one of countries. As the chains flow more smoothly, they speed up or add more chains.

Essentials. Build up the chains one at a time. First, the captain should give a color to someone. This person gives a color to a third person, and so on until everyone has a color and the last person gives a color to the captain. Now run the chain, just looping the same sequence of colors to the same people. Keep the loop going, and get as fast as you can. Stop, and build another chain with a different pattern, perhaps using animal names. When this one works well, try running both chains independently but at the same time. When it fails, debrief and try strategies to make it work. Keep adding new chains (three is enough for the first time) and debriefing. Finish by physicalizing the chains – for example, by high-fiving on every handover.

Outcomes: Warmed-up participants, and a great model of communication, shared responsibility, and trust

---

01   Always change all teams at the same time, so everyone starts and finishes each round at the same time, sharing the experience and building the dramatic arc.

WARM-UP
"Yes, and …" warm-up 🖑

A warm-up for a new mindset of additive creativity and cooperation demonstrating the principles of divergent and convergent activities.

Description: People stand in pairs. Taking turns within a pair, they plan a common activity – perhaps a party or a shared holiday. In the first round, their ritualized conversation is based on "Yes, but …"; in the second, it is based on "Yes, and …"

Essentials: Stand in pairs, face to face.[01] Explain the task (like planning a holiday), and the rules of the conversation: one person will make a suggestion, the second will respond to the suggestion, the first will respond in turn, and so on. In the first round, every response must start with "Yes, but …" After about a minute, stop the group and ask them to repeat the same exercise, but this time starting each response with "Yes, and …" Debrief the activity. Which attitude took them further? Which was more realistic? When is each useful? The links to convergent and divergent activities in innovation[02] are clear.

Outcomes: Fun, laughter, and a useful attitude change, especially when switching from convergent to divergent activities (or vice versa)

FEEDBACK
Red and green feedback 🖑

A simple but effective closed feedback system to maximize input and keep moving forward.

Description: A group of participants have just seen an idea, prototype, etc. and give concentrated feedback. They start by asking understanding questions, then briefly describe what they liked (green) and what they suggest as next steps (red).

Essentials: After a short presentation or proposal, there are three phases. In the understanding questions round, the audience can ask for any unclear points to be very briefly explained. Keep this short, and don't allow feedback disguised as a question. In the green round, the audience tell the team what they liked about the proposal, what should be kept or expanded in future iterations. Next, in the red round, the audience share concerns or suggestions about the proposal. Crucially, they cannot give red feedback unless it is constructive, including a clear proposal or suggestion for the team. In both red and green rounds, the feedback recipients take notes and may only say "thank you."

Outcomes: Plenty to think about for the team receiving feedback, as well as a brief overview of that team's work for the others

01 If someone is left without a partner, make one "triangle" group of three.
02 See especially Chapter 9, *Service design process and management*.

(A) The "three-brain" warm-up, a very powerful warm-up
with physical, cognitive, and spatial elements.

(B) A player in the color chain gets more physical in
his communication, and delivers his message more
effectively. Behind him, a second group are playing.

10
FACILITATION WORKSHOPS
CASES

→

These case studies show how unfamiliar methodology can help participants be more engaged and involved **(10.6.1),** and how flexibility in facilitation can lead to successful empathy building **(10.6.2).**

10.6.1 CASE: THE ENERGIZING POWER OF THE UNFAMILIAR

Redefining customer experience in the Philippines company

AUTHORS

Patti Hunt
Co-Founder and
Director, On Off Group

Kristin Low
Co-Founder and
Director, On Off Group

Joub Miradora
Chief Digital Officer,
Sun Life Financial

While service design is an emerging concept in the Philippines, the demand for improved customer services is ever-mounting. This is especially the case for the financial services industry, where it's widely acknowledged that no one provides outstanding customer experiences, with many companies frustrating customers with poor services and interactions.

Most companies tend to benchmark themselves against their competitors to discover "best practices." This often leads to average designs and a massive "meh" effect for customers. Instead of taking this path, Sun Life Financial (an insurance and financial services company) decided to take a stand and redefine the customer experience from the ground up, without worrying about what competitors were up to.

"It's a very different approach compared to how we usually do it. Normally we follow a set of specifications and let the technology do its job. I'm excited to see all this develop and really happen for my team now."

— *IT Manager and workshop participant*

Design Studio workshops and going "slide-less" for the first time

Inspired by the growing number of people against using slides as communication tools, the On Off team decided to go slide-less for the first time when facilitating "Design Studio" (applied design process) sessions with Sun Life. It turned out to be a great decision! Instead of slides, the facilitators used stories, whiteboards, and role-play to bring ideas and concepts to life as they went along. The energy in the room was completely different, people were much more engaged with what was happening and they weren't "zoning out." The Design Studio activities were being driven by "doing, not talking" and "thinking with your hands" – not by bullet points on a screen.

Observations and interviews

The team conducted interviews with existing and potential customers and observed them using Sun Life's digital platforms, such as websites and mobile applications, to find advisors and purchase insurance. This provided details about how easy it was for customers to find information online, as well as assessing their wants, needs, and motivations.

Outcomes

One of Sun Life's major goals is to create and deliver new standards of service in the Philippines. To prepare for that, several major internal

initiatives commenced in 2016 and were planned for 2017. Taking employees through a facilitated design process covering key stages such as research, insight generation, ideation, prototyping, and validating with customers enabled them to personally connect with the vision. The sessions provided a foundation on which to build on Sun Life's commitment to customer service and develop the organization's service design capability. The internal initiatives are aimed at preparing the entire organization to become more customer-centric, which means implementing significant organizational, structural, and cultural changes. The company is also aligning its digital transformation program to reflect customer needs and enable employees to deliver on them.

"I've not thought about life insurance yet. Neither have my friends. We Filipinos are carefree people."

Female interview subject, 36 years old

KEY TAKEAWAYS

 01 Don't make it about service design, make it about what service design does.

02 Design the day after the engagement ends. The best results are sustainable after you leave.

03 Use language as a design tool. Help your clients find a vocabulary that enables internal conversations to become more customer-focused.

04 Not every activity has to be collaborative or done as a team. Some of the best insights happen when you can think and work independently.

(A) Analyzing and grouping customer observations.

(B) Co-designing a customer-centric vocabulary.

10.6.2 CASE: PIVOT AND FOCUS

Setting up and rocking the day or the room

AUTHOR

Damian Kernahan
Founder and Head
of Experience Design,
Protopartners

Pivoting during a workshop

A few years ago while working with a rather large telco here in Australia, we hit a bit of a roadblock halfway through the project while trying to assist our clients to establish greater empathy with their customers. We had completed all the design research and it was compelling: customers were not too happy. But the senior management were finding it pretty hard to place themselves in the shoes of their most valued customers.

We decided that we could take the option to keep telling them how important it was or, maybe a better way, help them build greater empathy through a guided facilitation exercise. We explained to the lead on the project that we were concerned that, despite the amount of research, his team might not be connecting with the research well enough. We asked for and received his permission to have his team fill out the same research questions that their customers did.

Using the right tool at the right time with the right people

We decided to use a context mapping tool,[01] to great effect. Having already had our customers share with us how they felt about certain things like "control," "fairness," and "connection," we asked the senior managers in a workshop setting to fill out those very same pages in a diary format. We sent them outside for 30 minutes to reflect and write down how those things made them feel. While they did that, we placed up on all the walls the research in which their own customers answered those same questions.

Getting real with your clients

When the senior management team walked back into the room,

01 The context mapping tool used was Zilver Innovation's (see *http://7daysinmylife.com*).

we suggested that they read how their own customers felt. Our experience is that when people walk into their office, they forget that customers are people and feel the same way they do. This exercise quickly demonstrates that customers are real people with real feelings, not some figment that works only in our imagination.

Nothing beats empathy

As we helped the managers truly empathize with their customers, they began to understand from an emotional perspective not only the challenges their customers faced, but more importantly the validity of these challenges and the importance of addressing them. We have used this facilitation exercise many times to great effect across a range of categories. It never fails to help build the much-needed empathy that removes roadblocks and accelerates adoption of additional service design tools and techniques.

Within 5 minutes, all around the room, people who had found it hard to step into the shoes of their customers were spontaneously saying things like "They feel the same way I do," "He has the same experience I have had," and "I was surprised how similar I felt compared to our customers, it's all exactly the same."

KEY TAKEAWAYS

01 Don't tell your clients what they need to discover; instead, help them with the means to find it themselves.

02 Be ready and happy to pivot. Things don't always follow the path you intended, even when well designed up front.

03 Try to prove your findings from an emotional perspective first and a rational perspective second.

(A) The contextual mapping tool with real customer answers on the wall for all to read.

(B) Taking the insights and developing customer solutions once real empathy has been established.

11
MAKING SPACE FOR SERVICE DESIGN

Physical spaces for service design – from pop-ups to studios.

Expert comments ————————————————

| Birgit Mager | Doug Powell | Greg Judelmann | Maik Medzich |

11
MAKING SPACE FOR SERVICE DESIGN

WHY HAVE A DEDICATED SPACE?

A physical space for service design teams and projects is a common aspiration. Usually after the first few workshops and small projects have been successfully completed in meeting rooms, rented workshop facilities, and normal offices, the idea of a dedicated space comes up.

The hope is that a *lab, incubator, gym,* or suchlike will be inspiring, will enable better work, and will serve as a clear signal to the rest of the organization or the local business community. But how should these spaces be set up? What should they contain? How should they be used? And are they really necessary – or even helpful?

💬 COMMENT

"I think a dedicated working space is more than just an aspiration. The types of spaces described in this chapter are very purposeful – the work we do cannot be done in a traditional office with cubicles, heavy furniture, and small offices with walls."

– Doug Powell

This chapter also includes

11.1 TYPES OF SPACES

💬 **COMMENT**

"Service design spaces often evolve from *playground* to *serious play*. Playgrounds are seen as interesting and fun, but not everyone is able to see the potential impact on the business. Once a company reaches serious play the business impact of design-driven innovation is perceived, measured, and appreciated."[01]

– Birgit Mager

Physical spaces for creative work can be in-house or outside the normal working context, and can be permanent, temporary, or mobile. Often, organizations start with mobile solutions like toolboxes and carts, then experiment with temporary spaces before creating more permanent ones. Even if permanent spaces exist, the mobile solutions will always remain useful – you can use them in contextual project work (working in the physical context of the service), and when spreading the word about service design.

11.1.1 Mobile solutions: Kits, carts, and trucks

Simple, portable solutions are often the first step for service design initiators, and need not be complex or expensive. You can facilitate service design with the simplest of tools – so why not put them in a bag, cart, or even vehicle and take them where they are needed? Put some sticky notes, pens, cutters, scissors, glue, tape, modeling clay, figurines or paper cutouts, a big roll of paper, some cardboard, zip-ties, connectors, hole punches, templates, signage, a portable loudspeaker, and a few generally useful objects (rubber chickens are popular) on a cart or in a roller-suitcase, and away you go. Material presented in this way feels more approachable and attainable. You can

even make extra carts or cases and leave them behind after a project or session, empowering and encouraging the locals to keep going.

With more budget, you could outfit a trailer or vehicle and include more bulky tools for prototyping, like vinyl cutters, electronic maker equipment, costumes, or large card or foamcore panels for full-size prototyping.

11.1.2 Temporary/remote: The pop-up

It is possible to rent wonderful spaces for design projects off-site – this book was born in one of them.[02] They come with a great atmosphere and perfect furnishings, plenty of materials, and sometimes even facilitation. They are a great option for short projects and kickoffs – but if you want to be there for more than a few days, you are going to have to invest quite a lot of money. As the best ones are justifiably popular, it can also be quite difficult to get access at the time that suits you and the rhythm of your project. And there is a limit to how much you can customize the space to your process.

An interesting alternative is to set up your own temporary space. These "pop-up" design spaces have one tremendous benefit – they can be built and used in context. To do research or test a prototype with users, you

01 For more, see Mager, B., Evenson S., & Longerich L. (2016) "The Evolution of Innovation Labs," *Touchpoint* 8(2), 50-53.

02 The This is Service Design Doing executive school premiered at Launchlabs in Berlin (*http://www.launchlabs.de*).

**TYPES OF
SPACES**

IN-HOUSE	
MOBILE	CARTS, KITS, BOXES
TEMPORARY	SQUAT
PERMANENT	STUDIO

REMOTE	
MOBILE	TRUCKS, TRAILERS
TEMPORARY	POP-UP
PERMANENT	RETREAT, OUTPOST

💬 COMMENT

"When we asked for a room at our main head-quarters,[03] we were met with laughter because everybody wanted to have office space in that building. But there was a room which was not ideal for offices, but more or less perfect for us. Because it had few windows, it was diffi-cult to use as a regular office space, but gave us plenty of wall space for workshops. Once again, we learned – never give up, but take any chances you get!"

– Maik Medzich

can simply step out of the door. In retail or urban con-texts, it can be relatively easy to take over an unused shop or office (or shipping container) for a few months, set up a temporary studio, and work embedded in the context of your project. If you have a flow of users (customers, citizens, colleagues) through your own locations, why not temporarily co-opt some space there, and do some "open" service design with visitors to your shop, office, or airport?[04]

11.1.3 Temporary/in-house: The squat

A surprising number of service design initiatives in large organizations fly initially "under the radar."[05] That means there is no budget for an official space which can be

devoted to service design – but there is that underused room in the basement … With (or without!) explicit permission, almost any space can be turned into a useful service design facility. Meeting rooms, roof spaces, corridors, or underused offices miraculously lose cu-bicle walls, filing cabinets, and bulky shelving, before gaining whiteboards, prototyping materials, and more flexible furniture.

A temporary space like this even has some advan-tages over a permanent one. Because it is less polished, you are less likely to see it hijacked by the bosses for "presentations" and "events." And it is still flexible, so there is a great opportunity to experiment. What furni-ture works best? What balance of flexible and inflexible areas is useful? What technology is an aid, what is a hindrance? Start with trestles, old doors, even pallets. Encourage groups and facilitators to set up the space themselves, and to iterate and document their arrange-ments with each session.

03 See the whole story in 11.4.1, *Case: Sending a message in a major corporation.*

04 Pop-up studios where customers are invited to step inside might need to look more polished than less visible spaces. For a great example from a working airport, see 6.5.1, *Case: Opening the design studio to your customers.*

05 See Chapter 12, *Embedding service design in organizations.*

11.1.4 Permanent/remote: The retreat or outpost

Ringing phones, colleagues knocking on doors, "I'll just get something from my desk" – in an in-house corporate setting, distractions are a real problem and can even impact spaces which are "dedicated" to design work. The effects of these interruptions[01] and temptations are not trivial. They break trains of thought, puncture safe space, bring complex mental models crashing down – or simply remind us of that forgotten email.

For some organizations, the answer might be a creative space which is geographically separate from the everyday workplace. An owned space can come complete with your own research assets, familiar process tools, and even a facilitation team which really knows your business. Some organizations even make sure that the computer systems there do not connect to the company network, helping participants avoid the temptation of emails and familiar work platforms. Such *retreats* might be hidden away in the forest, in a hip part of town, or simply in a separate building on the same campus.[02]

Another type of permanent "external" space, the *outpost*, can have the opposite intent. Instead of isolating teams from distractions, it might be set up to thrust them into a more stimulating environment. Many technology firms have outposts in places like Silicon Valley, where they keep watch on innovations in the startup scene or high-tech companies.[03] Fashion companies might keep small teams of designers in hotspots like New York or Shanghai, scouting for trends on the street. Simply being present in an energetic community with easy access to specialists and outriders can be a valuable booster.

11.1.5 Permanent/in-house: The studio

Whatever you call it – studio, lab, workshop, gym, incubator – having a dedicated and enduring space is the ultimate ambition of many designers and creators. In many cases, simply being able to leave work hanging undisturbed from session to session can be enormously valuable – when our data and idea assets stay in the same place in the room, we seem to find it easier to build connections.

In a permanent space, equipment and resources can be kept near at hand, and distractions can be discouraged. For regular users, there can also be a ritual aspect to entering the space, which can easily shift them into a more creative mindset. And many first-time users will find themselves lifted into a different way of working by the change of context. The visible investment – both financial and personal – represented by a permanent setting always sends a powerful message about the intent, priorities, and values of the organization.[04]

💬 EXPERT TIP

"It was very difficult to convince management to let us have a room, as they were worried about the costs. But after they had worked in a similar environment, they said 'we think it could be a great idea to build a room at our headquarters.' In other words, don't explain it, but let them experience it."

— **Maik Medzich**

01 Unscheduled interruptions can actually help break impasses, but they reduce our powers of insight. See, for example, Beeftink, F., Van Eerde, W., & Rutte, C. G. (2008). "The Effect of Interruptions and Breaks on Insight and Impasses: Do You Need a Break Right Now?" Creativity Research Journal, 20(4), 358-364.

02 Example: *The Shed*, adidas. See Kuhna, C. (2014). "Physical Locations for the New Way of Learning and the Personal Future Workplace," at *http://blog.adidas-group.com/2014/04/*, April 25, 2014.

03 Example: Swisscom outpost in Palo Alto. See Leuthold, K. (2016). "A Trainee Project in Silicon Valley" (2016)," at *https://ict.swisscom.ch/2016/04/*.

04 Examples include the Hatch at Chick-fil-A, IBM Studios, and Swisscom BrainGym (this space has a coworking cafe which doubles as a large plenary space for events, smaller themed rooms for closed workshops, and an area of more secluded spaces where teams can "rent" a dedicated space for months at a time.

(A) The contents of a simple service design cart. Isobar's wheeled cart (like the kind used to serve coffee) includes catering supplies and a coffee machine. The black and white hats are for theatrical methods and for collecting feedback at the end of work sessions.[05]

(B) The "Shed" is a learning-by-doing space within adidas in Herzo, which incorporates many features of design studios. Although on a work campus, its striking visual style in dazzle camouflage makes it clear that what happens here is not "business as usual."[06]

(C) Part of a dedicated design space for visiting groups – the Launchlab in Berlin as it was when this book was conceived. This well-lit section is divided into group work pods with high tables, ergonomic stools, and prototyping materials in easy reach. Other parts of the complex have different heights and spaces for large group activities or individual retreats, with both space and furniture constantly evolving into new forms.

(D) A "squat" co-opted design space in a normal meeting room. Walls and windows are being used as work surfaces – no special furniture or facilities, but a space of your own.[07]

05   Photo: Isobar Budapest, Francis Cook.
06   Photo: Christian Kuhna, adidas Group.
07   Photo: Isobar Budapest, Judit Boros.

11.2 BUILDING THE SPACE

Creating a dedicated space for service design, whether permanent or temporary, is an exciting task. In fact, it is so much fun that you might be tempted to do it without really considering when (and if) it might be necessary. If you do decide to take the plunge and make a permanent space, there is plenty to think about.

11.2.1 Space

If possible, go for a well-lit space with a range of ceiling heights – but with generally high ceilings. Lots of natural light will help keep people awake and alert, and higher ceilings (not too high!) make us better at creative and abstract thought while lower ones can help us concentrate on details.[01] It's tricky to raise the height of most rooms, but it's easy enough to lower the perceived height in certain areas with dividers, strips of cloth, or hanging objects. Invest in good curtains, so you can dim the space to show a movie or promote concentration. A range of heights will also help divide the space into natural activity zones, without impacting on communication or line of sight, or making the space unsuitable for activities which need plenty of room.

> **💬 COMMENT**
>
> "One of the easy and cheap things we use in our studio is writable whiteboard paint on the walls, and corkboard for tacking and stapling."
>
> **– Doug Powell**

Selecting your canvas

If you are looking for a raw space to convert into your own service design studio, look for:

→ Lots of walls which won't get ruined by sticky notes and duct tape

→ Good acoustics so group work won't drown in the noise

→ Natural light and access to fresh air – high windows are ideal

→ A mixture of high and low ceilings (if you can't get that, go for a high ceiling)

→ Plenty of power sockets

→ Space and water connections for a kitchen and good toilets

→ Access to the outside world, but privacy while you are working

→ An atmosphere that feels like doing, not talking

11.2.2 Walls

You cannot have too much wall space. In service design projects, teams will pin up templates, cluster sticky notes, and hang much of their research on the walls to keep it visible and keep it working. It seems trivial, but it's often said that wall space is a critical success factor in service design. So make sure the walls are there to work – to be

01 See, for example, University of Minnesota. (2007). "Ceiling Height Can Affect How a Person Thinks, Feels and Acts. ScienceDaily," at *http://www.sciencedaily.com*.

pinned on, written on, stuck on. And if you have the height for it, provide a safe ladder so people can use the whole of the wall to display their work.

This will often not be enough, especially if several teams use the space – so use temporary "walls" which can be moved into storage and brought out again when the project continues.

If you work on flat boards, whether hanging from rails or hooks or simply propped up against a wall, you can stack them away when another team is using the space.[02] When you return, you can rehang the boards in the same order, and the workspace is re-created as if you had never left it.

11.2.3 Division of the space

COMMENT

"At *The Moment* in Toronto, we've experimented with different layouts for individual desk work, whiteboarding sessions, workshops, training, circle discussions, and so on. The ease of moving furniture around has enabled this practice of continuous experimentation and reformatting of our spatial environment."

— Greg Judelman

Varied ceiling heights and movable walls can help draw subdivisions which can take on various functions – reflection, sharing, movement, and more. You can create more subtle boundaries with changes in the color or texture of the floor and walls, with painted lines, light, movable furniture, or changes in the type and style of furnishings.

Think through the activities you will perform in the space (or better still, run a pilot and try them out).

02 This is great for confidential materials, which can then be locked away without breaking up their arrangement on the board.

Activities might include:

→ Arriving, hanging around (don't forget wayfinding support)

→ Having coffee and a chat

→ Listening for an extended period of time (a team presenting their work, for example)

→ Watching things on a screen

→ Making phone and video calls

→ Going online

→ Building and testing small, delicate things

→ Building and testing things which make a mess

→ Building and acting out full-size prototypes

→ Coming together in groups of various sizes for a quick huddle

→ Group activities involving all members (forming circles for introductions, energizers, campfires)

→ Working in teams, whether independently or in parallel

→ Welcoming guests

→ Taking a break, eating a meal or a snack

→ Meeting another team or the whole group for feedback

→ Working alone, or just being alone

→ Celebrating

Think in 3D – a "treehouse" will be a popular retreat for detailed solitary work or tiny teams. A set of bleachers or pyramid steps will attract groups in all kinds of situations, as well as being a great grandstand for a presentation.

(A) Movable walls come in many shapes; these were homemade using an aluminum frame, cardboard, and wheels from a furniture store.[01]

(B) Seemingly irrelevant objects in the space can be simply inspirational, but will often be used in prototypes or take on a connecting role in a team. They also help some people think better.

(C) Hanging walls, like in this railing system at an IBM Studio location, can be used by teams to create and re-create their own spaces, or pack work away between sessions.[02]

(D) Many connections, and no fear of technology in this IBM Studio. Appropriate tech can help you handle data, communicate your work, and simulate more complex devices. Or, like here, it can let you bring in expertise from around the world. Use technology where it helps, avoid it where it gets in the way.[03]

(E) Relaxed reflection at an improvised laptop "campfire." Mimic familiar topographies to summon up useful mindsets. Here, the campfire setting in this improvised pop-up space encourages storytelling and honesty. As one participant said, "You can feel the warmth of the flames."

01 Photo: Monica Ray Scott.
02 Photo: IBM.
03 Photo: IBM.

11.2.4 Sound

Consider the acoustics of the space. Large, light spaces often have challenging soundscapes and can be overly echoey or bright, especially when larger groups are busy talking. Soft furnishings, thick carpets, or other sound-catchers can help.

As much as you want to capture noise, sometimes you will want to make it. So make sure your space has a good sound system for music, film, and perhaps microphone – you won't regret it when you are facilitating. Encourage participants to co-create a playlist, and establish sound rituals to start and end sessions, to bring the group together or warn of a deadline approaching.

11.2.5 Flexibility

💬 EXPERT TIP

"Many of the collaborative spaces in the global network of IBM Studios use a system of movable whiteboards that are suspended from the ceiling from a tracking system. This enables our teams to reconfigure the space in a matter of minutes, from small team spaces to large all-hands meetings."

– Doug Powell

Service design includes many different activities, from silent reflection to high-energy group activities. Sometimes small teams work quietly or alone, sometimes dozens of people are moving through a full-size prototype. To meet all these challenges and many others you cannot foresee, keep the space flexible because you never know what you might need.

A flexible space has more than one advantage – when participants are allowed to change the space, they start to assume ownership of it, creating the physical and mental "safe space" they need for their best work. Let them do this a few times, and the ritual character of setting up the

space this way will get people into their design headspace even before they think they are working.[04]

So, look for furnishings which fold and stack safely out of the way. Make sure dividing walls pivot or collapse at need. Put wheels on pretty much everything,[05] but keep some fixed references or you will drive participants crazy. Most successful labs have a central store of key resources which never move, plus one eternal constant – the coffee machine.[06] And don't forget to add the best washroom facilities you can afford.

11.2.6 Furnishing

You probably need much less furniture than you think. Many service design tools work best when teams tape a template or arrange sticky notes on the wall and stand around them. Much prototyping is done standing up, but now and again your teams will want to reflect, or write, or build something delicate. Experiments at Stanford[07] suggest that the best furniture for group work is high tables and (not too comfortable) bar stools, combined with access to open spaces – the high seats encourage us not to keep sitting, but to perch for a while and move again. Choose tables with small, square tops, and move them together in different combinations

---

04 See 10.3.2, *Creating a safe space.*

05 McDonald's has a prototyping restaurant where all the kitchen equipment is on rollers. They can quickly experiment with different kitchen layouts, testing workflow and experience with piping hot food. (Byron Stewart & McDonald's, presented at the Service Design Global Conference, San Francisco, 2011.)

06 Our English co-author prefers a tea kettle.

07 See Doorley, S., & Witthoft, S. (2012). *Make Space: How to Set the Stage for Creative Collaboration,* Hoboken: John Wiley & Sons.

as needed. And mix in some low furnishings like sofas, stools, or soft floor rugs for more relaxed activities.

11.2.7 Connections

Your space does not stand alone. Even in a "retreats," make sure you have strong connections to the outside world. Your teams will need good internet connectivity for desk research and remote interviews or collaborations. But there will also be physical, human, and operational connections.

The ideal location has plenty of resources nearby – libraries, centers of excellence, specialist providers. It will have good opportunities for research and prototyping, and it will be easy to bring in or take out materials, prototypes, and guests.

Who is linked to your space? Who is likely to drop in, and perhaps stay a while? How do the activities in your space link to other activities in your organization? How are you linked to other innovation processes? To the customer experience team's workflow? To idea contests, culture work, open innovation? Is your space a central resource for key activities, or just a cul de sac in the organizational chart?

Think how you can encourage serendipitous encounters with the rest of your organization, your partners, your users. Plan events or offerings to encourage these visits and make them a habit.[02]

01 See 12.1.1, *Start with small projects.*

02 See 11.4.2, *Case: Sowing the seeds of innovation and change,* for a space which is part of an innovation ecosystem.

COMMENT

"A physical space is obvious evidence for a change, and can help get the people into the right mood – they experience something different in a totally different environment. It can help you to receive more visibility, especially if you have been flying 'under the radar.'[01] But it can build barriers to applying service design in any other space."

– Maik Medzich

11.2.8 Low and high tech

Creative spaces tend to be markedly or even dogmatically low-tech. It's true that in much of our service design process, a low-tech approach is quicker, easier, and will give us faster iterations. But restricting the space to purely low-tech approaches misses a valuable opportunity. Carefully chosen technology can help us get higher fidelity in our prototyping, and better examine the technical feasibility of our ideas. It can help us handle data better and make visualizations which open our work to a broader audience of contributors.

To a certain type of participant, technology is inspiring in itself. Look for technology which augments our smartphones, which lets us simulate interfaces and machines, and which can quickly turn rough mockups into more polished forms for presentation outside the group.[03]

11.2.9 Inspiration

Almost anything can be inspiring to your visitors, so fill your space with almost everything. While the traditional image of the design space is sparse and simplistic, a complex visual environment actually stimulates cognitive process, providing you with better ideas and

03 Also see the textbox *From specialized approaches to your own living prototyping lab* in 7.2.

04 See Davidson, A. W., & Bar-Yam, Y. (2006). "Environmental Complexity: Information for Human-Environment Well-Being." In A. Minai & Y. Bar-Yam (eds.), *Unifying Themes in Complex Systems, Vol. IIIB* (pp. 157-168). Springer, Berlin, Heidelberg.

05 If you use tech toys for prototyping in quick workshops, go for toys aimed at ages 6 to 9. That's usually simple enough for adults not to need an explanation.

decisions.[04] Walls need to be work surfaces, so don't fill useful bits of the wall with framed art. For visual inspiration, have the artist paint directly on the walls (and be happy about having the work covered in sticky notes) – or go for movable art and curious objects[05] instead, with space ready to hide them when they are in the way or you need clarity. Those gimmicks will often end up being passed around, fiddled with, or used as an ideation stimulus or prop in a service simulation.

Add to the inspiration by keeping your resources and tools clearly visible. Transparent boxes work well, or simply have plenty of cubbyholes and shelving – what is visible will be used.

11.2.10 Scars

Your space is a workshop, not a fashion boutique – so be prepared for it to suffer. Pens, paint, knives, glue, even power tools will all have an impact on their environment. So be prepared, and embrace the story that these scars can tell. Screw false tops to the tables, and replace them when truly needed – but not at the first scratch. Keep stain removers nearby – but don't be prissy about every spot. Signs of wear and tear give your teams permission to use the space fully, and to make their own mistakes to add to the story.

For inspiration, look to makerspaces, fablabs, and other open workshops. They are invariably clean enough and well organized, with clear areas for appropriate tool use – but they are also stained, cut, burned, with half-finished projects on shelves and crates of potentially useful junk in the corner. The combination of extreme organization and the marks of use makes a loud statement that this is a place for serious work.

11.2.11 Lay out the process?

Some of the most successful design spaces physicalize the design process in their architecture to help teams and co-creative partners orient themselves.

Chick-fil-A's "Hatch," for example, has a more or less circular arrangement of workspace around the outside of a large building. These peripheral zones are labeled and equipped for various stages of the design process, and teams move from one to the next (or drop back to iterate) as they work. In the middle is a large prototyping area, where you can build foamcore restaurants, try things out in working kitchens and eating areas, or even enter a virtual 3D simulation environment.

Amsterdam's Design Thinking Center attempts the same trick using pivoted walls which swing around to reveal the next stage of the process, as well as the appropriate equipment and resources.

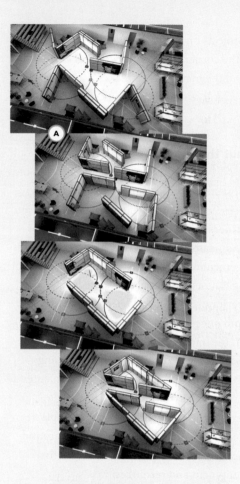

01 Illustrations: Design Thinking Center.

Holding the space

Once you have a space, expect to fight for it.

People looking for "inspiration" or "something different" will want to use your design space for meetings, presentations, "brainstorming" (meaning unstructured ideation), and the same old boring formats, thinking that the space itself will add some magic. They might not be totally wrong, and perhaps you should welcome them with open arms – or perhaps you should give them a firm "no."

Just like an expensive paintbrush does not make an artist, the space itself does not make creativity. Ask yourself, what is your space really for? What are your goals? How does your space and its output fit in the ecosystem of your organization? Then decide who and what to welcome into your space, and under what conditions.

It will be clear if you should allow others to use the space freely, or only with facilitation from your team. You will be able to decide if you limit use to certain formats, insist on co-design, or allow free rein.

Remember, the people visiting your space for these "other" events might be the ones who control your budget. You need them on your side – but you also need them to understand what the space is for, and what it can do. If they think it's just a wacky meeting room, you have already lost. ◄

11.3 SPACE OR NO SPACE?

Never forget that service design can be successful and hugely impactful without a dedicated physical space. "We don't have the space," is never an excuse for not doing service design – and while a good space can reduce the facilitation load, simply having a space will not make service design happen, or make it good. It needs to be populated with the right people, filled with the right knowledge and experience, and connected to the right processes.[02]

But a space can set a very clear signal, with two very contradictory messages. The first message is that the organization is investing in innovation, in co-creation, in customer experience and in the skills of its people.[03] If budget is how companies show love, investing floor space and cash in this kind of facility shows clearly that service design is loved by the organization. That's just the message you need to support your work.

The other message which a dedicated space can broadcast is much less helpful. It can suggest that service design – or even creativity – can only take place in special circumstances, far away from the everyday struggles of work. It can even suggest that this kind of work can only be done by certain special, selected people. That is the worst possible message you could spread – so every activity of your space will need to speak against it. Perhaps instead you should decide to spend your energies and budget on supporting people as they do service design in their usual offices and cubicles, not in a special space. Or perhaps you need both. Consider it carefully.

Or don't *think* about it at all. Approach your potential "service design space" as you should have done in the first place – as a service design project. Research the needs of your stakeholders; ideate possible solutions; prototype them, prototype them as you build your community, and iterate your way forward.[04]

And keep exploring the way forward into the physical ubiquity of a design-based approach – where it makes no sense to have a dedicated space, because the whole organization is set up to do service design anytime and anywhere.

Start cheap and rough, perhaps with mobile solutions to be used anywhere, or tools which can be used at any workstation. Try a range of kits and temporary spaces, learning from each one and building on each other's ideas. See what processes, tools, traditions, and rituals work best, and how each one can create a safe space. Any one of these prototypes could give the model for a permanent facility, or could prove that you do not need one.

02 See also the textbox *From specialized approaches to your own living prototyping lab* in 7.2.
03 See 11.4.1, *Case: Sending a message in a major corporation.*
04 See, for example, 11.4.2, *Case: Sowing the seeds of innovation and change,* for an explorative, iterative approach to space creation.

11
MAKING SPACE FOR SERVICE DESIGN

CASES

→

The case in this chapter show how a dedicated design space can send a strong message through an organization **(11.4.1)** and how it can be a catalyst for an ecosystem or even a country **(11.4.2)**.

11.4.1 CASE: SENDING A MESSAGE IN A MAJOR ORGANIZATION

Why space is more than just another playground

AUTHOR

Maik Medzich
Head of Customer
Experience,
Deutsche Telekom

Introduction: From process orientation to touchable customer orientation

When we started to transform Telekom Deutschland GmbH (Deutsche Telekom) into a more customer-centric company, our focus was on improving processes and regulations, or filling checkboxes for "customer centricity" within decision processes. At that time, this was the most appropriate action we could take, as the corporate culture was strongly influenced by a public authority. We were able to change a lot, but the end result always felt like a foreign object – we needed to take it to the next level. Moving from process orientation to action orientation, we started to actively help projects become more customer-focused through design thinking.

It's not just a room

It quickly became clear that design thinking works better when you have an appropriate (physical) environment. In a company like Deutsche Telekom, such a project meant we would have to bend all the regular processes to get where we wanted. In the end, we were able to lease a room that was considered too difficult to use for regular office spaces. It also helped a lot that we partnered with other departments in Deutsche Telekom, like HR Digital & Innovation, which facilitates transformative business challenges by applying design thinking, and the Creation Center,[01] which has a long history of setting up such spaces. This partnership made clear that we were not just a few nerds – the request was supported by different departments.

01 Learn more at *http://www.creation-center.de.*

Although a comprehensive physical space involves the risk that people see a high barrier in applying design thinking, for us it became necessary to have physical evidence of the changes that were happening within the company.

The impact of space

Our dedicated workspace helps us to better run projects with creative tools because we have materials on the spot, combined with an environment that supports "out of the box thinking." We clearly see that this has an impact on the people working in that environment. Although our colleagues are not accustomed to acting like curious children at work, the gadgets we provide are helping them let go of business behavior and start to play. We also see another phenomenon: usually our dress code suggests business casual, so suits and shirts are very common. We see a change here as well: the more often people

<table>
<tbody>
</tbody>
</table>

(A) Customer workshop: Co-creation by customers (here ideation with the Idea-Mixer).

(B) Customer dialogue: Customers talk directly to Telekom people.

(C) Flexible walls: We use paper walls to enhance flexibility during setup of group spaces.

(D) Flexible setting: With high and low tables, almost everything can be moved with little effort.

(E) Design thinking principles are permanently present.

work in the creative environment, the more they shift to embracing a casual dress code. It's like feeling "at home," where everybody maintains their own personality rather than being masked by a suit. You may ask yourself why this is big deal, but we believe it is important to get rid of classic business thinking like facts and figures and help to establish empathy, not only for teammates but also for customers.

Another important advantage of having a physical space is to support customer dialogues. In the past, this often happened via external agencies in spaces outside our headquarters, and in the worst case, even behind a mirror. We now have the chance to bring our customers to the heart of our company, directly to our project teams. From the customer's perspective, this feels like the opposite of a blank room where they are part of an artificial interview situation. Using the creative space makes it much easier to get in touch with customers and reduces barriers as the environment radiates a relaxing atmosphere. It is very interesting to see that at the end of a session, when

we say goodbye, our colleagues and the customers feel like "old friends" and they have fewer concerns about one another.

Last but not least, this room is also part of the marketing success story; we use it to communicate about what we do and how we do it. For example, the "opening" was designed like a vernissage (art exhibition) – so we not only provide access to the room, but we also spread the word about the things we do. We also try to get decision makers into the environment, as it helps to get support in other areas of our work.

For example, just six months later, another room was set up at this office. It was originally intended for a single project, which was so successful that the owner decided to keep the space for further usage. The continuous work of HR Digital & Innovation at the end also bore fruit, as they managed to set up a standard furniture set for creative spaces to be used in any similar setting throughout Deutsche Telekom.

KEY TAKEAWAYS

 01 Besides the obvious use case, physical spaces are a symbol for change and a place where employees and customers can meet at eye level.

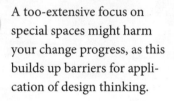 **02** A too-extensive focus on special spaces might harm your change progress, as this builds up barriers for application of design thinking.

 03 Experience is key – let managers, employees, and even customers experience what you are talking about, don't just tell them.

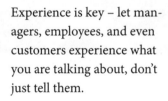 **04** In big corporate companies, you may need perseverance to reach your goals – look for like-minded partners and don't give up.

 05 Don't make it look too clean – a little bit of *hands-on* mentality helps to activate the users, as with prototyping.

11.4.2 CASE: SOWING THE SEEDS OF INNOVATION AND CHANGE

Spreading the co-creation culture in China

AUTHORS

Cathy Huang
Founder and Chairperson,
CBi China Bridge)

Linda Bowman
Service Designer,
CBi China Bridge

Angela Li
General Manager
and Partner,
CBi China Bridge

WECO is a co-creation platform that generates value for both the public and private sectors. In its first six months, WECO has already helped some 5,000 people to break down barriers between disciplines, industries, and generations, and contributed to helping turn ideas into sustainable ventures. To date, WECO has hosted 30 co-creation sessions, generating 100 new startup pitches to investors, with 3 of them already receiving a second round of investment. One of WECO's most prominent projects so far is the sustainability app called "Refuture." OpenIDEO selected this app to launch a global campaign that found successful backing on Indiegogo. By engaging diverse people to solve challenges, we unlock creativity, build communities, and make change happen.

Nowadays, unlocking innovation capabilities is an important challenge for China's economy and society. Innovation can play a catalyzing role in ensuring China's future success – this was one of the three themes that emerged from the World Economic Forum's Annual Meeting in September 2014. Both Prime Minister Li Ke Qiang (李克强) and Xi Jin Ping (习近平) are promoting "Shuangchuang" (双创). Double "chuang" means creativity, which refers to "innovation and startups" as keywords to encourage co-creation.

CBi China Bridge recognized this trend and started probing to discover the best methods, models, and practices of design for innovation. And moreover, they wondered, what is appropriate within the Chinese context?

Facilitating innovation

In 2015, together with SuccessfulDesign.org, CBi created WECO. The name is short for "We Co-create," meaning we bring together different kinds of people with various mindsets, backgrounds, and skills to turn ideas into reality.

With the lack of traditional methods or any established atmosphere of co-creation, we followed an iterative process that began with a raw collaborative model of space, along with methods that considered the fundamental aspects of openness and involvement.

Located in Jing'an district, the center of Shanghai's creative area, we found the perfect space – a former fashion warehouse. Starting from a 2D blueprint of the space we established the building's structural limits and possibilities; then, playing with drawings and paper models, we worked to create a flexible space that could reflect the basic principles of openness and inclusiveness. In this process, we quickly moved onto 3D, and once the space was physically empty we started to prototype hypothetical scenarios between people and available objects to simulate different types of interactions. Instead of starting with newly manufactured materials, we used

repurposed wood from our neighborhood to inject characteristics of warmth, with worn and natural surfaces on our desks, flooring, and in the kitchen area.

"We know that innovation is not about simply thinking harder; it also requires collaboration, creativity, and design in an open environment. Such environments are not very common or readily available in China, so we decided to develop one."

— Rudolph Wimmer, *Managing Partner and Innovator, CBi China Bridge*

(A) The heart of the WECO welcoming area is the kitchen table – as a symbol of conviviality, it is a great space for bringing people together.

(B) Key actors: people play a key role in WECO experience; mature companies, startups, and members of the community become part of the same ecosystem, bringing ideas to life.

(C) We believe kids will be the entrepreneurs of the future, so we embrace the chance to hold creative workshops with them.

(D) WECO is open to individuals and clubs for different types of gatherings that enable people with distinctly different backgrounds and hobbies – think watching sports, reading, reviewing movies, etc. – to come together, build relationships, and create some sparks while enjoying one another's company.

(E) WECO has hosted different interactive activities such as workshops, training courses, jams, creative camps, and brainstorming sessions.

(F) This creative space lends itself to a collaborative, cooperative mindset, making it perfect for workshops, team building, and innovative training.

A flexible and dynamic space

We wanted the WECO space to be flexible, a dynamic and inspiring environment that could allow people to reinvent the configuration depending on the hosted activity. Its features were initially selected according to the physical constraints of the space, building on event organization knowledge from *SuccessfulDesign.org* and CBi China Bridge facilitation and co-creation methodologies. A glass ceiling extends all the way from the kitchen to the guest area, where there are sofas and a public library. This is called 高架桥 (*gao jia qiao*), or the "expressway." It connects the entrance with CBi's studio and the observation room. Here is where most of the activities happen.

In the middle of the space is a projector screen that, when fully drawn down, transforms the space into a lecture room. This makes the space very flexible – it is, at once, a kitchen, an informal meeting room, a lecture hall, a dining room, and a welcome area. In other words, an open space for opening minds.

On one side of the *"gao jia qiao"* there are two smaller rooms, the "small bridge" and the "big bridge." This space is equipped for recording sound and video, but unlike traditional observation rooms, which usually have a one-way mirror, the activity is observed from another room. This creates a more comfortable feeling for the innovation team. The main room is connected with the big bridge by a door that, once opened, transforms the space into a bigger workshop or co-creation area.

CBi's studio also is open and connected with the common space. When external people are involved in projects that require a private space they can use the project rooms to immerse with the team and the material, while outside they can sit and collaborate with others.

"I think anything can happen in this place, and the space feels surprisingly free."
— Chen Zhang, CEO, Orient Landscape Group (张)

Creating an ecosystem

WECO was born as a space to host co-creation events, with the goal to encourage startups to test and iterate their products and services. But we soon realized, based on how people were interacting and communicating, that it was not simply about building a physical space, but also about creating an innovation ecosystem without boundaries.

"The kind of interaction and collaboration we were looking for made us realize that our goal should not be simply a physical space, but an innovation ecosystem without boundaries."
— Sissi Ren, Co-Founder of SuccessfulDesign.org

Every event is facilitated by experts who are able to support initiatives, follow up on projects, and assist brands in their design process. WECO's system and design methods can be applied to different organizations – while helping NGOs and social enterprises to use co-design to better confront important social issues and challenges, we charge companies for the opportunity to facilitate innovation, and engage their target customers, staff, and partners in the co-creation process, by adopting a design-driven approach with customer-centric perspectives of their business.

"It is so exciting for me just to look around this space, to know that there are spaces like this in China, because spaces like this can help great creative thinking, design, and product development."
— David Houle, Future Thinker, Strategist, Speaker

WECO is a tight ecosystem in which design and business are colliding in the same space. By combining CBi China Bridge design consulting knowledge and SuccessfulDesign.org's network, WECO overcomes the challenge of involving businesses in the design process to stimulate actionable creativity. It is an open environment for open minds. It goes beyond the physical space – through the WeChat platform, people can follow different activities, such as a weekly sharing session called "Hello Design" in which more than 300 people can listen, comment, and ask questions about the topic of the week.

For most of our offline activities we create online groups in which people can share their thoughts, news, and questions. These small communities that we create often remain active long after the event is over.

WECO was a needed space. The challenge was not only to make it relevant to the Chinese market, but for it to be useful and appealing at the same time. This friendly, inviting space contains various practical materials for notes, sketching, and prototyping, and a service design toolkit that serves as a reference for design thinking methodologies. CBi also developed a Workshop Toolbox, aimed at applying design methodologies to remote areas.

At WECO, ideas are nurtured and grow. We believe our space represents the future of collaborative working and that within 10 years, nearly all isolated spaces and cubicles will disappear. We are proud to be supporting co-creation as the means for becoming the standard way of working.

KEY TAKEAWAYS

01 In order to foster a creative environment you need tools and methodologies, but mostly you need an environment that enables people to gain their own "creative confidence."

02 Having a diverse group of people aligned around a common purpose, guided by a solid process, is like rocket fuel for innovation.

03 Diversity in backgrounds, expertise, and experience is so much more important than diversity around culture and race. Variety is important because differences attract open-minded people, which helps to create collision.

04 The business model itself will need to become more open and sustainable. Sometimes an innovation's success is linked to timing; the next iteration will be better designed, so it is prepared for changes in circumstances, resources, and other challenges of sustainable business.

05 It's important to find the right scale. Space around the world is expensive; we incubated our idea at home in a space we funded, and now we are situated to replicate our success by learning from our past failures.

06 A dedicated co-creation space and ecosystem is best suited for organizations that are able to provide a perpetual stream of challenges that can be rallied behind in order to co-create solutions that provide value to all.

◄

12

EMBEDDING SERVICE DESIGN IN ORGANIZATIONS

How to sustainably integrate service design in organizational structures and processes.

Expert comments ─────────────────────────────────────

Eric Reiss	Fernando Yepez	Hazel White	Klara Lindner	Maik Medzich
Mike Press	Ole Schilling	Sarah Drummond	Simon Clatworthy	

12
EMBEDDING SERVICE DESIGN IN ORGANIZATIONS

12.1 GETTING STARTED

EXPERT TIP

"One of the infuriating things about service design that I have experienced, is that people need to do it to understand it. So, the more you can get people to do service design, the better the understanding and uptake."

– Simon Clatworthy

This chapter also includes

How to introduce service design in an organization

Just acquiring service design capabilities is not enough to sustainably introduce service design in an organization. That process usually includes a cultural and organizational transformation that cannot be implemented within a few months.[01] It requires the alignment of the whole organizational system, including organizational structures, processes, practices, routines, and values. It is a change process in itself, and needs to be carefully designed and managed.

It's much easier to introduce service design if the organizational transformation builds on a supportive corporate culture. Signs of this are, for example, customer centricity, cross-silo thinking and doing, or an iterative way of working, such as early prototyping. While there's a lot of knowledge on how to change organizational structures, processes, and sometimes even culture, there's no silver bullet that works for all organizations.

Both a top-down approach and a bottom-up approach to introducing service design have potential pitfalls. While a pure bottom-up approach often lacks management buy-in and so also budget and approval, top-down approaches often lack support from employees as they feel that they are being forced to deal with "just another buzzword." The successful introduction of

01 In some cases, the introduction of service design can even be deliberately used as a vehicle of change to achieve cultural and organizational transformations.

Small projects, sometimes also called "island projects" or "stealth projects," that fly under the radar of an organization are a good way to get started with service design.

service design requires commitment on various levels: from the top and the bottom, but particularly also from someone in the middle who initiates the first project and connects top and bottom needs, expectations, and perspectives.

The involvement of influential middle managers can make the introduction of service design easier and more successful. They might be "influential" in terms of formal decision-making powers or because of informal social ties within an organization.[01] However, service design can only become a continuous success if top management approve the introduction and support it with enough resources like budget, time, and people, as well as some personal involvement. Some practitioners refer to this as the middle-top-bottom approach.

12.1.1 Start with small projects

Small projects are the ideal starting point as they can be detached from existing structures and processes, in particular from requirements to integrate with complex IT systems or business initiatives. Many things might cause your first project to drift away from the initial plan, and you need to limit both your expectations and those of your team – and in some organizations also the expectations of your superiors. Plan a mix of well-defined projects – ones where you are quite sure of success, and others where there is a chance they will go wrong.

It might help if you clarify up front what kind of results can – or cannot – be expected from a specific service design project, to make sure that everybody is aligned on the expected results. This will later help pinpoint unexpected positive or negative results. Luckily, service design projects usually provide a few unexpected quick wins that might help you to promote the approach within your organization and help you to get management buy-in.

This could also be a chance to bring "skeletons" out of the closet – projects that might be important from a business perspective but where nobody knows how to tackle the problem, or where someone has tried and failed before.

Try to choose first projects that include open and collaborative stakeholders to avoid wasting time and energy with unmotivated team members. Use these smaller projects to adapt the service design process and language to your organizational structures, processes, and culture. Focusing on just one project risks putting too much pressure on a team, and if this one project goes wrong, you might have "burned" the term service design (or whatever you call what you're doing) in the organization forever.

01 It might make sense to map the hierarchical structure of an organization to locate influential middle managers that act as hubs between the crucial departments you'll need to involve. Sometimes, using a simple tool such as a stakeholder map (see Chapter 3, *Basic service design tools*) and talking to some of your colleagues might be enough to find the right team.

EXPERT TIP

"Always be on the lookout for a champion or two within the organization. These are people with influence who can champion your case further up in the organization. Find them, and feed them regularly!"

— Simon Clatworthy

Indeed, it often helps if at first you give the service design approach a name which does not stand out in your organization.[02] A rather traditional project title helps you avoid too much early attention and gives you time to work out how to adapt service design to your organization, to fail in a safe space, to analyze what could be done better next time, and to understand where exactly in the process something went wrong. Perhaps you can even reuse the work done before the failure, and just try again from there – with the crucial lessons learned.[03]

12.1.2 Secure management buy-in

If needed, find someone from management to sponsor your initial projects. It is often said that "budget is how organizations express their love," but management buy-in is not only about financial backing, but also about political support within your organization. Often just a brief introduction from higher management will give a design team the credibility that you might need for your first projects.

It helps a lot if your sponsors have decent service design knowledge. Offer opportunities to experience service design through a hands-on approach, perhaps by involving higher management during research, running a pressure-cooker format like a mini-workshop or a short

EXPERT TIP

"To get senior buy-in, nothing beats showing them films of a user failing to use the service that they manage or have commissioned."

— Sarah Drummond

jam[04] with them, offering internal and external workshops and talks, or inviting visits from other companies who have introduced a more "design centric" approach within their business. Although top management don't need to be service design experts, they should be aware of the general process and potential benefits and pitfalls.

Try to speak a common language, understand their current goals and challenges, and remember that their time is often limited. Sometimes, "translating" project-specific details into the overall business strategy of a company helps to find a common ground; for example, by showing how a service design project relates to business and growth opportunities.

Up front, define a clear aim for the project with all team members and management. For small and well-defined projects, it is often even possible to agree on specific key performance indicators for a project.[05] Try to measure these before and after the project to understand and prove its impact. Document your project throughout the entire process using photos, videos, quotes from participants, and artifacts like personas or journey maps, as well as measuring potential impacts of your project. Remember to keep doing this as you approach the end of a project, when other things become very important. This is not only crucial to showcase your project and way of working to others, but also to celebrate the successes with your team.

---

02 See, for example, 12.5.1, *Case: Including service design in nationwide high school curricula*. The school subject is called "Business and Service Management." Although the content of the new subject very much focuses on service design, you'll only find the term "service design" in the fine print.

03 See Chapter 4, *The core activities of service design*, Chapter 8, *Implementation*, and Chapter 9, *Service design process and management*, for more information on the iterative character of a design process. Sometimes, when you introduce service design in an organization it helps to plan ahead for a minimum number of iterations within a project. This might help you to manage expectations up front and might give you more leeway for your first projects.

04 See the textbox *Innovation jams* in 12.2 for a detailed description of a jam.

05 These KPIs could focus on a specific product, process, or department and measure; for example, customer or employee satisfaction, sales or revenues, the duration of a specific process, conversion rates, up- and cross-selling, support tickets, and so on.

12.1.3 Raise awareness

When you have found "your" way of doing service design[01] through a series of small "stealth" projects and have developed management buy-in, you can start raising awareness within your organization. Good documentation of previous projects can help you do this organically. Project documentation should include the state of an experience before and after the project (if possible with a measurable impact) as well as the design process and how the team worked together.[02] Video summaries or short reports with plenty of photos usually work quite well, shared through a newsletter, an internal website, or a blog.

Another approach is to casually showcase high-fidelity journey or system maps that address a specific experience before and after a project – perhaps by hanging them in your office and even in hallways or coffee areas.[03] It helps if these maps are self-explanatory. Also, you can provide some general information on the project and particularly on the process the team went through.

Project participants from various departments and backgrounds can team up to educate others through demonstrations. The goal is not to up-skill non-designers to designers, but to create champions of the process throughout an organization. Explaining a project and the design process to others often brings better understanding for those who have to present, and stories from your own organization are better for promoting service design than cases from other companies. Make clear that service design works in your organization, in your structures, in your culture.

You can also use classic internal communication channels to celebrate achievements and showcase successes, such as posting an article in an employee newspaper, or asking someone from senior management to recap a project during a corporate event. It might make sense to explain the philosophy behind a project and what you hope to achieve with this. Also offer further reading, a listing of events, or contact details of someone within the organization so employees can learn more.

Both internal participants and management sponsors are often great advocates for service design in an organization and could act as a catalyst for further projects. You might raise enough interest that employees ask you for more information, and you can identify motivated people for your next projects.[04]

---

01 "Your" way of service design refers to the successful adaption of service design process, methods, tools, and language to your organizational structure, processes, and culture.

02 See 9.2.7, *Outputs and outcomes*, for some tips on possible outputs and outcomes of a service design process.

03 See Chapter 11, *Making space for service design*, for some more tips on how to use space for service design projects.

04 See 12.5.2, *Case: Introducing service design in a governmental organization*, for an example of of the importance of employee engagement in spreading service design in organizations.

12.1.4 Build up competence

As a next step, strive to build up and spread competence. Identify motivated colleagues from different departments and organize internal talks, workshops, masterclasses, jams, conference visits, and the like. These colleagues are often the best ambassadors within an organization and can help to diffuse service design knowledge organically by word of mouth. You can help them by offering them information they can share, such as an internal service design website or brochures showcasing projects, process, methods, and tools. Often they will convince new people who might show up to your events.

Sometimes, you will need to define a common language and standards for your organization. Often people think they are speaking the same language, but in fact have in fact understood service design differently. Inconsistent terminology makes collaboration inefficient and conflictual.[05] The aim should be to build up competence across different departments and to establish a network of like-minded people. Establishing a community of practice like this generates a safe space in which you can openly share lessons learned, success stories, and failures.

Give this community an easy way of sharing, such as a shared chat room or community page, but also establish regular face-to-face meetings to learn with and from one another. Invite your project sponsors and management and include them in your community.

The more management understand the process, tools, and methods, the more they'll realize that design needs a specific type of leadership. Micromanagement and uneducated decisions by superiors can demotivate a design team and ultimately kill innovation.

12.1.5 Give room to try

Three of the most quoted barriers to organizational change are employee resistance to change, management behavior that does not support change, and insufficient human and financial resources. Service design projects are rarely successful if employees have to run them on top of their daily work. This is no different to any other project.

"You get what you pay for" is a saying in many agencies, and the same is true for projects that are run internally. Empower employees with time, support, budget, and sufficient responsibility and decision-making power so they can really *do* a service design project. Ideally, a service design project is a separate activity outside of any other daily activity. Think, for example, of temporarily occupying a space outside the regular workspace, such as a dedicated creative space or design thinking center.[06] This ensures that your service design initiative will not get lost in day-to-day business and helps to bridge the spatial separation of departments.

05 See 12.5.4, *Case: Integrating service design in a multinational organization,* for an example of how to establish a common service design language across an entire company.

06 Chapter 11, *Making space for service design,* offers some tips on how to create – or borrow – a suitable physical space for service design.

Spotting the savvy:
Finding great service design staff

BY ERIK WIDMARK AND SUSANNA NISSAR, EXPEDITION MONDIAL

When we were in charge of scouting and recruiting talent for a rapidly growing service design company in Sweden, we struggled for seven years to find great talent. The service design scene was exploding and we needed to expand in order to meet market demands. The challenge was that there were no schooled service designers to choose from and many of Sweden's most experienced service designers were already in our company. These circumstances made us develop a strategy for looking beyond CVs in order to predict future potential. Service design talents are often full of contradiction, but there are some reoccurring clues to look for:

→ **Look for someone to hug.**
Service design is about interacting and understanding humans, and you need a people person to do this – someone who genuinely radiates empathy and interest in others. Huggable is highly employable.

→ **Look for a humble expert.**
The job of a service designer is 90% about listening, understanding, and adapting to the end users' and clients' needs. There is little room for big egos looking to push through their own ideas. Search for expert listeners, facilitators, and team players.

→ **Look for a philosophical craftsman.**
Service design is a craft. It's about doing, but also about contemplating and learning. So, you want a balanced mix of tinkering and thinking; someone who is learning by doing and doing to learn.

→ **Look for a zoom lens.**
An important skill for a service designer is the ability to change perspectives – from macro to micro, from technical platform to human needs, from system to touchpoint, from strategy to solution. Preferably, you want someone who can handle these various perspectives all at the same time.

→ **Look for meticulous simplicity.**
Life and humans are complex, often too complex to make complete sense of. A service designer has to have the ability to see the relevant patterns and simplify overwhelming information in order to deliver manageable results to enthuse the audience. If the design is too complex, you haven't done your homework.

→ **Look for spelling mistakes.**
Is the applicant's spelling really crappy? Great! A cover letter or CV full of misspellings is something that raises our interest. Dyslexics typically have had to find alternative ways of gathering knowledge and have developed their own strategies to learn, work, and achieve – skills that are great in a service design project. And hey, there's always spell check.

→ **Look for bipolar education.**
Has the person studied seemingly contradictory subjects? A combo of "rational," process-driven fields mixed with "creative," emotionally driven education shows an ability to be (and interest in being) both intuitive and logical and to switch between them – a great trait. Biochemistry (PhD)/Interactive Art Direction is one combo that developed a brilliant service designer. Business Admin/Product Design is another.

→ **Look for international lovers.**
It can't be a coincidence that many of the top service designers we've recruited have had partners from different cultures. Maybe it's a sign of curiosity about other people and perspectives. Extensive travelling is also a good sign.

→ **Look for humans.**
When browsing through an applicant's portfolio, can you see people? Too much focus on the details of the solution and little effort made to explain the benefit to users can be an indication of a person lacking the right perspective. We have to remember, a service designer's solutions are often mere puzzle pieces to facilitate users' lives.

And remember, if you happen to meet someone that ticks all of these boxes, hire them straight away! Great service design talent is a valuable resource and extremely hard to come by. ◀

12.2 SCALING UP

How to set up a service design team in an organization

Not everyone needs to be a service design expert, although a basic level of design knowledge for everyone – or at least an understanding of what design is for – has proved valuable in some great companies. Depending on the size of the organization, there's often a core service design team that keeps an overview of the end-to-end experience and coordinates all service design projects.[01] Each individual project, however, has its own extended project team built around the competencies needed for the specific project.

Service design projects are a great opportunity to give members of different departments a common focus and objective outside their normal work routines.

12.2.1 The core service design team

The members of the core team are usually experts on service design management, processes, tools, and methods, as well as facilitation. The role of the core team is to manage or support projects and perhaps facilitate them through workshops and activities. They do not necessarily need to be experts on specific products, processes, or departments.[02] Sometimes, it even helps if they are unfamiliar with organizational structures and processes or do not know how customers use certain offerings. They are often hired from outside the company to bring in know-how or are employees that are trained in service design and facilitation. In a small, private grocery market or a printing house business, this core team might have just one expert. In a government department or a multinational telco corporation, it might have hundreds. Members of this core team can be internal employees or external consultants; perhaps a service design agency that commits to a long-term relationship. External members are often better able to openly point out the inconvenient truths. Often, a mix of internal and external members is most promising.

12.2.2 The extended project teams

While the core team is rather small and focused on the service design process, most projects are also supported by extended project teams: larger groups of people with specific competencies related to the subject matter. These extended project teams should be as cross-functional and multidisciplinary as possible. The size of an extended

01 In this context, the end-to-end experience refers to the entire experience customers or users have with an organization, or the entire experience employees have within corporate structures and processes, or the experience the extended service design team has across multiple projects.

02 The term "products" describes anything a company offers – no matter if this is tangible or not. In academia, products are often divided into goods and services. However, products are usually bundles of services and physical/digital products. As "goods" is colloquially understood as referring to something tangible, we prefer to speak of the term physical/digital products. Read more on this in the textbox *Service-dominant logic* in 2.5.

project team can vary over time; it often even changes from workshop to workshop.

One aim of service design projects within larger organizations is to facilitate the organizational transformation toward a more customer-centric culture. Service design can help break down entrenched silos by connecting people from various departments.

Members of the extended project teams are often people that normally work apart from one another and sometimes even compete over budgets or KPIs. Working together in a project might help them to establish personal connections and ultimately get on the same page.[03]

"Where does the project brief come from?" and "Who needs to implement this?" are two questions you should always ask yourself when you start a project in an organization. You might, for example, learn about similar earlier projects and find people who were previously involved. They might be able to assist you in selecting your team members and managing stakeholders. As the size and composition of the extended project team can vary over time and depending on the project needs, the core service design team need to determine who to include and when.[04]

Extended teams should include people that are directly affected by the problem the organization is willing to solve – affected staff as well as users and/or customers. In the long run, across several projects, the people who were part of an extended team form a loose community of practice. With every project they pick up more and more, until some of them might eventually switch into your core service design team.

12.2.3 Choose a name that fits your culture

Often, it doesn't make sense to reinvent the wheel and raise expectations or even suspicions by using fancy names such as "Service Design Task Force" or "Design Thinking Squad." The core service design team should be named in a way which fits the corporate culture and strategy. Build on whatever exists already and only use a new name if you do this consciously.

A new department for service design might be useful if you want to push the approach internally and if this reflects your corporate strategy. However, this requires a corporate strategy that includes a commitment on service design; long-term management buy-in; internal service design competence; a shared language of service design; and a working process that is adapted to corporate structures, processes, and culture. If not, you might raise expectations that you probably cannot deliver with your first round of projects.

Name individual project teams according to the subject of their project, such as "call center improvement team" or "work group for online shopping experience." These unsuspicious names do not reflect the underlying method and help to reduce prejudices and barriers. Mentioning the subject matter also helps to generate a common understanding and identity. Members of the

💬 EXPERT TIP

"Organizations are complex systems. As such, it is hard for a system to change itself. An outside view seems to be a catalyst for aiding change to happen. Therefore, part of building a community of practice should include the knowledge and experiences of other outside subject matter experts and practitioners."

– Fernando Yepez

03 See 12.5.5, *Case: Creating a customer-centric culture through service design,* for an example of broad involvement of various stakeholders in a service design project from the beginning.

04 See also 9.2.3, *Project team and stakeholders,* for more information on who to include when in a service design project.

service design core team will usually not name service design as the underlying approach. The technical language of service design should remain within the core team, while extended service design project teams use the shared language of the subject matter.

12.2.4 Connect with the wider service design community

Working in cross-functional design teams is extremely rewarding but also demanding. The service design teams need to facilitate a process of organizational change, motivate stakeholders to look at things from different angles and distances, engage and inspire internal and external stakeholders, and often also break with or at least challenge an existing corporate culture. They will need to find ways to engage and inspire themselves at the same time. This can be triggered and nourished by connecting with the wider local and international service design community. Organizing and participating in community events, such as service design drinks, service design thinks, conferences, workshops, or jams,[01] connects the core team formally and informally with experts outside of the organization who can become crucial in future projects.

Sponsoring service design and innovation events like these increases employer branding and might attract further service design talents to your organization.

If you don't have a local service design community, you could be the one to start it. Look for like-minded people through social media and invite them for a first casual meeting. You'll find interested people in similar communities, like UX design, or at startup events. On a global scale, you'll find an active service design community in all common social media channels; just search for the hashtag or keyword *#servicedesign*. Use any opportunity you find to share your stories and learn from others. The wider service design community is delightfully open and happy to share success stories as well as lessons learned from projects that went wrong.[02]

01 See the textbox *Innovation jams* in 12.2 for an overview of what a jam in service design is and how this might be useful to connect your organization with the local community and beyond.

02 See 12.5.3, *Case: Increasing national service design awareness and expertise*, for an example of how to establish a community of practice around service design.

Innovation jams

BY MARKUS HORMESS AND ADAM LAWRENCE

Many of the working practices of service design – qualitative over quantitative, quantity not quality of ideas, building prototypes not comparing opinions – are contrary to the usual way people work in organizations. It's not enough for most people to hear about them, they need to use them themselves, see the results and feel them working.

So, many organizations that are introducing this approach look for formats which get as many people as possible to "touch" the design activities and tools. One of the most successful of these formats is jamming.

Jamming is a concept which comes from music, where musicians meet up without an agenda and play. They listen attentively to one another, picking up themes and adding to them, co-creating new music that none of them could have made alone. They don't discuss goals, they just play. They don't try to predict the success of a particular riff, they throw it into the mix and see how the audience responds. Often, they surprise themselves with the results.

A jam in an organization adapts this process to working on the organization's offerings, processes, or culture. There are no musical instruments, but a wide range of skills, attitudes, and experience. The group (usually 25 people or more, even hundreds) are given a theme and facilitated through a rapid innovation process over perhaps just two days. Research includes stopping passersby, or phoning colleagues. They try fast creative techniques to generate dozens of ideas. Then, like the musicians, they don't discuss ideas, but start building lo-fi prototypes. As the prototypes fail in testing, they iterate and move forward, building more prototypes to show to decision makers.

Some of these prototypes may be useful, and some may contain some valuable DNA and form the spark of a real service design project, but almost none will be implemented as they are. Although they are the most visible output, prototypes are not the main goal of jamming. Instead, jams are best used as a culture injection. They connect innovative people in an informal but productive context. They empower participants by giving them a crash course in useful methods.

Jams are also great fun, and that seems to be part of the success, as serious playfulness helps us let go of ideas and preconceptions – a crucial skill in design.

Jams have gained prominence in service design since the 2011 launch of the Global Service Jam, a volunteer event which takes place every year with physical locations in over 100 cities worldwide. Its success led to the Global GovJam, a similar event for public services, and others.[01]

The success of those events and similar initiatives has been largely responsible for the adoption of jamming as an innovation culture tool by a wide variety of organizations, from companies to governments. In 2015, BASF ran a series of jams around the world as part of a broad co-creative innovation program. The events involved customers, partners, employees, board members, and other stakeholders such as politicians and environmentalists.

It instigated cross-departmental and interdisciplinary conversations way beyond the jam itself and helped to ignite collaboration, looking outside the box and finding a solution *together*.[02]

Alongside similar hand-on formats like hackathons and design sprints, jams are widely used as effective transformational tools to help embed service design methods and mindsets into an organization or community.[03] ◄

01 See *http://www.globalservicejam.org*. In 2013, the event was awarded a Core77 Service Design Award (*http://designawards.core77.com*) for "significantly contributing to the spread of service design culture ... The challenging format, highly engaging and motivating, has contributed to add services to the global design agenda."

02 See Rangan, V. K., Billaud, E., & Dessain, V. (2016). "BASF: Co-Creating Innovation (A)." Harvard Business School Case 517-073, December 2016. (Revised April 2017.)

03 For further reading, see Kun, P., & Mulder, I. J. (2017). "Prototyping for Citizen Engagement: Workshop Outcomes, Design and the City Conference, 22 April 2016. See also Jade, M., Mirams, R., St. John Lawrence, A., Hormess, M., & Tallec, C. (2013). "Dragon Hunters: Jamming and Public Service." *Touchpoint* 5(2).

12.3 ESTABLISHING PROFICIENCY

How to lead organizations that integrate service design

Organizations of all sizes and sectors are affected by an ongoing digital transformation, with the increasing threat that their existing business models might be challenged or disrupted. This is one of many reasons why organizations are focusing more on customer centricity, innovation, and design in general. However, organizational structures, processes, and leadership approaches often still reflect a product-centric approach with many different silos, hierarchical structures, and processes. Their innovation process is often driven more by technology, by products, by engineering and learned behaviors, and less by human-centered design, by ethnographic research, and by co-creation with customers and employees. Many recent articles in business journals reflect the increasing awareness of service design,[03] but leadership[04] often struggles with such an open and fast approach, where you need more trust and less control.

Service design is not only a process and a toolset, but can be a management approach to innovation and business in general. It is an approach that is human-centered, that is based on value co-creation for multiple actors, that negotiates meanings and perspectives, that contributes to social innovation, and that proposes evidence-based solutions.

An organization that has integrated service design requires a certain kind of leadership. The following list presents some key suggestions for the leadership of such organizations.

Understand the design process

As a leader in a service design context, you should understand and value qualitative research and prototyping. You should appreciate the concept of a "sh!tty first draft,"[05] the importance of early stakeholder involvement, and the powerful process of early user feedback and iterative improvement. If you don't agree with this, you'll have a hard time working with a team doing service design.

→ **Tip: Learn by doing**
Participate in service design workshops to learn some basic tools and methods and to experience the process yourself. You can't learn to play football out of a book. Service design is just the same.

💬 **EXPERT TIP**

"In designing better services, we are also designing better work. Think of it as a new form of industrial democracy."

— Mike Press

💬 **EXPERT TIP**

"One particular side effect turned out to be the most relevant reason for applying customer-centric methodologies: project owners learned better arguments to fight back against *ifs* and *buts* throughout the decision process."

— Maik Medzich

---

01 Besides the term "service design," there are other names that describe iterative approaches, such as design thinking, UX design, CX design, experience design, business design, and Lean Startup. See Chapter 1, *Why service design?*, for some examples and figures on the increasing awareness of service design and other iterative approaches.

02 Leadership here refers to top/senior management of an organization.

03 See *sh!tty first drafts* in 10.3.4.

Lead through co-creation

Service design uses educated decisions based on research and prototyping. In the end, it is customers who decide if they want to use your product or not. The earlier you include them in your decision-making process, the more promising the outcome of your project is. To educate your decisions you need to understand customers and frontline employees.

→ **Tip: Lead by example.** Be part of research and prototyping and experience this firsthand. Go out to see yourself how customers react to a prototype instead of listening to presentations by your team.

Eat your own dog food

You should personally use the products offered by your organization. This is often one of the first steps in service design to help management understand a certain issue beyond mere reports and statistics.[01]

→ **Tip: Regularly become a customer of your own organization.** Use products your company offers – just as any other customers do. Do this at least once a month, quarter, or year. Some organizations incorporate this approach into their culture, and management meet afterward to share their experiences and discuss potential consequences. Some companies do the same with frontline work experience.

Practice empathy

It's important for service design leadership to understand the needs of people (employees, customers, stakeholders) and recognize critical situations (customer problems, team conflicts). If you understand your team, you will be able to give them the support they need. You'll establish mutual trust and empower your design team to achieve more.

→ **Tip: Dedicate time to train empathy.** Almost everyone has the ability to empathize with other people, but often we don't make use of it. Try to dedicate some time for this regularly: become aware of people you do not normally deal with in your organization, perhaps starting with the extended service design team. Be curious about their work routines, their lives, and their thoughts in general. Just ask them, show serious interest, and focus on listening – you want to learn something from them, not the other way around.

Look beyond quantitative statistics and metrics

You may have heard – or even repeated – the saying, "If you can't measure it, you can't manage it." This is an outdated myth from an era when management was restricted to quantitative tools. Customer experience is more than metrics. Numbers can help you identify that you have a problem and maybe where the problem is, but can't tell you why people like or hate something, or what their aspirations are.

04 For example, see the description of self-ethnographic approaches in 5.2, *Methods of data collection*.

→ **Tip: Focus on human experiences.** Look beyond mere numbers and use qualitative and mixed-method approaches to understand experiences more holistically, including the human and the business aspects. Use statistics and metrics to find problems or track developments over time, but use qualitative research to understand why people like or dislike something, to understand what they are trying to be, and to inspire your team.

Reduce fear of change and failure

Employees at all hierarchical levels often fear change because it happens too frequently, is initiated "top-down," and often has a negative impact on their own experience. Co-creation can lower this fear if you involve your employees in this process, embrace a culture of failure,[02] and are open to feedback and change yourself.

→ **Tip: Ask for prototypes instead of presentations.** Show that you use a design approach yourself. Support prototyping – for example, by relying less on shiny presentations and more on using sh!tty first drafts yourself. Encourage your employees to prototype their ideas together with customers and fellow employees. Allow them to test ideas and iteratively improve concepts with a clear and transparent innovation process and decision criteria.

Use customer-centric KPIs

Instead of only using KPIs that reflect the performance of single departments (silos) of an organization, add cross-silo KPIs that are based on customer experience. This can help departments to think beyond their boundaries. In order to impact these KPIs, departments need to work together and co-create with customers and employees. Reward those departments that take an active lead in impacting such customer-centric KPIs.

→ **Tip: Connect silos through KPIs.** Try out cross-silo KPIs that are based on customer events – for example, ones that can be described within the job-to-be-done (JTBD) framework. These KPIs might focus on customer satisfaction analysis regarding a specific JTBD, combining that with complaints, churn, and so on. Offer co-creative service design projects to the relevant departments so they can work together to impact these KPIs.

Disrupt your own business

Some organizations ask their employees to constantly challenge their own company, their own products. Waiting for other companies to find completely new ways of solving a customer's problem with a new, disruptive solution might ultimately put your company at risk.

→ **Tip: Empower employees to find problems and suggest projects.** Invite employees across your entire organization to look for new business

05 This does not mean that it is acceptable for whole projects to fail again and again. It means understanding that "failed" steps in a project (i.e., experiments with negative results) are necessary to learn, to improve, to iterate, and to innovate, and are always part of a successful innovation project or organizational change. Often it is middle management who are risk-averse and fear change, as they tend to be measured by their output. Leadership should embrace and accept failure on the road to success to lower this fear of change for middle management.

opportunities that might put your organization at risk. Establish a system for your employees to submit insights or ideas, to select the most promising, and to explore them outside of their daily routines together with your core design team.

Make design tangible

Instead of talking about what design is and how this can help an organization, follow a "doing, not talking" approach and constantly make design visible and tangible everywhere. Make your innovation and design process more transparent by exhibiting research data and insights, personas and journey maps, prototypes and workshop documentation.

Prototyping, for example, is a great activity to understand the feasibility and sustainability of a new idea, as well as a good way to test and understand the organization's willingness to change. Making design tangible lowers the barrier for others to participate in co-creative processes.

→ **Tip: Showcase the impact of design in your organization.** Exhibit journey maps showing the impact of service design projects in your own company. For example, show a journey map of before and after a project, and highlight the differences. Give some information on the process, tools, and methods, and add a contact from whom interested employees can learn more. This helps you to identify motivated people.

💬 **EXPERT TIP**

"A good measure of how the organization is absorbing service design is to listen for terminology changes within the organization, and the way terms are used. *Touchpoints* and *customer journey* quickly get absorbed, but you really feel you have cracked it when people in a project team start discussing what kind of experience an employee or customer will have at stages of a journey."

– Simon Clatworthy

Bring service design into the organizational DNA

If you aim to bring service design sustainably into your organizational DNA, you might decide to stop talking about service design. Instead, you and your team will work naturally with service design tools and methods, follow the basic principles, and work in an iterative, collaborative, and human-centered way without thinking about this as "service design." Thus, it stops being a special approach carried out by a dedicated group of people, and becomes everyday for everyone.

In the long run, when service design is part of your organizational DNA, you don't need a dedicated service design team.

→ **Tip: Do service design without talking about it.** Show your own passion for this way of working without mentioning service design, but simply by using the tools, methods, and principles in various situations – for example, by using prototypes instead of presentations, or by co-creating meeting documentation, perhaps even in a visual way through graphic recording, instead of sending around written meeting minutes that no one reads anyway.

Think about which decision rights your employees have; if your organizational structure allows them to work collaboratively, self-responsibly, and in an interdisciplinary way; if they know how their performance is assessed; and which objectives or incentives motivate them to follow this way of working.

Is design thinking a methodology?
No, it's a holistic change!

BY MAIK MEDZICH AND ANKE HELMBRECHT

When we started to put a stronger focus on customer experience at Deutsche Telekom, we followed an approach which we did not fully understand until a year later – "start small, but start."

In the beginning, there was no management assignment, no budget allocation, little knowledge about methodology, and just two people spending their time on an idea which looked impossible for a company of our size: to set up a community of volunteers who would spend 30% of their work time on projects outside of their job descriptions. These volunteers would become known as Customer Experience (CX) Navigators. Our idea was to bring CX to the people to whom it belongs, with the purpose to enable them to do a more customer-centric job.

Looking back, we would not have done anything differently. In the beginning, we had little to no visibility – hence, trying and failing was not a problem. It felt like everything we did was better than doing nothing. Eventually, the word spread and we started to grow. We were still a group of volunteers until Marc and Jakob introduced us to design thinking; that was when things began to change rapidly. While we were still experimenting with "the right way" to do things, we realized that a lot needed to change, and it reached beyond providing methodology expertise to our colleagues.

Applying an agile methodology like design thinking requires a complete change in how we:

→ **Lead projects:** Replace unproductive one-hour meetings with focused workshop sessions with a tangible result.

→ **Provide trust:** Hierarchy should be left outside, every voice is valuable.

→ **Think about staffing:** Experts are not the only ones for the job; rather, you need a diverse team of passionate people, coached by a facilitator.

→ **Think about humans:** People get motivated by taking on responsibility and meaningful work.

We had intuitively applied these principles to our community, which on the one hand made it more attractive for colleagues to join and on the other hand provided a prototype of an organizational set-up – hence, we became the symbol of the new working culture we were trying to establish. Management also realized our success, and we received support from our board – which was necessary in certain ways, especially to get backing for the 30% work-time issue. However, the management support we receive is by means of mentoring, not top-down decision making – we are still self-governed.

And, more importantly, we can see changes begin to manifest in the organization:

→ More business units/managers take on responsibility for CX; CX becomes an important part of the product development process.

→ Product ideas get rejected when the CX is not as desired.

→ Scaling in CX Navigators (from 4 to 30, to committed 100) and support requests (from around 5 to around 80 per year).

Design thinking as a mere set of tools and methods is not that important for us. We realized that we need to transform the entire organizational culture. To achieve this, the most important aspec is not the set of methods, but how you apply these methods, how you lead projects, how you set up diverse teams, or which principles you follow in general. The way of working is what makes up a more agile and customer-centric organization – not following methods out of a textbook. ◄

12.4 DESIGN SPRINTS

How to set up service design as an ongoing activity in an organization

One way to implement or introduce service design in organizations is as a sequence of design sprints.[01] Each sprint can be understood as a single service design project.[02] In larger projects, a sprint refers to one iteration within the project – for example, focusing on a specific step or stage of an experience. Once a project is implemented (or discarded), the next sprint starts with an evaluation of the overall customer or employee experience. Thus, the first step of any new sprint also includes an evaluation of the impact of the prior sprint.

Working with sprints can be effective because it gives teams a framework to work in. A design sprint provides a rough process structure with a specific deadline. The team need to deliver something at the end of each design sprint and receive feedback. However, within a sprint, the design team can adapt the process and iterate as needed. This also helps to manage the iterative service design process as you can work in a predictable structure. Often, a core service design team manages the sprints and builds the extended project team based on the specific topic of each sprint. The extended project team may vary within a sprint.[03]

Research[04]

Use qualitative and quantitative research to understand and review the existing customer and/or employee experience. Often previous sprints or a general roadmap guides the team to focus on a specific research topic. Research also includes evaluating the impact of previous sprints on the experience and business success. A design team then defines the next design challenge(s).

Typically, they use visualizations of their research data, such as system or journey maps to identify critical steps in the customer experience, often building on existing visualizations and adapting them based on their research. Journey maps and other visualizations should become living documents that are challenged in every new design sprint.

Research should also focus on the internal process of previous sprints and question team dynamics, problems, implementation challenges, and so on to iteratively improve the sprint process.

01   A design sprint describes a period of time in which a team works through at least one iteration of a design process. Sprints often have a duration of something like one to four weeks. The term "sprint" derives from agile software development, but the concept of timeboxed design processes has a long tradition in product/industrial design. Recently the design sprint approach has gained more attention; see, for example, Banfield, R., Lombardo, C. T., & Wax, T. (2015). *Design Sprint: A Practical Guidebook for Building Great Digital Products*. O'Reilly.

02   See also Chapter 4, *The core activities of service design*, and Chapter 9, *Service design process and management*, for an overview of the process of single service design projects. In particular, 9.2.4, *Structure: Project, iterations, and activities*, provides details on planning and reflecting planned iterations that also apply to design sprints as ongoing activities.

03   See 12.5.6, *Case: Building up service design knowledge across projects*, for a case study on how to balance the ongoing need for quick iterative cycles and the parallel need to build up more long-term value across sprints and projects in design research.

04   See Chapter 5, *Research*, for a detailed overview of how to do research in service design projects.

SERVICE DESIGN SPRINTS: IN THEORY

An archetypal structure of a service design sprint often looks like this.

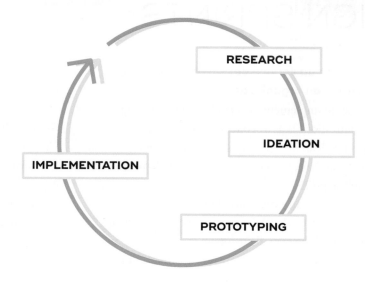

Ideation[01]

Based on the defined design challenge(s), a process of idea generation (diverge) and idea selection (converge) starts. If necessary, some more focused design research can be done to scrutinize the critical steps you identify. Ideation should take into account earlier ideas that have been "parked" (e.g., in an idea portfolio or on an idea wall). If organizational hurdles must be overcome to convince decision makers before prototyping, early ideas can be progressed into initial example concepts.

Prototyping[02]

Selected ideas are iteratively prototyped from low-fidelity concepts to high-fidelity prototypes and tested in context as early as possible. Prototyping can be focused on technical feasibility and look-and-feel, but here the main aim should be to test if an idea actually provides value to the customer, user, and/or employee. Prototyping and testing the value of an idea often provides a team with the arguments they will need to gain buy-in for further development and implementation. At any point during this stage, concepts can be discarded, iterated further, or "looped back" for additional research and ideation sessions.

01 See Chapter 6, *Ideation*, for guidelines on how to do ideation and idea selection in service design projects.

02 See Chapter 7, *Prototyping*, on how to prototype and test ideas and concepts in service design projects.

SERVICE DESIGN SPRINTS: IN PRACTICE

In reality, the design process within a sprint is iterative in itself. For example:

(A) **When you realize that you're missing research data, you can always go back and do more research.**

(B) **When you realize that an idea or concept doesn't work during prototyping, you go back to ideation or the last working prototype.**

(C) **When research brings up very obvious issues that need to be (or could be) fixed immediately, fix them.**

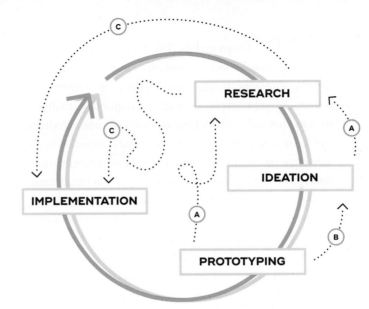

Implementation[03]

Once an idea has been successfully tested in context, and approved by the design team and (if needed) by superiors, it will be implemented and rolled out. Larger organizations often follow a step-wise implementation process from first local pilots to regional test rollouts to global implementation.

Sprints in organizations

The duration of service design sprints often depends on many factors. As a rule of thumb, small companies, such as startups, often work with sprints of 1–4 weeks based on their agile and lean structure. In particular, software startups can integrate a model like this seamlessly within their existing agile development workflows to define requirements as epics or user stories. Small- and medium-sized companies often use slightly longer sprint durations of 4–12 weeks, and some larger companies and governmental organizations even work in sprints of 3–6 months. Organizations use various names for sprints[04] depending on their individual context.

Some organizational structures and cultures tend to make it easy to work in sprints, while others make it much harder. Practice shows that a corporate entrepreneurship philosophy and intrapreneurship behaviors

03 See Chapter 8, *Implementation*, for a description of how a service design process is linked to implementation processes like software development, change management, engineering, and architecture.

04 Depending on the organization, there are various names for sprints, such as service design sprints, design thinking sprints, experience design sprints, customer experience sprints, user experience sprints, innovation loops, iterations, and journey projects, to name a few.

are helpful for design sprints. This type of managerial philosophy usually fosters employee empowerment and learning opportunities, and it promotes incentive systems, exemption phases, and serendipitous activities such as cross-silo networking, open innovation activities, and loose structures. For instance, some companies organize separated dedicated spaces to support experimentation with entrepreneurial ideas (e.g., internal incubators, accelerator programs, internal ventures). Employees get a chance to pitch their ideas (or better, their functioning prototypes) to a jury of external experts and internal decision makers. If accepted, they can continue the exploration with a small team of colleagues, supported by coaching and sometimes even funding to develop a minimum viable product (MVP).[01] If this succeeds, some programs even offer venture capital to start a spin-off outside of the existing organization. Through such initiatives, ideas can leapfrog the paralyzing structures of large organizations at the same speed as a startup.

Many organizations integrate design sprints within their existing innovation process – for example, a stage-gate process. In cases like this, it is important to review the existing decision criteria with a critical eye. It's hard to get better results if you change the innovation process but keep the same decision-making system. A system that stops projects before ideas can be explored further through an iterative design process is not helpful.

> **💬 EXPERT TIP**
>
> "At this stage, you need management buy-in. If you define new criteria and deliverables within existing processes this will lead to governance questions: *Who is responsible for developing deliverables? Who is checking the quality? Who is paying for the additional activities?* Key for us was that top management started to ask: *Where are the deliverables like personas and journey maps? Without them, I cannot decide.*"
>
> **– Ole Schilling**

---

01 For more on MVP, see Ries, E. (2011). *The Lean Startup: How Today's Entrepreneurs Use Continuous Innovation to Create Radically Successful Businesses.* Crown Books.

12
EMBEDDING SERVICE DESIGN IN ORGANIZATIONS

CASES

→

The following seven case studies provide examples of how service design can be embedded in organizations of various levels: how to include service design in the nationwide high school curricula of Austria **(12.5.1),** how to introduce service design in a governmental organization **(12.5.2),** how to increase the national awareness of and expertise on service design **(12.5.3),** how to integrate service design in a multinational organization **(12.5.4),** how to create a customer-centric culture through service design **(12.5.5),** and how to build up service design knowledge across projects in a large organization **(12.5.6).**

12.5.1 CASE: INCLUDING SERVICE DESIGN IN NATIONWIDE HIGH SCHOOL CURRICULA

Service design in secondary schools

AUTHOR

Helga Mayr
Teacher and
Course Coordinator,
Pedagogical
University Tyrol

Austria leads the way in disseminating service design by being the first country worldwide that has implemented service design in the national curriculum for all secondary schools with a business focus.[01]

Service design as a school subject

Since 2016, service design has been part of the Austrian national curriculum for secondary schools, integrated into a subject called "Business and Service Management."[02] There are approximately 90 secondary schools with a business focus in Austria and each school can individually define the scope of this subject, from 2 to 12 teaching hours per week. The work on the new curriculum started in 2011 with the objective of creating a subject addressing "business organization and implementation in reality." In 2012, a nationwide working group was established to support the introduction of the new subject. Four years later, in 2016, the new curriculum came into effect by decree. Business and Service Management is now taught nationwide.

By integrating service design in the curriculum, a space for "doing" as a promoter for sustainable learning has been created, with a strong focus on a multidisciplinary approach and applicability to business practice in the context of entrepreneurship education.

Meeting different goals

As graduates will predominantly find jobs in the relatively unspecific "service industry," they should be able to understand the nature of services as a whole. This includes knowing how services can be designed – including research, ideation, prototyping, and implementation – as well as identifying various stakeholders and considering backstage processes.

The subject in which service design is integrated was introduced in order to offer students the opportunity to link and practically apply what they had learned in different subjects.

Along with helping students acquire an entrepreneurial attitude, teaching service design will contribute to reaching the educational objectives of "active citizenship" and "employability." Integrating a seminal (trendsetting) innovation approach makes students fit for actively "designing" their (and our) future.

Implementation

The big challenge was – and still is to a certain degree – the question of how to anchor service design in the schools as it is still a relatively young discipline. Two years before the new secondary school curriculum was launched, the "concept" of service design was presented to a selected

---

01   This includes all secondary schools in Austria of the type "Höhere Lehranstalt für wirtschaftliche Berufe," abbreviated "HLW" or "HBLA," which could be translated as "secondary schools with a business focus."

02   The original German title of this subject is "UDLM - Unternehmens - und Dienstleistungsmanagement."

number of potential multiplicators, such as teachers and school principals. The audience were interested, but initially uncertain about how service design could be brought into the classroom.

Thanks to the internet, we realized that Marc Stickdorn was living just around the corner in Innsbruck, Austria. We contacted him to set up some further presentations and workshops to help us understand what service design actually is, how it can be beneficial for high school students, and how it could be taught in school. Then, we asked him and his colleague Markus Hormeß to set up nationwide teacher training in service design.

Nationwide teacher training

We set up these nationwide teacher training sessions as courses offered by the Pedagogical University Tyrol in Innsbruck exclusively to teachers that are responsible for this new school subject. There are two consecutive three-day courses: a "basic" course and a follow-up "advanced" course.

The three-day basic course includes basic service design tools, such as personas, journey maps, stakeholder maps, and prototypes, as well as the Business Model Canvas. It also includes some of the main service design activities: research, ideation, and prototyping. A big part of this first course is about the mindset and the iterative design process, as most of the teachers do not have a design background. The whole course is set up as a train-the-teacher course. As all participants are professional pedagogues, the course content focuses on service design in practice and gives the participants enough time to review and discuss how these tools and methods can be taught in school.

The three-day follow-up course adopts a more open "bar camp" or "unconference" approach.[03] Topics range from case studies, to exchanging first experiences, to trying out lessons and prototyping classroom materials.

03 A "bar camp" or "unconference" is a user-generated conference. The agenda of the event is co-created by the participants themselves on the day, so the content is based on their needs and interests.

"Our course topic was 'Street Food' and we prototyped the entire situation with a rented truck so that we could even produce and test our kitchen prototypes in the actual situational context."

— Marianne Liszt, Teacher at HBLA Oberwart/Burgenland

Gaining experience

In the winter semester 2016/2017, the third nationwide basic course and the second follow-up teacher training took place. More than 100 teachers in Austria have been through the training already and are passing on their knowledge to their students and colleagues, sometimes doing team teaching together with colleagues from other subjects.

Actually, implementing service design as a subject in secondary schools is a service design process on its own. Both teachers and students start with "sh!tty first drafts" and improve them iteratively: the teachers their lessons, the students the services they work on in their classes. In order to constantly improve this process, teachers can constantly exchange experiences and share

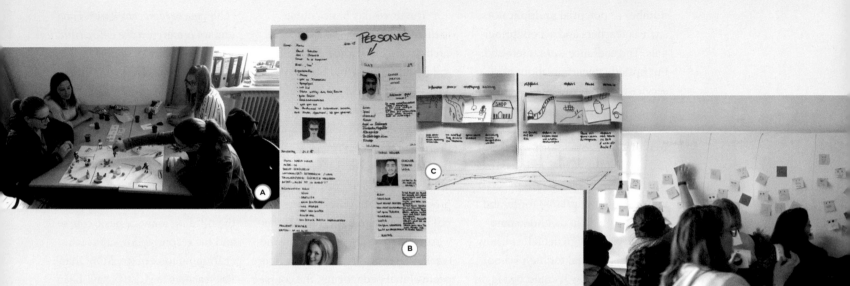

A Desktop walkthroughs are often a good start for prototyping and can help to visually connect customer experiences with frontstage and backstage employee processes.

B Assumption-based personas are easy and fun to do for students, but are only useful when they are backed with research data afterward.

C Creating first assumption-based customer journey maps to introduce journey mapping and emotional journeys in class.

D The Business Model Canvas is a great tool to connect service design with other business and economic subjects in school, like management, financing, or accounting.

E Using various warm-ups with students in class changes the relationship with the teacher and breaks out of routines that students are used to in classrooms.

F Students at the school HBLA Oberwart used service design methods to create a food truck service on campus.[01]

01 Photo: Marianne Liszt, HBLA Oberwart, 2016.

teaching material through an online forum shared with the growing community of service design teachers in Austria. In addition, we have received requests from teachers to establish an annual meeting fostering a living community of practice of service design teachers in Austria.

Prospects

Given the fact that service design is still in its infancy in schools, it will – without a doubt – stay exciting. We will academically monitor and evaluate the further process of implementing service design in secondary education in Austria during the upcoming years. One of our research questions is how students benefit from early service design education in their professional and maybe even in their private lives. Also, we hope with growing experience within our community to be able to offer profound guidance on how to effectively and successfully implement service design in secondary school curricula. Nevertheless, we can already see some initial results that we would like to share.

The individual degree of implementation at each school seems to depend on several influencing factors. One of these factors could be how service design is introduced to schools on a national level. In Austria, this is done through a mixture of a top-down approach (by including service design in the national curriculum of secondary education) and a bottom-up approach (by training teachers and establishing a community of practice), which seems promising so far. Another route to success might be to start with small projects and learn iteratively, tolerating – or even welcoming – errors as a source of knowledge for further improvement. Moreover, it is certainly helpful to raise awareness within the school (amongst all related stakeholders, such as teachers, students, parents, partners, and so on) and also between schools, by communicating about service design activities, exchanging experiences with colleagues, and staying open-minded about student involvement.

Indeed, one of the key drivers might be an open mindset and the willingness to share experiences and to learn from others. Finally, school principals are key stakeholders that also need some basic service design knowledge to understand the design process, methods, and tools. This knowledge will allow them to understand school projects related to service design, and how students and schools can benefit from these.

"Service design is also an attitude, an open, sensitive observation and perception of events that very often initiates a change process."
— *Bernadette Zangerl, Teacher at HLW Landeck/Tirol*

KEY TAKEAWAYS

01 Start with small projects, learn from errors and successes, and then iterate.

02 Be sure to keep an open mind and be willing to share experiences in order to learn from others.

03 Educate key stakeholders on service design to help them better understand and support your project. ◀

12.5.2 CASE: INTRODUCING SERVICE DESIGN IN A
GOVERNMENTAL ORGANIZATION

Unleashing creativity in an exhausted governmental organization

AUTHOR

Daniel Ewerman
Founder and
CEO, Transformator

Sophie Andersson
Senior Service
Designer, Transformator

Anton Breman
Senior Service
Designer, Transformator

Transformator design

⬥ Arbetsförmedlingen

With decreasing citizen trust and employees pushed to the limit of their engagement, Arbetsförmedlingen (the Swedish Public Employment Service) needed to find a new way forward and create a cultural change. At the time, Arbetsförmedlingen had 13,000 employees, 320 offices, and 27 million customer contacts every year.

Prior to this project, a line of projects had been done to design customer-centered solutions. The link between negative customer experience and internal problems was mapped. A clear prioritization for the changes was developed. But instead of simply commanding the offices to "implement these solutions and make them work," Arbetsförmedlingen took a brave turn and put frontline staff in charge of the change.

"The understanding of our trust problem had existed more or less for a long time, but the positive results as an effect of the understanding had been absent. We really had no choice other than to become more customer-centered in our approach, and that's why we turned to service design and decided to let our employers and our customers be a part of the development."

— Helena Engqvist, Former Director of Communications, Arbetsförmedlingen

"We didn't try to convince everyone, we started with those who were curious and volunteers. Today nearly the whole organization wants to be a Greenhouse."

— Pia Rydqvist, Customer Service Manager, Arbetsförmedlingen

Engaging employees

Offices were invited to participate, and seven with a range of conditions were chosen to become "Greenhouses." The staff got to attend a three-day crash course in service design, testing methods, tools, and the approach. The offices were introduced to the service solutions and got to perform the final iterations on a local scale.

They adapted the solutions to their everyday conditions and prototyped, interviewed customers, generated ideas for adjustments, and made the final designs. A central support function was set up, with service designers from Transformator Design and headquarters staff to moderate the process and coach the offices. So far 24 offices have become Greenhouses.

(A) Employee journey mapping to learn and adapt service design principles internally.

(B) Example of a customer journey made by the internal team being used as a tool for understanding and change management.

(C) Greenhouses as a tool for the employees to use their customer expertise, zoom out, and create space for creativity in their daily operations.[01]

(D) The management structure for coaching the organization toward full ownership and a mandate in the transformation process.[02]

01 Illustration: Per Brolund.
02 Illustration: Per Brolund.

"We thought maybe that solutions could be implemented without the employers having an understanding of the customers' needs and why we needed to change. This was a mistake, but that's the great part with this whole approach – it's based on making mistakes, but making them early, admitting them, learning from them, and adjusting as you go."

— *Pia Rydqvist, Customer Service Manager, Arbetsförmedlingen*

The result was a range of revised solutions that headquarters now knew would work well in large and small offices, in cities and in the countryside, and from the customers' and the employees' points of view. The changes were implemented with great buy-in from the front-line staff and created a sense of organizational ownership.

When the first concept was implemented in 320 offices it resulted in a reduction in time (from 50 minutes to just 10) spent on practical registration in the first meeting, freeing time for focusing on the individual's ambitions and needs. The decrease in citizen trust stopped, and employees say that the service design approach helped soften hierarchies and erase prestige, leading to drastically increased health and work satisfaction.

"Learning will take some extra time in the beginning, but we believe customer-driven development must be built in as a natural part of the everyday work."

— Pia Rydqvist, Customer Service Manager, Arbetsförmedlingen

Effects on organization

Customer-driven development is now seen as an essential part of the organization's future, and in June 2016 a permanent support function was implemented to establish the Greenhouse concept throughout the organization. So far 2,000 employees, including 400 managers, have been introduced to service design and the importance of a customer-centric approach, but the goal is to offer it to all employees. The support function will make sure that:

— Customer knowledge is shared and collected so that the development of services can be conducted in local offices.
— Future national development projects will be coordinated in Greenhouses.
— The Greenhouse framework continues to be relevant and contributes to creating better services, based on needs of the citizens.

"We can't go back to the way we worked before. Once you've learned the tools and methods, and more importantly adapted the approach, you can't keep [from] applying it to everything in your work"

— Anna Palmgren, Head of Arbetsförmedlingen, Växjö

KEY TAKEAWAYS

 01 Prepare a solid base of courage.

 02 Filter it through simplicity.

 03 Let it ripen through action learning.

 04 Practice what you preach.

05 Make sure to use a baking tin of persistence.

 06 Let it drip with reality.

07 Finalize it through organizational ownership.

12.5.3 CASE: INCREASING NATIONAL SERVICE DESIGN
AWARENESS AND EXPERTISE

The emergence of service design in Thailand

AUTHOR

**Waritthi
Teeraprasert (rAiN)**
Senior Design and
Creative Business
Development Officer,
Thailand Creative
& Design Center

Realizing the service economy's importance in creating value and improving the quality of life for Thai people, and boosting the country's competitiveness in the field of services, Thailand Creative & Design Center (TCDC) is the first Thai organization to introduce service design to Thailand, experimenting and applying it to various organizations in both the public and private sectors.

We initiated a Service Design Thailand program with the ambition to drive service design as a major part of improving existing services or boosting service innovation for businesses and public services in Thailand.

We first introduced service design in TCDC's annual symposium, Creativities Unfold 2012, by inviting Birgit Mager, President of the Service Design Network and Professor of Service Design at the Köln International School of Design, to

lecture on the value of service design. She presented ideas from countries such as Germany and Finland, which take a systematic and efficient public service development approach; this resulted in Thailand's first service design workshop. Participants included design professors, TCDC, and public service organizations, namely the Thai Post Office, the State Railway of Thailand, and the Office of Transport and Traffic Policy and Planning (OTP).

Workshops

The workshops created awareness among public service organizations of the role and importance of service design. Consequently, we have participated in two projects planning the future of Thailand's public transportation system:

1 The Service Design Research for User Insights and Needs in

High-Speed Trains (HST) Project, a co-creation project between TCDC, OTP, and Livework, resulted in the implementation of the design principles of space and services within the development of high-speed train stations. This project illustrated the importance of the design to the public sector, as the HST Service Design Principles were under the Terms of Reference of OTP, the organization that handled the Thailand HST feasibility study program.

2 The Hua Lamphong Train Station Improvement Study Project is a study of the unchanged, century-old Hua Lamphong train station. Our team applied service design, starting with field research, user studies, and moving on to a complete service design process. The result was physical improvements, including updates to the passenger waiting area and commercial area around the station, as well as a feasibility study of the new service design and the establishment of a new business model for Hua Lamphong Station in the future.

In 2014, we invited service design experts Marc Stickdorn, Markus Hormess, and Adam Lawrence to disseminate their knowledge more widely by hosting two types of service design workshops. First, a "Train the Trainers" program trained service design facilitators, who then acted as knowledge disseminators themselves, facilitating future service design workshops. Second, our guests facilitated co-creation workshops to initiate three projects in different service sectors: the healthcare sector with Bumrungrad International Hospital, the hospitality service industry with Thai Hotel Association, and the tourism sector with Designated Areas for Sustainable Tourism Administration (Public Organization). The concepts and prototypes derived from these workshops have been implemented in these organizations. Additionally, we set out to involve the education sector in supporting and amplifying service design. This initiated cooperation among five universities. Choosing the topic of "Service Design for Public Transportation," with a high-speed train as a service design development target, teachers and students from all five universities together learned the concepts and process of service design and created prototypes showcased in the "Service Design for Public Transportation" exhibition.

Training courses

We also created short-term service design training courses for the general public under the Bangkok Service Jam project, as well as hosting special service design training courses for 13 universities under the miniTCDC project, disseminating knowledge through workshop facilitation. The workshop results were service design prototypes in each local case.

After accumulating lessons, opportunities, problems, and obstacles from our service design program (which has mostly focused on the service sector in the past few years), in 2015, we challenged ourselves as well as the agricultural and manufacturing sectors with the question, "How can we transform Thai businesses from manufacturing and product-oriented companies to customer experience – and service-oriented companies using the service design approach?"

Large company adoption

We introduced the service design approach to two large-scale Thai companies – namely, STC Group, a leading company in the agricultural sector, and PTT Chemicals, a manufacturing company – and we were able to convince the executive boards of both companies of the importance and benefits of service design's principles, processes, and tools. We also initiated co-creative service design projects based within these two organizations by gathering the companies' staff and various stakeholders: we invited the production, product R&D, sales, and marketing departments, as well as top-level management, to join our service design workshops and training programs. We and our team

(A) Talking about the customer journey and touchpoints.

(B) Making and testing a low-fidelity prototype.

(C) A discussion on a customer journey during a service design workshop.

(D) A multifaceted collection of insights helps guide our projects.

facilitated the workshops, executed the whole service design process, and concluded with product and service prototypes.

This is a starting point in applying service design and the design thinking process. These companies may not have transformed themselves within a few years, but feedback from the companies is quite positive, as they have gained experience during these workshops and training programs. They have adopted new approaches which have given them a better understanding of their customers and the way their departments think and operate. They are creating prototypes and testing minimum viable products and services, comparing their prototypes with their existing business processes. The new approaches have led to changes in their manufacturing and in the organizations themselves.

Creative district

To promote TCDC moving to Charoenkrung and to apply design thinking and service design on a larger scale, we and our partners initiated the "Co-Create Charoenkrung" project. The project's aim was to revive and develop Charoenkrung district – once a significant economic and social area of Bangkok – to become a creative district of the future. The project, which ran from July 2015 to June 2016, was conducted using service design thinking and doing principles and processes, focusing on co-creation among experts on creative cities, architecture, and design, as well as key stakeholders in the district.

In co-designing the creative district, we invited designers and local people (who are not only users but participants) to express the problems and articulate the opportunities and needs of the community. This led to a concept of project development in various forms, steps, and processes: starting from design research, gaining insights, generating ideas, co-designing, making paper prototypes and 1:1 full-scale prototypes, and testing and evaluating with the local people in the real spaces. The ultimate goal of the project involves not only developing the creative district but also developing a "co-creation model" as well as the principles and processes of service design thinking and doing which can be applied to our beloved Thailand.

Our service design programs and schemes have just started; nonetheless, they have raised awareness among the public, business, and social sectors and provided essential outcomes. These include service prototypes for future investment and development. Our creation and dissemination of service design knowledge through workshop facilitation, together with project-based and co-creative schemes with other organizations and communities, have publicized and developed service design knowledge, as well as reinforcing the service design network and ecosystem that will create economic and social impacts in Thailand in the future.

As a result of these activities, we've seen major engagement with service design. From March 2013 through June 2016, 1,500 people attended our service design workshops. Additionally, our YouTube channel has logged more than 87,000 views. TCDC has encouraged 30 public and private organizations and 30 universities to participate in service design activities.

KEY TAKEAWAYS

 01 **The simplicity of service design and its process:** People are surrounded by services in almost every aspect of their lives. So, it is quite easy to educate, teach, train, and apply service design in either life or work.

02 **Co-creation in multi disciplinary projects:** Service design and the design thinking process can lead non-designers to understand design differently, as a method of solving problems and creating value. "Design" is not only for designers; it is the process of co-creation with people from various disciplines (whether they are experts or amateurs), blending experience and backgrounds and providing the appropriate solutions.

03 **Facilitation of workshops:** The best starting point for service design (for those people or organizations who are new to the approach) is to run through a service design workshop. This means that the intelligence and skills of the service design facilitator are the key to success. Even if they have great facilitation skills, good facilitators have to know or learn some specific content before they run workshops.

12.5.4 CASE: INTEGRATING SERVICE DESIGN IN A
MULTINATIONAL ORGANIZATION

Redesigning Deutsche Telekom

AUTHOR

Ole Schilling
Senior Design Manager,
Deutsche Telekom

Philipp Thesen
Chief Designer –
Lead Telekom Design,
Deutsche Telekom

The challenge

Deutsche Telekom operates in 14 countries, serves 160+ million customers, and has an annual turnover of around 70 billion euros. As a formerly state-owned company, we are mainly driven by technology and infrastructure. Just over seven years ago, the design department was established to challenge every product and service while driving customer centricity in order to achieve a best-in-class customer experience: a daunting challenge for a tech giant that used to be run by the government.

Our goal

From the 2016 World Economic Forum in Davos to the boardrooms of billion-dollar corporations, design thinking is a widely embraced approach to creative problem solving. Thanks to the increasing importance of customer experience as a key differentiating factor in most businesses, the role of design is changing – from form-giving to strategy-giving. Design has adopted a strategic leadership role and, by doing so, caused a major hiccup for large corporations in which design has traditionally played a less prominent role. We had one goal: a best-in-class experience for our 160 million customers. And we knew that in order to accomplish that, we needed a sustainable mind shift across major parts of our organization. This is the story of how it happened.

"Over the past few years we have successfully worked on more than 200 products and services for Deutsche Telekom and managed to climb the design ladder from a focus on form to focus on processes, slowly working our way up to a focus on strategy."
— *Philipp Thesen, Chief Designer,
Lead Telekom Design*

From doing to thinking

We leveraged the potential of design by integrating design thinking into the fundamental processes throughout the company. There are only about 100 designers in our team, so we could never hope to keep up with the increasing need for design. That's why we created tools and assets that would serve the organization while leveraging the potential of design and design thinking. We operationalized the processes and methods that we derived from our experience of *design doing*. Additionally, we analyzed existing design thinking methods while adopting approaches from various schools of thought, including from Stanford University and HPI.

Ultimately, we took external methods and hundreds of interviews and weighed them against our own internal expertise and experience in order to create a standardized set of methods and tools tailored for our organization.

This led to common ground, a clear understanding of responsibilities, and clean integration within the existing organizational structure. We created a selection of 17 methods, customized for our needs, along with detailed personas and practical tools and templates. It's the standard toolset of our daily work and it helps us to collaborate in a way that is both efficient and customer oriented. The toolbox is continuously extended and updated. It's available as a book and online within our corporate design tool, Brand & Design, a platform we created for our colleagues to distribute and leverage design.

"We aligned the design process and the integration of our methods and tools within the development process with our German and European colleagues that work on customer-facing products and services."
— Ole Schilling, Senior Design Manager

We strongly believe that visibility is key and we actively communicate and showcase our customer-centered ideal. This is also why we launched a new format for interaction called Customer Lab. On a regular basis we invite real customers, selected on the basis of our personas, to challenge existing products and proposed product innovations. This approach is especially powerful because it generates valuable feedback and insights which we embrace by inviting our colleagues across the company to share this knowledge and drive the visibility of our topic. Inviting the management team so that they can experience customer feedback firsthand is a simple, yet extremely powerful tool. Live and direct – customer-centric design.

Educational framework

Although we invited our colleagues at an early stage to engage with us and discuss how to implement customer experience KPIs with existing processes, the reality is that within large corporations change happens in baby steps. So, we need to foster a culture in which the principles of design thinking are largely embraced within corporate culture and values. The logical next step was to create an educational framework.

A

(A) Consistency leverages product experiences
      across products.

(B) Getting all stakeholders on board as early as possible.

(C) Testing and learning.

(D) Speedport Neo – customer-centric design.

(E) Prototyping early.

(F) Sharing experiences and creating ambassadors.

(G) Product experience is brand experience.

(H) "Design Thinking Doing" – the custom-
      tailored handbook for customer-centric design
      at Deutsche Telekom.

(I)   Establishing design as a leadership discipline for digital
      transformation.

In order to drive real change we created a space and program dedicated to focusing on design thinking: the Telekom Design Academy, a place where we teach our methods and the use of our tools but also support our colleagues with real project facilitation. We realized that the demand for project facilitation and on-the-job design thinking training can be applied to specific topics. Demand far exceeded our expectations, which is why we had to start staffing our internal and external teams immediately.

Learnings

We come from a strong legacy of design doing. This entitles us to create and implement processes and tools for our colleagues that will drive change within our company. Integrating design into processes ultimately brings us one step closer to integrating design into the corporate strategy. For now it's clear that we still have a long way to go to become a more design- and customer-oriented company, but we are well underway and design has taken a leadership position within the company.

KEY TAKEAWAYS

01 Integrate stakeholders and users as early as possible in order to help design thinking become a common approach. Start with the stakeholders who are most open to collaboration.

02 Make the approach as tangible as possible so it's clear how it works and what the benefits are. Create a clear target picture and work your way toward it. Don't waste time with theoretical discussions.

03 Integrate new processes into the existing context and make them as visible as possible. Make sure that there is a top-down pull toward the necessary deliverables. Leadership involvement is, however, very beneficial along the way in order to lay the foundation.

04 Design thinking is far too important to be left only to designers. However, the experience designers gain from a strong design doing background makes them the perfect ambassadors for design thinking. Building a community of experts has been especially beneficial for our European rollout, in which learning from and building upon on each other's experiences proved to be essential.

05 Don't expect results to be immediate. Change needs time.

◄

12.5.5 CASE: CREATING A CUSTOMER-CENTRIC CULTURE THROUGH SERVICE DESIGN

Toward a sustainable customer-centric organization

AUTHORS

Tim Schuurman
Co-Founder,
DesignThinkers Group
and DesignThinkers
Academy

Vladimir Tsaklev
Continuous
Improvement
Leader, Coca-Cola
Hellenic BSO

The Coca-Cola Hellenic Business Services Organization (BSO) is a fast-growing shared services center in Sofia, Bulgaria, operating on behalf of one of the world's largest Coca-Cola bottlers. Providing financial and HR support to 22 diverse countries, its 600 employees now aim to be best in class in terms of customer satisfaction. To realize this, BSO is leveraging the service design concept to introduce new ways of thinking and acting.

"If your business model became your prison, you've got to change your business."
— *Arne van Oosterom, Senior Partner and Co-Founder, DesignThinkers Group*

Changing the emphasis
BSO was originally set up with a focus on enhancing processes from a compliance and efficiency point of view, adding extra steps to gain the trust of the different country operations. "This often resulted in cumbersome processes spread over many departments," explains Business Services Director Simona Simion-Popescu. "This meant that the backbone of our services was not especially customer-oriented. And because the 22 country operations now see the added value of a shared service center, requests for even more services have added to the complexity of our operations."

The challenge for BSO was to change the approach and the setup of its processes. "We needed to find a way to get things right from the outset when launching new projects and services so as to respect compliance and governance while providing an excellent experience for customers," says Continuous Process Improvement Leader Vladimir Tsaklev, who is managing the project at BSO. "We needed to build an organization where there is a continuous focus on customer centricity and implementing in a sustainable way. This is where DesignThinkers Academy came in."

Learning by doing
The project kicked off with a workshop to establish proper ownership with relevant senior-level stakeholders from inside BSO and the client organizations. Further details of the program were developed with these leaders and a pilot customer journey workshop held on Service Management, a relationship management framework for internal customers. Similar workshops with other departments were set up within which customer journey mapping and employee journey mapping were key components.

"Workshops with relevant stakeholders from the country organizations and a number of external customers typically take two days," explains Tim Schuurman from DesignThinkers Academy. "We go

SERVICE SCENARIO and BUSINESS MODEL

WHAT IS THE CUSTOMER EXPERIENCING WHILE USING THE SERVICE?

STAKEHOLDER VALUE NETWORK MAP

VALUES	QUESTIONS

$ MONEY POWER EXPOSURE EXPERIENCE

INFORMATION CREDITS LOVE REPUTATION RIGHTS

! ATTENTION TRUST SERVICE PRODUCT

TOPIC

(A) Canvas tool used for sketching future or "What if?" scenarios.

(B) Canvas tool to visualize the value exchange between main stakeholders.

(C) Participants in action, mapping stakeholders and prioritizing relevance for the customer.

(D) Working with the customer journey map, building the stages first.

(E) Prototyping the imaginary scenarios and presenting to the team.

*design*thinkersgroup

**Coca-Cola
Hellenic Bottling Company**

BUSINESS SERVICES ORGANISATION
Partnership. Standardisation. Efficiency.

through the standard service design approach, including persona identification, interviews with customers, customer journey mapping, and the ideation part, prototyping. Where customer journey mapping focuses mainly on improving the services provided to customers and business partners, employee journey mapping aims to create an environment for them to work in a customer-centric way. In other words, customer centricity is approached from both an internal (employee) as well as external (customer) perspective."

An ongoing process

Periodic sessions with relevant stakeholders reflect on the process for building the customer-centric ecosystem. Focusing on *how* things are done is vital as new ways of collaboration basically determine the successful implementation of new service concepts.

"The idea is to turn this way of working into a regular routine that continuously builds on a customer-centric mindset in a sustainable way," adds Tsaklev. "You don't talk about change – you 'do change' and learn to collaborate in a way which leads to changes in mindset, and ultimately, genuine transformation which is anchored within the organization." A train the trainer model (as part of the workshops) assures capability building in tools and facilitation so that programs can be run independent of external trainers and consultants.

Broad involvement

In addition to internal (country organizations) and external customers, the senior management levels at BSO have also been involved from the outset, helping co-create the program and running a customer journey workshop on Service Management. Simion-Popescu welcomes this approach: "Employees are seen as customers and key stakeholders. By building empathy for one's colleagues and understanding how that empathy was developed, people understand each other better. This in turn means you automatically become a customer-centric organization and automatically collaborate in a way that is customer-centric."

"The initial skepticism about seeing service design as a means to build a customer-centric mindset quickly changed as we worked with tools such as the customer journey map. Together with proper facilitation, this creates a practical way of working which is understandable for all participants."

— Vladimir Tsaklev, Continuous Process Improvement Leader

Phased outcomes

An ambitious goal like becoming the best shared services organization in the beverage industry requires changing people's behavior – and that does not happen overnight. Tim Schuurman reinforces the importance of celebrating small wins at different phases of the project. "At the outset you have outcomes such as ensuring senior management commitment, engaging stakeholders in customer journey mapping, and sharing the customer journey narrative with employees. As the project evolves, the goals are improved employee satisfaction, enhanced customer satisfaction, better financial results, and a best-in-class shared service center."

The BSO project now has been handed over to the organization and is running independently of external consultants and trainers. Within the first year, the service design approach has achieved widespread support from stakeholders, along with a commitment to continuous involvement (design research) from customers in all major change initiatives.

Some 90 employees have shared the customer journey narrative and 2 customer (employee) journey workshops a year are planned for each service department. Last but not least, some 20 new short-term and 20 mid-term service concepts have been introduced across 4 service departments. The fact that the executive management of Coca-Cola Hellenic has now decided on an organization-wide scale-up of the service design project speaks volumes for its success.

KEY TAKEAWAYS

 01 Connect to end users and relevant stakeholders from the get-go.

 02 Ensure that minor short-term results are acknowledged and celebrated.

03 Put employees at the center of all your efforts.

 04 Integrate the new design-led modus operandi in the way you run projects as well as day-to-day operations.

05 Use a balanced set of KPIs to track progress throughout the project.

◄

12.5.6 CASE: BUILDING UP SERVICE DESIGN KNOWLEDGE ACROSS PROJECTS

Working with moving targets

AUTHORS

Geke van Dijk
Strategy Director, STBY

Katie Tzanidou
UX Research
Manager, Google

..STBY...

Google

Over the past few years STBY and Google have collaborated on a series of design research projects. Each project was focused on finding answers to a progressive set of specific questions from an internal team of developers, designers, and product managers who were working on a new service proposition. This string of research efforts also built up a repository of research assets across the individual projects, delivering more long-term value for the team and the wider organization. All of this happened in a fast-moving, agile context characterized by dynamic product strategy development – challenging the design research team to effectively cater for a moving target.

This continued strand of work has led us to jointly identify a few principles about agile collaboration with interdisciplinary teams in large organizations. Key to these principles is finding the right balance between the ongoing need for quick iterative cycles of design research efforts, during which data collection, analysis, and reporting happen in joint sprints, and the parallel need to build up more long-term value by documenting research activities in a structured way across the stages and projects in order to generate a "treasure trove" of design research assets. In this way design research contributes to a larger strategic value for organizations than just a probing resource in reactive mode.

"We jointly identified a few principles about agile collaboration with interdisciplinary teams in large organizations."

— *Geke van Dijk, Strategy Director,*
STBY London & Amsterdam

Various levels of questions

Often the starting point for design research projects consists of a few layers. Most urgent and obvious are the short-term and specific questions from the project team (e.g., developers and designers). They are working with an agile approach that entails developing new features in a fast-paced process. They are naturally most interested in specific answers to the questions they encounter in their current work, preferably to be delivered on short notice. The issues they face often change over time, so in various stages of the design research process new or altered interests and questions may come up and will get folded into the ongoing design research. It is of course very important to answer these questions, but gearing all of the design research toward answering them will limit the scope of the research to what is already in the focus. This risks not touching on more surprising angles on the topic that might have been discovered via design research.

Other stakeholders in the team and the wider organization (e.g., product managers and researchers) usually also have an interest in exploring more holistic overarching themes related to the type of product or service they are working on. Finding the answers to their more strategic and long-term questions needs a bit more open-ended exploration. Ideally the design research approach caters for both these types of stakeholders and their questions: while collecting data to answer specific short-term questions, it is also possible to collect data to answer more strategic and long-term questions.

"We need to cater for questions from different types of stakeholders, with different speeds and focuses."
— Katie Tzanidou, UX Research Manager, Google

Various speeds for exploration
Catering for a moving target through design research demands a process of regular quick update meetings to align the ongoing work with the progressive thinking of the various stakeholders. During these meetings the intermediary results from the design research are shared, even if they are still rough and unrefined. There

is no point in waiting until the end of the design research process before making the insights and research assets available, as the team may then already have moved on and no longer be engaged with the explorations. Meeting regularly and aiming for progressively informed conversations ensures that the results of the design research get better over time and are better aligned to the needs and interest of the stakeholders.

This is easy to say, but definitely not easy to do. It is a big challenge for researchers to work in such an open, transparent way while going through a few weeks of successive research stages. They need to open up the work process to produce and share intermediate results in quick joint cycles/iterations. This is a real challenge for researchers, as they usually tend to desire time to germinate thoughts and conclusions. Between STBY and Google we have tried, tested, and improved this process over time, based on a joint belief and trust that this would be the best way forward. From both sides we saw the benefits and decided to push for this. Of course, there were

moments of trial and error, followed by reflection on what worked best and what we wanted to change. For each project both parties were very flexible and open to adjusting our styles of working and trying different things.

This highly collaborative and transparent approach doesn't just ask a lot from the research team; also, the client team need to figure out how to best deal with this (e.g., the team need to decide who to involve in each stage). It can become quite messy, as stakeholders need to understand what stage the project is in and what the status of the intermediary deliverables is, so the process does need to be managed quite actively. It is important to guide expectations carefully as most of the materials shared are not yet finished. We have learned the value of sharing the research documentation at an early stage of the design research, even if we do not yet know exactly what may come out of it. The process of building on intermediary results, and jointly discussing the progressive filtering and prioritization process, helps to progressively refine the

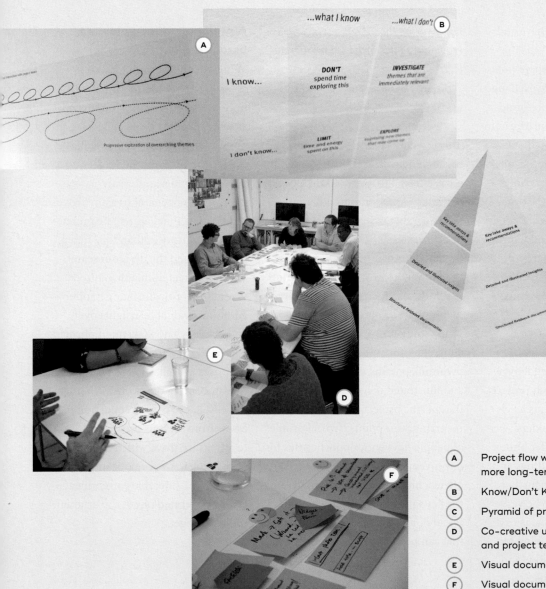

analysis and final results to better cater to the moving target the teams are working on.

"We have tried, tested, and improved this process of working over time, based on joint trust."
— Katie Tzanidou, UX Research Manager, Google

Working with shared online platforms

So, regular meetings are important, as is sharing the design research materials in a progressive and accessible way. We use shared online platforms

(A) Project flow with both quick iterations and more long-term explorations.

(B) Know/Don't Know matrix.

(C) Pyramid of project deliverables.

(D) Co-creative user lab with research participants and project team.

(E) Visual documentation of social context of use.

(F) Visual documentation of positive/negative user experiences.

for this, such as Google Drive and Google Sites. Google Drive is the shared project sandbox where notes and preliminary assets are exchanged and discussed with the core project team. Google Sites is the platform to share the more consolidated outcomes and assets from the various stages of the project with a wider group of stakeholders in the organization. To guide this process of continuous exploration and filtering, we use a simple matrix that indicates what findings may be most valuable to spend more time on (the Know/Don't Know matrix).

Various layers of deliverables

The intermediate and final deliverables of the design research project need to cater for the various levels and speeds of the stakeholders involved. They need to offer both a quick overview of key findings and a deep/rich repository for further exploration. They need to be very accessible and easy to scan, as some stakeholders are looking for actionable recommendations and others for more general inspiration or grounding.

"By layering the design research deliverables, we offer insights for different levels of interest."

— *Geke van Dijk, Strategy Director, STBY London & Amsterdam*

This is where layering of the design research deliverables is key. Different assets created throughout the design research process fit into different layers of what we call the "pyramid of deliverables."[01] The base of the pyramid consists of organized and structured fieldwork documentation (e.g., annotated customer journey maps, interview notes, diary or probe study returns, selected video clips, etc.), the middle layer of the pyramid contains the fully described and illustrated insights that answer the specific project questions (e.g., recurring pain points, typical profiles of people or events, opportunities for improvement, etc.), and the top layer offers a highly selective summary of the key takeaways from the design research and the recommendations that can be derived from those.

Additional added value across projects

While the middle and top layers of the pyramid answer directly both the more specific short-term and the more strategic long-term questions posed by various stakeholders involved in the project, the base layer of design research assets offers a more general treasure trove of materials that can also be mined for other purposes than the current project. When the design research assets are created in a structured way across projects, they can offer additional valuable insights over and above what is taken out of each project. They can be mined for other purposes as well, such as exploring new upcoming questions. When done well, the overall collection of assets from various projects adds up to a treasure trove with a more long-term value for an organization. This is where considerable extra mileage can be generated out of the original project budget.

01 See illustration C., *Pyramid of project deliverables.*

KEY TAKEAWAYS

01 Find the right balance between ongoing quick iterations and more long-term investigation of overarching themes.

02 Build in very regular update meetings to align the ongoing work through progressively informed conversations.

03 Be ready to share and discuss unfinished work, and benefit from this exposure.

04 Combine a transparent and collaborative approach with active management of expectations.

05 Layer the design research deliverables to cater for the needs of all stakeholders.

◀

CO-AUTHORS

These folks contributed to this book with case studies, expert comments, expert tips, and textboxes. We wanted to reflect the current status of service design as an evolving field with many different perspectives and ways of doing service design.

ALEX NISBETT
— SERVICE DESIGN CONSULTANT

Alex is a London-based service design consultant. For years he'd dreamed of being part of the Olympics, and in 2012 he was a member of the team that designed and delivered the spectator experience for 12.4 million ticketholders at the London 2012 Olympic and Paralympic Games.

ANDY POLAINE
— DESIGN DIRECTOR,
FJORD EVOLUTION APAC

Andy is a Design Director at the global design and innovation consultancy Fjord, where he divides his time between client work in Australia and Fjord Evolution across the Asia-Pacific region. He is co-author of the book *Service Design: From Insight to Implementation*.

ALEXANDER OSTERWALDER
— CO-FOUNDER, STRATEGYZER

Alex is the inventor of the Business Model Canvas and Value Proposition Canvas and the lead author of the global bestsellers *Business Model Generation* and *Value Proposition Design*. He is the C-Founder of Strategyzer, a software platform to design, test, and manage strategy and innovation. Alex won the Thinkers50 Strategy Award in 2015 and ranks among the world's top 15 business thinkers.

ANGELA LI
— GENERAL MANAGER, WECO

Angela is responsible for setting up business strategy, operational management, business development, and culture building at WECO. She has been invited by well-known organizations to act as a mentor in service design thinking workshops and has been a speaker and juror for innovation design events. In 2015, Angela was appointed as the Design Thinking Distinguished Expert of HPI and the Communication University of China.

ANKE HELMBRECHT
– PROJECT MANAGER DESIGN THINKING,
TELEKOM DEUTSCHLAND

Anke has a degree in Public Administration
and has been part of the Deutsche Telekom
group for more than 30 years. Since 2008, she
has been working for Strategic Projects Telekom
Deutschland GmbH and is responsible for management workshops and for design thinking and
optimization of customer service. She is also one
of two initiators of the CX Navigator community.

ARTHUR YEH
– REPRESENTATIVE AND
CO-FOUNDER, SERVICE DESIGN
NETWORK TAIWAN CHAPTER

Arthur focuses on creating value co-creation
service systems in social and business environments. He also runs training workshops for both
public and private organizations to spread the
impact of service design.

ANTON BREMAN
– SENIOR SERVICE DESIGNER,
TRANSFORMATOR DESIGN

Anton has degrees in both Industrial Design and
Business and Design. He works as a Business
Designer at Transformator Design, where he
uses service design thinking to coach and
support organizations in building their internal
capacity to become more innovative, efficient,
and user driven.

BARBARA FRANZ
– SENIOR DESIGN AND RESEARCH, IDEO

Barbara is a Senior Lead at IDEO's Munich studio.
A problem solver by nature, she is passionate
about designing holistic solutions bridging the
physical and digital space, allowing for a seamless
user experience throughout. At IDEO Barbara
guides clients from various industries through the
innovation process, with a strong focus on complex service systems. She studied in Stuttgart,
Paris, and Helsinki and holds a master's degree
in Industrial and Strategic Design from Aalto
University, Finland.

ARNE VAN OOSTEROM
– PARTNER/FOUNDER AND OWNER/
SENIOR FACILITATOR, DESIGNTHINKERS
GROUP AND DESIGNTHINKERS ACADEMY

Arne founded DesignThinkers Group and Academy
in 2007. DesignThinkers is a innovative network
company with clients like Coca-Cola, Samsung,
Philips, L'Oréal, and ING Bank. The company has
grown into a global organization with teams in
over 20 countries. Arne is a coach and innovation
facilitator and has a background in design, art,
theater, photography, and communications.

BELINA RAFFY
– CEO AND MASTER
COLLABORATOR, MAFFICK LTD

Belina is a global consultant, speaker, and
capacity builder with expertise in collaborative
change, sustainable innovation, and business
culture transformation. She is a world authority
on applied improvisation, and is currently
writing a book, *Using Improv to Save the World
(and Me)* about her round-the-world odyssey
delivering applied improvisation projects in
12 countries in 3.5 months.

BIRGIT MAGER
– PROFESSOR, TECHNICAL UNIVERSITY
KÖLN, KÖLN INTERNATIONAL SCHOOL
OF DESIGN (KISD)

Since 1995, Birgit has held the first European professorship on service design at the University of Applied Sciences Cologne, Germany, and has developed the field of service design constantly in theory, in methodology, and in practice. Her numerous lectures, publications, and projects have strongly supported the implementation of a new understanding of the economic, ecological, and social function of design in the domain of services. Birgit is the Co-Founder and President of the international Service Design Network, editor in chief of *Touchpoint – The international Journal of Service Design*, as well as Founder and Manager of sedes|research, the Center for Service Design Research at the University of Applied Sciences Cologne.

CHIRRYL-LEE RYAN
– GLOBAL DESIGN AND INNOVATION
PRINCIPAL, FJORD EVOLUTION

Chirryl-Lee is a designer who helps everyone from organizational giants to hungry startups solve complex problems and improve people's lives through purposeful and sustainable change.

CAROLA VERSCHOOR
– FOUNDER, GROH!

Carola is an innovator, growth agent, brand builder, creative doer, marketing strategist, and foodie. As the founder of Groh! innovation, she consults with some of the world's leading brands on strategic design challenges. She is the author of *Change Ahead: How Research and Design Are Transforming Business Strategy*, published in 2015.

CATHY HUANG
– FOUNDER AND CHAIRPERSON, WECO

Cathy is a respected thought leader in the design industry. Under her guidance, CBi has become the primary design research and innovation design consultancy in China. Cathy has judged numerous renowned design competitions and she is frequently invited to speak at international conferences regarding innovation and design. In addition, her design views have been featured in magazines and television shows around the world. Cathy has published two books: *Mobile Inspiration* and *Managing Design for Business Success: Readings & Case Studies on Design Management*.

CAT DREW
– SENIOR POLICY DESIGNER,
UK POLICY LAB

Cat is a hybrid policy maker and designer with more than 10 years of experience working in government, including at the Cabinet Office and No. 10. She also holds a postgraduate degree in Design. This allows her to seek out innovative new practices (such as speculative design, data visualization, and combining rich user insight and big data science) and experiment with how they could work in government.

CHRIS FERGUSON
– CEO, BRIDGEABLE

Chris is a service design leader and CX strategist who works with complex organizations such as Roche, TELUS, Genentech, RBC, and Mount Sinai Hospital to increase the impact of their services. He is the Founder and CEO of Bridgeable, a lecturer at the University of Toronto's Rotman School of Management, and the Co-Founder of the Canadian chapter of the Service Design Network.

CHRIS LIVAUDAIS
— CREATIVE DIRECTOR, INREALITY

Chris works across many aspects of the design process at InReality, from initial scoping and proposal storytelling to renderings, fabrication drawings, and UX wireframes. He enjoys turning seemingly wild ideas into tangible products, services, and experiences.

DAMIAN KERNAHAN
— FOUNDER AND HEAD OF EXPERIENCE DESIGN, PROTO PARTNERS

Damian believes that branding is the promise you make and customer experience is the promise you keep. He is considered one of Australia's leading experts on service design, having worked with both fast-growing and blue chip companies on how to harness the power of design to create intentional service experiences that customers love. As Owner and Founder of Proto Partners, Damian pioneered the introduction of service design to Australian business in 2008 to help Australian organizations keep more of their brand promises.

CHRISTOF ZÜRN
— CHIEF DESIGN OFFICER, DESIGN THINKING CENTER

Christof is the Chief Design Officer at the Design Thinking Center in Amsterdam and Founder of Creative Companion. He is also the initiator of MusicThinking.com.

DANIEL EWERMAN
— FOUNDER AND CEO, TRANSFORMATOR DESIGN

Daniel is the Founder and CEO of Transformator Design and Custellence. As a service design pioneer since the late 1990s, he is a board member of several cultural institutions, as well as an author, columnist, and frequent keynote speaker.

CLARISSA BIOLCHINI
— DESIGN CONSULTANT AND SERVICE DESIGN SPECIALIST, LAJE

Clarissa is a design consultant and service design specialist with 25 years of experience in Brazil, Europe, and Asia. She is the Co-Founder of Laje and a Partner at both Laje and Ana Couto Branding. She is also a lecturer at Pontifical Catholic University of Rio de Janeiro and Fundação Getulio Vargas in Brazil. Clarissa authored the preface of the Brazilian edition of the book *This is Service Design Thinking*.

DAVE CARROLL
— SINGER-SONGWRITER AND INNOVATOR, DAVECARROLLMUSIC.COM

Dave is an award winning singer-songwriter, professional speaker, author, and social media innovator based in Halifax, Nova Scotia, Canada. His video "United Breaks Guitars" was the #1 watched YouTube music video in the world in July 2009, has been called "one of the most important [videos] in Google's history," and became a metaphor for change and innovation.

DOUG POWELL
– DISTINGUISHED DESIGNER, IBM

Doug is responsible for scaling the practice of design and design thinking across IBM, one of the world's most established and enduring companies. A key part of this strategy is the global network of 36 IBM Studios, which are open, agile workspaces built for cross-disciplinary collaboration.

EDUARDO KRANZ
– SERVICE DESIGN LEAD, FJORD

Eduardo is a designer with a holistic approach that focuses on understanding the environment, framing problems, and connecting insights as he crafts joyful experiences for people while taking brands and governments on a design journey.

EMILIE STRØMMEN OLSEN
– SENIOR SERVICE DESIGNER,
DESIGNIT OSLO,

Emilie is a service designer who works mainly with the public and health sectors. She is an expert when it comes to research and visualizing information to create common understanding and excitement.

ERIC REISS
– CEO, FATDUX GROUP

Eric has been involved in service design projects since 1985. Today, Eric is CEO of the FatDUX Group in Copenhagen, Denmark, a leading UX company with offices and associates in more than a dozen cities worldwide. He also has several books to his credit, including the best-selling *Usable Usability*, which is now available in four languages.

ERICH PICHLER
– CEO AND CO-FOUNDER, SPLEND

Erich Pichler is a passionate solution designer. In 2016, he co-founded the company SPLEND. Erich has gathered more than 20 years of practical experience in the application of innovation and product management methods for the development of products, services, and the fitting business models in the area of industrial goods. He also lectures on innovation, product management, and design thinking at Austrian universities.

ERIK WIDMARK
– CO-FOUNDER AND SERVICE DESIGNER,
EXPEDITION MONDIAL

Erik has a Master of Fine Arts from Konstfack, or University College of Arts, Crafts and Design, in Stockholm, Sweden. With a lifelong curiosity for understanding people and the systems that surround us, Erik used his industrial design education to develop his first service design method and tools. For several years Erik worked as the Service Design Director for one of Sweden's largest service design agencies, in charge of recruiting, teaching, and further developing service design methods. Erik is also the Co-Founder of Expedition Mondial, a service design agency that investigates the frontiers of design thinking.

FERNANDO YEPEZ
– DIRECTOR OF GLOBAL SERVICES, PWC

Fernando Yepez is an economist and business strategy coach. Currently he serves as Director of Global Services for PwC, where he assists with the development of the firm's new internal organizational design and the deployment of a global digital supply chain for professional services.

FIONA LAMBE
– RESEARCH FELLOW, STOCKHOLM ENVIRONMENT INSTITUTE (SEI)

Fiona leads the Stockholm Environment Institute Initiative on Behaviour and Choice, a research program focused on understanding the factors influencing behavior in the adoption of new technologies and practices that aim to improve health and livelihoods in low-income settings.

FLORIAN VOLLMER
– PARTNER AND CHIEF EXPERIENCE OFFICER (CXO), INREALITY

Florian has years of experience in building creative teams and leading strategic CX/service design projects. In addition to his work at InReality, he teaches master's-level service design at the Georgia Institute of Technology. Florian is passionate about broadening the reach of design by moderating workshops and co-creation processes.

FRANCESCA TERZI
– SERVICE DESIGNER, DESIGNIT

Francesca is a Service Designer at Designit, a global strategic design firm that is part of the leading technology company Wipro. At Designit, Francesca has been helping to grow the discipline on a local level, with particular attention to finding the right way to develop user-centered service design solutions and creating seamless experiences with a "human touch."

GEKE VAN DIJK
– STRATEGY DIRECTOR, STBY LONDON & AMSTERDAM

Geke is the Co-Founder of STBY. She has a background in ethnographic research, user-centered design, and services marketing. She holds a PhD in Computer Sciences from the Open University in the UK and regularly publishes and presents on service design and design research. She is the chair of the Dutch chapter of the Service Design Network Netherlands, and the Co-Founder of the Reach Network for Global Design Research.

GIOVANNI RUELLO
– SERVICE DESIGNER, ROBERT BOSCH GMBH

Giovanni is a Service Designer at the Central Department of User Experience at Robert Bosch GmbH in Stuttgart, Germany. His background is in engineering and design and he previously worked as an IT consultant as well as an illustrator and comic artist.

HANNAH WANJIRU
– RESEARCH ASSOCIATE - ENERGY,
STOCKHOLM ENVIRONMENT INSTITUTE
AFRICA CENTER, NAIROBI, KENYA

Hannah has over 8 years' experience in the
energy and environment industry in Africa. Based
in Kenya, she has research interest in market
analysis, technology adoption, and policy development. She has designed and implemented
development and research projects with strong
community aspects and gender mainstreaming.

HENRIK KARLSSON
– CREATIVE DIRECTOR, DOBERMAN

As a Creative Director, Henrik is closely involved
in many different design projects at Doberman.
He is also responsible for the overall development
of the company's various design disciplines.

HAZEL WHITE
– DIRECTOR, OPEN CHANGE

Hazel has 25 years' experience in design practice, research, and education. She has delivered
Change by Design, an introduction to service
design for 350 Queen's Young Leaders run by the
University of Cambridge, and worked with clients
including the NHS, the Scottish Government, and
the National Library of Greece.

INGVILD STØVRING
– SERVICE DESIGNER, LIVEWORK

As a Service Designer at Livework, Ingvild has
worked with customers such as Transport for
London, Thailand Creative & Design Center,
Sykehusene i Vestfold (hospitals in Vestfold
County), Flytoget (airport train in Oslo), and
Gjensidige (an insurance company in Norway).
She joined the team following studies in industrial
design and service design at the Oslo School of
Architecture and Design and the École nationale
supérieure de création industrielle in Paris.

HELGA MAYR
– TEACHER AND COURSE COORDINATOR,
PEDAGOCIAL UNIVERSITY TYROL

Helga teaches business administration,
accounting, and management of organizations
and services at HLW Weinhartstraße/
Ferrarischule, a secondary school for the economic profession in Innsbruck, Austria. She is
also a lecturer in cost accounting at the Leopold
Franzens Universität Innsbruck and orga-
nizes teacher trainings for the Pädagogische
Hochschule Tirol.

ITZIAR POBES
– PROJECT BRAIN,
WE QUESTION OUR PROJECT

Itziar is the mastermind behind the projects
at We Question Our Project. Her hidden
goal is to pull clients into unknown waters;
but for that, she needs to assure them they
won't get lost. She crafts their work around
understandable methods and feasible actions,
with unexpected results.

IVAN BOSCARIOL
— INNOVATION AND BEHAVIOR LEAD, GOV.LAB - ELOGROUP

Ivan loves exploring the cracks in bureaucracy to help systems to evolve. He does this through service design + behavior science + lots of learnings in the public and social sectors.

JESÚS SOTOCA
— CONSULTANT AND STRATEGIC DESIGN DIRECTOR, DESIGNIT

Jesús has led innovation, user experience, and design projects for companies in the telecom, banking, insurance, health, entertainment, and consumer goods fields.

JAMIN HEGEMAN
— HEAD OF DESIGN FOR FINANCIAL SERVICES, CAPITAL ONE

Jamin is Head of Design for Financial Services at Capital One, where he leads design teams across multiple business units to support end-to-end service experiences and transform business operations to be more design-centric. He is a world-renowned speaker and teacher of service design. As a principal of the Service Design Network, he has helped the network grow and influence thousands of designers and business leaders around the world.

JOHAN BLOMKVIST
— SERVICE DESIGN RESEARCHER, LINKÖPING UNIVERSITY

Johan is a service design researcher working as a postdoc at Linköping University. His main research interest is service prototyping and, more specifically, how representations of services are made and used as prototypes of future situations.

JEFF MCGRATH
— OWNER/FOUNDER, DRTM VENTURES

Jeff is a lifelong learner who has had the benefit of working in and with a number of outstanding and innovative organizations ranging from startups to Fortune 500 companies in the US, Europe, and Asia. He considers himself very fortunate to have been able to learn service design from some of the brightest thought leaders in the industry.

JOHAN DOVELIUS
— HEAD OF SERVICE DESIGN, DOBERMAN

With 15 years in the design field, Johan has broad and deep experience in service design. Besides everyday work on design projects with clients, Johan is responsible for the art and practice of service design at Doberman as a design firm.

JOUB MIRADORA
– CHIEF DIGITAL OFFICER, SUN LIFE
FINANCIAL PHILIPPINES

Joub is the Chief Digital Officer of Sun Life
Financial in the Philippines. He is a change maker
and thought leader with 15 years of experience in
strategic marketing, customer insights, corporate
strategy, and corporate social responsibility in
the fast-moving consumer goods and financial
services sectors.

JULIA JONAS
– RESEARCHER, FRIEDRICH-ALEXANDER-
UNIVERSITY ERLANGEN-NÜRNBERG

Julia is a postdoctoral researcher and lecturer
at the Institute for Information Systems of the
University of Erlangen-Nuremberg. She works
with service innovation, including service systems,
open and interdisciplinary innovation, as well as
prototyping for digital solutions.

JURGEN DE BECKER
– VICE PRESIDENT, GLOBAL SOLUTIONS
CONSULTING, GENESYS

Jurgen is Vice President of Global Solutions
Consulting at Genesys, where he leads the
Genesys pre-sales team in helping customers
design and manage customer journeys
that maximize customer experience and
business results.

JÜRGEN TANGHE
– DIRECTOR, LIVEWORK BELGIUM

Jürgen is Director at Livework studio.
He specializes in service innovation and
transforming organizations. Jürgen is also
a faculty member at the Delft University of
Technology, where he researches and teaches on
service transformation through design.

KAJA MISVÆR KISTORP
– LEAD SERVICE DESIGNER, DESIGNIT OSLO

Kaja is responsible for the discipline and service
design team at Designit Oslo. She has worked
with service design at Designit since 2005,
and co-founded the Oslo office. She also does
research and teaches design for public services at
the Oslo School of Architecture and Design.

KATHRIN MÖSLEIN
– VICE PRESIDENT RESEARCH AND
CHAIR FOR INFORMATION SYSTEMS,
FRIEDRICH-ALEXANDER-UNIVERSITY
ERLANGEN-NÜRNBERG

Kathrin is Vice President of Research and Chair
for Information Systems – Innovation & Value
Creation at the Friedrich-Alexander-Universität
Erlangen-Nürnberg as well as Professor of
Management and Academic Director of the
Center for Leading Innovation and Cooperation
(CLIC) at HHL Leipzig Graduate School of
Management, Germany.

KATIE TZANIDOU
– UX RESEARCH MANAGER, GOOGLE

Katie is a UX research professional with a background in psychology and philosophy. She holds a PhD in Human Computer Interaction from the Open University in the UK. Before joining Google, Katie led the UX team in Europe, the Middle East, and Africa for PayPal. She is an active speaker at UX conferences and a mentor for startups.

KRISTIN LOW
– FOUNDER AND DIRECTOR, ON OFF GROUP

Kristin moved from Australia to Hong Kong in 2012, where he founded and built Hong Kong's largest design thinking network from the ground up (now over 2,000 members). He also co-founded the consultancy On Off Group and Design Thinking Asia, a training organization that meets the demand for human-centered design practitioners in Asia.

KLARA LINDNER
– HEAD OF CUSTOMER EXPERIENCE, MOBISOL

Klara strives to connect human-centered design with sustainable energy provision. She joined the solar company Mobisol in its infancy, led the pilot phase in East Africa, and developed its pioneering business model. Alongside improving Mobisol's customer experience, Klara has been part of the Research Program Microenergy Systems since 2013, investigating service design in the BOP/energy context. As a certified Design Thinking Coach, Klara has been using various workshop settings to teach making design thinking useful for the processes of innovation and change.

KRISTINA CARLANDER
– SERVICE DESIGNER, DOBERMAN

Kristina is a service designer with a background in cognitive science. Her experience ranges from clients such as PwC and Tele2 to Oscar, an insurance startup in the US.

KLAUS SCHWARZENBERGER
– CO-FOUNDER AND CTO, MORE THAN METRICS

Klaus Schwarzenberger is the Co-Founder and CTO of More than Metrics. In his role he combines service design and software engineering to build better products.

LAURA MALAN
– SENIOR CONSULTANT, USCREATES

Laura leads user insight, service design, and communication design projects for Uscreates, a 10-year-strong strategic design consultancy working to improve healthcare and well-being through embedding a design approach across organizations. She is experienced in working on projects relating to communicating complex information in simple and engaging ways, designing services and strategies, and producing high-quality digital and print outputs.

LAUREN CURRIE
– DESIGNER AND
ENTREPRENEUR, REDJOTTER.COM

Lauren, also known as Redjotter, is a designer and doer who works with people, teams, and organizations all over the world helping them be better. She is a catalyst, educator, and serial starter who turns ideas into reality, making masses believe in change and building networks around problems. She was recognized by *ELLE* magazine as one of 30 women under 30 changing the world and was awarded an OBE in 2017.

LINDA BOWMAN
– SERVICE DESIGNER AND INNOVATION
STRATEGIST, WECO

Linda is an Italian service designer based in Shanghai, China. She focuses on understanding and developing clients' business environment and strategy from a design point of view. By designing with people in mind, she challenges assumptions in order to achieve thoughtful innovation. Linda has a double master's in Product Service System Design and Innovation Design from Politecnico of Milan and Tongji University of China.

LISA GATELY
– SENIOR DIRECTOR,
CONTENT STRATEGY, GENESYS

Lisa is Senior Director of Content Strategy at Genesys, where she is responsible for the planning, creation, and curation of content that delivers useful and usable experiences.

MARCEL ZWIERS
– CO-FOUNDING PARTNER, 31VOLTS

Marcel is a co-founding partner at 31Volts based in Utrecht, the heart of the Netherlands. The 31Volts are proud to call themselves "strategic doers," helping organizations grow their business by designing meaningful services, always by putting people first!

MAIK MEDZICH
– HEAD OF CUSTOMER EXPERIENCE,
TELEKOM DEUTSCHLAND GMBH

Maik studied business informatics and has been part of the Deutsche Telekom group for more than 15 years. Since 2014, he has been responsible for implementing a customer experience culture within Telekom Deutschland GmbH (65,000 employees). He is also one of two initiators of the CX Navigator community.

MARC GARCIA
– PROFESSIONAL QUESTIONER,
WE QUESTION OUR PROJECT

As a serious service innovation consultant, Marc helps governments and businesses to involve users in creating new services. But at night, he goes back to good old days of drumming at Jacinto Uncle. He loves to rock! Or is it the other way around? He does crazy stuff at work. At night, he stays seriously at home.

MARIANNE ROLFSEN
– SENIOR SERVICE DESIGNER, LIVEWORK

Marianne joined Livework following an MA in Service Design from the Oslo School of Architecture and Design, and a career within the service sector prior to that. In her role as a Senior Service Designer, she has worked across a wide variety of sectors and businesses, both private and public, on projects ranging from improving services to creating overarching customer strategies. She currently works at Oslo Public Library, improving their digital services.

MARKUS DURSTEWITZ
– SENIOR INNOVATION MANAGER, AIRBUS

Markus is responsible for fostering a sustainable innovation culture across Airbus and building an effective innovation ecosystem that delivers value to the customer. He is working on establishing design thinking as basic approach for innovation across the whole corporation. He has over 20 years of experience in the aerospace industry and holds a PhD in Man-Machine Systems and Cognitive Engineering. Today, his focus is on data-driven services and digital transformation offering new ways of collaboration along the complete value chain of aviation in product development as well as in operations.

MARIE HARTMANN
– DESIGN DIRECTOR, DESIGNIT OSLO

Marie works as a Design Director at Designit Oslo and was the project manager in the Oslo University Hospital project. She is an experienced designer and user researcher and has led several service design projects within the public health sector.

MARIO SEPP
– FOUNDER, GASTSPIEL

Mario is the Founder of Gastspiel, a consulting company dedicated to service and experience design. He is a passionate and hands-on customer experience expert who helps companies to optimize or create services, products, and experiences that truly matter for customers, employees, and business results. His approach combines more than 20 years of international leadership experience, entrepreneurial spirit, and strong business acumen with his proven expertise in design thinking methods and takes an outside-in perspective to create the best customer experience possible.

MARINA TERTERYAN
– SERVICE DESIGNER AND DESIGN THINKING AMBASSADOR, THE WHY LAB, AND WHY SERVICE DESIGN THINKING PODCAST

Marina is a service designer with a deep love for design thinking, innovation, and all things human-centered. She hosts the world's first service design podcast, called "Why Service Design Thinking," teaches service design at General Assembly, and holds a master's degree in Strategic Design Management from Parson's School of Design. She believes that the world will be a better place if everyone works by the principles of design thinking, lives by the principles of jazz improvisation, and uses ergonomic standing desks.

MARTA SÁNCHEZ SERRANO
– HEAD OF COMMERCIAL STRATEGY AND OPERATIONS, VODAFONE

Marta has more than 10 years of experience in retail business and operations. She is responsible for the definition of in-store experience and Omnichannel strategy at Vodafone.

MAURÍCIO MANHÃES
– PROFESSOR OF SERVICE DESIGN,
SAVANNAH COLLEGE OF ART AND DESIGN

Maurício is a Professor of Service Design at
the Savannah College of Art and Design and
an Associate Design Researcher at the service design consultancy Livework. In 2015, he
obtained a doctorate in Knowledge Management
with a thesis titled "Innovativeness and
Prejudice: Designing a Landscape of Diversity for
Knowledge Creation."

MIKE PRESS
– DIRECTOR, OPEN CHANGE

Mike is a service design consultant, educator,
and Emeritus Professor of Design Policy. He is
also the author of numerous books and publications on design policy, and the Co-Founder of the
Service Design Academy.

MAURO REGO
– DESIGNER, BEING VISUAL

Mauro is a service and interface designer based in
Berlin. Since 2012, he has been teaching people
worldwide how to be more visual with the Being
Visual Workshop.

MICHAEL WEND
– SENIOR CUSTOMER
EXPERIENCE MANAGER, E.ON

Michael is an expert in customer care and
experience and has worked for large customer
care organizations. Since 2009, he has been
working for E.ON Germany. As Senior Customer
Experience Manager of the Customer Insights
and Innovation team, he is chiefly responsible
for service design. He previously worked as a
business consultant and project manager with
a focus on customer relationship management.
Michael studied intersectoral leadership and governance at Zeppelin University in Friedrichshafen,
studied sciences in Vienna, and graduated
with distinction from his studies in business consultancy.

MELISSA GATES
– COMMUNICATION DESIGNER, LIVEWORK

As Livework's Communication Designer,
Melissa works closely with the teams across
all Livework's studios to create communication
materials that facilitate understanding and
create internal buy-in for stakeholders. With a
background in both copywriting and illustration
and animation she's able to help Livework
explain and "sell" their work to clients and the
wider outside world.

MINKA FRACKENPOHL
– ARCHITECT AND SERVICE DESIGNER,
MINKAFRACKENPOHL.DE

Minka loves the interplay of tangible and
intangible elements. Working at the intersection
where space and service meet, she focuses
on the human scale, explores needs, and
accompanies change.

NINA WESCHENFELDER
– SENIOR SERVICE DESIGNER,
MINDS & MAKERS,

Nina is a trained graphic designer and graduate of Service Design program at Köln International School of Design (KISD) and University of Western Sydney, where she focused on design thinking and design research. In her stakeholder-centered research at the interfaculty Service Science Institute at Maastricht University she sought to understand and develop services as holistic systems. Since 2014 she has worked as a service designer and user researcher at minds & makers, leading projects in the private, social, and public sectors.

PATRICIA STARK
– CO-FOUNDER AND SOLUTION
DESIGNER, SPLEND

Patricia has worked as an international product manager since 2007 and due to her passion for creativity, service innovation, and technology co-founded SPLEND in 2016. Now, she works with industrial enterprises to unleash their creative potential in order to explore challenges and opportunities for the future.

OLE SCHILLING
– SENIOR MANAGER DESIGN,
DEUTSCHE TELEKOM AG

Ole was responsible for the development of the customer experience program across Deutsche Telekom AG as Head of Customer Experience Transformation. In addition to his background within the creative industries, he holds an Executive MBA in Design and Innovation Management and is committed to the field of change by design.

PATTI HUNT
– FOUNDER AND DIRECTOR, ON OFF GROUP

Patti moved from Australia to Hong Kong in 2012 and founded two service design and innovation companies that currently operate in the Asia Pacific region, On Off Group and Make Studios.

OZLEM DESSAUER-SIEGERS
– SENIOR SERVICE EXPERIENCE
DESIGN LEAD, VODAFONE

Ozlem is a principal multidisciplinary experience designer with an academic background in UX design and human interaction design. She started her career in the United States in 1997, moved to the Netherlands in 2010, and lives in Amsterdam, NL. During her career Ozlem has worked for Eastman Kodak Company, IBM Global Services, and Philips Design, and she currently works for Vodafone as a Senior Service Experience Design Lead.

PER BROLUND
– SENIOR CONCEPT DESIGNER,
TRANSFORMATOR DESIGN

Per has past working experience for the World Wide Fund for Nature, using design thinking to strengthen and develop a sustainable rattan industry in Cambodia. He is now the lead at Transformator in a department focusing on transforming complex service systems and abstract end-user value into comprehensive and intuitive visualizations.

PHILIPP THESEN
– SENIOR VICE PRESIDENT DESIGN,
DEUTSCHE TELEKOM AG

Philipp is Chief Designer and leader of the design
function at Deutsche Telekom. In this role he
is responsible for the design strategy, design
processes, and education and executive design
work for international products and services. With
15 years of experience as a designer, consultant,
creative director, and design strategist, he is
dedicated to driving innovation and digital transformation by strategic design. Philipp is a lecturer,
public speaker, and frequent member of international design juries.

PHILLIPPA ROSE
– SERVICE DESIGNER AND
FACILITATOR, CURRENT.WORKS

Phillippa has specialized in service design and
innovation since 2005, with particular interests
in design research and strategy. Alongside
client work with organizations like the Cabinet
Office's Policy Lab, the Open Data Institute,
the Met Office, and The App Business, Phillippa
also enjoys teaching in the master's program in
Service Design and Innovation at the University of
the Arts, London.

RENATUS HOOGENRAAD
– COLLABORATION SPECIALIST,
ORGANIZATIONAL DEVELOPMENT
CONSULTANT, AND COACH,
SPARKS TRAINING

Renatus helps shift organizational cultures
positively to face uncertainty in constantly
moving environments. By doing so he builds
agility whilst at the same time accelerating the
creation of value.

RUNE YNDESTAD MØLLER
– SENIOR BUSINESS DESIGNER, LIVEWORK

Rune joined Livework as a Senior Business
Designer following a career doing cross-sector
consulting in sectors such as financial services,
oil, gas, and transport. He has, among other
things, held responsibility for the development of
products, services, and processes. He also worked
as a researcher at Copenhagen Business School,
where he helped eight of the largest companies in
Denmark to improve their use of risk information
in decision-making processes.

SATU MIETTINEN
– PROFESSOR OF SERVICE DESIGN,
UNIVERSITY OF LAPLAND

Satu works in service design research and has
authored a number of books and research
publications. Her research interests in service
design include the areas of social and public
service development, citizen engagement, and
digital service development.

SARAH DRUMMOND
– CO-FOUNDER AND MANAGING
DIRECTOR, SNOOK

Sarah is the Co-Founder and Managing
Director of Snook, an award-winning design
consultancy working at the forefront of civic,
public sector, and democratic innovation.
Sarah focuses on making social change happen
by re-thinking public services from a human
perspective and regularly lectures and speaks
around the globe on service design, innovation,
and civic engagement. As a serial idea generator,
Sarah has co-founded MyPolice, CycleHack,
Dearest Scotland, and The Matter. She was
awarded a Google Fellowship for her work in
technology and democracy.

SIMON CLATWORTHY
– PROFESSOR, OSLO SCHOOL OF
ARCHITECTURE AND DESIGN

Simon has been researching and teaching service
design since 2004, and has a longer period of
service development behind him. He is keenly
interested in how design changes organizations
and their offerings.

SOPHIE ANDERSSON
– SENIOR SERVICE DESIGNER,
TRANSFORMATOR DESIGN

Sophie has a Master of Fine Arts, with a
major in Business and Design. In her current work she focuses on capacity building,
helping organizations to become more customer-centric in culture, business development,
and ways of working.

SUSANNA NISSAR
– CO-FOUNDER AND CEO,
EXPEDITION MONDIAL

Susanna has a diverse academic background
including an MSc in Computer Science and a
BA in Film Production. She found her way into
service design through UX for digital services. She
is today working with service design for a wide
range of Swedish and international organizations.
Susanna co-founded the social innovation agency
Expedition Mondial as a way to further explore
the boundaries of service design.

THOMAS ABRELL
– INNOVATION MANAGER, AIRBUS

Thomas is responsible for user-centered design in
the Airbus Corporate Innovation team. His work
includes involving users in designing experiences,
from the fuzzy front end to proofs of concept.
In addition, he currently conducts his PhD
research at the University of St.Gallen, Institute
of Information Management, with a focus on
customer and user knowledge in digital innovation. His background is mixed between design and
business, holding an MSc in International Design
Business Management (Aalto University, Helsinki),
and MA in Design (Tongji University, Shanghai),
and a Diplom-Betriebswirt (DH).

TIM SCHUURMAN
– PARTNER, DESIGNTHINKERS GROUP AND
DESIGNTHINKERS ACADEMY

Tim has an MBA and an MSc in Business and
Financial Management and extensive experience in designing and implementing product/
service concepts in diverse industries. A motiva-
tor and team player, he provides conditions for
professionals to be successful. Tim has extensive
experience in facilitating and developing service
design training sessions and master classes, and
teaches at universities.

VALERIE CARR
– CREATIVE DIRECTOR, SNOOK

Valerie is Snook's Creative Director, focusing on
co-designing health and social care services to
improve both the experience of the citizen and the
efficiency and effectiveness of the service delivery.
She has a PhD in Healthcare Service Design
and is motivated by creatively addressing the
challenges associated with engaging patients and
citizens in co-producing public services. In the
past, she has worked on projects for the Scottish
Government, NHS24, various health boards,
and Scottish councils.

VLADIMIR TSAKLEV
– CONTINUOUS IMPROVEMENT LEADER,
COCA-COLA HELLENIC BSO

Vladimir is an engineer by education and an inventor by nature who is inspired by curiosity and great design. He is leading a project for transforming his organization from a process efficiency–based to a customer- and value-centric one. He has been involved in every aspect of developing a full-scale continuous improvement program – from concept design and framework setup to training and project facilitation. He is interested in the integration of service design with other improvement methodologies and its implementation in new areas of business and people's lives.

WARITTHI TEERAPRASERT (RAIN)
– SENIOR DESIGN AND CREATIVE
BUSINESS DEVELOPMENT OFFICER,
THAILAND CREATIVE & DESIGN CENTER

Waritthi co-created TCDC's Service Design program and co-initiates it into Thailand's design and business communities. He started learning design from the personal question "How did the designer think like that?" He then finds the answers through design.

MAIN AUTHORS

Even though we wrote most parts of this book, all our texts were iteratively developed based on a lot of constructive feedback from our co-authors and contributors.

MARC STICKDORN
– CO-FOUNDER AND CEO,
  MORE THAN METRICS

Marc is the Co-Founder and CEO of More than Metrics, a company creating software for service design, such as Smaply and ExperienceFellow. With a background in strategic management and service design, he helps organizations to sustainably embed service design in their structures, processes, and culture.

In 2010, he published the award-winning book *This is Service Design Thinking* together with Jakob. Marc regularly speaks at conferences on service design and startups. He teaches service design at various universities and gives public and exclusive executive courses. He is pursuing a PhD at the University of Erlangen-Nuremberg in Germany in information systems based on design science, in which he has developed a new mobile ethnographic research approach. He is now almost finished, and has been for several years ...

If Marc is not working, he loves traveling with a backpack or in his VW van, going on sailing trips, or riding his classic Triumph Bonneville motorcycle. He lives in Innsbruck, Austria, surrounded by the European Alps.

Twitter: @MrStickdorn
Email: marc@tisdd.com

ADAM LAWRENCE
– CO-FOUNDER,
  WORKPLAYEXPERIENCE

Adam is the Co-Founder of WorkPlayExperience, a company which helps organizations worldwide change how their staff, partners, and customers work together to discover and create value. His background ranges from psychology, marketing, and product innovation to professional theater and stand-up comedy. Adam is fascinated by human interaction, so at WPX he focuses on the "front stage" of services and how groups of people from different backgrounds can work together effectively while having a great time. He has developed and adapted several theatrical tools and lenses and introduced them to the world of service design and facilitation.

In 2010, Adam co-initiated the award-winning Global Service Jam – which was soon followed by the Global Sustainability Jam and the Global GovJam – and he has been a leading figure in establishing the global community of practice and sharing around the Jams. He also teaches and gives keynotes on service design and human-centered innovation all over the world.

Adam lives in Southern Germany, enjoys nature and medieval re-creation, and rides a classic Japanese motorcycle.

Twitter: @adamstjohn
Email: adam@tisdd.com

MARKUS HORMESS

– CO-FOUNDER,
WORKPLAYEXPERIENCE

Markus is the Co-Founder of WorkPlayExperience, a service innovation consultancy. He loves to work and coach at the intersection of design, business, and technology – building on his experience of service design and business consulting, and on his background in theoretical physics. In his daily work, Markus helps organizations tackle complex business problems and make cultures more agile and human-centered. The focal point of his work is prototyping in service design, where he constantly pushes the boundaries of what a dedicated team can achieve with limited resources.

Markus is co-initiator of the Global Service Jam as well as the Global Sustainability Jam and the Global GovJam. He teaches service design at various universities and gives public and private executive courses.

Markus loves good design, human technology, practical experiments, authentic services, and playfulness in all things. In between project work and his growing family, Markus builds stuff in his local makerspace and occasionally performs as a DJ and bass player. He lives near Nuremberg, Germany.

Twitter: @markusedgar
Email: markus@tisdd.com

JAKOB SCHNEIDER

– CO-FOUNDER AND CCO,
MORE THAN METRICS
– PARTNER AND CREATIVE DIRECTOR,
KD1 DESIGN AGENCY

Jakob is a Partner and Creative Director at KD1 design agency, working in all fields of visual corporate communication. Being Co-Founder and CCO at More than Metrics, he also co-creates software for service designers, like Smaply and ExperienceFellow.

Working as an interdisciplinary designer since 2006, Jakob has had the honor to collaborate with clients such as Volkswagen, Daimler, Beiersdorf, Edeka, Siemens, and Deutsche Telekom. His scope of work ranges from rather designy stuff for cultural institutions to full-blown corporate projects – sometimes with, sometimes without human-centered thinking.

In 2010, he published (and designed) the business bestseller *This is Service Design Thinking* together with Marc. Jakob speaks at conferences, universities, and fellow agencies on service design, startups, and on the daily agency struggles.

Jakob lives in Cologne, Germany, enjoys urban life as much as the woods, and is seen on his old Dutch bike mostly.

Twitter: @jakoblies
Email: jakob@tisdd.com

INDEX

THIS IS SERVICE DESIGN DOING.

Marc Stickdorn/Adam Lawrence/Markus Hormess/Jakob Schneider

Editors	Marc Stickdorn, Adam Lawrence, Markus Hormess, Jakob Schneider
Main authors	Marc Stickdorn, Adam Lawrence, Markus Hormess
Creative Direction	Jakob Schneider
Graphic Design	Sarah Berenbrinker, Edie Freeman, Ron Bilodeau
Editorial assistance	Marina Terteryan
Development	Angela Rufino, Meg Foley
Technical Review	Mauricio Manhaes, Stefan Moritz, Chris Ferguson, Erik Flowers, Megan Erin Miller
Proofreading	Rachel Head
Typography	Minion, Ridley Grotesk
Photo credit	Unless otherwise credited, all photos within any case, chapter, or textbox belong to the author of the section where they appear. If no author is explicitly mentioned, the photos belong to the editors, Marc, Adam, Markus, and Jakob. Most workshop photos were taken during "This is Service Design Doing" courses – many thanks to the participants!

Co-authors (case authors and expert commenters)

Alex Nisbett, Alexander Osterwalder, Andy Polaine, Angela Li, Anke Helmbrecht, Anton Breman, Arne van Oosterom, Arthur Yeh, Barbara Franz, Belina Raffy, Birgit Mager, Carola Verschoor, Cat Drew, Cathy Huang, Chirryl-Lee Ryan, Chris Ferguson, Chris Livaudais, Christof Zürn, Clarissa Biolchini, Damian Kernahan, Daniel Ewerman, Dave Carroll, Doug Powell, Eduardo Kranz, Emilie Strømmen Olsen, Eric Reiss, Erich Pichler, Erik Widmark, Fernando Yepez, Fiona Lambe, Florian Vollmer, Francesca Terzi, Geke van Dijk, Giovanni Ruello, Hannah Wanjiru, Hazel White, Helga Mayr, Henrik Karlsson, Ingvild Støvring, Itziar Pobes, Ivan Boscariol, Jamin Hegeman, Jeff McGrath, Jesús Sotoca, Johan Blomkvist, Johan Dovelius, Joub Miradora, Julia Jonas, Jurgen De Becker, Jürgen Tanghe, Kaja Misvær Kistorp, Kathrin Möslein, Katie Tzanidou, Klara Lindner, Klaus Schwarzenberger, Kristin Low, Kristina Carlander, Laura Malan, Lauren Currie, Lennart Hennigs, Linda Bowman, Lisa Gately, Maik Medzich, Marc Garcia, Marcel Zwiers, Marianne Rolfsen, Marie Hartmann, Marina Terteryan, Mario Sepp, Markus Durstewitz, Marta Sánchez Serrano, Mauricio Manhães, Mauro Rego, Melissa Gates, Michael Wend, Mike Press, Minka Frackenpohl, Nina Weschenfelder, Ole Schilling, Ozlem Dessauer-Siegers, Patricia Stark, Patti Hunt, Per Brolund, Philipp Thesen, Phillippa Rose, Renatus Hoogenraad, Rune Yndestad Møller, Sarah Drummond, Satu Miettinen, Simon Clatworthy, Sophie Andersson, Susanna Nissar, Teresa Mang, Thomas Abrell, Tim Schuurman, Valerie Carr, Vladimir Tsaklev, Waritthi Teeraprasert

Contributors

The service design community and beyond, represented by 200 reviewers who volunteered to help us co-create this book. See preface.